What They Said® In 1978

The Yearbook of Spoken Opinion

•

Compiled and Edited by

ALAN F. PATER

and

JASON R. PATER

MONITOR BOOK COMPANY, INC.

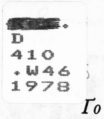
To

The Newsmakers of the World . . .

May they never be at a loss for words

TENTH ANNUAL EDITION

Printed in the United States of America

Library of Congress catalogue card number 74-111080

ISBN number: 0-917734-02-5

WHAT THEY SAID is published annually by Monitor Book Company, Inc., Beverly Hills, California. The title, "WHAT THEY SAID," is a trademark owned exclusively by Monitor Book Company, Inc., and has been duly registered with the United States Patent Office. Any unauthorized use is prohibited.

Preface to the First Edition (1969)

Words can be powerful or subtle, humorous or maddening. They can be vigorous or feeble, lucid or obscure, inspiring or despairing, wise or foolish, hopeful or pessimistic ... they can be fearful or confident, timid or articulate, persuasive or perverse, honest or deceitful. As tools at a speaker's command, words can be used to reason, argue, discuss, cajole, plead, debate, declaim, threaten, infuriate, or appease; they can harangue, flourish, recite, preach, discourse, stab to the quick, or gently sermonize.

When casually spoken by a stage or film star, words can go beyond the press-agentry and make-up facade and reveal the inner man or woman. When purposefully uttered in the considered phrasing of a head of state, words can determine the destiny of millions of people, resolve peace or war, or chart the course of a nation on whose direction the fate of the entire world may depend.

Until now, the *copia verborum* of well-known and renowned public figures—the doctors and diplomats, the governors and generals, the potentates and presidents, the entertainers and educators, the bishops and baseball players, the jurists and journalists, the authors and attorneys, the congressmen and chairmen-of-the-board—whether enunciated in speeches, lectures, interviews, radio and television addresses, news conferences, forums, symposiums, town meetings, committee hearings, random remarks to the press, or delivered on the floors of the United States Senate and House of Representatives or in the parliaments and palaces of the world—have been dutifully reported in the media, then filed away and, for the most part, forgotten.

The editors of *WHAT THEY SAID* believe that consigning such a wealth of thoughts, ideas, doctrines, opinions and philosophies to interment in the morgues and archives of the Fourth Estate is lamentable and unnecessary. Yet the media, in all their forms, are constantly engulfing us in a profusion of endless and increasingly voluminous news reports. One is easily disposed to disregard or forget the stimulating discussion of critical issues embodied in so many of the utterances of those who make the news and, in their respective fields, shape the events throughout the world. The conclusion is therefore a natural and compelling one: the educator, the public official, the business executive, the statesman, the philosopher—everyone who has a stake in the complex, often confusing trends of our times—should have material of this kind readily available.

These, then, are the circumstances under which *WHAT THEY SAID* was conceived. It is the culmination of a year of listening to the people in the public eye; a year of scrutinizing, monitoring, reviewing, judging, deciding—a year during which the editors resurrected from almost certain oblivion those quintessential elements of the year's *spoken* opinion which, in their judgment, demanded preservation in book form.

WHAT THEY SAID is a pioneer in its field. Its *raison d'etre* is the firm conviction that presenting, each year, the highlights of vital and interesting views from the lips of prominent people on virtually every aspect of contemporary civilization fulfills the need to give the *spoken* word the permanence and lasting value of the *written* word. For, if it is true that a picture is worth 10,000 words, it is equally true that a verbal conclusion, an apt quote or a candid comment by a person of fame or influence can have more significance and can provide more understanding than an entire page of summary in a standard work of reference.

The editors of *WHAT THEY SAID* did not, however, design their book for researchers and

iii

scholars alone. One of the failings of the conventional reference work is that it is blandly written and referred to primarily for facts and figures, lacking inherent "interest value." *WHAT THEY SAID*, on the other hand, was planned for sheer enjoyment and pleasure, for searching glimpses into the lives and thoughts of the world's celebrities, as well as for serious study, intellectual reflection and the philosophical contemplation of our multifaceted life and mores. Furthermore, those pressed for time, yet anxious to know what the newsmakers have been saying, will welcome the short excerpts which will make for quick, intermittent reading—and rereading. And, of course, the topical classifications, the speakers' index, the subject index, the place and date information—documented and authenticated and easily located—will supply a rich fund of hitherto not readily obtainable reference and statistical material.

Finally, the reader will find that the editors have eschewed trite comments and cliches, tedious and boring. The selected quotations, each standing on its own, are pertinent, significant, stimulating—above all, relevant to today's world, expressed in the speakers' own words. And they will, the editors feel, be even more relevant tomorrow. They will be re-examined and reflected upon in the future by men and women eager to learn from the past. The prophecies, the promises, the "golden dreams," the boastings and rantings, the bluster, the bravado, the pleadings and representations of those whose voices echo in these pages (and in those to come) should provide a rare and unique history lesson. The positions held by these luminaries, in their respective callings, are such that what they say today may profoundly affect the future as well as the present, and so will be of lasting importance and meaning.

Beverly Hills, California

ALAN F. PATER
JASON R. PATER

Table of Contents

PART THREE: GENERAL

About the 1978 Edition . . .

THIS is a special edition of *WHAT THEY SAID*. It marks the 10th anniversary of this yearbook of spoken opinion. Since its introduction in 1969, the series has grown, not only in circulation but in size and features.

Over the years, others, recognizing the importance of the *WHAT THEY SAID* concept, have tried to copy it. But none has succeeded in capturing the uniqueness of *WHAT THEY SAID*—the scope and range of subjects, the care in planning and format, the attention to detail, and the system of indexing and cross-indexing.

Now, with this 10th edition, *WHAT THEY SAID* is even more firmly established as the standard sourcebook for the world's spoken opinion, acknowledged as the sole authority in its field, the only serious, in-depth record of the spoken words of the world's most prominent individuals on virtually every aspect of contemporary civilization.

The Editors extend their appreciation to all who have helped make this 10th anniversary possible.

With no intention of being a complete news summary of 1978, following are some of the happenings reflected in many of this year's quotations . . .

Civil Rights:

The Supreme Court ruled, in the Bakke decision, that while race can be a factor in determining the admittance of students to college, there can be no arbitrary quota system for such admittance.

Commerce:

President Carter criticized the "three-martini" business lunch as an example of excessive corporate tax deductions.

The dollar rode a rollercoaster in world-wide exchange rates.

Farmers called a strike to protest low prices they receive for food products.

There were new calls for protectionism against what was termed unfair trading practices by foreign nations, particularly Japan.

The Justice Department voiced concern over a jump in corporate acquisitions and mergers.

Education:

Tuition tax credits and more emphasis on teaching the basic "three R's" were two issues in the spotlight in the field of education.

WHAT THEY SAID IN 1978

Economy:

President Carter issued wage and price guidelines as inflation failed to abate.

Energy:

U.S. dependence on imported oil continued to grow, as did the price of that oil.
Decontrol of natural-gas prices was debated.

Foreign Affairs:

Human rights continued as a controversial element of President Carter's foreign policy. A related issue was linkage (basing one's policy toward another country on that country's actions in other fields).

Government:

The size and cost of government became major issues facing voters and office-holders.
Proposition 13, California's controversial property-tax measure, won voter approval.

National Defense:

The U.S. cancelled the B-1 bomber and a nuclear-powered aircraft carrier, and delayed production of the cruise missile and neutron bomb.

Politics:

A Congressional influence-buying scandal involving South Korean businessman Tongsun Park culminated in investigations and hearings.
U.S. Attorney David Marston, in Philadelphia, was removed by President Carter amidst controversy regarding a case on which Marston was working.

Social Welfare:

Social Security taxes were increased.

Transportation:

The CAB relaxed its regulation of the airline industry, resulting in a fare war and a plethora of new route assignments.

Urban Affairs:

The Federal government agreed to guarantee bonds issued by fiscally troubled New York City.
Cleveland approached bankruptcy as Mayor Kucinich struggled to keep the city working.

Africa:

War between Ethiopia and Somalia flared, and Soviet and Cuban involvement became an issue.
Zaire claimed it was invaded by rebels based in Angola.
Rhodesia agreed to an "internal settlement" of its racial strife by formulating plans for black majority rule.

Americas:

The U.S. and Panama signed treaties which will gradually turn over control of the Panama Canal to Panama.
In Nicaragua, there was civil strife and demonstrations against President Somoza.

Asia:

The U.S. announced it will recognize mainland China and withdraw its long-standing recognition of Taiwan.
There were reported moves toward some liberalization of life in China.
Vietnam warred with Cambodia.

Europe:

In France, the Communists failed to win a majority in the national elections.
The Soviet tried, convicted and sentenced a number of dissidents.
The U.S. ended its arms embargo against Turkey.

Middle East:

Egyptian President Sadat and Israeli Prime Minister Begin met with U.S. President Carter at Camp David, Md., and announced a framework for peace between the two Middle Eastern countries.
Near year's end, civil unrest in Iran threatened to oust the Shah as leader of that nation. Moslem leader Ayatollah Khomeini prepared to return there from exile.

Journalism:

The Supreme Court allowed certain police searches of newsrooms.
New York Times reporter Stephen Farber was jailed in New Jersey for refusing to obey a court

order to turn over evidence he had collected as a reporter in a murder case.

In the Soviet Union, two U.S. reporters were tried for alleged libel.

Medicine:

HEW Secretary Califano launched a spirited campaign against smoking.

Medical costs continued to rise, and the possibility of national health insurance remained an issue.

Music:

Beverly Sills announced her pending retirement as a singer to become co-director of the New York City Opera.

Television:

Advertising on children's programs stirred criticism.

Religion:

In Guyana, San Francisco-based People's Temple members were involved in a mass murder-suicide.

Pope Paul VI died. His replacement, John Paul I, also died shortly after taking office. He was replaced by John Paul II, a Pole, the first non-Italian Pope in over 400 years.

Sports:

Football coach George Allen left the Washington *Redskins*, signed with the Los Angeles *Rams*, and was soon after fired.

Baseball player Pete Rose set a new National League consecutive-game hitting mark.

Women's Rights:

Women's-rights groups demanded extension of ratification time for the Equal Rights Amendment in one of the year's most controversial issues.

Editorial Treatment

ORGANIZATION OF MATERIAL

Special attention has been given to the arrangement of the book—from the major divisions down to the individual categories and speakers—the objective being a logical progression of related material as follows:

(A)   The categories are arranged alphabetically within each of three major sections:

Part One:	"National Affairs"
Part Two:	"International Affairs"
Part Three:	"General"

In this manner, the reader can quickly locate quotations pertaining to particular fields of interest (see also *Indexing*). It should be noted that some quotations contain a number of thoughts or ideas—sometimes on different subjects—while some are vague as to exact subject matter and thus do not fit clearly into a specific topic classification. In such cases, the judgment of the Editors has determined the most appropriate category.

(B)   Within each category, the speakers are in alphabetical order by surname, following alphabetization practices used in the speaker's country of origin.

(C)   Where there are two or more quotations by one speaker within the same category, they appear chronologically by date spoken or date of source.

SPEAKER IDENTIFICATION

(A)   The occupation, profession, rank, position or title of the speaker is given as it was *at the time the statement was made* (except when the speaker's relevant identification is in the past, in which case he is shown as "former"). Thus, due to possible changes in status during the year, a speaker may be shown with different identification in various portions of the book, or even within the same category.

(B)   In the case of speakers who hold more than one position or occupation simultaneously (or who held relevant positions in the past), the judgment of the Editors has determined the most appropriate identification to use with a specific quotation.

(C)   Nationality of speakers is normally not given unless this information is of interest or relative to the quotation(s).

THE QUOTATIONS

The quoted material selected for inclusion in this book is shown as it appeared in the source, except as follows:

(A)   *Ellipses* have been inserted wherever the Editors have deleted extraneous words or overly long passages within the quoted material used. In no way has the meaning or intention of any quotation been altered. *Ellipses* are also used where they appeared in the source.

(B)   *Punctuation and spelling* have been altered by the Editors where they were obviously incorrect in the source, or to make the quotations more intelligible, or to conform to the general style used throughout this book. Again, meaning or intention of the quotation has not been changed.

(C)   *Brackets* ([   ]) indicate material inserted by the Editors or by the source to either correct obvious errors or to explain and/or clarify what the speaker is saying.

(D)   *Italics* have sometimes been added by the Editors where emphasis is clearly desirable.

Except for the above instances, the quoted material used has been printed verbatim, as reported by the source (even if the speaker made factual errors or was awkward in his choice of words).

Special care has been exercised to make certain that each quotation stands on its own merits and is not taken "out of context." The Editors, however, cannot be responsible for errors made by the original newspaper, periodical or other source, i.e., incorrect reporting, mis-quotations or errors in interpretation.

DOCUMENTATION AND SOURCES

Documentation (circumstance, place, date) of each quotation is provided as fully as could be obtained, and the sources are furnished for all quotations. In some instances no documentation details were available; in those cases only the source is given. Following are the sequence and style used for this information:

Circumstance of quotation, place, date/ Name of source, date: section (if applicable), page number.

Example: *Before the Senate, Washington, Dec. 4/ The Washington Post, 12:6:(A)13.*

The above example indicates that the quotation was delivered before the Senate in Washington on December 4. It was taken for *WHAT THEY SAID* from *The Washington Post,* issue of December 6, section A, page 13. (When a newspaper publishes more than one edition on the same date, it should be noted that page numbers may vary from edition to edition.)

(A)   When the source is a television or radio broadcast, the name of the network or local station is indicated, along with the date of the broadcast (obviously, page and/or section information does not apply).

(B)   One asterisk (*) before the (/) in the documentation indicates that the quoted material was written rather than spoken. Although the basic policy of *WHAT THEY SAID* is to use only *spoken* statements, there are occasions when written statements are considered by the Editors to be important enough to be included. These occasions are rare and usually involve Presidential messages, Presidential statements released to the press and other such documents attributed to a person in high government office.

(C)   Two asterisks (**) after the (/) indicate the speaker supplied the quotation to *WHAT THEY SAID* directly.

INDEXING

(A)   The *Index to Speakers* is keyed to the page number. (For alphabetization practices, see *Organization of Material,* paragraph B.)

(B)   The *Index to Subjects* is keyed to both the page number and the quotation number on the page (thus, 210:3 indicates quotation number 3 on page 210); the quotation number appears at upper right-hand corner of each quotation.

(C)   To locate quotations on a particular subject, regardless of speaker, turn to the appropriate category (see *Table of Contents)* or use the detailed *Index to Subjects.*

(D)   To locate all quotations by a particular speaker, regardless of subject, use the *Index to Speakers.*

(E)   To locate quotations by a particular speaker on a particular subject, turn to the appropriate category and then to that person's quotations within that category.

(F)   The reader will find that the basic categorization format of *WHAT THEY SAID* is itself a useful subject index, inasmuch as related quotations are grouped together by their respective categories. All aspects of journalism, for example, are relevant to each other; thus, the section *Journalism* embraces all phases of the news media. Similarly, quotations pertaining to the U.S. Presidency, Congress, revenue-sharing, etc., are together in the section *Government.*

MISCELLANEOUS

(A)   Except where otherwise indicated or obviously to the contrary, all universities, colleges, organizations and business firms mentioned in this book are located in the United States; similarly, references made to "national," "Federal," "this country," "the nation," etc., refer to the United States.

(B)   In most cases, organizations whose titles end with "of the United States" are Federal government agencies.

SELECTION OF CATEGORIES

The selected categories reflect, in the Editors' opinion, the most widely discussed public-interest subjects, those which readily fall into the over-all sphere of "current events." They represent topics continuously covered by the mass media because of their inherent relevance to the changing world scene. Most of the categories are permanent; they appear in each annual edition of *WHAT THEY SAID.* However, because of the transient character of some subjects, there may be categories which appear one year and may not be repeated.

SELECTION OF SPEAKERS

The following persons are *always* considered eligible for inclusion in *WHAT THEY SAID:* top-level officials of all branches of national, state and major local governments (both U.S. and foreign), including all United States Senators and Representatives; top-echelon military officers;

college and university presidents, chancellors and professors; chairmen and presidents of major corporations; heads of national public-oriented organizations and associations; national and internationally known diplomats; recognized celebrities from the entertainment and literary spheres and the arts generally; sports figures of national stature; commentators on the world scene who are recognized as such and who command the attention of the mass media.

The determination of what and who are "major" and "recognized" must, necessarily, be made by the Editors of *WHAT THEY SAID* based on objective personal judgment.

Also, some persons, while not recognized as prominent in a particular professional area, have nevertheless attracted an unusual amount of attention in connection with a specific issue or event. These people, too, are considered for inclusion, depending upon the circumstances involved.

SELECTION OF QUOTATIONS

The quotations selected for inclusion in *WHAT THEY SAID* obviously represent a decided minority of the seemingly endless volume of quoted material appearing in the media each year. The process of selection is scrupulously objective insofar as the partisan views of the Editors are concerned (see *About Fairness,* below). However, it is clear that the Editors must decide which quotations *per se* are suitable for inclusion, and in doing so look for comments that are aptly stated, offer insight into the subject being discussed, or into the speaker, and provide—for today as well as for future reference—a thought which readers will find useful for understanding the issues and the personalities that make up a year on this planet.

ABOUT FAIRNESS

The Editors of *WHAT THEY SAID* understand the necessity of being impartial when compiling a book of this kind. As a result, there has been no bias in the selection of the quotations, the choice of speakers or the manner of editing. Relevance of the statements and the status of the speakers are the exclusive criteria for inclusion, without any regard whatsoever to the personal beliefs and views of the Editors. Furthermore, every effort has been made to include a multiplicity of opinions and ideas from a wide cross-section of speakers on each topic. Nevertheless, should there appear to be, on some controversial issues, a majority of material favoring one point of view over another, it is simply the result of there having been more of those views expressed during the year, reported by the media and objectively considered suitable by the Editors of *WHAT THEY SAID* (see *Selection of Quotations,* above). Also, since persons in politics and government account for a large percentage of the speakers in *WHAT THEY SAID*, there may exist a heavier weight of opinion favoring the political philosophy of those in office at the time, whether in the United States Congress, the Administration, or in foreign capitals. This is natural and to be expected and should not be construed as a reflection of agreement or disagreement with that philosophy on the part of the Editors of *WHAT THEY SAID.*

Abbreviations

The following are abbreviations used by the speakers in this volume. Rather than defining them each time they appear in the quotations, this list will facilitate reading and avoid unnecessary repetition.

ABC:	American Broadcasting Companies
ACLU:	American Civil Liberties Union
ACT:	Action for Children's Television
AMA:	American Medical Association
AP:	Associated Press
ATP:	Association of Tennis Professionals
BBC:	British Broadcasting Corporation
CAB:	Civil Aeronautics Board
CBS:	Columbia Broadcasting System (CBS, Inc.)
CEO:	chief executive officer
CIA:	Central Intelligence Agency
CPI:	cost-price index
D.C.:	District of Columbia
DH:	designated hitter
DIA:	Defense Intelligence Agency
DOE:	Department of Energy
EPA:	Environmental Protection Agency
ERA:	Equal Rights Amendment
FBI:	Federal Bureau of Investigation
FCC:	Federal Communications Commission
FDR:	Franklin Delano Roosevelt
FHA:	Federal Housing Administration
FOI:	Freedom of Information Act
FTC:	Federal Trade Commission
GAO:	General Accounting Office
GM:	General Motors Corporation

WHAT THEY SAID IN 1978

GNP: gross national product
GSA: General Services Administration
HEW: Department of Health, Education and Welfare
IBM: International Business Machines Corporation
ICBM: intercontinental ballistic missile
ICC: Interstate Commerce Commission
IRA: Irish Republican Army
KGB: Soviet secret police
MGM: Metro-Goldwyn-Mayer, Inc.
MIRV: multiple independently targeted re-entry vehicles
MPAA: Motion Picture Association of America
NATO: North Atlantic Treaty Organization
NBA: National Basketball Association
NBC: National Broadcasting Company
NFL: National Football League
NOW: National Organization for Women
OAU: Organization of African Unity
OPEC: Organization of Petroleum Exporting Countries
PBS: Public Broadcasting Service
PLO: Palestine Liberation Organization
PTA: Parent-Teachers Association
RCA: Radio Corporation of America
RFE: Radio Free Europe
RL: Radio Liberty
SALT: strategic-arms limitation talks
SWAPO: South-West Africa People's Organization
TV: television
UN: United Nations
UPI: United Press International
U.S.:   United States
U.S.A.:   United States of America
U.S.A.C.:   United States Auto Club
U.S.S.R.:   Union of Soviet Socialist Republics
VOA: Voice of America

Party affiliation of United States Senators, Representatives and Governors—

D: Democratic

I: Independent

R: Republican

The Quote of the Year

As a young man and as President, I have learned some things about leadership. One is that the fear of failure is one of the greatest obstacles to progress. How timid we are when we challenge some obstacle or engage in some contest or set a high goal for ourselves. How timid we are that we might fail in the effort and perhaps be the subject of ridicule or criticism or scorn. It is always a mistake to try for universal approbation, universal approval, because if you fear making anyone mad, then you ultimately probe for the lowest common denominator of human achievement.

JIMMY CARTER
President of the United States

Before Future Farmers of America, Kansas City

PART ONE

National Affairs

The State of the Union Address

Delivered by Jimmy Carter, President of the United States, to a joint session of Congress, in the House of Representatives, Washington, January 19, 1978.

Two years ago today we had the first caucus in Iowa, and one year ago tomorrow I walked from here to the White House to take up the duties of President of the United States. I didn't know it then when I walked, but I've been trying to save energy ever since. I return tonight to fulfill one of those duties of the Constitution: to "give to the Congress"—and to the nation—"information on the state of the union."

Militarily, politically, economically and in spirit, the state of our union is sound. We are a great country, a strong country, a vital and a dynamic country—and so we will remain. We are a confident people and a hard-working people, a decent and a compassionate people—and so we will remain.

I want to speak to you tonight about where we are and where we must go, about what we have done and what we must do—and I want to pledge to you my best efforts and ask you to pledge yours. Each generation of Americans has to face circumstances not of its own choosing, but by which its character is measured and its spirit is tested.

America's Spirit

There are times of emergency, when a nation and its leaders must bring their energies to bear on a single urgent task. That was the duty Abraham Lincoln faced when our land was torn apart by conflict in the War Between the States. That was the duty faced by Franklin Roosevelt when he led America out of an economic depression, and again when he led America to victory in war.

There are other times when there is no single overwhelming crisis—yet profound national interests are at stake. At such time the risk of inaction can be equally great. It becomes the task of leaders to call forth the vast and restless energies of our people to build for the future. That is what Harry Truman did in the years after the second World War, when we helped Europe and Japan rebuild themselves and secured an international order that has protected freedom from aggression.

We live in such times now—and we face such duties. We have come through a long period of turmoil and doubt, but we have once again found our moral course, and with a new spirit we are striving to express our best instincts to the rest of the world. There is all across our land a growing sense of peace and a sense of common purpose. This sense of unity cannot be expressed in programs or in legislation or in dollars; it is an achievement that belongs to every individual American. This unity ties together and it towers over all our efforts here in Washington, and it serves as an inspiring beacon for all of us who are elected to serve.

This new atmosphere demands a new spirit—a partnership between those of us who lead and those who elect. The foundations of this partnership are truth, the courage to face hard decisions, concern for one another and the common good over special interest, and a basic faith and trust in the wisdom and strength and judgment of the American people.

For the first time in a generation, we are not haunted by a major international crisis or by domestic turmoil, and we now have a rare and a priceless opportunity to address persistent problems and burdens which come to us as a nation—quietly and steadily getting worse over the years.

As President, I have had to ask you, the members of Congress, and you, the American people, to come to grips with some of the most difficult and hard questions facing our society. We must make a maximum effort—because if we do not aim for the best, we are very likely to achieve little. I see no benefit to the country if we delay, because the problems will only get worse.

Government's Role

We need patience and good will, but we really need to realize that there is a limit to the role and the function of government. Government cannot solve our problems. It can't set our goals. It cannot define our vision. Government cannot eliminate poverty, or provide a bountiful economy, or reduce inflation, or save our cities, or cure illiteracy, or provide energy. And government cannot mandate goodness. Only a true partnership between government and the people can ever hope to reach these goals.

Those of us who govern can sometimes inspire, and we can identify needs and marshal resources, but we simply cannot be the managers of everything and everybody. We here in Washington must move away from crisis management, and we must establish clear goals for the future—immediate and the distant future—which will let us work together and not in conflict.

Energy

Never again should we neglect a growing crisis like the shortage of energy, where further delay will only lead to more harsh and painful solutions. Every day we spend more than 120 million dollars for foreign oil. This slows our economic growth, it lowers the value of the dollar overseas, and it aggravates unemployment and inflation here at home. Now, we know what we must do: increase production; we must cut down on waste, and we must use more of those fuels which are plentiful and more permanent. We must be fair to people, and we must not disrupt our nation's economy and our budget. Now, that sounds simple, but I recognize the difficulties involved.

I know that it is not easy for the Congress to act. But the fact remains that on the energy legislation we have failed the American people. Almost five years after the oil embargo dramatized the problem for us all, we still do not have a national energy program. Not much longer can we tolerate this stalemate. It undermines our national interests both at home and abroad. We must succeed, and I believe we will.

Economy

Our main task at home this year, with energy a central element, is the nation's economy. We must continue the recovery and further cut unemployment and inflation.

Last year was a good one for the United States. We reached all of our major economic goals for 1977.

Four million new jobs were created—an all-time record—and the number of unemployed dropped by more than a million. Unemployment right now is the lowest it has been since 1974, and not since World War II has such a high percentage of American people been employed. The rate of inflation went down. There was a good growth in business profits and investment—the source of more jobs for our workers—and a higher standard of living for all our people. After taxes and inflation, there was a healthy increase in workers' wages.

And this year our country will have the first 2-trillion-dollar economy in the history of the world. Now, we are proud of this progress the first year, but we must do even better in the future. We still have serious problems on which all of us must work together. Our trade deficit is too large, inflation is still too high, and too many Americans still do not have a job.

Now, I don't have any simple answers for all these problems. But we have developed an economic policy that is working because it is simple, balanced and fair. It is based on four principles:

First, the economy must keep on expanding to produce new jobs and better income which our people need. The fruits of growth must be widely shared. More jobs must be made available to those who have been bypassed until now, and the tax system must be made fairer and simpler. Secondly, private business—and not the Government—must lead the expansion in the future. Third, we must lower the rate of inflation and keep it down. Inflation slows down economic growth, and it is the most cruel to the poor and also to the elderly and others who live on fixed incomes. And, fourth, we must contribute to the strength of the world economy.

Taxes

I will announce detailed proposals for improving our tax system later this week. We can make our tax laws fairer; we can make them simpler and easier to understand, and at the same time we can—and we will—reduce the tax burden on American citizens by 25 billion dollars. The tax reforms and the tax reductions go together. Only with the long-overdue reforms will the full tax cut be advisable.

Almost 17 billion dollars in income-tax cuts will go to individuals. Ninety-six per cent of all American taxpayers will see their taxes go down. For a typical family of four this means an annual saving of more than $250 a year—or a tax reduction of about 20 per cent. A further 2-billion-dollar cut in excise taxes will give more relief and also contribute directly to lowering the rate of inflation. And we will also provide strong additional incentives for business investment and growth through substantial cuts in the corporate tax rates and improvement in the investment tax credit.

Now, these tax proposals will increase opportunity everywhere in the nation, but additional jobs for the disadvantaged deserve special attention.

Jobs

We have already passed laws to assure equal access to the voting booth and to restaurants and to schools, to housing—and laws to permit access to jobs. But job opportunity—the chance to earn a decent living—is also a basic human right which we cannot and will not ignore.

A major priority for our nation is the final elimination of the barriers that restrict the opportunities available to women and also to black people and Hispanics and other minorities. We have come a long way toward that goal, but there is still much to do. What we inherited from the past must not be permitted to shackle us in the future.

I'll be asking you for a substantial increase in funds for public jobs for our young people, and I also am recommending that the Congress continue the public-service-employment programs at more than twice the level of a year ago. When welfare reform is completed, we'll have more than a million additional jobs, so that those on welfare who are able to work can work.

However, again, we know that in our free society, private business is still the best source of new jobs. Therefore, I will propose a new program to encourage businesses to hire young and disadvantaged Americans. These young people only need skills—and a chance—in order to take their place in our economic system. Let's give them the chance they need. A major step in the right direction would be the early passage of a greatly improved Humphrey-Hawkins bill.

Budget

My budget for 1979 addresses these national needs, but it is lean and tight. I have cut waste wherever possible. I am proposing an increase of less than 2 per cent after adjusting for inflation—the smallest increase in the federal budget in four years. Lately, federal spending has taken a steadily increasing portion of what Americans produce. Our new budget reverses that trend, and later I hope to bring the Government's toll down even further—and with your help we'll do that.

In time of high employment and a strong economy, deficit spending should not be a feature of our budget. As the economy continues to gain strength and as our unemployment rates continue to fall, revenues will grow. With careful planning, efficient management and a proper restraint on spending, we can move rapidly toward a balanced budget—and we will. Next year the budget deficit will be only slightly less than this year—but one third of the deficit is due to the necessary tax cuts that I proposed. This year the right choice is to reduce the burden on taxpayers and provide more jobs for our people.

Inflation

The third element in our program is a renewed attack on inflation. We've learned the hard way that high unemployment will not prevent or cure inflation.

Government can help us by stimulating private investment and by maintaining a responsible economic policy. Through a new top-level review process, we will do a better job of reducing Government regulation that drives up costs and drives up prices. But, again, Government alone cannot bring down the rate of inflation. When a level of high inflation is expected to continue, then companies raise prices to protect their profit margins against prospective increases in wages and other costs, while workers demand higher wages as protection against expected price increases. It's like an escalation in the arms race, and—understandably—no one wants to disarm alone.

Now, no one firm or group of workers can halt this process. It is an effort that we must all make together. I'm therefore asking government, business, labor and other groups to join in a voluntary program to moderate inflation by holding wage and price increases in each sector of the economy during 1978 below the average increases of the last two years. I do not believe in wage-and-price controls. A sincere commitment to voluntary constraint provides a way—perhaps the only way—to fight inflation without Government interference.

Farmers

As I came into the Capitol tonight, I saw the farmers—my fellow farmers—standing out in the snow. I'm familiar with their problem, and I know from Congress's action that you are, too.

When I was running Carter's warehouse, we had spread on our own farms 5-10-15 fertilizer for about $40 a ton. The last time I was home the price was about $100 a ton. The cost of nitrogen has gone up 150 per cent, and the price of products that farmers sell has either stayed the same or gone down a little.

Now, this past year—1977—you, the Congress, and I together passed a new Agricultural Act. It went into effect October 1. It'll have its first impact on the 1978 crops. It will help a great deal. It'll add 6½ billion dollars or more to help the farmers with their price supports and target prices.

Last year we had the highest level of exports of farm products in the history of our country: 24 billion dollars. We expect to have more this year. We'll be working together. But I think it's incumbent on us to monitor very carefully the farm situation and continue to work harmoniously with the farmers of our country. What's best for the farmers, the farm families, in the long run is also best for the consumers of our country.

Trade

Economic success at home is also the key to success in our international economic policy. An effective energy program, strong investment and productivity, and controlled inflation will provide our trade balance and balance it, and it will help to protect the integrity of the dollar overseas. By working closely with our friends abroad, we can promote the economic health of the whole world—and with fair and balanced agreements, lowering the barriers to trade.

Despite the inevitable pressures that build up when the world economy suffers from high unemployment, we must firmly resist the demands for self-defeating protectionism. But free trade must also be fair trade. And I am determined to protect American industry and American workers against foreign-trade practices which are unfair or illegal.

In a separate written message to Congress, I have outlined other domestic initiatives, such as welfare reform, consumer protection, basic education skills, urban policy, reform of our labor laws, and national health care later on this year. I will not repeat those tonight, but there are several other points that I would like to make directly to you.

Government Growth

During these past years, Americans have seen our Government grow far from us. For some citizens the Government has almost become like a foreign country—so strange and distant that we've often had to deal with it through trained ambassadors who have sometimes become too powerful and too influential: lawyers, accountants and lobbyists. This cannot go on.

We must have what Abraham Lincoln wanted—a Government for the people. We have made progress toward that kind of Government. You've given me the authority I requested to reorganize the federal bureaucracy, and I am using that authority. We've already begun a series of reorganization plans which will be completed over a period of three years. We have also proposed abolishing almost 500 federal advisory and other commissions and boards.

But I know that the American people are still sick and tired of federal paper work and red tape.

Regulations

Bit by bit, we are chopping down the thicket of unnecessary federal regulations by which Government too often interferes in our personal lives and our personal business. We have cut the public's federal paper-work load by more than 12 per cent in less than a year—and we are not through cutting.

We have made a good start on turning the gobbledygook of federal regulations into plain English that people can understand, but we know that we still have a long way to go.

We have brought together parts of 11 different Government agencies to create a new Department of Energy—and now it is time to take another major step by creating a separate Department of Education.

Civil Service

But even the best-organized government will only be as effective as the people who carry out its policies. For this reason, I consider civil-service reform to be absolutely vital. Worked out with the civil servants themselves, this reorganization plan will restore the merit principle to a system which has grown into a bureaucratic maze. It will provide greater management flexibility and better rewards for better performance without compromising job security.

Then and only then can we have a Government that is efficient, open and truly worthy of our people's understanding and respect. I have promised that we will have such a Government, and I intend to keep that promise.

Foreign Affairs

In our foreign policy, the separation of people from government has been in the past a source of weakness and error. In a democratic system like ours, foreign-policy decisions must be able to stand the test of public examination and public debate. If we make a mistake in this Administration, it will be on the side of frankness and openness with the American people.

In our modern world, when the deaths of literally millions of people can result from a few terrifying seconds of destruction, the path of national strength and security is identical to the path of peace.

Tonight I am happy to report that because we are strong, our nation is at peace with the world. We are a confident nation. We've restored a moral basis for our foreign policy. The very heart of our identity as a nation is our firm commitment to human rights. We stand for human rights because we believe that government has as a purpose to promote the well-being of its citizens. This is true in our domestic policy; it's also true in our foreign policy. The world must know that in support of human rights the United States will stand firm.

We expect no quick or easy results, but there has been significant movement toward greater freedom and humanity in several parts of the world. Thousands of political prisoners have been freed. The leaders of the world—even our ideological adversaries—now see that their attitude toward fundamental human rights affects their standing in the international community, and it affects their relations with the United States.

To serve the interests of every American, our foreign policy has three major goals.

The first and prime concern is and will remain the security of our country. Security is based on our national will and security is based on the strength of our armed forces. We have the will, and militarily we are very strong.

Security also comes through the strength of our alliances. We have reconfirmed our commitment to the defense of Europe, and this year we will demonstrate that commitment by further modernizing and strengthening our military capabilities there.

Security can also be enhanced by agreements with potential adversaries which reduce the threat of nuclear disaster while maintaining our own relative strategic capability.

In areas of peaceful competition with the Soviet Union we will continue to more than hold our own. At the same time, we are negotiating—with quiet confidence, without haste, with careful determination—to ease the tensions between us and to insure greater stability and security.

SALT/Proliferation

The Strategic Arms Limitation Talks have been long and difficult. We want a mutual limit on both the quality and the quantity of the giant nuclear arsenals of both nations, and then we want actual reductions in strategic arms as a major step toward the ultimate elimination of nuclear weapons from the face of the earth. If these talks result in an agreement this year—and I trust they will—I pledge to you that the agreement will maintain and enhance the stability of the world's strategic balance and the security of the United States.

For 30 years, concerted but unsuccessful efforts have been made to ban the testing of atomic explosives—both military weapons and peaceful nuclear devices. We are hard at work

with Great Britain and the Soviet Union on an agreement which will stop testing and will protect our national security and provide for adequate verification of compliance. We are now making, I believe, good progress toward this comprehensive ban on nuclear explosions.

We are also working vigorously to halt the proliferation of nuclear weapons among the nations of the world which do not now have them, and to reduce the deadly global traffic in conventional-arms sales. Our stand for peace is suspect if we are also the principal arms merchant of the world. So we've decided to cut down our arms transfers abroad on a year-by-year basis and to work with other major arms exporters to encourage their similar constraint.

Middle East Peace

Every American has a stake in our second major goal: a world at peace. In a nuclear age, each of us is threatened when peace is not secured everywhere. We are trying to promote harmony in those parts of the world where major differences exist among other nations and threaten international peace.

Mideast Role Is "Thankless and Controversial"

In the Middle East, we are contributing our good offices to maintain the momentum of the current negotiations and to keep open the lines of communication among the Middle Eastern leaders. The whole world has a great stake in the success of these efforts. This is a precious opportunity for a historic settlement of long-standing conflict—an opportunity which may never come again in our lifetime. Our role has been difficult and sometimes thankless and controversial, but it has been constructive, and it has been necessary—and it will continue.

World Economy

Our third major foreign-policy goal is one that touches the life of every American citizen every day: world economic growth and stability. This requires strong economic performance by the industrialized democracies like ourselves and progress in resolving the global energy crisis.

Last fall, with the help of others, we succeeded in our vigorous efforts to maintain the stability of the price of oil. But—as many foreign leaders have emphasized—to me personally and I'm sure to you, the greatest future contribution that America can make to the world economy would be an effective energy-conservation program here at home. We will not hesitate to take the actions needed to protect the integrity of the American dollar.

We are trying to develop a more just international system. And in this spirit we are supporting the struggle for human development in Africa, in Asia and in Latin America.

Panama Canal

Finally, the world is watching to see how we act on one of our most important and controversial items of business: approval of the Panama Canal treaties. The treaties now before the Senate are the result of the work of four Administrations—two Democratic, two Republican. They guarantee that the canal will be open always for unrestricted use by the ships of the world. Our ships have the right to go to the head of the line for priority of passage in times of emergency or need. We retain the permanent right to defend the canal with our own military forces if necessary to guarantee its openness and its neutrality.

Panama Canal Treaties: "Clear Advantage" to U.S.

The treaties are to the clear advantage of ourselves, the Panamanians and the other users of the canal. Ratifying the Panama Canal treaties will demonstrate our good faith to the world, discourage the spread of hostile ideologies in this Hemisphere and directly contribute to the economic well-being and the security of the United States. [Long applause]

Now I have to say that that's very welcome applause.

Foreign Policy Aims

There were two moments on my recent journey which, for me, confirmed the final aims of our foreign policy and what it always must be. One was in a little village in India, where I met a people as passionately attached to their rights and liberties as we are—but whose children have a far smaller chance for good health or food or education or human fulfillment than a child born in this country. The other moment was in Warsaw, capital of a nation twice devastated by war in this century. There, people have rebuilt the city which war's destruction took from them—but what was new only emphasized clearly what was lost.

What I saw in those two places crystallized for me the purposes of our own nation's policy: to insure economic justice, to advance human rights, to resolve conflicts without violence and to proclaim in our great democracy our constant faith in the liberty and dignity of human beings everywhere.

Summation

We Americans have a great deal of work to do together. In the end, how well we do that work will depend on the spirit in which we approach it. We must seek fresh answers, unhindered by the stale prescriptions of the past. It has been said that our best years are behind us, but I say again that America's best is still ahead. We have emerged from bitter experiences chastened but proud, confident once again, ready to face challenges once again, and united once again.

We come together tonight at a solemn time. Last week the Senate lost a good and honest man—Lee Metcalf of Montana. And today the flag of the United States flew at half-mast from this Capitol and from American installations and ships all over the world—in mourning for Senator Hubert Humphrey. Because he exemplified so well the joy and the zest of living, his death reminds us not so much of our own mortality but of the possibilities offered to us by life. He always looked to the future with a special American kind of confidence, of hope and enthusiasm. And the best way that we can honor him is by following his example.

Our task, to use the words of Senator Humphrey, is "reconciliation, rebuilding and rebirth": reconciliation of private needs and interests into a higher purpose; rebuilding the old dreams of justice and liberty, and country and community; rebirth of our faith in the common good.

Each of us here tonight—and all who are listening in your homes—must rededicate ourselves to serving the common good. We are a community, a beloved community—all of us. Our individual fates are linked, our futures intertwined. And if we act in that knowledge and in that spirit together, as the Bible says, we can move mountains.

Saul Bellow
Author

1

We Americans are in a peculiar position when it comes to brainwashing, because we've been spared the worst in modern history. We've been spared the holocaust—both wars—we've been spared totalitarianism, the forced-labor camps, the police regimes and all the rest of that. We are the *avante-garde* of safety, comfort, affluence, security. We're also witnesses to the horrible effects that safety, comfort, affluence, privilege can have. I sometimes think we're stuck somewhere in the middle. We no longer have nature and history to punch us in the nose. Other nations could safely depend on that punch in the nose to keep them realistic. I think we've lost that principle of realism in the United States—if we ever had it. Most of us are spoiled and blundering, and we believe, in a very shallow way, in the goodness of our intentions. I think that this is why many thoughtful Americans are so vigilant against Elsie Dinsmorism. They fear it and look upon it with the utmost suspicion, and I think rightly so, because we've been guilty of shallow, reprehensible optimism.

Interview/The Christian Science Monitor, 3-1:29.

Michael Caine
British actor

2

In the U.S., you have this incentive to work and to make money under a tax system which is not as penal as ours [in Britain]. You have this work ethic which I love—and this marvelous equality which made me feel instantly comfortable. I'm a great Americanophile as well as a tremendously patriotic Englishman. You have much more freedom in America than we have in England—or anywhere. I think in my most despondent moments about England that we

will all wind up in the United States if you have any room left.

Interview/U.S. News & World Report, 1-9:66.

Jimmy Carter
President of the United States

3

We all want something to be done about our problems—except when the solutions affect us. We want to conserve energy, but not to change our wasteful habits. We favor sacrifice, as long as others go first. We want to abolish tax loopholes—unless it's our loophole. We denounce special interests, except for our own. No act of Congress, no program of our government, no order of my own can bring out the quality that we need—to change from the preoccupation with self that can cripple our national will, to a willingness to acknowledge and to sacrifice for the common good.

*Before American Society of
Newspaper Editors, Washington,
April 11/The Washington Post, 4-12:(A)3.*

Rosalynn Carter
*Wife of President of the
United States Jimmy Carter*

4

[Responding to exiled Soviet author Alexander Solzhenitsyn who recently charged that the U.S. has grown weak and decayed]: Alexander Solzhenitsyn says he can feel the pressure of evil across our land. Well, I do not sense the pressure of evil at all. There is a pervasive desire among Americans to live a useful life, to correct the defects in our society, and to make our nation even greater than it is ... This is not a sign of a society that has lost its spirit ... Fifty million of us are volunteering freely of our time and talents as resources to fill a broad range of human and social needs. Last year the philanthropic contributions in our nation were over

WHAT THEY SAID IN 1978

$35-billion from private citizens, foundations and corporations. That is not a sign of "unchecked materialism." That is not "social irresponsibility."

At National Press Club luncheon,
Washington, June 20/
The Christian Science Monitor, 6-21:2.

Ramsey Clark
Lawyer; Former Attorney General
of the United States

1

I do believe that materialism is a great failing of the American people. Our whole value patterns are based on greed. We measure success in terms of accumulation of wealth. It's very destructive.

Interview, New York/Los Angeles
Herald Examiner, 11-26:(A)11.

James Dickey
Author

2

Anybody who wants to learn about the South should get to know her women. They are tough, loving, frail and powerful. They hold so many of our best secrets.

San Francisco Examiner & Chronicle,
10-29:[This World] 2.

Oriana Fallaci
Italian journalist

3

In America I like the telephones that work so well, even for long-distance calls; and the conditioned air system and the splendid heating system; and the cabs where you can smoke; and the New York-Washington, New York-Boston shuttles—something the Italians will never learn to install even between Rome and Milan; and the incinerators where you can throw the Sunday *New York Times* and even the Sunday *Los Angeles Times* and *The Washington Post*; and my food shop which is open till one in the morning; and the TV which has so many channels giving you a choice—and in the night if you suffer insomnia you can always see a good old movie; and the milk half-and-half which is the best in the world; and Lark cigarettes which are the only ones I've smoked for the past 15 years; and Walter Cronkite and Central Park and Arizona.

Interview, Rome/
Los Angeles Herald Examiner, 5-7:(F)6.

Gordon (Bud) Filer
"King of the Hoboes"

4

[On the state of hoboing today]: ... hoofing is finished. Now if you're broke you go on welfare. You don't have to grab a freight and move on to somewhere else where there might be work. And if you do have the wanderlust, who would want to travel in a box-car when he can hitch a ride on the highway and travel in an air-conditioned car?

Interview, Anchorage, Alaska/
The Washington Post, 9-29:(D)14.

Eric F. Goldman
Professor of American history,
Princeton University

5

The '60s left a profound legacy in the country. There is a new quasi-isolation, a new role for women—not just women's lib but the fact that 50 per cent of the women are working—a new upper middle class, and other factors affecting government and life. This period was a watershed as important as the American Revolution or the Civil War in causing changes in the United States.

Interview/The New York Times, 3-10:(C)27.

Alex Haley
Author

6

Almost all black people in this country are comprised of part African blood, part European and part Indian. I feel it reflects democracy in America more than anything else. When you see us in our various complexions ranging from black to white, and when you reflect that those Africans who were brought here were consistently African black, you realize that what one looks at today is really walking genetics.

Interview, Los Angeles/
The Christian Science Monitor, 1-19:25.

Shearon Harris
*Chairman, Carolina Power & Light
Company; Chairman, Chamber of
Commerce of the United States*

1

I am very much of a fundamentalist, and I have a tremendous appreciation for the value of experience. Most everything we do as a democratic society has evolved out of some kind of experience. I believe that we, as a country, need to concern ourselves more with some of the fundamentals that we may have departed from.
Interview/Nation's Business, May:59.

Eric Hoffer
Philosopher

2

Courage is the quality I most admire. I pray that the American people get angry, because anger is a prelude to courage. The majority has been bused, bamboozled, brainwashed and bullied—and they don't strike back!
Interview, San Francisco/People, 1-16:31.

Jesse L. Jackson
*Civil-rights leader; President,
Operation PUSH (People United to
Save Humanity)*

3

We're in a civilizational crisis ... Americans have been traumatized by distrust. This generation of adults hasn't gained the confidence of the current generation of youth. We've got too many doctors who put personal wealth ahead of the public health, too many lawyers who are more concerned with judgeships than justice. The result has been an ethical collapse.
Parade, 3-19:4.

Howard Jarvis
*Co-author of California property-tax
limitation measure (Proposition 13)*

4

We think that the people who own homes in the United States are the most important people in this country. We think that the most important thing in this country is to preserve the right to own private property because it is the Number 1 extension of human rights in the United States. Without the ownership of private property in the United States, freedom will disappear. You hear the President [Carter] talking all over this world about human rights, but he never says what they are. And the reason I think he doesn't say what they are is that so many countries we are trying to cozy up to don't have property rights. ... the people who wrote the Constitution of the United States said the people of the United States shall be protected in their life, liberty and property. They didn't say life, liberty and welfare, or life, liberty and food stamps. They said life, liberty and property. The ownership of property and the right of free people to acquire property is the most important part of human rights, and without that right we don't have any other right.
*TV-radio interview/"Meet the Press,"
National Broadcasting Company, 6-18.*

Reginald H. Jones
Chairman, General Electric Company

5

Unfortunately ... [in the U.S. today] there is a growing aversion to risk. Having learned the trick of self-sustaining economic progress through capital formation, we begin to overestimate our powers. We start to believe that, if we really want to, we can protect everybody from the risks and vicissitudes of life. We dream of Utopia. Unfortunately, the road to Utopia leads to bankruptcy. Here in the United States, the fastest-growing element of the Federal budget is that portion designed to protect us against the risks of unemployment, sickness and old age—the so-called transfer payments by which money is transferred from the producers to the non-producers in our population. In 10 years, this item has increased from 25 per cent to 40 per cent of the Federal budget. It is the major driving force that has brought our Federal budget to the astounding level of half a trillion dollars a year ... The whole structure of government is directed toward the redistribution rather than the creation of wealth. The impulse to reduce everyone to a common level, to assure not equality of opportunity but equality of results—no matter how poor the results—is in many places the prevailing philosophy ... What we must avoid is a loss of nerve. What we must resist is the stifling of the human spirit. What

13

WHAT THEY SAID IN 1978

(REGINALD H. JONES)

we must maintain is our faith in the human adventure.

The Dallas Times Herald, 12-17:(G)2.

Mike Mansfield
United States Ambassador to Japan;
Former U.S. Senator, D-Montana

1

We [the U.S.] have to bring about a restoration of American pride. We have to rejuvenate our knowhow and go-get-'em and get-ahead psychology. We have to quit blaming other people and look at the motes in our own eyes; and if we blame other people, we ought to do it on an equitable basis.

TV-radio interview/"Meet the Press,"
National Broadcasting Company, 10-29.

William J. McGill
President, Columbia University

2

... human-rights ferment now continues at fever pitch in the United States. New constituencies appear almost monthly. Within the last two years we have seen the emergence of gay people, the handicapped and the elderly as organized constituencies, each with a special psychological identity and each with its own agenda for social change. Once again dramatic conflict, this time on behalf of human rights and the special interests of a multitude of small constituencies in the United States, has created amazement and awe throughout the world. Others wonder as they watch us how we can absorb all these unprecedented strivings without tearing ourselves apart.

At University of Nevada, Reno, Oct. 6/
Vital Speeches, 12-1:103.

George S. McGovern
United States Senator, D-South Dakota

3

We worry about defending our nation as a physical entity; we must also defend it as a source of justice and mercy. National security includes the condition of our national spirit as much as the size of our nuclear arsenal. The gravest threat today is not a foreign adversary, but an enemy within. That enemy is not a conspiracy or a fifth column; it is inside ourselves and among our leaders. It is the sense of futility. It is the dulled conscience. It is the lost vision.

Before Americans for Democratic Action, June 17/
The Washington Post, 6-25:(D)6.

Richard M. Nixon
Former President of the United States

4

We shall have to admit, there has been some weakening of will among some leaders in some very important areas of American life ... Others simply have given up on America even though they won't say it that bluntly, because they are so blinded by those things that are wrong they can't see so much that is right. They want us to turn inward and away from the leadership that has been imposed upon us whether we want it or not.

At dedication of recreation complex in his
honor, Hyden, Ky., July 2/
Los Angeles Times, 7-3:(1)9.

Herbert Passin
Sociologist, School of International
Affairs, Columbia University

5

We used to think of this as a lean, free-enterprise country, but we're becoming second-rate, as Britain did. Their problem was national featherbedding to benefit unions. We're heading for national equalizing to accommodate our civil divisions.

U.S. News & World Report, 11-27:56.

Ronald Reagan
Former Governor of California (R)

6

... if we [the U.S.] are not to shoulder the burdens of leadership in the free world, then who will? The alternatives are neither pleasant nor acceptable. Great nations which fail to meet their responsibilities are consigned to the dustbin of history. We grew from that small, weak republic which had as its assets spirit, optimism, faith in God and an unshakable belief that free men and women could govern themselves wisely. We became the leader of the

(RONALD REAGAN)

free world, an example for all those who cherish freedom. If we are to continue to be that example—if we are to preserve our own freedom—we must understand those who would dominate us and deal with them with determination. We must shoulder our burden with our eyes fixed on the future, but recognizing the realities of today, not counting on mere hope or wishes. We must be willing to carry out our responsibility as the custodian of individual freedom. Then we will achieve our destiny to be as a shining city on a hill for all mankind to see.

Before Conservative Political Action Conference, Washington, March 17/Vital Speeches, 5-1:425.

Mstislav Rostropovich
Cellist; Musical director, National Symphony Orchestra, Washington

1

[On his leaving the Soviet Union to come to the West] : I have to tell you that I love America very much. I sit in my Watergate apartment in Washington the other day and the telephone rings and it is [President] Jimmy Carter. We had a very nice and interesting talk. Now America is my second *patrie*. Even my daughter, Olga, has become an American. She called me yesterday from New York and said, "Papa, I'm depressed." I ask why. She says, "Because the weather is bad." Well, if at her age she can be depressed over bad weather, that means she must be an American. In Russia, young people get depressed over many things, but never about the weather.

Miami Beach, Fla., Nov. 26/ The New York Times, 11-28:(C)6.

Arthur M. Schlesinger, Jr.
Historian; Professor of humanities, City University of New York

2

The yearnings of today's society aren't any different from those of other periods in our nation's history . . . There's no inexorable moral decline in America. We're in a period of moral growth, not decay. Public sensitivity to

corrupt behavior is greater than ever before. Maybe too great.

Parade, 3-19:4.

3

If you look at American history in this century, there has been a cyclical rhythm—two active decades early in the century: the progressive era and World War I; that left the nation in a period of exhaustion. Then there was a period of repose in the 1920s, followed by two more active decades in the '30s and '40s with the New Deal and World War II. Once again, that left the nation exhausted and you had the 1950s, the years of Eisenhower stagnation, followed by the 1960s, with the turbulence of the civil-rights movement, the black rebellion, the war in Vietnam, the disaffection of the young. After that, came the utter exhaustion of the 1970s. These periods of repose give time for the national batteries to be recharged and also mean that a lot of problems accumulate. So I can imagine that, in the 1980s, the dam will burst again and we will have another period of forward movement.

Interview, New York/The Christian Science Monitor, 10-23:(B)18.

Richard L. Strout
Political columnist (TRB), "The New Republic"; Reporter, "The Christian Science Monitor"

4

We have a clumsy form of government. We deserve a better one. You see it in various ways: We elect a President first, and then find out who he is. There's been a national failure of nerve, of will-power, over the energy problem. We can't seem to make ourselves do what we have to do. I don't want to be too pessimistic, but the last 30 years have seen a decline in American preeminence . . . Also, I see a failure in the national nerve on this question of illegal immigrants. Mexico City is on the way to becoming the biggest city in the world. We have a million illegal immigrants a year coming in, taking jobs—mainly from black people—and we don't know how to deal with it.

Interview, Washington, March 14/ The Washington Post, 3-15:(B)4.

WHAT THEY SAID IN 1978

Barbara Tuchman
Author, Historian

1

[On the future of the U.S.]: I have such a tremendous faith in the virtues and values of political freedom that I cannot believe that a nation that does enjoy and does value political freedom will go down before the Russians or the Chinese. I just cannot in my guts believe that.

Interview, Cos Cob, Conn./
The Wall Street Journal, 9-28:22.

Jack Valenti
President, Motion Picture
Association of America

2

I am neither a Republican nor anti-government nor stagnant cynic. I am a liberal Democrat who believes devoutly in the worth and common sense of the individual. In my judgment, the largest asset of America is the very one that is so easily squandered. It is the enterprising entrepreneur, the risk-taker, the competitive antagonist, the builder of plants and factories, the creator of new enterprises and the expander of old ones, the people who make better mousetraps, cheaper and faster. If our economy is not strong, we will have neither the zest nor the vitality for other adventures, however useful and attractive they may be. Our economy is strong only if there is work to be done and jobs to be filled. And there is work available only if some men and women have the zeal and courage to risk their imagination, their energy—and their capital—in the marketplace.

Before Harvard Business School Club/
The Washington Post, 6-21:(A)24.

Andrew Young
United States Ambassador/
Permanent Representative to the
United Nations

3

[Clarifying his recent statement that there are thousands of political prisoners in U.S. jails]: There is nobody in prison in the U.S. for criticizing the government. There is no one in prison for writing a style of literature or for having a monitoring system of our human rights . . . I do think there are some people who are in prison much more because they are poor than because they are bad. But that's a problem we are working on and one on which we are making great progress. There are problems in our system which send intelligent, aggressive, poor people to jail and in which intelligent, aggressive and rich people have opportunities.

Interview, Geneva, July 12/
The New York Times, 7-13:(A)3.

Morris B. Abram
Former president, Brandeis University

1

I learned American history, I majored in it, but when I had gotten my degree in American history I didn't really know that American history was more shaped by the confrontation between blacks and whites in this country than by any other factor. American history is the product of the interactions of these two people, and the cruelty of the one toward the other and the ever-forgiving nature of the other toward the one.

At Tougaloo (Miss.) College commencement/
The New York Times, 6-2:(B)17.

E. L. Bing
Deputy Superintendent of Education,
Hillsborough County (Tampa), Florida

2

"Desegregation" can be relatively easily accomplished because it is administrative in nature; it simply involves the moving of people and things. While "integration" is much more difficult; it involves, among other things, the changing of attitudes of people.

Washington/The New York Times, 3-13:(A)15.

Tom Bradley
Mayor of Los Angeles

3

[Saying he believes in integration] : I think that until people begin to interrelate with each other in a normal fashion, where it becomes a natural event for them, they're not going to have the values that can come from intercultural social change, not going to have full and mutual respect, one race for another. Until that happens, there will continue to be disparity in terms of opportunity, in terms of equality of treatment, jobs opportunity and all the rest.

Interview, Los Angeles/
Los Angeles Times, 12-29:(1)24.

Joseph A. Califano, Jr.
Secretary of Health, Education and
Welfare of the United States

4

Busing [of schoolchildren for racial balance] will solve fewer and fewer problems as we go down the road, for two reasons: One, we have over-burdened the schools with all of the political freight of our failure to provide an economic system in which everyone has an equal opportunity. The schools are plagued by the same problems that any single institution would have in trying to integrate society. Two, the school populations of the center cities are increasingly minority-dominated, with some urban school systems having more than 90 per cent minority enrollment. It becomes very difficult to see how busing can resolve that kind of development.

Interview, Washington/
U.S. News & World Report, 1-9:44.

Jimmy Carter
President of the United States

5

When I was growing up on a farm in Georgia . . . an invisible wall of racial segregation stood between me and my black playmates. It seemed then as if that wall between us would exist forever. But it did not stand forever. It crumbled and fell. And though the rubble has not yet been completely removed, it no longer separates us from one another, blighting the lives of those on both sides of it.

Before Indian Parliament, New Delhi/Time, 1-16:11.

6

I grew up in a society struggling to find racial harmony through racial justice . . . I know that progress can best be found if the determination to see wrongs righted is matched by an understanding that the prisoners of injus-

WHAT THEY SAID IN 1978

(JIMMY CARTER)

tice include the privileged as well as the power-less.

Lagos, Nigeria/Newsweek, 4-10:31.

James S. Coleman
Professor of sociology,
University of Chicago

1

[Supporting a tuition tax credit for parents sending children to private schools]: Parents and children have a better sense of what's a good school context for them than do professionals who must deal with a very large number of children. I trust the parents and children more than the professionals. I think the stronger the private schools are the better it will be for the public schools, because the public schools will be forced to be better to stay in business.

At forum on desegregation, Washington, June 19/
The Washington Post, 6-20:(A)3.

2

It is not the case that school desegregation, as it has been carried out in American schools, generally brings achievement benefits to disadvantaged [black] children... Desegregation has turned out to be much more complicated than any of us ever realized. There appear to be beneficial effects for some black kids, those who are better students, and harmful effects for blacks who are poorer students. It all seems to balance out.

Interview/The Dallas Times Herald, 9-18:(A)1.

Alan M. Dershowitz
Professor of law, Harvard University

3

[On the Supreme Court ruling in the Bakke case that the University of California Medical School's rigid minority-admission quotas discriminated against whites and was thus illegal]: The decision will go down in history not for what it did but for what it didn't do. It neither legitimized racial quotas nor put down affirmative-action programs. The decision will make the job of admissions offices a lot harder. It will

make them look at people as persons, not as members of a group and not as computerized ciphers.

June 28/The New York Times, 6-29:(A)22.

Ernest G. Green
Assistant Secretary for Employment
and Training, Department of Labor
of the United States

4

... what the country hasn't focused on is that the issue in the '60s clearly was that no blacks, regardless of economic class, could do certain things... Now, legally, that's been thrown out and what that did was to open up access for those who had a certain amount of income and economic security. But still, for large numbers of people, that didn't matter. Making that legal change didn't gain them any more access than they had before.

Los Angeles Times, 6-22:(1)16.

Maxwell Greenberg
Lawyer; Chairman, national executive
committee, Anti-Defamation League

5

When you begin to define minority for special favors by color of skin, or by ethnic origin, or by religious affiliation, you begin to get some very severe problems. We would have to begin to create a Disadvantage Quotient. Who is more disadvantaged? Is it the Soviet Jewish emigre? Is he more disadvantaged than the recent immigrant from Naples? He learned to read in the Soviet Union; is he less disadvantaged than the Navajo who lives in Window Rock [Ariz.] and who did not have a very good education, who is functionally illiterate? Then there is the assumption—the very, very racist assumption—that being black is a form of automatic disadvantage. That is the problem of the racial quota. It is a complete *non sequitur;* it is irrational and it is racist... By the way, in our Disadvantage Quotient, are we going to rate blacks by the tint of their skin? Black blacks are much more discriminated against than light blacks. Do we give light blacks, say, two points to get into medical school, but to really black blacks we will give five points? What about the

(MAXWELL GREENBERG)

children of widowed mothers? They are disadvantaged, terribly disadvantaged. What about physically handicapped people? What kind of Disadvantage Quotient do we give them?

The Center Magazine, March-April:52.

Alex Haley
Author

1

I know a lot of words; I am a writer. I am a good writer; I have a tremendous vocabulary. But I do not know the words that would start to describe the loss that the society of the United States of America has suffered . . . for practically pouring down the drain the potential abilities of the various minorities.

Before National Association of Broadcasters,
Las Vegas, Nev./Los Angeles Times, 4-14:(4)26.

Lionel Hampton
Jazz musician

2

When I first played with Benny Goodman in the 1930s, it was the first time black and white ever played together on the stage. There was really a big social injustice going on because blacks were excluded from a lot of the entertainment world. Blacks did not act on the Broadway stage. Blacks were not used in the movies, except as servants or maids. And there were no blacks on the baseball, football or basketball teams. The Benny Goodman Quartet . . . was such a sensation and was so popular and closely followed that people couldn't discriminate against it. The Goodman Quartet was a door-opener for Jackie Robinson and all the wonderful things that are happening in sports today.

Interview/U.S. News & World Report, 10-2:86.

Patricia Roberts Harris
Secretary of Housing and Urban
Development of the United States

3

. . . busing [of schoolchildren for racial balance] probably should be even more extensive, from a justice point of view. The worst thing

that can happen in this society is that there should be a privileged sanctuary from black people—that white people should be able to find a place where there will be no black people. With busing, I happen to believe that we should eliminate our privileged sanctuaries. I would prefer a much more active governmental process in the area of fair housing. This is a place where we've really run into a stone wall. I don't think we've yet reached the point where we're prepared to work at integration in this country. There's certainly a lot more acceptance of it than there was when I was a young woman. But we are still a society in which, for white people, whiteness is very important and in which blackness is very threatening.

Interview/Los Angeles Times, 5-24:(1)20.

4

I don't think any black person in this country has any reason to be grateful to any white person in this country, because black people have, as has been pointed out for a long time, been in this country since before the *Mayflower* and, by reason of their genetic background, have been excluded—deliberately excluded—from what was accepted as normal opportunity for people who are not black. So white people think that, because in 1960 they decided to stop doing the wrong things—desperately mean things—to black people, that black people should have been grateful. Many black people, and I am among them, simply said, "But this is what you should have done 300 years ago."

Interview/Los Angeles Times, 5-24:(1)20.

Richard G. Hatcher
Mayor of Gary, Indiana

5

There has been a reluctance, on the part of the media itself, to take a hard look at itself, to recognize that it could only have a segregated kind of perspective based on the fact that it is a segregated industry itself. I think a meeting of black television executives in this country could probably be held in a very small phone booth. Until we can move in on a management level, until there are black persons in the board rooms of the major dailies and television stations who

WHAT THEY SAID IN 1978

(RICHARD G. HATCHER)

are able to present their own perception of the news, which gets translated into what people see on a daily basis, the false notion of minorities having moved too fast too soon is going to persist.

Before National Urban League, Los Angeles/
Los Angeles Herald Examiner, 8-12:(B)2.

S. I. Hayakawa
United States Senator, R-California

1

[Saying he is impatient with special pleadings among minorities today]: Right now, if you're a well-behaved, well-spoken black with skills, the world is your oyster. You don't need affirmative action. If you're ignorant and lazy and can't do arithmetic and then sit around and complain that there are no opportunities, you're not seeing the world as it really is. One has to start at the bottom of the ladder. I made my first two bucks playing mandolin at a Polish wedding when I was 5 years old!

People, 10-2:50.

Benjamin L. Hooks
Executive director, National
Association for the Advancement
of Colored People

2

We're [blacks] no longer arguing about riding on the back of the bus, but being the bus driver or the president of the bus company. We're not pushing for the right to buy the hot dog, but selling the hot dog and the right to own the hot-dog franchise.

Interview, New York/
The Washington Post, 6-23:(B)10.

3

[Criticizing the Supreme Court ruling in the Bakke case that the University of California Medical School's rigid minority-admission quotas discriminated against whites and was thus illegal]: How can there be "reverse discrimination" as long as 91 per cent of the medical-school seats go to whites? How can there be reverse discrimination when less than 3

per cent of all doctors in California are minority, with a black and brown population of over 25 per cent? We do not accept tokenism, and we will not accept any interpretation of this Supreme Court decision which encourages the opponents of affirmative action. We profoundly regret that the Court has issued an ambiguous decision at a time this nation needs clarity, precision and determination to achieve and enforce affirmative action.

At NAACP convention, Portland, Ore./
Los Angeles Times, 7-5:(1)8.

4

Nearly 80 per cent of the white people in America feel that enough has been done for black people, and that we have reached the place where it is no longer necessary to give any special attention to the racial problems that still exist. And 80 per cent of the black people feel exactly the opposite. This poses a collision course of unpredictable, disastrous dimensions.

At NAACP convention, Portland, Ore./
Los Angeles Times, 7-5:(1)8.

Roy Innis
National director, Congress of
Racial Equality

5

The leadership of black people in the United States has always been overwhelmingly of mixed ancestry. The whiter you look, the more qualified you are to be a black leader. Going back to slavery, the abolitionists who allegedly were fighting for our rights always selected mulattoes, the children of slave masters, to educate and to force on us as leaders . . . Today, in the late '70s, the same thing exists. Most black leaders do not look like me. I look African. I can pass in any country as African. The average black leader cannot.

Interview/Los Angeles Herald Examiner, 10-9.(A)1.

Jesse L. Jackson
Civil-rights leader; President,
Operation PUSH (People United to
Save Humanity)

6

Despite all of the publicity about the new South, the election of a Southern President

(JESSE L. JACKSON)

[Carter], no more riots, no more demonstrations, there is still hostility. I'm impressed with the fact that blacks and whites are associating in social ways, but beneath that sugar-coating there is that hostility—and the black middle class, the educators, are being severed.

Interview, Chicago/
The New York Times, 3-22:(A)20.

1

... blacks are intelligent enough and patriotic enough and have worked long enough to be entitled to run for any [political] office. The onus is on the white population to appreciate our worth and to stop devaluing us based upon race. We were ready to play baseball before 1947, but white America was not ready. We were ready to sit in the front of a bus before 1955; white America was not ready. We were ready to use public facilities before 1964, but white America was not ready. We were ready to vote before 1965; white America was not ready. And we are ready to be President now. The question really becomes: Is white America ready to appreciate our worth?

Interview/U.S. News & World Report, 4-10:66.

2

[On the Supreme Court's Bakke-case ruling against the University of California Medical School's rigid racial quota system]: We have gone from the protection of the law to a situation where we must depend upon the will of the American people, and history has taught us that it is basically ill will, not good will. This decision represents another external threat to our attempt to gain educational economic equity and parity. Legally, the Bakke decision represents the end of the period of the second Reconstruction, and lays the predicate for another century of struggle around the issue of race discrimination and separation ... [It sets] in motion a principle for erosion from the top down.

Before National Education Association, Dallas,
July 3/The Dallas Times Herald, 7-4:(A)1.

Daniel James, Jr.
General, United States Air Force (Ret.);
Former Commander, North American
Air Defense Command

3

When I was in the ghetto I was dadgum bitter. But I learned that bitterness and fighting against the system was not going to do it. You've got to realize that any time you're in a confrontation with authority or [with] a rule, you've got to work within the system to get change and not go for unconditional surrender.

San Francisco Examiner & Chronicle,
2-12:(This World)2.

Vernon E. Jordan, Jr.
President, National Urban League

4

Behind the discussion about what the real nature of today's civil-rights movement should be is a lingering nostalgia for those good old days of clear-cut moral decisions and easily defined issues. But that phase of the movement is over. The basic rights were won through judicial decisions, legislation and executive orders. But the reality behind those rights has not kept pace. Black people today can check into any hotel in the country, but most do not have the wherewithal to check out. It is too often forgotten that the 1963 March on Washington was for more than just abstract rights. It was for jobs and freedom. To a large extent, we won the freedoms, but we still don't have the jobs. There are today half a million more black people unemployed than at the time of the March on Washington ... Despite some gains in employment and education, the masses of black people did not witness significant changes in their lives because of the rights they won in the 1960s. We were poor then, we're poor today; we were disadvantaged then, we remain so today.

Before National Press Club, Feb. 14/
The Washington Post, 2-21:(A)16.

5

Civil rights don't take place in a vacuum. They are meaningful only in the real world, the world where people have to survive, to work, to raise their families, to instill in their children hope for the future and the skills to function in

WHAT THEY SAID IN 1978

(VERNON E. JORDAN, JR.)

a society where a broad back and a desire to work are no longer enough. That is why we insist there is a vital moral component to the current struggle. The struggle for equality is identical with the struggle for jobs, for housing, for education, for urban vitality, and that struggle is, above all, a moral struggle ... I am here to say that the moral banner is still unfurled; it still waves high above the current struggle. The issues are more complex, and the resistance more entrenched. But the civil-rights movement is still about the business of bringing America's minorities into the mainstream of our national life, with all of the rewards and responsibilities others take for granted. In the 1960s we fought to build an integrated, open, pluralistic society. That is still our goal, still our moral burden.

At Atlanta University, April 18/
Vital Speeches, 7-1:552.

1

By any measure, equality for the majority of black people remains an elusive ideal, and this explains the continuing impatience so many black people feel toward the Carter Administration. It is clear, however, that the Carter Administration is the first in a decade whose doors have been truly open to black people, whose concern is evident and whose policies have been tilted toward meeting the needs of America's poor and minorities. This Administration has, in the past year, reorganized civil-rights enforcement, moved against redlining, tried to target urban-development monies, proposed welfare reforms and an urban policy. It has endorsed the Humphrey-Hawkins bill and increased public job programs that have been directly responsible for preventing even greater unemployment in the black community. But for all its concern, this Administration can lapse into insensitivity, and though it supports many of the things we want, it does not fight hard enough for them and apparently lacks the will to put its power and its prestige on the line for issues vital to minorities or poor people. [Nevertheless,] despite our impatience with the Administration, we have greater problems with a callous Congress marked by inaction and intransigence.

This Congress is trying to weaken the Humphrey-Hawkins bill with irrelevant and crippling amendments. This Congress has one of the worst equal-opportunities records of any American institution ...

At National Urban League convention,
Los Angeles, Aug. 6/
The New York Times, 8-7:(D)10.

2

Let's face it: Blacks have a lot of different, sometimes conflicting, interests. The blacks who went into unions 15 years ago have different notions about seniority than those who have just managed to get in. Black entrepreneurs are concerned about such things as the capital-gains tax. The views of black bankers on interest rates are likely to be very different from those of black borrowers or civil-rights organizations. The issues that concern blacks often transcend race.

Time, 12-18:15.

Alvin M. Josephy, Jr.
Editor, American Heritage magazine

3

Unhappily, the Carter Administration seems to be on its way to being the worst Administration for American Indians since the Eisenhower Administration in the early 1950s ... The Carter Administration has no understanding of American Indians, of Indian history or Indian policies. It has nothing to do with sympathy. The Carter Administration is full of people who think they're warm and sympathetic. But if they can't even understand why Indians want reservations, they're going to continue to move in an ignorant way.

At Writer West conference, Sun Valley,
Idaho/The New York Times, 7-10:(B)2.

Coretta Scott King
Civil-rights leader

4

Many of the gains of the civil-rights movement are being threatened by the shocking levels of joblessness among minority citizens ... Joblessness is a cancer eating away at

(CORETTA SCOTT KING)

the black community, destroying our hopes, our aspirations and even our most valuable asset, our youth. While experts talk about economic recovery, I see the gains of the last two decades being washed away in the aftermath of recession.

Before House Employment Opportunities Subcommittee, Washington, Jan. 18/ The Dallas Times Herald, 1-19:(A)15.

1

[Saying the main goal of the civil-rights movement today is economic justice for minorities] : A whole range of social problems can be solved if people can have meaningful employment. All people seeking work should be able to find a decent job at decent pay. We have the resources and the skills to solve this problem; what's lacking is the national will. We've come a long way since the movement began in 1955. Things are not what they ought to be, but they're not what they used to be either. Let us continue to dream big dreams and go out and work to fulfill them.

Before high-school students, Oakland, Calif., March 4/The Washington Post, 3-5:(A)18.

Walter J. Leonard
President, Fisk University

2

We know that civil rights is no longer considered one of the urgent and national issues. There has been a deliberate and well-orchestrated program to derail the movement toward equality and opportunity. Such obscurants, racist propaganda and empty shibboleths as "preferential treatment," "benign neglect," "quotas," "reverse discrimination" and others have been used to stall the dramatic and intensive drive toward separate and unequal existence in the United States. In a real sense, we face the same problem—if not the same odds—to which Frederick Douglass spoke some 125 years ago: "Having despised us, it is not strange that Americans should seek to render us despicable; having enslaved us, it is natural that they should strive to prove us unfit for freedom; having denounced us as indolent, it is not

strange that they should cripple our enterprises."

At Black Seniors Dinner of Harvard-Radcliffe/ The Christian Science Monitor, 7-13:23.

James E. Lowery
President, Southern Christian Leadership Conference

3

The [civil-rights] issues are the same as in the '60s, except now we're [blacks] not talking about sitting down on the customer's side of the counter. We're talking about sharing in the operations of the counter.

Los Angeles Times, 11-17:(1-B)4.

Peter MacDonald
Chairman, Navajo (Indian) Tribal Council

4

If you believe what you read, we [Indians] are all millionaires. We are taking back the whole Eastern United States, starting with Maine and working our way down the Eastern seaboard. We are destroying tourism in the Northwest by asserting our fishing rights. We are holding the entire Southwest hostage with our water rights and energy resources. Americans find it useful and convenient to believe that Indians are rich. It wipes out any need to feel guilt or concern; it provides a justification for taking our resources, destroying our tribal sovereignty and ignoring our problems. The media projects our feeble efforts to pull ourselves up by our own bootstraps as the biggest menace since Little Big Horn.

Window Rock, Ariz./ Los Angeles Herald Examiner, 4-17:(A)1.

Thurgood Marshall
Associate Justice, Supreme Court of the United States

5

Be careful of the people who say [to blacks], "You've got it made. Take it easy. You don't need any more help" ... Today we have reached the point where people say, "You've come a long way." But so have other people come a long way. Has the gap been getting smaller? No. It's getting bigger. People say we're [blacks]

23

WHAT THEY SAID IN 1978

better off today. Better off than what? ...
[Anti-blacks] in every phase of American life
are still laying traps for us. The [Ku Klux] Klan
never dies; they just stop wearing sheets because sheets cost too much ... Don't listen to
that myth that it [inequality] ... has already
been solved. Take it from me, it has not been
solved.

At Howard University, Nov. 18/
The Washington Post, 11-19:(A)2.

Maurice B. Mitchell
President, Center for the Study of
Democratic Institutions; Chancellor,
University of Denver

1

... I have seen no evidence that the education of any non-minority student has ever suffered because of busing [of schoolchildren for
racial balance]. There are no statistics ... that
indicate that a student gets hurt intellectually
in an integrated system. The normal, average
white student who is sent to a minority school
suffers no apparent damage. Minority students
do not seem to get hurt, either, by being bused.
Also, there is some evidence that minority students in desegregated classrooms are more likely to go on to college, that the ones who go to
college are more likely to graduate, and that the
ones who graduate are more likely to do reasonably well in their careers. If you talk to these
students at any stage in this process, they reflect far less hostility to the white community
than they did before. Thus, even if nothing else
happens, some of the racial tensions, barriers
and cross-hatreds seem to diminish as a result of
desegregation.

Panel discussion, at Center for the Study of
Democratic Institutions, Santa Barbara, Calif./
The Center Magazine, Nov.-Dec.: 75.

Walter F. Mondale
Vice President of the United States

2

In many ways, the challenges we face in civil
rights [today] are even more difficult than
those in the past. The issues are less dramatic
than the right to sit at a lunch counter or the
right of every citizen to vote. The brutality is
less visible when a black teenager can't find
work than when a civil-rights marcher is set
upon by dogs. Yet you and I know the damage
is just as real. [The late civil-rights leader] Martin Luther King Jr.'s dream lives on. But we can
go to many communities where despair and
poverty exist. Dreams are dying there in neighborhoods with no hope, in families without
work, in drug abuse and suicide and crime. So
the challenge we face ... is to summon up a
new constituency of conscience in America
around the broad issues of economic justice and
human rights, which are the agenda of the civil-
rights movement today.

At Leadership Conference on Civil Rights,
Washington/The Christian Science Monitor, 4-4:31.

Aryeh Neier
Executive director, American
Civil Liberties Union

3

Rarely are centrist groups denied their First
Amendment rights. It is almost always fringe
groups—people who are provocative, who select
that place where they are disliked the most
because that is where they can get the most
attention. Isn't that what [the late civil-rights
leader] Martin Luther King did at Selma? For
that very reason it is the extremes that have the
greatest interest in protecting the rights of their
enemies. Once the freedom of one group is
abridged, that infringement will be cited to
deny the rights of others. The people who most
need the ACLU to defend the rights of the [Ku
Klux] Klan are the blacks. The people who
most need the ACLU to defend the rights of
Nazis are the Jews.

During debate at Brooklyn (N.Y.) Law School,
April 20/The New York Times Magazine, 7-9:10.

Eleanor Holmes Norton
Chairman, Equal Employment Opportunity
Commission of the United States

4

Affirmative action [by companies in hiring
minorities] is far more complicated, more subtle and ultimately more effective than an occasional quota case. For, if correctly done, affirmative action brings permanent institutionalized

(ELEANOR HOLMES NORTON)

change to the total personnel system of a company.

At NAACP conference, Chicago, May 6/
The New York Times, 5-7:(1)30.

1

... there has been in the main, despite some backlash in this decade, remarkable acceptance of affirmative action. In jobs, for example, we do not see a major protest by workers when minorities come in pursuant to a consent decree. Even in education ... a poll revealed that most Americans believe that people ought to be taken into colleges based on qualifications, and an almost equal majority believes that special attention should be paid to minorities. The fact is that Americans—and I speak now of white Americans—are of two minds on these questions. The period of the 1960s indelibly made plain what black people in particular had suffered in this country, and most Americans of good-will want to undo this. On a person-by-person basis that will mean some inconvenience and even some pain for some. There simply is no way to move from a period of racism to a period where racism is no longer part of the American life without some dislocation in the society, at least for a limited period of time.

TV-radio interview/"Meet the Press,"
National Broadcasting Company, 7-2.

John U. Ogbu
Anthropologist, University of
California, Berkeley

2

Better access to jobs and real dismantling of discrimination in such areas as health care and housing are as essential as better schooling for improving the educational performance of large number[s] of black children. The economic reality of most adult blacks' lives is still more discouraging than that of whites and at virtually all income levels. This discouraging reality profoundly shapes black children's skills and attitudes, including their skills and attitudes for learning.

News conference, New York/
The Washington Post, 3-5:(A)15.

Joseph L. Rauh, Jr.
Vice president, Americans for
Democratic Action

3

[On the Supreme Court's Bakke-case ruling against the University of California Medical School's rigid racial quota system, but which also upheld the use of race as a factor in college admissions] : I think we won. The important thing about the decision is not that Allan Bakke can go to medical school, but that the racists who wanted to turn back the clock on minority progress have received a stunning blow. The Supreme Court's decision that race is a proper factor in admissions decisions is the legal concrete on which further affirmative-action progress can be made.

Los Angeles Herald Examiner, 6-29:(A)10.

Alexander I. Solzhenitsyn
Exiled Soviet author

4

[In the West,] the defense of individual rights has reached such extremes as to make society as a whole defenseless against certain individuals. It is time, in the West, to defend not so much human rights as human obligations.

At Harvard University commencement, June 8/
Newsweek, 6-19:43.

Steve Suitts
Executive director, Southern
Regional Council

5

What the civil-rights movement has got to figure out now is how to go beyond statutory guarantees of equality. It's not enough just to have a voting-rights act and an accommodations law and people no longer living in fear. People also have to have something that they can put their hands on, a decent living standard. You have to follow through on laws that you pass. We've had progress since [civil-rights leader Martin Luther] King died. But nowhere near enough.

San Francisco Examiner & Chronicle,
4-9:(This World)26.

WHAT THEY SAID IN 1978

George C. Wallace
Governor of Alabama (D)

1

In all my political career, no speech or book can be brought forward in which I ever made light of black people or made fun of them or cast them in an inferior rank among whites. Of course, I stood for segregation at that time [the early 1960s], and if you call that offensive to blacks, then, of course. [But] segregation is over. And it's better that it is over. And there's no need to go back to it or try to talk about it because it's never coming back . . . But it wasn't a fight against the blacks. It was just the government we were fighting. We lost those battles, and we adjusted and went ahead. We're now looking ahead instead of behind.

Interview,
Montgomery, Alabama/
Los Angeles Herald Examiner,
12-7:(A)2.

C. Vann Woodward
Emeritus professor of American history, Yale University

2

So much of the [civil-rights] movement's ambitions have been realized. If there is a reason that it is quiescent, it is its very success. This makes the crusading movement irrelevant. I would agree that the chief beneficiaries of the civil-rights movement have been the black middle class. So many were the leaders of it. But I would not agree that no benefits accrued to the mass of blacks. They are not subject to the same Hindu-like caste system of the past. I

don't mean to say that their salvation is at hand either.

Interview, Washington, May 3/
Los Angeles Times, 5-4:(1)13.

Andrew Young
United States Ambassador/Permanent Representative to the United Nations

3

All of the small-business ventures that have developed out of the [civil-rights] movement and needs of black Americans—who are an undeveloped nation within a highly affluent society—are going to prove to be extremely relevant as we begin to take on the task of world-wide development. Somehow we are the bridge as black Americans between the "haves" and the "have nots" of the world. We are beginning to build the kind of economic bridges that will enable the dream of [the late civil-rights leader] Martin Luther King to be fulfilled in a world-wide manner.

At memorial conference for the late Martin
Luther King, Atlanta, Jan. 14/
The Dallas Times Herald, 1-15:(A)15.

Evelle J. Younger
Attorney General of California

4

I believe very strongly that forced busing [of schoolchildren for racial balance] is a very bad idea. I don't think it will do very much to achieve integration; indeed, the evidence and data indicate that it may actually be counter-productive and lead to re-segregation, rather than integration.

To newsmen, Los Angeles, Aug. 30/
Los Angeles Times, 8-31:(1)3.

Mark Anthony
President, Kaiser Steel Corporation

1

[Lamenting the U.S. government's allowing cut-rate imported steel to be sold in America]: We've got imports from Belgium, Japan, Italy, Taiwan, West Germany, France, South Africa, Korea and Romania—all of them selling lower than Kaiser. Now, you tell me how the [U.S.] West Coast is a natural market for Romania, and I'll eat everything they sell.

Newsweek, 11-20:105.

Les Aspin
United States Senator, D-Wisconsin

2

Junk phone calls [those for the purpose of selling to the call's recipient] should be banned to anyone who doesn't want to receive them. They are a terrible nuisance and can be terribly inconvenient. They rob you of your privacy—interrupting you in the middle of dinner, when you're taking a bath, or when you're gardening in the back yard. And there's no way to know by the ring whether it's a serious call or some salesman soliciting your business. At least with junk mail, you can go the mailbox when you want or open the letter at your convenience.

Interview/U.S. News & World Report, 9-11:43.

Robert A. Bandeen
President, Canadian National, Ltd.

3

The company of today is a faceless institution. The public does not know who the heads of its corporations are or what they think and stand for . . . Industry spokesmen spend far too much time talking to each other. It's all too easy to accept comfortable speaking engagements where the audience is composed of business people and where your message gets picked up by business writers to appear the next day in the business section of the paper. It feels good, but it doesn't accomplish much. Instead, it's time to search out and ask to speak to those groups who are *not* converted—the environmentalists, the consumer groups, the people who do not read the financial pages.

Before Canadian Chamber of Commerce, Halifax, Nova Scotia, Sept. 17/Vital Speeches, 10-1:763.

Bob Bergland
Secretary of Agriculture of the United States

4

I want to broaden the [Agriculture] Department—not just for political reasons, but for humanitarian reasons. I believe in the food-stamp program, and I'm hiring the best people to work on it. I decided to hire the Department's biggest critics, because I figure if they can seriously criticize they know a lot about the problem. I know what it's like to be poor, because I represented one of the poorest districts in the country when I was in Congress. I shouldn't say this, but I think [former Agriculture Secretary] Earl Butz wanted to purify this place. He wanted to get it so that it would only have to deal with the large, mechanized agricultural businessman. I think that's wrong. The basic conservation of the family farm is critical to the basic well-being of the United States.

Interview, Washington/ The Dallas Times Herald, 1-15:(F)1.

5

[On whether the government owes farmers a guaranteed profit]: We can't bail out everybody who makes a poor business judgment. If we do it for farmers, then we will have to do it for homeowners and service-station operators, and it will never end. What we need to provide farmers is some protection against the vagaries of weather at home and abroad and economic forces over which they have no control.

TV-radio interview/"Meet the Press," National Broadcasting Company, 3-19.

WHAT THEY SAID IN 1978

C. Fred Bergsten
*Assistant Secretary for
International Affairs, Department
of the Treasury of the United States*

1

[Criticizing subsidies and concessions by foreign governments to induce U.S. firms to locate new production in or purchase materials from their countries]: We believe that subsidies represent one of the most critical problems for the world trading system in the decade ahead, because governments are increasingly tempted to export their problems to others through direct financial and other types of help to favored industries.

*Washington, Aug. 1/
The Dallas Times Herald, 8-2:(E)3.*

Christopher S. Bond
*President, Great Plains Legal Foundation;
Former Governor of Missouri (R)*

2

Too much government regulation of agriculture has made farmers saddlesore, but consumers have a stake in it, too. Just as housewives found beef shortages following on the heels of ceilings on beef prices, they can find higher prices or even shortages in their markets if government continues to pile regulation upon regulation without weighing the costs of each additional layer ... No one argues about the need for common-sense regulations to assure a safe food supply and protect our environment, but increasingly questionable regulations are being forced on American farmers, with no effort to weigh the supposed benefits against the real costs to the food-production system. These regulations may just be the straw that breaks the camel's back. If it does, consumers will feel the weight.

*At Farm Management Recognition Program,
Kansas City, March 8/Vital Speeches, 4-15:404,405.*

Benjamin C. Bradlee
Executive editor, "The Washington Post"

3

I'm sure that the press has not had enough respect for business, and I am even more sure that has been true coming back the other way.

Respect for one's opposite number is in one's self-interest.

*At business seminar, Houston/
Nation's Business, April: 77*

Joseph Brooks
Chairman, Lord & Taylor stores

4

Show me a country, a company or an organization that is doing well and I'll show you a good leader. Show me a country or a company that is not doing well and I'll show you a bad leader.

Interview/"W": a Fairchild publication, 2-3:2.

Yale Brozen
*Professor of business economics,
Graduate School of Business,
University of Chicago*

5

There is a strange notion brewing in the Antitrust Division [of the U.S. Department of Justice] and the Federal Trade Commission—a notion which will be suicidal for the country if we adopt it. That notion is that we must penalize any firm, or small group of firms, which, by operating efficiently and producing greater values for consumers, wins a large share of a market. Perhaps that notion emerges from the passion for equality of results that has come to pervade public policy; perhaps it is simply envy; or perhaps it is the final erosion, perversion or transmutation of democracy from individual sovereignty into mobocracy—tyranny by majority ... Once we gave high regard to those who created great enterprises by designing desirable products, producing them at low cost and offering them at such attractive prices that they won a large body of customers. Henry Ford, in his day, was looked upon as an industrial hero. Today, he would be regarded as a monopolizing fiend upon whom the antitrust prosecutors should be unleashed. The 1921 Ford Company, with its more than 60 per cent share of the market, would today be called a dominant firm and charged with violating the antitrust laws.

*Before Ashland (Ky.) Economic Club, Sept. 15/**

Chester Burger
Management consultant

1

The typical successful executive is overwhelmingly interested in his work; he doesn't play very much. If he gets out on the golf course, it's to win. He doesn't dally. Most CEOs I know aren't widely read either. What they do have is a tremendous drive—so they aren't heavy drinkers. They're not heavy anything except heavy workers. They have a desire to prove to themselves that they really can overcome impossible obstacles.

Interview/U.S. News & World Report, 7-10:81.

Arthur F. Burns
Former Chairman, Federal Reserve Board

2

I feel a great deal of anguish about the international position of the dollar, both for the sake of this country and for the sake of the international economy. We must give far more serious attention to assuring the integrity of the dollar than we have done. That is vital not only to the international economy, including our own, but to healthy political relations among the great powers of the world.

Interview, Washington/
Los Angeles Herald Examiner, 3-29:(A)11.

3

. . . we do not have a healthy environment for investment at the present time. Venture-capital investment is virtually dead in our country. Investment in large new projects is not proceeding at all rapidly. The spirit of innovation, of business enterprise, of capital investment is not what it was at that time [after 1962]. I think that persistent inflation, which has led to a deterioration of profits since the mid-1960s, has weakened the spirit to invest.

Discussion, at American Enterprise Institute,
June/The Washington Post, 7-30:(B)5.

Jack W. Carlson
Chief economist, Chamber of
Commerce of the United States

4

Some foreign manufacturing companies are dumping in the U.S. They are running plants full steam to avoid unemployment and then selling their products abroad, particularly in the U.S., for anything they can get. This is classic dumping, and stagnant foreign economies contribute to this bad situation.

Nation's Business, August:33.

Donald C. Carroll
Dean, Wharton School of Business,
University of Pennsylvania

5

Not so long ago, the stereotypic business executive was a hard-driving supersalesman, an efficiency expert, a bottom-liner, a bit of a pirate, the man who actually thought that what was good for his company was good for his country. The most noble concern of this breed was probably, "Whither the price of my stock?" Such people are going the way of the dinosaur; they are simply not equipped for business leadership today. Society has imposed, and will continue to impose, constraints in response to abuses committed by socially irresponsible businesses and business executives. Several of these spring to mind: equal economic opportunity, environmental protection, occupational safety and health, toxic-substances control, truth in advertising, truth in lending, new strictures on political contributions, and so on and on. These rocks and shoals consequently demand a much different kind of business leadership today: Leaders now must be *valid participants* in the formulation of public policy or else be victims of it. A contemporary leader must genuinely understand the public interest, as well as his or her personal economic interest.

Before University of Pennsylvania undergraduates/
The Wall Street Journal, 4-25:20.

6

. . . we live today with laws written largely by dewy-eyed idealists—by people with little understanding of the economic or even the technological consequences of these laws. How much better, I submit, had we, corporate America, recognized the legitimacy of the public interest and brought our technical and economic expertise to the drafting table. What I am suggesting is a proactive, rather than a re-

WHAT THEY SAID IN 1978

(DONALD C. CARROLL)

active role—as partners, not adversaries. To do this, we must have an ability to anticipate social interest and validly to participate in the search for solutions to social problems. Educationally, this says tomorrow's managers must comprehend law, sociology and political science as well as technology, economics and management disciplines. I do not suggest that we all rush out and take graduate degrees in sociology or political science. I do suggest that we must raise our sights beyond the comfortable limits of our day-to-day operations. We must become society-watchers and students of the non-business world around us; and furthermore, we must master ways of influencing our social environment.

At Business Writers Seminar, Philadelphia,
October/The Christian Science Monitor, 11-8:23.

Jimmy Carter
President of the United States

1

If a working man or woman takes a lunch to work, say a $1.50 or $2 sandwich and something to drink and buys it in a local store, a restaurant, you can't mark it off as a business expense. But if a salesman or someone else has a very fancy lunch and has a customer with them, then they can mark all of that off, maybe a $25 or $30 lunch as a business expense. The same thing is applicable with tickets to sporting events, tickets to the theatre. If they carry a customer with them, then they can mark it all off as a business expense. I don't think that is right. And I think we ought to do away with it.

At town meeting, Bangor, Maine/
The Dallas Times Herald, 2-26:(A)10.

2

[Criticizing a bill now before the House which would raise support payments for a variety of farm products]: I will veto any farm legislation, beyond what I have already recommended, that would lead to higher food prices or budget expenditures ... The Senate has just passed a bill that would raise food prices by 3 per cent and the over-all cost of living by four-tenths of a per cent, shatter confidence in the

crucial export markets for America's farm products, and cripple American farm families through increased costs. It is bad for farmers, bad for consumers and bad for our nation.

Before American Society of
Newspaper Editors, Washington, April 11/
The Dallas Times Herald, 4-12:(A)17.

Emanuel Celler
Former United States
Representative, D-New York

3

I think there ought to be an amendment ... that provides that where a corporation does a business of $10-million it should be precluded from buying another corporation that does $1-million, [because conglomerates] have become tremendously powerful ... and they can do a lot of things which are just within the legal limits but which are immoral ... While it is true that we're a big nation, we have big business and big unions; and I'm not opposed to bigness—it's what bigness does which is detrimental. When they keep growing and growing, there must be a stop somewhere. There must be some brakes put on them.

Interview, New York/
The Washington Post, 9-17:(B)4.

Coy G. Eklund
President, Equitable
Life Assurance Society

4

To cater only to maximization of profits is to invite corporate doom. In this country, we've developed corporate enterprise by reason of the will of the people. The only way that we will continue to have the support of the people who enfranchised us is to perform in ways that are socially desirable. If we do not, somebody will blow the whistle on the corporate-enterprise system.

Time, 5-15:77.

Charles D. Ferris
Chairman, Federal
Communications Commission

5

I believe in zero-based regulation. I want to go back and find out right from the beginning

30

(CHARLES D. FERRIS)

the value of each rule and regulation to see if it still has validity. If it doesn't, let's get rid of it. I think that the regulatory scheme we have now has, to a great extent, gone stale. The purpose of regulation should not be to protect the status quo. It's there only to assure that the marketplace forces can work.

Interview, Washington/TV Guide, 7-15:9.

Montague Finniston
Director, Sears Holdings, Ltd.
(United Kingdom); Former chairman,
British Steel Corporation

1

I don't think the public really understands nationalization. It is relatively new—since 1947 is barely a generation. And I don't believe we're ever going back [to when there was no nationalization]. If you look at the United States itself, you can hardly boast of being the exemplar of the private-sector economy. There's more hidden nationalization in the U.S. than there probably is in this country [Britain]. Companies [in the U.S.] are supported by government funds for so long they may just as well be a part of the government—Lockheed, General Dynamics, even your railways. They're not nationalized in the sense of the government sitting on their boards or being legally committed to them, but if you've got big contracts at stake you're not likely to stand out very much against them. We're living in a world where the mixed economy is here to stay, and there's no point in making a pig's breakfast of it. You might just as well make it a success.

Interview/The New York Times, 5-28:(3)2.

Alec Flamm
Senior vice president,
Union Carbide Corporation

2

... most businessmen are not asking how we can rid ourselves of [government] regulation, but, rather, how much do we need and what form should it take. We have reached the point where nearly every aspect of our business operations is subject to some form of regulation. The cost to business and to the public is astronomical. ...

business has a checkered history, and we continue to labor under a legacy of mistrust. That mistrust, I believe, is the most serious obstacle in the way of reducing the burden of regulation. The fact is that few are willing to believe business can be counted on to do what is right ... unless pressured to do so. Surveys continue to show that most Americans believe that business puts profits ahead of morality. They feel business cares little about the consumer; that we care little about the environment. In sum, says one research group, most Americans feel that business needs more watching over. So while Americans have been saying they have no taste for further government intrusion in business, they are unlikely to signal a halt unless they trust business to do what is right without it.

Before Commercial Development Association,
New York, March 7/Vital Speeches, 4-15:387.

Joseph P. Flannery
President, Uniroyal, Inc.

3

I have said that no responsible businessman can oppose reasonable [government] regulations, and I do not. I am no more opposed to government regulation than I am to police protection. But I am as opposed to over-regulation as I am to the police state. And over-regulation is just that—an economic police state. Over-regulation has cut down productivity. Over-regulation has impeded growth. Over-regulation has held down employment. Over-regulation has lowered living standards. It has clamped down on the housing supply, prolonged the energy crisis, put the brakes on research and development, stifled enterprise and fueled inflation and weakened us in world market competition.

At National Postal Forum XII, Washington,
Sept. 11/Vital Speeches, 10-1:750.

Malcolm S. Forbes
Economist; Editor, "Forbes" magazine

4

[Businessmen] are as honest as any given segment [of society], and perhaps more honest than most. It's like motorcyclists. They are not all Hell's Angels. But there is a per cent in

WHAT THEY SAID IN 1978

(MALCOLM S. FORBES)

business, and it varies from 2 per cent to 10 per cent, depending on your definition of dishonesty.

Interview/Los Angeles Herald Examiner, 11-17:(A)6.

Gerald R. Ford
Former President of the United States

1

I wish some people in high places would stop talking [against] the three-martini [business] lunch. I happen to think that the three-martini lunch is the epitome of American efficiency. Where else can you get an earful, a bellyful and a snootful at the same time?

Before National Restaurant Association, Chicago/
Los Angeles Times, 5-23:(1)2.

Douglas A. Fraser
President, United Automobile
Workers of America

2

We receive many reports of company use of subterfuge in efforts to avoid citations [from Federal job-safety inspectors]. Some companies do this by ordering special plant cleanups, temporarily replacing guards and activating safety devices, changing chemicals, handing out respirators or shutting down operations temporarily. If this has occurred with unannounced inspections—in the time it takes the inspector to go from the front office to the plant floor—how often will it occur when employers have prior notice?

Detroit/The Christian Science Monitor, 6-7:25.

Malcolm Fraser
Prime Minister of Australia

3

It will take an unusual amount of political determination and courage on the part of all countries to take the steps necessary for a broad liberalization of trade. Above all, we need a trading world that is structured to benefit all nations. The test of this determination will come if nations show willingness to break down the barriers to their imports of agricultural and other commodities. We then will have a truly open world market and can look to the

future with confidence. If not, we face a period of tensions and difficulties.

Interview, New York, June 2/
The New York Times, 6-3:26.

John Kenneth Galbraith
Professor emeritus of economics,
Harvard University

4

There is not the slightest reason to believe that after being absorbed by the conglomerate, the small enterprise is more innovative, more efficient, more effective or more profitable than before. If anything, the evidence is in the other direction. [The usual motivation for acquisition is] empire-building. And no one doubts that it is frequently to get hold of the cash reserves that have been acquired by the smaller enterprise.

Before House Antitrust Subcommittee, Washington,
May 17/The Washington Post, 5-18:(D)15.

Jonathan Galloway
Professor of political science,
Lake Forest College

5

... what happens when the corporation undertakes to carry out its own independent and autonomous "foreign policy"? What happens when it engages in bribery not just for some economic purpose, i.e., to get sales, but because it really is acting as a kind of quasi-government, dominating the whole local economy of another country and, along with it, its political structure? That, too, has happened in the past. I don't think you can deal with this problem by laws from the Congress on bribery. It is a fact of life that Firestone was dominant in Liberia, that the copper companies were dominant in Chile, and that the oil companies, before the rise of OPEC, were dominant in the Middle East.

Discussion sponsored by Center for the
Study of Democratic Institutions,
Chicago/World Issues, April-May:25.

Allan Grant
President, American
Farm Bureau Federation

6

Of course, we are in sympathy with the plight of farmers who call for a strike. Farm

(ALLAN GRANT)

income is a severe problem. The "tractorcades" have identified and dramatized a real problem—but have done so without presenting any real solution. A strike isn't practical. You can't strike a biological industry like agriculture. Who plants the crop? Who milks the cows? Farmers produce about 80 per cent of the nation's commercial crop. They're thinking about planting and harvesting—and not striking. A strike is self-defeating. Farmers can strike—and go broke. That is no solution . . . We can't in good conscience talk about shutting off a nation's food supply. Food must not become a weapon.

News conference, Houston, Jan. 8/
The Dallas Times Herald, 1-9:(A)9.

W. T. Grimm
Authority on business mergers

1

Today's [corporate] acquisitions are pursued with greater care than the "buy for diversification" attitude during the late '60s. Buyers are purchasing companies which will complement or expand their existing business area. Corporations are adopting acquisition strategies as a way to fulfill various business needs, particularly growth goals. Financially sound companies are acquiring other successful firms, resulting in consolidations which will enable both parties to meet the demands of the future.

U.S. News & World Report, 10-23:45.

Wilhelm Haferkamp
Vice President and
Commissioner for External Affairs,
Commission of the European Community

2

It is claimed, I know, that the open trade policies we have been following are now out of date. What we need, the seductive argument runs, is a new doctrine—"organized free trade." I am only too aware of the temptations of this doctrine for governments. In these difficult economic times they face a wide range of pressures, not least of which comes from interest groups within business and organized labor seeking protection in domestic markets. But I think it would be a perilous road to set

out on. For what is "organized free trade" but limited protectionism? And when has the infection of protectionism, once established, failed to spread? So the very use of the phrase "organized free trade" reminds me of the sinister euphemisms of George Orwell's *1984,* where there was a Ministry of Peace and a Ministry of Truth, both concerned with things very different from peace and truth.

Before German-American Chamber of Commerce,
New York/The Wall Street Journal, 1-6:6.

Armand Hammer
Chairman, Occidental
Petroleum Corporation

3

Throughout my life, I have fervently believed that trade is one of the basic common denominators of communication. We businessmen must leave to the statesmen the enormous and delicate problems related to diplomacy in the international arena. But, in our own way, I hope and sincerely believe that we are able to assist the statesmen by establishing our bonds of mutual interest.

Accepting the Order of Friendship Between Peoples,
Moscow, May 25/Los Angeles Times, 5-26:(1)6.

Thomas A. Harnett
Senior vice president and counsel,
Travelers Insurance Company

4

[Saying regulators should allow insurers fair prices] : Unless a profit is made from underwriting and investment operations, the insurers will be unable to provide for the growing needs of the insuring public. It is hypocritical of public figures to demand that insurance be made available and, at the same time, to deny the insurer a profit which can provide the capacity—the funds—to assume new risks.

Nation's Business, November:108.

S. I. Hayakawa
United States Senator, R-California

5

Our rules on commissions or finders' fees or bribes paid to the agents of foreign governments who place large orders are far more strict than any other nation's. Purchasing agents

(S. I. HAYAKAWA)

come to this country and want to place an order; they expect a little gift or finder's fee or "bribe." They find they are going to be investigated and held up to disgrace in the American press for doing this, so they go to Germany, Japan, France, Canada, etc., and place their orders. We lose business. In a sense, we are trying to export a business morality we do not live up to anyway.

At Sacramento State University,
Dec. 1/Los Angeles Herald Examiner, 12-3:(A)1.

Frank E. Hedrick
President, Beech Aircraft Corporation

1

Really, I stick pretty close in my philosophies to the basics—honesty, hard work, sincerity, appreciation of the other fellow's viewpoint, understanding. And listen, listen . . . What you want to do in business if you want to progress is to be like an asparagus patch, except you want to be a three-foot stalk of asparagus while everybody else is 18 inches. So when anything happens they can't overlook you.

Interview, Wichita, Kan./
Los Angeles Herald Examiner, 7-21:(A)13.

Robert Hessen
Historian, Graduate School of
Business, Stanford University

2

. . . corporations are able to attract capital from investors precisely because the shareholders won't be required to play any active role in managing the enterprise. What investors seek is a *sideline* opportunity to earn profits on their money. Corporate shareholders, in other words, are deliberately and intentionally inactive. Although the separation of ownership and control in giant corporations is frequently denounced, it merely represents a widening specialization of function, or division of labor. There is no reason why a shareholder must personally manage his own wealth instead of entrusting it to managerial specialists, as investors do when they become limited or silent partners, or buy mutual funds, or deposit money in savings banks or purchase corporate bonds. None of these other opportunities car-

ries *any* voting rights or voice in management. The primary safeguard for corporate shareholders, the most effective protection they possess, is their ability to instantly sell their shares if they are dissatisfied with the performance or policies of the officers. Through the mechanism of the stock market there is a daily plebiscite which allows shareholders to register their approval or disapproval.

Broadcast commentary/
The Wall Street Journal, 4-27:20.

Lee A. Iacocca
President, Chrysler Corporation

3

[On his becoming president of Chrysler, which has been faltering, after being fired by Ford Motor Co.]: I really believe that if we can turn this company around, then I will have capped a career. I will have helped 200,000 people in their livelihoods. We are the biggest private employer in Detroit; I would have helped the city. They won't know it, but I will have helped GM and Ford compete more. So what the hell more would you want to do to end an auto career? The only other option, I guess, was to take all my money and run.

Interview/Time, 11-20:91.

Peter Jay
British Ambassador to the United States

4

[On import tariffs]: I think history shows very clearly that the most fertile source of conflict in human affairs is economic nationalism. I think that if we destroy the fabric of a fairly liberal international economic order which was established after World War II, we shall destroy the harmony in terms of the Western nations in response to any threat from the East. Even looking quite a few years down the track, it would be the most disastrous mistake we could make.

Interview/Los Angeles Herald Examiner, 3-6:(A)6.

Roy Jenkins
President, European
Economic Community Commission

5

In my view, the United States would be wise to welcome Europe taking more [financial] re-

(ROY JENKINS)

sponsibility—with a view to moving, in the future, toward a world monetary system in which the dollar would always be a leg in the tripod. The European currency—the European Currency Unit—would form an important second leg, and the yen the third.

Interview, Brussels/
Los Angeles Times, 12-11:(3)16.

Eugene Jennings
Professor of management,
Graduate School of Business,
Michigan State University

1

[Saying business executives are under more stress than ever before] : The number of voluntary quits is astronomically high, and the number taking 180-degree turns and walking away from business is phenomenal. It's becoming an infinitely more perverse world out there, with more and more ways to screw up, and it ain't going to get better.

The Dallas Times Herald, 11-15:(B)1.

Donald M. Kendall
Chairman, PepsiCo, Inc.

2

. . . what the Soviet Union needs and wants is advanced-technology goods, equipment and know-how available here in the United States—if we are willing to sell it to them on the same commercial terms and credits we offer to nearly every other trading partner in the world . . . I am not talking about defense-related technology and equipment. I am talking about industrial goods of commercial value, which are the leading and most profitable edge of trading among all the great industrial nations of the West. . . . it is very much in the U.S. self-interest to expand our exports wherever we can. A sizeable export growth is the only arithmetic that will reduce our intolerable trade and payments deficits, and will salvage the value of the dollar in world money markets. The Soviet Union offers us an opportunity to expand our exports, cut our trade deficit and reduce unemployment. However, these opportunities are not going to be realized unless we normalize our trade relations with the Soviets, grant them most-favored-nation status, and give them access to Ex-Im Bank credits on the same terms as our other valued trading partners. For the foreseeable future, that trade will not only be profitable for the American firms engaged in it, but will also contribute positively to our national accounts, since *their* capacity to absorb our exports greatly exceeds *our* capacity to absorb theirs.

Before National Press Club, Washington,
Feb. 21/Vital Speeches, 4-15:391

Edward M. Kennedy
United States Senator, D-Massachusetts

3

It doesn't take much antitrust sense—just common sense—to see that there is something wrong with antitrust enforcement when major cases take decades to complete . . . Trial of an antitrust suit . . . is much like conducting a war. Our oversight hearings revealed that the Antitrust Division's supply lines are stretched thin, their equipment is antiquated, and their command posts are never in the same place nor manned by the same people . . . Legislation which prevents the gobbling up of independent businesses by increasingly large and aggressive conglomerates should be a matter of high antitrust priority. [There should be legislation that] makes clear that the Sherman Act does not require the elaborate search for corporate intent that mires so many antitrust suits in a decade-long search for why something was done, instead of the far easier and more important fact of *what* was done.

Before Computer and Communications
Industry Association, Washington, Feb. 28/
The Washington Post, 3-1:(D)9,10.

4

I am especially concerned with the ease with which the major conglomerates and large multi-national oil companies can swallow up major chunks in any other domestic industry . . . The potential for additional mergers and acquisitions is staggering. Exxon, for example, could tomorrow buy the J. C. Penney Company, Du Pont, Goodyear and Anheuser-Busch, using only its accumulated cash and liquid assets.

U.S. News & World Report, 10-23:45.

WHAT THEY SAID IN 1978

Martha E. Keys
United States Representative, D-Kansas

1

[Saying the tax deduction for business meals should be cut in half]: The deduction is one of the most obvious symbols of inequity in our tax code. Everyone has to eat. And many who can less afford to eat at lunchtime than the select few who can take a business deduction for meals and entertainment enjoy no such deductions ... I think that cutting the deduction by 50 per cent is a reasonable change in a traditional policy. There is no finding fault with the fact that people do like to do business at lunch or with entertainment. There's nothing wrong with that, and there may be times when you can do business only at lunch. So it seems reasonable that, by allowing half the deduction, you can probably lessen the inequity while preserving recognition that the cost of doing business is a legitimate deduction.

Interview/U.S. News & World Report, 2-27:57.

George J. Kneeland
Chairman, St. Regis Paper Company

2

[On how much of his professional time is spent in dealings with government and its regulations]: I would estimate at least 50 per cent goes for work on government issues. Ten years ago, a business leader in my sort of position spent about 10 per cent of his time on government problems. There are reports, hearings in Washington and state capitals, efforts to get our message across to the people who make laws ... A lot of laws we must comply with are a waste of time. I'll cite one: For the safety and health of employees, wastepaper baskets in restrooms must be so-and-so inches high; if they are as much as half an inch off, you can be fined $25 per basket. Another problem: We must deal with state and local governments, and sometimes their laws conflict with Federal laws. So no matter whose laws you comply with, someone is going to get mad at you.

Interview/Nation's Business, June:76.

Juanita M. Kreps
Secretary of Commerce of the United States

3

I think people in the government are getting rid of the notion that if you made business pay for improving the quality of life, somehow you buried the cost. Now regulators are paying attention to the cost, because they realize that it's going to be passed on to buyers.

Interview, Los Angeles/
Los Angeles Times, 9-18:(3)16.

Ray A. Kroc
Chairman, McDonald's Corporation

4

[On success in business]: It's all a matter of having principles. It's easy to have principles when you're rich. The important thing is to have principles when you're poor.

Interview/Los Angeles Herald Examiner, 2-15:(A)12.

William M. LeFevre
Vice president,
Granger & Company, securities

5

There are only two emotions in Wall Street: fear and greed. For most of 1977, we had an excess of fear. The last few days [when the stock market advanced more than 55 points on 63.5 million shares], greed has come back with a vengeance.

Time, 5-1:42.

Richard L. Lesher
President, Chamber of
Commerce of the United States

6

Our business system is marvelously adaptive. But the one thing that it cannot handle is continual uncertainty. Business will play by the rules of the game—whatever they are—as long as those rules are not changed halfway through the game. But today, the government is changing the rules with bewildering frequency—rules dealing with hiring practices, investment practices, environmental practices, marketing practices, pay practices, energy use, political action, advertising, taxes ... you name it and the fickle winds of political fashion have changed it. Not once, but several times. Today's corporate steward has very little idea of what to plan on five years from now, 10 years from now, 30 years from now. So he does what you would do if you found yourself in an unfamiliar place with

(RICHARD L. LESHER)

no light: he moves very slowly and very cautiously.

Before Toledo (Ohio) Area Chamber of Commerce,
Jan. 3/Vital Speeches, 3-1:319.

1

We surveyed our members as to what's troubling them. Number 1 is government. Number 2 is government. Number 3 is government. And Number 4 is government.

Interview/"W": a Fairchild publication, 4-14:2.

Arthur Levitt, Jr.
Chairman, American Stock Exchange

2

My information from investment bankers around the country is that well over 50 per cent of their acquisition assignments are currently on behalf of foreign clients . . . While we should certainly do everything we possibly can to encourage foreign portfolio investment in the United States, surely it is not in our best interest to have our innovative and technologically oriented small business under foreign control.

Before House Ways and Means Committee,
Washington, March 7/The New York Times, 3-8:(D)11.

3

[On business' attitude toward the Carter Administration]: There is a general malaise out there. Businessmen don't sense that there is the kind of leadership we need. If a way isn't found to create an interest in greater capital formation, we might stumble into capital allocation. If the key to the question of business confidence is a revitalization of the entrepreneurial appetite, there will be a disenchantment and a fortress mentality [*vis-a-vis* Carter] until we make progress in feeding that appetite.

Interview, Washington/
The Washington Post, 3-9:(A)23.

Sydney Lewis
Chairman, Best Products Company

4

One of the greatest enemies of the free-enterprise system in the United States is the business corporations of this country. The free enterprisers of America are committing free-enterprise suicide. . . . the simple truth is that too many businessmen are afraid to compete . . . Although the fair-trade laws have been outlawed, there are manufacturers still today who refuse to sell to us for fear we will discount their suggested selling prices, which have been set and maintained by collusion with retailers and distributors . . . It used to be that the proper competitive response to soft demand was to lower prices. Nowadays there is no need to cut the price. You can ask the government for a subsidy—like farmers; or an import quota—like steel, textiles, shoes and televisions. And if these avenues are closed to you, then try an antitrust suit. . . . at the very least, you can persuade your state legislature that your particular occupation needs licensing.

At Best Products annual meeting/
The Washington Post, 11-29:(D)7.

James B. Longley
Governor of Maine (I)

5

There is need for better understanding of business problems by law-makers. It is sad and dangerous that politicians, too many legislators and members of Congress feel that a tax break for business is not as politically popular as a social-welfare program. There are far too many people holding seats in legislatures who know absolutely nothing about business and who are far more interested in winning the next election than they are in looking to the future to improve the long-range economic stability of a state or nation.

Interview, Augusta, Maine/
U.S. News & World Report, 8-7:79.

Ben Love
Chairman, Texas Commerce Bancshares

6

I can tell you what will be the topic of conversation in any luncheon with business executives. It will be the burden of regulations coming from Washington. We are being hit from behind with a two-by-four, and we're worrying that Congress will make it a four-by-four. We know they won't make it a one-by-one.

U.S. News & World Report, 2-6:17.

WHAT THEY SAID IN 1978

J. Paul Lyet
Chairman, Sperry Rand Corporation

1

[Supporting trade with the Soviet Union by U.S. firms] : I'm no politician. I'm just a businessman trying to make a living—and so you may think this is self-serving—but I would think that trade builds bridges. When you think back to the situation in the '40s and '50s at the height of the cold war—well, it's a lot better now. As bad as it is, it's a lot better. I don't subscribe to the Russian system. But eventually there's going to be a coming together—peaceful coexistence, if you want to call it that. I think that the more their people see our system and how it works, the more it's going to moderate their views. There just somehow seems to be more human freedom in nations where economic progress is stressed. I would like to assume that economic growth in the Soviet Union will lead—even if slowly—toward more freedom for the people of that country as well as a more accommodating attitude toward world peace.

Interview/U.S. News & World Report, 12-18:24.

W. A. Mackie
Executive vice president,
Ingersoll-Rand Company

2

Sometimes I wonder just how many people are aware of the importance of the multinational [corporation] to our own economy. In our country, the world economy absorbs the products of one out of every three acres of U.S. farmland; it is the source for nearly one of every three dollars of U.S. corporate profit; and it keeps one out of six Americans employed in manufacturing. I might add that, despite the claims of organized labor, multinationals effectively *increase* employment at home by building overseas businesses and plants which become markets for many ancillary and domestic products. In addition, our international markets serve as a balance against the effects of variations in domestic supply and demand. Each of these contributions add to the betterment of our living standards—and that is the Number 1 ethical obligation of any business.

At Bentley College, April 7/
Vital Speeches, 6-1:512.

David J. Mahoney
Chairman, Norton Simon, Inc.

3

The populace has a one-sided view of business—and it's negative. We have to balance the scales in the minds of the public by being more aggressive about our position on key issues—backed by facts, figures and well-reasoned analyses and position papers. Too often, we are defensive and reactive, and by the time we respond to criticism, it's too late—the public has already made up its mind.

Before American Association of
Advertising Agencies, Scottsdale,
Ariz., April 27/Vital Speeches, 7-1:548.

John Marks
Chairman, Development Finance
Corporation, Sydney, Australia

4

The principal portent of possible future disaster is the clearly apparent trend toward increased trade protectionism throughout the world. Trade protectionism can only add to inflationary pressures, which must in the ultimate destroy the industrial muscle of any nation.

At International Business Outlook Conference,
Los Angeles/Los Angeles Herald Examiner, 5-24:(A)10.

James P. McFarland
Director and former chairman,
General Mills, Inc.

5

I sincerely believe that every individual involved in an organization should expect, and deserves, clearly defined communication of what is expected of him or her. And further, good performance and productivity should be rewarded with genuine appreciation and recognition. Of course, the reverse is also true—mediocre results or unnecessary failure should be noted and discussed with the individual or individuals responsible. Well-ordered, but relaxed, discipline within an organization avoids looseness, idleness and unnecessary arguments. And when it is understood that the element of human dignity is a genuine concern of the leaders of an organization, people develop the feeling that fairness, equity and understanding are

(JAMES P. MCFARLAND)

the main ingredients of decision-making—and a great deal of conflict will be avoided.

Before Episcopal Church Foundation,
Minnesota Advisory Council, Minneapolis,
Sept. 30/Vital Speeches, 11-15:80.

Robert S. McNamara
President, International
Bank of Reconstruction and
Development (World Bank)

1

... the rising number of protectionists amongst us are clearly unaware that the health of our economy is increasingly a function of our exports, that export trade in relation to gross national product has almost doubled in the past 10 or 15 years. Today it is a source of one out of eight of all of our manufacturing jobs. It takes the product of one out of every three acres of our farmland. Over a quarter of this export trade is with developing countries.

Interview/The New York Times, 4-2:(4)3.

George Meany
President, American Federation of
Labor-Congress of Industrial Organizations

2

We don't have free trade today ... We're trading in a world where practically every country in the world has various devices and methods of protecting their own people. We [the U.S.] are theoretically the only free-traders left, and we feel the time has come that we no longer look at the word "protectionism" as a bad word—that we are looking for protection.

Miami Beach, Fla., Feb. 21/
The Dallas Times Herald, 2-22:(A)8.

G. William Miller
Chairman, Federal Reserve Board

3

A declining dollar disrupts world trade, and that hurts the United States and its economic growth. A weak dollar hurts international investment, and that adversely impacts the United States. A weak dollar introduces inflation into our economy ... Because of cheaper dollars, Japanese cars are now higher priced,

and so makers of other cars that are sold in competition have been able to raise their prices. That's also true of television sets and other things. Also, as a responsible nation, it's not in our interest to have a weak dollar. It is the principal reserve asset of the world. Eighty per cent of foreign-exchange reserves are held in dollars. A substantial proportion of world trade is conducted in dollars. And for us not to take a responsible attitude toward the value of the dollar can weaken our own leadership in the world, our political impact in the world and even our own security in the world.

Interview/U.S. News & World Report, 8-7:21.

Daniel P. Moynihan
United States Senator, D-New York

4

The great corporations of this country were not founded by ordinary people. They were founded by people with extraordinary energy, intelligence, ambition, aggressiveness. All those factors go into the primordial capitalist urge.

Time, 6-19:27.

John M. Murphy
United States Representative, D-New York

5

[Saying there should be legislation reserving 9.5 per cent of imported oil for transport by American tankers]: I think some form of cargo equity is inevitable. Cargo equity may run counter to the classic principles of international free trade, but the United States cannot continue to watch the death of its merchant marine and do nothing.

At Posidonia Forum, Athens, June 9/
The New York Times, 6-10:26.

Thomas A. Murphy
Chairman, General Motors Corporation

6

The Japanese sell more than 1 million vehicles a year in the U.S., but they import fewer than 50,000 vehicles from all countries. They have a way of operating to make sure that their markets are served by their own manufacturers. When I look at the value of the yen today compared with its value three years ago, I have to conclude that their autos are not fairly

WHAT THEY SAID IN 1978

(THOMAS A. MURPHY)

priced, because the value of the yen has appreciated a heck of a lot more than they have raised their prices. In the U.S., we have to take a hard look to make sure that we are not victims of our own desire to continue on a free-trade course. Any alternative would be bad for the U.S. and bad for the world, but I don't think the game should be rigged against us.

Interview, Detroit/Time, 3-27:70.

1

... we need [government] regulation [of business] to preserve order in our society and to prevent abuses—but let it be reasonable regulation, let it be cost-effective regulation. That is our plea—and hopefully, the people of this country will recognize that their own interest is at stake here. That—just recently—has been motivation enough to move the American people to revolt on the issue of paying taxes. The grass roots in this country are stirring. The people are angry. And we are encouraged that the American people can act, will act and have acted, on matters that directly affect their welfare—such as this issue of wasteful government regulation. And not only that. We are encouraged that responsible members of our government are ready to listen—that they will join the people as they are doing on the tax issue, and that we will see an end to the adversary relationship and a new birth of cooperative action between the two principal sectors of our society that serve the people—American business and American government.

Before Business-Government Relations
Council, Hershey, Pa., September/
Los Angeles Herald Examiner, 10-21:(A)9.

Ralph Nader
Lawyer; Consumer advocate

2

[Criticizing the House for voting against creating a Federal consumer-protection agency]: The corrupting influence of big-business [political] campaign contributions, promised or withdrawn, has never been more clear than in the last few days. That is why big-business' massive lobbying defeated a measure supported by a 2-to-1 public margin and by 150 consumer, labor, farm and elderly groups. But those members who today voted against the consumer should know that consumers will organize to vote against them tomorrow.

Feb. 8/The Washington Post, 2-9:(A)1.

Joseph L. Oppenheimer
Vice president,
Standard & Poor's Corporation

3

The average [stock] investor is not a professional. He is not on Wall Street. There is no way that he is going to avoid the occasional drops that will hit the market—even with good advice. The stock market has a history of moving to irrational extremes because, on a short-term basis, stock prices are often more a reflection of fear, greed or other psychological factors than of business and monetary fundamentals.

Interview/The New York Times, 11-14:(D)2.

Paul F. Oreffice
President, Dow Chemical Company, U.S.A.

4

Government intervention in all forms, but particularly the growing dictatorship of the regulators, is the most serious threat faced today by the American economy. The President [Carter] has said, "We must do a better job of reducing government regulation that drives up costs." But will the government really police itself? Can the regulators really regulate themselves? I, for one, doubt it. About the only way the job can get done is if the American people rise up and say, "Enough is enough" ... Indeed, if labor and management together can't reverse the present trend of Federal government intervention, American industry will be stifled and American jobs will continue to be lost by the thousands. Furthermore, we need to get strong support from academia to help bring scientific and economic logic to the world of regulation. I am not saying that all regulations are bad. Certainly, some guidelines are needed. But just like the speed limits and stop signs we put on our highways and streets, they must be logical, workable and economically feasible. We don't put stop signs in the middle of a busy

(PAUL F. OREFFICE)

highway, but we do put them in the path of American business.

Before Commonwealth Club, San Francisco/
Los Angeles Times, 5-28:(7)3.

Ellmore C. Patterson
Chairman, Morgan Guaranty
Trust Company, New York

1

. . . the occurrence of some bank failures and the admission that there are "problem bank" lists have stirred demands in Congress and elsewhere for more regulation. These demands seem to be based on a belief that somehow regulation, if only it were tight enough, could make it impossible for any bank to get into difficulties. That, of course, is not so. Nor should it be the aim of public policy to make banking a no-risk business. The usefulness of banks to society depends in large part on their ability to evaluate risks and their willingness to accept them. This is their function. This is how they contribute to the efficient allocation of economic resources. Banking without risk-taking would be a sterile, even a parasitical, business.

Before Robert Morris Associates, New York/
The Wall Street Journal, 3-6:16.

Jeno Paulucci
Founder, Chunk King
Corporation and Jeno's, Inc.

2

Where else but in America could an Italian-American by the name of Luigino Francesco Paulucci go into the Chinese food business in the Scandinavian country of Minnesota, can chop suey practically in the shadows of the iron-ore dumps, sell that company for millions to a tobacco company—and I don't even smoke—and then go into the pizza business, where mama said I should have been in the first place, and with the help of a dedicated core of people make that business Number 1 in the world in seven years?

Interview, Washington/
The Dallas Times Herald, 10-15:(G)12.

Michael Pertschuk
Chairman, Federal Trade Commission

3

When I first came to Washington in the early '60s, the regulators invariably looked over their shoulders at business and the friends of business. Today, for most agencies it's reversed—the sensitivities are to the public interest, the people and the press. It's an extraordinary change and no one has tracked it.

The New York Times, 2-15:(A)21.

4

Unrestrained conglomeration could conceivably result in the concentration of an enormous aggregation of economic, social and political power in the hands of a small number of corporate leaders, responsible in a formal sense to stockholders but in a real sense only to themselves. This vision of a relatively few companies dominating the private sector is not so far from reality.

Before Senate Antitrust and Monopoly Subcommittee,
Washington, July 27/The Washington Post, 7-28:(E)1.

Carl Reichardt
President, Wells Fargo Bank,
San Francisco

5

[On the poor image of banks as a result of loan losses, bank failures and the Bert Lance affair] : . . . we have had obvious problems at American banks. But the fact that the system has come through the worst economic recession since the early '30s, in the fashion that it has, is a hell of a tribute to the system. In general, our reserve levels are quite high, our leverage ratios are low, the quality of earnings is generally quite good and, as you can see, actual loan losses and provisions for loan losses were down substantially last year and will go down even further this year. The Bert Lance thing [in which the Federal Budget Director resigned amidst controversy about his past bank dealings] is unfortunate. It is such a unique situation that to paint the banking system as a whole with that brush is really unfortunate because it just isn't true.

Interview/
San Francisco Examiner & Chronicle, 4-16:(C)9.

WHAT THEY SAID IN 1978

John B. Rhodes
President,
Booz-Allen & Hamilton, International

1

In the history of business, the 1960s are likely to be characterized as the decade in which American enterprise ventured overseas most forcibly . . . The 1970s may be thought of as the decade of interdependence and the era in which the great corporations of Japan and Europe took their rightful place. This represents a major shift . . . with the likelihood that there may be a change of similar magnitude on the way over the next 10 years. This change concerns the new phenomenon of governments acting as entrepreneurs and taking a place alongside private enterprise as owners of multinational enterprises . . . Increasingly, states—and this includes the market-economy states—are assuming roles as active, multinational competitors of private businesses. Clearly, we can no longer use the term "multinational corporation" and assume that we are talking about private enterprise alone . . . The state-owned enterprise is emerging as a significant factor in international competition . . .

Before International Chamber of Commerce,
Orlando, Fla., Oct. 2/Vital Speeches, 11-15:89.

David M. Roderick
President,
United States Steel Corporation

2

There can never be a full resolution of the steel import problem unless and until every foreign company that competes for business in the American market is required to compete under the same disciplines of the marketplace and laws that apply to our domestic industry.

At steel industry symposium, Pittsburgh,
Dec. 27/The Washington Post, 12-28:(D)12.

Murray Roman
Chairman, Campaign
Communications Institute of America

3

. . . I object to the description of phone [sales] solicitations as "junk calls." I think that's a vulgarization of the truth. Phone marketing is an acceptable, tried, tested, desired and necessary form of communication—one which elicits very few complaints from the consuming public. The public is happy to find an easier way to shop for a product or service. If people weren't, they would be saying, "Thank you very much, and goodbye." They wouldn't be purchasing the products they now are buying. The market place, not the government, should decide whether these calls should continue.

Interview/U.S. News & World Report, 9-11:43.

John H. Shenefield
Assistant Attorney General,
Antitrust Division, Department of
Justice of the United States

4

. . . the ingenuity of counsel and the flexibility of existing rules of civil procedure have created a seeming inability to force major [antitrust] cases to decision. Antitrust law, particularly in the monopolization area, can easily be subverted in favor of endless searches down back alleys for testimony that does not stand witness to anything, for mountains of documents that do not prove anything, and for lengthy briefs in support of legal theories that do not really mean anything.

Before Senate Select Committee on
Small Business, Washington, Jan. 24/
The Washington Post, 1-25:(D)8.

5

. . . as industries come to be dominated by just a few companies, it becomes relatively easy for them to fix prices—not through clear-cut conspiracies, where businessmen get together in a room to decide on prices and markets, but through price "signaling." Prices are agreed on tacitly through speeches, frequent press conferences or unnecessarily complete reports to trade journals—reports that go far beyond what customers and investors need to know. I see several industries that bargain on price levels in this manner. One company says there ought to be a 7 per cent increase. A second announces that 7 is too high, but 5 3/4 would be just about right. This kind of give-and-take seems to go on in the headlines. . . . I'm not saying that press conferences, as such, are illegal. Not all of

(JOHN H. SHENEFIELD)

them are part and parcel of conspiracies to restrain trade. But I question the kind and detail of information that is provided at them. We want to see whether these statements go further than necessary. If they do, they may be in violation of the antitrust laws.

Interview/U.S. News & World Report, 3-20:68.

William E. Simon
Former Secretary of the
Treasury of the United States

1

Hilton Kramer, writing in *Commentary* magazine recently, spoke of "the liberals's craven fear of being stigmatized as a conservative." There are businessmen like that, and they can be found in high places in our biggest corporations. Indeed, I am very sad to observe that it is in those very executive suites that there seems today so little inclination to take on the battles of principle. Perhaps this has come with the age of the non-owner manager, with the disappearance of the entrepreneurial spirit that once characterized our culture and informed our system of values and morality. How often in recent years have we heard the soft voices from the biggest of big business counseling against speaking out, urging upon us the virtues of a "low profile." We hear them scoffing at the ideal of a free market as an idea that is *passe*. In point of fact, the real problem is that our so-called business leaders suffer from a lack of conviction, a lack of courage, and an obsession to be in tune with the trendy liberal notions of our time.

At conference sponsored by
National Chamber Foundation, New York/
The Wall Street Journal, 2-14:18.

Edgar B. Speer
Chairman,
United States Steel Corporation

2

There seems to be no willingness to protect business. Government over-taxes us, and we run a country with wide-open borders permitting any foreign country to ship any and all products into this market with absolutely no restrictions ... We don't seem to have the willingness to establish the rules and regulations that permit our industries in this country to compete world-wide, let alone compete in our own market. We permit the predatory pricing of products coming into the market [from abroad], and we tax the hell out of domestic producers, which makes them less and less competitive.

Interview, Pittsburgh/
The Washington Post, 9-10:(F)6.

William S. Sneath
Chairman, Union Carbide Corporation

3

... there is simply no escaping individual company responsibility for setting and maintaining high ethical standards. Many companies that value their standing in the community have recognized the task as one of merging ethics and policy in a way that leaves no doubt about management's concern for the corporate reputation, and no room for shady practices. That may not be easy in a complex, world-wide business, but it can be done ... The task of management is to decide what is proper when questions arise, and to make absolutely certain that no individual in the corporation finds any reason or incentive to depart from the standards it has set. How can that be accomplished? Few would deny that a clear and specific code of ethics, the route that many concerned companies have taken, can provide useful guidelines for people in doubt about corporate standards. Such a code should be a living document, written in plain language, that has clear and precise application to real business situations. And it must be discussed, circulated and reaffirmed among every employee group wherever the company does business.

At Southern Assembly, Biloxi, Miss.,
Jan. 5/Vital Speeches, 3-1:302.

4

Business is an integral part of society. Our employees are part of the community. Therefore, we must share its goals and share the work of achieving them. That's true whether the goal is energy conservation, environmental protection or increased opportunity for women and minorities. Business has helped with all of these

WHAT THEY SAID IN 1978

and with others, and we must be part of further progress. The issue is rather one of balance. Few of the corporations I know about seek to avoid their responsibilities. However, many do resist the efforts of activist groups to have them address a single cause or a narrow issue in advance of a broad consensus in the community about the direction to take or the speed at which to move. In my view, we would create more problems than we solved—for the corporation and the community—by doing otherwise.

At Southern Governors Conference, Hilton Head, S.C., Sept. 18/Vital Speeches, 10-15:18.

J. Paul Sticht
President, R. J. Reynolds Industries

1

At times, the demands of government [on business] are so contradictory or idiotic as to give you a feeling of schizophrenia, since every pull of every bureaucratic demand may be accompanied by the shove of being denounced for the very ability to meet the demand. On Monday, you are exhorted, as a major multinational, to marshal your resources abroad to help close the growing balance-of-payments gap; but—on Tuesday—you, along with every other multinational, are denounced as imperialists threatening to undermine democracy. On Wednesday, you are importuned, as the provider of 80 per cent of all jobs, to bend every effort to provide still more; but—on Thursday—you confront a corporate income tax that impairs your ability to increase employment or modernize your plants. On Friday, you are urged, as a company engaged in oil production, to stretch every muscle to increase supplies and thus help meet the energy shortage; but—on Saturday—you are prevented from doing anything about it because the regulators refuse to believe anything the oil and gas companies say. On the seventh day you rest—if you can.

At University of Pittsburgh School of Business, Aug. 4/Vital Speeches, 9-15:718.

2

It is appalling that there are now so few business leaders within the Carter Administra-

tion. In fact, we often find that key elements of our overgrown, unresponsive Federal bureaucracy are headed by yesterday's hard-shell anti-business activists. Business leaders have the skill and experience to help contribute to our society's progress. Perhaps they can be encouraged now to regain the determination to serve in and with government. We need a new era of business statesmanship to enable the United States to reach beyond yesterday's achievements.

At University of Pittsburgh School of Business, Aug. 4/ Los Angeles Herald Examiner, 10-16:(A)11.

Robert S. Strauss
Special Representative for Trade Negotiations of, and Adviser on Inflation to, President of the United States Jimmy Carter

3

Open trade implies access for U.S. exports to foreign markets. The same as those foreign producers have to our markets. We cannot and will not, and Congress will not let us, tolerate predatory pricing or dumping or other actions that prejudice unfairly American working men and women. The voices of protectionism in this country are loud and shrill. The answer is not to close our doors and shut off markets. The answer is to create better agreements, to export more, improve export possibilities and insist on the right to reach foreign markets.

At International Business Outlook Conference, Los Angeles/ Los Angeles Herald Examiner, 5-24:(A)10.

William Sullivan
President, Steel Communities Coalition

4

We are the only nation that insists on playing by a free-trade policy. That's like playing basketball with football gear.

Los Angeles Herald Examiner, 12-28:(A)14.

Ryohei Suzuki
Chief executive director, Japan Trade Center

5

. . . American business is losing confidence in itself, and especially confidence in its future.

(RYOHEI SUZUKI)

Instead of meeting the challenge of the changing world, American business today is making small, short-term adjustments by cutting costs and by turning to government for temporary relief. This loss of confidence of American business may also be related to a shift in the attitude [toward] work in the United State. To reverse this development, it may be necessary to consider the Protestant work ethic more seriously and to strengthen cooperation between labor and management. In Japan, we have learned that labor and management have common as well as conflicting interests. In the United States, new ways must be found to develop mutual interests—for example . . . in the fields of pensions, profit-sharing and employee stock ownership.

Before The Conference Board,
New York, Oct. 5/Vital Speeches, 12-1:122.

Herman E. Talmadge
United States Senator, D-Georgia

1

We were founded as a nation of farmers. It remains true that the welfare of the whole community depends on the welfare of the farmer.

U.S. News & World Report, 4-17:27.

Preston Robert Tisch
President, Loews Corporation

2

Twenty years ago, we were all bewitched by the concept of corporate image. It was innocent enough in the beginning. It makes perfect sense to find out as accurately as possible what the public thinks about a company or a product or a candidate. And it makes sense to respond to public priorities, to correct misconceptions, to present oneself to the public accurately. But then we began to perceive that image could be separated from reality—that an image could be shaped independently of reality. Business began to concern itself not with how to present itself to the public most accurately, but whether to maintain a "high profile" or a "low profile." We began to think more about the impact of alternative synthetic images than the authentic-

ity of our image . . . And so we in business, whether we like it or whether we deserve it or not, find ourselves in the public consciousness with the politicians and planners who make decisions in secret, who shade the truth, who view public opinion as something to be managed and manipulated. All this was based on a subliminal suspicion that the public could not be trusted with the whole truth.

Before Dallas Assembly, Feb. 10/
The Dallas Times Herald, 2-11:(C)6.

Morris K. Udall
United States Representative, D-Arizona

3

Today, less than 1 per cent of all U.S. corporations, about 200 big firms, control two-thirds of all manufacturing assets. And 2 per cent of all U.S. corporations control some 90 per cent of all net profits. That's an incredible statistic—and a very troubling one.

The Dallas Times Herald, 12-16:(C)2.

Alain Vernay
Deputy editor, "Le Figaro," Paris

4

To the average American, the weakness of the dollar doesn't matter as much as the price of a hamburger. In a nation where only 6 per cent of the GNP comes from foreign trade, people can't get worked up about the dollar unless they travel [abroad]. Then when they find the dollar is not worth as much as they thought, they think they are being robbed, and decide to stay home.

Panel discussion, Warrenton, Va./
Atlas World Press Review, November:27.

Paul A. Volcker
President,
Federal Reserve Bank of New York

5

Today, more than ever before in the postwar period, we need to recognize and cope with the risk that . . . nations will turn inward for solutions, seeking relief for themselves by closing markets to others. In this country, a week hardly passes when the case in not put that foreign competition has contributed to the closing of a plant or sizeable layoffs . . . The mis-

WHAT THEY SAID IN 1978

(PAUL A. VOLCKER)

take we could make is to forget that these pressures are not unique to the United States and that the countries from which we import are usually also large markets for our export industries. Jobs are at stake at both ends—here and abroad—in export--as well as import-competing industries. We stand on strong ground when we insist that competition be fair as well as open, when we guard against dumping and export subsidies. We need to insist that our open markets are matched by others ... The dividing line between those policies and unilateral decisions to close certain markets may sometimes seem thin, but maintaining that distinction is vital to world economic stability and prosperity. Difficult as it is, the line needs to be drawn. Upon that basic distinction rests much of the hope for world economic progress and order.

The Washington Post, 3-14:(A)16.

Joe D. Waggonner
United States Representative,
D-Louisiana

1

[Arguing against reducing the tax deduction for business meals] : Senator Russell Long has put this in some perspective. He says entertainment expenses are to sales what fertilizer is to farming. And that is what a business lunch is intended to do—to increase sales and production ... President Carter is caught up in campaign rhetoric when he indulges in these horror stories about the $55, three-martini lunch, and contrasts it with the truck driver's nondeductible $1.50 hamburger. It might well be that this $1.50 is a fringe benefit, too, because in many instances the employer provides living expenses for some of these people. But nobody can demonstrate that anything like the $55, three-martini lunch is typical. It's not an accurate portrayal of the situation. And again, no matter what the cost, if it's a necessary and ordinary expense of doing business, it is fair.

Interview/U.S. News & World Report, 2-27:57.

Murray L. Weidenbaum
Director, Center for the
Study of American Business,
Washington University, St. Louis

2

Government regulation often has yielded important benefits—in terms of less pollution, fewer product hazards, reduced job discrimination, and other socially desirable objectives. It should also be realized that these government programs were established in response to rising public expectations about business performance. But the worthiness of these social objectives should not make the specific methods being used in attempting to achieve them totally immune from criticism ... Government leadership—Federal, state and local levels—needs to take a dramatically different view of the regulatory mechanism than it does now. Rather than relying on regulations to control in detail every facet of private behavior, the regulatory device needs to be seen as a very powerful tool to be used reluctantly, and with great care and discretion. The emphasis should be placed upon identifying the least costly and most effective means of achieving social objectives.

At conference sponsored by
Federal Home Loan Bank of San Francisco/
San Francisco Examiner & Chronicle, 1-8:(TC)8.

3

Defensive research, what companies call defending themselves against government, is a rising share of corporate research and development. In many ways, regulations are creating a subtle bureaucratization of industry. You don't take risks; you think like a bureaucrat.

U.S. News & World Report, 11-27:58.

Clay T. Whitehead
Former Director, Federal Office of
Telecommunications Policy

4

The biggest problem with American business is that it's terribly inarticulate. In many ways it's its own worst enemy in national policy debates. You look at the amount of money and effectiveness with which they advertise their product, then look at the work they do in

(CLAY T. WHITEHEAD)

putting across their political philosophy and participate in public debate about business-policy ethics. With the growing involvement of government in business affairs, businessmen are just going to have to become articulate.

Interview/Los Angeles Herald Examiner, 2-6:(C)2.

Thomas R. Wilcox
Chairman and president,
Crocker National Bank, San Francisco

1

There has been a lot of activity in the business community to write and publish corporate codes of ethics. I suppose publishing such a code may silence some critics of business, and certainly publishing a code does no harm. It certainly responds to several of our constituencies. It is kind of cosmetically therapeutic and gives management and boards of directors a warm feeling—a feeling that if what they fear might happen does happen, they are on record as having foreseen the problem. But I suggest to you that the business community, of which banking certainly is a part, could not have accomplished what it has if unethical behavior had been rampant. Indeed, I suggest to you that in our society no institution, be it business, education or government, can long survive if it is fundamentally unethical. My only quarrel with the current corporate fad for publishing codes of ethics is that it implies an absence of prior ethical conduct. Despite all the recent disclosures of instances of unethical behavior in some companies, I submit instances of high ethical behavior outnumber them thousands to one ... I would be the last to argue that bankers are always ethical, but I will be the first to argue that ethical conduct is absolutely essential for a banker to be successful.

Before Commonwealth Club, San Francisco,
Jan. 20/Vital Speeches, 2-15:284.

Harold M. Williams
Chairman, Securities and Exchange
Commission of the United States

2

... I question whether there can, over time, be such a thing as "corporate morality" or "corporate ethics," as distinct from that of the society of which it is a part and the people who make up that society. I believe there is only a corporate environment that responds to, and impacts upon, the individual behavior, morality and ethics of those who inhabit that environment. Government may have a role in creating an environment which facilitates and encourages accountability. It should not, as a general matter, dictate the way in which managerial decisions are reached, or demand that a certain balance be struck between the conflicting groups affected by corporate action.

At Securities Regulation Institute,
San Diego, Jan. 18/Vital Speeches, 5-15:468.

3

One of the most important challenges facing business is to come to grips with the implications of life in an environment in which annual inflation of 6 per cent or more is conceivable—an environment in which costs double every 12 years, and triple every 19. A basic consequence of that environment is the fact that the traditional income statement, by itself, no longer serves to portray the full economic realities of business operations. To the extent that that fact is not grasped, or is ignored, it will have radiations which seriously, and perhaps permanently, jeopardize public confidence in private enterprise ... Public unease with the perceived level of corporate profits and disbelief of claims that earnings are insufficient to meet capital needs are only elements in a larger erosion of confidence in business.

At forum sponsored by Pitzer College,
Beverly Hills, Calif., Feb. 7/
Los Angeles Times, 2-8:(3)12.

Walter B. Wriston
Chairman, Citicorp (Citibank, New York)

4

One of the few scientific edges that we still have on the rest of the world is in computer hardware and software. So the government is suing to dismember IBM. The question is: What is the public good of knocking IBM off? The ultimate conclusion to all this nonsense is that

WHAT THEY SAID IN 1978

(WALTER B. WRISTON)

people will cry, "Let's break up the *Yankees* [baseball club] —because they are so successful."

Time, 5-1:44.

Lewis H. Young
Editor-in-chief,
"Business Week" magazine

1

A business executive once asked me how did I or any business journalist have the brass to criticize the management of companies when journalists have almost never managed anything. The answer to that is the same that drama critics give complaining producers of plays. Because a critic has not or cannot write a successful play does not mean he cannot tell a bad one when he sees it on the stage. Similarly, a good business journalist can spot poor management and can chronicle the results of such effort without having run a company.

At ITT Key Issue Lecture Series, Columbia, Mo.,
Sept. 21/Vital Speeches, 11-15: 78.

Crime • Law Enforcement

John E. Ackerman
Dean, National College of Criminal
Defense Lawyers and Public Defenders

1

Crime causes fear, and people have got to find a way to deal with crime. If they believe that criminals will be rounded up and herded into prison for a great deal of time, it helps them to deal with that fear. But we're ignoring 200 years of history. Prisons don't help the crime problem. They create criminals. It's absurd to believe that, by putting someone into a place with a lot of other people who are criminals, they're somehow going to decide not to commit crimes any more. It's like putting someone into a society made up entirely of Shriners, and expecting them to somehow not wear a funny hat.
The Christian Science Monitor, 11-28:16.

2

We don't any longer see the Bill of Rights as the thing that keeps me free, that keeps me from living under a police state. We see it as a thing that allows criminals to go free. That kind of thinking has the subtle effect of making people think freedom is not as important as other things; that maybe freedom is not as important as safety; that maybe, in order to keep away a lot of people that I'm scared of, I can sacrifice freedom. As a result, invasions of privacy are growing more rapidly than efforts to curb them. If the trend doesn't reverse, life in this country as we know it won't exist 50 years from now.
The Christian Science Monitor, 11-30:13.

Allen H. Andrews
Superintendent of Police of
Peoria, Illinois

3

The [Federal] Law Enforcement Assistance Administration really has been a good thing.

Local government just doesn't provide money for research, experimentation and demonstration in this area, and law enforcement has suffered from the notion that "everybody knows" what to do in this area. Well, everybody doesn't know, and this money has enabled us to mount experiments that help us know a lot more about how to do our jobs better.
The New York Times, 7-17:(A)11.

F. Lee Bailey
Lawyer

4

[On capital punishment]: Emotionally, I share the view of a lot of people when I'm outraged by a crime: an eye for an eye. I particularly believe in it for people who shoot me. But on a logical basis, it just doesn't wash. The risks are so horrendous—the damage it does to society, perceiving this legal murder as a fair means of remedying a bad act. And, in some cases, they have convicted people and executed them, and had the victim walk back in . . . Perhaps somebody who kills a policeman or guard during a riot—you may have to execute him because the only thing that can deter those who are in prison already is the fear of death.
Interview/
Los Angeles Herald Examiner, 12-7:(A)12.

Roger Baldwin
Founder, American Civil Liberties Union

5

One of the most striking things about the times in which I have lived is the decline of violence. We don't have the industrial warfare we had between unions and employers. Nor the racial warfare, both in the South and in the North. Remember, there were lynchings, and then they called out troops time and time again. So the regime of law is in effect.
Interview, New York/
Los Angeles Times, 7-23:(1)4.

WHAT THEY SAID IN 1978

Griffin B. Bell
Attorney General of the United States

1

Surely the investigative forces of the Federal government should not be monitoring the legitimate First Amendment activities of our citizens because the views they are expressing are controversial or even antithetical to our constitutional system. But, just as surely, the FBI should not stand idly by while terrorist groups seize hostages or set off bombs, merely because the terrorists purport to act in the interest of a "cause."

Before Senate Judiciary Committee, Washington,
April 20/The Washington Post, 4-21:(A)3.

Julian Bond
Georgia State Senator (D)

2

I go out to the Federal pen here a lot and people tell me that the age has just dropped so radically. The average age of the prisoners used to be in the late 30s; now it's in the mid-20s. This is the Federal system we're talking about, not the state system. The black-white ratio has almost reversed from being 20 per cent black some years ago to being 40 per cent white now. And you see it in all these young guys out there—Vietnam vets, bank robbers, drug people and such. Small-time—all of them small-time. The prison used to be filled with organized-crime figures. Now it's filled with bank robbers. It used to have a lot of moonshiners in it—white country moonshiners. Now it's got black bank robbers. Bank robbery is the crime of choice among black youth. Big money. And that's what happens to those people.

Los Angeles Times, 6-22:(1)17.

Anthony V. Bouza
Bronx borough commander,
New York City Police Department

3

You look at the average policeman, and he comes from the lower middle class or upper lower class, and suddenly he's going to become a policeman. He wants security; he wants a nice-paying job; he wants to work out of doors; he wants to help people. And that is the psychology. And he goes to the police acad-

emy, and he is taught how to help people. He's going to be preserving the fabric of our society. He's going to be preserving life and property and maintaining peace. And then he gets out there, and he suddenly discovers that he's regulating human behavior, that he is bitterly resented. And he's shocked. The police officer's reaction to this is absolute shock—that a citizen, and I mean the citizen generically, should resent his presence. And it *is* resented. And it is resented rightly. We all bridle at control. The policeman has great difficulty assimilating that knowledge. He becomes a bit cynical. He becomes a bit hardened. He cannot permit every emotional contact to drain him; he has to have emotions for his life and for his family. So like the prostitute who cannot afford to become emotionally, romantically involved with every client, the policeman cannot afford to become emotionally or romantically involved with every client. And the result is that he develops calluses over his emotions. As a matter of fact, that hardness and that cynicism permit him to cope with what he encounters. I think that if you maintained the involvement of the philosopher in the ghetto in a policeman, he'd disintegrate after a very little while.

Television interview, New York/
"The Police Tapes," Public Broadcasting Service

Harry D. Caldwell
Chief of Police of Houston

4

Policing used to be a fairly simplistic trade. It was deputize the posse, jump on the horses and go after the bad guys. Now it requires much greater response to the human condition.

U.S. News & World Report, 4-3:37.

Norman A. Carlson
Director,
Federal Bureau of Prisons

5

The basic reason why I think [inmate] furloughs are effective is that family ties—or the lack thereof—are the prime determinant in recidivism. If an inmate goes out without a family, without a place to go—no home, nobody to turn to—the chances of recidivism are far higher.

Los Angeles Times, 4-10:(1)7.

Jimmy Carter
President of the United States

1

I have inspected many prisons and I know that nearly all inmates are drawn from the ranks of the powerless and the poor. A child of privilege frequently receives the benefit of the doubt; a child of poverty seldom does.

Before Los Angeles Bar Association, May 4/
The Dallas Times Herald, 5-5:(A)6.

Benjamin R. Civiletti
Deputy Attorney General of
the United States

2

[On white-collar crime]: Imposition of heavy prison terms joined with appropriate fines should be the rule, with probation and early parole reserved only for the most exceptional cases. We must increase the cost of such crimes by ensuring punishment more severe than only the possible loss of reputation and community standing ... Only by "recriminalizing" white-collar-crime offenses can we hope to deter would-be offenders ... It is hard to justify incarcerating the ghetto youth for theft of a car while simultaneously admitting to probation the corrupt government official or corporate officer who has betrayed his trust and milked the public for millions of dollars.

Before House Crime Subcommittee, Washington,
July 12/The Dallas Times Herald, 7-13:(A)9.

Terence Cardinal Cooke
Roman Catholic Archbishop of New York

3

Terrorism has the potential to destroy the whole fabric of society and diminish the hope of men and women, as it deprives them of the peace and safety they need to raise their families. The tactic of achieving political results through the direct striking out at innocent people is evil and threatens all society and every family and person in their daily activity.

At memorial mass for
slain Italian Premier Aldo Moro, New York, May 12/
The New York Times, 5-13:7.

Donald R. Cressey
Criminologist; Professor of sociology,
University of California, Santa Barbara

4

It seems safe to conclude that our white-collar crime problem stems directly from the divisiveness and multiple moralities which have developed over the years. Today, learning how to accommodate one's moral principles to such practices as price-fixing, false advertising and bid-rigging is as easy as learning how to drive a car faster than 55 miles an hour. Once this is acknowledged, we are faced with the task of developing a single morality, one which makes it unethical to ignore the requirements of the public interest, the common good, the general welfare. This task is beyond the capabilities of the sociologist and criminologist. It is probably beyond the capabilities of Congress, too. Still, it is just possible that either Congress or a Presidential commission on white-collar crime may be able to stimulate American businessmen to move toward the development of a nationwide sense of community which would make white-collar crime unthinkable.

Before House Judiciary Subcommittee on Crime,
July/The Center Magazine, Nov.-Dec.:48.

Edward M. Davis
Chief of Police of Los Angeles

5

I've gotten in trouble with many of my critics in saying that all those things that are laws [against crimes] which traverse the sanctity of the family, to destroy it, are the kinds of laws that I am going to enforce, in addition to the other laws. There is a liberal trend of thought that says: Do not enforce "victimless" crimes; do nothing about pornography; do nothing about prostitution; do nothing about open, ostentatious homosexuality; forget about this, forget about that—and I've said, baloney.

At Garden Grove (Calif.) Community Church
The New York Times, 1-14:8.

Bob Dole
United States Senator, R-Kansas

6

Up to 28 per cent of all murders and 19 per cent of all rapes are committed by persons on

WHAT THEY SAID IN 1978

(BOB DOLE)

conditional release [from jail] . . . Persons who are victimized by criminals out on bail rightly feel that the criminal-justice system has failed to protect them.

The Washington Post, 1-24:(A)6.

Jim Estelle
Director, Texas Department of Corrections

1

In my opinion, until we are willing to invest in . . . youth . . . what we really owe, or what we owe ourselves, we are not going to answer the question of criminal activity with any degree of effectiveness . . . I have some reason to be hopeful; I have seen some dramatic improvements in [youth] activities and programs just in the last six or seven years. The expansion of juvenile probation and effective diversion programs in some of our larger communities for juveniles I have some hope for . . . We are not going to manage the commitment rate because that is set by the community and their courts, but I think we can devise ways of handling the population a little more effectively and a little more economically than we are now. If those things don't come about, obviously we are going to have to continue to build prisons as we are now. We are overcrowded now. We are playing a catch-up game, and, very honestly, we are going to be playing a catch-up game unless there are some alternatives to prison.

Radio interview, Feb. 25/
The Dallas Times Herald, 2-26:(A)23.

Louis Harris
Public-opinion analyst

2

It is entirely conceivable that small towns will inherit many of the apprehensions that have beset the cities for over a decade now. It took close to 15 years for the cities to build a reputation for being havens of crime. And it will take some further time, even if the crime rate for cities is declining in fact, for the cities to outgrow that reputation. But these latest [poll] results . . . are sensitive indicators that in the future crime may be every bit as much or

more a problem in the small towns of the South and West as any parts of the country—at least in the perception of the people who live there.

Before Congressional Joint Economic Committee,
Washington, May 17/The Dallas Times Herald, 5-18.

Philip B. Heymann
Assistant Attorney General, Criminal Division, Department of Justice of the United States

3

[The use of informers is] a most important investigative technique—one that we need in our efforts to combat organized crime and white-collar crime, official corruption, narcotics and violence. Many crimes could not be solved but for the information furnished by informants.

Before Senate Judiciary subcommittee,
Washington, July 12/
The Dallas Times Herald, 7-13:(A)10.

Eric Hoffer
Philosopher

4

I am not afraid to walk around this city. I ask to be mugged. They can smell my courage. But there is so much violence now. My cure for it is to make the authorities act. You have to punish those who do evil. Otherwise they will not learn. I am not very good at taking abuse. By nature I am a savage. I believe in retaliation.

Interview, San Francisco/People, 1-16:31.

Brian Jenkins
Authority on terrorism, Rand Corporatioon

5

I see terrorism as violence calculated to create an atmosphere of fear and alarm which will cause people to exaggerate the strength of the terrorists and the importance of the cause. The violence is not aimed at the victims in the planes or buses; it is aimed at the people watching, the media. Terrorism is a form of theatre, and that is why you find terrorists almost choreographing acts of violence to make them deliberately more dramatic in order to get the most media attention. Terrorists are telling the world: "See how desperate we are. We are will-

(BRIAN JENKINS)

ing to do even this to command your attention, and we will continue to cause you such pain even though it may be a vicarious pain. We will continue to make your world intolerable unless we get what we want, what we feel we deserve."
Interview/The Christian Science Monitor, 3-20:46.

Edward M. Kennedy
United States Senator, D-Massachusetts

1

The idea of independent juvenile courts ... has backfired. There has been a notorious lack of rehabilitation. The violent juvenile is often let off with a slap on the wrist. [Instead,] some significant punishment should be imposed on the young offender who commits a violent crime. This should translate into jail in a special juvenile facility for the most serious violent offender ... Age cannot justify treating the 17-year-old rapist or murderer differently from his adult counterpart. The poor, the black, the elderly—those most often victimized by crime—do not make such distinctions. Nor should the courts.
Before International Association of Chiefs of Police, New York, Oct. 8/
Los Angeles Herald Examiner, 10-9:(A)6.

Edward I. Koch
Mayor of New York

2

I believe that city government has an obligation to assist [crime] victims by lessening the inconvenience, cost and trauma imposed on them through crime. In studying the criminal-justice system over the years, I have been dismayed by the treatment accorded to victims of crimes ... No one tells them what is happening ... they have no one to provide them with assistance, while the defendant has a lawyer.
The Christian Science Monitor, 6-21:13.

Robert H. Kupperman
Chief Scientist, Arms Control and
Disarmament Agency
of the United States

3

... terrorism has received so much coverage from the media that it has become a spectator

sport for the public. When the public becomes bored with one type of terrorist tactic, it loses its appeal and drops from the front page. Modern terrorism is theatre. To keep the public sufficiently enthralled requires an occasional upping of the ante—a new tactic, more violence, more disruption.
Interview/U.S. News & World Report, 3-6:68.

Walter Laqueur
Historian, Center for Strategic and
International Studies;
Authority on terrorism

4

As a rule of thumb, the more dangerous your terrorist enemy, the less you should make concessions. The less dangerous the terrorists, the more you should consider concessions. Let me give you an example: The Hanafi Muslim seizure of hostages in the city hall and another building in Washington. This was not a big, dangerous terrorist movement but a small group of people with a grievance. This was an occasion when concessions should have been considered since it did not involve the risk of inviting more actions by this group in the future. But it's a different matter when you're dealing with people like the Baader-Meinhof in Germany or the Red Brigades in Italy. With such terrorists, the rule should be never to give in—however important the victim [hostage].
Interview/U.S. News & World Report, 5-22:36.

Patrick V. Murphy
President, Police Foundation

5

To those of us concerned about the right of the American citizen to the best possible police service at every level, [the late FBI Director] J. Edgar Hoover's transparent program to divide and conquer made him and his Bureau the biggest single bureaucratic obstacle in the country to better law enforcement. His half-century on the Mount Olympus of American law enforcement turned into an American nightmare.
San Francisco Examiner & Chronicle,
1-29:(This World)2.

6

What's been lost since the automobile and the two-way radio started to come in is the

WHAT THEY SAID IN 1978

contact with the people. Police officers ride around in cars and they don't know anyone. The foot officer knows the business people and he gets a head full of good information. And information's the life-blood of police work.

Interview/Los Angeles Times, 3-19:(1)2.

David Ross
President, Los Angeles Association of
Deputy District Attorneys

1

The bottom line is that the criminal-justice system—all these marble palaces and high salaries—exists for one thing: to protect the public. And it's not doing the job.

The Christian Science Monitor, 11-27:12.

Stanton E. Samenow
Clinical psychologist; Director,
Center for Responsible Living

2

[On using insanity as a defense plea in criminal court]: It is a charade participated in by the courts, some psychiatrists and criminals ... If a person commits a felony and faces a conviction, there is a lore in the District of Columbia, in the streets and among lawyers that if you can convince a court and a psychiatrist that you're insane, you go to a hospital and not to prison. In the hospital, the conditions are better. If you play the psychiatric game, you can get out sooner and beat the charge.

Interview, Washington/
Los Angeles Times, 6-9:(1)14.

Laurence H. Silberman
Senior fellow, American Enterprise
Institute; Former Deputy Attorney
General of the United States

3

The fact that a group has not yet crossed the line between legal activity and criminal conduct should not prohibit the FBI from collecting *any* information concerning that group if it can be reasonably expected that they may cross the line.

Before Senate Intelligence Committee, Washington,
July 18/The Washington Post, 7-19:(A)12.

James R. Thompson
Governor of Illinois (R)

4

It's time to put to rest the notion that prisons are for rehabilitation. When they can accomplish that end, it is good. But the primary purpose of prison is to separate criminals from the rest of us and to punish them so as to deter other people from similar behavior.

Time, 2-20:20.

William H. Webster
Director, Federal Bureau of
Investigation

5

[Saying there were mitigating circumstances involved in the indictments of several former FBI officials charged with illegal break-ins]: I don't say it's a legal justification. I've never said that. But I do say it would have to be considered in terms of mitigation. If a person is convicted, he's entitled to make that argument in terms of punishment, if any is received ... We've isolated these acts [break-ins] from their setting, and we tend to forget the riots in the streets, the bombs that were blowing up people, the Capitol—I was here the night that the Capitol was bombed. We tend to forget that that's the group that ... the Bureau was trying to identify—who they were, where they were.

To reporters, Washington, April 28/
Los Angeles Times, 4-29:(1)3.

6

[On the late FBI Director J. Edgar Hoover]: I think each Director ought to be remembered in terms of the times in which he lived and how he responded to those times. I always think of Mr. Hoover as a great builder. He built this organization into one of the most effective law-enforcement agencies in the world, and that reflected certain talents—discipline, determination, steadfastness. Sometimes along the way—what was it, 48 years?—there were some ups and downs, and it would be hard not to recognize those. But I tend to feel that history will make a more accurate evaluation of his contribution. I think his most lasting effect on the

(WILLIAM H. WEBSTER)

Bureau is what I call the "can do" attitude of all the men who serve here, including the younger agents. It's a responsiveness to leadership and a confidence that we can do the job, and that's important.

Interview, Washington/
The Christian Science Monitor, 6-22:(B)2.

1

[On white-collar crime]: In most cases, all these crimes are committed without violence, but they attack the very trust that is so essential to the American economic system. Because of the highly sophisticated nature of the schemes employed, white-collar crimes comprise one of the most difficult challenges facing law enforcement today.

Nation's Business, November:35.

2

[Saying that while he is dismissing two FBI supervisors who were involved in allegedly illegal break-ins, wiretaps, etc., in the early 1970s during the Bureau's investigation of radicals, he is not taking action against 59 street agents who were also involved]: It seems clear to me that, to discipline the street agents at this late date for acts performed under supervision and without needed legal guidance from FBI headquarters and the Department of Justice, would wholly lack any therapeutic value either as a personal deterrent or as an example to others. It would be counter-productive and unfair.

News conference, Washington, Dec. 5/
The New York Times, 12-6:(A)1.

Marvin E. Wolfgang
Professor of sociology and law,
University of Pennsylvania

3

[On the decline in the number of people of crime-committing age, 15 to 24]: No matter what we may otherwise have done—increased the number of police, tried to control, prevent or deter crime—the changing age composition is extremely important. We have found that the rates of crimes of violence are likely to decline in the late '70s, continue to decline in the '80s, just on the basis of changing age composition alone.

Before House subcommittee, Washington/
San Francisco Examiner & Chronicle,
7-2:(This World)14.

Evelle J. Younger
Attorney General of the United States

4

I think the level of respect for law enforcement was at a low ebb in the '60s. I think the pendulum is swinging back now. I don't know if it will swing back to where it was in the '50s, and I don't know if that's necessarily good. I don't want to return to the McCarthy era, but I would like to return, and we are returning, to a point where people are generally held responsible for their own acts.

Interview/Los Angeles Times, 10-30:(1)20.

Education

Mortimer J. Adler
Author; Former professor of philosophy, University of Chicago

1

We have an increasing and heterogeneous student population. The college receives students from high schools who are ill-equipped to go to college. The high school receives students from the elementary schools in the same condition. The system requires that they all be passed through from grade to grade, and so the standards have had to be lowered. To find a college graduate who is competent as a reader and writer is very difficult.

Interview, New York/
Book Digest, May:22.

Grace Baisinger
President, National Parent-Teachers Association

2

[Arguing against tax credits for parents of private-school students]: In going the route of the tax credit, the Federal government abandons its long-standing policy that you provide aid on the basis of need. A family can qualify regardless of income. This will deny substantial assistance to those less well off, because there is only so much money in the Treasury ... We are very concerned that passage will mean that Federal support for private and parochial education will increase at the expense of public education. Passage would be saying, in effect, that the Federal government is placing a greater emphasis on private than on public education. That would make a complete turnaround in the way America has looked at how to best educate masses of people.

Interview/
U.S. News & World Report, 5-1:69.

Robert A. Bandeen
President, Canadian National, Ltd.

3

From their very beginnings, universities have always been under attack. In the early days it was from religious zealots and dictatorial regimes. More recently we have seen the anti-intellectual forces on the campus itself, destroying computer centers and occupying the offices of the administration. Now some of these forces seem to have switched from blue-jeans to three-piece suits as they seek to have universities become more and more merely technical training centers. Universities have always been the well-springs of our culture, the nurseries of our new ideas. As you build a better world, make sure that the primary role of these institutions is not forgotten, that the well-springs are not polluted, nor new ideas allowed to become an endangered species.

At Dalhousie University, Halifax, Nova Scotia,
May 11/Vital Speeches, 8-1:612.

William S. Banowsky
President, Pepperdine University

4

I've heard critics say I spend too many hours in the outside world, moving around the business community. But I have to do an enormous amount of fund-raising. I have management responsibility for a corporation, a university that spends $40-million a year. We have budgets to balance, just like any business. We have personnel situations to deal with, purchasing and cash flow and banking problems. I also deal with a board of regents. I try to lead the faculty, and this is entirely separate from dealing with regents. I also try to have a relationship with the students—they, after all, are the reason for the university.

Interview/Los Angeles Times, 6-4:(Home)49.

Thomas Berg
Minnesota State Representative

1

Despite all the problems involved in financing public education, the one thing most politicians and voters agree on is that public education is important—not only to school kids and parents, but to the future of the country. If the tax-limitation movement grows out of control, serious damage to the nation's future well-being could be the outcome. Cuts in educational budgets can and should be made, but a scalpel may well be more appropriate than the meat-axe currently being wielded by some politicians and commentators.

At United Press International Conference of
Editors and Publishers, San Diego/
The Christian Science Monitor, 12-28:23.

Leonard L. Berry
Chairman, department of marketing,
Georgia State University

2

One of the truly significant forces for change in America today is the rising level of education for vast numbers of its population. When you add up the number of students, teachers and administrators now engaged full-time in formal education in this country, you end up with nearly a third of the entire population—a figure that doesn't include the millions who are taking courses part-time in the evening. Or to view the rising level of education in America in another way: Those now retiring from the labor force average about 9 years of formal education, while those now entering the labor force average over 12 years of formal education. The number of adults completing four years of college rose from 1 in 14 in 1950 to 1 in 7 in 1975 . . . What is most significant about these educational trends is that education changes people. Educated men and women expect more . . . from themselves, from their institutions, from society. Educated men and women are quicker to challenge traditional values and behavior, harder to convince with superficial answers, more inclined to self-examination, e.g., who am I, where am I headed, where should I be headed. In sum, the rising level of education

in America is helping to fuel a new set of values . . .

Before American Association of
Advertising Agencies, New Orleans, Feb. 17/
Vital Speeches, 6-1:490.

George Blakley
Chairman, department of mathematics,
Texas A&M University

3

[On the use of the new small calculators by students in doing homework and other math problems]: Like sex and automobiles, they're here to stay, but if you get involved with them too early you might get hurt. For certain kids, calculators can be the best thing in the world because they use them to discover things and be stimulated. But let's face it, most grammar-school math is pretty dull, and if you can avoid it by using a calculator you're going to do it . . . I like the idea of exploiting them at the university level, but you have to control the rate at which young kids learn to use these new tools. It's like giving a kid a power-saw too soon. A power-saw is a great tool, but if you give it to him too soon you have to supervise very carefully . . . We can disagree and test the ways of teaching with and without them, but sooner or later everyone is going to have one and their very bulk is going to force their way into the classroom.

Interview, Austin, Texas/
The Dallas Times Herald, 7-2:(A)41.

Ernest L. Boyer
Commissioner of Education of
the United States

4

[On television as an educational medium]: Today, the traditional teacher is not the only source of knowledge. The school has become almost incidental to some students. The classroom has less impact and receives less respect. To put it bluntly, a new "electronic classroom" has emerged . . . The separate sources of information which educate our children must somehow be brought together . . . Surely the various

WHAT THEY SAID IN 1978

sources of information need not be in competition with each other.

At "Television, the Book and the Classroom"
seminar, Washington/
The Washington Post, 4-28:(B)2.

Jimmy Carter
President of the United States

1

I don't favor tuition tax credits under any circumstance, even if it was at a very slight level, because this would inevitably rapidly grow with each succeeding budget and the first thing that you know, tuition tax credits would be the major Federal expenditure for all education in the United States. And so I think the tuition tax credit itself as a subject is very detrimental to the future of education in our country. It gives the credit to those who need them least and it makes the average parent, who is a working-class person, particularly who has his children in public schools, pay for high tax benefit for families in a higher tax group who have their children in private schools. So I think the whole concept is fallacious and I don't like it.

Before American Society of Newspaper Editors,
Washington, April 11/The New York Times, 4-12:35.

Lisle S. Carter, Jr.
President, University of
the District of Columbia

2

It is most often those who have made it as a result of higher education who appear to want to pull up the ladder of opportunity behind them and to question the value of education, for any but a limited number, to either the individual or society. It is those who have made it who appear to view much of public higher education as a residual welfare system rather than as a central strand in a network of educational pluralism. The fundamental questions those individuals raise are not about higher education but questions about our commitment to freedom, equality and opportunity in this society; questions which tend both to encourage the individual self-centeredness that is all

too prevalent among us today and to discourage belief in the future possibilities in America and in our common purposes.

At inauguration of David Knapp as president of
University of Massachusetts, Oct. 29/
The Washington Post, 11-15:(A)18.

Charles Collingwood
News commentator, Columbia
Broadcasting System

3

There is a general public perception that something is very wrong with our public-school system, and people are beginning to realize that it cannot be corrected simply by the schools or government alone. It has to involve parents, citizens, everyone. Everybody has got to understand it, care about it, put some personal effort into improving it . . . From 13 to 15 per cent of our high-school graduates are unable to read road signs, look up names in a phone directory, add up a bill. That, in itself, is an indictment of our educational system. Some people feel that our educational system is a monolith, not subject to change. But I have found it to be volatile, amenable to pressures and changes—perhaps too much so. In the 1960s, whole new theories came into the foreground and led to a proliferation of elective courses, a concentration on making school relevant and fun, with reading and writing almost secondary. Those theories are being reversed now to a great extent. There is a strong movement to return to the basics.

Interview, New York/
The Christian Science Monitor, 8-21:22.

Michel J. Crozier
Founder and director, Centre de
Sociologie des Organisations, Paris

4

Universities in France were, in the past, always considered a bourgeois milieu so that proletarians never thought of sending their children there. Those attitudes are changing, but the social barrier still persists. There is still a feeling among working-class parents and children that they are out of place in the universities.

San Francisco Examiner & Chronicle,
12-31:(This World)2.

E. T. Dunlap
Chancellor for Higher Education
of Oklahoma
1

[Federal agencies] require a lot of meaningless paper work [and are] indirectly affecting and influencing educational policy even though the Constitution says it is up to the states.
U.S. News & World Report, 6-12:43.

Charles Frankel
President, National Humanities Center;
Professor of philosophy and public
affairs, Columbia University
2

Scholarship cannot and should not be shackled to problem-solving. It must be free to follow crooked paths to unexpected conclusions.
Interview, New York/
The New York Times, 7-2:(1)34.

William P. Gallagher
Executive director, New York State
Federation of Catholic School Parents
3

[Advocating a tax credit for parents of private-school students]: Parents should have the right of choice in education. The way things stand now, the choice is being eliminated because people can't afford to pay tuition at private schools. The tax credit would give people a choice, and it would be very easy to administer ... Diversity and pluralism are good for the country. The tax credit would foster these values in education. The Supreme Court said in 1925 that parents could fulfill the mandatory-attendance laws by sending their children to non-public schools. All we want is a share of our tax dollar so we can exercise a right already guaranteed to us by the Supreme Court.
Interview/U.S. News & World Report, 5-1:69.

David Pierpont Gardner
President, University of Utah
4

In our compassion for students, we sometimes confuse personal growth and academic progress in our evaluations. The "inward journey," personal growth, is, let us hope, the inevitable accompaniment of education, but it is largely ineffable. Academic progress can and must be measured, judged by standards appropriate to the discipline. We want both personal growth and academic progress. We want compassion and humanity in our students and in ourselves. No supply of it from us toward them or from them toward themselves, however, will take the place of knowledge—any more than that knowledge, once mastered, can save us without grace and wisdom in the use of it.
Before Western Association of Schools and
Colleges, Newport Beach, Calif., March 9/
Vital Speeches, 5-1:446.

A. Bartlett Giamatti
Professor of English and comparative
literature, Yale University;
President-elect of Yale
5

The interesting thing to me is that this generation of students is much more wary of, or less susceptible to, the rhetorical as opposed to the substantive appeal of social issues. I hope they never become unresponsive to the substantive appeal. But I'm delighted that they're a little more skeptical about the rhetoric. Part of that is, not only do they have older brothers and sisters who went through it and got very disillusioned and they've learned, but also because they've got younger brothers and sisters—from a very different point of view—for whom it is going to be difficult, given the cost of going to college, to have the same shake they have. And, therefore, I find this a very responsible group of kids. They aren't grinds, but they really have (a) sense of the need to make the most of this time in college. And they're very upset when cutbacks and consolidations occur, because they don't want to get shortchanged.
Interview, Chicago/
Los Angeles Times, 5-7:(8)19.

A. Bartlett Giamatti
President, Yale University
6

Within a dozen years, there will be just about a million fewer 18-year-olds in America than there were three years ago. The competition [among colleges] for potential college ap-

WHAT THEY SAID IN 1978

(A. BARTLETT GIAMATTI)

plicants will increase dramatically, and no institution will be immune. For even those universities whose colleges will still attract a greater pool of applicants than there will be places in a class will feel this shrinkage because their doctoral candidates will find, as so many are now finding, that there is no market for their skills. Indeed, of all the immediate challenges facing the major research universities—to sustain research libraries, to support academic science in the context of a university population that will shrink, to plan the direction of medical education, to finance graduate students, and to embrace part-time or older students in new patterns—of all these challenges, the most difficult and internally consequential will be the need to attract into the academic profession the ablest and most dedicated young men and women. Nothing we do in colleges or universities, or that the country wants done, is possible without the next generation of teachers and scholars.

Inaugural address as president/
The Washington Post, 11-23:(A)15.

Ira Goldenberg
President, Franconia (N.H.) College

1

Alternative colleges began as this one did as an alternative to large, impersonal, highly structured educational institutions. What we offered was an education that presumed respect for the individual in an atmosphere of closeness. But most alternative colleges—including this one—fail to look at the basic contradiction within themselves. Who went there? Rich, spoiled, narcissistic, white, middle-class students. You had people from one social strata, one economic class and one race. And they got here in the '60s, basically because they wanted to avoid the draft and preached and spouted rhetoric about social change. Almost all colleges serve to perpetuate the existing social and economic order. But alternative colleges that are elitist are just as dangerous as the established ones. That was the contradiction here. Don't talk to me about social change when you're running a school that

has no poor people, no blacks, no Hispanics. It's absurd.

Interview, Franconia, N.H./San Francisco
Examiner & Chronicle, 3-12:(Sunday Punch)7.

Timothy S. Healy
President, Georgetown University

2

College is essentially a time of growth, of change. The major part of that change takes place in you. If the college you go to is any good, it will hit you like a ton of bricks. It will lead you to question every conclusion you have ever reached; it will lead you to deny lots of assumptions and remake them; it will refuse to answer many of your questions, because you're asking the wrong things. It will shake your strong places and blow tons of cold air into all your warm hide-outs. It will laugh at your emotions and cry at your humor. It will be a tough and cruel place—only because it cares for you but seldom bothers to show it. It will torture you into the best you think you can do and, by mocking the results, make you do better. For perhaps the only time in your lives, you will know, existentially, that the life of the mind is soul-sized. You will be stretched till you squawk. And if you're not—transfer.

Before graduating class of Georgetown
Preparatory School, Washington/
The Washington Post, 6-4:(B)7.

Terry Herndon
Executive secretary,
National Education Association

3

I do not quarrel with the importance of reading, writing and arithmetic. Those who speak about three Rs—back to the basics—are not all wrong. But they are wrong when they isolate these from high-school subjects such as science, history, literature, music and the arts.

At National Education Association convention,
Dallas, July 3/The New York Times, 7-4:5.

Eric Hoffer
Philosopher

4

The education explosion is producing a vast number of people who want to live significant,

(ERIC HOFFER)

important lives but lack the ability to satisfy this craving for importance by individual achievement. The country is being swamped with nobodies who want to be somebodies.

Before employees of Phillips Petroleum Co.,
Bartlesville, Okla./
The Wall Street Journal, 3-23:14.

John R. Hubbard
President, University of
Southern California

1

A great university, which is perhaps the most delicate and complex mechanism ever devised by man, is not built by political combustion but by love of learning. And that love has thus far been able to transcend all the slings and arrows that American educational establishments have been heir to—depressions, wars, anti-intellectualism. Now it must transcend another threat of doom, and I refer to raging inflation.

Interview/Los Angeles Times, 11-12:(Home)84.

Jesse L. Jackson
Civil-rights leader; President,
Operation PUSH (People United to
Save Humanity)

2

... it is not for soulful reasons that we develop great athletes, but for very scientific reasons. They practice an average of three hours a day without radio, television and telephone. And whatever people do most and do much, they do well. If we apply three hours of uninterrupted time at night or in the afternoon to reading and writing and counting, our cognitive skills will be as great as are our motor skills.

News conference, Washington, Jan. 5/
The Washington Post, 1-6:(A)2.

3

[On today's students]: The choice is theirs: They can put dope in their veins or hope in their brains. Motivation must be seen as important and a critical element in turning this crisis in education around. We must teach our children that if they can conceive it and believe it,

they can achieve it. They must know it is not their aptitude but their attitude that will determine their altitude ...

At Howard University/
The Washington Post, 5-21:(A)5.

4

Too many of our schools are infested with a steady diet of violence, vandalism, drugs, intercourse without discourse, alcohol and television addiction. The result has been to breed a passive and superficial generation.

Time, 7-10:45.

Herman Kahn
Director, Hudson Institute

5

For 10 years the American public has known the schools were going downhill. Did HEW worry? No ... they didn't even know about it until six months ago. They did a study. In New York the reading and arithmetic scores are going down. What does HEW think the problem is?—the racial balance of faculties and the need for women principals. That is ridiculous.

San Francisco Examiner & Chronicle,
6-11:(This World)2.

Douglas T. Kenny
President, University of British Columbia

6

... the centuries-long history of universities has indicated that higher education's purpose has been, is and always must be unbiased critical enquiry. The university deals in ideas. That is what we produce and what we provide. It has often been said—and cannot be said too often—that a university is dedicated to *learning.* This sounds thin, quaint, dull and limited. On the contrary, it is the one true and reliable source of intellectual excitement. The joy of the chase, the drive to discover, is the fundamental reason for our existence. Without a strong commitment to first-class learning, a university will be committed to a second-class future. Our foremost precept has to be: what facilitates learning is beneficial, what hinders learning is harmful. There is no better guarantee against the undermining of this maxim than the "grit" to maintain and strengthen standards. This test of ex-

WHAT THEY SAID IN 1978

cellence has to be the watch-concept of the university community in the allocation of resources, in setting entrance and promotion standards, in the approval of the curriculum, and in the recruitment and retention of faculty. In assessing the relative merits of competing needs within a university, the answer can usually be ascertained by comparing the standards each claimant has. What is important is that the side of high standards wins out.

At Commonwealth Universities Congress,
Vancouver, B.C., August/Vital Speeches, 10-1:753.

Peter J. Liacouras
Dean, Temple University Law School

1

[Students] are increasingly being judged on the basis of artificial, "objective," standardized tests rather than on [their] total merit and practical performance . . . Kids are being stereotyped more and more, even in pre-school, as either "bright" or "hard to teach" on the basis of some test score.

The Dallas Times Herald, 11-5:(G)10.

Rosalind K. Loring
Dean, College of Continuing Education,
University of Southern California

2

People come back [to school] for a variety of reasons. There are people who come to school because they need the contact of other thinking human beings. They don't have any goal other than to communicate with somebody who wants to talk about the same issue they do. That's a valuable thing to do in our society, because we're talking about a fairly alienated group of adults these days. We are frightened; we don't know where the world is going; we seem to have lost control over our fate. Education is one of the places where you can understand what the issues are and what some of the proposals are.

Interview/
Los Angeles Herald Examiner, 12-11:(A)1.

John J. Lo Schiavo
President, University of San Francisco

3

. . . I don't think Roman Catholic education is coming to an end. Of course, the small schools with small alumni organizations will have problems. But there are still people who will want a Catholic education. There are still people who want the distinctive and quality education that we can provide. The religious and moral aspect is important.

Interview, San Francisco/
Los Angeles Times, 5-28:(1)3.

Frank J. Macchiarola
Chancellor, New York City
Public School System

4

[On the success of many parochial schools with problem and ghetto children compared with public schools] : . . . the parochial schools by and large take the children their parents bring and they really exhaust themselves in trying to cope with those children before they give up. [Parochial schools] can also mandate certain performance standards with the threat of throwing a kid out, a threat of discipline, which we don't have. That's a part of it. Another part of it is a system of recognizing the need of the whole child, a value system in which the child's place exists. There is a family system. A public school system in many cases does not like families. The [parochial] system is built on families. There are values; there is the value of right and wrong. The Constitution somehow seems to make people afraid of confronting; they think that good conduct is so closely connected to religious values that we don't even promote good conduct. We're gunshy about confronting the issue of behavior.

Interview/The New York Times, 11-26:(4)5.

William F. May
Chairman, American Can Company

5

. . . [university] trustees should spend as much time as they possibly can on campus—yes, even on occasion sleeping in an uncomfortable dorm and eating in the college cafeteria. Nothing is quite as exhilarating to a grey-haired

(WILLIAM F. MAY)

business executive who serves as a college trustee than to spend a few hours in a frank exchange of ideas with students half or less than half his age. It's a great stimulus to middle-age thinking, and is undoubtedly ample compensation for all those hours volunteered at college board meetings and spent getting to and from a distant campus. The contact between an older mind and younger ones is, for me, a very important part of the intangible income from being a college trustee.

At University of Rochester (N.Y.), Sept. 23/
Vital Speeches, 10-15:24.

George S. McGovern
United States Senator, D-South Dakota

1

It is intolerable, but true, that on International Literacy Day in 1978, America's standing in world literacy ratings is falling sharply. The United States, the first country to provide public education for all, has now been surpassed by the Soviet Union in effectively educating its citizens. According to the United Nations in 1970, the U.S. illiteracy rate was three times higher than that of the Soviet Union; 2 million Americans of at least normal intelligence were illiterate, according to the UN count. In fact, even this estimate of America's illiteracy rate is too low. The results of new and more accurate tests reveal that one out of every five Americans is reading with serious difficulty; they cannot read a newspaper intelligently, understand directions on household articles or comparison-shop for value. But nowhere is the evidence more frightening than among our youth. In 1977, Gilbert B. Schiffman, Director of the Federal Right-to-Read Program, reported that "at least one out of 10 students nearing the end of high school is still not able to do basic, everyday tasks ... In certain low socio-economic areas, the ratio exceeds one out of five." Even many prospective teachers are not truly literate. For example, in 1976 one-third of the applicants for teaching jobs failed an eighth-grade general-knowledge test in Florida. And, as the problem worsens, educational agencies do less and less about it, even though study after study continues to document the dimensions of our failure.

Before the Senate, Washington/
The Washington Post, 9-8:(A)12.

John Meyers
President, National Catholic
Educational Association

2

[Calling for Federal aid to Catholic schools] : Realistically, we have always known that the main support for Catholic schools is going to come from Catholic parents. But it's a question of justice. Our argument is that the government ought to aid parents in the education of their children.

The Washington Post, 3-19:(A)12.

Maurice B. Mitchell
Chancellor, University of Denver

3

Essentially, the university is run by the faculty. The administrator is honored as though he runs it, and his title suggests that he runs it, but the faculty really runs the university. The faculty decides who gets admitted, and who gets turned down at the doors. The faculty decides who is on the faculty and who is not on the faculty. The faculty decides who gets tenure and who does not get tenure. The faculty determines what books are bought for the library. And to a great extent, the faculty even determines which buildings are built. The great problems in the administration of higher education occur when people come from other fields and think they can just transfer the power associated with, say, top business administration to university administration.

Interview, Center for the Study of
Democratic Institutions, Santa Barbara, Calif./
The Center Magazine, March-April:10.

4

There is no longer in today's rapidly changing, very disturbed society a clear consensus about the place in the scheme of things of a college education. For example, what had become a generally understood educational destination for the majority of children, beginning with kindergarten or the first grade, is no longer

WHAT THEY SAID IN 1978

universally so. There is also great confusion in our society as to the purpose of higher education. One does not speak today of higher education as rapidly progressing and growing—a clearly developing enterprise. Even its own research about itself is scattered, uninformative and confusing... The capability of our institutions of higher learning to do pure research has also been blunted by Federal policy whose basic premise is that support should be restricted to positive cost-benefit projects. This has dashed the hopes of countless young men and women who developed their academic skills in the expectation that someday they would do basic research in the tradition of the university of earlier decades... One has the feeling that our institutions of higher education are like actors in a pageant which has become frozen in its tracks. The lights have dimmed; the stage has darkened. It is difficult to know whether the performance is over or whether, when it starts again, it will be any different.

Lecture, University of California,
Santa Barbara/The Center Magazine, July-Aug.:2.

Robert A. Nisbet
Professor of sociology, Columbia
University

1

The collective autonomy once taken for granted by universities in this country, even, in substantial degree, public universities, has been jeopardized not by malevolence but—much more dangerous—benevolence that manifests itself through rules and regulations which daily increase in number and become ever more constricting... Government covers the surface of university life with a network of small, complicated rules, minute and uniform, through which the most energetic characters and original minds find difficulty penetrating... Such a power does not destroy, but it prevents existence. It does not tyrannize, but it compresses, enervates, extinguishes and stupifies a university administration and faculty till each university is reduced to nothing better than a flock of timid and industrious sheep, of which the government is shepherd.

Talk sponsored by Hoover Institution, Stanford,
Calif./The Wall Street Journal, 9-19:18.

Dallin H. Oaks
President, Brigham Young University

2

Educators should not oppose all government laws and regulations affecting higher education. In some respects an educational institution is relatively indistinguishable from other employers. Thus, I believe the government can legitimately lump educational institutions with factories and other employers for purposes of assuring employees a safe place of work and a financially secure savings and pension fund. But there are respects in which government regulation should not lump the business of education with retailing, manufacturing and other business activities. The market for ideas is sufficiently different from the markets for goods and services that education should receive different treatment from government regulators when the issue is the manner in which the business is conducted. Thus, the Food and Drug Administration may prescribe standards for prescriptions, but HEW should not prescribe standards for textbooks or the college curriculum.

Before Pennsylvania Association of Colleges and
Universities, Hershey, Pa., Sept. 25/
Vital Speeches, 11-1:36.

Glenn A. Olds
President, Alaska Methodist University

3

Education in the country so far has been totally influenced by Western Europe, but in my view there is a comprehensive shifting of influence from the Atlantic to the Pacific. The exploration and the future lies in the Pacific, and the four great powers will be our country, Russia, [mainland] China and Japan.

Interview, Dallas/
The Dallas Times Herald, 5-18:(C)8.

Eleanor Ott
President, Eastfield College

1

I've been a little defensive from time to time about the community colleges because people often compel us to defend ourselves. It is not true that we can be all things to all people, but I do believe that we have some things for all people and all things for some people. It makes me feel good that a serious student can study two years here and go on to any university. One thing I personally do is help qualified students make a smooth transition to a fine university. Then, we provide an extremely valuable service to women who are exploring new dimensions for their lives and an excellent way for a career-bound student to learn a specific skill in a short time.

Interview, Dallas/
The Dallas Times Herald, 10-19:(F)6.

J. W. Peltason
President, American Council on
Education

2

The closer the program of intercollegiate athletics is tied to the rest of the activities of the educational world, the stronger it will be and the more likely it will be to prosper. [College] presidents, no matter how much they might wish otherwise, now exist in environments in which the chain of command between them and their athletic directors will be strengthened.

Before National Association of Collegiate
Directors of Athletics, Denver, June 19/
The Dallas Times Herald, 6-20:(D)5.

Max Rafferty
Dean, School of Education,
Troy State University

3

The two worst things in American education are study-hall and the intercom. Nothing good ever happened in study-hall. Nothing good was ever announced over an intercom. It's absolutely shattering on the good teacher's morale. The teacher will have established rapport with the class as the hour comes to an end and a horrible voice from Mount Sinai will say, "Now Hear This!" And some jackass of a principal or vice principal will have some knotheaded announcement that could have been conveyed with a simple mimeographed sheet.

Interview, Troy, Ala./
The Dallas Times Herald, 8-6:(I)4.

4

Progressive education, utilitarianism, or whatever you call it, is the fault for nearly everything that is wrong with education . . . nation-wide. "Relevance," slop like that—and the teachers colleges are still teaching that pap—is the trend which has increased illiteracy.

Interview/Los Angeles Times, 11-3:(2)1.

Diane Ravitch
Historian, Teachers College,
Columbia University

5

Our present trouble derives from the fact that schools have been expected to take over the responsibilities of the home, the workplace and the community. They have been expected to equalize people's intellectual skills, to make up for economic and social hangups, even to cause everyone to end up with the same income. Like every other human institution, the schools are flawed, and there is plenty of room for criticizing them and improving them; but it is not fair to measure them against a utopian standard and then to declare them failures.

At conference sponsored by American Jewish
Committee, New York/
The Wall Street Journal, 5-3:18.

Wilson Riles
California State Superintendent of
Public Instruction

6

We have no right to diminish [college admission] standards just because excellence is hard to attain and maintain. We can't afford to waste the development of the human mind. Any society which takes that path is on the high road of extinction.

San Francisco Examiner & Chronicle,
11-26:(This World)2.

WHAT THEY SAID IN 1978

Olin Robison
President, Middlebury (Vt.) College

1

[On the trend toward vocational and specialized education]: I think that liberal education will remain an integral part of American higher education, but it will be a tough struggle. There will be fewer purely liberal institutions, and society will suffer.

Newsweek, 2-6:70.

Henry Rosovsky
Dean, Harvard University

2

An educated person should be able to control our language, to read and write English effectively, to express ideas, to communicate. The person should have a critical appreciation and an informed acquaintance with the three major ways in which we understand ourselves, our society and our universe: in the sciences, through mathematics and experiment; in the social sciences, through quantitative and historical analysis; in the humanities, through the study of great traditions ... The person cannot be provincial but has to have some understanding of other cultures, other times. And there should be a serious encounter with moral and ethical questions, and some knowledge in depth. Our hope is that education doesn't end with a degree but is a lifetime process.

Interview/People, 9-25:45.

William V. Roth, Jr.
United States Senator, R-Delaware

3

[Supporting tax credits for college tuition]: It's the easiest, simplest method of helping the big group that now gets no educational aid. Middle America is finding it increasingly difficult to send their children to college. This approach will help the greatest number for the least money ... This is money families have earned and should keep rather than give to the government. The problem is people in Washington think all earnings belong to the government. In fact, the opposite is true. All I am saying is: Let those who earn it keep more of their own money to spend on college expenses. They're not asking for a handout.

Interview/U.S. News & World Report, 4-3:61,62.

John Ryor
President, National Education Association

4

[On the passage of California's Proposition 13 which reduced property taxes]: Too many Americans seem willing to risk sacrificing the very foundation of our future as a free people, namely our public schools, in order to achieve financial relief. But the problem does not lie with the schools. The problem lies with our system for financing them. [Proposition 13] not only threw the baby out with the bath—it destroyed the bathroom.

*At NEA convention, Dallas, July 4/
The Dallas Times Herald, 7-5:(C)1.*

5

Taking a look ... at the sort of property-tax issues that are coming before taxpayers all over the country and the great disparity in the amount of money spent per child in the public schools of this country—some local school districts are spending as much as $3,200 per child, others spending as little as $550 per child—that kind of inequality makes it all but impossible to afford each child an equal educational opportunity. And because the money is flowing so fast to the Federal level, and because children and families are mobile today and moving from district to district, we believe it is important that the Federal government assume a very vital role in financing public education and reduce reliance on the property tax.

*TV-radio interview/"Meet the Press," National
Broadcasting Company, 8-27.*

John C. Sawhill
President, New York University

6

[On corporate support of universities]: Some would have you limit your support to particular ideas and points of view in an attempt to silence detractors and assure the creation of a favorable cadre of future "opinion-

(JOHN C. SAWHILL)

makers." This concept of giving is inimical to the basic concept of a university, where ideas must be given free expression so that time-tested values may be preserved and, through critical reflection, constructive change may occur . . . And then there is the school of thought that urges corporations to restrict their dollars exclusively to people, projects and institutions that most closely parallel their own products or fields . . . While this practice has been a valuable and much appreciated source of support, it serves only a limited purpose. It does not recognize the larger cultural or social context in which companies operate the interrelationship of all areas of knowledge, and the wider intellectual context in which business activities can be understood.

At conference sponsored by National Chamber Foundation, New York/ The Wall Street Journal, 1-10:18.

John E. Sawyer
President, Andrew W. Mellon Foundation; Former president, Williams College

1

The intrusion of Federal regulation [of education] offers a warning of the pressures that a separate national Department of Education could set in motion. Given the dynamics of government and the ambitions of men, one need not be a hardened conservative to anticipate the drift toward centralized planning and control that would follow; or the ways in which this could undercut the diversity and initiative, responsiveness, flexibility and independence of the network of private public institutions, locally governed, that history has given us. . . . whatever the deficiencies of existing educational forms and practices—and they are many—let us resolve them without installing an overarching authority and attendant bureaucracy that will almost inevitably bring remoteness and rigidity in place of the ranging, rambling resiliency of our present pluralism. In a country as diverse as ours and in a field as sensitive for a free and open society as higher education, the unintended consequences of centralization could be

both regrettable and, once in place, difficult to reverse.

At inauguration of Elizabeth Kennan as president of Mount Holyoke College/ The Christian Science Monitor, 10-27:27.

2

The most distinctive feature of higher education in this country is surely its diversity and extent, and the absence of any single, integrated national control from above. Though the United States offers more educational opportunities to more people than any nation has ever attempted, it has done so without any central plan or governing authority. Given the complexity and sensitivity of the field, the variety of our needs, and the size and divergent interests of different sectors and regions, I feel that this is a good thing, and that we should strive to keep it so . . . The increasing intrusion of Federal regulation offers a warning of the pressures that a separate national Department of Education would inevitably set in motion. Given the dynamics of government and the natural ambitions of men, one need not be a hardened conservative to anticipate the drift toward centralized planning and control that would follow, or the ways in which this could undercut the diversity and initiative, the adaptability and responsiveness of the vigorous, flexible, competitive network of private and public institutions, locally governed, that history has given us.

At Mount Holyoke College/ The Washington Post, 12-16:(A)15.

Hugh Scott
Dean for programs in education, Hunter College

3

Morality is the connecting rod that binds a society together. And teachers are dealing with morality when they help pupils learn how to live with each other. I can't see a special lesson teaching children not to steal; but a teacher can declare that stealing is wrong, and could show by logic that society can't exist with people violating each other's rights.

Interview, Hunter College/ The Christian Science Monitor, 11-6:(B)6.

WHAT THEY SAID IN 1978

Albert Shanker
President, American Federation of Teachers

1

I favor toughness; I think the schools have gotten soft. We used to have very rigid schools that did all sorts of stupid things, that kept hundreds of thousands of students out of college because they didn't learn Greek or they didn't learn Latin. We opened up, thank God, and allowed people to go to college who would never have gone to college under the old standards. But we went too far the other way, and now this argument is being over-politicized. We ought to bring help to students at a very early age. All the research that's around—at least a preponderance of research—shows that the mere act of leaving children back doesn't do anything. [But if] you're going to leave somebody back *and* give them help simultaneously, I don't know who would be opposed to that.

Panel discussion/The New York Times, 4-2:(4)20.

2

[Arguing against a U.S. Department of Education]: Education has never been a national responsibility in our country, and school systems should not be operated by an agency in Washington. Public schools must continue to be largely a responsibility of state and local governments ... Our members feel very strongly that education should not be isolated from other functions of government. We think that we're much stronger being represented by the head of a massive Department of Health, Education and Welfare than we would be by a Cabinet member who's the head of a department with a relatively small staff and budget.

Interview/U.S. News & World Report, 5-29:75.

John R. Silber
President, Boston University

3

Academics often think that academic life is superior, but I haven't seen the evidence of it yet. A good life depends on moral and spiritual qualities and one's relations to loved ones and how he fits into his community. Intellectual life has little to do with these things, but it should be related to it.

*Interview, Boston/
The Christian Science Monitor, 1-27:15.*

4

[Saying his school has asked families of newly admitted students for financial gifts to aid less-privileged students]: ... how do we come by that kind of money to help the poor and minorities? I'll tell you. It's by going to the parents of the wealthy students who can pay more and by saying to them, "Will you not make a contribution to Boston University so that we can educate some children of the poor and some minority students who don't have any money?" If that's an educational and a moral practice that's offensive to some people, then that's too bad. I think it's exemplary as an ethical proposition. So why the hell should I be ashamed of that?

*Interview, Boston/
The Washington Post, 3-16:(A)5.*

Robert L. Sinsheimer
Chancellor, University of California, Santa Cruz

5

The humanities can teach us about the nature of man, the enduring qualities of man, whether they derive from our genes or from the long-lived, very slowly changing elements of our nature.

*San Francisco Examiner & Chronicle,
11-5:(This World)2.*

Charles E. Taylor
President, Wilberforce University

6

It is unfair to the students and to the institution to carry youngsters who for one reason or another are not prepared to function at the college level. Opportunities in graduate and professional schools are open, and if we want our students to compete, we must be sure they are prepared.

The New York Times, 2-8:(B)3.

Daniel B. Taylor
*West Virginia State Superintendent
of Schools*

1

[Advocating a U.S. Department of Education]: It is time to give education the status within the U.S. government that it deserves. Education represents the nation's second-largest fiscal commitment and directly involves some 65 million Americans. Not only has education historically been central to the functioning of a democratic society, but there has been a Federal presence in education since the government's inception—and it is growing larger each year ... [But] I don't think it gets the proper attention from the White House and the Office of Management and Budget. Too often, I think, education is played off against the needs of health and welfare [in HEW] —and it gets short-changed in the process. I don't think that is the correct arena in which educational priorities ought to compete.

Interview/U.S. News & World Report, 5-29:75.

John S. Toll
President, University of Maryland

2

Our [higher education's] emphasis will shift more toward paying attention to the needs of people who want continuing or advanced education. Ever since World War II, the universities have been expanding in response to a growing demand of high-school graduates. In the future, our goal will be increasing our contribution to the social and economic development of the region and the state.

The Washington Post, 9-14:(DC)1.

Barbara Tuchman
Author, Historian

3

I think what is happening in education is perhaps the most disturbing symptom. Students really are not required to learn; they are not required to study. There is no discipline. Many are living without rules, without authority, without respect for authority. How are these people ever going to acquire the habits and the knowledge that can run the country, or run the businesses, or produce the works of art? All that means discipline. I don't write without working eight hours a day, sitting up there and working hard. Among many of these students there's no sense of work, no respect for work, no sense of the satisfaction you get out of it.

*Interview, Cos Cob, Conn./
The Wall Street Journal, 9-28:22.*

Carolyn Warner
*Arizona Superintendent of Public
Instruction*

4

Yes—there are Johnny's who can't read, Lisa's who can't write and Dina's who can't add two plus two. There have been in the past, there are now and there always will be. That's reality, but it is also the exception. The problem is that the exceptions are publicized on a day-to-day basis as the rule and, since our friends in Oz-on-the-Potomac seem to believe only what the media tells them about education in America, therefore they are going to take over education and fix it for us. But let me tell you the truth about the United States of America and our public education system. Let me tell you where we *really* are. The United States is the most productive nation in history. With only about 7 per cent of the world's land and less than 6 per cent of the world's population, the United States produces more than 25 per cent of the world's total goods and services. The entire world envies our technical expertise and seeks to acquire it. They try to emulate our system, not because they have believed the exceptions, but because education in the United States of America is the institution that has enabled our nation to accomplish most of the objectives we aspire to as a free and productive people. Education in the United States of America is the one thing that causes us to differ so greatly from so many other nations on our planet. American education *works.*

*Before National Parent Teacher Association,
Atlanta, June 20/Vital Speeches, 9-15:709.*

WHAT THEY SAID IN 1978

Clifton R. Wharton, Jr.
Chancellor,
State University of
New York

1

The truth is that the public versus-private higher-education funding controversy is a foolish and bogus one. As long as there is equity in treatment and in accountability, there should be no dispute. Unity, not dissension, should then prevail. For Americans ... there can be only one issue: good public and private education versus ignorance and decline. Not merely as chancellor of the State University of New York, but as a student of higher education and a taxpayer, I firmly believe the best system of higher education is when both the public and private sectors are strong.

At State University
of New York-at-Buffalo
commencement/
The New York Times, 6-2:(B)17.

Jerome B. Wiesner
President, Massachusetts Institute of
Technology

2

[Criticizing government intrusion into the affairs of universities, such as a new regulation placing a ceiling of $47,500 on the salary of a faculty member who works on government contracts): People are tired of it and I know personally of some new Federal requirements that have been almost despotic. What we need and what the country needs is regulation of regulation ... To say that a Nobel Prize winner should have a ceiling on his salary and his value to the world is absurd. I think it's wrong for the Federal government to tell universities what kinds of salaries they can pay. We can't allow our best people to have their salaries pegged by the Federal government.

Before National Council of University Research
Administrators, Nov. 9/
The Washington Post, 11-10:(A)8.

The Environment

Cecil D. Andrus
Secretary of the
Interior of the United States

1

There are more environmentalists out there [west of the Missouri River] than there are big miners or oil drillers or timber cutters. The days of the old rape-ruin-and-run approach to using our natural resources are dying, because the people see what that means and they don't want it. They know they can have development in the West that doesn't have to be at the expense of their environment . . . When I insist that we can have more growth in the West and Southwest without destroying the things that make them such great places to live in, then the developers call me a crazy environmentalist. When I don't bring everything to a screeching halt, the environmentalist community says I've "sold out to industry."

Interview, Washington/
The New York Times, 5-23:(A)16.

Barbara Blum
Deputy Administrator,
Environmental Protection
Agency of the Unites States

2

Since 1972 almost 12 million—or one in five—new motor vehicles sold in the United States have been recalled because they were violating exhaust air-pollution standards. As a record of compliance with the law and as an expression of concern for public health, this marks a dismal showing by auto-makers.

News conference, Washington, May 10/
Los Angeles Times, 5-11:(1)6.

3

It is pretty obvious, I think, that a healthy environment and health economy are both necessities. You can't have sick people or a sick environment and you can't have a weak economy, constantly wracked by inflation or unemployment. What you *can* have . . . is an environment that is sound enough to support a productive economy and an economy that makes good use of, but doesn't use up, the environment. Frankly, I find it tiresome to have our work constantly judged in terms of "selling out the environment to make life easy for industry" or of "ignoring economic realities in pursuit of some super-idealistic concept of the environment"—sometimes attacked in both sets of terms for the very same decision . . . We think it's possible to clean up the environment and do it in a way that avoids unnecessary costs, in a way that takes account of the difficulties that the sudden changes or adjustments compelled by environmental laws impose.

The Washington Post, 11-24:(A)18.

Barry Bosworth
Director, Federal Council on
Wage and Price Stability

4

We have, as a national goal, increased reliance on coal. But people die in coal mines, so we have a set of regulations that makes deep mining more expensive. If you turn to surface mining, there are problems with environmental regulations. Now we have pending regulations that would require all utility plants to install scrubbers, whether or not they burn high-sulfur coal. These conflicts in regulatory policy have become very expensive. We have problems of energy, of job safety, of environment. We don't have to pick one over the other, but we do have to make rational choices.

The Christian Science Monitor, 10-12:11.

David Brower
President, Friends of the Earth

5

Environmentalists try to be broadly concerned with everybody's problems. We would

WHAT THEY SAID IN 1978

join coalitions to help city people, but that cannot be the focus of our efforts. We speak for those who don't have a voice. We speak for animals, trees and flowers.

San Francisco Examiner &
Chronicle, 5-14:(This World)2.

Edmund G. Brown, Jr.
Governor of California (D)

1

I mentioned two years ago that we were in an era of limits, and that was construed by some business quarters as an attempt to limit economic expansion. I meant it in a much more comprehensive sense and that is that as we fill up the space that we have, the cowboy ethic becomes less and less appropriate. We have more people occupying the same amount of space, taking the finite amount of resources and rubbing up against each other in a more continuous manner . . .

Before State Bar of California, San Francisco,
Sept. 11/Los Angeles Times, 9-12:(1)3.

John H. Chafee
United States Senator, R-Rhode Island

2

One of the great problems of our country has been the disappearance of our wetlands at what has been a very alarming rate. In hearings conducted by the Committee on Environment and Public Works it quickly became apparent that, if our remaining swamps and marshes were not given a greater measure of protection, those areas would continue to vanish at an ever-increasing rate. The Committee's research revealed the astonishing fact that we are losing wetlands at a rate of 300,000 acres per year . . . What are wetlands, and why do we care? Wetlands are really the start of the chain of life . . . [They] are critical to the survival of most fish and wildlife species, as well as being an important factor in maintaining good water quality and in protecting our coastal areas from the destructive forces of storms.

Before the Senate, Washington, Aug. 8/
The Washington Post, 8-13:(C)6.

Ira G. Corn, Jr.
Chief executive officer,
Michigan General Corporation

3

It was the productivity of [the American] economy that literally deluged the U.S. with pollution and environmental problems. It was as if overnight we had learned the secret of producing wealth for our vast population. In producing that wealth, however, we overlooked the tremendous waste which accrues from production. No one opposed the production of the wealth because it has made the lives of our citizens fantastic in regard to ease, comfort, health, job opportunities, social and economic mobility, personal freedom, travel, education, and all the things associated with affluence. So we must not overlook, as our forecasters did in the past, that the by-products of an improved and larger society sometimes backfire.

Before National Association of
Corporate Real Estate Executives,
San Francisco, April 12/Vital Speeches, 8-15:665.

Douglas M. Costle
Administrator,
Environmental Protection
Agency of the United States

4

People don't calculate the benefits when they look at the costs of environmental regulation, because they can't—they don't know how. And we have found that the American public, according to recent polls, is willing to pay the price to improve the quality of life.

To reporters, Washington, Aug. 10/
The Washington Post, 8-11:(D)2.

5

[Environmental groups] have had a tremendous influence in shaping the laws. One of the things they have done is shape the laws in ways that allow them a continuing participation [after the law is passed]. Environmental laws are marked by a characteristic of allowing access by private citizens to compel enforcement of Federal and state laws . . . Environmentalism is now a permanent part of our political value system. It is institutionally a part of our [government] at the state level, the local

(DOUGLAS M. COSTLE)

level, the Federal level. It is a part of American society.

Los Angeles Times, 11-23:(6)4,5.

John C. Culver
United States Senator, D-Iowa

1

The Endangered Species Act was a recognition—and a woefully late one—that our developmental activities were responsible for destroying forms of life that were present as a result of processes that began with the first appearance of life on earth 3 1/2 billion years ago. All species present today have been shaped by those forces, and they have evolved and developed for ages, which, in contrast, makes the length of our lifetimes insignificant. This has been a continuing saga. Species and life-forms appear, flourish for a time, and then disappear forever ... And yet, events shaped by our industrialization over the past few hundred years have led to a sharp acceleration in the rate of extinction, to the point where the natural process may be increased by a factor of hundreds or even thousands. The chilling tragedy of this massive loss of species from our ecosystems and biosphere will never be fully understood, because among the species irreversibly lost are some whose existence we never realized, and whose contribution to science and mankind will never be known. The Endangered Species Act is a first, a belated and a noble attempt to reduce these losses by requiring that our citizens and our government be aware of threatened or endangered species, and that they plan future activities to prevent these losses.

At debate on Endangered Species Act/
The Washington Post, 7-21:(A)12.

Allan Grant
President, American
Farm Bureau Federation

2

[Criticizing current wildlife-protection laws]: If farm people did not love wildlife, we wouldn't be tolerant of so much wildlife damage. [But] the "public's deer" feed on our hay, soybeans and corn. The "public's" coyotes, wolves and bobcats feed on our sheep, calves and chickens ... We cannot understand the narrow-mindedness of the environmental purist who seems to think that evolution can be frozen; that no species or creature—animal or plant—must ever be endangered no matter how many billions in economic loss may be suffered by people.

Before Indiana Farm Bureau, Indianapolis/
The Christian Science Monitor, 1-3:13.

Adlene Harrison
Regional Administrator (Dallas),
Environmental Protection
Agency of the United States

3

We have misused and mistreated our land and air. We have been careless and, in a strange way, uncaring about having an environment fit to live in. Everybody gives lip service to the decline of quality of the air and water. Their desire to clean up pollution is deeply felt. Yet the heart of the discontent about pollution is that it challenges the talent of technology—in terms of the working person and industry itself—which is so central to the complex economy and society that America has become. The young who feel strongly about air and water pollution at the same time find the automobile an indispensable part of their lives. Those who live comfortably and those who are educated get upset over the ravaging of the environment, but nonetheless live in a maze of electronic gadgets which are the output of the same industrial system which also produces pollution. Unfortunately, there is little concerned effort and outcry to plan, to preserve, to use wisely.

Before Dallas Pastors' Association/
The Dallas Times Herald, 2-12:(I)3.

Walter J. Hickel
Former Secretary of the
Interior of the United States;
Former Governor of Alaska (R)

4

Growth is not a dirty word. God never made this world to be locked up. God made this world for the living, to be used for the benefit of all the people.

San Francisco Examiner &
Chronicle, 8-20:(This World)44.

WHAT THEY SAID IN 1978

Philip Johnson
Architect

1

Today the public is saying: "Hold it! Let's preserve the scene around us." Look at the brownstone movements in Brooklyn and other areas around the nation. There's growing interest in saving landmarks, such as Grand Central Station [in New York]. Thirty or 40 years ago you wouldn't have seen any interest in saving the Station. People are looking to have their region preserved. For example, they want the Boston Back Bay area left the Boston Back Bay. And if you're building in Georgetown in Washington, D.C., you had better build consonant with what's in Georgetown already. And there's a move to symbolism: Why shouldn't a church look like a church—with a steeple? And why shouldn't a house look like a shelter and like other houses people are used to seeing?

Interview/U.S. News & World Report, 6-5:74.

George E. Mueller
Chairman and president, System Development Corporation; Former Director, Manned Space Program, National Aeronautics and Space Administration of the United States

2

The costs imposed by EPA have become mindboggling. The National Commission on Water Quality . . . concluded that the public and private capital expenditures needed to meet just the water-pollution control laws could be as high as $670-billion. For that amount of money, we could create an atmosphere around the moon, and thus make productive an area equal to the entire land area here on earth.

Before Town Hall, Los Angeles/ The Wall Street Journal, 5-23:20.

Edmund S. Muskie
United States Senator, D-Maine

3

What does it mean for a human being to be "productive"? To make such calculations, economists limit their view to items defined in dollars. But society must not be burdened by such blinders. Economists speak of goods and services. Let's look at environmental protection for a moment not as a "cost," but as an investment for production of the environmental goods—unmeasured environmental goods—that Americans have indicated they want to have produced. If a company invests in equipment that demands less energy, that investment will preserve energy for future generations. Isn't that a "good"? If a worker in an occupation with a high cancer risk sees that risk eliminated—isn't that a "good"? If raw sewage is no longer dumped into streams but is returned to the land as a nutrient—isn't that a "good"? . . . Consider the reverse. If a firm makes a product through the wasteful use of energy because it is cheap, will future generations say that was "productive"? Suppose a company could produce 10 per cent more photographic film if it could dump its waste chemicals directly into the water. Are we to consider such action "productive"? It isn't productive for recreation reasons. It isn't productive for fishing fleets. It isn't productive for towns downstream that must remove those pollutants to purify drinking water. Likewise, it is not productive to allow the annual events of the *Argo Merchant* and the *Amoco Cadiz* [tankers which leaked oil into the oceans] to continue simply because industry argues that pollution controls and safety controls cost money.

At Washington Journalism Center/ The Washington Post, 4-23:(D)6.

Vladimir Ossipoff
Architect

4

[Saying environmental regulations stymie the work of an architect]: The focus of the architecture moves away from design and into a labyrinth of rules and regulations, a sort of torture chamber where the daily challenge is to prove one's endurance. The architect arrives home at the end of a long day, clutching his head and talking to himself. He has nightmares about environmental-impact studies. Maybe he's designed a building that will purify the air for its occupants and improve the entire neighborhood by adding some much-needed beauty. But before the architect can convince those who preside over environmental-impact studies,

(VLADIMIR OSSIPOFF)

he'd better be sure he'll make it to a ripe old age.

Interview, Honolulu/
Los Angeles Times, 4-9:(Home)25.

Dixy Lee Ray
Governor of Washington (D)

1

There is no way of making peace with the extreme environmentalists. There are those who are zealous, who insist that things must be their own way. Unfortunately, they have a very strong voice in the Sierra Club and the Friends of the Earth and certain other environmentalist organizations. If, in fact, they should get their way, it would be the end of the industrial age, and I do not accept that . . . We cannot destroy the industrial age.

Interview, Olympia, Wash./
Los Angeles Times, 3-5:(1)3.

Sargent Shriver
Former Director,
United States Peace Corps

2

No question [exists] that there are limits to the number of people who can be accommodated on this earth. But this alone does not mean population crisis. It does require that we seek a balanced and fair world economy in which families and nations will match available resources with population so that they can achieve a decent standard of living based on an equitable sharing of those resources. That's not a population crisis. That's an economic crisis. Greed, not sex, is the cause. "Wealth control" as much as "birth control" may be the answer . . . Yet much of government population policy continues to focus on birth-control services. This goes on despite the agreement of both developing and advanced countries that such birth-control services had to be viewed as one part, and only one part, of a comprehensive program of social and economic development. Too little attention has been given to the other elements that have direct effects on population.

Before House Select Committee on Population,
Washington/The Washington Post, 2-14:(A)18.

Fred Smith
Member, National Environmental
Development Association

3

Like all national movements for reform or improvement, however sound in the beginning, environmentalism was destined sooner or later to become exploited by individuals and groups for what is essentially private personal gain—votes, money, notoriety, sometimes to promote a point of view or an ideology. Even the most constructive urge has a way of becoming a destructive, divisive influence—an assault on the underbelly of our democratic system. When this happens, the common people, prodded by their common sense, inevitably turn sour. There are an overwhelming number of common people, and a broadening majority of them has already tired of environmental extremism; they distrust it, they are sick of hearing about it. Vast damage has been done to the economy and to the workings of the private sector by the excesses of enthusiasts and exploiters, and more will be done before the entrenched Federal and local bureaucracies and the self-seeking professional environmental establishment finally reach the end of their string.

Before National Press Club, Washington,
March 14/Vital Speeches, 4-15:411.

Gus Speth
Member, Federal Council on
Environmental Quality

4

. . . the CPI is not a satisfactory measure of the inflationary impacts of Federal environmental regulations; a measured increase in the CPI does not mean that such requirements, on balance, cause inflation. Inflation is best understood as an increase in price without a corresponding increase in value. It follows that as long as the full benefits of environmental regulations exceed the full costs—and I believe that this is clearly the case today—these regulations cannot be considered truly inflationary . . . In 1952, London experienced a five-day episode of extreme air pollution. Annual pollution damages to health and property resulting from that incident were estimated at $700-million—and there is, of course, no method for quantifying

WHAT THEY SAID IN 1978

the value of a human life in terms that make sense to anyone but an insurance company. We have had plenty of analogous incidents more recently, ranging from the Kepone disaster in Hopewell, Virginia, to the destruction of the *Amoco Cadiz* off the coast of Brittany. Such dramatic events help us gauge the costs of environmental disaster or *weak* regulation. Perhaps even more important, they suggest the unmeasured but nonetheless real benefits of properly drawn and properly enforced environmental statutes that *prevent* damage. Our economics counts up the money we *have* spent; it is not beginning to take account of the money that we did *not* have to spend to repair the consequences of our carelessness.

Before American Bar Association, New York/
The Christian Science Monitor, 8-18:22

Russell E. Train
President, World Wildlife Fund-U.S.;
Former Administrator, Environmental
Protection Agency of the United States

1

[There is a] progressive deterioration of natural systems world-wide brought about by growing human populations, spreading human settlements, the cutting of forests, the deterioration of grasslands, the erosion of soils, chronic pollution, the over-exploitation of fisheries and other living resources, etc.... I have spent most of my time over the past several years working on a variety of pollution problems—air, water and chemical, among others ... The real "bottom line" of all those efforts is the maintenance of life on this earth ... Time is running out rapidly on the natural systems of the earth, and particularly on the survival of species. The loss of genetic diversity which threatens everywhere, and the resulting biological impoverishment of the planet, have grave implications for our own long-term future.

The Washington Post, 4-7:(A)16.

Shirley Williams
Secretary of State for Education and
Science of the United Kingdom

2

An economy which begins by being throwaway in goods ends up by being throw-away in human beings ... We waste energy. We waste raw materials. We waste the goods we import on a colossal scale ... Consider, because it's directly linked to unemployment, how many people could be engaged in the business of recycling, the business of saving, the business, for example, of insulating homes and public buildings and all the rest of it, which could be financed out of the savings that we can certainly make. Because we still are essentially a throw-away economy.

At British Labor Party conference, Blackpool,
England/The Christian Science Monitor, 10-6:7.

ENERGY

Brock Adams
Secretary of
Transportation of the United States

1

The motor vehicle is the prime mover of our society, and our mobility and much of our economy depend on a fragile alliance with the Organization of Petroleum Exporting Countries. The recent OPEC price rise and events in Iran reinforce my belief that we must have a new type of propulsion unit. The government is going to have to be involved very heavily in the basic and advanced research because the automotive companies say they just do not have the resources or the inclination to get into it . . . I don't want to get into a situation where we have a set of government engineers independently developing some great new thing, and then having the auto-makers who have to commercialize it calling it the dumbest thing they ever heard of. It's the same kind of thing we did when we said, "Okay, we'll put a man on the moon." We used a lot of different resources in the government and industry.

Interview, Washington/
Los Angeles Herald Examiner, 12-27:(A)8.

William M. Agee
Chairman and president,
Bendix Corporation

2

. . . after the Arab oil embargo of 1973, this nation proclaimed its intention to become energy independent. The program was launched with predictable hullabaloo, tied to the patriotism of the Bicentennial celebration and named, appropriately, Project Independence. Without detailing all that happened, let me point out that before we embarked on this program, we imported 35 per cent of our oil. Last year we imported about 50 per cent of the oil we use—and sent $45-billion to other countries to pay for it. If we had been as successful when we launched the first Project Indepen-

dence in 1776, we'd still be paying taxes to the King of England.

Indianapolis, Ind., March 30/
Vital Speeches, 6-15:541.

Carl E. Bagge
President, National Coal Association

3

The greater availability and use of coal would relieve much of the pressure on oil supplies and help slow down the price mechanism that is threatening to bankrupt the free world economy. But most importantly, coal can give all nations—rich and poor—access to an abundant and widespread midterm fuel resource that will provide the priceless time needed to develop new, more exotic energy technologies. And, at the risk of sounding melodramatic, time in this instance . . . could eventually mean the difference between war and peace—between survival and holocaust.

At World Conference on
Future Sources of Organic Raw Materials,
Toronto, July 11/Vital Speeches, 9-1:701.

Howard W. Blauvelt
Chairman, Continental Oil Company

4

Almost 20,000 permanent employees work for the [U.S.] Department of Energy. The annual budget for both regulatory and non-regulatory functions—including research-and-development programs and the program for the strategic stockpiling of petroleum—runs close to $10-billion. Ten billion dollars is significantly more than the major oil companies earn in this country in a year. Moreover, the oil companies employ the equivalent of 10,000 people full time at a cost now estimated at between $400-million and $500-million a year to handle DOE regulations. That is 10,000 man-years and roughly half a billion dollars *not* helping to meet the industry's primary responsibility of developing energy supplies. With half a billion

WHAT THEY SAID IN 1978

(HOWARD W. BLAUVELT)

dollars, the oil companies could drill approximately 3,300 new wells in states like Texas and Oklahoma. It may seem to be a contradiction in terms—and against the laws of physics—but the regulatory process also has a characteristic of becoming "frozen" even as it acquires momentum. It's an inflexibility that Dr. Laurence Peter identified in one of his lesser-known principles, the one that states: "Bureaucracy defends the status quo long past the time when the quo has lost its status."

Before American Institute of Chemical Engineers,
Philadelphia/The Wall Street Journal, 6-26:10.

Thornton F. Bradshaw
President, Atlantic Richfield Company

1

The major reason the United States does not have a coherent energy policy is that the Americans have no real sense of energy crisis. It is very difficult for democratic people to come to grips with a problem of the future. It would be very difficult to make the sacrifices which would be inherent in any energy policy for the benefit of future generations if the people are not convinced that there is a crisis—and they are not convinced . . . In any situation in which the crisis is still pending, in which it is a crisis of the future, it requires leadership to bring the people to recognize that the crisis is brewing. If the crisis is upon us, if the bombs are being dropped on Pearl Harbor, anyone can see that. But during the 1930s, during the build-up of militarism and Fascism, not many people saw it, and therefore we were most unprepared for that particular situation, as we are now most unprepared for an energy crisis when it does arrive.

Interview/Los Angeles Herald Examiner, 7-6:(A)1.

Peter J. Brennan
Chairman and president, New York
State Committee for Jobs and Energy
Independence; Former Secretary of
Labor of the United States

2

A recent poll shows that the Number 1 issue—way ahead of any other on most Americans' minds—is the economy. They don't know what "GNP" means, but they do know that it costs them a big chunk of their paycheck for energy—to heat their homes, to drive their old car, to keep the lights on and to buy the essentials of life—almost all of which keep getting higher due to energy costs. Someone once said, if you laid all the economists end-to-end, you still couldn't reach a conclusion. I can. Increase our supply of energy using home-grown energy resources which we *already* have at hand. That will keep the price of energy in check. That will stabilize inflation. That will help reduce unemployment. That will open the door to whatever kind of future we and our children choose to have. If we do not follow these simple facts of life, that door will be slammed shut to us, and we will be faced with the prospect of a second-rate nation, fighting over crumbs of an energy pie too small to go around.

Before Public Utilities
Association of the Virginias, Pipestem
State Park, Va., May 19/Vital Speeches, 7-1:570.

Jimmy Carter
President of the United States

3

I remember the almost unbelievable change the coming of electric power made in the farm life of my childhood. Electricity freed us of the continuing burdens of pumping water, sawing wood and lighting fires in the cooking stove. But it did even more: It gave us light by which to read and study at night. It gave us power— not just to perform the old exhausting tasks, but power to make more of our own choices. Because electric power came to us through cooperatives, in which we all had to share the responsibility for decision, it changed our lives in other ways. Farmers began to meet to discuss local needs and national issues, and to decide how to influence government and to negotiate with large, far-off companies that provided their supplies. I have seen the farm life I knew and the fields of my childhood transformed by energy and technology and increasing knowledge, and by the opportunity to participate in the decisions that affect ourselves and our families. I can understand the unfulfilled yearnings of other people in the developing nations to share these blessings of life.

Venezuela, March 29/
The Washington Post, 3-30:(A)22.

(JIMMY CARTER)

1

Of all the major countries in the world, the United States is the only one without a national energy policy; and because the Congress has not acted, other nations have begun to doubt our will. Holders of dollars throughout the world have interpreted our failure to act as a sign of economic weakness. And these views have been directly translated into a decreasing value for our currency. The falling dollar in international monetary markets makes inflation worse here at home . . . That's why we simply must have meaningful energy legislation without further delay. Our security depends on it, and our economy demands it.

Before American Society of Newspaper Editors, Washington, April 11/ The New York Times, 4-12:34.

2

The question is no longer whether solar energy works. We know it works. The only question is how to cut costs so that solar power can be used more widely . . . We must begin the long, tough job of winning back our economic independence. Nobody can embargo sunlight; no cartel controls the sun. Its energy will not run out. It will not pollute our air or poison our waters. It is free from stench and smog.

At Solar Energy Research Institute, Golden, Colo., May 3/Los Angeles Times, 5-4:(1)15.

3

[Criticizing Congress for not adopting comprehensive energy legislation]: We created a Department of Energy and have failed to give it the tools it needs to do the job. For the last 14 months we have been talking energy, and, while we have been talking, America has suffered economically. Talk is cheap, but energy is not.

At Democratic Party fund-raising dinner, Houston, June 23/The New York Times, 6-24:7.

4

Our influence and prestige in the global economic community are tarnished and U.S. leadership is seriously weakened without a policy to reduce waste and bring energy costs in line with the cost of replacement. It is time for us to become responsible caretakers of the bounteous world we inherited.

Before Mexican-American leaders, Houston, June 23/The Dallas Times Herald, 6-24:(A)3.

5

There are four basic ways . . . where we can increase the price of oil—just to the world-level price—to discourage waste. One is to let the oil companies decide how much they should raise the price of oil, which I think would be very bad for the American consumer. Two other ways are for me to impose quotas or oil import fees, which would result in administrative difficulties, but which is presently permitted under the law. The fourth way is much preferable—to impose a crude-oil equalization tax to raise the price of oil, and within that act of the Congress to restore that money—collect it—immediately back to the consumers of this country. There would be no net shift away from the consumers of money, but the price of oil would be raised to encourage conservation. That's my preference, and I still hope and believe that the Congress will take action accordingly.

News conference, Washington, July 20/ The New York Times, 7-21:(A)6.

Gordon R. Corey
Vice chairman, Commonwealth Edison Company, Chicago

6

[On the opposition to nuclear power]: At the root of it all is the ubiquitous questioning by some critics of the need for any new products or services at all. In the eyes of these critics, any uncertainty, however small, related to a new technology is often deemed unacceptable. . . . if we had not already developed the technology of electric-power generation, transmission, distribution and utilization, we would find it difficult to bring it about in today's climate. We would be required to prove in a public adversary proceeding: a) that enormously large quantities of electrical energy could be transported through our streets and distributed throughout residential subdivisions and high-rise buildings without massive electrocutions; b) that no alternative sources of energy could do the job so well as electricity; c) that small, decentralized installations like neighbor-

WHAT THEY SAID IN 1978

(GORDON R. COREY)

hood foundries, Corliss engines and water wheels would not be preferable—perhaps more in keeping with a democratic society—than central-station electric generation; d) that all possible contingencies had been accounted for and safeguarded against; and e) that the future products of our infant electric and electronic technologies would indeed provide desirable additions to the quality of life. In view of the foregoing, is it any wonder that the nuclear era is having difficult sledding?

Before Congressional committee/
The Wall Street Journal, 3-7:20.

Millicent H. Fenwick
United States Representative,
R-New Jersey

1

The President [Carter] has not conveyed the seriousness of the energy problem. He should serve notice to every Governor of the 50 states that in 60 days he wants them here for a White House conference on energy. He should go on TV with the Governors and talk about energy. He should set specific goals, such as cutting oil imports by 5 per cent each year. He should force the country into action.

Interview, Washington/
U.S. News & World Report, 2-6:20.

E. J. (Jake) Garn
United States Senator, R-Utah

2

Imposing import fees [on foreign crude oil] would have the same impact on prices as decontrol of oil. But instead of encouraging more domestic production, it would take revenues from consumers and give them to the government. Who knows what Washington would do with the money? One thing is certain: The bureaucrats wouldn't find any more oil for us.... [there is still] a great deal of oil in the U.S., but it is expensive to obtain. Decontrolling oil would bring a lot more oil on to the market and decrease our dependency on foreign sources. If consumers are going to have to pay higher prices for oil through either decontrol or import fees, why not choose the method that

will encourage more exploration and production in the U.S.?

April 10/**

Maurice F. Granville, Jr.
Chairman, Texaco, Inc.

3

To really schedule a decontrol of oil, both old and new will give proper recognition to companies such as ours who spent our money to develop crude oil long ago, and are being deprived of the proper compensation for it now. I have a very strong feeling there is a growing awareness, even within the government, that the solution to this thing has to lie with a phase-out of price controls on crude oil. There is still a hang-up that goes with it of so-called windfall profits for the oil companies. But the fact of the matter is that as soon as you get through with royalty payments, and the regular taxation of the industry, that the percentage of profit that would go to the producer is relatively small—certainly less than 40 per cent. And that's money that's really needed.

Interview, Harrison, N.Y./
The Washington Post, 10-20:(D)9.

Michel T. Halbouty
Consulting geologist

4

... I would like to clarify a flagrant misconception by making it perfectly clear that there is absolutely no energy crisis in the United States. This country has a tremendous amount of energy potential. But there is a very, very serious energy problem—in fact, the problem is the crisis!—namely, Washington has politically manipulated, interfered and imposed dictatorial controls and regulations which severely stymied discretionary productive efforts by the energy industries.

Before American Association of Petroleum Landmen,
Houston/The Wall Street Journal, 8-11:10.

Shearon Harris
Chairman, Carolina
Power & Light Company

5

We cannot afford to ignore the nuclear [-power] option. Nuclear power is the most economical alternative known today for the

(SHEARON HARRIS)

generation of power in countries lacking significant reserves of fossil fuel or sufficient opportunities for the development of hydropower. It is equally essential for countries that need to reduce their reliance on costly petroleum imports.

Nation's Business, December:29.

Gary W. Hart
United States Senator, D-Colorado

1

The dangers inherent in accumulated nuclear wastes impose a threat to civilization greater even than the terrible plagues of the Middle Ages. For while an epidemic runs its course over a span of several years, this threat is continual and growing. There is no known way to neutralize these wastes to render them less dangerous. We can't burn them. We can't treat them with chemicals. We have only the most primitive choice of all: to bury them, hide them away—for literally tens of thousands of years ... We have thus far settled for temporary answers and unfulfilled promises. We must now insist on an end to holding actions and stopgap solutions. We must have real answers that work. The stakes involve more than our environment. Our energy future is at stake, too. Sixty-seven nuclear reactors are operating in this country today. By the year 2000, we could have 500 helping to meet our growing energy needs. If an acceptable solution to radioactive waste disposal is not developed, we may be forced to look seriously at halting further development of this important energy resource. The political climate is changing. The public, through its elected representatives, will demand a halt to nuclear-energy development if answers are not provided.

Before National Wildlife Federation/
The Christian Science Monitor, 5-10:35.

Brooke Hartman
President, Pennsylvania
Electric Association

2

Our problem in Pennsylvania is not a [coal] shortage; we have plenty of coal. Our problem is with the regulations that prevent us from using that coal. Until we find out how well all these regulations shake down, the utilities have an awfully critical decision to make about taking care of the future.

Nation's Business, December:32.

Denis Hayes
Senior researcher, Worldwatch Institute

3

Society is far behind schedule in making the transition to a solar-powered economy. If we are to get most of our energy from solar resources within 50 years, we must begin immediately to build millions of solar collectors and solar cells and thousands of wind turbines each year. We can meet five-sixths of the anticipated world energy budget with solar energy by 2025. To get there from here, however, requires a considerable commitment at the national, neighborhood and even individual level. The payoff will be a sustainable energy system that would last as long as the earth is inhabitable.

Washington, April 22/
The Dallas Times Herald, 4-23:(A)14.

Henry M. Jackson
United States Senator, D-Washington

4

The oil industry is not just another business. It's a business affecting the public interest, and there's going to be more regulation [by government] unless ... [oil] companies have the ability to meet and keep pace with the requirements of the public. The oil companies appear to be offering the public a choice between shortages and ever-rising gasoline prices. I can think of no strategy less likely to gain the industry's objective of decontrol.

At Senate Energy Committee hearing, Washington,
Dec. 11/The Dallas Times Herald, 12-12:(A)7.

Alfred E. Kahn
Counsellor on Inflation to President
of the United States Jimmy Carter

5

I think the OPEC countries may themselves come to regret so sharp an increase [in the price of their oil exports] in view of the harmful effect that it will have on the world economy.

WHAT THEY SAID IN 1978

(ALFRED E. KAHN)

You can't enact a 15 per cent increase in the price of the world's most important fuel, and not expect the customers on whom you depend to suffer and that suffering to reflect back on you.

The Dallas Times Herald, 12-23:(B)2.

Herman Kahn
Director, Hudson Institute

1

... there's no shortage of energy yet. Everybody complains that the average American doesn't appreciate the fact that we have an energy crisis. Well, I think the man in the street has this thing pegged exactly right. He has to pay more for his gasoline, but he gets all he wants, and he knows it. Four years have passed, and his government hasn't done one thing about it. So why should he? We haven't got an energy crisis—we've got an energy problem.

*Interview, Croton-on-Hudson, N.Y./
The New York Times, 2-26:(3)1.*

Llewellyn King
Publisher, "The Energy Daily"

2

In today's political climate in the United States, if you're in favor of organized labor, redistribution of income, a more egalitarian society and other noble goals, then you are axiomatically, as part of that political creed, likely to be opposed to nuclear power. Likewise, if you subscribe to a conservative political philosophy, you are likely to believe in high technology, in continued ownership of the Panama Canal and in maintaining national defense at a high level—and in nuclear power as a cornerstone of the future energy development of the United States. I deplore this polarization because it presents technology in political and ideological terms, where I believe it does not belong. I think hanging labels around technology, as has happened with nuclear power, is a piece of intellectual mischief for which the United States and possibly the world will pay. That the alternative technologies to nuclear are known as "appropriate technologies," and the Department of Energy has institutionalized this piece of semantic legerdemain by using that phrase, shows the extent to which the mischief has taken hold. To explain why nuclear development is in a hiatus is to explain the existential nature of the new class philosophies in opposing growth and protecting the environment at all odds. It is also to deny the empirical evidence that America's well-being is symbiotic to its technological success.

*At Uranium Institute, London,
July 12/Vital Speeches, 9-15:716.*

Seymour Lampert
*Professor of solar energy,
University of Southern California*

3

I'm high on solar energy, but I do not have one on my house. Right now, it does not pay off. The strong economic reason to install one simply is not there for the mass of people ... Also, people seem to respond only when there is a crisis situation, like there not being enough natural gas to go around or at too expensive a price. But what is too high a price? A few years ago when the price of gasoline started to go up, many people said they wouldn't pay 50 cents a gallon. Now we pay over 60 cents, and a neighbor told me he'd pay $1 a gallon if he had to do it.

Los Angeles Times, 4-29:(1)26.

Ulf Lantzke
*Executive director,
International Energy Agency*

4

The intervals between [oil-supply] crises are shortening. We've faced two serious supply disruptions in the Middle East in the past five years: the 1973-74 Arab oil embargo, and again in 1977 when Saudi Arabian production was interrupted for a short time by an explosion at a pumping station. And now we have [the turmoil in] Iran. The economic stability of the world relies to a large extent on a region which is very sensitive to policy changes and unrest. We should be carefully watching our growing dependence on oil from the Middle East. The Iranian situation shows how fragile the world balance of oil supply and demand has become.

Interview/U.S. News & World Report, 11-27:33.

R. J. Munzer
Chairman, Petrolane, Inc.

1

Perhaps the most vivid and long-term example of ill-advised, poorly conceived and ineptly administered government policy has been the regulation of the price of natural gas since the mid-1950s. This policy, which held the price of natural gas down to artificially low levels, produced an abnormally large market for this fuel, while discouraging drilling for new reserves. The net result was the extraordinary growth in consumption, while the number of wells drilled *decreased* by 50 per cent over the 17 years that followed the implementation of this inspired piece of policy-making. When will government learn that regulation of oil and gas prices is the cause, not the solution, to our energy problem?

At Town Hall, Los Angeles, May 23/
Vital Speeches, 7-15:586.

Rene Ortiz
Secretary general, Organization of
Petroleum Exporting Countries

2

[On OPEC's just-announced price increase for its oil exports]: Those countries that have reservations about our decision should realize that we are building for the future of our peoples. The OPEC member states have got responsibilities toward the coming generations. They would never forgive us if we failed them.

San Francisco Examiner &
Chronicle, 12-24:(This World)18.

Mana Saeed Oteiba
Minister of Petroleum of the
United Arab Emirates

3

[On why OPEC is increasing the price of its oil exports]: We have been freezing the price of oil. We did this of our own free will. We agreed to freeze the price of oil for two years because we want to play a constructive role in the world economy. [But the fall of the dollar and the increase in the price of imports are] affecting our revenues and investments.

Abu Dhabi, Dec. 16/
The Washington Post, 12-17:(A)1.

Stanley Ragone
President, Virginia
Electric and Power Company

4

Lots of people are saying let's conserve energy instead of building more [nuclear] power plants, but they don't run electrical systems. Conservationists never really give you solutions. They just talk about the problems ... When you cut back on power use, industry goes first, and that means jobs. . . . the conservationists, they've already got theirs. They overlook the economic needs. They say wait for wind and solar power. But what do the poor people do in the meantime?

San Francisco Examiner &
Chronicle, 3-26:(This World)36.

John J. Rhodes
United States Representative, R-Arizona

5

I am in hopes that [we] will come up with some sort of a bill which will take the first step that is necessary in this particular time-frame, and that is to deregulate new natural gas. I would like to see [it] go further and deregulate all natural gas and even all oil, because I am satisfied if you did, the marketplace would take care of the price. But my colleagues, particularly the ones on the Democratic side, are so price-conscious that they have completely forgotten about supply. They would rather have a scarcity that is cheap than a plentitude that is a little bit more expensive.

· *TV-radio interview/"Meet the Press,"*
National Broadcasting Company, 1-22.

W. F. Rockwell, Jr.
Chairman, Rockwell International

6

If America is going to act with a long-range energy program, we must realize that the movement from inspiration to reality is a function of applying technology. And here I mean, very simply, we must push ahead in the development and the utilization of nuclear energy while continuing our long-term development of more exotic energy sources, such as fusion, solar, wind and geothermal energy. Development of nuclear power is essential because it will bridge

WHAT THEY SAID IN 1978

(W. F. ROCKWELL, JR.)

the gap that exists between today's dwindling fossil fuels and the bringing on stream of exotic energy sources 25 to 40 or more years from now. Nuclear energy has proved its effectiveness in filling this gap by literally saving our bacon during the last two energy crises.

*Before American Textile Manufacturers Institute, San Francisco, March 17/***

James R. Schlesinger
Secretary of
Energy of the United States

1

The energy problem ... is a test of our system, because what we're asking everybody to do—politicians, businessmen, ordinary citizens—is take painful action now in order to avoid much greater difficulties at a later point. So our ability to cope with the energy problem is indeed a test of our institutions, a test of democracy.

Interview/U.S. News & World Report, 7-10:24.

James R. Schlesinger
Secretary of
Energy of the United States

2

What we face in the middle 1980s is a national world-wide shortage of about 5 million barrels [of oil] a day. Obviously we will not consume more than we produce. The effect would be either to shoot up prices or, more likely, to slow down economic activity to balance the available supplies against demand. But even if the world has a slowdown in economic growth, it will only postpone the day of reckoning. A few years later, we will be in a position where supply cannot sustain burgeoning demand at prevailing prices.

Interview/U.S. News & World Report, 7-10:26.

3

The notion of physical limits, of something being in finite supply, is hard for Americans to appreciate. We've always had things in abundance. But just as land ran out in the 1890s and water shortages are now being felt in the west-

ern states, the nation must realize that the days of cheap, limitless energy are disappearing.

Parade, 9-10:4.

4

Obviously solar [energy] has a great attraction, environmentally speaking. It does not put out any combustion products ... There is no waste disposal problem. But we must make solar energy—like any other energy source—something that can be fitted into the family budget.

Interview/The Dallas Times Herald, 10-2:(D)8.

5

... the energy problem will be a continuing one. Really, it's a set of problems. First, as of now, we are dependent on foreign sources of supply to the extent that it creates a severe balance-of-trade strain which weakens the U.S. dollar. Secondly, it imposes constraints on our foreign policy and creates national-security problems. Nevertheless, even if we were able to pay for the oil and didn't worry about oil sources from a foreign-policy standpoint, in the longer run the energy problem would arise from the fact that there simply is not a sufficient prospective oil capacity world-wide to permit us to continue to expand its use in preference to other fuels.

Interview/U.S. News & World Report, 10-16:69.

John E. Swearingen, Jr.
Chairman, Standard Oil
Company (Indiana)

6

The fact is that we are well-supplied—even over-supplied—with oil on this 11th of January, 1978. Our inventories are high, partly as a result of the arrival of Alaskan oil and partly because of large-scale purchases early last year in anticipation of OPEC price increases. While this is all very well for 1978, it offers little more than a breathing spell in our long-term effort. But neither the American people nor their representatives in Congress regard it as such. We act as if the problem of the next 25 years has been solved ... The onus today is on Congress to look beyond 1978, to recognize our true priorities and to take the steps neces-

(JOHN E. SWEARINGEN, JR.)

sary to secure continued energy growth and economic health over the next 25 years and into the century beyond.

Before business officials, Dallas, Jan. 11/
The Dallas Times Herald, 1-12:(C)11.

Robert D. Thorne
Assistant Secretary,
Technology, Department of
Energy of the United States

1

... the fallacy that most people have been tripping over is the idea that we have to have a single national solution [to energy problems], the so-called big fix; that we must do here in Texas exactly what we do in New England; that there is only one way for the whole country to go. And that concept, in turn, often leads people to the conclusion that they're going to rape their region because of what another region needs, or that our country is ready to accept *laissez faire,* and its needs transcend local or regional cultures and traditions. But I don't see why there has to be only a single national solution to our energy problems. On the contrary, I can think of a lot of reasons why we ought to have many different energy solutions for many different places in our country, depending on their energy needs, their available energy resources, and the tastes, customs and traditions of the people who will be affected. And interestingly, in following that course, I believe we can continually upgrade the environmental posture of the country as a whole. And that is what makes all of these technologies mutually supportive and linked together. It should be obvious that what I am talking about is a more local and regional approach to our energy problems.

Before Institute of Environment Sciences, Fort
Worth, Texas, April 18/Vital Speeches, 8-1:627.

Peter M. Towe
Canadian Ambassador to the United States

2

[Saying the U.S. should enact an energy policy]: We face physical shortages which imply severe economic dislocation and political dislocation, if one of the major consumers doesn't have a meaningful energy program, doesn't fulfill its treaty commitment under the International Energy Agency to reduce its dependence on imported oil ... More than that, it's quite obvious that lack of a U.S. energy policy today in part is contributing to the substantial balance-of-trade deficit of the U.S., which is growing as oil imports grow.

At luncheon sponsored by Canadian Society,
Los Angeles, Feb. 3/Los Angeles Times, 2-4:(1)25.

John G. Tower
United States Senator, R-Texas

3

[Criticizing a compromise natural-gas bill which he says extends Federal controls rather than deregulates gas prices]: ... distressing is the fact that this measure clings to the silly notion that Federal controls—somehow—will be more effective in increasing supplies than free-market forces. How many more winters of real hardship must we endure before this Administration and members of Congress who profess worries about rip-offs realize once and for all that, without plentiful supplies of natural gas, the nation as a whole and each individual consumer suffers? This compromise is no solution at all. It is complete resignation to the falsehood that the past should have little bearing on the future.

News conference, Stephenville, Texas,
Aug. 5/The Dallas Times Herald, 8-6:(A)27.

Pierre Elliott Trudeau
Prime Minister of Canada

4

Canadian policy recognizes that the era of cheap energy is behind us. ... we now know that new sources of oil supply and alternate sources of energy are costly, more costly than you [the U.S.] or we are yet paying. We must, therefore, allow rising prices to constrain demand and to stimulate new supply. Conservation of energy must become a way of life—in our personal lives and in commerce and industry. Our ingenuity must be invested in alternate energy sources and alternate technologies which are oil-conserving.

Before Economic Club, New York, March 22/
The New York Times, 3-23:(A)12.

WHAT THEY SAID IN 1978

Thomas A. Vanderslice
Senior vice president and
sector executive for power systems,
General Electric Company

1

... unless we recognize increasing energy consumption as a reality, at least for a while yet, we are irresponsible planners and do a disservice to the nation and the world community. There is a relationship between energy consumption and economic growth. While the connection may not be a basic law provable for all times, we do know that we cannot change it overnight without very disruptive consequences. There is no acceptable alternative to the increasing use of energy as a basic reality in human existence on this increasingly small planet. And we'd better get on with it.

Before Birmingham (Ala.)
Rotary Club/
Los Angeles Times,
6-4:(4)3.

Carl Walske
President,
Atomic Industrial Forum

2

Nuclear energy scored solidly in power-plant performance in 1977. The enviable public safety record of nuclear energy continues intact, even though more plants are coming into operation and production is soaring.

The Dallas Times Herald,
4-24:(A)5.

Frank Zarb
Former Administrator,
Federal Energy Administration

3

The energy crisis is not merely a set of numbers on the bottom line of a ledger. It is the dilemma faced by every working person who stops at a gas station to refuel the car he needs to take him to and from his job every day. It is the choice faced by the housewife selecting a can or a package from the shelf of her supermarket. It is the decisions every homeowner is faced with in determining how best to heat his home and protect his family's health. It is an issue faced by every investor and producer as well as each factory manager who must keep costs down to compete. It is the question every student faces wondering what new kinds of careers and jobs companies may be planning for him a few years from now, and how he can best prepare to fill one of them. The energy crisis is the option faced by the voter trying to decide which candidate makes the most sense in representing a point of view on foreign and domestic policy. It is the challenge to the local schoolteacher trying to project just what it is that students must learn today to cope with the problems this country will face tomorrow. The energy crisis is, in fact, the totality of all the factors that make up the human condition. It is the determinant of the way of life and the standard of living this country will experience—and hopefully continue to enjoy—in the years ahead.

Before National Energy Foundation, Los Angeles,
Dec. 8/Los Angeles Herald Examiner, 12-8:(A)17.

Foreign Affairs

Georgi A. Arbatov
Director, Soviet Institute of
U.S.A. and Canadian Affairs

1

As you [the U.S.] have your right to believe in God or manifest destiny, we [Soviets] have the right to believe that the trends and laws of social and economic development in the world cannot work for very long in the framework of the free-enterprise, capitalist system. Even the brightest future will never bring the day when every American will like what is going on in the Soviet Union, and vice versa . . . The problem is not for the Soviet Union to begin to love the United States, or vice versa. It is a matter of understanding one's own interest.

Interview, Moscow/Los Angeles Times, 5-21:(1)4.

Howard H. Baker, Jr.
United States Senator, R-Tennessee

2

[On the U.S. response to the latest political trials of dissidents in the Soviet Union, in the face of U.S. President Carter's plea for human rights]: [Carter should] pick up the telephone and call the Russians and say, "Look, we're really upset about this . . . We ain't going to be pushed around this way. And just so you know that it's all linked together, we're going to temporarily suspend the SALT talks; we're going to suspend any other talks we can lay our hands on" . . . I think the Russians are thumbing their nose at us and enjoying every minute.

To reporters, Washington, July 11/
The Washington Post, 7-12:(A)13.

Menachem Begin
Prime Minister of Israel

3

. . . the free world is under constant on-slaught. You can see what is happening around us. Aden, Southern Yemen, Ethiopia, Angola, Mozambique—all these countries were actually taken over by the Soviet Union. There is a plan in Moscow to take over country after country, usually by proxy. The whole free world is in danger. We are an integral part of it and we are interested in keeping liberty alive. From this point of view, the prestige of the President of the United States is very important to us.

Interview, Jerusalem/Time, 9-11:15.

Lucy Wilson Benson
Under Secretary for Security Assistance,
Department of State of the United States

4

[Saying President Carter's desire to reduce U.S. arms sales abroad could be a slow process]: I don't think there is any point in not selling arms just for the sake of not selling arms. The President believes that arms are part of the international currency, and they probably will be until such time as the world decides it's not going to have any arms at all. The best thing you can do is to accept that as a fact and then try to control it and organize it to suit your own foreign-policy goals.

Boston, Jan. 18/
The Christian Science Monitor, 1-20:6.

Lloyd M. Bentsen
United States Senator, D-Texas

5

[On agreements with the Soviet Union, such as the SALT treaty]: We simply do not feel that we can enter an agreement of such evident significance with a nation we cannot trust, with a nation that speaks of accord while seeking out confrontation.

Before the Senate, Washington, June 28/
Los Angeles Herald Examiner, 6-28:(A)6.

WHAT THEY SAID IN 1978

C. Fred Bergsten
Assistant Secretary for International Affairs, Department of the Treasury of the United States

1

[Two factors have thrust developing nations] into the forefront of U.S. policy concerns. One is our increasing dependence on the rest of the world for our security and our prosperity—as our preoccupation with Middle East policies and the continuing oil crisis depict so vividly. The second is the leap of the developing nations into world prominence—by achieving nuclear capabilities, pivotal positions in regions of political turmoil, and an ever-growing role in the world economy.

At International Development Conference, Washington/The Christian Science Monitor, 2-16:15.

Charles W. Bray III
Acting Director, International Communication Agency of the United States (formerly U.S. Information Agency)

2

We Americans have in recent years understated the importance of ideas in human history and have unnecessarily deprecated the currency of our own ideas—their power—in the international marketplace. I have found it significant in recent travels to three continents that to a remarkable extent, given the traumas of American society in recent years, other societies continue to look at us as a model—not a perfect model, to be sure, but a relevant model in an imperfect world ... [And] if it is true that it is ideas that most importantly affect the course of history, then it is important that we have an institution whose sole function is to engage with ideas. Is it worth the $400-million that the President [Carter] proposes to spend via the International Communication Agency next year? I believe it is. Could those $400-million be better spent for one submarine? I think not. Not if one agrees with Lenin that ideas are more fatal than guns.

Before American Newspaper Publishers Association/The Wall Street Journal, 9-26:20.

Kingman Brewster, Jr.
United States Ambassador to the United Kingdom

3

[On being Ambassador]: The most important things you can achieve are, you might say, somewhat negative. You try to make the U.S. government more sensitive to the impact of what it does on the British and to make the British government more sensitive to the impact of what it would like to do [on] the Americans. There's only a very small area where you can create, where you can offer a solution that someone else hasn't thought of. But it's hard to keep score because an Ambassador's job is to brief people; and, after they've made up their minds, how do you weigh your input against all the other inputs? Occasionally, you can see that your rifle might have hit the duck in the shooting gallery, but there's such a hail of bullets it's hard to tell which one is yours.

*Interview, London/
"W": a Fairchild publication, 9-15:37.*

Leonid I. Brezhnev
President of the Soviet Union; Chairman, Soviet Communist Party

4

Trying to distort the meaning and goals of Soviet foreign policy, imperialist propaganda maintains that there is a contradiction between our policy of detente and peaceful coexistence, and our relations with countries that have thrown off the colonial yoke. [The Soviet Union] and other socialist countries are being falsely accused of interference in the affairs of young states ... [But] the facts show that the peoples of the young states defend their independence and vital interests all the more successfully, the more solid their unity and solidarity and the more solid their friendship with the countries of the socialist world, on whose support they can rely in their just struggle.

*Before Young Communist League, Moscow, April 25/
Los Angeles Times, 4-26:(1)16.*

Bill Brock
Chairman, Republican National Committee

5

The basic fallacy of the Carter Administration in foreign policy has been their refusal to

(BILL BROCK)

accept the concept of "linkage." The fact is that all international relations are linked. [The Administration should] state publicly that there is linkage, and that we will view [Soviet] action in any part of the world within the context of their relationship with this country.

News conference, Washington, March 22/
The Washington Post, 3-23:(A)20.

Zbigniew Brzezinski
Assistant to President of the United
States Jimmy Carter for National
Security Affairs

1

We did not go out of our way to identify our human-rights policy as one directed at the Soviet Union. Events—particularly in the first two weeks of the new Administration—created that identification to some extent, although we wanted our support for human rights to be a generalized, global principle. After we began to emphasize more and more the global character of our interest, we were accused of having compromised and of having backtracked. Our concern for human rights neither exempts nor focuses exclusively on the Soviet Union.

Interview/U.S. News & World Report, 2-13:31.

2

My job is to think about the national security of the United States. That's what I have to think about every day, every morning and every night . . . I think it is very important that there be a clear voice in this Administration that points to the national-security implications of trends and developments. It is very easy to be drawn to attractive solutions which generate good atmospherics . . . On the whole, my views are strategically consistent, tactically very fluid. I'm perfectly willing to change tactical positions, because the world changes. Anybody who maintains that one has to be constant in one's views in every respect for decades is a jerk.

Interview, Washington/
The Washington Post, 3-14:(A)11.

As far as detente is concerned, I think it is terribly important for all of us to understand what it is and what it is not. There is a tendency to assume that detente is the equivalent of a comprehensive, indeed total, accommodation between the United States and the Soviet Union. That has never been the case. Detente really is a process of trying to contain some of the competitive aspects in the relationship, competitive aspects which I believe still are predominant, and to widen the cooperative aspects. In that process, at one time or another, either the cooperative or the competitive aspects tend to be more predominant. I would say that today the competitive aspects have somewhat surfaced, and I would say categorically that this is due to the shortsighted Soviet conduct in the course of the last two or so years.

TV-radio interview/"Meet the Press,"
National Broadcasting Company, 5-28.

4

Previous to our [Carter] Administration, the tendency was, in part because of the highly personal nature of the diplomacy, to focus on a small number of issues. Thus, a number of other issues festered. We have tried to work on a wider front because we had no choice. I can't think of a single issue we're tackling we should have left alone. What would one drop and not deal with? SALT, or southern Africa, or Panama? We thought we had to move on all. The fact that we're dealing on a wide front does create certain problems; but on balance, by and large, I believe we've made progress.

Interview/Time, 5-29:18.

5

A big country like the U.S. is not like a speedboat on a lake. It can't veer suddenly to the right or left. It's like a large ship. There's continuity to its course. There's continuity between our [Carter] Administration's foreign policy and the policy of our predecessors and, indeed, between them and their predecessors. However, each Administration imposes its own stamp on foreign policy, by turning a little bit from one side to the other.

Interview/Time, 5-29:18.

WHAT THEY SAID IN 1978

(ZBIGNIEW BRZEZINSKI)

1

I think we are now beginning to realize that there is no such thing as simply maintaining the status quo in order for American values and the American system to survive. I believe strongly that more people appreciate the fact that to make the world congenial to ourselves, to prevent America from being lonely in the world, we have to be very active in shaping wider and new global institutions, wider and fairer patterns of global cooperation. This is why [U.S. UN Ambassador] Andy Young has been a very constructive force in the United Nations. This is why the President [Carter] has struck a responsive chord with his human-rights policy. This is why we have to shape new arrangements to give so many new participants in the global political process a genuine opportunity to participate.

Interview/The New York Times Magazine, 12-31:9.

George Bush
Former Director of Central Intelligence of the United States; Former U.S. Ambassador/Permanent Representative to the United Nations

2

If I ever popped off as much as [current UN Ambassador] Andy Young, I'd have been fired [as Ambassador]. P.S.: I'd have deserved to be fired. I'm appalled by some of the things Young is doing. This kind of statement, for example: "Cubans are a stabilizing influence in Africa." Cubans are Russian surrogates in Africa and you don't need to have been head of the CIA to see this. On the other hand, I'm not hypercritical of Young himself. This is the President's [Carter] foreign policy. He wants this, so why fault Young? I fault the President.

Interview, Houston/
"W": a Fairchild publication, 4-28:22.

Robert C. Byrd
United States Senator, D-West Virginia

3

[On U.S.-Soviet relations in the wake of Russia's involvement in the Horn of Africa]: [The Soviets are] meddling in what is strictly an African affair. I think these things raise serious questions as to the credibility of the Soviets and as to their interest in many other areas of mutual interest to our two countries. They want American grain, they want American technology, they want loans and credits on the one hand. And yet they want to do, with the other hand, that which undermines the interest of the United States and the peace of the world.

San Francisco Examiner & Chronicle,
3-5:(This World)21.

Jimmy Carter
President of the United States

4

[On the human-rights aspect of U.S. foreign policy]: I don't intend to back down ever. As long as I am in the White House, human rights will be a major consideration of every foreign-policy decision that I make, and, I might say, also domestic.

Interview, Washington/
The Christian Science Monitor, 2-3:4.

5

Less than three decades from now, four-fifths of all the world's people will live in Africa, Asia and Latin America—in the sorts of developing nations that I have [just] visited. Only three decades ago, many nations of these continents were largely colonies of foreign powers. Their rise to independence means a world in which we must treat each other as equals, and one of the purposes of these trips has been to demonstrate the genuine respect my nation feels for its partners around the world and our opposition to the continuation or re-establishment of colonialism in any form whatsoever.

At arrival ceremony, Monrovia, Liberia, April 3/
The Washington Post, 4-4:(A)16.

6

I have no fear of Communism and no inordinate concern about Communism. I'm not preoccupied with the Soviet Union; I don't fear them. I see the inherent strength of the United States, economically and politically and militarily, and I'm determined as President to main-

(JIMMY CARTER)

tain that strength, which is in almost every respect superior to that of the Soviet Union.

News conference, Chicago, May 25/
The New York Times, 5-26:(A)10.

1

The word "detente" can be simplistically defined as the easing of tension between nations. The word is in practice, however, further defined by experience as those nations evolve new means by which they can live with each other in peace. To be stable, to be supported by the American people and to be a basis for widening the scope of cooperation, detente must be broadly defined and truly reciprocal . . . Our principal goal is to help shape a world which is more responsive to the desire of people everywhere for economic well-being, social justice, political self-determination and basic human rights. We seek a world of peace, but such a world must accommodate diversity—social, political and ideological. Only then can there be a genuine cooperation among nations and among cultures.

Before graduating class, U.S. Naval Academy,
June 7/The New York Times, 6-8:(A)22.

2

My government will not be deterred from our open and enthusiastic policy of promoting human rights, including economic and social rights, in whatever ways we can. We prefer to take actions that are positive, but where nations persist in serious violations of human rights we will continue to demonstrate that there are costs to the flagrant disregard of international standards.

Before foreign ministers of members of
Organization of American States, Washington,
June 21/The New York Times, 6-22:(A)17.

3

. . . we've never tried to threaten the Soviet Union; we've never held out the prospect of increased or decreased trade if they did or did not do a certain thing that we thought was best. We've tried to pursue peace as the overwhelming sense of our goals with the Soviet Union . . .

I believe that [Soviet President Leonid] Brezhnev wants the same thing I do. He wants peace between our country and theirs. We do, however, stay in a state of competition. This is inevitable. I think it's going to be that way 15 or 20 years in the future. We want to have accommodation when we can mutually benefit from that accommodation. We're willing to meet the Soviets in competition of a peaceful nature. When the Soviets commit acts with which we disagree, I have to make a judgment whether to be quiet about it or to speak out openly and acquaint the American people with the facts, so that Americans can understand the interrelationship between us and the Soviet Union.

News conference, Washington, June 26/
The New York Times, 6-27:(A)12.

4

If the Soviet Union chooses to join us in developing a more broad-based and reciprocal detente, the world will reap untold benefits. But genuine detente also includes restraint in the use of military power and an end to the pursuit of unilateral advantage, as in Africa today. And detente must include the honoring of solemn international agreements concerning human rights and a mutual effort to promote a climate in which these rights can flourish. But whatever the Soviets decide, the West will do whatever is necessary to preserve our security while we continue the search for a lasting peace.

At City Hall, Bonn, West Germany, July 14/
The Washington Post, 7-15:(A)8.

5

I do not contemplate, short of a direct threat to the security of my own nation, the sending of troops to another country to solve an internal conflict as we did in Vietnam in the past . . . [But] just because we don't send troops, as we did in Vietnam, doesn't mean we have abandoned freedom or that we will sit back and let local conflicts bring suffering to those in whom we are deeply interested and about whom we are concerned.

At town meeting, West Berlin, July 15/
The New York Times, 7-17:(A)2.

WHAT THEY SAID IN 1978

(JIMMY CARTER)

1

[On whether his credentials in foreign-policy matters have been enhanced since the success of his Camp David summit with Israeli Prime Minister Menachem Begin and Egyptian President Anwar Sadat]: I think so. There is a general sense, looking at it from as objective a point of view as I can, that I am more to be trusted on making difficult decisions on international affairs than before. I don't say it with a semblance of pride, but it is a fact.

To reporters, Washington, Sept. 27/
Los Angeles Times, 9-28:(1)20.

2

I don't know of anyone in the Administration of Jimmy Carter who has done more for our country throughout the world than [UN Ambassador] Andy Young.... as long as I am President and Andy Young is willing to stay there, he'll be the United Nations Ambassador.

Before Congressional Black Caucus, Washington,
Sept. 30/The Washington Post, 10-1:(A)2.

3

The effectiveness of our human-rights policy is now an established fact. It has contributed to an atmosphere of change that has encouraged progress in many places. In some countries, political prisoners have been released by the hundreds, even thousands. In others, the brutality of repression has been lessened. In still others, there is movement toward democratic institutions or the rule of law. To those who doubt the wisdom of our dedication, I say: Ask the victims. Ask the exiles. Ask the governments which practice repression. Whether in Cambodia and Chile, in Uganda or South Africa, in Nicaragua or Ethiopia or the Soviet Union, governments know that we care—and not a single one of those who is actually taking risks or suffering for human rights has asked us to desist. From the prisons, the camps, the enforced exiles, we receive one message: speak up, persevere, let the voice of freedom be heard.

At 30th anniversary ceremony of Universal
Declaration of Human Rights, Washington, Dec. 6/
The New York Times, 12-7:(A)10.

4

We live in a difficult, complicated world, a world in which peace is literally a matter of survival. Our foreign policy must take this into account. Often a choice that moves us toward one of our goals moves us farther away from another. Seldom do circumstances permit us to take actions that are wholly satisfactory to everyone.

At 30th anniversary ceremony of Universal
Declaration of Human Rights, Washington, Dec. 6/
The New York Times, 12-7:(A)10.

5

My experience in negotiating sensitive and complicated agreements with foreign leaders ... is that to negotiate through the news media, through public pronouncements, and with wide divergencies of views expressed by different leaders of a country, is not conducive to success.

Television interview, Washington, Dec. 19/
The Christian Science Monitor, 12-22:1.

Frank Church
United States Senator, D-Idaho

6

[Saying the U.S. should sell food to foreign countries regardless of their type of government]: Fat Communists are less dangerous than hungry ones ... As far as I'm concerned, I am for selling food to any country that needs it and can pay for it—whether I approve of its government or not. I am for selling anything that can't shoot back.

Before National Farmers Union, Salt Lake City,
March 4/The Dallas Times Herald, 3-6:(A)2.

William E. Colby
Former Director of Central Intelligence of
the United States

7

[On the U.S.' lack of response to Soviet and Cuban intervention in last year's guerrilla war in Angola]: The Soviet Union has, through that inaction, discovered an apparently effective foreign-policy weapon, in its use of Cuban troops, that the U.S. either cannot or will not challenge. It is probably the most effective strategy they [the Soviets] have had since the days

(WILLIAM E. COLBY)

when [Soviet Premier Nikita] Khrushchev discovered the wars of national liberation.

Dallas/The Dallas Times Herald, 5-25:(A)20.

1

[Saying the main threat against the U.S. is from "have not" nations such as Mexico] : The greatest danger of violence and difficulty in the world is between the "haves" and the "have nots" ... You cannot stop the [population] growth at this point. The women are alive today who are going to bear those children. So you can have all the birth control you want between now and the end of the century. It isn't going to change those figures in real terms. So what's going to happen to that extra 60-odd million Mexicans? Twenty [million] of them are going to be right here [in the U.S. as illegal aliens].

Interview, June 5/Los Angeles Times, 6-6:(1)11.

2

As Clausewitz said, war is an extension of policy by other means, and in a world of state sovereignties you're going to have problems with other countries. Some of those could be met by alliances, and some of them have to be met by deterrence, and sometimes you have a danger of having to meet those problems with your armed force. But sometimes a preliminary covert support of some group in that country can avoid problems.

Panel discussion/The Washington Post, 11-12:(B)5.

John Conyers, Jr.
United States Representative,
D-Michigan

3

[On U.S. UN Ambassador Andrew Young's controversial outspokenness] : If President Carter wants to throw away his fast-diminishing chance of re-election, all he has to do is to fire Andy Young. Andy still dares to bring freshness and candor to a diplomatic post. He is keeping alive the new politics Carter campaigned on and was elected on.

The Washington Post, 7-14:(A)16.

Alexander Dallin
Professor of history and political
science, Stanford University

4

The code of detente is unwritten, and each side reads something else into it. In the early '70s, there was a feeling we were stabilizing the status quo. [Then-Secretary of State Henry] Kissinger oversold that idea in this country, but the Soviets never bought it. As far as they are concerned, parity means equal opportunity to meddle in international affairs. I'm not as alarmed as some people. I don't see any great Russian master plan. They are interested in asserting their influence so long as there is no great risk involved. And, so far, there isn't.

Interview/Newsweek, 6-12:41.

Alexander De Conde
Professor of history, University of
California, Santa Barbara

5

I am not particularly alarmed about what has happened to detente. As far as I can see ... never in the history of Soviet-American relations have they been so good, in the sense that while there will always be crisis, always some kind of conflict, Americans and Communists are not killing each other. There may be some problems in Angola ... But I really can't see cause for alarm. I can't see why stability has to be linked with an active foreign policy.

Discussion at Center for the Study of
Democratic Institutions, Santa Barbara,
Calif./World Issues, April-May:12.

Patricia M. Derian
Assistant Secretary for Human Rights,
Department of State of the United States

6

Human rights is one of the basic elements of [U.S.] foreign policy. But it's not the only element. National security is also an element, and its importance has not diminished. In the case of South Korea, the national-security interests of the United States require that South Korea be able to defend itself. And it is obvious that our security interests there are critical and that certain kinds of military aid are required. That doesn't mean that we ignore human-rights

WHAT THEY SAID IN 1978

concerns in South Korea because we have this overriding security interest. It's the same with Iran. We have vigorously pursued our human-rights policy there at the same time that we've continued large military sales and maintained very close military and security cooperation .... there's no grid that we just slap on every country and say, "It all has to conform like this." We try to be sensitive to varying factors in each country.

Interview/U.S. News & World Report, 12-4:35.

Marian Dobrosielski
Polish delegate to Belgrade conference on the Helsinki Agreement on European Security and Cooperation

1

This whole campaign on human rights in the press, and started by the U.S. delegation, has not helped one single person in this respect. Rather, it has hardened positions and increased suspicions. No socialist country can permit itself to be dictated to as to what they have to do with this or that person or group.

Belgrade/The Washington Post, 2-23:(A)16.

Bob Dole
United States Senator, R-Kansas

2

This [Carter] Administration's foreign policy is a pattern of inconsistencies. The rhetoric of human rights is followed by the reality of retreat. To the south, they're cuddling up to [Cuban Premier Fidel] Castro. To the east, they're still looking for a face-saving device to withdraw relations from the government of Taiwan. Not too far away from Taiwan, they're trying to retreat from our security position in Korea ... In the Middle East, we have managed to confuse nearly everyone, by insisting that Israel accept pre-conditions ... And in our negotiations with the Soviet Union, they have already given away one of our most crucial negotiating points—the B-1 bomber.

The Wall Street Journal, 3-7:20.

Gerald R. Ford
Former President of the United States

3

Congress in recent years has gone too far in many areas in trying to assume powers that belong to the President and the Executive Branch. From experience, I can say that when the Congress hobbles the President in the execution of delicate foreign-policy decisions, the United States inevitably pays a heavy price. We should never send a President of this great country to the bargaining table with one hand tied behind him.

Before American Enterprise Institute for Public Policy Research, Washington, Dec. 13/ The New York Times, 12-14:(A)22.

Valery Giscard d'Estaing
President of France

4

Detente implies a certain code of behavior on the part of all those who participate, and all regions of the earth must be adapted to the necessity of detente ... It appears to me fundamental at the present time to underline the global nature of detente, and that it cannot be accompanied by a quest for, or even the acceptance of, a change in [the world] balance ... It is not compatible with detente at the present time to have the crossing of frontiers between sovereign states by armed forces. It is not possible for these incursions to be supported by this or that partner in detente.

News conference, Paris, June 14/ Los Angeles Times, 6-15:(1)9.

Arthur J. Goldberg
United States Ambassador to Belgrade conference on the Helsinki Agreement on European Security and Cooperation

5

... the relaxation of tension, which is what detente is all about, has to be a product of agreement in many areas: business, scientific, cultural, military confidence-building measures, flow of information, as well as human rights. Let me make clear that I see no direct linkage between the pursuit of human rights at Belgrade and negotiations on SALT, multilateral force reductions in Europe, limitation of con-

(ARTHUR J. GOLDBERG)

ventional armaments, Indian Ocean problems, or even grain deals. But if we are going to strengthen detente, it must encompass humanitarian progress. As I have always said, detente must have a human face.

Interview, Belgrade/
U.S. News & World Report, 3-13:31.

Marshall I. Goldman
Professor of economics,
Wellesley College

1

The one thing I think the [Carter] Administration is doing well is using its China card. That's fine. Let the Soviets feel a little pressure from China. There are some other things it could be doing in Eastern Europe—for example, Hungary is being considered for most-favored-nation treatment, and that should be pushed. Some of the other East European countries should be approached in the same way. I would do everything I could to encourage the Mongolians to open diplomatic relations with us. In other words, the U.S. should let the Soviets know that they have flanks that are vulnerable, too.

Interview/Newsweek, 6-12:41.

Barry M. Goldwater
United States Senator, R-Arizona

2

[On President Carter's emphasis on human rights in foreign affairs]: For such a policy to have any credibility anywhere in the world, it has to be applied universally without regard for political considerations of any kind; in this, my country is sorely lacking. It has adopted a set of standards which it applies to many nations, including some of our best friends, while never mentioning their application to countries on the left-hand side of the political spectrum. For example, the American Administration is quick to yell "foul" when appraising human rights in places such as South Africa, Rhodesia and Latin America, but we hear little if anything about the gross repression and violation of human rights in countries like Communist China, Cuba,

Uganda, Cambodia and Vietnam. I, for one, am sick of this hypocrisy, this selective application of a policy which could stand for something in the world but, instead, has become nothing but a tool for politicians grinding their own domestic political axes.

At Rand Afrikaans University, South Africa,
March 28/Vital Speeches, 5-15:455.

3

[President] Carter is a nice fellow, but he is the most poorly equipped man ever to sit in the White House. He has no grasp of foreign policy, and [U.S. UN Ambassador] Andrew Young has less. Andrew Young is the most despised man we ever sent anywhere.

Interview/San Francisco Examiner & Chronicle,
5-7:(Sunday Punch)3.

4

[On the effect on U.S. foreign affairs of President Carter's decision to cancel the defense treaty with Taiwan without Congressional approval as part of establishing full relations with mainland China]: Aside from its immediate effect upon a friend and ally [Taiwan] ... the treatment of Taiwan calls into question the honor—the very soul—of America's word in the field of foreign relations. For years we made much of how worthless were treaties and agreements entered into by the Soviet Union. We told the world that *our* commitments were matters of honor, while commitments made by the Soviets were matters of expediency. Now, in this crucial era, we have come down on the side of expediency and thrown honor to the wind.

Television broadcast, Dec. 23/San Francisco
Examiner & Chronicle, 12-31:(This World)22.

Otis L. Graham, Jr.
Professor of American history,
University of California,
Santa Barbara

5

There is a long and rather discouraging American record of trying to influence the ideological, political and economic patterns inside other societies. I happen to be interested in our effort to try to influence—in the late 1930s—the Japanese government in directions

WHAT THEY SAID IN 1978

(OTIS L. GRAHAM, JR.)

we thought it ought to be going. We tried to promote moderate regimes and pragmatic politicians in Japan who, if not pro-Western, would be at least acceptable to us. We did not do very well in that case. Everything we did seemed to strengthen the "bad guys," and finally we had a war. In Vietnam, we misunderstood the situation. In China, we have the whole record of Chiang Kai-shek to look at. So there are many chapters in this, on the whole, unsuccessful American effort to influence others—always, of course, in the context of the cold war.

Panel discussion/World Issues, Oct.-Nov.:5.

Orrin G. Hatch
United States Senator, R-Utah

1

If [President Carter is] going to talk of human rights, then he should have more respect and appreciation for those dictators who respect and love us and have a little less for those who hate us.

Interview/U.S. News & World Report, 2-6:20.

2

One of the more controversial issues of the day deals with the selling of modern [U.S.] technology to nations that would be considered adversaries of the United States. In particular, the Soviet Union is mentioned as the main target of those who would like to stem this ever-increasing flow of know-how . . . It becomes apparent to even the novice in foreign affairs that those nations who operate under a closed society have had problems maintaining a reasonable rate of growth in the area of technology. They are then forced to turn to the West for the information they need to serve as a catalyst for their own sluggish programs . . . The Soviet Union is a nation that is rich in natural resources. It does not make sense for the United States, a nation that is so dependent upon foreign suppliers of many critical resources, to provide the technology—know-how, if you will—to develop those resources. The clearly stated goal of the Soviet Union is to surpass the United States. By giving away the one major advantage that we possess, we only

assist in the propaganda campaign that they promote, extolling the virtues of a socialist state over a capitalist one.

Before the Senate, Washington, Aug. 8/
The Washington Post, 8-15:(A)10.

S. I. Hayakawa
United States Senator, R-California

3

I am very much ashamed at the present time that the United States is frightened of Russia. Damn it, Russia should be frightened of *us.* But every move we take we say, "What will the Russians say? What will the Russians say?" The hell with what they say. They should be asking about every move *they* make, "What will the Americans say?"

Interview/U.S. News & World Report, 10-30:32.

Hua Kuo-feng
Chairman, Communist Party of China

4

The forces that once dreamed of setting up a world empire have long ago turned to dust under the iron blows of the people. Today, those who hold in vain the thought of ruling the world will—even if they briefly enjoy their folly—meet with the same fate.

At state dinner, Bucharest, Romania/
Time, 8-28:25.

Huang Hua
Foreign Minister of the People's
Republic of (mainland) China

5

There are some people in the West today who are cowed by Soviet military threats and are afraid of war, or who indulge in a false sense of security and deny the existence of a serious danger of war. Politically, they seek peaceful cooperation to accommodate the Soviet hoax of detente. Economically, they offer big loans and technical equipment to pacify the Soviet Union. Militarily, they seek a respite through compromises and concessions. They even dream of averting the danger threatening themselves by sacrificing the security of others.

Before United Nations General Assembly special
session on disarmament, New York, May 29/
The New York Times, 5-30:(A)10.

(HUANG HUA)

1

There is need for unity now that there is a common enemy [the Soviet Union], a common danger. West Europe and the Third World countries have no choice but to cooperate and unite to defend their independence, security and territorial integrity ... It is the Soviet Union which wishes to conquer the whole world.

Interview/San Francisco
Examiner & Chronicle, 6-18:(A)2.

Samuel P. Huntington
Director, Center for International
Affairs, Harvard University

2

Look at our situation over-all, and it's quite clear that we are certainly the most powerful country in the world. Doubtless, the Soviet Union is the second most powerful. But if you look at the next five countries, four are our allies, and the fifth is the deadly enemy of the Soviet Union. I'd say we are in a fairly good position.

Interview/U.S. News & World Report, 11-27:64.

3

Perhaps one of the most important roles which American leadership can play in the world today is precisely that of attempting to resolve many of the regional conflicts which exist in the world. This is a role which, at least in the Middle East, has been played successfully by both the previous Administration and this [Carter] Administration. It is a role which the Soviet Union clearly cannot play, either in the Middle East or in southern Africa or elsewhere.

Interview/U.S. News & World Report, 11-27:65.

Henry M. Jackson
United States Senator, D-Washington

4

It is high time we stopped the dangerous practice of entering into unequal deals with Moscow in the misguided notion that Soviet leaders will reward our generosity with restraint in international affairs ... An American willingness to enter into such a manifestly unequal agreement [the currently-being-discussed SALT treaty] is certain to persuade the Russians that we are weak, however strident the rhetoric in Presidential speeches. How are the Russians interpreting the [Carter] Administration's proclivity for one-way concessions and one-sided retreats? It is clear that the Soviet leaders are increasingly confident that they can bully us and get away with it. They are becoming bolder in their policies and more prepared to take risks.

Before the Senate, Washington, July 10/
Los Angeles Times, 7-11:(1)5.

5

If neither trade nor the transfer of technology nor negotiated agreements give us leverage over the Soviets, why on earth should we continue to help them solve their economic problems, modernize their industry and obtain from us agreements that are politically, militarily and economically favorable to them? If, however, these various components of American policy do make it possible for us to affect Soviet policy, then we should use them consistently to uphold Western interests and to achieve arrangements with the Soviets based on genuine reciprocity and mutual forbearance. The basic error many people make in analyzing this question is to look for instant results.

Interview, Sept. 11/Los Angeles Times, 10-1:(6)2.

6

Our human-rights [foreign] policies cannot consist of punishing small countries and merely exhorting large nations. If we adopted such a course, we would inevitably—and justly—be accused of cynical hypocrisy.

Interview, Sept. 11/Los Angeles Times, 10-1:(6)2.

Abdurahman Jama Barre
Foreign Minister of Somalia

7

[Urging a boycott of the summit of non-aligned nations next year if it is held in Havana]: Cuba is a de facto member of the Warsaw Pact. Cuba wants to be both a non-aligned and an aligned nation at the same time. That contravenes the principles of our organization ... Cuba has been used by the Soviet Union as a force of aggression against one member after

WHAT THEY SAID IN 1978

(ABDURAHMAN JAMA BARRE)

another of this organization. It has become an instrument of Soviet strategic policy.

Interview, Belgrade, Yugoslavia, July 26/
Los Angeles Times, 7-27:(1)1,10.

Neville Kanakaratne
Ambassador to the United States
from Sri Lanka

1

... diplomacy has no agenda of limited scope; it embraces within its compass every aspect of man's existence in this world; it intrudes itself into ever-widening areas of international co-existence; it deals with serious economic disputes between nations; it exerts its efforts in fields which can only be described as "diplomatic functions" by the widest interpretation of its classic definitions; it seeks to prevent not only the march of armed forces across recognized national boundaries but also the over-population of the earth by man, the contamination of the oceans, the rivers and the air common to all of us; it seeks to prevent hunger and malnutrition; it aspires to touch the moral conscience of mankind in demanding respect for human rights, recognition of basic human needs, the equality of men and women everywhere. In short, diplomacy has become global and universal in its manifestations and takes within its province almost the entire field of activity of the international community as one human family.

At George Washington University, Feb. 20/
Vital Speeches, 5-1:431.

Henry A. Kissinger
Former Secretary of State of the
United States

2

[On Secretary of State Cyrus Vance]: I have extremely high regard for Vance. I like him enormously as a human being. He's done a very good job in conducting foreign policy. His strengths are his fairness, his sound judgment and his patience. If he has any weakness it's that he doesn't assert himself enough. There can be free debate within the government, but there has to be one recognizable voice that speaks for American foreign policy.

Time, 4-24:13.

3

It is time that one overcomes the ridiculous myth of the invincible Cubans ... We cannot conduct our foreign policy under the threat of possible intervention of Cuban troops. It is a sign of the decline of our world position that we have inflicted on ourselves ... and it is a proposition that is bound to undermine our position around the world ... Let us justify our foreign policy by arguments other than the fear of Cuban military intervention. We must make clear to other countries that we will not be blackmailed by Cuban troops or by Soviet arms. Whatever arguments can be advanced for conducting our foreign policy, we will not accept the proposition that, if we do not accede to the arguments of individual countries, they will then call in the Cubans, or the Soviets will then send arms.

Before International Radio and Television
Society, New York/San Francisco
Examiner & Chronicle, 5-7:(B)7.

4

Modern foreign policy, by its very complexity, does not lend itself to instant successes. In domestic affairs the timeframe of new departures is defined by the legislative process; dramatic initiatives may be the only way to launch a new program. In foreign policy the most important initiatives require painstaking preparation; results may be months and years in becoming apparent. Foreign policy, if it is to be truly an architectural endeavor, is the art of building for the long term, the careful nurturing of relationships, the elaboration of policies that enhance our options and constrain those of potential opponents. It requires the coherence that can only come from national unity, a strong leadership and a political process that reflects the recognition that we are all—the Administration as well as its opponents—part of a permanent national endeavor.

Lecture, New York University/Los Angeles
Herald Examiner, 5-7:(E)4.

(HENRY A. KISSINGER)

1

[On the recent Camp David meetings between Israel and Egypt]: You can't imagine how painful it was to me to see how much could be accomplished without me.

Time, 11-13:77.

2

... we [cannot] accept the proposition that the Soviet Union has the right of unlimited intervention, directly or by proxy, in every part of the world, while in the name of relaxation of tensions we do not react. In other words, I believe in linkage. Russia must choose between expansionism and relaxation of tensions. It cannot have both.

Interview, New York/Newsweek, 12-11:56.

3

[On his term as Secretary of State]: When you're in office, you react to things like an athlete: You do this, you do that. But now I have the chance to reflect on it all and to think about why. There are painful episodes. I was in office during a period when America really tore itself apart. I had to conduct foreign policy under near-civil-war conditions. That was a difficult period in our history, and when you see now the bitterness that existed then, it's sad to review it—sadder than actually living it . . . Nobody can go through eight years like that without some tactical things you would do differently. But the main lines of policy I would do again the same way.

Interview, New York/
The New York Times, 12-29:(B)1.

Walter Laqueur
Historian, Center for Strategic and
International Studies;
Authority on terrorism

4

Terrorism needs a certain amount of freedom. In the kind of police state that the Communists run, the terrorist groups cannot organize effectively. If they manage to organize, they are smashed by the secret police, who are not constrained by civil-rights laws. Neither a

Communist state nor a reasonably effective military dictatorship has anything to fear from terrorism.

Interview/U.S. News & World Report, 5-22:36.

Paul D. Laxalt
United States Senator, R-Nevada

5

[On the emphasis on human rights in U.S. foreign policy]: Concern for individual liberties of the citizens of other lands is a longstanding, legitimate objective of U.S. foreign policy. But empty rhetoric in cases where we have very little leverage helps neither our over-all image nor the unfortunate victims of human-rights violations overseas. Yet what should we do about those states such as the Soviet Union that are militarily powerful, economically largely independent and utterly oppressive of the individual rights of their citizens? I admit that this is a serious question and one to which I have no ready answer. However, I can say what I think we should *not* do. As a responsible government, the United States should not indulge in empty posturing. Warnings, admonitions and even threats emanating from Washington need to be seen to carry weight. Just as it is hazardous to bluff too often in Vegas, so it is dangerous for a government to have its bluff called when it gets involved in matters over which it has very little control.

At Total Force II 1978 program, Las Vegas, Nev.,
Aug. 3/Vital Speeches, 10-1:742.

Wilbert J. Lemelle
United States Ambassador to
Kenya and the Seychelles

6

A credible stance in the international arena is necessarily one that reflects what we believe in for ourselves and how we behave toward one another at home. We recognize our domestic shortcomings and we criticize ourselves and each other for lack of consistency in pursuing the ideals—based on the principle of human rights—to which we subscribe. There is no reason why this same principle should not be applied in our dealing with other countries and other peoples. Quite the contrary. If the ideal of human rights is a central thread in the fabric

WHAT THEY SAID IN 1978

(WILBERT J. LEMELLE)

of American society—and I am convinced that it is—then it is neither honest nor practical to omit that thread in the weaving of our policies with regard to the rest of the world's people. To do so is to imply that somehow their rights are less than ours. Such an attitude smacks of the worst kind of arrogance, condescension and callousness.

Before Black Catholic Ministries and Laymen's Council, Pittsburgh, Feb. 26/ Vital Speeches, 4-1:369.

Clarence D. Long
United States Representative, D-Maryland

1

There's no way you can convince me you can somehow get peace in a section of the world in which you are pumping vast arms. The United States is the great supermarket of arms in this world. We have become the merchants of slaughter in this world.

At House Foreign Operations Appropriations Subcommittee, Washington, Feb. 24/ Los Angeles Times, 2-25:(1)4.

Richard Lowenthal
Professor emeritus of international relations, Free University of Berlin

2

Soviet leaders are pursuing an ambitious program of power expansion with resources that are still limited. The U.S. must seek to influence their choices by making Soviet expansion more risky and costly, and Soviet restraint and cooperation more rewarding. It must convince them of our determination to match and out-match their armaments, and to react to Soviet intervention in crisis areas either on the spot or by reduction of the forms of economic cooperation most vital to Moscow, such as credits and technology transfers. But it must also seek to convince them of our ability and willingness to carry out a negotiated policy of arms control and to reward restraint with an increase of those forms of cooperation.

Interview/Newsweek, 6-12:38.

Clare Boothe Luce
Former American diplomat and playwright

3

Common sense tells us—or should tell us—that the primary goal of a sound foreign policy can never be peace. To be sure, a nation that makes the avoidance of war its supreme goal will always find that goal easy to achieve. All any nation needs to do in order to avoid war is to yield to every demand that its enemies make on it. And even if war nevertheless comes, it can still obtain peace by surrender.

Vital Speeches, 8-15:645.

Joseph Luns
Secretary General, North Atlantic Treaty Organization

4

There is an unwillingness of the Soviet Union to accept that detente is indivisible, and an unease among all of us over the continued build-up of Soviet arms and Soviet actions in Africa and elsewhere. We had all hoped that detente would lead to restraint on the part of the Soviet and Warsaw Pact powers, but that has not happened. A new SALT agreement is not just around the corner. And when it comes to human rights, I need only mention the name Orlov [a Soviet dissident sent to jail] to show that neither the spirit nor the letter of the Helsinki [human-rights] agreements is being observed by the Soviet Union.

News conference, Washington, May 29/ Los Angeles Times, 5-30:(1)5.

Georges-Henri Martin
Editor-in-chief, "Tribune de Geneve," Geneva

5

East-West coexistence is of great interest to small countries. Superpowers like the U.S. and the Soviet Union are so powerful that, whatever the tensions, they are bound to survive. But to small countries, international cooperation is crucial because with their limited power they would be crushed unless there was some respect for the rule of law. In recent years, the Swiss have been very active in trying to bring imagina-

(GEORGES-HENRI MARTIN)

tion to foreign relations and finding new ways of getting along.

Interview, New York/
Atlas World Press Review, August:22.

Lawrence P. McDonald
United States Representative, D-Georgia

1

The American people are tired of foreign-policy planners who find beauty in retreat and glory in defeat.

Los Angeles Times, 1-22:(1)26.

George S. McGovern
United States Senator, D-South Dakota

2

No National Security Adviser wants to appear faint-hearted in the face of genuine crisis. But to avoid being chicken, one need not become Chicken Little. We cannot conduct foreign policy as though every stirring in Africa, Asia or the Indian Ocean is another Cuban missile crisis. Foreign policy must be selective in centering upon the few fundamental interests of the nation—not the minor distractions.

Before Americans for Democratic Action,
Washington, June 17/
The Washington Post, 6-18:(A)6.

Robert S. McNamara
President, International Bank for
Reconstruction and Development
(World Bank)

3

It has become almost a cliche to say that we live in an increasingly interdependent world. But it is a fact, and the trend toward increasing interdependence I believe will shape our future in ways that we are just beginning to understand. Few among us realize that food shortages in sub-Saharan Africa or in Bangladesh will stimulate inflation in the United States, will cause bread prices to rise in the supermarkets and will lead to wage increases in the auto industry. Even less are we aware that within our lifetime population growth in Mexico is very likely to cause the Spanish-speaking population in this country [the U.S.] to multiply several-

fold and to become the largest minority group in the nation, with all that that implies for social stress and institutional change.

Interview/The New York Times, 4-2:(4)3.

Sig Mickelson
Chairman, Radio Free Europe/
Radio Liberty

4

The Communist regimes are greatly disturbed by the fact that we have large audiences in their countries. They go to great lengths to jam us, to discredit us, to prevent citizens from listening to what we have to say ... [RFE/RL's most important contribution] is not in stimulating opposition which can be put down by government power. It is rather by stimulating thoughtfulness on the part of the citizen. An informed citizen is less likely to be manipulated by his government. This is the philosophical underpinning of our effort and our approach. We believe that peaceful relations between nations should rest on some basis of shared facts and ideas. Radio Free Europe and Radio Liberty intend to continue to build toward that mutual understanding and all the benefits that go with it: detente, responsible governments, informed publics exercising influence in government decisions, human rights, civil rights and political rights.

Before Cincinnati Rotary Club, May 25/
Vital Speeches, 7-1:576.

Donald O. Mills
Jamaican Ambassador to the United States

5

What we [the developing nations] say to the developed world is this: Don't underestimate our seriousness. Too many still think of us as a bunch of impractical, poor countries with our hands out begging for assistance. Listen to us. We have put forward our proposals. What are you waiting for? Are you still afraid that you're going to lose all your marbles? Join us in creating a world that is really going to benefit all countries, and take the developing countries out of this situation we've been in for so long. The world is not going to remain the way in which history has left it, with a small group of

WHAT THEY SAID IN 1978

countries dominating a much larger group that is in a secondary position. You either bring about an equitable world by conscious device, or risk the emergence of a world which will be a very uncomfortable place for all of us. Certainly it will not remain as it is today.

Interview/U.S. News & World Report, 7-31:62.

Milos Minic
Former Foreign Minister of Yugoslavia

1

The superpowers are carrying out bigger penetration into the non-aligned movement than ever before. They want to tie as many non-aligned countries as possible to their blocs and thus finally paralyze and break up the non-aligned movement forever.

At Yugoslav Communist Party Congress, Belgrade, June 21/The Dallas Times Herald, 6-22:(A)7.

Parren J. Mitchell
United States Representative, D-Maryland

2

[On the controversial outspokenness of U.S. UN Ambassador Andrew Young]: Ambassador Andy Young does have a fault—his fault is he is an honest and moral man attempting to tell the truth to a world which is immoral and dishonest.

U.S. News & World Report, 7-24:56.

Walter F. Mondale
Vice President of the United States

3

[On Secretary of State Cyrus Vance]: He's an old government pro. I don't know of any member of the Cabinet who tries harder to avoid poisonous disputes over minor matters. He doesn't indulge in backbiting, and he won't tolerate adults with graduate degrees behaving like children fighting over a toy ... He fights on principle. But he doesn't run up the flag five times a day to show who's boss.

Time, 4-24:14.

4

We must show by our actions that we cherish human rights, and above all the rights of other people to determine their own destiny.

Without reckless interventionism ... we can make it clear that we are on the side of human freedom and majority rule, even when that challenges powerful economic and political interests.

At University of Michigan commencement, April 29/The New York Times, 4-30:(1)26.

Richard M. Nixon
Former President of the United States

5

There is no nation in the free world today, except the United States, that has the strength and the power to save not only freedom for ourselves but for others and to stem the tide of dictatorial aggression in other parts of the world ... The question is whether the United States is going to meet that responsibility ... or whether we're going to shirk that responsibility because of the disappointments we've had in places like Vietnam and Korea and so forth.

At dedication of recreation complex in his honor, Hyden, Ky., July 2/Los Angeles Times, 7-3:(1)9.

Mohammad Reza Pahlavi
Shah of Iran

6

[On U.S. foreign policy]: You have no policy anywhere. You only react when something happens. The other side is planning something for 50 years. If the West wants to die slowly, that is your business.

Interview, Teheran, Iran, March 5/ The Washington Post, 3-6:(A)16.

Carolyn R. Payton
Former Director, United States Peace Corps

7

[Criticizing current Peace Corps policy which resulted in her forced resignation as Director]: I believe it is wrong to use the Peace Corps as a means of delivering a message to particular constituencies in the United States, or to export a particular political ideology. Those now responsible for the Peace Corps seem to wish the organization to be engaged in a kind of political activism and advocacy. They would be pleased to have Peace Corps volunteers demonstrate overseas against corporations

(CAROLYN R. PAYTON)

that engage in practices with which they disagree, or that market products they see as harmful. They would see the Peace Corps as a vehicle to allow unemployed black ghetto youth, as short-term volunteers, [to] learn about life in a black socialist country ... The Peace Corps has strayed away from its mission. As Director, I could not—because of the peculiar administrative structure under which the Peace Corps operates—do anything about this situation. As an ex-Director, I am free to sound the alarm.

Before Eastern Association of College Deans,
Washington, Dec. 7/
The Washington Post, 12-8:(A)8.

William Proxmire
United States Senator, D-Wisconsin

1

The President's [Carter] arms-sales restraint policy right now is more smoke than substance, more exemptions than rules, more sales than reductions ... The fine print allows sales to continue and even grow. Surely that is not what the public thinks of when considering arms restraint. This is akin to Orwell's doublethink.

The Christian Science Monitor, 2-10:6.

Sinnathamby Rajaratnam
Foreign Minister of Singapore

2

We [non-aligned nations] have become so used to putting the blame for our difficulties on others that we have lost the capacity to take a hard look at our own shortcomings. All we can hope for is occasional acts of charity, but no rich nation I know is prepared to undergo great distress and sacrifices to help the poor, no more than poor nations are willing to make sacrifices on behalf of nations poorer than themselves.

At non-aligned nations ministerial meeting,
Belgrade, Yugoslavia, July/
The Washington Post, 9-1:(A)20.

Ronald Reagan
Former Governor of California (R)

3

If the Carter Administration "stands with the victims of repression," the people of Cuba,

Panama, Vietnam, Cambodia and the mainland of China have yet to hear about it. The fact is ... [the Administration has] ceaselessly scolded authoritarian governments that are friendly [to the U.S.] and ignored authoritarian and totalitarian countries that are not.

At Conservative Political Action Conference,
Washington/The Christian Science Monitor, 3-22:3.

4

Many people in high places—academic, political and business—learned the wrong lesson from [U.S. involvement in the war in Vietnam]. When they say, "Never again," they mean we should never again oppose Communist aggression. The right lesson that should have been learned from the Vietnam war was never again should this country ask young men to fight and die for their country unless it's for a war we intend to win.

At dinner for former U.S. Vietnam prisoners of
war, Los Angeles/San Francisco
Examiner & Chronicle, 6-4:(This World)14.

John E. Reinhardt
Director, International Communication
Agency of the United States (formerly
U.S. Information Agency)

5

I believe it imperative that other societies know clearly where we [the U.S.] stand and why—as a government and as a people—on issues of concern, just as I believe it inevitable that other societies, in their own interests, will want to know. An important part of our [the Agency's] mandate continues to be the obligation to explain American policies as clearly and effectively as we can ... I believe, above all, that the work we do can and does make a difference. Surely there will always be real conflicts of interest among peoples. But I believe that we can play a profound role in helping to reduce a multitude of conflicts that arise largely, if not entirely, from misunderstandings and misperceptions among people. And I believe we can make an essential contribution to the creation of an international environment in which

WHAT THEY SAID IN 1978

real differences are worked out rationally, sensitively and peaceably.

At inaugural ceremonies of International
Communication Agency, April 3/
The Washington Post, 4-5:(A)14.

Abraham A. Ribicoff
United States Senator, D-Connecticut

1

[On his current visit to the Soviet Union]: Out of it came the realization of how deeply people can feel about the same circumstances and facts and still reach opposite conclusions ... Each gets a distorted view of how the other looks at the same set of facts. The overriding tragedy is that there is such basic suspicion between the United States and the Soviet Union that it clouds the clarity that should exist between two great powers. [It] prevents men of responsibility from getting at the heart of complicated problems.

Interview, Moscow/
The Dallas Times Herald, 11-19:(A)30.

2

[The Soviets] may not want to address the problem of linkage, but any strategic-arms-limitation treaty requires 67 affirmative [U.S. Senate] votes. And any Senator considers all the factors affecting Soviet-American relations. So the problems of SALT can't be separated from the issues of human rights, emigration, trade, Africa, the Cubans and the Middle East.

Interview, Moscow/
Los Angeles Times, 11-19:(1)11.

Donald W. Riegle, Jr.
United States Senator, D-Michigan

3

[On U.S. relations with the Soviet Union in the wake of Soviet prosecution of dissidents]: I cannot imagine a SALT treaty I could support with a nation that terrorizes its own people. I cannot see the value of an expanded trading relationship with a government that brutalizes dissenters who act within the bounds of the Soviet Constitution. I must urge my own gov-

ernment to do nothing that would give aid and comfort to a Soviet regime that would devour its own people.

Before the Senate, Washington, July 11/
Los Angeles Herald Examiner, 7-12:(A)6.

Eugene V. Rostow
Professor of law, Yale University;
Former Under Secretary of State of
the United States

4

The [U.S.] government is in a strange mood, a mood which reminds me of the '30s, when we and the British hesitated between action and inaction until it was too late to prevent World War II. [There are still people] who do not yet believe that Soviet military power exists and is being used to promote political ends. They are somnambulists, still bemused by lullabies of detente.

Before Senate committee/
Nation's Business, July:58.

Helmut Schmidt
Chancellor of West Germany

5

... after Vietnam, [U.S.] Presidents are not as successful with Congress [in foreign policy] as before, and it is far more difficult to read the long-term political lines of Congress than the concepts of the Administration. We have to deal with Congress directly more than ever before. Our Embassy is not enough. Members of our Parliament go over to Washington more and more to talk to the new generation in American politics, who have neither emotional ties toward Europe nor specific experience in American-European cooperation. Thus, the whole process of inter-allied decision-making becomes far more complex than in the past—in strategy, energy, trade and monetary policies. Horrendously complicated. Cooperation between democracies is becoming more and more difficult to manage.

Interview, Hamburg/Newsweek, 5-29:46.

6

[On telephone talks he has had with U.S. President Carter]: [He] does not even turn off the music when he calls. All those violins and

(HELMUT SCHMIDT)

drums make it impossible to understand him ... No useful purpose is served by talking with Carter. During our next telephone conversation, I will read out to him the Cologne-Euskirchen railroad timetable. He does not listen anyhow.

Los Angeles Times, 5-29:(1)5.

1

[Warning against sanctions and other tough measures against the Soviet Union resulting from that country's persecution of dissidents]: In a showdown they will be tough as well, and two guys just shouting at each other will not lead to an improvement of the situation ... I think the more we pursue [the] policies [of detente] ... the more we can expect a further opening up of their society. It is a slow process, I would accept, but it is a process, and one should not provoke its interruption.

TV-radio interview, West Berlin/"Issues and Answers," American Broadcasting Company, 7-16.

John W. Sewall
Executive vice president, Overseas Development Council, Washington

2

The common perception in the industrialized countries is that North-South economic relations are most often an area where the costs exceed the benefits. But this perception ignores the reality that the developing countries now are rapidly becoming more integrated into the global economy. The image of all developing countries as needy recipients of aid has been overtaken by events. A number of developing countries collectively—and in some cases individually—have become important participants in the world economy, and their impact on the economies of the industrial countries is significant. As a result, policy-makers will have to consider the impact of the progress—or lack thereof—in the developing countries on the prospects for resumed growth, higher employment and less inflation in the industrial world.

At seminar, West Berlin/ The Christian Science Monitor, 12-22:11.

Dimitri Simes
Director of Soviet studies, Georgetown University

3

Detente affected the rules of the superpower game, adding a greater element of cooperation and crisis management. But it did not affect the name of the game, and the name still is rivalry. The problem with Soviet actions is not that they don't fit the code of detente, but that they represent a serious challenge to the legitimate U.S. strategic interests and, indeed in the long run, to the very security of the U.S.

Interview/Newsweek, 6-12:41.

Alexander I. Solzhenitsyn
Exiled Soviet author

4

A decline in courage may be the most striking feature which an outside observer notices in the West in our days ... Political and intellectual bureaucrats get tongue-tied and paralyzed when they deal with powerful governments and threatening forces, with aggressors and international terrorists. Should one point out that, since ancient times, decline in courage has been considered the beginning of the end?

At Harvard University commencement, June 8/ Newsweek, 6-19:43.

R. Peter Straus
Director, Voice of America

5

We [the VOA] are not going into the propaganda line in our news presentation. We are indeed "telling it like it is." I think we've learned that the only sensible way to get an audience is by convincing people that when they tune into the VOA, they're tuning into the most credible and reliable news-and-information service available to them. Will we also do other things? Yes, but the fundamental ingredient in VOA is hard news and background—and it accounts for about 50 per cent of our total time. That is played as straight as we know how. Nobody else is responsible for its content, and the mistakes we make are editorial-judgment mistakes, not dictated by the Secretary of State or the Defense Department or anyone else.

Interview/U.S. News & World Report, 6-12:56.

WHAT THEY SAID IN 1978

Josip Broz Tito
President of Yugoslavia

1

No other political force in the post-war period has striven and fought so consistently and perseveringly as the non-aligned [nations] movement for better and more just international relations. It is precisely the non-aligned countries that have, through their view of the world and joint political action, brought to light the real problems facing mankind and charted the avenues and possibilities leading to their resolution . . . In essence, the policy of non-alignment is directed against imperialism, neo-colonialism, racism and all other forms of foreign domination and exploitation. It is directed against power politics, political and economic hegemony, and every kind of external interference and dependence . . . The non-aligned movement has pledged itself, and will continue to dedicate its energies, to active and peaceful coexistence, implying consistent struggle for peace and equality in the world, and against the imposition of social and political systems or ideologies.

At conference of foreign ministers of
non-aligned countries, Belgrade, July 25/
Vital Speeches, 9-15:706.

Cyrus R. Vance
Secretary of State of the
United States

2

People expect immediate successes [in foreign affairs] and when that doesn't happen, criticism is bound to follow. People have got to recognize that these are terribly difficult, long-term problems. You've got to give necessary time to work through them and not stick down a thermometer each week and say: What in hell have you done this week? . . . Opinion is very, very fickle. What people want to see is coonskins on the wall, and they don't see enough coonskins on the wall at this point.

Interview, Washington/Time, 4-24:20.

3

. . . our strength in the world does not rest on our military power alone. Remaining strong also involves putting our economic house in order, by controlling inflation and by implementing a comprehensive energy policy. Our strength is also based on the vitality of our alliances, and we are broadening our joint efforts for mutual and sustained economic growth and for development programs for the Third World. Finally, the bedrock of our strength is our heritage as a free nation, our democratic institutions, and what we stand for as a people. Our ideals are the most powerful in the world.

Before House International Relations Committee,
Washington/The Christian Science Monitor, 6-30:23.

Charles E. Wiggins
United States Representative,
R-California

4

. . . Congress has become much more intimately involved in the formulation of foreign policy. And, by and large, its efforts have been close to disastrous. Congress has legislated in such foreign-policy areas as Angola. Its decision to lend no support at all to the established government was tantamount to supporting the radical elements that ultimately took over. Angola now is a base of operations for further destabilizing activities in south and central Africa; witness the excursions into Zaire. Congressional intervention in the dispute between Greece and Turkey over Cyprus is another illustration with profound consequences for United States policy and the North Atlantic Treaty Organization.

Interview/U.S. News & World Report, 6-5:24.

Peter Wiles
Professor of Russian studies,
London School of Economics and
Political Science

5

[On U.S. dealings with the Soviet Union] : I think [U.S. President] Carter has performed no better and no worse than [former President Gerald] Ford and [former Secretary of State Henry] Kissinger would have. Now, with [for-

(PETER WILES)

mer President Richard] Nixon, I think that the U.S. would have fared better toward the Soviet Union. He was a bastard, and perhaps you need a bastard when you are dealing with the Soviet Union.

Interview/Newsweek, 6-12:41.

Andrew Young
United States Ambassador/Permanent Representative to the United Nations

1

I don't know what to believe about Soviet President Leonid Brezhnev's health, but I certainly think that the climate in which a new Soviet Administration will emerge is being established now. If that Administration is established in a climate of detente, we have the possibility of building on it toward a more peaceful world. On the other hand, if that succession is established in a climate of missile rattling, we are pointing to the possible destruction of our planet. I don't believe in playing games like that. I don't think it's in America's military interests. I know it's not in our political interests. I always look at what the U.S. interests are, and make decisions on the basis of how I perceive U.S. interests. I think it's unwise to have a reactive policy. Foreign policy has to be based on a nation's self-interest, and we ought not automatically react until we determine what our interests are.

Interview/
U.S. News & World Report, 6-12:25.

2

[On criticism of his outspokenness and controversial statements]: I'm certainly not, you know, what people's traditional notion of a diplomat happens to be. But I don't represent a country like that. I became a diplomat and was appointed to this position because I was politically active in a human-rights movement, and in an anti-war movement, and because I fought for the things that I believe in, and I did not fight to be a diplomat. Whether I'm a diplomat or not, I am going to continue to fight in any way I know, short of violence, for the things that I believe in. And I really don't care what people think about it. The only thing that's important is that they think. And if I am a wrong kind of diplomat, maybe diplomats for the last 50 years should have been making people think a little more and we might not have had some of the trouble that we've had for the last half century.

Interview/The Washington Post, 7-19:(A)22.

3

We do not find more and more people in the Third World moving into the Communist camp. We find exactly the opposite. We find countries in which a decade ago the Soviet Union appeared to have tremendous influence—[and] are now demonstrating a fierce independence. More and more, they are realizing that rigid socialist prescriptions will not enable them to meet their development goals.

Before American Bar Association, New York,
Aug. 10/The Christian Science Monitor, 8-11:2.

INTELLIGENCE

William F. Buckley, Jr.
Political columnist;
Editor, "National Review"

1

[On those who make public CIA classified information]: There ought to be some penalty. You can go to jail if you reveal somebody else's income taxes, but not if you print your country's secrets.

New York/"W": a Fairchild publication, 8-4:6.

George Bush
Former Director of Central
Intelligence of the United States

2

I'm offended by the way [President] Carter continues to publicly flog the Agency [CIA] for political purposes by linking the CIA to Watergate. We have the best foreign-intelligence capability in the world. What needed to be cleaned up has been cleaned up. Instead of trying to continually weaken our intelligence community through outrageous attacks on the CIA and FBI, we ought to look to our own national interest to find ways to strengthen it.

Interview, Houston/"W":
a Fairchild publication, 4-28:22.

3

I think that there is an underlying feeling on the part of the American people that we must have clandestine services. Some things in an open society must be kept secret and I think there's more awareness of this fact coming back ... Some covert capability is essential. It should be sparingly used and properly supervised and properly conceived. Heads of various departments must meet and discuss it with the President. It must then be reported to the Congress. In my view, there are too many committees of Congress involved, and I favor more consolidated oversight. But covert action is necessary and it's very much misunderstood.

Quiet support for a friend is probably more of what covert action is really about than harassing some opposition someplace; much more of it, I'd say.

Panel discussion/
The Washington Post, 11-12:(B)1,5.

Jimmy Carter
President of the United States

4

[Addressing CIA employees]: There is a growing appreciation for what this Agency does, for what you individually do for our nation. There is now a stability in the CIA. There have been too many shocks, too many rapid changes in the past. But the policies that have now been established ... will give you a much surer sense of what the future will bring ... I appreciate what you are, what you do— the high professionalism, training, education and experience which you bring to your job. You have to be even more pure and more clean and more decent and more honest than almost any person to serve in government, because the slightest mistake on your part is highly publicized and greatly magnified, whereas your great achievements and successes quite often are not publicized and not recognized.

At Central Intelligence Agency, Langley, Va.,
Aug. 16/Los Angeles Herald Examiner 8-17:(A)5.

William E. Colby
Former Director of Central
Intelligence of the United States

5

I believe that you can't run an army if every lieutenant decides which order to follow. You can't run an intelligence service if every junior officer decides which secret to keep.

Television interview/"60 Minutes,"
Columbia Broadcasting System, 5-14.

Gerald R. Ford
Former President of the United States

1

Yes, there were abuses in those agencies [the CIA and FBI], but the corrective measures of the past two years have been so extreme that apparently our best sources of intelligence out of Iran are public newspaper stories. That is an outrageous state of affairs. A nation without eyes and ears is a nation wandering in the dark.

Before American Enterprise Institute for Public Policy Research, Washington, Dec. 13/ The New York Times, 12-14:(A)22.

Richard Helms
Former Director of Central Intelligence of the United States

2

[Criticizing Congressional attempts to control the CIA and other attacks on the Agency, including leaks of secrets, etc.]: If it continues, this country is going to be at a serious disadvantage. The Russians are putting things into place. This is a time when our intelligence can't possibly be too good and when we can't have enough of it. To coin a phrase, we're certainly fiddling while Rome burns.

Before Senate Intelligence Committee, Washington, May 16/The Washington Post, 5-17:(A)1.

3

Assassination [as a foreign-policy tool] is not a way for the American government. It is not a way for the CIA. I was never in favor of it. It will always, eventually, leak around in some fashion that it was done.

Television interview/"Headliners with David Frost," National Broadcasting Company, 5-31.

4

I am personally convinced that the [CIA] got a bit overextended in the past in terms of covert action, but I would not like to see this capability done away with. The current war against the CIA, however, is something quite different from reducing covert-action activity. Many of our critics want an elimination of any meaningful intelligence operation, and not just a housecleaning operation.

Panel discussion/The Washington Post, 11-12:(B)5.

Thomas Karamessines
Former Director of Clandestine Activities, Central Intelligence Agency of the United States

5

In light of what's happened to our country in the last few years and the manner in which we've managed to tear our intelligence services apart, if I were the head of the KGB sitting in Moscow, I would be absolutely delighted.

Interview/The Dallas Times Herald, 6-15:(A)9.

Richard H. Leonard
Editor, "Milwaukee Journal"

6

The straight truth, and there is no way around it, is that any relationship with the CIA will either impair or destroy the credibility of a journalist if that relationship is discovered. Further, the knowledge that the CIA has a relationship with any journalist, American or foreign, casts suspicion upon all journalists.

Before Senate Intelligence Subcommittee, Washington, May 4/ The Dallas Times Herald, 5-5:(A)13.

Stansfield Turner
Director of Central Intelligence of the United States

7

If you want happy spies, I am not out here to give you that as a primary goal. If you want effective spies under close control, I'll give you that. I deny the scurrilous reports that I am not a good leader. I have made a career of leading men and women and I am good at it.

To reporters, Washington, Jan. 31/ Los Angeles Times, 2-1:(1)7.

8

The Soviet military is the Number 1 intelligence issue and must remain so. But without neglecting the cardinal line of defense, we've got to be able to tackle a much wider range of subjects. Today we've got to look at most of the 150-odd countries of the world. We have legitimate needs for good intelligence information on many of them. That transcends military matters. It gets into the economic as well as the

WHAT THEY SAID IN 1978

political area. So the character of the whole organization has got to shift to accommodate these new factors.

Interview/Time, 2-6:18.

1

There is not a morale problem in the CIA today ... This place is producing. The President of the United States is pleased with it. And the product is high. People work twelve-, sixteen-hour days out here. I have people, at the drop of a hat, working all day Sunday, coming over to my house Sunday night with the results. They are dedicated, wonderful, inspired people. Now, there are complaints. There's griping. There is in every organization of the government. And when you're in a period of transition to new objectives, new methods, new management systems, new styles of openness, of course there are people who are complaining because it isn't being done the way it was yesterday.

Interview, Washington/Newsweek, 2-6:29.

2

... the advent of new technological means of collecting intelligence is one of the factors that is creating change in the process of intelligence in a very substantial way. The trouble is that, in a general sense, technical intelligence tells you what happened yesterday. Ever since the Battle of Jericho in Biblical times, the human intelligence agent has helped you to find out what's likely to happen tomorrow. I find that the more technical intelligence data I give to the policy-makers, the more often they ask me what is going to happen tomorrow—the intentions of the other side. And I must turn to the human intelligence people of the CIA for those answers. So ... the advent of better tech-

nical collection has led to greater demands for the kind of collection which is done by the human intelligence element.

Interview/U.S. News & World Report, 2-6:51.

3

I happen to believe that good intelligence is more important to America today than at any time in its history. Because of detente and the situation now facing the nation, what happens in foreign countries has more importance. But, at a time when our leaders need good intelligence, I'm sorry to have to report to you how much of our time is not spent collecting good intelligence but defending ourselves [the CIA] against false accusations.

Upon acceptance of Veterans of Foreign Wars' Americanism Award, Dallas, Aug. 21/ The Dallas Times Herald, 8-22:(C)1.

4

The most significant change in American intelligence in recent years ... and one that is truly revolutionary, is the introduction of effective external oversight from both the Executive and Legislative Branches. The Congressional oversight committees are now in the process of legislating guidelines, prohibitions and injunctions and further refining the oversight procedures themselves in what will be known as charters for the intelligence community. I strongly support this undertaking. In the first place, it will provide the legal foundation for our activities. In the second place, it will provide guidance so that the U.S. intelligence officer on the street in a foreign country, and those of us in the headquarters, will have a better idea of what is expected, what may not be done and what, if done, must be justified convincingly to our overseers.

At National Press Club, Washington/ The Christian Science Monitor, 11-15:27.

William M. Agee
Chairman and president,
Bendix Corporation

1

I sometimes think that we need a Secretary of the Future in government, as an antidote to our current practice of legislating in crisis and regretting at leisure . . . I see this Secretary of the Future as being responsible for weighing *all* the implications of a particular piece of legislation, so that Congress makes an informed decision instead of a hasty one. And the additional responsibility would be to announce—well in advance—that there's a problem on the way. Does anyone doubt that there was plenty of time to see the energy crisis coming? And yet, the program to deal with it had to be born when Americans found themselves lined up in their cars at gas stations.

Indianapolis, Ind., March 30/
Vital Speeches, 6-15:540.

Peter Bachrach
Professor of political science,
Temple University

2

[Arguing against a proposal to permit voters to enact Federal laws directly through national initiatives]: It would stimulate the rise of hate-and-fear issues. Issues that were more liberal would be resoundly defeated. It would help vested interests more than lower-income groups. So, on the one hand, it would endanger democracy; and, on the other hand, it would create cynicism among a group of voters who thought they could have a role in enacting new programs . . . We live in a mass society in which a significantly large number of people are politically isolated, apathetic, powerless and lacking in political experience—not being involved with their peers in formulating and defining community issues. Too many citizens have little

basis upon which to form intellectual opinions, to articulate their interests, to gain insights. In the last national election, for example, 46.4 per cent of the people who were eligible to vote did not vote. Would these non-participants become politically active because of issues raised through the initiative? With the exception of hate-and-fear issues, I think not.

Interview/U.S. News & World Report, 6-12:69.

Howard H. Baker, Jr.
United States Senator, R-Tennessee

3

At a time when many are claiming that the Congress is living in an "ivory tower," let me suggest that just the opposite may be true. Increased television exposure, perhaps even audio and/or video transmission of the proceedings of this body and the effectiveness of mass-mail communications, have come together with the telephone and other mechanisms to make us more accessible than ever before.

Before the Senate, Washington, Jan. 27/
The Washington Post, 2-2:(A)18.

Roger Baldwin
Founder, American Civil Liberties
Union

4

Because of a government's relation to its people, a government intruding on its people's private rights is opposed to people's instincts to be let alone. We want to be let alone in our speech, our opinions, our thoughts, our private lives, our sex lives, our freedom from interference with what we naturally want to do. These are our natural rights; these are not just Constitutional rights. The Constitution just wrote them down on a piece of paper. They are there in the nature of man; they're not something the state gives us. And that's the great virtue of a democracy like ours—that we proceed on the

WHAT THEY SAID IN 1978

(ROGER BALDWIN)

theory that these rights we give to government to exercise these controls are limited and that we keep all the rest of the rights to ourselves.

Interview, New York/Los Angeles Times, 7-23:(1)4.

Daniel Bell
Professor of sociology,
Harvard University

1

Our political institutions do not match the scales of economic and social reality. The national state has become too small for the big problems of life and too big for the small problems.

Before American Jewish Congress/
The New York Times, 11-12:(1)1.

Griffin B. Bell
Attorney General of the United States

2

I believe that the confidence of the American people has been restored in their government, at least to the extent that they are now willing to give those in government an opportunity to perform as public servants in the traditional sense. When I say traditional sense, I mean traditional in that all Americans, including public officials, have been presumed to be honest, and the burden of proof is on those contending otherwise ... My perception is based on my visits over the country and in Washington with people from all walks of life. Their views and hopes are a good deal more charitable than those of a few of our opinion-givers who unfortunately are holding fast to the Watergate syndrome and are not yet ready to face the reality that our country must put suspicion and carping behind us. The alternative, as I see it, is something approaching the McCarthy era of the 1950s, but this time using the Watergate lexicons of obstruction of justice, cover-up, aider and abettor and the like in a loose, unethical and non-due-process approach toward those who have the audacity to serve in high public positions. We can do better than this. Indeed, we are better.

Before Atlanta Rotary Club, April 3/
The Washington Post, 4-12:(A)26.

Robert F. Bennett
Governor of Kansas (R)

3

There has been a Federal-government trend of using the buck by telling the states, "We'll give you the money if you do what we want." There is an attempt to control the administration of state government itself.

U.S. News & World Report, 6-12:42.

W. Michael Blumenthal
Secretary of the Treasury of
the United States

4

People come in here and sit in that chair and I notice they can't talk very well. They're tongue-tied because they're in the presence of the Secretary of the Treasury. Well, they're awed by the job, and therefore they think I must be some kind of genius. [But] I'm just like they are. And it just might be that, if they took away all my paraphernalia and power, that they might do better than I would. You see, they just don't know that.

Interview, Washington/
The Christian Science Monitor, 8-3:(B)2.

William F. Bolger
Postmaster General of the United States

5

We're [the Postal Service] bound to make mistakes. You can't handle almost 100 billion pieces of mail a year without making mistakes. In most service businesses, if you can get a tolerance of 1 per cent you'd be delighted. A tolerance in our business of 1 per cent is almost 1 billion pieces of mail. We would not be delighted. I think most people take the Postal Service for granted. They have a right to. They should expect that we're there every delivery day. We're the government agency that gets closest to the people. They see their government in action when they see the Postal Service. Surveys show the public thinks we do a pretty good job. I don't say we're perfect, but we're very good at our job.

Interview, Washington/
The Christian Science Monitor, 4-17:13.

(WILLIAM F. BOLGER)

1

The postal system of the past, a welfare dependent of the Federal treasury, has been transformed into a modern, responsible, basically self-sufficient government service . . . After struggling through some trying transition years, the Postal Service is an awakening giant—lean and trim and revitalized. These career professionals . . . have rejuvenated the old, failing Post Office Department into the most operationally sound postal system America has ever known.

At National Press Club, Washington, Dec. 6/
The Dallas Times Herald, 12-7:(A)16.

Edmund G. Brown, Jr.
Governor of California (D)

2

If the people, by saying government should be reduced, are also prepared to perform [by private and voluntary means] the role of nursing homes, child-care centers, alcohol-abuse clinics, child-abuse programs, special-education programs—if that's the direction people want to return to and if they're prepared—then very significant cuts in government can be made. But there's no free lunch. The tremendous ability to go where you want, to do what you want, to change your particular living arrangements almost at will, is made possible by a government that will pick up the pieces.

Before United Press International editors,
Palo Alto, Calif., June 15/
Los Angeles Times, 6-16:(1)32.

3

Government has never been cut back—never. And I perceive a major credibility crisis in American politics. Starting with Johnson, Reagan, Ford, Nixon—a whole group from the Democratic and Republican parties—people have been talking about curbing inflation, creating full employment and cutting government spending. And it hasn't happened. And I identify that as the root cause of public cynicism and discontent with politicians, including myself . . . Political figures from both parties with the best of intentions in the world have been

talking about curbing government spending at election time. Now the Democratic Party has pre-empted this spending issue. All the commentators are sitting back in their very intelligent way and saying, "Look how clever the Democrats are. They have promised all the voters that they would cut spending." And what I'm saying is: If the Democrats don't follow through and actually bring about a leaner government, this party will suffer a massive erosion of public confidence.

Los Angeles, Nov. 8/
Los Angeles Times, 11-9:(1)20.

Theodore A. Bruinsma
President, Harvest Industries, Inc.

4

Many people view those who consistently advocate bigger government as the saviors of the modern world out to rescue the persecuted underdog. On the other hand, those who advocate less government and the strengthening of free enterprise are often dismissed out of hand as greedy exploiters out to make a fast buck for themselves or their companies. Because image is so all-important and bad news is big news, those who supposedly "care" are often afforded greater media exposure to expound on all our social ills and to claim they can cure them by increasing government spending. There's no question it makes for a much more colorful news story; but in reality, of course, this is no cure at all. It is this same destructive approach that is at the very root of the problem we are struggling with today. Big government isn't the solution: It is the problem.

At Town Hall, Los Angeles, March 21/
Vital Speeches, 6-15:528.

James MacGregor Burns
Professor of political science,
Williams College

5

The test we must apply to great leaders is whether, in the end, they actually change the lives of people, as they propose. It's a very harsh test. If you judge Gandhi, for example, by the tens of thousands of Indian villages that are hardly different today from what they were 50 years ago, something obviously was lacking

WHAT THEY SAID IN 1978

in an otherwise transforming leader who was concerned about the plight of the poor ... That's where a Franklin Roosevelt, despite his many foxlike evasions, meets the test of great leadership—because at the end of his Presidency, by his standards, we had a government much more effective in dealing with human problems and facing up to its international obligations. We have not repealed the New Deal or interventionism, so I think he meets that test. So, probably, do Jefferson and Lincoln. But it's a harsh test.

Interview/U.S. News & World Report, 11-27:64.

Willard C. Butcher
President, Chase Manhattan Bank,
New York

1

I would like to see government adopt a goals-oriented approach to regulation. Instead of telling us *how* to do things, tell us instead what it wants *accomplished*. There's nothing new in this approach. As early as the 18th century B.C., in fact, King Hammurabi had a simple building regulation that if a house collapsed and killed the occupant, the builder would be executed! While this may be a bit harsh by today's standards, the law rightfully sets goals rather than the means of reaching them.

Before Commonwealth Club, San Francisco/
The Wall Street Journal, 10-18:16.

Robert C. Byrd
United States Senator, D-West Virginia

2

[Criticizing filibusters and other rules that tend to delay action on Senate business]: I have become so fed up by what I consider to be the abuse of some of the rules here, which have been used to hamstring and straitjacket the Senate from getting on with its business, that I am ready to change some of those rules so that the Senate can act.

Before the Senate, Washington, Sept. 21/
The Washington Post, 9-23:(A)3.

Hugh L. Carey
Governor of New York (D)

3

[On his experience as Governor]: I didn't play the Albany game. I found the Albany game was a trade post. "You trade me a job here and I trade you a job there." Everybody was brokering. . . . and who paid for it? The people. The Albany game is what's breaking all of us.

Interview, New York/
The Washington Post, 10-24:(C)3.

Jimmy Carter
President of the United States

4

While civil and political liberties are good in themselves, they are much more useful and much more meaningful in the lives of people to whom physical survival is not a matter of daily anxiety. To have sufficient food to live and to work, to be adequately sheltered and clothed, to live in a healthy environment and to be healed when sick, to learn and to be taught— these rights, too, must be the concerns of our government(s).

Before Indian Parliament, New Delhi, Jan. 2/
Los Angeles Herald Examiner, 1-3:(A)2.

5

I came to Washington with the promise—and the obligation—to help rebuild the faith of the American people in our government. We want a government that can be trusted, not feared; that will be efficient, not mired in its own red tape; a government that will respond to [the] need[s] of America and not be preoccupied with needs of its own. Taxpayers who work hard for their money want to see it spent wisely. We all want a government worthy of confidence and respect. That is what reorganization is all about. We have no illusions that this task will be easy. Our government and its bureaucracy have evolved over many generations and the work of reform cannot be completed in a single year or a single Administration. But we have begun. We have adopted zero-based budgeting. We have cut the burden of paperwork on the public, and excessive government regulation, replacing it with free-mar-

(JIMMY CARTER)

ket competition ... We have cut significantly the number of employees in the Executive Office of the President and abolished hundreds of unneeded advisory committees. But all that is not enough. The single most important step we can take is a thoroughgoing reform of the civil-service system. Civil service reform will be the centerpiece of government reorganization during my term in office.

At National Press Club, Washington, March 2/
The Washington Post, 3-3:(A)18.

1

I would like to go out of office having accomplished a resurgence of idealism in our country, acknowledging our mistakes, having the American people believe their governments are basically good people—not dishonest, not thieves, not trying to steal—dedicated to the decent commitment of serving others.

At town-hall meeting, Spokane, Wash., May 5/
The Dallas Times Herald, 5-6:(A)24.

2

I am still frustrated by the Federal bureaucracy. There are few levers a President can pull to bring immediate action. There are too many agencies, doing too many things, overlapping too often, coordinating too rarely, wasting too much money—and doing too little to solve real problems.

Before Illinois General Assembly, Springfield,
May 26/The Washington Post, 5-27:(A)2.

3

While some material must be classified, the government classifies too much information, classifies it too highly and for too long. These practices violate the public's right to know, impose unnecessary costs, and weaken protection for truly sensitive information by undermining respect for all classification.

Washington, June 29/
The New York Times, 6-30:(A)7.

4

Anyone who depends on the belief that I will not veto a spending bill that breached the

integrity of my budget is laboring under a serious misapprehension. I will not hesitate one minute to veto the bill. I think this year is going to see a good many disputes resolved only through the veto process.

Interview/San Francisco
Examiner & Chronicle, 7-9:(This World)2.

5

[On his wife's diplomatic role]: She is not an official of government ... She cannot negotiate or speak for government, but precisely because of that she has a flexibility that a professional often does not have. She can explore and probe positions ... She can convey the spirit and philosophy behind a policy, because she knows me better than anyone else.

U.S. News & World Report, 7-31:44.

6

[The Presidency] is not an office which can be conducted on the basis of looking for approbation. It is an office that is inherently a difficult one, but it is an exciting and challenging responsibility. I can tell you in the most complete honesty and candor that I feel at ease with it. I enjoy it. Every day when I come over here, I look forward to the day. I don't dread the decisions that I have to make ...

Interview, Washington/Newsweek, 8-28:20.

7

I have found it much more difficult to be a leader in a time of calm than in a time of crisis. Leaders are very popular in a time of crisis because it is easy to arouse support for the interests of those who are concerned with the crisis itself. But to take action to prevent a future crisis that can't be easily detected nor proven is a very difficult task indeed.

Before Future Farmers of America, Kansas City,
Nov. 9/The Washington Post, 11-10:(A)4.

8

For too many years, the most open society in history had a government that operated in secrecy. When government operates in the shadow and is complicated, bloated and impossible to understand, then the best financed, most powerful and sometimes most selfish lobbies

WHAT THEY SAID IN 1978

(JIMMY CARTER)

have every advantage. The government of the United States today belongs to the people of the United States, not to the power brokers.

At Democratic Party mid-term convention, Memphis, Tenn., Dec. 8/ Los Angeles Herald Examiner, 12-9:(A)2.

John H. Chafee
United States Senator, R-Rhode Island

1

[Criticizing the new under-construction Senate Office Building which will cost an estimated $122-million]: My strong feeling is that we've got to draw the line somewhere on this constant, constant expansion. I'm a firm believer in Chafee's law—that staff expands to fill the space available.

The New York Times, 8-4:(A)6.

John Conyers, Jr.
United States Representative, D-Michigan

2

Congress used to be a lifetime career. You died in Congress, or you tried to become Governor or Senator. On a clear day, some guys even saw the White House. Now members are cashing in early. Congressmen are being watched more closely, criticized more and prosecuted more. And the pay is not that munificent. Lobbyists make twice as much.

Time, 1-23:11.

Douglas M. Costle
Administrator, Environmental Protection Administration; Chairman, Federal Regulatory Council

3

[Government] regulations are not inflationary if the benefits exceed the costs . . . Consider regulations that require power plants to stop spilling sulfur dioxide out of their smokestacks. If those near the plant save more through reduced medical-care charges, less crop loss or lost wages than they pay in higher electric bills to amortize the investment in smokestack scrubbers, clearly the regulations are not inflationary. And that . . . doesn't even take account

of the benefits of not being sick, or not dying sooner. Economists have proven far more skillful in analyzing the costs of regulation than the benefits.

The Washington Post, 11-5:(D)6.

John A. Durkin
United States Senator, D-New Hampshire

4

[President] Carter must start rewarding his supporters and blackballing his opponents. He has got to get down in the world of the Senate and—figuratively speaking—start to mix it up. He is not the kind to do horse trading. He thought issues made their way on their own merit. But he has to realize that we [in Congress] are the grease monkeys of democracy and he is the head grease monkey.

Interview/U.S. News & World Report, 2-6:20.

Stuart E. Eizenstat
Assistant to President of the United States Jimmy Carter for Domestic Affairs and Policy

5

I still believe that government has a positive role to play in making people's lives better. I'm not one who believes that Washington is the enemy of the people. But we've learned in the last 10 years that there are limits to government's resources and to its capacity to solve problems.

Time, 4-3:14.

Joseph F. Fletcher
Professor of medical ethics, University of Virginia

6

It seems absurd to have laws that require candidates or public office-holders to disclose their bank accounts, but allow them to pursue office or function in office, while secretly suffering illnesses that could interfere with their performance. I'd rather have a rich man, with some temptation to favor his investments, in public office than I would a man with a brain tumor.

The Dallas Times Herald, 7-16:(H)1.

Milton Friedman
Senior research fellow, Hoover
Institution, Stanford University;
Former professor of economics,
University of Chicago

1

Everyone knows that you simply do not get your money's worth for what you pay the government. If government has $7-billion less to spend, the public will have $7-billion more to spend, and will spend it more wisely.

San Francisco Examiner & Chronicle,
4-9:(This World)2.

Jack Fuller
Washington correspondent,
"Chicago Tribune"

2

[On his experience when he worked for then-Attorney General of the U.S. Edward Levi]: I learned how government operates in fact, which is often very different from what it appears. I learned all the restrictions and limitations people in government operate under, how little leeway they sometimes have. I came to realize that many things which appear to outsiders—especially skeptical reporters—to be clever schemes are often just a random sequence of events or a result of coincidence or oversight or inefficiency.

Los Angeles Times, 2-28:(1)14.

Paul Gann
Co-author of California property-tax
limitation measure (Proposition 13)

3

[On his tax measure's effects]: [People are] going to see a tremendous change in their tax bills, but they aren't going to see tremendous cutbacks in services. What people will see is simply that we're going to reduce the number of employees in the governments of the state of California—not just the state but local governments as well. We want to do it through attrition so that there's no mad layoff of people. We want the featherbedding in government to go. That's where you don't go to work; you just draw a salary. And we would get rid of the deadwood. You see, we have public employees running out of our ears. We elect officials to go down and carry a title, but it's bureaucrats who run things.

Interview/U.S. News & World Report, 6-26:20.

John W. Gardner
Founder, Common Cause

4

In government, old programs never die; they just go on and on. The government in Washington is a mausoleum of old programs.

Interview/Los Angeles
Herald Examiner, 9-22:(A)13.

E. J. (Jake) Garn
United States Senator, R-Utah

5

Certain Greek cities, we are told, had a policy that anyone proposing new laws had to do so from a platform in the public market—with a rope around his neck. If the law was adopted, they removed the rope. If it was rejected, they removed the platform.

Before the Senate, Washington/
The Wall Street Journal, 10-6:16.

Michael J. Harrington
United States Representative,
D-Massachusetts

6

[Supporting a proposal to permit voters to enact Federal laws directly through national initiatives]: In the proposal that I am supporting, 8 per cent of voters, in three quarters of the states, could sign a petition suggesting that they have significant interest in a particular piece of legislation. Then the proposal would go on the ballot, and, if it were passed by a prescribed majority, it would become law ... The value has to be appreciated in the context of a profound alienation of people in this country from government. The public has been telling us in Congress for years that we're not effective. The initiative would signal to people that Congress isn't totally isolated and insensitive but is willing to try to make the institution of government more responsive and effective.

Interview/U.S. News & World Report, 6-12:69.

WHAT THEY SAID IN 1978

Shearon Harris
*Chairman, Carolina Power & Light
Company; Chairman, Chamber of
Commerce of the United States*

1

We have looked to the central government to do more and more, and people seem to think that, because the central government can do something, it doesn't cost something. People, it seems, will opt for the easy, cheap way out today without regard for the inevitable expense that they are going to bear a little later. I believe in public understanding not only of the short-term benefits of government action, but of the long-term costs.

Interview/Nation's Business, May:62.

Gary W. Hart
United States Senator, D-Colorado

2

Congress is a different institution, and it's composed of a different breed of cats, than in Lyndon Johnson's time, Dwight Eisenhower's time, or even Richard Nixon's time. There are a lot more independent people up here, a lot of people less willing to follow party leadership or Congressional leadership or White House leadership . . . I happen to think that's what Congress should be. I probably wouldn't even want to serve in a Congress where the President could call me up and say, "You're going to vote for this—or else."

The Christian Science Monitor, 1-27:3.

3

[Disputing the idea that members of Congress should vote the way their constituents desire even when the Senator or Representative feels he should vote otherwise on a specific issue]: [Some say] that our role . . . is simply to convert [our constituents'] emotions and opinions into a vote. But surely representation is not so simple. Otherwise, this profession would scarcely appeal to men and women of character, of judgment, of thoughtfulness. Otherwise, why would Thomas Jefferson have stressed the need for the representative to educate his constituents? And otherwise, would

not a republican form of government be useless? We would need only conduct referenda or polls and to consider the opinions of those who felt strongly enough to write letters. But that is most surely not our system of governing. It was not the role of a parliamentarian before this government was founded, nor has it been in the 200 years since Edmund Burke reminded his British constituents that he owed them more than his industry; he owed them also his judgment. No one, before or since, better described the awesome burden of this job, particularly when our own conviction and our own judgment persuades us that what is best for our country—what is our moral imperative—may conflict with the popular view.

*Before the Senate, Washington, March 16/
The Washington Post, 4-4:(A)18.*

Paul Hays
*Chairman, Republican Party of the
District of Columbia*

4

[Advocating full representation in the House and Senate for the District of Columbia]: I know that some have reservations about these proposals . . . The first argument is that D.C. is not a state, and therefore should not be represented in the Senate. The fact is that the citizens of Washington bear all the burdens of citizenship. There is no excuse . . . denying them any of the rights enjoyed by all other [Americans]. Constitutional scholars . . . have concluded that there is no impediment to granting voting representation to the citizens of the District . . . Another objection raised is that the District is so poorly managed that its citizens should not be granted any additional rights. I submit that, while it is certainly true that this government leaves much to be desired, this argument is completely irrelevant to the issue at hand . . . A final argument . . . is that this measure would simply ensure two additional Democratic Senators and one or two more Democratic Representatives. If an election were held today, that would undoubtedly be true. We in the local Republican Party are working to change that . . . Whether we succeed or not, I feel quite strongly that the principles on which

(PAUL HAYS)

this country was founded demand that partisan considerations be put aside.

Before Senate Judiciary Committee on the Constitution, Washington/ The Washington Post, 5-5:(A)18.

Jesse A. Helms
United States Senator, R-North Carolina

1

[Introducing a bill to freeze Congressional salaries]: Thomas Paine called it tyranny when the English monarch imposed taxes on the American colonies that people in England did not have to pay. The Congress is equally guilty when it imposes the "tax" of inflation on the American people and then makes itself immune from inflation by automatically increasing the salaries of its own members.

The Wall Street Journal, 4-27:20.

Al Hofstede
Mayor of Minneapolis

2

The California vote [for Proposition 13, reducing property taxes] should be no surprise ... People everywhere are frustrated with government; and in government, we had better redefine government's role, or someone will do it for us.

At Minnesota League of Cities meeting, Minneapolis/The Washington Post, 6-11:(H)1.

Leon Jaworski
Lawyer; Former Special Counsel, House Ethics Committee

3

Any time members of one branch of government are investigated by other members of that same branch, that is tantamount to self-investigation—and you will find public skepticism and cynicism. However thorough and honest such an investigation may be, it is difficult for the public to accept it as being conducted in good faith. If that cynicism can be avoided, it should be avoided ... I would separate the investigative function from the prosecutorial function. I would have the investigation done by a commission, a group of people not appointed by the branch under investigation. Let that commission have the authority to conduct a full investigation. Its job would be to find out the facts, but it would not handle the prosecution. Once the facts are determined by an independent commission, I would not be particularly concerned as to who does the prosecuting, because the commission—familiar with the facts—can always look over the shoulder of the prosecutor.

Interview/U.S. News & World Report, 8-14:16.

Barbara Jordan
United States Representative, D-Texas

4

Much of the criticism of Congress stems from conditions beyond our control. The lumbering, slow movement of legislation—that's how Congress is constructed, and I don't think it can move more quickly than it does. The reforms that we've brought about, such as the limitations on chairmanships, are good; they have cured a lot of what was wrong when seniority was the premier feature of service in Congress. But I'd like to see more changes in the committee system. We don't need as many committees as we have. You've got members with a vested interest in the fiefdom of the committee, and they get their friends to help defeat any meaningful changes. But more changes will be made because they have to be made.

Interview/U.S. News & World Report, 6-5:24.

Hamilton Jordan
Assistant to President of the United States Jimmy Carter

5

Americans want it both ways: They want to pay less taxes and have less government interference, but they want more government services. They want detente, but they want us to be tough with the Soviets. They want us to have more weapons systems, but they want us to cut the defense budget. You have to reconcile all these things when you're President.

Interview, Washington/ U.S. News & World Report, 5-22:22.

WHAT THEY SAID IN 1978

Jack Kemp
United States Representative,
R-New York

1

[Saying that while he supports a tax cut, he doesn't think it should cut too deep into government operations] : You need to protect people from the vicissitudes of economic contradiction and catastrophe. Government has a legitimate role to play in providing a network of social service[s] and [a] level of support under which people shouldn't be allowed to fall.... the reason that I don't talk about $100-billion spending cuts and meat-ax approaches is that you would hurt people. You're going to hurt some very legitimate needs of our society by just meat-axing away a chunk of the Federal government.

Interview/Los Angeles Times, 9-21:(1)18.

Edward M. Kennedy
United States Senator, D-Massachusetts

2

Professional skills must be harnessed in public service of the sort comparable to those required for law or medicine or business. An unskilled Senator or Congressman or Cabinet secretary is as great a danger to the body politic as an unskilled surgeon is to a patient on the operating table.

At dedication of John F. Kennedy School of
Government at Harvard University/
The Washington Post, 10-22:(A)3.

Dale E. Kildee
United States Representative,
D-Michigan

3

[President Carter] needs to improve his relations with Congress and needs a broader base of advisers. Carter is affable, warm and bright, and, when he is contacted personally, all goes well with Congress. But then you run into those advisers who have this disdain for Congress. Southern legislatures don't meet too often or too long, and the Governor runs the state. Carter realizes that the Federal government doesn't operate that way, but his staff doesn't realize it.

Interview/U.S. News & World Report, 7-24:23.

Juanita M. Kreps
Secretary of Commerce of the
United States

4

While we are considering the role of the Federal government, we must build greater capacity among local governments to set their own course toward economic self-sufficiency. We must look to the states to shoulder their share of the responsibilities. Any proposed new directions for growth policy that failed to draw on the resources and authorities of our balanced state governments will surely fail.

At White House Conference on Balanced National
Growth and Economic Development, Washington,
Jan. 29/The New York Times, 1-30:(A)13.

Richard D. Lamm
Governor of Colorado (D)

5

The day of big Federal solutions to our problems is gone. The Democratic Party is on the wrong side of the Federal-vs.-state issue. Resentment is building against Washington. States' rights can be a big issue—and I'm not talking about that tattered flag waved in the civil-rights struggle. Franklin Roosevelt saved us in the '30s, but those days are behind us. Beware of solutions tied to the past but disastrous to the future.

Interview, Denver/U.S. News
& World Report, 4-3:53.

Paul D. Laxalt
United States Senator, R-Nevada

6

My office received a press release the other day from the General Services Administration. At first I thought I was being subjected to some sort of joke, but as I read on I realized that the Federal government was indeed concerned about the welfare of my hair, and wanted to make sure that I used the right shampoo when I was moved to wash my hair. I was relieved to learn that the bureaucracy has analyzed—and published the results of its analysis—not only the various sorts of shampoos available on the market, but after-shampoo conditioners, additives in shampoo, their respective functioning in hard and soft water, and a host of other little-

(PAUL D. LAXALT)

known facts about keeping my hair soft and shiny. I was told in the press release, for example, that I should not look toward protein or other additives to feed my hair, or make my hair alive, since my hair is dead and cannot be fed. I was told, in addition, that I would need to use a special after-shampoo conditioner to mask the problems caused by the use of dyes, bleaches, waving or straightening mixtures, or from the intense heat used to curl or straighten my hair strands. I am certainly glad to know that the Federal government has taken it upon itself to use its resources to come to grips with these acute problems of our society. I am sure, as well, that the voters in California who voted for Proposition 13 [tax relief] would be equally happy to know how their tax dollars are being spent.

Before the Senate, Washington, Aug. 21/
The Washington Post, 8-27:(D)6.

Anthony Lewis
Political columnist,
"The New York Times"

1

... I can remember no period of our history, or any other country's history, when [government] information was in fact freer, when more issues of defense and foreign policy were disclosed, and leaked. If you were, say, a representative of a foreign government in the United States these last few years, you would have to assume that if you talked to a U.S. official about something this week, you would read it on all the wire services the next week. That doesn't always happen, but it happens to a considerable extent.

Panel discussion/The Center Magazine, July-Aug.:14.

R. Robert Linowes
President, Metropolitan Washington
Board of Trade

2

[Calling for regular Congressional representation for D.C.]: The District of Columbia now has a resident population larger than that of the state of Alaska, Delaware, Montana, Nevada, Idaho, New Hampshire, North Dakota, South Dakota, Vermont and Wyoming. District residents pay a per-capita Federal income tax greater than that of most citizens residing elsewhere. District residents serve in the armed forces of this nation and are subject to military conscription. Yet District residents are denied the basic privileges other citizens of this nation enjoy ... In a period that has seen this nation celebrate more than 200 years of freedom premised on representative government, and now a renewed and aggressive policy in support of human rights and dignity, it is unthinkable that the people who live in the nation's capital should be without these fundamental rights.

Before Senate subcommittee, Washington/
The Washington Post, 4-30:(B)6.

Seymour Martin Lipset
Professor of political science,
Stanford University

3

While the public wants lower taxes, it still wants big government. All the polls indicate people want health insurance, they want government to take responsibility for unemployment, they want all sorts of things that government does. The only thing they don't want government to do is support welfare. And by welfare they don't mean helping poor people. They mean helping chiselers. Because if you say, "Should the government spend more money on helping poor people?" the people say yes. If you say, "Should the government provide jobs for the unemployed?" the people say yes. They prefer [Senator] Teddy Kennedy's health bill to [President] Carter's. ... the public wants its cake and wants to eat it, too. It wants lower taxes and big government.

Interview/
Los Angeles Herald Examiner, 11-11:(A)10.

James B. Longley
Governor of Maine (I)

4

California's Proposition 13, putting a limit on property taxes, is a message to elected officials that "you're not doing your jobs." It's a message to officials that are spending and to bureaucrats that are taking advantage of the spending. I think it's a modern Boston Tea

WHAT THEY SAID IN 1978

(JAMES B. LONGLEY)

Party. The concept of changing laws by petition and referendum [by which Proposition 13 was adopted] is not a new one in America but one which I submit has been under-utilized. The real changes are going to come in America through a combination of an independent movement that will make the two parties more responsive to the will of the people and, through a far greater utilization of the petition and referendum process, to amend our Constitution and change our laws.

Interview, Augusta, Maine/
U.S. News & World Report, 8-7:79.

George H. Mahon
United States Representative, D-Texas

1

The Federal government is out of control. The tendency is to determine what you need— you have to do more for the poor, more for the handicapped, more for education, more for public roads. In other words, all of these things are pressing for consideration, and the tendency of the Administration and Congress has been that we've got to have these things, and whether or not you've got the money doesn't receive adequate consideration. I've preached the doctrine that we shouldn't expand old programs and originate new expensive programs unless we had the money in hand or in sight. But that philosophy is disregarded in so many instances.

Interview, Washington/
The Dallas Times Herald, 10-22:(A)34.

James R. Mann
United States Representative,
D-South Carolina

2

[On being a Congressman]: It's no longer the power, fun and glory job our fathers once knew. It's a tough, political, nitty-gritty service job—especially when public expectations are of equality of condition in life instead of opportunity.

Interview/Parade, 11-5:11.

J. W. Marriott, Jr.
President, Marriott Corporation

3

I suggest a revolt—a taxpayers' and business-leaders' revolt against far more government than we need. Or deserve. Or want. Or will stand for. Or will pay for . . . When you think of how government has grown, consider this: The average taxpayer has to work until May [each year] to pay his taxes. If that's not madness, I don't know what is.

St. Louis, Feb. 24/The Washington Post, 7-21:(E)1.

Charles McC. Mathias, Jr.
United States Senator, R-Maryland

4

Every new Administration charges into office full of ideas and immediately suspects the Federal establishment of trying to slow it down. We have all heard horror stories of bureaucratic delay and inefficiency, and many of them are true. But I've been around Washington for nearly 20 years now, which is long enough to learn that bureaucracy is made up of sedimentary layers, like the volcanic ash that buried Pompeii and the blown dust that once covered the Parthenon. But stir it up with good ideas, and it responds. It will even produce some astonishingly valuable artifacts. With rare exceptions, career executives have reached the top by repeatedly proving their ability to perform well under difficult conditions. They are the glue that holds the government together in times of political transition. They are our ancestral memory. We tamper with their status at our peril.

Before California Republican League/
The Washington Post, 6-4:(B)6.

George S. McGovern
United States Senator,
D-South Dakota

5

Timid officials are repeating and reinforcing a despair of democracy. Last January the President [Carter] himself announced that the state of the union was one of powerlessness—that government cannot solve our problems . . . define our vision . . . eliminate poverty . . . or reduce inflation. A President reaps disapproval

(GEORGE S. MCGOVERN)

not because he is set back in the cause that is right, but when he is lukewarm in a course that is confused. We elected leaders to set goals and solve problems, not to plead that they are insoluble.

Before Americans for Democratic Action, Washington, June 17/ The Washington Post, 6-18:(A)6.

1

Inflation is really beginning to pinch, and since the only part of it the voters can control is the government, they lash out at the liberals they associate with deficit spending. Personally, I think that's misplaced blame, but it does put a special burden on us. We are going to have to be more cautious about Federal outlays—not abandon our commitment to full employment and health insurance and the rest, but both military and domestic spending have to be scrutinized more closely. And we have to get out front on government corruption, like this GSA mess. Maybe Congress is going to have to spend more time on its oversight [of the Executive Branch] and less time unleashing new legislation.

Interview/Los Angeles Times, 9-26:(2)5.

James T. McIntyre, Jr.
Director, Federal Office of Management and Budget

2

It is very clear to me that we must constrain the growth in the Federal budget. That is the appropriate direction toward which fiscal policy should be shifted. I believe the Federal government must show a willingness to conduct its own affairs in a more disciplined manner, if it is going to ask other parts of our society to do the same.

Before Federal Executive Board, Dallas, Aug. 9/ The Dallas Times Herald, 8-11:(A)16.

Lloyd Meeds
United States Representative, D-Washington

3

There is a loosening of idealism in the House. The last two groups that came in here ask first on every issue, "How is this going to affect me politically?" Not whether it's right or wrong. They probably got a pretty good lesson from the group I came in with in 1964. We lost about 60 per cent of them in 1966, much of it from voting idealistically on Taft-Hartley and other tough issues. Added to that is the disenchantment I'm beginning to have with people. What I consider to be a healthy skepticism has turned into a very unhealthy cynicism where people shoot first and ask questions later. One night I was signing mail in my home and I came across this very angry letter from a woman who raked me over the coals for not opposing a pay raise. She said I didn't work enough to deserve it. And there, at 1:30 a.m., I'm signing goddamned letters.

Interview/Los Angeles Times, 5-1:(1)7.

Helen S. Meyner
United States Representative, D-New Jersey

4

People say [Jimmy Carter] is not up to the job [of President]. But who is? It has become an impossible job. A father complex exists among the people. We want to look to daddy to handle things.

Interview/U.S. News & World Report, 7-24:23.

G. William Miller
Chairman-designate, Federal Reserve Board

5

I prefer to see the government's role as providing the atmosphere in which the private sector and the individual can flourish. Still, I recognize that there are issues that only the government can resolve. Actually, when I look at myself I'm a rather strange mixture. I would like to see social justice and I would like to see equal opportunity for all. I would like to see all the barriers to achievement removed. But, at the same time, I would like to see the government become less involved.

Interview, Bahamas/Newsweek, 1-9:54.

WHAT THEY SAID IN 1978

Toby Moffett
United States Representative,
D-Connecticut

1

The yardstick used in measuring a Congressman's success has changed. It used to be the number of bills you introduced. Now our constituents think that perhaps too many bills are introduced. What counts with our constituents is the service we give them and how well we oversee laws already on the books. The public is certainly less deferential to any office-holder, including Congressmen.

Interview/Time, 1-23:16.

Walter F. Mondale
Vice President of the United States

2

In the Senate, you have friends; in the Executive, you interface. There's a wonderful thing about the Legislative Branch that is missed too much in the Executive Branch: If someone is pompous or posturing, your colleagues can hardly wait to deflate you. There's no way, if you've got friends, that you can avoid getting blasted if you're making a fool of yourself. I think there's a lot of strength in that. In the Executive Branch, they tend to be very serious, very dignified, very programmed—19 points on every argument. It almost gets to be too much.

Interview, Washington/
The Dallas Times Herald, 2-26:(E)7.

John E. Moss
United States Representative,
D-California

3

I've preached oversight [by Congress] as long as I've been here. We don't need new laws half as much as we need sound administration of existing laws. And when we find an agency or department failing to administer the laws, then they ought to be called to account for it. From its oversight, Congress should derive the guide for the bulk of its legislation. If we can get into that pattern, we will have a great improvement.

Interview, Washington/
San Francisco Examiner & Chronicle, 9-24:(A)22.

4

Congressmen used to want to be right. Now they want to be popular. They are not as easy to work with. There have been too many changes here in too little time—Congress hasn't paid enough attention to itself as an institution. Our laws are being written by tired people.

Interview/Parade, 11-5:12.

Peggy Musgrave
Visiting professor of economics,
University of California, Berkeley

5

Recent public-opinion polls show that the more centralized and the higher the level of government, the more confidence people have in the government. There is more confidence in the Federal government than in state and local governments. These confidence levels vary markedly by social group. The urban, non-white, low-income apartment dwellers have vastly more confidence in the Federal government than they have in local government. The middle-income suburbanites have much more confidence in local government.

Discussion at Center for the Study of Democratic
Institutions, Santa Barbara, Calif./
The Center Magazine, May-June:47.

Richard A. Musgrave
Visiting professor of economics,
University of California, Berkeley

6

If we are to live peacefully with each other, then we have to accept that society can no more function without public services than it can without private enterprise. Those who are better off have to help those who are disadvantaged. It worries me that much of the support for tax cuts does not come from people who have legitimate complaints, but from people who feel, wrongly I think, that there is no need for a governmental role in a good society.

Interview/People, 6-26:99.

Edmund S. Muskie
United States Senator, D-Maine

7

The Federal government now operates more than a thousand different programs touching

(EDMUND S. MUSKIE)

every aspect of our daily lives. Few, if any, ever end. And every year there are more.

At Chamber of Commerce of the U.S. annual meeting, Washington/ Nation's Business, June:35.

1

We in Congress are increasingly hampered from doing an effective job in the future because our hands are so bound by the past.

Los Angeles Herald Examiner, 10-12:(A)10.

2

I think [Federal] budgetary restraint is a must. But I think to try to tie oneself to a specific number like the deficit . . . could well prompt us to take actions that would trigger economic results we would not like . . . I think the $30-billion deficit figure is an over-preoccupation with a number and that we ought rather to look at what the program needs are—and I'm talking about rock-bottom program needs—and fairness.

TV-radio interview/"Meet the Press," National Broadcasting Company, 12-31.

Ralph Nader
Lawyer; Consumer advocate

3

[On the Freedom of Information Act]: More than any other law, the FOI Act gives the U.S. citizen parity with his government. Can there be any doubt that such a law is a cornerstone of democracy?

Newsweek, 6-19:86.

Mary Rose Oakar
United States Representative, D-Ohio

4

The President [Carter] has got to do more communicating with Congress. It is very important for his supporters up here to know when he's shifting positions. Very often we don't find out about the change until we've jumped off the bridge.

Interview, Washington/ U.S. News & World Report, 2-6:20.

Dallin H. Oaks
President, Brigham Young University

5

A clever leader can nearly always take public insistence on government economy and turn it to his own advantage. For example, most of us can recall some candidate for public office who has campaigned on a platform of reduced government spending and employment. Elected to office, such a politician may achieve reductions, but the more likely outcome is further increases in public employment and spending. The conventional way to promote economy in government is to hire experts to analyze the problems and recommend solutions, hire others to evaluate the suggestions, hire others to write regulations to implement them, hire others to supervise their enforcement, and hire others—public-relations specialists—to praise the results and persuade the public of their success. This is the way of most government economy drives. A government official makes himself a hero, and the people—both taxpayers and spectators—think they see a great improvement. In fact, there has been an increase in both government regulation and government employment. The process is endless, which brings to mind my favorite aphorism about pointless activity: "When you're doing nothing, you never know when you're through."

At College Board Western regional meeting, Colorado Springs, Colo., Jan. 22/ Vital Speeches, 3-1:297.

6

. . . a government's bureaucratic army is never demobilized. If a government agency is created or a government worker is employed to accomplish a task that is later accomplished, experience teaches that the public-employment rolls will not be reduced. The bureaucratic army will be transferred to another front, and if there are insufficient conflicts to justify their continued mobilization, they will start some. When this happens, we realize that the agency's formal goal of giving the service desired by taxpayers and citizens has been displaced by the controlling goal of providing continued employment for the workers and a secure

WHAT THEY SAID IN 1978

(DALLIN H. OAKS)

power base for the leaders. All of this ensures that law and government activity expand in proportion to the resources available for their enforcement.

The Washington Post, 3-24:(A)20.

Edward W. Pattison
United States Representative, D-New York

1

Almost every citizen wants, in general, to reduce government spending, lower taxes, balance the budget, whip inflation. But individually, those very same citizens are interested in the one or two programs that provide benefits to him or her individually, and want expenditures increased in those one or two categories. My constituents are no different ... I am not sure whether they are more interested in holding the national debt down or getting their individual projects funded, because they say both things. But it is up to us to keep reminding them—as hard as it may be politically—that we cannot have it both ways.

Before the House, May 10/
The Washington Post, 5-17:(A)14.

James B. Pearson
United States Senator, R-Kansas

2

When I came here [to the Senate] there were a lot of powerful men here. In the early years, when Dick Russell was here, and Bob Kerr was here, and Lyndon Johnson had just left, and Everett Dirksen was here, there were people with a great deal of power—the kind of guy who would speak and change your vote. They simply aren't down here any more. There are some capable men, but we've become so institutionalized and we've been so fragmented and the workload has become so much greater that the Senate has turned into a group of technicians and specialists. The generalists were the strong people, and we don't have them any more. I can't name powerful people in the Senate any more.

Interview, Washington/
San Francisco Examiner & Chronicle, 3-5:(A)14.

Shirley N. Pettis
United States Representative,
R-California

3

[In Congress,] there is a heavy responsibility to make the right decision. Each time you vote, there are only three buttons to press: yea, nay and present. There isn't any "maybe." I had the luxury of "maybe" when I was a Congressman's wife.

Interview/Parade, 11-5:12.

Otis G. Pike
United States Representative,
D-New York

4

[On a new rule requiring members of Congress to disclose their personal financial details]: Having fought and voted for years against people having their phones tapped, their mail opened, their tax returns publicized, their bank accounts examined and for their right of privacy, I am expected to give up all of my own. Public servants are people, too. I would rather give up my public life and get out of the goldfish bowl.

The New York Times, 3-27:(A)15.

5

This may be a function of age, but I feel increasingly uneasy with the never-ending fiscal irresponsibility of the majority of my own party, and the absolute indifference of both political parties to inflation, the size of our annual deficit, our national debt, or any obligation to pay our bills and balance our budget. The Republicans pay lip service to these things, and then vote overwhelmingly to increase defense spending, start new pension programs, revenue-sharing programs, increase tax credits and increase tax cuts, every one of which must, of course, increase both the deficit and the debt. The Democrats vote to increase welfare programs, education programs, health programs, and recognize every national need except the need to pay our bills. In your community people who do not pay their bills are not

(OTIS G. PIKE)

well thought of, and in the international community nations aren't either.

The Wall Street Journal, 4-21:16.

Joseph J. Pinola
Chairman, Western Bancorporation

1

... the government reflects all of us—and all of our interests, individual and collective. The government might not do what *I* tell it to do, or what *you* tell it to do. But the government does follow *its* perception of what we *all* are telling it to do.

At American Textile Manufacturers Institute, San Francisco, March 17/Vital Speeches, 5-1:442.

David Pryor
Governor of Arkansas(D)

2

[On Federal restrictions on the use of funds given by Washington to local governments]: The Federal government follows the golden rule of politics and administration—those with the gold do the ruling.

U.S. News & World Report, 6-12:42.

Gerald Rafshoon
Assistant to President of the United States Jimmy Carter for Communications

3

... the Presidency will never have the awe it once did; not because Jimmy Carter has "de-pomped" or because of anything he's done, but because [former President] Richard Nixon brought about a diminishing of respect for the President. . . . it's just harder to be President in the post-Watergate atmosphere. Also, a lot of people are dissatisfied with their lot in life, with inflation and other problems. We said in the campaign what was wrong with eight years of Republican rule and people expected the President [Carter] to change everything. People are impatient with the President the way Carter is impatient with Congress.

Los Angeles Times, 8-27:(1)7.

Hyman G. Rickover
Admiral, United States Navy

4

The public is more critical of those in high office than it has ever been. It is easier to point out the flaws and fallacies of a great man than to be one.

*At ship commissioning/
The Dallas Times Herald, 8-28:(D)3.*

5

We don't have a fundamental understanding of what government is all about. We expect the President of the United States to be pluperfect, even more perfect than the Lord. We don't understand. We put a man in a job with little power, little authority, and we expect him to do everything that every citizen wants.

*TV-radio interview, Washington/"Face the Nation,"
Columbia Broadcasting System, 9-3.*

Floyd M. Riddick
*Staff Member, Senate Rules
and Administration Committee*

6

[On the Senate filibuster procedure]: Coming from the House to the Senate, it is like going from prison to freedom. This procedure of the filibuster, when the Senators restrain themselves and do not abuse the privilege, is more edifying and constructive. I'm talking about the freedom of time to develop what you are trying to get over . . . I just can't imagine debates in the Roman senate ever being developed under the House procedures [of limited legislative discussions].

The Washington Post, 6-15:(A)3.

Alan Rosenthal
*Director, Eagleton Institute of
Politics, Rutgers University*

7

A big problem [of state legislatures] is that of "Congressionalization," the process by which a legislative institution becomes more and more like Congress: full-time members, each chairing a subcommittee with a narrow focus, backed up by armies of professional staff. Professionalization, specialization, individualization, rationalization, bureaucratiza-

WHAT THEY SAID IN 1978

(ALAN ROSENTHAL)

tion, computerization in state legislatures are all well under way.

Before National Conference of State Legislatures/
The New York Times, 11-12:(1)74.

Richard M. Scammon
Public-opinion analyst

1

While Congress as an institution excites very little praise, people tend to have an entirely different perspective when it comes to their own Senators and Representatives. People will rail against Congress as a bunch of fakers and phonies and worse, but then turn around and say: "Our own Representative is different from the rest of them." They probably feel that way because the Representative has performed some special service for them. Basically, they feel their own man is all right; it's those other guys who are the problem. If people really had the low view of individual members of Congress that they have of the body as a whole, Republicans would win a two-to-one majority this fall. All the Democrats, who now hold two thirds of the seats, would be thrown out and replaced by Republicans; all the Republicans would be replaced by Democrats. Of course, that's not going to happen.

Interview/Nation's Business, July:24

Eileen Shanahan
Assistant Secretary for Public Affairs,
Department of Health, Education and
Welfare of the United States

2

While there are many highly competent, dedicated civil servants, the percentage of the civil servants who are not earning what the taxpayers are paying them is almost as high as any figure you ever heard by any right-winger you ever hated. There is a very substantial number of people on the civil-service rolls who are literally bilking the taxpayer.

Before Women's National Democratic Club/
Time, 3-6:13.

Howard K. Smith
News commentator, American
Broadcasting Company

3

[In his State of the Union address, President Carter] said, "Government cannot solve our problems. It cannot set our goals, define our vision, eliminate poverty or reduce inflation," and he went on to list so many things, [that] he made government sound helpless and useless. I can't think of a wronger statement by a President in recent times. In fact, only government can solve those problems. Without FDR's New Deal for relief, we might have had a revolution in this country . . . [The late civil-rights leader] Martin Luther King's fight for rights would be a mere memory of a lost hope had not [then-President Lyndon] Johnson made rights a government law, governmentally enforced . . . The Carter statement sounded too much like a self-apologism. Well, if he and the present Congress can't solve these problems, we must elect others who can. For in the end, only our elected, representative government can set national goals and mobilize the public to achieve them.

Commentary, Jan. 30/
The Washington Post, 2-1:(A)18.

Jay Solomon
Administrator, General Services
Administration of the United States

4

The fraud, the corruption, the thievery, the mismanagement and downright abuse of the public trust that have been exposed to this date [in GSA] are only the beginning. GSA is today sitting in exile like a wounded animal. It is surrounded by the vigilant media, the disgruntled, the corrupters, and by turf-conscious bureaucrats from other agencies [who] would like to put an end to the cost-effective concept of centralized administrative services envisioned by the Hoover Commission in creating GSA.

San Francisco Examiner & Chronicle,
9-24:(This World)2.

Adlai E. Stevenson
United States Senator, D-Illinois

5

I just wonder if the Senate and other institutions of self-government are equal to the de-

(ADLAI E. STEVENSON)

mands of government in the late 20th century ... It is getting harder than ever to get anyone with sense to run for office.

Time, 5-8:65.

Sid Taylor
Research director, National
Taxpayers Union

1

President Carter didn't cut [the Federal pay raises] enough. What's really needed is a pay freeze. The issue no longer is pay comparability. The issue now is taxpayer affordability. There aren't enough taxpayers to support an automatically escalating Federal payroll. We are printing funny-money in Washington like drunken sailors.

U.S. News & World Report, 9-11:34.

Strom Thurmond
United States Senator, R-South Carolina

2

[Advocating full voting representation in Congress for the District of Columbia]: Recently, much has been made of the issue of human rights. The President [Carter] has predicated a portion of his foreign policy on this issue. So has the Congress on various occasions. I say we cannot talk about human rights to others in the world until we here at home can show we are recognizing basic human rights. Through the world community, only two other Federal districts deny their residents full voting representation in their national legislatures: Brazil and Nigeria. Citizens of London, Paris and Bonn are represented in their national legislatures. Are we to be considered less democratic than England, France or West Germany? I would hope not. Human rights begin at home, here in the nation's capital. The fact that more than 700,000 people do not have a voice in the election of those who write the nation's laws is not a very good position from which to preach human rights.

Before the Senate, Washington, Aug. 16/
The Washington Post, 8-18:(A)19.

Stansfield Turner
Director of Central Intelligence
of the United States

3

How will [government] openness help us preserve secrets? Well, simply by reducing the excessive corpus of secrets that now exists within our government. Today so much information is unnecessarily classified that we have lost respect for the classified label. By making as much as possible available to the public, we reduce the amount that is kept secret. In turn, this makes it easier to engender respect for that which remains classified.

At National Press Club, Washington/
The Christian Science Monitor, 11-15:27.

Malcolm Wallop
United States Senator, R-Wyoming

4

From the time I got here last year, I worried about the influence of [Congressional] staffs. My first eye-opener was watching staffs at committee sessions. Some make decisions, and one time a staffer even made a motion.

U.S. News & World Report, 5-15:21.

William F. Walsh
United States Representative, R-New York

5

Congress is a disappointment. I don't see movement or progress. When I was Mayor of Syracuse, I could watch downtown being rebuilt. The legislative process here [in Washington] is cumbersome; the system isn't designed to take on major reforms.

Interview/Parade, 11-5:12.

Jack H. Watson, Jr.
Secretary to the Cabinet and Assistant
to President of the United States
Jimmy Carter for Intergovernmental
Affairs

6

In essence, we need an aroused public to help us make government work better. [However,] what I fear is that a healthy and appropriate skepticism about what government can do is turning sour. It seems to me that, as a nation, we have become preoccupied with what

(JACK H. WATSON, JR.)

we are against and momentarily lost our vision of what we are for. [Americans seem engaged in] a kind of inexorable, ritual destruction of our political leaders, starting with the President but extending to the leaders at all levels of government. It is almost as if we have lost the capacity to believe or trust anyone once we have invested them with the authority and responsibility to lead.

Before National Association of Counties, Atlanta,
July 9/Los Angeles Times, 7-10:(1)3.

Theodore H. White
Author; Political historian

1

The power of the Presidency has been countermined by two of the worst Presidents we ever had—[Lyndon] Johnson and [Richard] Nixon. That's 12 years, actually, when the people and Congress learned to distrust the President. Jesus, Congress has achieved an authority that it hasn't reached since the 1870s and '80s. Congress has its own budgetary forces, its own immense bureaucracy checking on the Executive bureaucracy.

Interview, San Francisco/
San Francisco Examiner & Chronicle, 10-1:(Scene)3.

Charles E. Wiggins
United States Representative,
R-California

2

Congressmen now are children of the media market. Their education level is higher, but they are neophytes in politics. There's too much response to people's often irrational demands that make government bigger. I don't give a damn what my constituents want. I vote the way I want. And procedurally we haven't helped ourselves with all these sunshine laws. Government in the hallways is repugnant to me. Maybe I am out of style, but today's Congress is not a better Congress.

Interview/Parade, 11-5:12.

Thomas R. Wilcox
Chairman and president, Crocker National Bank,
San Francisco

3

The [Federal budget] deficit could be $80-billion in the next fiscal year. What the Federal government has to do is the same thing a private corporation would have to do if it were imperiled, as the United States government is now. It would have to cut back its operations drastically and slash costs. For the United States, it means that the boom will have to be turned off a bit, interest rates will have to rise, and unemployment will have to go up some. The world wants us to do this.

Interview/The New York Times, 4-12:52.

Charlotte Williams
President, National Association of
Counties

4

[On citizen tax revolts, such as the recent passage of Proposition 13 in California which limits property taxes] : People are going to suffer for tax cuts. If they have to cut back on services the people feel that they need, they're going to put people in office who will give them what they had ... Counties will feel tax cuts more than any level of government because counties are responsible for the people programs, such as human-services programs, and many of these are mandated by state and Federal statutes ... There's an awful lot government can do. We must sit down together and spend better that which we are charged with spending.

At National Association of Counties convention,
Atlanta, July 8/
The Dallas Times Herald, 7-9:(A)19.

David Wise
Political writer; Lecturer, department
of political science, University of
California, Santa Barbara

5

... there is a conflict in society between First Amendment values and the values we associate with national defense and national security. If we grant the premise—and I do grant it—that some types of information must be

(DAVID WISE)

kept secret by the government, at least for a limited time, then important questions arise. Who shall decide what information shall be kept secret: the Executive Branch of government? the Congress? the courts? the press? What criteria should be used to define the information to be kept secret? Who shall define national security? Can national security be defined? Perhaps even more important questions arise once secret information has escaped the control of the government. Should there be prior restraint of the press in some circumstances? Should there be prior restraint in circumstances involving "national security"? Should there be subsequent punishment of newspapers, magazines or reporters who publish information that had been secret? Should the espionage laws be applied to journalists? Should there be criminal or administrative sanctions applied to officials who leak secret information? Here we get into a difficult area. Do sanctions against reporters, or their sources, abridge the First Amendment or raise First Amendment questions? It would be gratifying if we could settle these questions. I don't think we can. I am not even sure there are answers to some of these questions.

Panel discussion/The Center Magazine, July-Aug.:8.

Lester L. Wolff
United States Representative, D-New York

1

[On Congressmen who personally travel and investigate problems facing the U.S. and its citizens): I think we have a whole new breed of Congressmen here. The new breed's not just a cigar-puffing individual who's a political hack someplace in the boonies, decides he wants to go to Congress and some political party puts him in. These young people who come into Congress now just will not take the dog-and-pony shows that the various government agencies put on for them. They want to determine for themselves what the true facts are ... making themselves part of the situation that causes the problem, to learn what it's all about.

Los Angeles Times, 12-3:(1)22.

Labor · The Economy

Gar Alperovitz
Co-director, National
Center for Economic Alternatives

1

It's very clear that the final quarter of the 20th century is going to be very different from the period we all thought was normal, the post-war boom. The boom is over. We're in for slower growth, more stagflation, resource problems. Our position in the world economy is slipping. All of that means traditional solutions are failing. Self-evidently, it's a new ballgame.

San Francisco Examiner & Chronicle, 7-16:(B)5.

Robert O. Anderson
Chairman, Atlantic Richfield Company

2

What do we mean by "balanced growth" in the economy? If it is all "balanced," there is no growth. I don't see how an economy such as ours can avoid growth if we are to meet our social goals. A large segment of our society has to have better opportunities, better chances for social improvement. It is difficult to see how minority and disadvantaged groups can improve themselves in a static society. At the same time, growth has created a lot of problems, particularly environmental problems. How can we continue to grow with a minimum of intrusion on our physical environment? How can we have a growth that is consistent with our resources, and with our monetary constraints? I think we must realize the international impact of our actions. Look at the condition of the dollar in the world today.

Panel discussion/
The Center Magazine, July-Aug.:60.

Charles G. Bluhdorn
Chairman, Gulf & Western Industries

3

I don't see where [President Carter's economic] program does anything to inspire confidence in the business community ... One gets the impression that the President is trying to change our system without knowing what to change it to. There is nothing wrong with being a populist President, but if he doesn't know what road he is traveling, how should the rest of the country know which way to go?

U.S. News & World Report, 2-6:17.

W. Michael Blumenthal
Secretary of the
Treasury of the United States

4

[On President Carter's proposals to eliminate certain business tax deductions]: We're not taking anything away from business that it really needs. But our whole tax system has to be fair. We have to have the respect of all taxpayers if our voluntary system of paying taxes is to keep on working. When people read about the businessman who deducted 338 lunches in one year, or the dentist who deducted $14,000 a year for a yacht for entertaining other doctors, no wonder that they become cynical about government. Deductions for meals and entertainment cost more than $2-billion a year in lost revenues. That's not an incidental tax item.

Nation's Business, April:34.

5

I know of no problem that is potentially any more threatening and more serious to the average American than the problem of inflation ... But inflation is more than just this country's problem. We live in a world that is much more interrelated than even 15 to 20 years ago: a world of floating exchange rates, dependence on OPEC oil, growing importance of trade; a world in which no country, including the U.S., has predominance. We're all tied together.

Interview/U.S. News & World Report, 4-24:21.

(W. MICHAEL BLUMENTHAL)

1

Massive tax reduction in an economy already suffering from inflationary pressures is sheer waste. We do not have the financial or physical resources to absorb such stimulus without adding to inflationary pressures.

Before House Budget Committee, Washington, July 12/Los Angeles Herald Examiner, 7-12:(A)10.

2

[Author Theodore H. White] summed it up precisely when he wrote: "Inflation is the hidden threat that disorganized government holds over those who try to plan, who try to be prudent." Our problem is that we are living with the heritage of neglect and inappropriate treatment of the economy by the Federal government. Previous Administrations and Congresses have allowed inflation to become a way of life; it has been built into the price and cost decisions of all sectors of the economy, producing a vicious circle of inflationary reactions. This process has been building over the past decade ... The responsibility for exorcising the evils of inflation from our economic system falls squarely on the government.

Oct. 23/The Washington Post, 11-2:(A)20.

Barry Bosworth
*Director, Federal Council on
Wage and Price Stability*

3

[On the wage and price situation] : There are absolutely no signs—going the way we're going now—that we're going to get where we want to go. We've had some cooperation from business in holding down prices, but there is no indication that that's more than words. With labor, we're stymied. I think you have to have your head in the sand not to realize where we're going. If inflation keeps up, we're headed straight for another recession.

Newsweek, 7-10:51.

4

Businessmen explain inflation as being caused by government and labor; labor blames business and government; and government blames business and labor. Each group is probably about two-thirds right. We are all part of the problem and, unless everyone contributes to the solution, inflation will continue ... If we don't succeed, we will inevitably find ourselves going back to the old way of trying to break the back of inflation by putting millions more on the unemployment rolls and shrinking the output of our plants and factories. Not only would that be very painful; there are no guarantees that it would succeed.

*Before Economic Club of Detroit, Nov. 13/
The Dallas Times Herald, 11-14:(A)16.*

Robert Brandon
*Director, Public Citizen
Tax Reform Research Group*

5

Taxes are easy to understand. They can be easily explained to the general population. The problem is that we have perpetuated the myth that they are very complicated ... Demystifying the tax system is simple. It gets down to a question of politics. It is not difficult to explain what the property tax is, how it is levied, how it is administered. It is not difficult to explain what an income tax is, how that tax is levied, and how it is administered. And it is not difficult to show the interaction between the two. What is difficult is trying to explain the thousands of pages of regulations and the thousands of special, unique deviations from that over-all tax system. Those are the things that most destroy equity. And those are the things in which there is a stake in making sure people do not understand them.

*Discussion at Center for the Study of
Democratic Institutions, Santa Barbara, Calif./
The Center Magazine, May-June:50.*

Harry Bridges
*Former president, International
Longshoremen's and Warehousemen's Union*

6

The strike is the only weapon labor has. You can make it work if you strike on a broad enough basis. When they were trying to form a newspaper guild in San Francisco and ran into trouble, we refused to unload newsprint at the docks. You have to stick together. Labor may

(HARRY BRIDGES)

be divided today, but if you get the right issue at the right time, labor will mobilize within 24 hours and join together and fight till hell freezes over. I don't know what the issue will be, but it will come.

Interview, Washington, Jan. 16/
The Washington Post, 1-17:(B)3.

Robert J. Brown
Under Secretary of
Labor of the United States

1

There are ... cases when management and labor fail to reach an agreement which would avoid a strike. It is during those instances when the role of the government ought to be clear, consistent ... and absent. The failure to reach an agreement is the problem of management and of labor. The Federal government ought not to be involved in solving the problems of men and women who are perfectly capable of solving their own problems. This Administration's consistent attitude toward the collective-bargaining process is that we will not do anything which would relieve the tension placed upon the two concerned parties to reach an agreement. If we were to make a practice of interfering where we are not needed, then management and labor would rely on the government to impose some solution. They would delay their efforts, expecting the government to intervene. They would work less hard. They would not rely as strongly on their own best efforts. And that would mean more strikes of longer duration. This Administration believes that where government is not needed, government should not be involved.

At Georgia State University,
April 4/Vital Speeches, 6-1:497.

Theodore A. Bruinsma
President, Harvest Industries, Inc.

2

Those who consistently look to government have never asked themselves why a country like the Soviet Union, with some of the largest, richest tracts of grainland in the world, but

with a government-owned and operated agricultural system, cannot even feed its people without turning to American farmers who own their own land, make their own decisions guided by the incentives of a free marketplace and feed not only our own people, but millions of others around the globe as well ... The proposition that we who advocate the free market "lack compassion" is ironic. Even the most cursory glance at history shows us that the American economy is the most successful the world has ever known—precisely because it is an essentially humane creation of the people, by the people, for the people.

At Town Hall, Los Angeles, March 21/
Vital Speeches, 6-15:528.

Arthur F. Burns
Former Chairman,
Federal Reserve Board

3

The Federal government is fully capable of leading our country out of the inflationary morass. The government could, for example, cut back on our huge and persistent budget deficits. Again, instead of raising the pay of Federal employees by 7 per cent—as the government did last October and may do again this year—the increase could be limited to 3 per cent or 4 per cent, thus setting an example for American businessmen and their employees. Again, the President might cut his own salary by some 10 per cent and invite all Presidential employees and perhaps Congressmen to do likewise, thus dramatizing his leadership in unwinding the inflation that is plaguing our country.

Interview, Washington/
The New York Times, 3-29:(D)10.

4

People in the middle class—which is the more creative and the more productive part of our economic society—feel that they have been neglected. And, to a large degree, they are right. To be sure, we have had cuts in income taxes at the Federal level, but these reductions have applied to people in the lower income brackets. Taxes for the middle and upper income groups have been rising. And people at all income levels have been suffering from inflation. More

(ARTHUR F. BURNS)

and more people are therefore saying to themselves: "We see our government doing more, spending more, taxing more, but our problems —economic and social—are not going away; they are not being solved." So there is a great deal of unhappiness and frustration in our country, particularly on the part of the middle class.

Discussion at American Enterprise Institute,
June/The Washington Post, 7-30:(B)1.

August A. Busch, Jr.
Chairman and president,
Anheuser-Busch, Inc.

1

... just look at some of the countries where competition has been forgotten. You can see the decay of the entire business system and the people within it. The executives go stale. The whole system goes stale. Profit, free enterprise and competition are what makes the system run. Without them, there is no incentive for a guy to get up in the morning and move, and push, and be creative, and take chances. None whatsoever. There is always competition to be Number 1, and there always should be competition. That's what makes Ford run against General Motors, Heinz against Campbell, and any corporation run to remain the leader. You give consumers a better product, and inform them about that product through competitive advertising. It's our economic system, and thank God for it.

Interview/Nation's Business, November:68.

Willard C. Butcher
President,
Chase Manhattan Bank, New York

2

[Wage and price guidelines] historically have been a failure and they won't work this time either. Controls or guidelines merely shift the emphasis from what really causes inflation— excessive [government] spending—to what doesn't. If you put a lid on prices, you squeeze profit margins. That, in turn, discourages investment even more.

Interview, Chicago/
The Dallas Times Herald, 10-15:(L)3.

Fletcher L. Byrom
Chairman, Committee for
Economic Development

3

The most destructive consequence of our current inflationary addiction is the liquidation of the nation's capital base. This insidious process is eroding our international competitiveness. It depresses the international value of the dollar. It mortgages our capacity to create future wealth and jobs. It hastens the transformation of our private-enterprise system into a government-administered economy, with the eventual threat of government ownership. It fattens the inflationary worm that feeds upon it.

Before New York Financial Writers
Association, June 28/Vital Speeches, 8-1:638.

Hugh L. Carey
Governor of New York (D)

4

[Saying President Carter should invite more business leaders into his Administration]: Roosevelt kept businessmen around him—like Frank Knox and Jesse Jones. Truman followed the same model. Who would be like that on the scene today? I'll be very blunt: Henry Ford II. He knows how to handle labor. He writes good wage pacts. He enjoys the respect and admiration of minority groups. He is gutsy, no doubt about that. A businessman, a czar, has to be in charge of the economy. Nothing is going to be accomplished until the people overseas see that somebody is in charge. Also, there are elements of leadership in the [House] Ways and Means Committee, and they will listen to someone who speaks their language. Ford is the kind of man to do it.

Interview/Time, 11-27:27.

Raymond N. Carlen
Chairman, Joseph T. Ryerson & Son, Inc.;
Senior vice president,
Inland Steel Company

.5

From both a business and a human standpoint, inflation hurts more Americans, destroys more of our values and is potentially more damaging to our social fabric than any other problem we face, including unemployment.

Nation's Business, June:28.

WHAT THEY SAID IN 1978

Jimmy Carter
President of the United States

1

[Announcing the invoking of the Taft-Hartley Act in the coal strike]: As Americans, we all share the responsibility for preserving the health and safety of our country, which is now in danger. The labor laws of our country, of the United States, have been written to protect our nation and at the same time to protect the rights of workers. In times of crisis the law binds us together. It allows us to make decisions openly and peacefully, and it gives us through the courts and legal procedures means to resolve disputes fairly. Respect for the rule of law insures the strength of our nation. The law will be enforced. As President, I call on the mine workers, the coal-mine operators and all Americans to join in a common effort under the law to protect our country, to preserve the health and safety of our people, and to resolve fairly the differences which have already caused so much suffering and division in our land.

Broadcast address to the nation,
Washington, March 6/The New York Times, 3-7:24.

2

Inflation has now become imbedded in the very tissue of our economy. It has resisted the most severe recession in a generation. It persists because all of us—business, labor, farmers, consumers—are caught on a treadmill which none can stop alone. Each group tries to raise its income to keep up with present and anticipated rising costs and eventually we all lose the inflationary battle together. There are no easy answers. We will not impose wage and price controls; we will work with measures that avoid both these extremes.

Before American Society of Newspaper Editors,
Washington, April 11/The New York Times, 4-12:34.

3

... we're not slackening off at all on the unemployment question. The programs that we've put into effect are still in effect. They're getting more and more specifically effective with different groups as time goes on. My belief is that the unemployment rate will continue to decrease ... and at the same time we can tackle inflation with a much higher concentration of our own effort and commitment and public awareness. The two are not in conflict. We've seen that when the last [Ford] Administration, which happens to have been Republican, concentrated on inflation by letting unemployment go up, it did not work. So I believe the best thing is to do what we've already done and that is to try to hold down inflation and bring down unemployment at the same time.

News conference, Washington, April 25/
The New York Times, 4-26:(A)20.

4

[On a proposal to decrease the capital-gains tax]: This proposal would add more than $2-billion to the Federal budget deficit. Eighty per cent of its tax benefits would go to one-half of one per cent of the American taxpayers who make more than $100,000 a year. Three thousand millionaires would get tax reductions averaging $214,000 ... The American people want some tax relief from the heavy burden of taxation on their shoulders. But neither they nor I will tolerate a plan that provides huge tax windfalls for millionaires and two bits for average American.

News conference, Washington, June 26/
The New York Times, 6-27:(A)12.

5

The fight against inflation becomes nearly impossible when the pressures of special-interest lobbyists are successful. These lobbyists care nothing about the national interest—as long as they get theirs. We will never win the fight against inflation unless we help the Congress to resist these pressures.

Before Midcontinent Farmers
Association, Columbia, Mo./Time, 8-28:11.

6

In the last 10 years, in our attempts to protect ourselves from inflation, we have developed attitudes and habits that actually keep inflation going once it has begun. Most companies raise their prices because they expect costs to rise. Unions call for large wage settlements because they expect inflation to continue. Because we expect it to happen, it does

(JIMMY CARTER)

happen; and once it's started, wages and prices chase each other up and up. It is like a crowd standing at a football stadium: No one is willing to be the first to sit down. Except for our lowest-paid workers, I am asking all employers in this country to limit their total wage increases to a maximum of seven per cent per year. From tonight on, every contract signed and every pay raise granted should meet this standard. My price limitation will be equally strict. Our basic target for economy-wide price increases is 5 3/4 per cent. To reach this goal, I am tonight setting a standard for each firm in the nation to hold its price increases at least one-half of a percentage point below what they averaged during 1976 and 1977.

Broadcast address to the nation, Washington,
Oct. 24/The Washington Post, 10-25:(A)11.

1

We know that government is not the only cause of inflation. But it is one of the causes, and government does set an example. Therefore, it must take the lead in fiscal restraint. We are going to hold down government spending, reduce the budget deficit and eliminate government waste. We will slash Federal hiring and cut the Federal workforce. We will eliminate needless regulations. We will bring more competition back to our economy. And we will oppose any further reduction in Federal income taxes until we have convincing prospects that inflation will be controlled.

Broadcast address to the nation, Washington,
Oct. 24/The Washington Post, 10-25:(A)11.

2

I think the standard of living is determined by many things—the assurance of peace, stability, the strength of families, the quality of education, the enhancement of basic human rights, harmony among dissident groups. This will certainly continue to improve. But if you measure quality only by how fast someone's income goes up, then I think there is going to be a difference in the future compared to what it has been in the past.

To reporters, Washington, Dec. 7/
Los Angeles Times, 12-8:(1)7.

Leonel J. Castillo
Commissioner,
Immigration and Naturalization
Service of the United States

3

[On illegal aliens in the U.S.]: . . . most of the people who come to the U.S.—with or without documents—are the more ambitious, the more daring, the more active. The destitute are not coming; the elderly are not coming. We're primarily getting young men who are aggressive, in good health and who are hard workers. So we're finding that many employers want to hire them.

Interview/U.S. News & World Report, 2-20:34.

A. W. Clausen
President, Bankamerica Corporation

4

Government deficits are the principal contributor to our present inflation. We've got to have tax cuts to keep the economic expansion going, but I don't think we'll get enough tax reforms to offset the tax cuts. So the deficit is likely to be $70-billion instead of $60-billion. Nineteen seventy-eight is a good year, and we are still running a deficit in that magnitude. No wonder business doesn't have much confidence in the future.

Interview/The New York Times, 4-12:52.

Alex Comfort
Gerontologist

5

I don't think you want to make a fetish of non-retirement, because some people would like to retire. But you've got to remember that if you're going to have compulsory retirement at 65, with the present demography, you're going to have an enormous reserve of unused talent. There aren't going to be enough young people to do everything.

Interview/Los Angeles Herald Examiner, 9-7:(A)14.

Albert H. Cox, Jr.
President,
Merrill Lynch Economics, Inc.

6

The Carter Administration really doesn't have an anti-inflation program. If you set aside the

WHAT THEY SAID IN 1978

speeches, almost everything is pro-inflationary—higher government spending, higher minimum wage, higher farm subsidies, a protectionist policy that keeps out some cheap imports. The only thing I can think of that has been done that is anti-inflationary is the attempt to deregulate the airlines. But until President Carter and Congress face up to the fact that we've got to cut Federal spending—and I mean cut it, not just slow down the increase—we'll never get inflation under control.

Interview/U.S. News & World Report, 5-15:27.

Walter Cronkite
News commentator,
Columbia Broadcasting System

1

I regret that there has to be mandatory retirement in any circumstances. You're only as old as you feel. On the other hand, I can understand that we have to spread the benefits of improved technology around and that means shortened work weeks and shortened work lives of individuals. However, mandatory-retirement policies in the arts are silly. I think to retire [news commentator] Eric Sevareid, whose wisdom and great insight improve every day with age, is absolutely ridiculous. On the other hand, I'll be very pleased that I won't have to make the decision about myself when I reach 65, because there are so many other things I want to do.

Interview, New York/
The Christian Science Monitor, 3-24:21.

Paul R. Ehrlich
Professor of biology,
Stanford University

2

If you listen to the average economist or politician, you would get the idea that the ultimate end is economic growth at any cost. That's how they define progress: How big is the GNP? Even though the GNP is probably negatively correlated with the quality of life and the standard of living by any rational measure, people still pray the GNP will go up each year, even

if it's necessary to shove it up by producing electric eyeball massagers, or what have you.

Interview, Palo Alto, Calif./
The Dallas Times Herald, 6-23:(E)14.

Malcolm S. Forbes
Economist; Editor,
"Forbes" magazine

3

There is a growing awareness that, for all its faults, all its need for whistle-blowers for abuses and abusers, it [capitalism] is the one system where incentive can be rewarded. Rather than greedy exploiters or people with inordinate amounts of wealth, today's capitalists are only those with sufficient income to feel they do have equity in the United States. That's what was significant about Proposition 13 [the California initiative recently passed by voters to lower property taxes]—that enough people have equity now and want to keep it and are concerned about a government that insists it can do a better job with your income than you can.

San Francisco Examiner &
Chronicle, 10-8:(This World)2.

4

I'm something that's out of fashion these days. I'm a liberal. You conserve by coping with change, not by opposing it. I hate to use silly words, but for the economy to stay alive the system has to be dynamic. That means coping with changes, mores, attitudes and preferences. The conservative, to me, is somebody who wants to keep things as they were, or to keep his niche. That's a hopeless case.

Interview/Los Angeles Herald Examiner, 11-17:(A)6.

Henry Ford II
Chairman, Ford Motor Company

5

As I look at our country today, I see a powerful but uncertain and unsteady giant trussed up in a growing web of rules and regulations to the point where it can no longer exert its strength freely and effectively . . . Maybe it's only a coincidence that the recent period of rapidly rising government spending and roughshod regulation [of U.S. business] also has been

(HENRY FORD II)

a period of high unemployment, slow productivity improvement, slow growth in personal income, soaring government deficits and unprecedented peacetime inflation. But I don't believe it's a coincidence at all ... Despite a mounting record of failure and frustration, our leaders have failed to grasp the fact that too much government inevitably leads to economic decay.

At White House Conference on
Balanced Economic Growth, Washington,
Jan. 30/Vital Speeches, 3-1:305.

Abe Fortas
Lawyer; Former Associate Justice,
Supreme Court of the United States
1

[On the law, effective January, 1979, increasing the minimum mandatory retirement age from 65 to 70]: These changes are going to present some very serious problems to labor and employers next January. These changes will have a very important impact on collective-bargaining contracts, upon the operation of and effect of seniority practices, upon insurance and the funding of pension plans. The amended legislation in effect nullifies retirement provisions which have been in existence or customary for a long time. [While commendable and necessary,] these laws present a new challenge to America, to its government and to its private sector—a challenge to provide more job opportunities for useful and productive employment, a challenge we must resolve. We must absolutely provide employment for our young people, for the women who seek employment and for a newly liberated black population as well as our older people who are eager and able to work.

At National Conference on Age and
Employment, Rosemont, Ill., April 12/
The Dallas Times Herald, 4-13:(A)15.

Douglas A. Fraser
President, United Automobile
Workers of America
2

As sure as I'm standing here, the American worker is going to have a four-day work week

without a cut in pay. I strongly believe the U.S. economy is capable of performing in that fashion. But it's going to be a struggle, and the battle is going to be won on the picket lines and the bargaining tables and not in the halls of Congress ... When we go to the table in 1979, we'll be seeking a shorter work week. It won't happen immediately or simultaneously in all industries. But eventually, workers will be working four days in factories that are operating six days a week.

At meeting of All Unions Committee to
Shorten the Work Week, Dearborn, Mich.,
April 11/The Dallas Times Herald, 4-12:(A)14.

3

No labor leader in any union can just go to his membership and say, "I want you to sacrifice." We're willing to sacrifice, but only if there's an equality of sacrifice—if every segment of the economy sacrifices equally. We've been saying for a long time that there is not a wage-price spiral at all now but a price-wage spiral. Look at any inflationary surge in the last 50 years and you find the same thing: Prices go up and then wages start chasing them. If we want a downward spiral in the cost of living, then the first move really should be made by industry. They should start to contain themselves in terms of price increases. If you can arrive at an eminently fair proposition in which all segments of society make equal sacrifices, I don't think the labor movement could or would object.

Interview/U.S. News & World Report, 9-11:88.

4

[On the adoption of California's recent Proposition 13, which reduced property taxes]: ... I don't believe we have yet had a test on the real Proposition 13, because in Proposition 13 the people of California have not yet had to pay the piper because they had a $5.5-billion surplus [in the state treasury], as you know, and they will have another one next year, so they will not feel the impact of Proposition 13 at all. I would like to see the situation where, if people vote for a Proposition 13-type piece of legislation, and that passes and they have to pay the consequences of that action by reduced

WHAT THEY SAID IN 1978

services in terms of teachers, in terms of firemen, in terms of policemen and other public services. If that happens, my suspicion will be that the people of the United States in almost every community will turn right around and enact a tax increase to fill that void.

TV-radio interview/"Meet the Press,"
National Broadcasting Company, 10-1.

1

I am opposed to strikes by firemen and policemen. However, you have to provide for a substitute by which they can get redress of grievances. But I am against strikes by firemen and policemen. I think strikes in the public sector are tolerable, providing they only cause inconvenience; but when they jeopardize the community, I don't think anyone has that right.

TV-radio interview/"Meet the Press,"
National Broadcasting Company, 10-1.

Audrey Freeman
Labor specialist,
The Conference Board

2

The issue of income and job security is like Brigadoon—it materializes out of the economic mists after every severe recession . . . As unemployment increases, preserving both job and recall rights becomes paramount to the worker who has found a niche inside the system. Currently there is a longer line of unemployed— now including young people, women and blacks —all just waiting to compete for the incumbent's job.

The Christian Science Monitor, 3-20:12.

Milton Friedman
Senior research fellow, Hoover
Institution, Stanford University;
Former professor of economics,
University of Chicago

3

The Federal government is the engine of inflation—the only one there is. But it has been the engine of inflation at the behest of the American public, which wants the government

to spend more but not raise taxes—so encouraging resort to the hidden tax of inflation. The public objects to inflation—but I have yet to hear any group object to a rise in the price of something *it* sells!

Interview/Newsweek, 5-29:81.

4

We have to bear in mind that tax-limitation laws are not cure-alls; they are temporary stop-gaps . . . The real problem for the future is to stop the growth in government spending . . . Tax-limitation amendments are a way of trying to hold back the tide until public opinion moves in the direction that those of us who believe in limited government hold to be desirable.

San Francisco Examiner &
Chronicle, 6-18:(This World)2.

5

There is only one way to cure inflation. There aren't any alternatives. The only way to cure inflation is for the government to spend less and to print less money. It is the increase in the amount of money in circulation that is the primary cause of inflation. That comes from Washington and nowhere else. The attempt to impose voluntary price and wage controls is simply, in my opinion, an attempt on the part of the government to shift the responsibility for its own mistakes to labor and to business.

TV-radio interview/"Meet the Press,"
National Broadcasting Company, 11-12.

Takeo Fukuda
Prime Minister of Japan

6

I was highly dissatisfied with the attitude of the American government in letting the dollar fall last year by failing to take aggressive measures to protect it. Because the dollar is the key international currency, wild fluctuations of the dollar will lead to chaos in the world economy. A decline in the value of the dollar also invites inflation. Then, with inflation, the dollar declines further. And the fear of a vicious cycle occurs.

At luncheon sponsored by Japan Society
and Foreign Policy Association, New York,
May 4/Los Angeles Times, 5-5:(1)19.

John Kenneth Galbraith
Professor emeritus of
economics, Harvard University

1

[On wage and price controls]: I keep noticing that the majority of the American people think that they are necessary, and as far as the statement that they are unworkable is concerned, they worked marvelously for us during World War II, under wartime conditions. They broke the inflational spiral in the Korean War, and they got Mr. Nixon re-elected [President] in 1972. He got unemployment and inflation down, both of them, to less than five per cent. That is an extraordinary good record. But I am not saying that they are pleasant things. I am merely saying that they are better than either unemployment or inflation... The economic policy of the twenty years, say up until... the end of the '60s, the beginning of the '70s, was a rather lovely thing. The economy was working at less than capacity. Inflation was not yet a serious problem, so economic policy was: cut interest rates, cut taxes, increase expenditures, and economists could come into the Oval Office and the President was glad to see them. Now an economist is a man who has to talk about a choice between tighter money, tighter budgets... price and wage restraints—every one of them reprehensible, nasty, disagreeable.
TV-radio interview/"Meet the Press,"
National Broadcasting Company, 7-9.

2

I have always felt that the essential problems of economic policy are capable of being put in clear English. But much of the complexity that surrounds the subject is of two sorts. It's first to build a priestly wall around the subject, to keep out the unwashed and the uninitiated, which is what lawyers, physicians, psychiatrists also do. And secondly, which is more serious, much unclear expression in economics is the result of unclear thought. It's impossible to state simply and clearly what you haven't thought through. To be fair, there are problems of refinement having to do with techniques of economic measurement and computer technology, where the language becomes a kind of shorthand, but that I think is very rarely a

barrier to understanding. There is also the possibility that the individual, in turn, has never learned to speak good English.
Interview/Los Angeles Herald Examiner, 7-16:(A)7.

E. J. (Jake) Garn
United States Senator, R-Utah

3

What will it mean if we achieve a four per cent unemployment rate and we still have 10, 12, 15 per cent inflation? This Congress is not willing to address itself to [inflation]. We continue to go on wildly spending... Until we start attacking inflation, the poor are going to be poor and the elderly are going to be poor, and the people are going to suffer... I suggest it's time this Committee and this Congress and the special-interest groups pay a little more attention to inflation. We might start accomplishing something.
Before Senate Banking Committee,
Washington, June 22/**

Robert J. Genetski
Vice president and
economist, Harris Bank, Chicago

4

There is a strong relationship suggesting that above-average increases in a state's tax burden can lead to below-average economic growth, while below-average increases in a state's tax burden can lead to above-average growth... The relationship suggests that for every one-per-cent increase in a state's relative tax-burden growth over the period analyzed, relative income growth declines by approximately .5 per cent, and vice versa. As time passes, resources in the form of both investment capital and workers tend to move to those states where relative burdens are falling.
The Dallas Times Herald, 11-6:(D)11.

Eli Ginzberg
Chairman, National Commission for
Manpower Policy of the United States

5

[On the work ethic in the U.S.]: In this country's early days, the Southern plantation owners didn't work very hard; their slaves did

WHAT THEY SAID IN 1978

the heavy jobs. We had a million hobos riding the rails around the time I was born early in this century, so obviously that was a group not too much addicted to the work ethic. What was true about the United States was that, if you worked hard in those days, the opportunities to get ahead were unequivocally clear. Moreover, if you were part of a frontier family and you didn't work, you'd starve to death. There were real pressures to reinforce a belief in hard work. Today, of course, our affluent society offers more people a chance not to work, if that's their inclination. Still, you're likely to find in any organization perhaps 1 ambitious person out of every 5 or 6 who is an eager beaver.

Interview/U.S. News & World Report, 1-23:47.

C. Jackson Grayson, Jr.
Chairman, American Productivity Center;
Former Chairman, Price Commission,
Federal Cost of Living Council

1

Don't install [wage and price controls]. They are self-defeating. They don't get to the root of inflation. All they do is suppress, by coercion, the basic causes. Eventually, when controls are removed, inflation breaks out at a more virulent rate than ever ... [Jawboning] doesn't get results—and since the government doesn't like to admit defeat, it will have to resort to mandatory controls to make up for what wasn't accomplished by the jawboning process. So we come back to the fact that improving productivity is the only real answer to fighting inflation. Every other route says the government should do something. The private sector has to do the job, and productivity is its chief hallmark.

Interview/U.S. News & World Report, 5-1:95.

2

I've heard all the rhetoric about we-don't-want-to-work-hard-any-more, and I don't believe it. The work ethic has not been lost. What has happened is that autocratic, bureaucratic organizations in business and public service have suppressed the desires and ability of the individual to feel that he or she is contributing. People do not mind contributing to the success of an enterprise, so long as they feel that they have a hand in helping to shape it and are rewarded.

Time, 9-25:69.

Alan Greenspan
Former Chairman, Council of
Economic Advisers to the President
of the United States (Gerald R. Ford)

3

It is always the moment for a tax cut in the sense that taxes are too high and, I think, do inhibit investment in the country. And I think to the extent that we build up taxes, it causes an extraordinarily heavy burden on the average American. The problem is to reduce taxes by curbing the rate of growth in Federal spending. If you ask me, do I think we should allow Federal spending to rise indefinitely and cut taxes indefinitely, I would say that is playing a shell game with the American people and that, while they may appear to have a tax cut, the inflation which would occur as a consequence would be the much sharper implicit tax on their real incomes.

TV-radio interview/"Meet the Press,"
National Broadcasting Company, 4-9.

4

... the way the President [Carter] manages economic policy is in my view the cause of his problems. He tries to resolve each issue on its merits, so there is a lack of central focus around which economic policy can emerge ... The President's advisers string all across the lot [in terms of economic philosophy]. He is getting advice from conflicting policy viewpoints and he does not have the economic knowledge to choose. Of necessity, he chooses on the basis of personality. When he tries to dig into detail, he runs out of time. It is okay to have conflicting views presented, if the President has the ability to choose.

Interview, Chicago/
The Christian Science Monitor, 6-7:8.

Walter E. Hanson
Chairman, Peat, Marwick,
Mitchell & Company

1

We have become so accustomed to the capital-gains tax that we accept it as part of the income tax. This is wrong. For the exchange of an asset for cash does not produce income, and the tax upon such an exchange is not an income tax, but a sales tax ... If the Treasury sets the transfer tax on such exchanges at unreasonable levels, I cannot afford to make the transfer, and it is the Treasury that loses revenue.

Before New England Council, Boston/
The Wall Street Journal, 3-21:16

Shearon Harris
Chairman, Carolina Power & Light
Company; Chairman, Chamber of
Commerce of the United States

2

... I am terribly disappointed with President Carter's proposed $500-billion budget that contemplates a $60-billion deficit. Deficits are one of three major factors fanning inflation. The others are wage increases which are not matched by increases in productivity, and the hidden costs of over-regulation. I have a philosophy that a responsible citizenry can't defer obligations to later generations ... I just don't think it is acceptable, in a time of strong economic activity, to continue deficit financing of the government and go on piling up our national debt.

Interview/Nation's Business, May:59

S. I. Hayakawa
United States Senator, R-California

3

The economically disadvantaged in our society will never achieve economic success if there are no bottom rungs of the ladder to start from. What we must do is restore some bottom rungs so that the person who is willing to work, who is ambitious, who is determined to make his place, can find a place to start.

Washington/San Francisco
Examiner & Chronicle, 8-6:(A)13.

Harold J. Haynes
Chairman, Standard Oil Company of
California

4

A phased return to the principles of a free competitive market is not only compatible with our tradition of economic freedom, it is also the most effective way of getting the job done—in energy or in any other type of individual enterprise. In the final analysis, all of us should remember that the inherent strength and power of our nation is not based solely on our abundant material resources, nor on our sophisticated technology. Our country's real strength is the ability of its people and the freedom they have enjoyed to develop their own talents, to seek their own economic goals. America did not develop from a small, backward agricultural country into the world's greatest industrial nation by strangling business in red tape, by limiting competitive opportunities through government restrictions, or by adhering to the strange but widespread idea that earning a reasonable profit is somehow a social sin. Even Lord Keynes conceded that profit is the engine ... of enterprise. Instead, our country's economic prosperity, our industrial growth, was made possible by providing a maximum degree of economic freedom. Because enterprise was encouraged rather than penalized, America created history's most advanced industrial nation—with greater freedom and economic opportunity for the individual than any other society that ever existed.

At National Computer Conference, Anaheim,
Calif., June 6/Vital Speeches, 7-15:604.

Walter W. Heller
Professor of economics, University of
Minnesota; Former Chairman, Council of
Economic Advisers to the President of
the United States (John F. Kennedy)

5

[On the recent passage of California's Proposition 13, which reduced property taxes] : ... what happens to services when you have a tax revolt like this? What services are cut down eventually? In the California case, they will buffer it for a year or so, but in the last analysis, who wins? Who loses? Is it the poor? Is it

143

WHAT THEY SAID IN 1978

(WALTER W. HELLER)

the aged? Is it the ill? Is it the disadvantaged?—
at the expense of preserving services for the
middle class? . . . The questions of fairness in
the distribution of tax burdens, efficiency in
the delivery of services, inadvertent tax increases that arise from inflation—in other words,
where inflation takes the place of the legislature, in effect, and stealthily and inadvertently
increases taxes—I think those questions need to
be faced. We have a big agenda there. I just
don't think that this slashing and crashing
about in taxes, the way [California's] Jarvis-
Gann [Proposition 13] has done, is the way to
go about it.

Discussion at American Enterprise Institute,
June/The Washington Post, 7-30:(B)5.

1

There is no doubt that our rate of productivity increase has slowed down. Partly it's because of two recessions, one of them very deep,
in the '70s. It's partly because we're investing
more in safety, in a decent environment and in
health; those things don't count as part of the
gross national product or add to profits. They
improve the quality of life, but they don't
improve U.S. competitiveness. But the most
disturbing development is the slowdown in innovation and technological advance. We are
devoting a smaller share of our national income
to research and development than we did even
five or 10 years ago, while our competitors are
devoting a larger share of theirs. Unless we can
reverse that trend, this country's economic
leadership of the world will be threatened.

Interview/U.S. News & World Report, 11-27:65.

Alexis M. Herman
Director, Women's Bureau, Department
of Labor of the United States

2

Some women work out of economic necessity, some to improve their families' living standards, some for self-fulfillment. Unfortunately,
most people assume that the increased participation in the labor force is by women who
don't need work. "If they'd just go back home,
we wouldn't have this unemployment prob-

lem," they say. But that's not so. Cinderella
doesn't live here any more. We need to know
that today nine out of 10 women will work at
some point in their lives. We don't have just a
casual flirtation with the job market.

Interview, Washington/Los Angeles Times, 9-4:(4)1.

Richard D. Hill
Chairman, First National Boston
Corporation

3

Price and wage controls—even jawboning—
merely treat the symptoms, but fail to cure the
disease. The disease is caused by an insidious
narcotic which raises our expectations of good
things for all beyond our ability to manufacture
or pay for them. As the disease spreads in
classic fashion, wealth flows from the private to
the public sector, and employment tends to do
likewise. Perhaps this will produce the desired
benefits, but we will have to undergo some
drastic political changes to a more socialistic
and centralized government, which Americans
are not yet ready to accept.

Nation's Business, June:30.

Wayne L. Horvitz
Director, Federal Mediation and
Conciliation Service

4

I view the collective-bargaining system as
working best when we [mediators] work
least . . . I've never seen the value of going 72
hours without a break and getting everybody so
damn tired they have to live with a lousy
[labor] contract for the next three years.

Interview, Washington/Los Angeles Times, 4-23:(1)9.

Thomas E. Huebner
City Manager of San Antonio, Texas

5

The basic reason for denying at least some
government employees the right to strike is the
necessity of the services that are being provided
to the public. Fire and police are two of the
essential services that the public ought to have
24 hours a day, every day of the year. But it
really goes beyond that. A lot of serious problems are created by other government workers

144

(THOMAS E. HUEBNER)

striking, such as teachers and people who work in sewage-treatment operations. There are a whole host of services that ought not to be interrupted. Government employees should not be able to dictate to their employers.

Interview/U.S. News & World Report, 9-25:81.

Richard J. Jacob
Chairman, Dayco Corporation

1

[On labor unions that press for shorter working hours]: If they can do the same amount of work or more in fewer hours, I don't give a damn. If they can't, forget it. A 40-hour week is a pretty practical approach for a working-man's life. I think our nation's productivity would drop off considerably if a 38-hour or 36-hour week became customary. I don't know that for certain. I'm not an expert in this area. But I do know that you can improve productivity through innovative methods of talking to your personnel—telling your hourly people what productivity is, what it does for them, and what it does for the company they work for.

Interview, Dayton, Ohio/
Nation's Business, April:68.

Neil H. Jacoby
Founding dean and professor emeritus of business economics and policy, Graduate School of Management, University of California, Los Angeles

2

[On California's Proposition 13, which sharply reduced property taxes]: The stimulative effects of a sharp tax reduction on an economy are well-established in both economic theory and history. Because Proposition 13 has raised the rate of return on investment in property conservatively by 20 per cent, most of the dollars kept in the private sector will be invested in the construction and improvement of property. These investment dollars will have a much higher multiplier effect upon California income and employment than they would had they been transferred to government, where most would have been paid to employees and

spent on consumer goods. Although it is difficult to quantify the expansionary effects of tax reduction, one may be confident that they are positive and large ... Adjustments to Proposition 13 will produce manifold benefits to California: more efficient government, more equitable taxation, less social tension, an improved business climate with rising investment, and less price inflation.

Before Joint Conference Committee of
the California Legislature/
The Center Magazine, Nov.-Dec.:30.

Howard Jarvis
Co-author of California property-tax limitation measure (Proposition 13)

3

We want to cut income tax to the amount government *has* to spend—not *wants* to spend. This is a movement that will restructure the government of this nation.

TV-radio interview/"Meet the Press," National
Broadcasting Company, 6-18.

4

We have seen the trauma of high taxes on older people. The deteriorating state of mind. The disease. The ulcers. When elderly people get those tax bills on their meager homes that demand another $1,500 a year, they get a cloud over their heads. Many of them give up the spirit and quickly die. One woman had a heart attack in front of me back in 1962 right in the assessor's office. That means something to me. Even the Russians don't do that, run people out of their homes for no reason. It is a goddamned crime. It is grand-felony theft.

Interview, Los Angeles/Time, 6-19:13.

5

[On the vote passing Proposition 13]: The millions who voted for this amendment will not be trifled with. We will not put up with it! To ignore us is political suicide! Tonight we know how our forefathers felt as they hurled crates of tea into Boston Harbor and paved the way for freedom and liberty in the United States. The fight for Proposition 13 is the opening battle in the New American Revolution. We have a new

WHAT THEY SAID IN 1978

revolution against the arrogant politicians and bureaucrats whose philosophy of tax-tax-tax, spend-spend-spend and elect-elect-elect is bankrupting the American people. And the time has come to put a stop! Our victory tonight is a taxpayers' victory, and we have just begun!

Los Angeles, Nov. 7/Newsweek, 12-25:

Jack Jones
Leader, Transport and General Workers Union of Britain

1

I'm a democratic socialist. But unlike the American trade-union movement, we have tried to keep the door open to our comrades in Eastern Europe and [mainland] China. We don't accept their philosophy, but we try to treat with the world as it is. That makes it possible for us to raise issues of mutual concern, like the operations of the multinationals in Eastern Europe, for example. I agree with Churchill: It's better to jaw, jaw than war, war.

Interview, London/The New York Times, 2-25:2.

Alfred E. Kahn
Counsellor on Inflation to President of the United States Jimmy Carter

2

[On his new job as inflation counsellor]: I'm not a price-and-wage fixer. That doesn't mean that I feel it violates my sense of intellectual integrity to see what you can do to affect strategic wage and price bargains, but it isn't my forte. I'm not an arm-twister. I'm not a jawboner. So if the job is defined principally as being the Administrator of a wage-price guideline program, it's really not for me. If, instead, it is defined as the President's adviser on inflation, so that it enables me to play an important role in the whole range of government programs that inflate costs, that obviously is congenial to me.

Interview, Washington, Oct. 23/
The Washington Post, 10-26:(A)4.

3

[On President Carter's wage-price guideline program to fight inflation]: If the program flops, the only alternatives are a deep recession or mandatory wage and price controls. If inflation is permitted to accelerate, sooner or later there will be a tightening, a total breakdown of the organization and morale of our economy—and that will lead to recession. The other alternative is mandatory controls, and I hope everybody realizes that having to impose such controls would constitute failure. We've got an incredibly big stake in not being forced to face that dilemma. That's why the Administration is firmly committed to making the program a success. I know the President is determined, because he understands the consequences to the country and that it will be extremely damaging to him if the program doesn't work.

Interview/U.S. News & World Report, 11-27:21.

4

I began [as CAB Chairman] with the ideological conviction that airlines could stand to be as competitive as possible. Open up the doors— that was the principle. But with inflation, there is no easy principle. Licking this one involves exhortation, moral suasion, walking a balance of fiscal restraint on every side. It's the peculiarity of inflation that it feeds on itself. It's the nebulae, the amorphousness of it, that will defeat you.

Interview/The Washington Post, 11-27:(B)3.

Garson Kanin
Author, Playwright

5

[On mandatory retirement at age 65]: I don't think it's right for *anyone* to be forced out just because he's committed a birthday. The United States of America watched CBS News for years, watched Eric [Sevareid, the commentator who was recently retired by CBS when he reached 65]. No longer. CBS didn't tell us he lost his marbles or got drunk or came in late every night. No; they're saying he got to be 65 and so he had to get out. This visible act conveys to all of us that at 65 a man is no longer useful. A disgraceful myth. I think it *takes* someone of 65—or 70 or 75—to do Eric's job.

Interview, New York/Publishers Weekly, 1-23:276.

Jack Kemp
United States Representative, R-New York

1

[Advocating cutting taxes across the board]: This issue goes beyond conservative-liberal or Republican-Democratic dialogues. It even goes beyond taxes. It has to do with putting rungs back on that ladder, with removing barriers between your efforts and your rewards. The real issue is government promoting a climate for increase and growth. It's about hope and ... *opportunity* ... I haven't been trained in the modern school of economics. But I understand incentive. I know why those guys go into Bethlehem Steel with their lunch pails every morning: for income after taxes. And the problem is, that income is being taxed away. People are thinking on the margin. I may not totally be on the right track—but I'm not far off.

Interview, Washington/
The Washington Post, 6-22:(B)3.

2

My constructive criticism of my [Republican] Party is that we've put the balanced budget ahead of the type of economic growth that *leads* to a balanced budget. We've always said we were the party of lower tax rates, but we added that we couldn't lower them until we balanced the budget. So we've become, in effect, the tax collectors for Democratic spending programs. We came across as being negative, as more interested in dollars and budgets than people. The Democrats offer the voters a banquet menu of soup, salad, nuts, wine and beef—and you know you're going to pay for it through the nose in terms of inflation and taxes. But the Republicans have said: "Come to our table, and we'll tighten your belt. You can have a bone and crumbs, but someday we'll have a good meal for you if you can just hold on." That is not a very appetizing menu—and I want to change it.

Interview/U.S. News & World Report, 7-3:19.

Edward M. Kennedy
United States Senator, D-Massachusetts

3

If we are going to bring relief to the hard-pressed taxpayers of this nation, let us do so in ways that do not destroy local tax systems that are the cornerstone of local control over local services. If we are going to stop the hemorrhage of revenues wasted in massive spending designed to help the many who are poor, let us do so in ways that also stop the hemorrhage of revenues wasted in massive spending through tax loopholes designed to help the few that are rich.

At U.S. Conference of Mayors convention, Atlanta,
June 19/The Dallas Times Herald, 6-20:(A)7.

4

The one thing that [the late Senator] Hubert Humphrey and [the late Presidents] John F. Kennedy and Franklin D. Roosevelt understood—and that we hope [current President] Jimmy Carter understands—is that you cannot meet the needs of the nation without a strong economy.

At Democratic fund-raising dinner, Bloomington,
Minn./Los Angeles Times, 10-23:(2)7.

Lane Kirkland
Secretary-treasurer, American
Federation of Labor-Congress of
Industrial Organizations

5

Exhorbitant interest rates and tight money are not going to solve the problems of inflation. They are going to cause unemployment and economic stagnation. In fact, I think they will add to the problems of inflation. In a highly capitalized society, the cost of money is extremely significant to the cost of living. I fail to see how you can expect to reduce the rate of price increases by raising drastically the price of one of the central ingredients of the economy—the cost of money.

Interview, Washington/The Arizona Daily Star,
Tucson, 11-29(A)2.

Loren E. Klaus
President, Shawnee College, Ullin, Ill.

6

Militant teachers claim public employees ought to have the same collective-bargaining rights as private employees—and that would solve most problems. Nonsense! Here's what happened in the 34 states that require collective

WHAT THEY SAID IN 1978

bargaining by public agencies: 1) The number of public employees boomed. 2) Unionization grew everywhere. 3) State legislators caved in to union demands for power. 4) And strikes against the people flowered everywhere. In Pennsylvania, strikes rose from six before collective bargaining to an average of 73 four years later. Generally, states with collective-bargaining laws have more strikes than those without. And finally, the national unions are calling the shots for the local unions.

Before Wyoming School Boards Association, Cheyenne/The Wall Street Journal, 7-26:14.

Lawrence R. Klein
Professor, Wharton School, University of Pennsylvania

1

[On President Carter's 1977 economic record]: I grade him a 70. The main thing is that economic policy should be steady, and Carter's policy hasn't been steady. He proposed a stimulus program, then dropped the $50 tax rebate. Tax reform was in, then out again. Now there's a big tax cut proposed for 1978. People feel that policy is in too much of a state of flux.

Interview/The Washington Post, 1-5:(A)21.

Arthur B. Laffer
Professor of economics, Graduate School of Business, University of Southern California

2

The most immoral act a society can perpetrate on its citizenry is to destroy the production base on which all beneficence ultimately rests. I think we have a very strong need for public services. The only way I can see government spending increasing, however, is to have a very large tax base. I would much rather see full employment than very high spending on unemployment compensation . . . The inner cities are deteriorating because of the failure to recognize the role played by incentives. [The late President John] Kennedy recognized that a rising tide raises all boats. I see in this country a tax on the rich as opposed to help for the poor. I

see the moral equivalent of war on the oil companies. And I see soak-the-rich policies throughout the entire country. The correct policy is—let's expand the base. Let's get everyone employed, and then use those revenues for very needed public services.

Interview/The New York Times, 6-17:30.

R. Heath Larry
President, National Association of Manufacturers

3

We are in an era when inflation will make productivity uppermost in [labor-management] bargaining. If that means hard-nosed, so be it.

U.S. News & World Report, 4-17:82.

Richard L. Lesher
President, Chamber of Commerce of the United States

4

. . . we still have people who have no jobs and say they want them. For them, you may wonder, what's wrong with creating public-service jobs? It sounds like a simple solution, on the surface. The problem is this: When the government creates a job, it takes the money to do it from the private sector. So the jobs the government "creates" are subtracted from the private sector. There's no net gain, only the illusion of a gain. Worse yet, the jobs that would have been created by the private sector are productive, economically useful jobs, whereas jobs created by the government are notoriously inefficient.

Before Toledo (Ohio) Area Chamber of Commerce, Jan. 3/Vital Speeches, 3-1:319.

Russell B. Long
United States Senator, D-Louisiana

5

One thought has been kicking around awhile but hasn't been bought at the White House—it would be that we might suggest giving business a tax cut if they would hold prices down . . . That pitch always appealed to me, to say, "All right, if you hold the prices down, don't let your price go above the average of all the other

(RUSSELL B. LONG)

prices, we will give you a tax break that otherwise you wouldn't get." That just might work. I would like to see us experiment.

Interview/The New York Times, 5-4:61.

James B. Longley
Governor of Maine (I)

1

I am concerned about the programs which are being advocated almost daily in our legislatures; these programs would push us closer and closer to a society where half the people will be working to support the other half. I am concerned about the strong resistance I have seen . . . to tax-relief efforts that would benefit business. It is disturbing to me to see the attacks on small, medium and large businesses and industries which provide jobs for our people. I ask myself whether those who constantly advocate more and more welfare spending and, at the same time, attack the businesses which provide the jobs which pay for the welfare, are not, in fact, advocating a socialistic, divide-the-wealth approach.

Nation's Business, October: 74.

Donald C. Lubick
Assistant Secretary-designate for
Tax Policy, Department of the
Treasury of the United States

2

[Arguing against a cut in capital-gains taxes] : First, the Steiger [tax-cut] amendment involves a tremendous loss in tax revenues. We estimate that it would reduce tax revenues by $2.2-billion. Second, it would have very serious effects on the progressivity of the tax system: The relief would be focused almost entirely upon taxpayers with incomes over $100,000 a year. Third, there are much more efficient and effective ways to assist capital formation . . . [And] you've got to bear in mind that a very large part of any reduction would be in the taxes on existing gains in real estate, timber holdings and farmland. Already there are many tax provisions that give very liberal investment incentives for that sort of investment. I don't

see any evidence that cutting taxes on the capital gains that come from the sale of stock is going to be a big stimulus to new productive investment.

Interview/U.S. News & World Report, 6-26:81.

3

Fairness requires that taxpayers with equal incomes be treated equally for income-tax purposes. Compensation received in kind may be just as valuable as compensation received in cash. When fringe benefits are exempted from tax, taxpayers with equal incomes pay unequal taxes. Exempting fringe benefits from tax produces unfairness not only among employees at the same income level, but also among employees at different income levels. When a fringe benefit is exempted from tax, the exemption is of greater value to a high-income taxpayer than to a low-income taxpayer. For a person in the highest tax bracket, an exemption provides 70 cents in tax savings for every dollar's worth of fringe benefits received. For a person in the lowest tax bracket, the exemption is worth only 14 cents. For a person with income too low to be taxed, the exemption is worth nothing.

Before House Ways and Means Committee Task Force
on Employee Fringe Benefits, Washington, Aug. 14/
Vital Speeches, 9-15:719.

Cornell C. Maier
President, Kaiser Aluminum &
Chemicals Company

4

Our national leaders attract attention to their jousts with windmills like three-martini lunches, snail darters and human rights in Chile, while the real problems [inflation, unemployment, energy] are gnawing our legs off up to our knees.

San Francisco Examiner & Chronicle,
9-24:(This World)2.

J. W. Marriott, Jr.
President, Marriott Corporation

5

. . . it is becoming more and more popular to tear down the free-enterprise system, the system that made this country the most pro-

WHAT THEY SAID IN 1978

ductive, with the highest standard of living in the history of the world. We're letting government run away with the football. In our democracy I thought government was supposed to be an impartial referee. But somehow they're in there trying to change the rules and calling the plays, as the special interests cheer for more points to be scored against business. But in our system the field of play is the free market. The players come from the private sector. The game is called competition. The stars are the best innovators, entrepreneurs, strategists and marketers. The goal is profit and growth, and employment and a good living for everyone. The public referees represent the public interests. They help assure safety, security and fair play. They must be conscientious, well-informed, objective and practical. But they've got to get their mitts off the football. They've interfered too deeply in the way the game is played. And they're distorting the outcome. And so, I suggest a revolt. A taxpayers' and business-leaders' revolt against far more government than we need. Or deserve. Or want. Or will stand for. Or will *pay* for.

Before American Marketing Association, St. Louis,
Feb. 24/Vital Speeches, 5-1:427.

Alfred J. Marrow
Industrial psychologist; President,
National Academy of Professional
Psychologists

1

The vast majority of workers these days are demoralized. They aren't producing at their potential. The result is high labor turnover, low productivity, frequent absenteeism, wildcat strikes and lowered product quality ... A major cause is poor bossing. Too many managers don't have a scientific understanding about how to get along with employees. They try to run their plants and stores and offices autocratically, with no real attempt at two-way communication. This causes psychological stress and great inefficiency on the part of workers ... Most employers think in terms of the economic man—"pay him a little more money and he'll work a little faster." Well, you can give your car a little more gas and it will go faster, but you

can't give a worker a little more money and expect him to respond. People want more than economic rewards from their jobs. They want self-esteem, recognition, satisfaction in what they're doing to earn a living. For many workers, quality of life is more important than money. That's why the absentee rate is so high on Fridays in many plants.

Interview/U.S. News & World Report, 2-13:75.

F. Ray Marshall
Secretary of Labor of the United States

2

Concern over unemployment is not restricted to just those who are currently looking for work. Somewhere between one-third and one-half of all Americans have current, direct and personal contact with the effects of high unemployment. The implication is clear. Most Americans, whether employed or not, expect both a job and stable prices. While the relative importance of inflation increases when prices rise rapidly, providing jobs continues to be a top priority.

Los Angeles Herald Examiner, 9-11:(A)1.

William McChesney Martin
Former Chairman, Federal Reserve Board

3

Inflation is still the biggest problem of the free world. We have all found how easy it is to step on the accelerator, but we haven't learned that we must also apply the brakes. All nations in the Western world have been moving their economies too fast. I know you're very unpopular when you say that, but it's true.

Interview, Washington/
The New York Times, 1-25:(D)1.

W. Howard McClennan
President, International Association of
Fire Fighters; President, AFL-CIO
public employee department

4

[Saying public employees should have the right to strike]: [No strikes] was the philosophy in the 1930s and 1940s. This is 1978, and nobody today—regardless of where he works—should have to give up his rights. Even though they work for a city or the Federal government,

(W. HOWARD MCCLENNAN)

they still have a right to vote like everybody else. If drafted, they must serve their country like anybody else. There should be no differences just because they work as public employees. It used to be said that a civil-service job was great because it guaranteed you a job for the rest of your life. Well, that's not true any more. Policemen are laid off; fire-fighters are laid off. They've cut back on city employees, school teachers and sanitation workers. They used to say that anybody in public service had better pensions and better benefits. But all of those things are gone now. The people in the private sector are way ahead of most workers in the public sector. In fact, public employees today are always playing catch-up.

Interview/U.S. News & World Report, 9-25:81.

Paul W. McCracken
Professor of business administration,
University of Michigan; Former
Chairman, Council of Economic Advisers
to the President of the United States
(Richard M. Nixon)

1

... what consumers and business need most is to see in 1978 a discernible tendency toward a lower rate of inflation—not an immediate and total solution to that problem, but so that people could be saying by the end of this year that it looks as if the rate of inflation has moved down from about 6 per cent a year to, say, about 5. I doubt there is anything that would do more to restore business confidence or the confidence of people generally than that. Why? Because if people really thought the rate of inflation was moving down, this would have a very therapeutic effect on interest rates. Therefore, it would have a favorable effect on the stock market and on the international standing of the dollar.

Interview/U.S. News & World Report, 2-6:19.

George S. McGovern
United States Senator, D-South Dakota

2

[On the passage of California's Proposition 13, which will reduce property taxes]: While the tax revolt expresses profound legitimate anger, it also has undertones of racism . . . Sixty per cent of the [government] employees who may be laid off in Los Angeles are members of minority groups. It is unfashionable now to worry about the poor and minorities and to defend the idea that they, too, deserve an opportunity. Perhaps property-taxpayers ought to remember, if only for a moment, how many of them would never have owned a home without a governmental loan and a mortgage tax write-off. To give up on government now, to turn our backs on those who have been left behind . . . is to give up on our own best instincts. It is un-American; it is unacceptable. At stake is whether America will become a parcel of geography drained of ideals, a collection of selfish, competing economic persons whose highest purpose is the bottom line.

Before Americans for Democratic Action,
June 17/The Washington Post, 6-25:(D)6.

3

I would recommend very strongly that the first order of business when Congress comes back into session in January ought to be for the President [Carter] to request mandatory wage and price controls on concentrated industries. I am not talking about the little stores up and down Main Street, the little farmers, the ordinary retailer. I am talking about those major corporate concentrations, in oil, in automobiles, in steel, in chemicals, that are driving up the prices and the cost of living. There is no other way that I know of to deal with these inflationary pressures that I think have put liberals on the defensive in this country except to come out four-square for mandatory wage and price controls.

TV-radio interview/"Meet the Press,"
National Broadcasting Company, 10-15.

George Meany
President, American Federation of
Labor-Congress of Industrial
Organizations

4

. . . the American trade-union movement today is more deeply involved in politics than its most politically oriented critics could have believed possible a few decades ago. Our com-

WHAT THEY SAID IN 1978

mittee on political education is the single most effective political machine in the country . . . I don't know whether this is "pure and simple unionism" or "business unionism" or "social unionism" or "political unionism." None of these labels tell the true story of what the trade-union movement is today. One thing is for sure: It is a more sophisticated, effective, broad-based, democratic and involved movement today than it was 10, 20 or 30 years ago . . .

Accepting Eugene V. Debs Award from Social Democrats, U.S.A., Washington/ The Wall Street Journal, 2-1:16.

1

Labor, I am sure, will cooperate with the President of the United States and the authorities in Washington in trying to fight this matter of inflation. We are sufferers. [But] under no circumstances will we give up our right to go to the bargaining table and make our conditions and to tell the employer just how much we hope to get or expect to get, with the government sitting behind our shoulder and setting wages or conditions.

Before AFL-CIO building and construction trades department, Washington, April 17/ Los Angeles Herald Examiner, 4-18:(A)8.

2

In the past, workers have been called upon to sacrifice first to fight inflation. And they have. But the corporations and the bankers never did their share and there is no evidence that they will do so now. I don't think it is too much to ask of those who have reaped the most from the American economic system—the wealthiest individuals, corporations and banks—to take the first step in combating the economic evils of inflation . . . Workers are among the hardest-hit by inflation. That is why—on this Labor Day—workers are still willing to sacrifice as much as anyone else, as long as anyone else. But workers cannot and will not sacrifice alone.

Labor Day address, Sept. 3/San Francisco Examiner & Chronicle, 9-10:(This World)8.

3

We believe the [Carter] Administration is already headed in the direction of over-all [wage-price] controls in piecemeal and ill-designed stages. America might just as well do it now and do it right . . . We believe the time has come for mandatory legislated economic controls.

The Christian Science Monitor, 11-2:4.

David I. Meiselman
Professor of economics, Virginia Polytechnic Institute and State University

4

The primary thing [in fighting inflation] is to break the printing press. The Federal Reserve has just been creating money too fast. It should announce that it is going to reduce the rate of growth of the money supply by about 1 percentage point a year over a period of, say, five years, or until it reaches its goal of stable prices and then stick to this timetable. That's important. Because, if the Federal Reserve stays on this course for a while and then gives up when the going gets tough, it will lose any gains it has made in fighting inflation. It is possible that the Federal Reserve will have to push the rate of money growth down to zero in order to achieve price stability. But money growth should probably settle in the zero to 2 per cent range eventually.

Interview/U.S. News & World Report, 10-2:51.

G. William Miller
Chairman-designate, Federal Reserve Board

5

Once an inflation rate becomes an accepted floor, any abnormal events—business booms, commodity shortages, dislocations abroad, energy problems—are likely to lift that inflation to disastrous levels. In addition, inflation is a serious disease that erodes the savings of people and the earning power of all Americans—not only those who live on fixed incomes, but also those whose earnings appear to keep up with inflation. The whole malaise that comes from inflation is so serious over the long term that

(G. WILLIAM MILLER)

we have got to give high priority to bringing the rate down progressively in the next few years.

> *Interview, Nassau, Bahamas/*
> *U.S. News & World Report, 1-16:29.*

G. William Miller
Chairman, Federal Reserve Board

1

Show me a nation that has let inflation get out of control, and I'll show you a nation that has gone bankrupt.

> *To reporters/*
> *The Christian Science Monitor, 4-10:4.*

2

During the last decade, it has become apparent that government spending does not always produce results—economically or socially—and may not be the most effective way of reaching our desired objectives. Amidst growing disenchantment, a more promising course would be to return more of the spending decisions to individuals and to businesses, where the cumulative effect of thousands and millions of private initiatives would be more efficient in sustaining and expanding economic progress.

> *Before National Press Club, Washington, June 7/*
> *U.S. News & World Report, 6-19:72.*

3

Even if compensation [wage] increases had remained stable—and of course they did not— the productivity slowdown would have added fully two percentage points to the rise of unit labor costs and, very likely, a commensurate impetus to inflation. Increased productivity is the best prospect to break the cycle of wages chasing prices and prices chasing wages ... A successful effort to improve productivity will directly offset upward cost pressures on prices; it will tend to make output more competitive in international markets, and thus improve our balance of trade and help stem the deterioration of the dollar in the currency-exchange markets. We need a change in attitude among managers, workers—among all citizens. I am convinced that a substantial cooperative effort in the private sector coupled with the reorientation in tax and regulatory policy ... will stimu-

late productivity growth and will help ease inflationary pressures without curtailing growth.

> *At conference sponsored by "Business Week"*
> *magazine and American Productivity Center,*
> *New York, Oct. 3/Los Angeles Times, 10-4:(3)14,17.*

4

If the media is the message, and we hammer every day that there is going to be a recession, then we'll have one, because every one of us will hole up from his normal activities and fear will replace confidence. But there is no *economic* reason to have a recession.

> *People, 12-25:49.*

Parren J. Mitchell
United States Representative,
D-Maryland

5

The principal fuel on which inflation feeds is money ... Once we recognize that rapid money growth can unleash inflation but cannot solve our unemployment problem, we can break through the psychological barrier which has prevented us from developing a full-employment, non-inflationary ... strategy that works ... Business and labor leaders alike would know that exhorbitant, monopolistic price increases and wage demands were not going to be financed by a new run of the printing presses, and hence they would temper price increases and wage demands. In turn, this would quicken the reversal of inflation.

> *At University of Wisconsin*
> *Graduate School of Banking, Madison,*
> *Aug. 21/Los Angeles Times, 8-22:(1)9.*

Walter F. Mondale
Vice President of the United States

6

Jobs are an investment in human beings—the best investment this country can ever make. Jobs mean everything. They are essential to self-respect.

> *Before National Urban League, Los Angeles, Aug. 7/*
> *Los Angeles Herald Examiner, 8-7:(A)1.*

7

If we don't solve inflation, this society will suffer terribly. Everything we stand for will be

WHAT THEY SAID IN 1978

(WALTER F. MONDALE)

eroded. Inflation can destroy everything we believe in. When we press for real income improvement, inflation burns up the increase. When we push for growth, our standard of living deteriorates; when we expand personal opportunity, inflation lays its damp hand on our dreams of a more prosperous future.

At Democratic Party mid-term conference, Memphis, Tenn., Dec. 10/ The New York Times, 12-11:(D)11.

Thomas A. Murphy
Chairman, General Motors Corporation

1

The best economic and social and political system—and in my mind the most Christian—is the one that enables man not only to survive but to create sufficient wealth to reward the successful competitor, and sufficient surplus to provide adequate care for the citizen who has failed or who was unable to compete.

At Metropolitan YMCA Good Friday Prayer Breakfast, Los Angeles, March 24/ Los Angeles Times, 3-25:(3)7.

2

Too much attention is being focused on the stock market and what is happening there, rather than the true economic picture. The stock market only reflects the number of buyers and sellers at any one time, and right now the sellers outnumber the buyers. But the economy is really in pretty good shape and I hate to see everyone reacting to what happens in the stock market. We shouldn't be concerned with what happens there and should be concentrating on the Number 1 problem facing our country, which is controlling inflation . . . It is absolutely essential that organized labor as well as business cooperate fully with the President's [Carter] voluntary guidelines. Union leaders have been demanding and receiving annual increases of 10 per cent or more in total compensation for their members at a time when the inflation rate in our economy had been averaging around 8 per cent. [This is] clearly inflationary. If we seriously hope to succeed in containing inflation, everyone must do his share.

At General Motors plant, Van Nuys, Calif., Oct. 30/Los Angeles Herald Examiner, 10-31:(A)12.

3

Other countries have legislation to protect the environment and to promote safety [on the job], but their legislation is not nearly so stringent as ours [in the U.S.]. They are far more prudent in this area. They assess how much legally enforced public protection their economies can afford, and they don't permit concerns for the environment to dominate and dictate every decision. In America, on the other hand, our industry has been compelled to invest far heavier sums to meet environmental, health and safety rules. As a result, it has been estimated that our national productivity gains in recent years have not been as great as those of competing nations because capital which otherwise could have been earmarked for productivity improvement, greater competitiveness and more jobs has been diverted, instead, to the meeting of government regulation.

Before Industrial Association of San Fernando Valley, Los Angeles, Oct. 30/ Los Angeles Times, 10-31:(3)14.

4

[On President Carter's plan of voluntary wage and price restraints to fight inflation]: [The voluntary concept,] coupled with the kind of anti-inflationary monetary and fiscal policies promised by the President, is a viable one. It not only has a very good and distinct possibility of succeeding, it *can* succeed, it *must* succeed and it certainly is worthy of the best effort we as a people can put into it . . . Mandatory wage controls are as abhorrent to organized labor as mandatory price controls are to industry. I think it is safe to say that we all have learned—or at least a great majority of us have—from our mutual and bitter experience with such controls . . . To reduce inflation to more livable dimensions will require concerted action by everyone . . . I cannot believe that the extremely few negative voices that have been

(THOMAS A. MURPHY)

raised are representative of the responsible union leadership we have in this country.

Before New York Chamber of Commerce and Industry, Nov. 21/Los Angeles Herald Examiner, 11-22:(C)1,2.

Richard A. Musgrave
Visiting professor of economics, University of California, Berkeley

1

I have serious doubts about the role of [labor] unions in public employment. The function of unions in private enterprise is to get employees fair wages relative to profits. This simply does not apply to public employees. It is a different situation altogether when unions can hold up essential services like garbage collection. This is socially not acceptable. Union policy has overreached itself in public employment and some correction is needed.

Interview/People, 6-26:90.

Arthur M. Okun
Senior fellow, Brookings Institution; Former Chairman, Council of Economic Advisers to the President of the United States (Lyndon B. Johnson)

2

I think it is very unlikely that the President [Carter] can balance the [Federal] budget in fiscal '81 ... [because] it is very unlikely that business capital spending or foreign demands for our goods in the form of exports from the United States will strengthen enough to make a balanced budget desirable. It is not that he can't control Federal spending or anything of the sort. It is that a balanced budget would be bad medicine for the economy over that near-term horizon. I think we can begin to get our deficits down if things go well and if he does have an anti-inflation program in place after fiscal '79, but I think one should really postpone the target date for the balance into the second term of the Carter Administration.

TV-radio interview/"Meet the Press," National Broadcasting Company, 1-1.

The incentive system of the marketplace uses both a carrot and a stick, offering large rewards to the outstanding winners of the competitive race and imposing heavy penalties on some of the losers. The operation of the stick is often ugly—indeed inhumane. The unmitigated verdict of the marketplace would condemn millions to deprivation. When our economy is depressed, many skilled workers cannot find jobs. Even when our economy is prosperous, there are not enough jobs to go around for the young and others who have not had the opportunity to develop skills. And there are never remunerative jobs for many with severe physical or emotional handicaps. Small farmers are exposed to serious deprivation at the whim of nature. Technological progress exacts its toll; as we recognize Edison's contribution, we must also recognize that it indirectly destroyed the livelihoods of many owners, workers and investors in the kerosene-lamp business ... Deprivation and misery need not be inherent in a democratic capitalistic society *if* it uses its budgetary resources to eliminate them. Today, one-third of our Federal budget is devoted to that end, largely through a reshuffling of progressive taxes into benefit payments. If not for that, the number of Americans living below the poverty line would be at least double the actual figure ... Correcting deprivation and preserving economic efficiency are both desirable goals, which unfortunately sometimes conflict with each other. Of necessity, we must live with compromises between the two. We cannot aid low-income groups to the point of destroying the incentive system of the market that marshals the effort and economic activity to fill the bucket. Nor can we tolerate kids with empty stomachs, adults selling apples and oldsters with begging cups, in the name of a greater aggregate of real gross national product.

Columbia University/McGraw-Hill lecture/ The New York Times, 12-29:(A)23.

Robert Perry
Chief economist, Security Pacific National Bank, Los Angeles

4

There is little you can do about inflation unless you take strong legislative action to cut

WHAT THEY SAID IN 1978

(ROBERT PERRY)

into some of the Federal spending programs . . . The [Carter] Administration is forecasting a budget deficit of $35- to $40-billion in 1980. I think it could be higher, and this will be in the fifth year of the economic recovery. The Administration considers the 1980 budget an austerity budget, which makes me pessimistic.

The Christian Science Monitor, 5-26:7.

Ronald Reagan
Former Governor of California (R)

1

The limits-to-growth people who are so influential in the Carter Administration are telling us, in effect, that the American economic pie is shrinking, that we all have to settle for a smaller slice. I believe . . . Americans want . . . a crack at a decent job, a home, safety in the streets and a good education for our children; and the best way to have those things is for government to get out of the way while the rest of us make a bigger pie so that everybody can have a bigger slice.

At luncheon sponsored by Citizens for the Republic, Atlanta, Jan. 21/ The Washington Post, 1-22:(A)12.

2

We are faced with a great economic bellyache in the not-too-distant future if we don't get [tax] reductions. We've had three opportunities in this century to see what an across-the-board tax cut will do—under Harding, Coolidge and John F. Kennedy. And in every instance the government wound up getting more revenue—not less—because of the broadening of the base of the economy. Granted, it will take a little while for the revenues to catch up. But the only way that a tax cut is going to hurt economically is if everybody runs out and buries the money they save in a tin can in the back yard. That isn't going to happen. When people start using the money they save in taxes, you get a multiplier effect. History shows that then both the government and the people get more.

Interview/U.S. News & World Report, 8-14:23.

3

Inflation is as violent as a mugger, as frightening as an armed robber, and as deadly as a hit-man.

At Republican fund-raising dinner/ Los Angeles Times, 10-20:(1)16.

Henry S. Reuss
United States Representative, D-Wisconsin

4

We will never, I hope, return to the bad old days of deliberately engineered recessions as the cure for inflation—with all the human and social consequences that such a strategy has produced in the past. But we cannot expect the high-employment economy we desire to be inflation-free: The world simply is not so nice. I think you will see increasing recognition of this basic, unpleasant truth as time goes on.

At College of Commerce, DePaul University/ The Christian Science Monitor, 3-16:39.

Markley Roberts
Research economist, American Federation of Labor-Congress of Industrial Organizations

5

Whether it's a *Thor-Delta* rocket to Japan, an International Harvester tractor factory to Russia or a Piper airplane plant to Brazil, we [the U.S.] are exporting technology to a dangerous degree that also exports production, services and jobs.

At meeting sponsored by American Association for the Advancement of Science, Washington/ The Washington Post, 6-21:(A)15.

Felix G. Rohatyn
Chairman, Municipal Assistance Corporation of New York

6

Our economy is out of control, our currency is in danger, our institutions of government [are] unresponsive or inept . . . We are at war today. With inflation, with unemployment, with lack of education, with racial discrimination. We are, furthermore, not winning. If we lose, our system of government may not sur-

(FELIX G. ROHATYN)

vive . . . The hour is very late, almost as late for the U.S. as it was for New York in 1975. In the city, we fought against bankruptcy; in Washington, they are fighting the same thing under different names: controlling inflation, protecting the dollar, avoiding a recession. If the President loses this fight, if, collectively, we cannot create the climate to help him to win, the result will not be note-holders with a moratorium imposed on them, or a wage freeze on the unions; but it could be the end of a form of government which, since the days of the French Revolution, has done more for more people than any other system ever invented. There will be no winners or losers then, simply the history of another nation that was unable to count its blessings and lost sight of its values.

Before French-American Chamber of Commerce, New York, Dec. 1/The New York Times, 12-3:(1)60.

Lawrence K. Roos
President, Federal Reserve Bank of
St. Louis

1

In the private sector, there is a clear understanding that satisfaction of current desires requires some future sacrifice. Individuals and business cannot afford to ignore the future consequences of their actions, because they personally will be held accountable. The same is true of government, in principle. There is one major difference, however—the government can print money and thereby appear to avoid the accumulated debt. The cost is avoided only for a time, however. What is really happening is that we are taking out an ever-larger mortgage on the future standard of living of our nation.

Nation's Business, June:28.

2

The Fed [eral Reserve] doesn't operate in a vacuum. It is subject to all sorts of pressures—pressures to monetize the Federal debt, pressures to keep interest rates low, pressures to recognize the widespread view that interest rates are the way to control the economy. The Fed is a creature of Congress. If the Fed ignored all these pressures, some say the traditional independence of the Fed might be lost. But independence is worth very little if policy is not conducted in an independent fashion.

Interview, St. Louis/
The New York Times, 11-16:(D)2.

Walt W. Rostow
Professor of economics and history,
University of Texas, Austin

3

. . . we have come to a time when, in my judgment, we cannot return to sustained full employment simply by having a slightly soft-hearted fellow at the Federal Reserve or balancing the Federal budget just a bit more. This time we are going to have to go back to full employment by investment on the supply side in those sectors where there is degeneration. And this is, for most of the economists of this generation, quite a revolutionary change. They had thought of investment in aggregate terms, along with consumption and government outlays, as determining the over-all level of effective demand. They are not used to thinking in terms of sectoral requirements. I sense that the economists—be they Friedman, Greenspan or what have you, Samuelson and Schultze—are obsessed with what worked in the '50s and '60s. And they are in great danger of producing a protracted period of stagflation, with a loss of social and political cohesion that will damage the prospects of our society.

Interview/Los Angeles Herald Examiner, 5-27:(A)11.

Walter Rybeck
Special Assistant to the Chairman of
the U.S. House of Representatives
Committee on Banking, Finance and
Urban Affairs

4

In one sense, there is no alternative to the property tax. It is unique. It performs good and necessary functions that no other tax duplicates. Yet none of us would claim that the property tax in its present form is a model of perfection. In that sense, the best alternative to the property tax is a better property tax . . . It cannot be emphasized too much that the property tax is one of the best taxes in our fiscal kit

WHAT THEY SAID IN 1978

of tools. Property values grow as the community grows, providing a kind of natural income for it. Tapping a local source of revenue, the property tax can prevent communities from becoming too dependent on distant, centralized governments. The property tax alone enables the city or county to recoup values which they create through public works and services. And the tax is one of the few that citizens can readily speed up or slow down to exercise control over their officials.

At International Conference on Assessment Administration, Toronto, Sept. 19/ Vital Speeches, 12-15:149,150.

Helmut Schmidt
Chancellor of West Germany

1

I have personally been warning the world of such a danger [a world depression] for the last four years.... leadership from the U.S.—financial, commercial, monetary, political—is sorely needed. But the lack of an American response following the fivefold increase in oil prices, and the inability even to live up to the promises and obligations which had been undertaken ... have contributed significantly to the threat of a world depression. If the biggest and richest nation in the world [the U.S.] is producing a current-account deficit of $35- to $40-billion a year, one cannot expect that the rest of the world will get back on its feet. There is no cure without the stabilization of the world's most important currency. We have been as helpful as we could in steadying dollar-exchange rates by bilateral agreement with the U.S. But I think it's just ridiculous that some people believe that medium-size countries like Japan and Germany should be the physicians at the sickbed of the world's economy, or the locomotives, or what have you. The U.S. economy is four times as big as ours.

Interview, Hamburg/Newsweek, 5-29:56.

Charles L. Schultze
Chairman, Council of Economic Advisers to President of the United States Jimmy Carter

2

[On President Carter's recently introduced program of wage-price guidelines]: ... it is not true that wage-price programs in the past have been necessarily ineffective. They had some effect in the '60s, and they have had effect in other countries more recently—in Britain, for example.... the standards this Administration has worked out are not intended to stand out there all by themselves. They are accompanied by the other two elements of the program ...: the government's over-all anti-inflation policies and its moves in specific areas such as regulation. Inflation stems from a number of causes, and this is an attempt to have a balanced program relying on a number of different approaches—not just budgetary austerity, not just wage and price guidelines, not just other government actions, but a combination of all three. They depend upon each other.

Interview/U.S. News & World Report, 11-13:29.

William E. Simon
Former Secretary of the Treasury of the United States

3

I think the country is in a mood now to accept tough [economic] leadership. I think the President [Carter] could go to Congress and propose a budget for a three- or four-year period that would end up in balance. He could put proper emphasis on monetary policy. He could propose a reduction in taxes, with stress on capital formation rather than on three-martini lunches. He could begin to seriously trim regulation—though that's pretty difficult when Carter has placed [consumerist Ralph] Nader-ites in top positions in all the regulatory agencies. If this sort of tough, forthright approach were taken, you'd see the stock market soar, and you'd watch our dollar regain its respect as the reserve currency of the world.

Interview/U.S. News & World Report, 4-24:23.

(WILLIAM E. SIMON)

1

Most Americans have been trained to see the state as economically omniscient and to blame all evil on "business." The sadly ignorant public really believes that the bureaucrats and politicians in Washington have the keys to the economic kingdom. Should a great economic disaster come, out of panic they will demand a take-over of the major means of production by the state ... We have plenty of legal precedents for such a take-over. Then this economy will be exactly like the socialist British economy—stone-dead ... In the full context of human history, individual liberty was a bizarre new idea, but not as bizarre as the idea of a free market—the discovery that allowing millions upon millions of individuals to pursue their material interest as they choose, with a minimum of interference by the state, will unleash an incredible outpouring of prosperity. If we return to that philosophy, our problems are licked.

Interview/People, 10-16: 72, 79.

Gus Speth
Member, Federal Council on
Environmental Quality

2

Inflation is best understood as an increase in price without a corresponding increase in value.

Before American Bar Association, New York/
The Christian Science Monitor, 8-18: 22.

Robert S. Strauss
Special Representative for Trade
Negotiations of, and Adviser on
Inflation to, President of the United
States Jimmy Carter

3

What we are seeking is a deceleration in the rate of inflation in each and every industry. This means that if the individual worker should agree to accept a smaller rate of wage increase in 1978 and subsequent years than in prior years, he has the right to expect to benefit from a lower rate of price increase for the goods and services he buys ... The time for action is now—1978. If we are to achieve wage deceleration, we will have to demonstrate to unions bargaining this year

and next that we are making equal progress on prices not only in the supermarket but in housing, doctor's and hospital costs and the like ... [Inflation] has been with us for many years. It will be with us for a long time in the future. Any proposed solution must be capable of being applied over a significant period of time. We just have to keep chipping away.

At dinner of Columbia University
Graduate School of Business, New York,
April 26/The New York Times, 4-27: 53.

4

There is in this country today a psychology of "I'll grab mine and run." That is what we have to stop if we are going to turn back the [inflationary] curve. The expectation of inflation causes each sector to reach for more and more as insurance against the future. It's self-defeating as it feeds upon itself.

New York, May 16/The New York Times, 5-17: (D)2.

Nancy Hays Teeters
Member, Federal Reserve Board

5

What's been going on in the last year is alarming. Every group is trying to grab as much for itself as it can. Business says the problem is wages; labor is saying it's always [the workers] who pay. Officers of corporations give themselves 12 per cent higher salaries. The auto industry likes to raise prices more than it worries about beating out the foreign competition. There has to be a general realization that everyone is involved in this inflation fight.

San Francisco Examiner & Chronicle,
12-3: (This World)2.

Studs Terkel
Author

6

People want their work to be an extension of themselves. The anonymous steelworker says "I'm nothing," but he has a dream: "Someday if I could pass a tall building, like the John Hancock in Chicago, I'd like to see a strip of metal from the top story to the bottom and on it the name of every bricklayer, every plumber, every tool- and die-maker, as well as the architect, so I could say to my kid, 'I put in

(STUDS TERKEL)

that brick; I laid that pipe.' " As things get bigger and bigger, people get more anonymous.

Interview/The Christian Science Monitor, 5-15:27.

John G. Tower
United States Senator, R-Texas

1

I oppose the reimposition of mandatory wage and price controls. I oppose giving the President stand-by authority to impose wage and price controls at his discretion. We've tried that. It created all sorts of anomalies and inequities and shortages. The question is always how long do you keep them on, and what happens when you take the lid off?

Interview/The Dallas Times Herald, 11-5:(K)1.

2

The decision [by President Carter] to impose wage and price guidelines, with the clout of the Federal government to achieve compliance, was made in the face of inflation rates that are far too high for a stable economy. No one can quarrel over the need to reduce the rate of inflation. But one can certainly question the means of achieving that goal . . . Wage and price guidelines ignore [the] fundamental sources of inflation. Actually, they make it easier to avoid policies that are needed to bring inflation under control. They relieve the pressure from the Federal government to reduce the growth in Federal spending, lower the Federal deficit and bring the rate of monetary growth under control.

Before Dallas Home and Apartment Builders Association, Dec. 11/
The Dallas Times Herald, 12-12:(E)6.

Pierre Elliott Trudeau
Prime Minister of Canada

3

Governments must remove themselves as agents of inflation. They must not, through their access to the printing press, ratify excessive deficits through expansion in the money supply. They must be conscious that over-regulation of industry can breed inefficiencies. They

must be careful in their social policy pursuits not to damage incentive. They must, with respect to their own employees, arrive at responsible and non-inflationary wage bargains.

Before Economic Club, New York, March 22/
The New York Times, 3-23:(A)12.

Rexford G. Tugwell
Economist; Senior fellow, Center for the Study of Democratic Institutions

4

I think the American people have been spoiled. I sometimes put it this way: We are unwilling to produce as much as we want to consume. Now, spread this all over, and it's a very elaborate kind of a theory. But, actually, we hold back as much as we can when we are producing, and we get as much as we can when we are consuming. That is what is the trouble with the economy at the present time . . . That is what causes inflation. There are two ways to cure inflation. One is to reduce the number of dollars. The other is to increase the amount of goods. We don't increase the amount of goods.

Interview/The Center Magazine, Sept.-Oct.: 71.

Al Ullman
United States Representative, D-Oregon

5

When people realize that every dollar of a tax cut is another dollar of [government] deficit, and when they relate that to inflation, I think that, by and large, they would rather have less cuts and therefore less deficit.

Time, 5-8:55.

Paul A. Volcker
President, Federal Reserve Bank of New York

6

Sometimes we still hear the argument that in time we can learn to live with inflation. But experience suggests the contrary—that this powerful economy of ours will simply not work smoothly or at anything like maximum efficiency or output when there is pervasive uncertainty about the price level . . . Labor pushes for wages beyond productivity gains, business protects profit margins, government finds it

(PAUL A. VOLCKER)

simpler to embark on new spending programs than to raise taxes, farmers want protection from the pressures of the marketplace, we raise the minimum wage higher than the productivity of some of our young and unskilled may warrant, we want to improve the incomes of the elderly, and on and on ...

Address at start of savings-bond campaign,
New York, Feb. 1/The New York Times, 2-2:(D)3.

Charls E. Walker
Chairman, American Council for Capital
Formation; Former Deputy Secretary of
the Treasury of the United States

1

[Supporting a cut in capital-gains taxes]: The substance of the legislation will have a very early and strongly positive impact on decisions of savers, investors and businessmen to increase real productive investment in new plant and equipment. It's been lagging very badly in this country, relative to both our past rates and to our competitors abroad. It is this investment that increases productivity and brings you all those things that should be revered like home and mother: jobs, economic growth and inflation control. The psychological effect—if not discounted in advance—could be a tonic for the stock market and a signal to people around the world that we've not only diagnosed one of our fundamental economic maladies, we're going to do something about it.

Interview/U.S. News & World Report, 6-26:81.

Henry C. Wallich
Member, Federal Reserve Board

2

Inflation has ended the dollar's role as a trustworthy measure of values. Dealings and contracts based on the dollar have become deceptive. This is not simply a cause of economic injury. It is a moral as well as an economic issue. Without honest money, our economic dealings will be neither efficient nor even honest. If our contracts were made in terms of frequently shrinking measures of weight, time or space, as we buy food, sell our labor or

acquire real assets, we would probably regard that as cheating and as intolerable. Yet the case is much the same when we are dealing with monetary values. Nothing that is expressed in dollars any longer means what it says. Inflation is like a country where nobody speaks the truth. It introduces an element of deceit into all our economic dealings.

At graduation exercises of Fordham University
Graduate School of Business Administration/
The New York Times, 8-3:(A)21.

Murray L. Weidenbaum
Director, Center for the Study of
American Business, Washington
University, St. Louis

3

The government is the nation's largest employer. Clearly the pay raises of government employees and postal workers have been leading the inflationary parade for years. Somehow, Congress got sold on the notion of "pay comparability" between the public and private sectors, ignoring the high Federal fringes. And who makes the computations of the "comparability"? Surprise, surprise! It's the civil servants themselves—which is like having the foxes guard the henhouse.

Interview, St. Louis/Time, 5-29:76.

Mark H. Willes
President, Federal Reserve Bank of
Minneapolis

4

... new [anti-inflation] policies should be announced in advance, so that people can better plan for the future. If the policies are inflationary, people will no doubt try to protect their incomes—and a new round of inflation will hit earlier than it might have. But if the policies are anti-inflationary, people will see that they don't have to keep raising prices and wages frantically just to stay even—and the rate of inflation will come down sooner than it otherwise would have ... [The government should] stick to its announced policies fastidiously. If it announces that the Federal deficit will be cut by $30-billion, it needs to cut it by $30-billion—with no excuses. If its tax revenues

WHAT THEY SAID IN 1978

(MARK H. WILLES)

are not as high as expected, then its public services must be trimmed. Should it announce policies and fail to carry them out, it will have less credibility and its future announcements will not have the desired effect. Once it announces one or two policies and carefully follows through, however, it will be able to reduce inflation without causing much of a drop in employment or production.

The New York Times, 12-10:(3)18.

H. Johannes Witteveen
Former managing director, International Monetary Fund

1

... I think the risk of depression is ... closely related to the exchange-rate situation. My worry is that, if there is insufficient growth of demand in the surplus countries, their surpluses will continue and their currencies will go on appreciating. This, in turn, makes it more difficult for these countries to ever get growth going, because it makes their export industries less competitive and businessmen won't invest. There's a kind of vicious circle here. At the same time, the depreciation of the dollar makes it more difficult to bring inflation in the U.S. under control, and that leads to a more restrictive monetary policy in the U.S., which also depresses recovery.

Interview/The New York Times, 7-12:(D)6.

Walter B. Wriston
Chairman, Citicorp (Citibank, New York)

2

The taxpayers are in revolt. You see that in the Jarvis Initiative in California, which would drastically cut property taxes. You see it in people leaving New York State by the thousands and fleeing Massachusetts for New Hampshire. The attraction of the Sunbelt is not just the sunshine but that there is no income tax in Texas. Just about anywhere in the country, if local authorities try to raise taxes, citizens come over the wall in protest.

Time, 5-1:44.

Jerry Wurf
President, American Federation of State, County and Municipal Employees

3

[On California's Proposition 13, which reduced property taxes]: Proposition 13 was a natural reaction by California voters to an intolerable property-tax burden. The tax burden is absolutely unbearable for low- and moderate-income families because they pay too much, and the wealthy and the corporations pay too little ... When the elected officials delayed tax relief, demagogues stepped in with Proposition 13. When budgetary chaos hits California, public employees won't be the principal victims. Everyone depends upon public services to provide a livable environment. Only the irresponsible sponsors of Proposition 13 can afford to retire to their comfortable estates and shut out the rest of the world. Proposition 13 should not be viewed as the edge of a burgeoning national revolt against any and all taxes. But California voters have sent a clear message. It's time for government to stop relying so heavily upon unfair property taxes. And it's time to devise tax systems that place the heaviest burden upon those who can best afford to pay.

The Washington Post, 6-13:(A)20.

4

... I agree that inflation is among America's Number 1 domestic problems. President Carter is asking [Federal government workers] to hold down wage demands and wage settlements. All I am saying is that if President Carter is able to get the kind of cooperation from those who fix prices—business, corporations, banks who fix interest and so on—so that when a worker gets a 5.5 per cent increase as proposed by President Carter—not only Federal workers, but state and local workers—and as a result of that 5.5 per cent increase, their standard of living doesn't regress in an economy that is running somewhere between 8 and 10 per cent in an inflationary spiral, then we are perfectly willing to cooperate in stabilizing the situation. At this moment Carter is asking for sacrifice from labor and has not been able to persuade those who fix prices, who fix interest rates, who control

(JERRY WURF)

other economic activity, to limit their profits, limit their income.

TV-radio interview/"Meet the Press,"
National Broadcasting Company, 9-3.

Kenneth Young
Director, department of legislation,
American Federation of Labor-Congress
of Industrial Organizations

1

We think the whole idea of combatting inflation by undercutting wages is very unfair and inequitable. The same problem seems to exist in the minimum wage where we hear talk of deferring minimum-wage rates or creating a subminimum wage for youth. These are two other ways of placing the entire burden of inflation upon the working poor. It seems to us that deferring the minimum-wage rate, undercutting wage rates, changing the benefits of Social Security, denying funds for programs to other groups of disadvantaged people in this country, all lumped together, are an attack on the people who can least afford to maintain any standard of living. This places the burden of fighting inflation on those who cannot help themselves and are most in need of help from society.

Interview, Washington/
The New York Times, 12-28:(D)2.

Law · The Judiciary

Anthony G. Amsterdam
Professor of law, Stanford University

1

I don't think it's useful to talk about percentages when discussing lawyer competency. It depends on one's standards for competency. If the standard is that of lawyers who shouldn't practice at all, the incompetency rate is maybe 5 per cent. If the standard is room for improvement, that would include 99 per cent of all lawyers and 99.9 per cent of all judges.

Los Angeles Times, 11-5:(1)21.

F. Lee Bailey
Lawyer

2

[On his reputation for being flamboyant]: In or out of court? There is a big difference. I mean, this is serious business. We don't go around making jokes and doing wild things [in the courtroom], letting the jury think this is a game. That doesn't mean you don't look for a little comic relief, especially on the defense side. It's like the old maxim in a rape case: If you can get laughter, you won't get a conviction. The two just don't mix.

Interview/Los Angeles Herald Examiner, 12-7:(A)1.

3

In the military, the jury system is at its best. The number of jurors is between five and 11, and there is no requirement for unanimity, which is a fiction anyway. Two-thirds or better is a conviction; anything less is an acquittal. They never hang, and they are usually back in a couple hours. They are a high caliber of jurors in terms of education and so forth, because they are all officers. If I were innocent, I would rather be tried by a military jury than a civilian one.

Interview/Los Angeles Herald Examiner, 12-7:(A)12.

Ivan E. Barris
Vice president, Michigan Bar Association

4

If a lawyer is worth his salt, has done his investigation on the suit, talked to the experts and has grounds to believe his client's claims, he should proceed full-steam-ahead with the lawsuit. This will be a deterrent to any lawyer with an ounce of brains to stop filing any frivolous suits.

Los Angeles Times, 8-27:(1)28.

Griffin B. Bell
Attorney General of the United States

5

[Saying he is prohibiting Justice Department staff from discussing pending cases with Congress and Congressional and White House staff]: It is improper for any member of Congress, any member of the White House staff, or anyone else, to attempt to influence anyone in the Justice Department with respect to a particular litigation decision, except by legal argument or the provision of relevant facts ... The problem is that their positions of power create a potential for unintentional influence upon a decision, or, more often, may give rise to the broad appearance of improper influence ... I acknowledge that this set of procedures will seem unduly restrictive to some of our colleagues in government. But I believe that these restrictions are a small price—and a necessary one—for restoring and maintaining public confidence in the Department of Justice.

Before Department lawyers, Washington, Sept. 6/
Los Angeles Times, 9-7:(1)12.

Rose E. Bird
Chief Justice of California

6

... [Critics] would paint judges as politicians in black robes who make law while pretending to interpret it, as privileged elitists who

(ROSE E. BIRD)

are paid exceedingly well for doing little or no work, and as cunning opportunists who decide cases in whatever manner seems most in tune with their own self-interest ... History has taught us well that when emotions are stirred without thought to consequences, and when individuals such as judges, who cannot respond in kind, are denigrated and publicly vilified, an entire system of government may be threatened. If our courts lose their authority and their rulings are no longer respected, there will be no one left to resolve the divisive issues that can rip the social fabric apart. When the courts are destroyed, so too is the Bill of Rights. The courts are a safety valve without which no democratic society can survive.

Before State Bar of California, San Francisco,
Sept. 10/Los Angeles Times, 9-11:(1)3.

1

The more the courts are asked to handle political issues, the more their fragility is exposed. To some extent, the questioning of the courts is simply part of the increased attention that has been paid to all our institutions over the past several years. What concerns me is that the focus of this questioning of the courts seems to be not on matters of substance but rather on points of prejudice and personal pique. A judge's integrity, fairness, temperament and knowledge of the law are all pertinent areas for public inquiry. The people have every right to express their views on these matters and engage in public dialogue about them. However, what is happening, instead, is that judges are being perceived as easy targets and are being portrayed in a manner calculated to create prejudice in the public mind and then play on it.

San Francisco Examiner & Chronicle, 10-22:(B)3.

Warren E. Burger
Chief Justice of the United States

2

As legislation is proposed to Congress—and it is being proposed, and it is pending—to accom-

plish piecemeal shifts of jurisdiction away from state courts and into Federal courts, these efforts must be examined critically by you [state judges] and answered thoughtfully and effectively ... Many problems of people can be justly and fairly disposed of more swiftly and less expensively in the state courts than in Federal courts.

At state courts conference, Williamsburg, Va.,
March 19/The New York Times, 3-20:(B)12.

3

If law-school graduates, like cars, could be recalled for failure to meet commercial standards, the recall rate would be very high on those who go into the courts without substantial added training. It is ... very encouraging to find that the ... academic profession is coming to the conclusion that our present mode of legal education is ripe for re-examination and restructuring ... We must require some form of internship before lawyers claim a right to represent clients in the trial courts. There are cases being tried that an experienced, well-trained lawyer would have settled ... Cases are being tried for as much as four, five or six days which truly competent, well-trained lawyers would try in as little as two days. In civil cases, this means that there are delays which increase the costs ... In criminal cases, it means that there are some people on the streets under our very liberal bail-release concepts ... who are ultimately going to be found guilty and confined ... The public is placed in serious jeopardy.

Before American Bar Association, New Orleans/
U.S. News & World Report, 8-21:73.

4

We should get away from the idea that a court is the only place in which to settle disputes. People with claims are like people with pains. They want relief and results and they don't care whether it's in a courtroom with lawyers and judges, or somewhere else.

Before American Bar Association, New Orleans/
Los Angeles Times, 8-27:(1)32.

WHAT THEY SAID IN 1978

(WARREN E. BURGER)

1

The number of [Federal] judges has grown from those first 19 [in 1789] to 397 authorized district judges, 97 judges of the courts of appeals, and another 21 judges of three specialized tribunals—a total of 515. At least as important as the need to examine the increase in the size of the Judicial Branch is the need to examine the powers exercized by the judiciary. The authors of the Constitution did not contemplate that the judiciary would be an overseer of the other two branches. At most, they expected that the judicial function would be confined to interpreting laws and deciding whether particular acts of the Congress or of the Executive were in conflict with the Constitution; but even that was not explicit. We make a large point of the independence and separateness of the three branches, but the authors of the Constitution also contemplated that there would be coordination between the branches deriving from a common purpose. The uniqueness and true genius of the document is that it had precluded any one of the branches from dominating any other. This will continue so long as we are faithful to the spirit and letter of the Constitution.

At Seminar on Legal History, National Archives, Washington/The Christian Science Monitor, 11-29:27.

William J. Campbell
*Judge, United States District Court
for the Northern District of Illinois*

2

Today, the grand jury is the total captive of the prosecutor who, if he is candid, will concede that he can indict anybody, at any time, for almost anything, before any grand jury.

U.S. News & World Report, 6-19:65.

Jimmy Carter
President of the United States

3

Access to justice involves issues that lie beyond the scope of any single group. The law is not the private property of lawyers, nor is justice the exclusive province of judges and juries. In the final analysis, true justice is not a matter of courts and law books, but of a commitment in each of us to liberty and mutual respect.

The Dallas Times Herald, 4-26:(A)2.

4

No resource of talent and training in our society, not even medical care, is more wastefully or unfairly distributed than legal skills. Ninety per cent of our lawyers serve 10 per cent of our people. We are over-lawyered and under-represented ... When a poor family is cheated by a merchant, unfairly threatened with eviction, falsely accused of a crime, it can rarely take advantage of skilled legal talent at reasonable rates. But adequate legal help is often beyond the reach of most of the middle class as well.

Before Los Angeles County Bar Association, May 4/The Washington Post, 5-5:(A)1; Los Angeles Times, 5-5:(1)1.

5

If I didn't have to get Senate confirmation of my appointees, I could just tell you flatly that 12 per cent of all my judicial appointments would be blacks, 3 per cent would be Spanish-speaking and 40 per cent would be women, and so forth.

To reporters, Washington, Dec. 7/ The Dallas Times Herald, 12-20:(C)2.

Leonel J. Castillo
*Commissioner, Immigration and
Naturalization Service of the
United States*

6

Laws that are not enforced, that are not consistently missed, are bad laws.

Interview/Los Angeles Herald Examiner, 3-24:(A)1.

William P. Clark, Jr.
Justice, Supreme Court of California

7

People are concerned about the courts' abuse of power. In our decisions we've wandered over into the traditional provinces of the legislative and executive branches of government too often. Without question, more accountability is called for. I question the validity

(WILLIAM P. CLARK, JR.)

of the argument that opening up the process would subject us to political pressure ... The court is a political institution. All of us here were appointed by Governors—politicians—and none of us can deny we were chosen in part for our political belief. To suggest that doesn't influence our thinking now that we're judges is just naive.

Los Angeles Times, 11-23:(1)3.

Donald R. Cressey
Criminologist; Professor of sociology,
University of California, Santa Barbara

1

One of the difficulties in criminal cases is the insistence of the legal system that a person is either guilty or not guilty; that either the murderer had a criminal intent, or it is not murder. Things in law tend to be black and white.... [But] we all know that some people are a little bit guilty, while other people are guilty as hell. Some people have a little bit of criminal intent; some have a lot of it ... However, once you get into the courtroom, you are doomed to do battle; then it becomes yes or no, guilty or not guilty. You cannot bring in a verdict that the defendant is a little bit guilty.

Discussion at Center for the Study of Democratic
Institutions, Santa Barbara, Calif./
The Center Magazine, May-June:61.

Alan M. Dershowitz
Professor of law, Harvard University

2

Judges are the weakest link in our system of justice, and they are also the most protected.

Newsweek, 2-20:76.

Jack P. Etheridge
Senior Circuit Court Judge,
Fulton County (Atlanta), Georgia

3

The state trial judges are being asked to make moral judgments. On abortion. On the question of when death occurs. These shouldn't be a judge's decisions. These should be scientific or theological decisions.

The Christian Science Monitor, 11-27:13.

Macklin Fleming
Judge, United States Court of Appeals
(Ninth Circuit, Los Angeles)

4

We've lost sight of the basic purpose of criminal law, which is to protect our fundamental rights. We look at criminal law as something that interferes with our freedom and imposes onerous duties on us, whereas the true way of looking at criminal law is as the protection of our rights to life, liberty, the security of our person and the security of our property.

Interview/San Francisco Examiner & Chronicle,
7-30:(This World)38.

Marvin E. Frankel
Judge, United States District Court for
the Southern District of New York

5

... we [lawyers] must alter our prime axiom—that we are combat mercenaries available indifferently for any cause or purpose a client is ready to finance. Our ethical canons now enjoin upon us duties to the client and to the adversary process. There is nowhere among the canons—but there should be—an explicit duty to seek justice. We should all be what I would term "ministers of justice." As such, we would have to reconsider and revise a system of loyalty to clients that results too often in cover-ups, frauds and injury to innocent people. A favorite quotation in the legal profession, a cliche among advocates, is Lord Brougham's declaration that an advocate "knows but one person in all the world, and that person is his client ..." for whom, Brougham said, the advocate would stand against the world and "involve his country in confusion," if necessary. Lord Brougham was wrong; we should be less willing to fight the world and sow confusion for all manner of clients, right or wrong, and more concerned to save our own souls. As ministers of justice, we would find ourselves more positively concerned than we now are with the pursuit of truth. When our witnesses took the stand promising to tell the truth, we would not have coached them to make certain that they avoided telling more of the truth than might be agreeable or beneficial for the client we were

WHAT THEY SAID IN 1978

(MARVIN E. FRANKEL)

serving. We would not negotiate for our clients if negotiation meant, as it so often does, stating untruths and concealing misinformation. We would not draft the contracts, the forms and the laws that are designed to outsmart or over-reach those we are hired to discomfit. We would not consider it sufficient to avoid directly lying or cheating. We would help others less than we now do in their courses of lying and cheating.

At Boston College Law School commencement/
The Washington Post, 5-7:(B)8.

William P. Hogoboom
Presiding Judge, Superior Court of
Los Angeles

1

Usually, the courts are asked to step in where the society has failed. All these things—cleaning up the rivers or the skies, running the schools systems—shouldn't be done by the courts ... People have the feeling that if they beat on the door of city hall and nothing happens, they can merely file a lawsuit.

The Christian Science Monitor, 11-27:13.

Leon Jaworski
Lawyer

2

Whether the legal system survives depends on how it functions from day to day. What must never be forgotten is that adjudications by the courts must be observed without deviation, whether we like them or not.

Before Houston Bar Association, April 28/
The Houston Post, 4-29:(A)19.

Irving R. Kaufman
Chief Judge, United States Court of
Appeals for the Second Circuit

3

The manifold protections against judicial aberrance that have already been molded into our system make change unnecessary ... More-over, to allow any simpler process for judicial removal, even one under the control of judges themselves, would eviscerate the independence

of the individuals on the bench ... Both logic and history compel the conclusion that the Constitution intended impeachment to be the only permissible procedure for judicial removal ... We must abide some judges without whom the system would be better off, because the dangers are greater on the side of an overly potent removal power. Even apparently innocent attempts to rid the bench of its disabled members—those suffering from senility, drunkenness, mental instability or other unfortunate "status" defects—may mask something more sinister. We must realize that judgments of inability still involve a crucial subjective element, and that equating unorthodoxy with mental illness has therefore often been the easiest means of eliminating intellectual ferment in totalitarian countries.

Benjamin N. Cardozo lecture, at Association of
the Bar of the City of New York, Nov. 1/
Los Angeles Times, 11-3:(1-A)7.

Thomas M. Kavanagh
Chief Justice, Supreme Court of Michigan

4

Civil laws against adultery and fornication have been on the books forever, in every country. That's not the law's business; that's God's business. He can handle it. A lot of people look to the state to save their souls. You can't make people good by passing a law.

San Francisco Examiner & Chronicle,
3-5:(This World)2.

Edward M. Kennedy
United States Senator, D-Massachusetts

5

Our legal system has failed the individual because it has done too little to equalize the power of the people to obtain satisfaction from the institutions with which they deal. In fact, the legal system is in part responsible for [the] very size and growth [of both big business and big government]. And too often when the individual finds himself in conflict with these forces, the legal system sides with the giant institution, not the small businessman or private citizen.

Before American Bar Association, New York,
Aug. 7/The Washington Post, 8-8:(A)6.

Robert J. Lipshutz
Counsel to President of the United States Jimmy Carter

1

Most of us engaged in the practice of law spend the bulk of our time protecting the property rights of our clients. A very small proportion of our collective time is spent protecting the liberty of our citizens. One of the principal reasons for this is that many of the citizens whose personal rights and liberties are threatened simply do not have the money available to employ competent legal counsel to defend them . . . I suggest that the American Bar Association—working through both legislative and judicial processes—strongly advocate a program which will require that all practicing lawyers participate substantially in the financial support of an adequate indigent-defendants legal representation.
Before American Bar Association, New York, Aug. 7/The Washington Post, 8-8:(A)6.

Lee Loevinger
Lawyer

2

What [happens] to society when the laws and regulations that are supposed to govern become so voluminous and arcane that nobody can possibly know all those that may be applicable to his activities and only a few can afford the time and expense of learning what some of them are? Obviously, this puts the power of selective enforcement in the hands of officials who may exercise it arbitrarily, punitively, for political purposes or merely eccentrically. How then do judges enforce the laws and regulations fairly, impartially and with justice? There are no good answers to such questions. What these questions do suggest is that it is quite possible to have too many laws and regulations; that the whole legal apparatus of government may collapse from its own weight; and that too many laws and regulations may paralyze society so that we have a condition approximating anarchy. Too much may be the equivalent of none at all.
Lecture, New York University, Oct. 25/ Vital Speeches, 12-15:144.

Wade Hampton McCree, Jr.
Solicitor General of the United States

3

[On lawyers' advertising] : I would obviously think that there should be some control of it. We don't want a shoddy professional product packaged by advertising so the people would be hurt; but at the same time, as the Supreme Court pointed out, the public should know that it has choices. I am not certain that our problem is any different from the other problems in the other professions. There should be some guidelines about what is acceptable advertising and what isn't.
Interview/Los Angeles Herald Examiner, 3-29:(A)1.

James R. Mills
California State Senator (D)

4

Whether the courts and judges are in trouble depends on the degree to which courts enter into the political fray . . . [For instance,] people don't understand that freedom of the press meant one thing from 1791 to 1959, and then [because of court rulings] something else. They don't understand that something which was legal and proper for a police officer is no longer [as a result of court rulings] . They look on that as legislating. The people who wrote the Constitution didn't have any idea that courts would play the role they are playing today. Because they didn't anticipate it, the system works imperfectly. Nobody knows where they stand. If courts are to have the respect they should have, some attention has got to be paid to this problem.
Panel discussion at California Judges Association meeting and State Bar convention, San Francisco, Sept. 13/Los Angeles Times, 9-15:(1)23.

Louis Nizer
Lawyer

5

[Preparation] is the be-all of good trial work. Everything else—felicity of expression, improvisational brilliance—is a satellite around the sun. Thorough preparation is that sun.
Newsweek, 12-11:100.

WHAT THEY SAID IN 1978

Lewis F. Powell, Jr.
*Associate Justice, Supreme Court of
the United States*

1

The [Supreme] Court is ... perhaps one of the last citadels of jealously preserved individualism. For the most part, we function as nine small, independent law firms.

Los Angeles Times, 7-9:(1)1.

Irving S. Shapiro
*Chairman, E. I. duPont de Nemours
& Company*

2

Lawyers in this country have always worn two hats. One is that of the counsellor, guiding clients through the legal maze, steering people away from harm to themselves or others. The other hat is that of the advocate, ready to do battle to defend the clients' interests in court. Both functions are needed, but for a variety of reasons the art of the advocate has become paramount. I believe the system is out of balance. Litigation has come to be regarded as the natural order of things, as though it were the only way to go. It's not just lawyers who think this way; it's their clients, too. Often, people don't even seek legal counsel until a dispute has gone so far that the gladiators have to fight it out in court. Litigation should be a last resort, not a knee-jerk reflex. Lawyers ought to think more like counsellors and less like advocates. After all, what's the basic mission? Not to win trials, but to seek justice for clients.

*At Delaware Law School/
The Christian Science Monitor, 12-5:23.*

Alexander I. Solzhenitsyn
Exiled Soviet author

3

People in the West have acquired considerable skill in using, interpreting and manipulating law—though laws tend to be too complicated for an average person to understand without the help of an expert. Every conflict is solved according to the letter of the law and this is considered to be the ultimate solution. If one is right from a legal point of view, nothing more is required; nobody may mention that one could

still not be entirely right, call for sacrifice and selfless risk—this would simply sound absurd. Voluntary self-restraint is almost unheard of; everybody strives toward further expansion to the extreme limit of the legal frames ... I have spent all my life under a Communist regime, and I will tell you that a society without any objective legal scale is a terrible one indeed. But a society with no other scale but the legal one is also less than worthy of man. A society based on the letter of the law and never reaching any higher fails to take advantage of the full range of human possibilities. The letter of the law is too cold and formal to have a beneficial influence on society. Whenever the tissue of life is woven of legalistic relationships, this creates an atmosphere of spiritual mediocrity that paralyzes man's noblest impulses. And it will be simply impossible to bear up to the trials of this threatening century with nothing but the supports of a legalistic structure.

*At Harvard University commencement, June 8/
Vital Speeches, 9-1:680.*

William B. Spann, Jr.
President, American Bar Association

4

[On the emergence of neighborhood storefront legal "clinics"]: Many comparatively simple matters can well be handled by lawyers through the clinic method. This [method] probably will prove more effective and less expensive because they'll be streamlined to handle this type of matter. This is sound; it presents an opportunity to young lawyers, and we will likewise see it develop rapidly.

Los Angeles Times, 2-12:(4)7.

5

[On President Carter's recent criticism of the legal profession]: It is clear that Carter has taken the popular course of attacking the professions at a time when our foreign allies are concerned over his policies, when we again appear headed for double-digit inflation, when challengers are appearing for the 1980 Presidential nomination and when his ratings in the polls are at a historic low ... There are no

(WILLIAM B. SPANN, JR.)

instant solutions to the problems of decades for him or for us. We hope name-calling will cease.
News conference, Washington, May 10/
Los Angeles Herald Examiner, 5-10:(A)12.

1

... I have ambivalent feelings about [TV] coverage of trial-court proceedings. Trials are often very long and cover several days or weeks. Naturally, few television stations would be interested in covering a trial in full. Therefore, editing becomes a major concern and there is an extreme danger that edited selections will show the sensational or the reluctant witness and not give the public the full flavor of what is transpiring in the proceedings. Also, trials involve a great number of people who are not legal professionals, such as witnesses and jurors, and there is a great danger they will be intimidated by the news coverage or distracted from the proceedings at hand. Because of these reasons, I believe that we must proceed with great caution in removing or modifying our prohibition of cameras on the trial level. But the public needs to be involved, and visual communication, television in particular, is one of our best mediums for doing so if fair and intelligent standards can be worked out for its use and strictly adhered to.
Before West Virginia State Bar Association/
The Christian Science Monitor, 5-23:27.

2

It is a growing tendency on the part of the individual to demand compensation from someone for almost any kind of misfortune that befalls him. One social researcher calls it the psychology of entitlement. For example, one man lost a finger operating his power lawn mower and sued the manufacturer. It didn't matter to him—and it apparently didn't matter to the jury, either—that his injury occurred when he was using the lawn mower to cut a hedge. He was entitled to compensation for his suffering. The most obvious results of this trend toward drop-of-the-hat litigation are economic. Juries hand down large judgments, seemingly

regardless of blame. Insurance companies pay the judgments, then raise their premiums to the insureds. Finally, the insureds pass along the higher premiums to the rest of us in the prices of their products and services ... If we persist in believing that somewhere there is a mysterious "they" who will pay for everything, then eventually that burden must become intolerable. For the society we live in is a precariously balanced and delicate instrument, founded upon the belief that rights and wrongs are distinguishable and that in the end fairness and honesty will prevail. Fairness and honesty are finding it increasingly hard to prevail in a judicial system clogged with frivolous lawsuits.
At University of Georgia School of Law/
The Wall Street Journal, 6-20:20.

John A. Sutro
Lawyer

3

[Arguing against television news coverage of trials] : ... the purpose of trials is to provide a forum for the administration of justice. Trials are not for public entertainment. They aren't a drama to be played for the public, but are held to ascertain the truth ... There isn't a television station that would show a court proceeding from the moment the judge takes the bench until the jury is discharged. That could take from a day or two to a matter of weeks. The only portions that are going to be televised are those that are dramatic—where the accused takes the stand or where the principal witness testifies or when some lawyer is making a big speech ... Courtrooms are open to the public. A person attending a trial sees exactly what goes on in the courtroom. If you're looking at TV, you see only what the camera pictures, and there's no camera that can show you everything that goes on in court.
Interview/U.S. News & World Report, 4-17:51.

Jack B. Weinstein
Judge, United States District Court
for the Eastern District of New York

4

[Supporting the use of television in news coverage of trials] : ... I don't think the public is getting the information [about courts] it needs through the written media alone ... I

WHAT THEY SAID IN 1978

(JACK B. WEINSTEIN)

think television would improve matters. Putting the eye of the public into courtrooms, so to speak, may improve the work of courts at every level—even the U.S. Supreme Court, where I think it's perfectly clear that arguments ought to be televised. Many of the arguments before the Supreme Court are substandard. A city or state official who wants the publicity and prestige of arguing a case before the Supreme Court when he's not competent to do so would be seen on television. People back home would see what's going on, and there would be pressure to let the best-qualified make arguments at the Court.

Interview/U.S. News & World Report, 4-17:51.

Sam Williams
President, Los Angeles Bar Association

1

Unfortunately, one does not learn how to try a lawsuit in law school. I'm not sure that you can adequately construct a law-school setting on how to try a lawsuit. It may very well be that the answer here is some kind of internship similar to the medical profession in terms of a program that requires that a lawyer who wants to specialize in the trial practice spend some time working with some accomplished trial lawyers. Then, before being allowed to try lawsuits on his own, the lawyer could be certified by those trial lawyers as possessing the minimum qualifications.

Interview/
Los Angeles Herald Examiner, 4-17:(A)10.

Franklin E. Zimring
Professor of law, University of Chicago

2

Because of plea-bargaining, I guess we can say, "Gee, the trains run on time." But do we like where they're going?

Time, 8-28:47.

Lew Allen, Jr.
General and Chief of Staff,
United States Air Force

1

The Air Force supports a reasonable SALT agreement—and I believe negotiations are moving us toward such an agreement. It must be recognized that we live in a world of competition and cooperation with the Soviets. Negotiation and strength are not contradictory—they are complementary. We have not lost ground to the Soviets because of arms limitations, but because the Soviets have pursued force modernization within the limits of those agreements more aggressively than we have. To continue to seek lower aggregate force levels—while maintaining a verifiable and equitable balance—does not serve our national interest. Maintaining that balance, however, is an imperative. Soviet arms are the reality of the threat. Negotiations qualify and help to contain the threat, but they should not obscure the need for strength.

The Washington Post, 10-17:(A)16.

Les Aspin
United States Representative,
D-Wisconsin

2

The dangers of Soviet violations of SALT II arise if there is a significant military advantage to be gained by cheating . . . But that is impossible. The United States under SALT II will have a very formidable strategic arsenal: almost 2,000 launchers and roughly 10,000 independently targetable warheads. To upset the balance of terror would require very large numbers indeed—numbers that would be impossible for the Soviets to acquire without cheating on so massive and pervasive a scale as to be detectable with certainty.

March 26/The Washington Post, 3-27:(A)10.

Howard H. Baker, Jr.
United States Senator, R-Tennessee

3

On the question of remaining superior to the Soviet Union, I think you get caught in the semantics of the equation. My own test is: I want the United States to remain so undoubtedly strong that Russia would never dare to challenge her. That does not necessarily mean a great superiority of arms, nuclear or otherwise, but it does mean strong *enough*. I very much fear that President Carter's defense posture so far has raised doubts in the Soviet mind, and I think this latest cancellation of the [aircraft] carrier will greatly strengthen those doubts in the Soviet mind that we have the will, the resolve and the determination to stay undoubtedly strong.

TV-radio interview/"Meet the Press,"
National Broadcasting Company, 8-20.

Frank Barnaby
Director, International Peace
Research Institute, Stockholm

4

It's obvious to most of us that increased military spending threatens the very existence of Western society. There's absolutely no sign of restraint—the $50-billion M-X [missile] program in the United States, what may be tens of billions of dollars in expenditures by the North Atlantic Treaty nations over the next few years, and many billions of dollars spent by the Soviet Union for defense against the cruise missile. If we continue to do what we are doing, unemployment is going to be much greater because of inflation. If you look at industrial investment in the United States and compare it with the possible $50-billion cost of the M-X, you will see that a private-enterprise system can't go on. You'll have to move to Draconian controls and eventually to something like the Soviet

WHAT THEY SAID IN 1978

(FRANK BARNABY)

Union ... I personally believe in the common sense of the man in the street. If people know that the world's nuclear arsenals contain a million Hiroshimas and that the use of even a small part of them would reduce the Northern Hemisphere to a radioactive desert, if they know the facts about inflation, they will demand disarmament.

Interview, United Nations, New York/
Los Angeles Times, 6-21:(1)13.

Leonid I. Brezhnev
President of the
Soviet Union; General Secretary,
Soviet Communist Party

1

A number of statements in favor of disarmament has been made lately in the West, the U.S.A. included. But the people judge not by word but by deeds. Very indicative in this respect is the question of neutron weapons. This is a new type of mass-destruction weapons. The talks that such weapons are allegedly "defensive" in character is not true to fact. These are nuclear offensive weapons, weapons designed chiefly to destroy people. This weapon increases the risks of a nuclear war ... It is high time some leaders of the West ponder in earnest on their responsibility to their own peoples, to all peoples for the destinies of the world, and show in deed the readiness to take effective steps toward curbing the arms race.

Before sailors of Soviet Pacific fleet,
Vladivostok, April 7/The New York Times, 4-8:6.

2

We are approaching the negotiations on the limitations of the feverish arms race with maximum seriousness and honesty. There does not exist such a type of weapon the Soviet Union would not be willing to limit and prohibit on the basis of agreement with the United States. What is important is that the wish to stop the arms race be sincere and not only pretended ... It is our ardent endeavor to bury the war ax so deeply into the ground that no dark forces would ever be able to dig it out again. The time

has come to realize that the feverish arms race will bring profit to nobody. It is necessary to put an end to it and honestly work for disarmament.

Before Czechoslovak Communist Party
representatives, Prague, May 31/
The Dallas Morning News, 6-1:(A)16.

3

... the principle of equal security of sides must be observed at all the stages of the struggle to achieve this goal [disarmament]. We shall not agree to the weakening of our defenses in the face of the growing military might of imperialism, no matter by what demagogic arguments such calls are camouflaged. This would bring about irreparable consequences for the cause of socialism, for the cause of the peoples' freedom and independence.

At dinner for Afghan leader Noor Mohammad Taraki,
Moscow, Dec. 5/The Dallas Times Herald, 12-6:(A)5.

Harold Brown
Secretary of Defense
of the United States

4

Deterrence and stability, not overbearing military power, are what we seek. The world remains turbulent and dangerous. The Soviets, despite all those internal handicaps and external problems, have become a serious military competitor. But they have not suddenly achieved the status of Goliath any more than we have ended up abruptly as a David at the end of an inoperative slingshot. Although both of us are heavyweights, I am confident that we remain the more agile of the two.

Before House Armed Services Committee,
Washington, Feb. 2/The New York Times, 2-3:(A)1.

5

[Saying quantity of aircraft is militarily important]: You need F-14s to defend carriers against massive air threats, such as the [Soviet] *Backfire* bomber or cruise missiles. But in other situations, in a sea-control situation, somewhat more distant from the Soviet land mass, you need lots of planes to fight other planes, to deliver air-to-ground missiles. We've had some

(HAROLD BROWN)

recent combat tests to show, to a substantial degree, that aircraft numbers count. It's not enough to have an airplane with a lot of capability if you have five, eight or 10 targets. Numbers count. So it's important to have substantial numbers, and you're only going to do that if you have relatively low-cost F-18s, which are cheaper than F-14s.

Interview, en route to Honolulu,
Feb. 16/The New York Times, 2-17:(D)11.

1

[The neutron bomb would be] an improvement and a real addition to our present nuclear armory. [It would be] useful militarily, providing a way to attack massed tank forces . . . and it does it effectively. [But] there are other ways to do the same thing . . . I would not want anyone to think it is the [only] new idea in warfare and that it would make a difference in itself.

TV-radio interview/"Face the Nation,"
Columbia Broadcasting System, 4-9.

2

The greater our strength, the less likely that it will have to be proven in combat.

Memorial Day address, Arlington, Va.,
May 29/The Dallas Times Herald, 5-30:(A)6.

3

We don't necessarily care whether the Soviets have more tanks than we do. We do care whether, in the event of a Soviet attack, we are able to throw it back. We assume that if we can produce that kind of result, we will have produced a powerful deterrent to attack. And that, rather than simply outdistancing the Soviets in numbers of tanks or any other single item, is what you should demand of the U.S. and allied defense establishments . . . We could, of course, go out and simply try to duplicate Soviet capabilities, but it would not make sense to do so. Our interests are different. We do not need four million men, 45,000 tanks or 10,000 surface-to-air missile launchers. We need whatever it takes to protect our interests. Basically, we want to

forestall or deter conflicts that could jeopardize those interests . . . It is no secret that a quarter of the Soviet non-nuclear capability is on the Chinese border; that many aspects of the Soviet logistic capability remain fragile; that current Soviet operating doctrines require larger forces than we could use for the same purposes; and that we have stronger, more reliable allies than the Soviets. The simplistic comparisons ignore all this.

Before Commonwealth Club, San Francisco,
June 23/The New York Times, 6-24:22.

4

If deterrence of nuclear war is our most fundamental defense objective—and it surely is—what counts is what Soviet civilian and military leaders believe. On that score, unfortunately, we face another uncertainty. What we see as sufficient for security may appear as quite inadequate to them. What would deter us might not deter them. What some of us consider credible as a deterrent, they may dismiss as a bluff. Great caution and careful hedging are essential in the face of these uncertainties.

Nation's Business, July:57.

5

[On the all-volunteer armed forces] : There's a lot of talk about how the volunteer force isn't working. It does have some deficiencies. But I think there have not been very many, if any, serious attempts by legislation to reintroduce the draft. So I think we have to take as a given that there are strong and, in my view, justified political inhibitions against the draft. You have to weigh those inhibitions against the deficiencies in the all-volunteer service. And I think we can live with the deficiencies in the present circumstance. If you look to the '80s, when there will be fewer people of military age, it's harder. You have to ask what you can do to make up that difference. If you can't do those things or if you can't think of anything to do, then you'll have to reconsider the all-volunteer force. But I don't think that's the situation now.

Interview/U.S. News & World Report, 7-17:35.

WHAT THEY SAID IN 1978

(HAROLD BROWN)

1

[Saying a new nuclear aircraft carrier should be eliminated from the next defense budget]: There are two reasons for that. First of all, the Congress and the President have agreed that we need to spend more on defense in fiscal '79 than in fiscal '78. They've also agreed that there's a limit to how much we can spend. That makes it very important that we spend it for the things we need the most. The nuclear carrier does not fall in that category. To stay within the budget limits, the Congress [by supporting the carrier] is taking out of the President's requests far-more-important things—things that deal with readiness, with our ability to reinforce NATO quickly, with Army ammunition, with Air Force electronic warfare, with ships and planes that aren't working because they don't have spare parts.

Interview/U.S. News & World Report, 8-28:25.

2

. . . once one starts to use nuclear weapons, even in a tactical way, it is quite likely that it will escalate. There is a kind of power train [that goes into motion] even if both sides do not want it to happen. The compression of the time for decision, the lack of information that would be available on both sides, the expected great advantage that a military commander might think would come from being the first to get in his blow, all push for rapid escalation. On the other hand, I do not think it is entirely inevitable. For that reason I think we need a spectrum of different kinds of nuclear weapons and close command and control so that if, for example, Europe is being subjected to a massive conventional attack, a few nuclear weapons can be used with the thought that perhaps—and it is only perhaps—that will be a strong enough signal so that the two sides will stop and try to find some other solution. I do not have great confidence in that at all, but I think it is worth preserving the option, providing we remember that it is by no means assured—in fact, in my view unlikely—that things could stop that way.

Before House Appropriations Subcommittee, Washington/The Washington Post, 11-11:(A)2.

3

[On the U.S. decision to recognize mainland China]: Normalization will probably make the political-military situation more stable. I think the Japanese and the [South] Koreans should and probably will feel more secure because this is a sign that the People's Republic of China has an interest in peace in the Far East. It will probably inhibit the North Koreans. It probably will reduce chances that the Soviets will take a rash military action in Northeast Asia and therefore, by reducing the threat, probably make our military capabilities there more adequate than they would otherwise be.

Interview, Washington, Dec. 28/ The New York Times, 1-3('79):(A)11.

Zbigniew Brzezinski
Assistant to President of the United States Jimmy Carter for National Security Affairs

4

SALT fits into our broader effort to enhance national security, an effort which we pursue not only through improving our own forces, but also, where appropriate, through arms control . . . I can assure you that we will never constrain our ability to meet our national-security needs. A satisfactory SALT agreement will allow us to maintain the effectiveness of the United States strategic arsenal as a deterrent against nuclear war, based on a credible retaliatory capability in the event that war should break out.

Before Foreign Policy Association, Washington, Dec. 20/The New York Times, 12-21:(A)3.

Eric Burhop
Professor of nuclear physics, University College, London

5

[On the neutron bomb]: It is the weapon *par excellence* of the aggressor who is determined to take over intact cities and industries of another country.

San Francisco Examiner & Chronicle, 5-21:(This World)28.

Jimmy Carter
President of the United States

1

Our central security problem today is maintaining our will to keep the military strength we need, while seeking every opportunity to build a better peace. Military power without detente may lead to conflict, but detente would be impossible without . . . popular support for a strong defense.

Before French American organizations,
Paris, Jan. 4/The New York Times, 1-5:(A)8.

2

. . . some believe that because we possess nuclear weapons of great destructive power, we need do nothing more to guarantee our security. Unfortunately, it is not that simple. Our potential adversaries have now built up massive forces armed with conventional weapons—tanks, aircraft, infantry and mechanized units. Those forces could be used for political blackmail and could threaten our vital interests—unless we and our allies and friends have our own conventional military strength as a counterbalance.

At Wake Forest University,
March 17/The New York Times, 3-18:9.

3

[On the Soviet Union's offer not to build a neutron bomb if the U.S. does likewise]: The Soviets know, and President [Leonid] Brezhnev knows, that the neutron weapon is designed to be used against massive and perhaps overwhelming tank forces. In the Western and Eastern European areas, the Soviets over a period of years have greatly built up their tank forces, and others, stronger than have the NATO allies. The neutron weapons are designed to equalize that inequality, along with many other steps that our country is now taking. The Soviets have no use for a neutron weapon, so the offer by Brezhnev to refrain from building the neutron weapon has no significance in the European theatre, and he knows it.

News conference, Washington,
April 25/The New York Times, 4-26:(A)20.

4

The Soviet Union and other Warsaw Pact countries pose a military threat to our [NATO] Alliance which far exceeds their legitimate security needs. For more than a decade, the military power of the Soviet Union has steadily expanded and it has grown consistently more sophisticated. In significant areas the military lead we once enjoyed has been reduced. Today, we can meet that military challenge; but we cannot be sure of countering the future military threat unless our Alliance modernizes its forces and adds additional military power.

At NATO conference, Washington,
May 30/The New York Times, 5-31:(A)14.

5

Efforts will continue [by the U.S. and Soviet Union] with negotiations toward a SALT II agreement . . . We must be willing to explore such avenues of cooperation despite the basic issues which divide us. The risks of nuclear war alone propel us in this direction. The numbers and destructive potential of nuclear weapons has been increasing at an alarming rate. That is why a SALT agreement, which enhances the security of both nations, is of fundamental importance. We and the Soviet Union are negotiating in good faith almost every day because we both know that a failure to succeed would precipitate a resumption of a massive nuclear arms race.

Before graduating class of U.S. Naval
Academy, June 7/Vital Speeches, 6-15:515.

W. Graham Claytor
Secretary of the Navy
of the United States

6

Before becoming Secretary of the Navy, I gave very little thought to the year 2000 and beyond. But we must think about that timeframe now, or our citizens of that era will judge us harshly, and with good reason. We cannot be the "now" generation or the "me" generation. We must, as Americans did in the past, make some tough decisions and some sacrifices to benefit those who follow us. The ships of the Navy we authorize today will be delivered in

WHAT THEY SAID IN 1978

(W. GRAHAM CLAYTOR)

the early or mid-1980s and spend nearly, or in some cases more than, half their service life in the 21st century. We must plan a balanced force that is capable of a full range of possible naval missions. We intend to follow one very old U.S. Navy tradition, and that is to go in harm's way. We must plan as Lewis and Clark did—to take along whatever we might need for a whole range of unforeseen contingencies. We can't do otherwise because we just don't understand the wars we haven't fought yet, especially the ones in the 21st century.

At Naval War College, March 27/
The New York Times, 3-28:10.

1

Today, the submarine poses the single most dangerous threat to our lifelines at sea. Covert by design, a modern submarine contains the power to cripple these lifelines quicker and more effectively than any other threat. It is a fact that Russian submarines suited for anti-shipping roles number over 260, while we have 78 attack submarines. It is also a fact that the prospect for near-term improvement in this ratio is poor. [But] we are more capable in this area than any enemy. The qualitative edge that we hold over the Soviets in both equipment and personnel is awesome, and our ability to orchestrate the many components [of the U.S. anti-submarine team] into an effective submarine-killer force has enormously improved in recent years.

Before National Security Industrial Association,
Washington, May 24/The New York Times, 5-25:(A)6.

Bob Dole
United States Senator, R-Kansas

2

In a tense and armed world, we have given up the B-1 bomber. We are cutting back drastically on our Navy, and the neutron bomb reportedly will be abandoned. 1600 Pennsylvania Avenue has been turned into 1600 Madison Avenue, the public-relations capital of the world.

At Republican fund-raising dinner,
Detroit, April 6/The New York Times, 4-7:(A)6.

Robert K. Dornan
United States Representative, R-California

3

[Criticizing the House vote to kill the B-1 bomber project]: If the Russians broke out the vodka bottles on June 30 when President Carter first attempted to destroy the B-1 project, they are really having a party now.... we now have a hamstrung cruise missile and a dead B-1.... this vote will come back to haunt this House over and over again.

Los Angeles Herald Examiner, 2-23:(A)3.

Thomas J. Downey
United States Representative, D-New York

4

[On the House Armed Services Committee, on which he serves]: The Committee is tremendously frustrating. The Committee will listen to facts and opinions that would lead reasonable men to conclude that we need to end the arms race, yet the Committee comes to the reverse conclusion and says we need to spend more on arms. The frustrating thing is to have the DIA or Air Force intelligence give a security briefing and explain how the Russians are ahead of us, and the Committee chortles with delight. But when they hear a briefing, as they did the other day from [CIA Director] Stansfield Turner, who gave a realistic assessment of where we were ahead and where we were behind, these people who would have us spend infinite amounts on arms seem almost depressed. They're depressed when they find that there are areas in which we surpass the Russians. It's an amazing situation.

Interview, Washington/
The New York Times, 3-16:75

Charles W. Duncan, Jr.
Deputy Secretary of
Defense of the United States

5

Despite the momentum of the Soviet [arms] build-up, all of us need to recognize a third reality. It is that where it counts, the worldwide military balance remains favorable to us ... I see no grounds for believing that today we are any worse off militarily than we were

(CHARLES W. DUNCAN, JR.)

five years ago. We were Number 1 [where it counts] five years ago; we are still Number 1 today.

Before Association of the U.S. Army, Washington, Oct. 18/The Dallas Times Herald, 10-19:(A)9.

Ralph Earle
United States Ambassador to strategic arms limitation talks with the Soviet Union

1

[On negotiation with the Russians] : It's frequently tedious and frustrating. The importance of the exercise is its reward. It goes slowly partly because the chips are so large—although I find it's more like chess than poker because of the complex interrelationship of the issues. Obviously we're negotiating on different sides of the table from the Soviets, but we're in a common endeavor. It's not a race which one will win and the others will lose. It's more like two climbers trying to get to the summit at the same time.

Time, 8-14:11.

Richard H. Ellis
General, United States Air Force; Commander-in-Chief, Strategic Air Command

2

To me, the alternatives to a SALT agreement are unacceptable: appeasement, economic exhaustion resulting from an arms race, or a nuclear holocaust. But to achieve an equitable SALT agreement will require many years of patience, determination and resolve. And while we are pursuing SALT, it is vital that we be strong. I am convinced that if a meaningful SALT agreement is to be forthcoming, our negotiators must be backed by a strong, modern, deployed nuclear deterrent force, together with new systems in development . . . The men and women of the Strategic Air Command will meet the challenges of deterrence. We have lived with that responsibility for more than 30 years. Entrusted with the proper resources, we can and will continue that heritage

so that SALT negotiations can have a full opportunity to succeed.

At New York Union League Club, New York, July 27/Vital Speeches, 9-1:704.

E. J. (Jake) Garn
United States Senator, R-Utah

3

[On U.S. SALT negotiations with the Soviet Union] : It's inconceivable to me that the U.S. could, or would, continue to negotiate in good faith with the Soviets while they violate the spirit of detente and cooperation all over the globe. . . . to a large extent, verification depends on good-will and trustworthiness. And the refusal of the Soviet Union to moderate its action does nothing to increase my confidence in their good-will and trustworthiness.

At Conservative Political Action Conference, March 18/**

4

While the U.S. has reduced its military manpower levels to around two million, the Soviets have increased theirs to over four million. We continue to cut our Navy at a time when the Soviet Navy is rapidly increasing. [President] Carter has delayed the M-X missile again, killed the B-1 bomber and badly bungled the decision of the neutron bomb. Conversely, the Soviets continue to build the *Backfire* bomber and develop a new generation of ICBMs with throw-weight advantages that exceed our missiles by 7-1. . . . we can't bury our heads and hope the Soviet challenge will simply go away.

Before World Anti-Communist League, April 29/**

Andrei A. Gromyko
Foreign Minister of the Soviet Union

5

[Criticizing U.S. proposals to produce and deploy the neutron bomb]: Some people express surprise at a powerful wave of protest on the European continent and throughout the world against the plans to produce these weapons in the U.S.A. and to subsequently station them in Western Europe. But the peoples and the world public have been quick to realize that this is a particularly vicious and cruel means of

WHAT THEY SAID IN 1978

(ANDREI A. GROMYKO)

mass destruction, intended specially to annihilate all things living ... The Soviet Union does not intend to begin the production of neutron weapons unless the United States or any other state does so. Our country declares this with full clarity: Neutron weapons must be banned once and for all. We put it straight to the peoples of certain countries where sometimes support is voiced for neutron weapons: Beware lest you be deceived; be on your guard; it is reason rather than folly that must triumph.

At disarmament conference,
United Nations, New York, May 23/
U.S. News & World Report, 6-5:22.

Alexander M. Haig, Jr.
General, United States Army;
Supreme Allied Commander/Europe

1

With respect to Soviet intentions, that's a political question. I'm concerned with capabilities. And by any objective measure or criterion, Soviet [military] capabilities far exceed what they need for defensive purposes ... The bottom line is that there are profound differences at all levels between Moscow and its allies and the Western world—political, economic, sociological—which are all grist for confrontation ... Now, we have to improve all across the board. All three elements of our triad system of defense—strategic and tactical deterrents and conventional forces—require some sense of urgency. The conventional area is a source of particular concern, and there are no cheap solutions.

Interview/Newsweek, 1-9:39.

2

[On the neutron bomb]: The utility of the weapon, its usability, its credibility generally in deterrence terms, contributes to the reality that it will not have to be used ... It's our military view [that the neutron warhead] raises, not lowers, the nuclear threshold ... [From a] purely military point of view, we feel it is a

most desirable modernization step to be undertaken by the [Atlantic] Alliance.

News conference, Washington, March 21/
The Washington Post, 3-22:(A)14.

Orrin G. Hatch
United States Senator, R-Utah

3

[President Carter] has got to stop being naive about the Russians. He needs some arms advisers to protect this country. The SALT negotiators are selling us down the river by causing us to give up our great deterrent systems. Russia's goal is still world-wide domination.

Interview/U.S. News & World Report, 2-6:20.

Elizabeth P. Hoisington
Brigadier General,
United States Army (Ret.);
Former Director, Women's Army Corps

4

[On the use of women in combat]: I have no personal experience in a combat unit, but my male colleagues tell me—and I believe—"War is hell." Heads are blown off; arms and legs are maimed; suffering is so intolerable it affects men for years. It is bad enough that our men have to endure this. But do we want young women to suffer it, too? I do not doubt the Army has women who can complete a combat course, endure three days or three weeks under field conditions, and shoot as straight as any man. But in my whole lifetime, I have never known 10 women who I thought could endure three months under actual combat conditions in an Army unit. I think we should continue to have a legal bar against women in combat units—not because they are women but because the average woman is simply not physically, mentally or emotionally qualified to perform well in a combat situation for extended periods. Nor should our country allow women to subject themselves to this experience that is so devastating and leaves such dreadful wounds—mentally and physically.

Interview/
Los Angeles Herald Examiner, 2-12:(A)11.

Jeanne M. Holm
Major General, United States
Air Force (Ret.); Former Director,
Women in the Air Force

1

I see no reason for any restrictions on the use of women as members of combat air crews. I see no reason why they should not serve aboard combat ships. The bottom line is obviously infantry. There I have a little difficulty. I think the services have to be very cautious in what they do in that regard because there are unique problems. Remember, only 8 per cent of the people in the armed forces are infantrymen. There are other forms of combat without being in the infantry ... Any reticence that the military has about increasing the numbers of women is, I am convinced, a genuine, deepseated concern about combat effectiveness. There is a concern that a potential enemy would see this as a weakening of our resolve, a weakening of our armed forces. But it's interesting to note that the Russians in World War II used large numbers of women as combatants in the military—even as pilots of combat aircraft.

Interview/Los Angeles Herald Examiner, 2-12:(A)11.

Huang Hua
Foreign Minister of the People's
Republic of (mainland) China

2

The history of the strategic-arms limitation talks since they began in 1969 has been the history of a strategic-arms race between the Soviet Union and the United States, no more and no less. The previous SALT agreement, reached after hot bargaining, provides neither for a reduction in quantity nor restriction in quality ... They have vied with each other in improving their strategic arms and rapidly developing MIRVs, and they have worked hard to develop new types of strategic weapons, such as the [Soviet] *Backfire* bomber, the [U.S.] cruise missile and [Soviet] multiple-warhead missiles. In the eight years of SALT, the Soviet Union has brought its once backward nuclear arsenal up to a par with that of the other superpower.

At United Nations, New York, May 29/
Los Angeles Times, 5-30:(1)11.

Henry C. Huglin
Brigadier General,
United States Air Force (Ret.)

3

The Soviets do not seek [military] equivalence; they are seeking a clear superiority for the political ends they believe it will achieve. I don't think that the Soviets are building up to wage a war against us, although that cannot be ruled out if they achieve a certain degree of superiority ... One may well presume, then, that if the Soviets do achieve a clear strategic superiority, they could very well have freedom of action almost anywhere in the world ... Our cancellation of the B-1 bomber was [a] unilateral initiative on our part. We didn't ask the Soviets for any trade-off on this. [Some] say that we are already looking like suckers and that, if the Soviets just stonewall it, the United States will keep giving them things.

Panel discussion, Center for the Study of
Democratic Institutions, Santa Barbara,
Calif./World Issues, June-July:15.

John H. Johns
Brigadier General,
United States Army; Director,
Pentagon drug-abuse program

4

[On the extent and effects of drug abuse in the military]: [There] is no deliberate attempt to try to beg the question or to stick our head in the sand and say that there is no impact on combat readiness. [But] when we go out to commanders and ask what are the most serious problems that impede combat readiness, this one comes far down the list. In Europe, I think the commanders list drug abuse as Number 20 of the number of things that impact on combat readiness.

U.S. News & World Report, 8-14:18.

David C. Jones
General, United States Air Force;
Chairman, Joint Chiefs of Staff

5

We've [the U.S.] never been ready for war. We weren't ready for World War I or World War II or Korea. We certainly weren't ready to fight the type of war we fought in Vietnam ... Too

WHAT THEY SAID IN 1978

(DAVID C. JONES)

often we look at readiness through binoculars, and I believe we have to look at readiness through bifocals . . . I intend to spend a great deal of time in the non-glamorous areas of readiness, of making sure we have the plans and the command and control, and the hardware and the spare parts, and that we can get our forces to Europe, and that we can do these things which are much less glamorous than buying a new aircraft or a new tank . . . It's very important that we have new systems and modernization. I'm not trying to say that "readiness now" is more important. I'm just saying that in my role as Chairman I can be a great advocate for "readiness now" . . .

Interview, Washington/
The Christian Science Monitor, 9-28: (B)2,3.

John Killick
Permanent British representative
on the North Atlantic Council

1

. . . we live with a paradox in NATO. We need more military force than is in fact required to deter the Soviet Union, in order to persuade ourselves that we are in fact deterring the Soviet Union. I don't know how to find a way out of this dilemma . . . There must be a cutoff point in NATO. We are exclusively a defensive alliance. We do not want to increase our conventional arms capability so greatly that it then looks as though we are contemplating fighting a conventional war and not using nuclear weapons, or that we are trying to acquire some kind of superiority. This kind of thing spirals. Where do you end? In all of this, it is not how we assess the things that matter, but how the other side perceives it. It is how we perceive what the other side is doing, and how they perceive what we are doing.

Interview, Center for the Study of
Democratic Institutions, Santa Barbara,
Calif./World Issues, Dec.-Jan.:3.

Henry A. Kissinger
Former Secretary of
State of the United States

2

In the crises in which I was involved, the use of naval power—particularly of [aircraft] car-

rier power—turned out to be almost invariably the crucial element . . . I cannot imagine reducing the number of our carriers. If anything, I think we should increase it.

At Naval War College/
U.S. News & World Report, 9-18:21.

3

For the greater part of the post-World War II period we could defend most threatened areas by our nuclear superiority . . . For a variety of reasons, that superiority has eroded . . . That means that we and our allies must have a capacity for regional defense inside and outside the NATO area. If we don't develop this, then in the '80s we're going to pay a very serious price. The first installments are already visible.

Interview, New York/Newsweek, 12-11:56.

Clare Boothe Luce
Former American
diplomat and playwright

4

The United States has a gross national product, or income, of almost $2-trillion. Its problem is to decide how that money should be best spent for the well-being of the United States. The first job of a President is to protect the well-being and security of his own country. Now, we have quite enough money—if we haven't, who has?—to maintain a defense that will keep ourselves and the West secure. We have preferred to spend our money on all kinds of benefits rather than on the protection of our own country. I hope that will change. It ought to change because the United States is very rapidly becoming the Number 2 power in the world; and anyone who reflects on the nature of the Number 1 power, the Soviet Union, has no reason for satisfaction.

Interview/
Los Angeles Herald Examiner, 7-2: (A)13.

5

Central to idealistic pacifist thought has always been the totally irrational belief that armaments are the cause of war. And that a nation whose intentions are sincerely peaceful can, by disarming itself, produce a similar re-

(CLARE BOOTHE LUCE)

sponse from its enemies. History does not offer a single example of a nation that ever preserved its independence by rolling over and showing its belly.

Vital Speeches, 8-15:645.

George H. Mahon
United States Representative, D-Texas

1

[Arguing against development of the B-1 bomber]: Both countries [the U.S. and Soviet Union] have far more than is needed to obliterate each other, B-1 or no B-1.... let's put it to bed.

Los Angeles Herald Examiner, 2-23:(A)3.

2

[Arguing against the building of a new nuclear aircraft-carrier]: Does anybody think that the building of a new nuclear carrier will deter war with the Soviet Union? I don't think so. If war comes, it will be fought with missiles—bang, bang, bang. There is no sense in appropriating more than two billion [dollars] for the carrier.

Before the House, Washington/
The New York Times, 8-8:(A)1,16.

Michael M. May
Associate director,
Lawrence Livermore Laboratory

3

The need for sufficient invulnerability has been recognized for many years. By far the larger fraction of money we have spent on strategic systems has gone to improving the survivability and reliability of silos, submarines, aircraft, to less vulnerable communication *systems*, and not to the nuclear weapons themselves or to the missiles ... No one knows what the answer is as of now. Maybe it will be mobile missiles of some kind, maybe in tunnels, maybe more silos for the Soviets to shoot at than we have missiles, maybe better-defended missiles. But I can tell you that, whatever the answer, it will be costly and difficult to carry out. It will have an environmental impact, a political im-

pact, an impact on SALT negotiations. It will surely have many opponents, who will say that we have enough weapons already and ask how long are we going to continue the arms race. There will be no popular answer. No one will find it easy to say that a piece of the arms race must go on—that some changes have been and will continue to be necessary if we are to maintain any deterrent capability.

Before Commonwealth Club, San Francisco,
March 10/Vital Speeches, 6-1:487.

George S. McGovern
United States Senator,
D-South Dakota

4

I argued in 1972 that the United States should take the lead in [arms] reduction—cuts of $10-billion a year for three years in the Pentagon budget. Since that time we've moved in the opposite direction. We're now approaching a military budget of $130-billion, with proposals for $10-billion more in the coming fiscal year. I think the nature of the Soviet leadership has changed. Cautious, conservative, albeit tough-minded men, are running the Kremlin today. And we ought to act accordingly.

Interview/San Francisco
Examiner & Chronicle, 1-29:(This World)48.

Robert Moskin
Author; Former foreign editor,
"Look" magazine

5

The question is repeatedly raised whether we still need a Marine Corps. I think American imperialism in military form is over. It began very early, and ended in Vietnam. I don't think this country will seek territorial conquest in the future. Therefore, I don't feel the Marine Corps will seize and hold territory for acquisition. But there has been hardly a year in our history when Marines weren't put ashore someplace to do things like protect the rights of American seamen. I think it will continue to be a need to have a force that can project power and intervene when American interests are at stake. It is extremely difficult to mass armies and tanks any more. We'll see warfare between highly

WHAT THEY SAID IN 1978

(ROBERT MOSKIN)

mobile, very skilled fighters. This is what the Marine Corps is all about. Their job is to kill and win battles. They do that job very well.

*Interview/ San Francisco
Examiner & Chronicle, 1-8: (Scene)3.*

Charles C. Moskos, Jr.
Sociologist, Northwestern University 1

[On the type of people enlisting in the all-volunteer Army]: Whereas the black soldier is fairly representative of the black community in terms of education and social background, white entrants of recent years are coming from the least-educated sectors of the white community. My stays with Army units also leave the distinct impression that many of our young enlisted white soldiers are coming from non-metropolitan areas. I am even more impressed by what I do not often find in line units: urban and suburban white soldiers of middle-class origins. In other words, the all-volunteer Army is attracting not only a disproportionate number of minorities, but also an unrepresentative segment of white youth.

Lecture/Los Angeles Times, 8-16: (1-A)4.

Paul H. Nitze
*Former Deputy Secretary of
Defense of the United States;
U.S. delegate to SALT talks, 1969-74*

2

Today almost no one says that the SALT agreement that we are negotiating [with the Soviet Union] will do much for us. They merely say it could be worse if we don't have an agreement and that you really have to look to SALT III. But somehow or other they assume that, while negotiating SALT III, the U.S. negotiating position is going to have greater power behind it than now, so that we will be able to negotiate things that are not negotiable now. I don't see what is going to bring that about. As my Russian friends say, "We are not philanthropists." I think the focus has been on the wrong point in the last five years. The focus of almost everybody's attention has been on a SALT agreement. Relatively little attention has gone

into the much more fundamental problem. That is: How do we maintain rough equivalence with the Soviet Union's great effort? How do we avoid an instability in the strategic nuclear situation? How do we minimize the dangers of a nuclear war? This is where our effort ought to have been focused. SALT, I believe, has taken our eye off that.

Interview/U.S. New & World Report, 3-13:56.

Richard M. Nixon
Former President of the United States

3

What we [the U.S.] have done or seem to have done up to this time by canceling the B-1 [bomber], by not going forward with the cruise [missile], is to go up to the Soviets and say, "We're not going ahead; now we want you to stop this and that." And all they'll do is thumb their nose at us.

*Interview, San Clemente, Calif., Aug. 18/
The Dallas Times Herald, 8-20: (A)12.*

Sam Nunn
United States Senator, D-Georgia

4

Aided by a strategic-force budget twice as large as ours, the Soviets have introduced no fewer than eight new strategic ballistic missiles, compared to only two for the United States during the same period. Also during the same period, the Soviets have expanded and modernized their ground forces, transformed their navy from a coastal defense force into an offensive fleet and rebuilt what was once a limited tactical air force into a powerful, aggressive air armada ... I have slowly and sadly come to the conclusion that, for the Soviets, their strategic programs drive their arms negotiations while, for the United States, our arms negotiations drive our strategic programs.

*At Warner Robins Air Force Base, Georgia,
July 17/The New York Times, 7-18: (A)8.*

Bernard W. Rogers
*General and Chief of Staff,
United States Army*

5

Our mission is to take the funds made available and to use them as effectively as we

(BERNARD W. ROGERS)

can. We're going to have the kind of Army and armed forces the people of this country want. And the way they express their will is through their elected representatives. It is the people who have to make up their minds on our priorities.

U.S. News & World Report, 7-17:37.

The Soviets have surpassed us militarily and will continue to threaten us. Furthermore, they are disarming us at SALT. Every proposal weakens the U.S. and strengthens the Soviets. This is of particular danger to NATO. The Soviets might soon be able to do anything they want just by threat. It's kind of like this: Where does an 800-pound gorilla sit? Anywhere he wants.

Interview/People, 7-10:26.

John K. Singlaub
Major General, United States Army;
Chief of Staff, Army's Forces Command

1

[Criticizing President Carter's decision to postpone production of the neutron bomb]: I think the decision not to produce the neutron bomb without some compensating concession from the other side is like throwing your trump card away in a game of bridge. I think it's ridiculous ... To give that up, I personally feel, is militarily unsound. I think it's wishful thinking to suggest that the Soviet Union might, through the goodness of its heart, also do something like it.

Before ROTC cadets,
Georgia Institute of Technology,
April 27/Los Angeles Times, 4-28:(1)4.

Robert N. Smith
Former Assistant Secretary for
Health Affairs, Department of
Defense of the United States

4

[On the effects of drug abuse in the military]: As far as I am concerned, any use, whether drug or alcohol, is too much and has an adverse impact on personal and unit effectiveness. The effects could range from none to inability to muster, to mistakes leading to personal death or injury or to critical tactical-decision mistakes that could hazard entire units ... We may not find out the real answers to combat effectiveness until it is too late in a literal trial by fire.

U.S. News & World Report, 8-14:19.

John K. Singlaub
Major General, United States Army
(Ret.); Former Chief of Staff,
Army Forces Command

2

[On the all-volunteer armed forces]: The overall-quality of the soldier is as good as can be expected considering the declining reading and writing skills of Americans. But, in another way, it's a disaster. We have to have a total Army, with adequate numbers of National Guard and Army Reserves. The absence of the draft has eliminated the incentive to join the Reserves and has reduced our manpower pool to a dangerous level. The volunteer Army isn't working, and some form of selective service should be restored.

Interview/People, 7-10:26.

John C. Stetson
Secretary of the
Air Force of the United States

5

We have reduced our actual training and flying to the point where, if we reduce it further, it's going to get counter-productive. We're using simulators, and they're good, they're excellent, but they're still in the last analysis no substitute for actual flying experience. It's not only a matter of training, it's a matter of psychology. It's a little difficult to bring people along in the Air Force and the other services, and tell them they're pilots, and then they don't fly very much.

News conference, San Francisco,
May 5/Los Angeles Times, 5-6:(1)20.

WHAT THEY SAID IN 1978

James B. Stockdale
Admiral, United States Navy;
President, Naval War College

1

Management skills are not the essence of a military man's profession. The winning of wars is more a matter of national and personal commitment than the acquiring of the ability to administer technology.

Interview, Naval War College/
Los Angeles Times, 7-30:(1-A)2.

Malcolm Toon
United States Ambassador to the
Soviet Union

2

No SALT agreement we arrive at [with the Soviet Union] is going to rest on the element of trust. [U.S. arms negotiator Paul] Warnke and others have made it perfectly clear, and I agree with them, that any SALT agreement—any agreement at all, for that matter—with the Soviets must be verifiable and self-enforcing. By the latter, I mean that, if the Russians don't live up to whatever bargains or commitments they make, then we are relieved of our commitments as well.

Interview, Moscow/
U.S. News & World Report, 1-9:28.

John G. Tower
United States Senator, R-Texas

3

[Criticizing President Carter's decision not to proceed with production of the neutron bomb]: The very survival of Western Europe depends on the availability of every weapons system modern technology can provide to our NATO forces. I find it totally incomprehensible that the President, in the face of reported virtual unanimous opposition among his advisers ... would give even the most casual consideration to such a move as the arbitrary cancellation of this important addition to our tactical arsenal.

Washington, April 5/
The Dallas Times Herald, 4-6:(A)11.

Cyrus R. Vance
Secretary of State of the United States

4

New weapons systems acquired by one side stimulate the other side to develop more-sophisticated counter-measures. The net effect is the expansion of weapons systems on both sides without real increase in the security of either.

Before American Society of
Newspaper Editors, Washington,
April 10/The Dallas Times Herald, 4-11:(A)2.

5

... in both our defense efforts and our arms-control negotiations, our basic aim is to strengthen the security of the United States and that of our allies. This has been and will always be the fundamental touchstone of our policy. That is why we are involved in SALT—because a sound agreement will improve Western and global security. Without an agreement, our technological and economic strength would enable us to match any Soviet strategic build-up. But a good agreement can provide more security with lower risk and cost.

Before Royal Institute of
International Affairs, London,
Dec. 9/The New York Times, 12-10:(1)22.

Yuli M. Vorontsov
Soviet delegate to Belgrade
conference on the Helsinki Agreement on
European Security and Cooperation

6

[On U.S. development of the neutron bomb]: It is those who are hawking the neutron bomb to Europe and peddling the extermination of human beings without damaging houses, cars and other property who speak the loudest about human rights. One cannot imagine anything more cynical than that.

At the Belgrade conference, March 9/
The New York Times, 3-10:(A)3.

John Patrick Walsh
American diplomat

7

In the past 10 years, while we drifted in somnolence, [the Soviets] have out-produced

(JOHN PATRICK WALSH)

us in all aspects of strategic and conventional weaponry. We have surrendered our strategic superiority of a decade ago and now shakily maintain some form of parity or equivalence. "Second to none" as a description of our military posture has a hollow ring for the richest and the most innovative country in the world. American defense expenditures as a percentage of national production and the Federal budget are at the lowest level in the past quarter century. With a far smaller economy, Soviet military outlays substantially exceed ours. The arms race is accelerating and our will and wisdom are being put to the test. The Soviets cannot reach their evident goal of military superiority unless we permit them to do so.

Before English Speaking Union, Montgomery, Alabama, Feb. 17/Vital Speeches, 6-1:504.

Paul C. Warnke
Director, Arms Control and Disarmament Agency of the United States

1

A SALT treaty is not a reward for Soviet good behavior. It's a way in which we advance our own interests.

To reporters, Washington, March 1/ The Washington Post, 3-2:(A)21.

2

[If there were no SALT treaty,] that would mean an unrestrained nuclear-arms competition. At the present point, the Soviets have a whole fifth generation of strategic weapons under development. They unquestionably would go ahead and deploy them. Under those circumstances, they would go up to something like 3,000 strategic nuclear-delivery vehicles. Now, we could match that. But some experts have estimated it would cost us something like $20-billion additional within the next few years to do it. But, more important than cost, if the nuclear-arms competition continues, strategic stability may be damaged. You could then have a situation in which one side or the other could

feel that it was in its interests—maybe essential to its interests—to start a nuclear war at a time of crisis.

Interview/U.S. News & World Report, 3-13:55.

R. James Woolsey
Under Secretary of the Navy of the United States

3

We have no better idea today what specific wars or crises we are going to have to deal with between now and 2010—32 years from now—than we had in 1946—32 years ago—about the crises of today. Who of you here foresaw in 1946 that in 1978 our thinking about when and how we might need naval forces could be significantly influenced by a commitment to Israel, the need to protect sea lines of communication to Persian Gulf oil, a split between Communist China and the U.S.S.R., and U.S.-Soviet parity in strategic nuclear weapons?

At Naval War College, March 28/ The New York Times, 4-4:16.

4

Naval forces may be the most acceptable form of military presence in crisis situations. They can convey, if the policy-maker chooses, calculated ambiguity and calibrated response. Their presence does not irrevocably commit the United States to a given course of action. They do, however, seriously complicate the calculations of opposing parties. U.S. fighting forces can be assembled for action without using bases in other nations. Indeed, naval forces help make us comparatively indifferent to the vicissitudes of other nations' policies about base rights, whether for us or for hostile countries, and naval forces thus help make us more able to tolerate shifts in political winds without feeling our vital interests are injured. If a crisis is resolved satisfactorily, naval forces can be withdrawn with limited fanfare. In sum, naval forces provide a policy-maker with important flexibility and a tool for orchestrating events.

At Naval War College, March 28/ Vital Speeches, 7-1:566.

Politics

James Abourezk
United States Senator, D-South Dakota

1

I personally happen to think President Carter is a man decently motivated, and if I compare him with past Administrations that I have worked here at the same time in Washington with—and that is the Nixon and Ford Administrations—I would have to say they are decent, they are not mean, they are not vindictive, by and large. I think they make a great many mistakes in their decisions. He shouldn't listen to [Energy Secretary James] Schlesinger on energy policy, for one thing. I don't think he ought to listen to [National Security Affairs Adviser Zbigniew] Brzezinski on policies *vis-a-vis* the Soviet Union. Those two people are very hardlined people, and I think they give him the wrong advice. I think, left to his own instincts, he would do an excellent job of being President. Unfortunately, he is not trusting his own instincts; he is listening to some very bad advice.

TV-radio interview/"Meet the Press,"
National Broadcasting Company, 8-6.

Herbert E. Alexander
Professor of political science,
University of Southern California

2

The public is quite cynical [about the amount of political spending]. But consider this: In 1976, all elective and party politics cost some $540-million. It sounds like a lot of money, but it is very little measured against the gross national product or against disposable personal income. It is peanuts—less than 1 per cent of the combined Federal, state and municipal budgets. It is less than the two largest corporation advertising budgets.

Interview/
U.S. News & World Report, 10-16:29.

John B. Anderson
United States Representative,
R-Illinois

3

The great failure of the Republican Party in my mind to date is that somehow the country, and I believe in many cases wrongly, perceives us to be less compassionate, less humane in our approach to the issues than the Democratic Party. And, as a result, I think a moderate has to emphasize that even though he is in favor of a balanced budget, even though he thinks we have got to cut back on Federal spending, eliminate some of the waste in government programs, particularly the programs that had developed in the last 10 or 15 years, that we cannot ignore the plight of America's cities; we cannot ignore the fact that this [Carter] Administration, after two years, still has an unemployment rate of almost 35 per cent among the teen-age blacks of America. I think Republicans have got to be talking about human problems and indicate that even though they don't think all of the answers to those problems lie at the Federal level—that we have to look to the private sector, that we have to look to state and local government to make their contribution, to share in the solution of these problems—that we are not turning our back on the plight of minorities, on the plight of unemployed young people, on the plight of our cities, some of the other great social problems that still lie untended on the nation's doorstep.

TV-radio interview/"Meet the Press,"
National Broadcasting Company, 12-10.

Griffin B. Bell
Attorney General of the United States

4

[Defending the Carter Administration's controversial ouster of Philadelphia U.S. Attorney

(GRIFFIN B. BELL)

David Marston]: It is not wrong that a new President and Attorney General should seek to appoint persons of high quality who, in general, share their philosophy and views on the major issues involved in effective law enforcement.

Before House Subcommittee on Courts, Civil Liberties and Administration of Justice, Washington, March 13/ The Dallas Times Herald, 3-14:(A)6.

1

[On those convicted of Watergate crimes who are writing books]: I never thought you ought to profit out of crime. But it seems to be one of the big things in our country—to turn these people into heroes. We have a strange bent of mind in America: You get into some kind of trouble and you can write a book. You do very well indeed. You can also become a campus lecturer.

Before Stanford Sloan Executive Fellows, Washington, March 28/ Los Angeles Times, 3-29:(1)8.

2

People ought to worry about the Presidency. It is a vital institution. Nobody ever suggested 435 House members and 100 Senators could direct the government. Remember President Lyndon B. Johnson? We drove him out of office because of the Vietnam war. [Richard] Nixon was the "imperial President" and resigned when he was about to be impeached. [Gerald] Ford was liked by the average person and the press seemed to like him. But he was made into a joke; he was always pictured as falling down or bumping his head. As far as I know, they haven't pictured [President] Carter falling down or bumping his head, but they're systematically weakening the Presidency by paying so much attention to the polls. The press and many politicians pay too much attention to the polls and not enough attention to the substance of what Carter has done.

Interview/ Los Angeles Times, 8-27:(1)7.

Julian Bond
Georgia State Senator (D)

3

Politics is not the art of the possible, as it is taught in high-school civics, or even the art of compromise, as you learn in Pol. Sci. 101. It is a much more serious art—the art of seeing who gets how much of what from whom.

The Dallas Times Herald, 5-4:(E)5.

Peter G. Bourne
Former Special Assistant to President of the United States Jimmy Carter for Health Issues

4

[Comparing his just-announced resignation as Special Assistant, because of the revelation of a drug prescription he wrote illegally for a White House employee, with last year's resignation of Bert Lance as Federal Budget Director because of controversial past financial dealings]: I'm hesitant to draw the Lance analogy. But after watching what happened to him, I know this [Bourne's resignation] is the best way. Maybe I wouldn't feel this way if I hadn't seen what Bert went through. But I did—God, didn't we all?— and I'm not going to go through it, too.

Interview, Washington, July 20/ The New York Times, 7-21:(A)8.

Dolph Briscoe
Governor of Texas (D)

5

Some candidates for public office will promise anything to get political support. That always has been the case and I'm sure it always will be. When they talk with school teachers, they promise massive pay raises for school teachers. When they talk with any organization interested in state spending, the sky is the limit on the promises they make. Then they have the audacity to claim these promises will not result in new taxes . . .

Victoria, Texas, Feb. 15/ The Dallas Times Herald, 2-16:(A)19.

Bill Brock
Chairman, Republican National Committee

6

It is very difficult these days for us to defeat a sitting Democrat, because the Congress in the

(BILL BROCK)

last 10 years has passed so many bills to advantage itself, to make it impossible to challenge a sitting member of Congress. They have the frank, where they use the taxpayers' money to write every constituent once a week if they want to. They increased their own pay $13,000 a year; they increased their staff allowances. They have got huge advantages over a challenger. That does bother me. It really does, because it makes it more difficult for all of us who consider ourselves just people to freshen the process with some new faces.

TV-radio interview/"Meet the Press,"
National Broadcasting System, 1-8.

1

It is very disturbing to see the evolution of single-issue groups, because it can lead to a very negative kind of politics where people vote "no" on one topic and ignore the whole complex of issues that affects us. Candidates should be judged on the sum total of all their parts: their ability, integrity, their stance on a whole range of problems. This trend is growing, though, because both parties have failed to respond to some very fundamental concerns that people in this country have. Voters are fed up with having a candidate come home and say one thing, then go to Washington and do something very different. The solution is to get the parties back to where the people are.

Interview/U.S. News & World Report, 9-4:22.

William F. Buckley, Jr.
Political columnist; Editor,
"National Review"

2

[On the upcoming 1978 national elections]: Any Democrat who adopts the Republican platform can't lose.

Nov. 6/Los Angeles Times, 11-8:(1)1.

James MacGregor Burns
Professor of political science,
Williams College

3

TV, plus the tendency of politicians to build and rely on their own organizations, has pul-

verized the party system. Now we have a bunch of Chinese war tongs.

Newsweek, 11-6:58.

Robert C. Byrd
United States Senator, D-West Virginia

4

[On President Carter's accomplishments in office]: Unemployment is down. Housing starts are up. Real income is up. The number of people who are employed is the highest ever: 94.5 million people. We have passed a minimum-wage bill. We shored up the Social Security system, which was about to collapse. We passed a major farm bill. And look at the international initiatives: NATO has been strengthened; the Turkish embargo has been lifted; there has been a new momentum in our movement toward normalization with the People's Republic of China; the Panama Canal treaty has been passed, which improves our relations with South America; the President is going for the [Egyptian-Israeli] summit at Camp David. There is much to his credit that is overlooked, and I think that when one focuses on the record he will say, "Yes, he is competent. He has made mistakes, but he is getting good support from the Congress. This is good for the American people."

TV-radio interview/"Meet the Press,"
National Broadcasting Company, 8-13.

Bruce F. Caputo
United States Representative, R-New York

5

[On the Korean influence-buying scandal involving U.S. Congressmen]: We covered the most odious episode in the story today [during committee testimony]. It was a conspiracy of American businessmen, Congressmen and Koreans to make blatantly improper payments over a sustained period with U.S. taxpayers' money. The details are revolting.

To reporters, Washington/
Los Angeles Herald Examiner, 3-3:(A)6

Jimmy Carter
President of the United States

6

[On the firing of Philadelphia U.S. Attorney David Marston, who claims it was politically

(JIMMY CARTER)

motivated due to his corruption inquiry involving U.S. Congressmen] : I see nothing improper in the handling of the case. I made a campaign commitment that any appointee to a position as U.S. Attorney or a judgeship would be appointed on the basis of merit, and this campaign commitment will be carried out. There has also been a statement made by me during the campaign that, all other factors equal, I would choose someone for those positions, or even for the Supreme Court, whose basic political philosophy was compatible with mine ... I think that the Attorney General [Griffin Bell] has handled the [Marston] case as well as possible ... and, so far as I know, there is no impropriety at all.

News conference, Washington, Jan. 30/
The Washington Post, 1-31:(A)9.

1

[On his decline in the popularity polls] : ... I don't agree that there is a dramatic shift in image. I think the poll results have been fairly stable for four or five months and, as has been the case with previous Presidents, after the flush of victory is over and the very difficult responsibilities descend on the shoulders of a President, the high expectations of the people that problems would be resolved overnight tend to cause a deterioration in public expectancy and sometimes a feeling of discouragement.

Before American Society of Newspaper Editors,
Washington/San Francisco Examiner
& Chronicle, 4-16:(A)2.

2

[Saying political candidates do not ride a President's coattails very much any more] : I think there is a minimal amount of coattail-riding these days, not just because of me but also my immediate predecessors. The new classes in Congress are ... highly independent. They ran their campaigns in 1974 and 1976 basically the same way I did, on priding oneself on not being part of the establishment, not being dominated by the political leaders, being tied directly to the constituents, being inde-

pendent in attitude and in the legislative process ... There is much less interrelationship between individual members of Congress and the popularity or unpopularity of an incumbent President.

Interview, Washington/
The Christian Science Monitor, 5-9:11.

3

My esteem in the country has gone up substantially. It is very nice, now, that when people wave at me, they use all their fingers.

At Democratic fund-raising dinner, Baltimore/
Time, 10-30:32.

Charles W. Colson
Former Special Counsel to the
President of the United States
(Richard M. Nixon)

4

I suppose that we are all idealistic, as Americans. We would like to think that everybody [in government] thinks, first thing every morning, what they can do best for their country. But the reality is that politics are always going to creep into it. There will always be guys around thinking of ways to cut corners and [give] expedient answers, how to look good in the eyes of the President. How to gain favor with the President. If anybody read George Reedy's book about the twilight of the Presidency in the [Lyndon] Johnson years, there should have been a very good warning about what was coming in the Nixon years. But we somehow feel that when you change people you somehow change the nature of man. That just isn't so.

Interview/Los Angeles Herald Examiner, 4-18:(A)8.

Silvio O. Conte
United States Representative,
R-Massachusetts

5

[President] Carter has got to stop drifting, take a stand, take his lumps and battle on through. He's been too much like New England weather. It changes quickly.

Interview/U.S. News & World Report, 2-6:20.

WHAT THEY SAID IN 1978

Justin W. Dart
Chairman, Dart Industries

1

[Saying business should get more involved in politics] : We feel that the first responsibility of a corporation, the first social responsibility of a corporation, is to participate in the political process. The United States is the last bastion of free enterprise on the face of the earth, and if we don't set an example here, we've not only let down our children and our grandchildren, but we've let down the rest of the world.

Before businessmen, Minneapolis/
Los Angeles Times, 6-18:(1)4.

True Davis
Former United States Ambassador to
Switzerland

2

I cannot associate blue-jeans with the White House. I have been very disappointed with the lack of decorum there ever since [President] Carter got in. Discipline of mind goes with discipline of dress.

Interview/"W": a Fairchild publication, 3-31:2.

John D. Ehrlichman
Former Assistant to the President of
the United States (Richard M. Nixon)
for Domestic Affairs

3

[On his just getting out of prison after serving time for the Watergate affair] : I have done my time. I don't think he [former President Nixon who resigned from office but did not go to prison] is ever going to stop doing *his* time.

Time, 5-15:67.

Gerald R. Ford
Former President of the United States

4

[On President Carter's performance in office] : Using golf phraseology, he's hit a few out of bounds, had a number of double bogeys, quite a few bogeys, a few pars and not many birdies. His constant flip-flopping is his fundamental difficulty. The inconsistencies and uncertainties worry people. One day he's here and

the next day he's there. It's a pragmatic approach that has no ideological consistency.

Interview, Vail, Colo./Newsweek, 8-14:18.

Douglas A. Fraser
President, United Automobile Workers
of America

5

I think that the labor movement should be much more exacting and demanding when they are endorsing [political] candidates, and I believe that we have to tighten up the process of endorsement. As you know, the freshmen and sophomore class that entered the Congress—not all of them by any means, thank goodness—just have no principle; they have no direction; they have no commitment. The only commitment they have is for their own re-election.

TV-radio interview/"Meet the Press,"
National Broadcasting Company, 10-1.

6

The strategy we propose aims to make the Democratic Party in fact what in principle it has proclaimed itself to be since the New Deal— a progressive party struggling against the reactionary capitalist money power of the Republicans; to transform America into a fair and decent society.

At social conference, Detroit, Oct. 17/
U.S. News & World Report, 10-30:40.

Fred W. Friendly
Professor of journalism, Columbia
University; Former president,
Columbia Broadcasting System News

7

Jimmy Carter understands the impact of the media but not that the President is, in the words of Walter Lippmann, the nation's teacher. Thus far he has not explained the biggest issues—energy, disarmament, the Panama Canal—to the American people. There is too much exposure of a non-substantial nature— appearances at editors' conferences, arrivals at airports—and too many gimmicks. On the call-in show, [newscaster] Walter Cronkite looked like the President, Carter like the other fellow. I

(FRED W. FRIENDLY)

want to see the President in a cardigan sweater because he has been playing golf or shooting marbles with [his daughter] Amy—not when he's talking to 45 million people about energy. He was probably wearing a suit and changed into a sweater.

People, 1-9:12.

Curtis Gans
Chairman, Committee for the Study of the American Electorate

1

Over the last decade, events such as Vietnam and Watergate have led to a disillusionment on the part of the electorate that their vote can make any difference in their lives or the course of the country. There hasn't been anything to rekindle the feeling that their votes have some efficacy.

Nov. 9/Los Angeles Times, 11-10:(1)16.

John W. Gardner
Founder, Common Cause

2

... the 96th [Congress] will float in on the greatest flood of special-interest money in history. The Johnstown Flood will look like a trickle when you see that money pouring in. That means, in the coldest terms, we're going to get a Congress that's heavily indebted to heavy donors. Campaigns cost enormous amounts of money these days, and you can't really blame Congressmen. They have to get the money if they are going to run; it's the system that forces them into this.

Interview/
Los Angeles Herald Examiner, 9-22:(A)13.

Valery Giscard d'Estaing
President of France

3

Do not believe those [candidates] who promise too much. You do not in private life. Why should you in public life?

Los Angeles Times, 3-8:(1)17.

Floyd K. Haskell
United States Senator, D-Colorado

4

Incumbents do have an advantage [at election time]. But they also have a disadvantage— they've got a voting record.

The Washington Post, 2-18:(A)10.

5

[On his recent loss in his bid for re-election]: Incumbency didn't help me. I don't think incumbency, *per se,* means a damn thing. People would keep telling me to talk about being subcommittee chairman of this and subcommittee chairman of that—frankly, I don't think people could care less about it. People don't care. The guy mowing his lawn, he doesn't give a goddamn whether some clown is chairman of some subcommittee on the Energy Committee. He'll have a visceral reaction, a tummy reaction, as to whether that guy more clearly has his interest at heart than the other fellow.

Interview, Washington/
The Washington Post, 12-4:(A)1.

John A. Howard
Director, Rockford College Institute

6

The advent of the welfare state has ... fundamentally skewed the basis on which the voters judge who is the best candidate for national office. To an increasing extent, honesty, breadth of knowledge, good judgment and the other sound and honorable qualities which one would hope to find in candidates for high office are being subordinated to a very different set of characteristics. In the new order, when voters are concerned about what benefits the elected officer will provide for them, promises, hypocrisy, deceit, log-rolling and clout are fast becoming the characteristics of electability.... of 21 Congressmen linked in one way or another with political wrongdoing or personal scandal prior to the 1976 election, 19 were re-elected. Criminal activity and flagrant immorality have

WHAT THEY SAID IN 1978

become insignificant in the view of the ever-greedier voters of the welfare state.

At American Farm Bureau Tax and Spending
Limitation Conference, Chicago, Sept. 18/
Vital Speeches, 11-1:40.

Eugene Ionesco
Playwright

1

There are three types of men: politicians, scientists and humanists. The politicians are the origin of all the evil in the world. Politics create rhinoceroses and fanaticism. Politicians are neither scientists nor humanists. The world certainly will be better off when political men begin to deal with the administration of things more than the administration of men. The best leaders would be computers because computers have no passions. We should be more occupied with culture and art than politics. Then the world would be a better place.

Interview, Los Angeles/
Los Angeles Herald Examiner, 10-1:(F)8.

Jesse L. Jackson
Civil-rights leader; President,
Operation PUSH (People United to
Save Humanity)

2

Black people need the Republican Party to compete for us so that we have real alternatives for meeting our needs. The Republican Party needs black people if it is to ever compete for national office or, in fact, to keep it from becoming an extinct party. Hands that picked cotton in 1966 did pick the President in 1976, and could very well be the difference in 1980.

Before Republican National Committee,
Washington, Jan. 20/
Los Angeles Times, 1-21:(1)15.

3

The only protection people have politically is to remain necessary. We [blacks] must pursue a strategy that prohibits one [political] party from taking us for granted and another party from writing us off. The only protection we have against political genocide is to remain necessary.

Before Republican National Committee, Jan. 20/
The Christian Science Monitor, 5-4:18.

Leon Jaworski
Lawyer; Special Counsel, House Ethics
Committee; Former Special Government
Prosecutor for Watergate

4

[On Watergate]: Still fresh on my mind is the sadness of seeing one of the great tragedies of modern history—men who once had fame in the hands sinking to infamy, all because their goals were of the wrong dreams and aspirations. The teaching of right and wrong had been forgotten, and little evils were permitted to grow into great evils, and small sins to escalate into big sins.

Before Houston Bar Association, April 28/
The Houston Post, 4-29:(A)19.

5

[Saying he is quitting as Special Counsel and terminating his investigation into the Korean influence-buying scandal in Congress]: The fact that we investigated the circumstances, got all the testimony we could have gotten, is going to have in the end a salutary effect, because it's going to be known, by any public official, especially Congressmen, that there was something different about the receipt of these gifts and monies, that this was wrong. And this is going to be a warning to anyone who might in the future be inclined to stray from the right, that these are unethical acts. And they are going to think twice about it next time. I feel it was worthwhile to go as far as we did. And actually, we went a lot further than we ever expected to go. That we couldn't finally resolve the issue is, of course, to be deplored; but we've made every conceivable effort. There is nothing more we can do. When you're through, you're through.

Interview, Houston, July 27/
The New York Times, 7-29:20.

Merrill Jensen
Professor of history, University of
Wisconsin, Madison

1

If these 18th-century [political] figures were alive today, they could give cards and spades to any of our present-day politicians. They could take the game away from any of them. When it comes to logrolling, dirty politics, hanky-panky, bribery—you name it—our Founding Fathers often behaved in a way that would make many 20th-century politicians look like saints.

Interview, University of Wisconsin, Madison/
The New York Times, 3-16:(A)18.

Nicholas Johnson
Chairman, National Citizens Committee
for Broadcasting; Former Commissioner,
Federal Communications Commission

2

Broadcasters elect and defeat [public] officials, and there are a million ways they do it. For starters, stations determine how much people in their areas know about public issues. They can accept or reject that half-hour on weekend television of *Your Congressman Reports.* When he comes back to his district, they can treat that as newsworthy or ignore it. They can give air time to those who might challenge him. And finally, they can editorially endorse.

U.S. News & World Report, 1-30:40.

Hamilton Jordan
Assistant to President of the United
States Jimmy Carter

3

My own reading of the political situation is that we've got an activist President when the mood of the country is somewhat passive. The options for a President are to adjust to the popular mood, or to go on and face some of these tough issues that should be faced. We obviously have chosen the latter course. So, to that extent, it can be argued that maybe we're a little bit out of synch with the country.

Interview, Washington/
U.S. News & World Report, 5-22:22.

Vernon E. Jordan, Jr.
President, National Urban League

4

... I think black people ought to be involved in both [political] parties. Blacks were pretty much in the Republican column until 1932, and the trend has been Democratic since then. But I reject the notion that blacks only vote for Democrats. We are not wedded to any one party or any one candidate. But rather, we vote our interests, our needs, our aims and our aspirations ... I think it has been a political mistake for the Republicans to ignore us. That's what happened in 1976, and the results were disastrous for [then-President Gerald Ford's reelection hopes].

Interview/U.S. News & World Report, 4-10:66.

Jack Kemp
United States Representative, R-New York

5

[Former California Governor] Ronald Reagan is not a fanatic; he is a conservative. He is a thoughtful, able individual. ... and isn't it interesting that [current California Governor] Jerry Brown now is talking about some of the things that Ronald Reagan [has] talked about for a long time. To call Reagan a fanatic is to label [the late liberal Senator] Hubert Humphrey a fanatic.

Interview, New York/
The Christian Science Monitor, 9-18:6.

6

They've [Democrats] been Santa Claus and we've [Republicans] been Scrooge. They said yes and we said no. They said more and we said less. The Republican Party has to define its role ... It has to be the party of real economic growth. The Republican Party, if it doesn't get timid, can dominate the political scene for the next 10 to 20 years.

Interview/Los Angeles Times, 9-21:(1)18.

Jeane Kirkpatrick
Professor of the foundations of American
freedom, Georgetown University; Resident
scholar, American Enterprise Institute

7

While we still have a two-party system—certainly at the Presidential level—it is significant

WHAT THEY SAID IN 1978

that the number of people who identify with neither party has increased dramatically since 1964. Even more important: Among party identifiers, party loyalty has grown steadily weaker. We're seeing more split-ticket voting and indifference to what the party thinks about issues and candidates. That's important, because party loyalty is probably the greatest protection a political system can have against surge movements: men on horseback and various kinds of demagogic, sudden-flash parties . . . One reason [for the decline in party loyalty] seems to be the declining strength of the family. People traditionally inherit their party identification from their parents, but as intergenerational ties have weakened, that's not happening to the same extent it used to. Also, changes in party rules and the increased importance of primaries have affected party loyalty. Some of the most exciting, closest contests now are taking place within parties, not between them.

Interview/U.S. News & World Report, 9-18:55.

Richard D. Lamm
Governor of Colorado (D)

1

When the party is riding high, as the Democrats have been in recent elections, it is in a time of greatest danger. It is no longer lean and hungry. Political parties have to evolve, or they are in for grievous losses at the polls.

Interview, Denver/
U.S. News & World Report, 4-3:53.

Seymour Martin Lipset
Professor of political science,
Stanford University

2

There is no question there is a conservative mood in the country, but it is not benefiting the party which could best take advantage of that swing [the Republican Party]. At the same time that the Democrats have formed as broad a coalition as you can think of, the Republicans are finding it difficult to get beyond their own enclaves. They don't know whether they want

to be right [about the issues] or whether they want to win elections.

Interview, Los Angeles/
The Christian Science Monitor, 10-20:3.

Clare Boothe Luce
Former American diplomat and playwright

3

. . . I have not changed my [political] views since I was in my 20s, at which time I was considered a liberal. I campaigned for Congress as a liberal Republican. Now I'm still where I was, but the country has moved much further to the left. And as the country moves to the left, it obviously calls anybody that hasn't moved with them "on the right" or "conservative." So having been all my life a liberal, I'm now called a conservative.

Interview/Los Angeles Herald Examiner, 7-2:(A)13.

David W. Marston
United States Attorney for Philadelphia

4

[Saying he is being fired from his job as U.S. Attorney because of political pressue due to his corruption inquiry involving U.S. Congressmen]: We know from what the President [Carter] said at his news conference that it was Congressman [Joshua] Eilberg's phone call that expedited the decision to remove me, and I think that raises very grave questions. A Congressman called the President of the United States and said, "Get that prosecutor out of there." A Congressman called at a time when he didn't have a candidate for the job. He just said, "Anybody but Marston. Get that guy out of there." And that's why I'm gone.

To reporters, Washington, Jan. 20/
Los Angeles Times, 1-21:(1)1.

Eugene J. McCarthy
Former United States Senator,
D-Minnesota

5

[On President Carter]: You can't go into the Presidency with so little background and experience. Carter was so inexperienced that no one could make up such lack of information unless he was a genius, which he hadn't demon-

(EUGENE J. McCARTHY)

strated. Then, when he said that he was going to take up speed-reading, I knew the cause was lost.

Interview/The Dallas Times Herald, 8-25:(C)3.

George S. McGovern
United States Senator, D-South Dakota

1

They [the political right] are not against waste; they are against government, good or bad, except when it is paying for B-1 bombers and neutron bombs. Their loyalty is not to hard-pressed taxpayers, but to the ideology of McKinley, Harding and Hoover.

San Francisco Examiner & Chronicle,
6-25:(This World)2.

2

It does take a rather large ego to run for President. In a sense, it's almost an act of arrogance to say that you are qualified for the most powerful office in the world.

Television interview, Philadelphia/
The Dallas Times Herald, 8-27:(L)6.

Thomas J. McIntyre
United States Senator,
D-New Hampshire

3

[On the New Right]: These people are different from traditional conservatives. I know the traditional conservatives of my own state. I have competed with them in the political arena. I have worked with them in behalf of our state. They are people of honor, civility and decency. The New Right cannot comprehend how people of opposing viewpoints can find common ground and work together. For them, there *is* no common ground. And this, in my judgment, is the best indication of what they truly are— radicals, whose aim is *not* to compete with honor and decency, *not* to compromise when necessary to advance the common good, but to annihilate those they see as "enemies."

Before the Senate, Washington, March 1/
The Washington Post, 3-3:(A)23.

George Meany
President, American Federation of
Labor-Congress of Industrial
Organizations

4

[On President Carter's re-election chances in 1980]: If the election were today, I don't know how he could win New York. Pennsylvania doesn't augur well for him. No one can say he'd be guaranteed to get Minnesota or Wisconsin. If he loses a couple of those, where does he get 270 electoral votes [needed for victory]? Ohio and Delaware are doubtful now. There's no indication he's any stronger now in the West than he was in 1976. Just take one big state away from him . . . From my experience, the greatest thing Carter has going for him is the Republicans.

Interview, Washington, Nov. 9/
The Dallas Times Herald, 11-10:(A)8.

Lloyd Meeds
United States Representative,
D-Washington

5

[On his decision not to run for re-election]: The post-Watergate period produced a healthy skepticism of politics and politicians, but that has now turned into an unhealthy cynicism. It's not just me, it's all politicians. People shoot you down first and ask questions later, instead of giving you some credence or credibility. Let's be realistic. Most of us are not in this for the money. We get some sort of ego satisfaction in serving, or prestige, or the opportunity to go on to something higher. I gave up on higher office long ago, so when you remove the ego satisfaction and the prestige, what's left?

Interview, Washington/
The New York Times, 2-12:(1)24.

William G. Milliken
Governor of Michigan (R)

6

We [Republicans] preach the policy of the open door but, as a party, we don't always practice it nor deserve it. As a party, we have yet to offer real hope to urban Americans and a real commitment to the revival, or even the

(WILLIAM G. MILLIKEN)

survival, of our cities large and small. [It] would be premature to claim that our victories [in the recent national elections] signaled any real resurgence to the Republican Party nationally. Despite our regional victories, we have yet to prove that, as a national party, we really have kicked the habit of snatching defeat from the jaws of victory.

At Republican Governors Conference,
Williamsburg, Va., Nov. 27/
The Dallas Times Herald, 11-28:(A)14.

Walter F. Mondale
Vice President of the United States

1

[On President Carter]: He's a brilliant man, and he's a decent man. No one ever occupied that office that tried harder and with more ability and decency than that man. He is such a decent man. I have never seen a mean streak in him. I have never seen a dishonest streak in him. I have never seen anything except a man trying to do his absolute best.

Interview, Los Angeles/
The Christian Science Monitor, 8-8:6.

John E. Moss
United States Representative, D-California

2

There is a class of legislator developing who places a premium on job security ... who becomes very sensitive to being popular on each issue, rather than right on each issue. They like to use their polls ... When I first came here, men were a lot more interested in voting right. That meant right for themselves, too—rather than taking the popular stand. It was partly a conviction that if it was popular today it might not be popular tomorrow—but if it was right today it would continue to be right.

Interview, Washington/
San Francisco Examiner & Chronicle, 9-24:(A)22.

Daniel P. Moynihan
United States Senator, D-New York

3

[On speculation that he will run for President in 1980]: What has happened here is a strong new perception on the left that public opinion is moving back to our position in the center. If you accept their view that the center now isn't where the center was, persons such as I seem more of an electoral threat than in recent years.

Interview, Washington/
The New York Times, 8-1:(A)10.

Richard M. Nixon
Former President of the United States

4

[On the Watergate affair]: I am not one of those who believe in a conspiracy or that I was a victim of some attempted *coup d'etat.* The responsibility was mine. The Watergate break-in did nobody any harm but it did harm to the democratic process. It has been done in America before, but two wrongs don't make a right. After it happened, I did not take the decisive action which should have been taken. I tried to limit the damage so it would not hurt us politically and also rub off on my friends who might have been implicated. In essence, I was the one responsible. Grave mistakes were made, and the best I can characterize it is a quotation from Talleyrand who said in criticizing Napoleon for something he did: "It was worse than a crime; it was a blunder."

Television interview, Paris, Nov. 28/
Los Angeles Times, 11-29:(1)10.

5

Being controversial in politics is inevitable. If an individual wants to be a leader and isn't controversial, that means he never stood for anything. In the world today, there are not many good choices—only choices between the half-good and the less half-good. If a leader doesn't stand up on a great issue, he's not going to be great. If he does stand up, he will be controversial. The mark of leadership is not how a leader can take a popular position and ride with it, like a poll, or Congressional sentiment. The real test is to take the unpopular position, if he thinks it is right, and make it popular.

Interview, New York/
The Dallas Times Herald, 12-10:(A)8.

David Owen
Foreign Secretary of the United Kingdom
1

There are some who know me well who will say I am one of the least ambitious people. Others, if you choose the right ones, will say I am a very political animal, and I won't dissent from that. Most Welshmen are. Anyone who comes into politics wants to be the one who has the greatest influence.

People, 3-6:67.

Tongsun Park
South Korean businessman
2

[On the scandal involving payments he made to U.S. Congressmen]: Lobbying is a dirty but essential business . . . Labor unions and teacher associations have lobbies. Why shouldn't foreign countries have lobbies?

To reporters, Seoul, South Korea,
Jan. 19/Los Angeles Times, 1-20:(1)4.

Gerald Rafshoon
Assistant to President of the United
States Jimmy Carter for Communications
3

I think it's a bum rap for people to say that [President Carter] is not competent. The two things I've always known about him are his competence and his toughness. I'd like people to see more of that side. I'd like people to understand that he is making tough decisions for the public good, that he's committed to social programs—but to well-managed programs that take into account economic realities. That's the way I see him; that's what I see in this Administration, and I'd like to see it communicated more.

Interview/U.S. News & World Report, 7-24:22.

Ronald Reagan
Former Governor of California (R)
4

Politics is supposed to be the second-oldest profession. I have come to realize that it bears a very close resemblance to the first.

At business conference, Los Angeles, March 2/
Los Angeles Herald Examiner, 3-3:(A)11.

John J. Rhodes
United States Representative,
R-Arizona
5

Every person elected to public office should have integrity and wisdom—the integrity to keep every campaign promise and the wisdom not to make all those fool promises.

Washington, April 13/
The Dallas Times Herald, 4-14:(A)6.

Nelson A. Rockefeller
Former Vice President of the
United States
6

[Saying he is out of politics for good]: I just decided it was time to get out of politics. Quitting wasn't hard. I've spent my life changing jobs. So I've got no problem. I just pulled the curtain down.

Interview, New York/
The Washington Post, 3-6:(B)11.

Felix G. Rohatyn
Chairman, Municipal Assistance
Corporation of New York
7

In the last election, almost two out of three Americans of voting age did not exercise their franchise. The 37 per cent of the people dragging themselves to the polls were sold candidates through TV commercials. During news programs and football games, we were bombarded with 30-second spots which turned each candidate into an actor. With opinion polls telling the candidates what the voters want to hear, a minority of the electorate gives power, with few exceptions, to men and women who follow rather than lead. Once in office, the same process is continued: If saying what the polls tell you to say gets you elected, why not do what the polls tell you to do to stay in office? The trouble is that polls cannot teach you to lead in crisis.

Before French-American Chamber of Commerce,
New York/The New York Times, 12-7:(A)23.

WHAT THEY SAID IN 1978

James R. Sasser
United States Senator, D-Tennessee

1

[President Carter's] first 18 months have been more good than bad, certainly better than is reflected in those opinion polls. His problem there is the perception people have of him as weak and vacillating. People will forgive just about anything but weakness in their leaders, and that's the paradox because Carter has very strong convictions and fights furiously for what he believes in.

Interview/U.S. News & World Report, 7-24:24.

Arthur M. Schlesinger, Jr.
Historian; Professor of humanities,
City University of New York

2

[On whether John, Robert and Edward Kennedy can be considered a "dynasty" because of their quests for the Presidency]: [If] a dynasty implies people aspiring to the Presidency because they are born in a certain family, it's a terrible idea. But I don't think that people should be disqualified if they have proven on their merits that they should be considered. In the past, the Adamses and the Roosevelts made very valuable contributions. I think to disqualify somebody because they are related to someone else who became President would be a mistake.

Interview, New York/
The Christian Science Monitor; 10-23:(B)16.

Ian Smith
Prime Minister of Rhodesia

3

I have always believed in qualifications for the vote—a kind of meritocracy, as opposed to democracy. I think it leads to better government. I am critical of the system [in which] a man who is an absolute rotter, a crook, has the same say as the best man in your land, the most brilliant man. I wonder whether democracy will survive under those circumstances.

Interview, Washington/Time, 10-23:54.

Adlai E. Stevenson
United States Senator, D-Illinois

4

[On his investigation of the South Korean-U.S. Congress influence-buying scandal]: What the public will see, I think, is some political expedience, some human weakness, campaign contributions from questionable sources. But it will not see . . . money from [South Korean businessman] Tongsun Park in return for favors and a policy friendly to South Korea.

Interview, May 18/The Washington Post, 5-19:(A)14.

I. F. Stone
Journalist

5

[President Carter] just doesn't have the gift of greatness, the capacity to speak to the hearts and souls of men. He gets bogged down in details, like a mechanic taking apart an engine. Nobody really understands either his energy or his welfare programs. They invite caricature by their complexity. They are Rube Goldberg contraptions. His rhetoric is inane, and its cadence insipid. He twirps.

San Francisco Examiner & Chronicle,
1-29:(This World)2.

Robert S. Strauss
Special Representative for Trade
Negotiations of, and Adviser on
Inflation to, President of the
United States Jimmy Carter

6

[On President Carter's decline in public popularity]: He's not going to come out of the funk in the polls for some time, but it doesn't disturb him much. There's some witch doctor in me and I like to gamble, so I know there's a lot of luck involved. For two years luck went his way, but now nothing seems to work. That is going to change. He's going to get some breaks soon. I'm with him walking or riding, right or wrong. But we've got to improve our act.

Interview, Washington/
U.S. News & World Report, 8-7:16.

Jack Valenti
President, Motion Picture
Association of America

1

[On similarities between politicians and actors]: Both are egotistical. Both depend on the reaction of the public, either at the voting booth or the box-office. And both function "on stage." The unquestioning adoration entertainers attract from the public intrigues politicians more and more in these post-Watergate days of tarnished images.

Parade, 2-19:2·

Guy Vander Jagt
United States Representative,
R-Michigan

2

We [Republicans] should not be tarred as the party of big business. In fact, over half the contributions of business and industrial political money in 1976 went to Democrats and not Republicans. As a party, we have many programs and proposals that indicate our genuine concern and ability to deal with the problems people face daily.

Interview/U.S. News & World Report, 6-12:50.

Joe D. Waggonner
United States Representative,
D-Louisiana

3

Congress is not facing up to the issues. The average member is much more political now. He is thinking mostly about getting re-elected. For example, the Ways and Means Committee was considering rescinding the Social Security tax increases, not because of fiscal responsibility, but for pure political reasons—no others . . . You can't react to political expedience day in and day out. Political expedience is a shifting-sands proposition. It's one thing one day and something else another.

Interview/U.S. News & World Report, 6-5:23.

John White
Chairman, Democratic National Committee

4

Our party stands for diversity, and dissent is part of our process. I wouldn't urge any Democratic candidates to accept or be silent on any part of the President's [Carter] program if they disagree with it. What I have objected to is taking personal potshots at the President. [The late Senator] Hubert Humphrey once said that every American ought to have some public official they could cuss out with comfort. I agree with that, but I think most people reserve for themselves the right to criticize the President.

Interview/U.S. News & World Report, 9-4:22.

Theodore H. White
Author; Political historian

5

[On former President Richard Nixon, who resigned from office in 1974]: I've never been able to get inside that man's mind. I think he'd love some bit of honor. I think he'd love to be an elder statesman. I do not think he thinks of himself as a morally repugnant person; I think he thinks he made a mistake [in the Watergate affair, which forced him from office]. I don't think he feels he needs to purge his conscience. Hell, you do not require in our day and age that a man stand up in public confession and beat his chest. I just want him to be silent. I do not want to humiliate or imprison him . . . I'd like to see him play with his grandchild in San Clemente and maybe go out to football games, which he seems to like. I'd like to have him go his grandfatherly way into the sunset.

Interview, San Francisco/
San Francisco Examiner & Chronicle, 10-1:(Scene)3.

Social Welfare

Julian Bond
Georgia State Senator (D)

1

...we've developed this permanent underclass. You know, the American myth and fact used to be that people sort of moved in and out, went up and down. There's always been this little knot at the bottom. But now this little knot of people at the bottom has become larger, Number 1, and has become permanent, Number 2. The mother's a welfare case, the child is a welfare case, the child's child is a welfare case, and they all live with the grandmother, who's a welfare case.

Los Angeles Times, 6-23:(1)21.

2

Nothing is going to be done about poverty in this city [Atlanta]. There's no movement out there ... It's sad. I feel like I am a cheerleader and the game is over. And I am still out in front of the stands, and the crowd is leaving. I am out in front of the stands, saying, "Come on, one more time, let's hear it," and the crowd is leaving. The players have already left the field, but I have my back to them, so I don't know. All I can see is the crowd.

Interview, Atlanta/
Los Angeles Times, 11-20:(1)31.

Alice M. Brophy
Commissioner, New York City
Department for the Aging

3

For the majority of women, to be old is to be poor. Their Number 1 problem is income, followed by forced unemployment, job discrimination, sex discrimination, poor housing, lack of transportation, which denies them the rights and benefits that they must have if they are to survive, and, in more recent years, crime victimization. It is important to remember that coming into the 65-and-over age group are not only those who all their lives have been victims of poverty but also multitudes of people, especially women, who become poor only on becoming old. Although older people represent 10 per cent of the total population of our country, they represent 25 per cent of the poor. And the majority are women.

At symposium on aging, New York/
The New York Times, 5-26:(A)15.

Robert N. Butler
Director, National Institute on Aging

4

There has been some improvement in nursing homes in the last few years. But we're just beginning to look beyond the basics of fire-safety and sanitation requirements to the quality of life they offer, and we have a long way to go in that area ... Even more than cancer, what people fear most is growing old, losing their mind and being put away. Once the baby-boom generation reaches 65, our nursing-home population will double to 2 million.

U.S. News & World Report, 4-24:56,58.

Joseph A. Califano, Jr.
Secretary of Health, Education and
Welfare of the United States

5

[Saying he does not want $3.6-billion added to HEW's budget] : Continuing to pour money into HEW appropriations not only threatens to over-burden the prudent management of some programs, it could add to the risk of inflation, which ultimately exacts a cruel toll on the same vulnerable people we are trying so hard to help—the poor, the old, the handicapped.

Washington, May 2/The New York Times, 5-4:51.

Jimmy Carter
President of the United States

6

[Saying he does not favor a rollback this year of the new, higher Social Security taxes] :

(JIMMY CARTER)

The Congress, I think, last year very coura-geously passed Social Security legislation that would bring order out of chaos and put the Social Security reserve fund back on a sound basis for 25 or 30 years in the future. They were on the verge of bankruptcy. Also, those who are particularly affected with higher Social Security payments beginning next year ... are those in a higher income group who will have their retirement benefits increased.

Before American Society of Newspaper Editors, Washington, April 11/The New York Times, 4-12:35.

1

When a [social] program is poorly man-aged—when it is riddled with waste and fraud—the victims are not abstractions but flesh-and-blood human beings. They are the unemployed teen-agers who get shut out of a job; they are the senior citizen deprived of a needed medical service; they are the school child who goes without a nutritious meal; or they are taxpayers whose hard-earned dollar goes down the drain ... Those of us who believed that our society has an obligation toward its weakest members have the greatest stake in improving the management and efficiency of the programs that are designed to meet that obligation. This is especially true when the battle against infla-tion makes it impossible to bring vast new re-sources to bear on our social problems. There is no room any longer for waste. At such a time—indeed, at any time—efficient management is in itself an act of compassion, for it unlocks new resources to be used for human ends.

At HEW conference, Washington, Dec. 13/ The Washington Post, 12-14:(A)6.

John H. Chafee
United States Senator, R-Rhode Island

2

Over the years, the Congress and state and local governments have responded to the needs of older citizens with numerous programs aimed at providing for their special needs. There are now about 50 separate programs in the Federal government alone, administered by approximately 17 different departments and agencies. But the shocking fact is that, with all these programs, so many needs are still not being met. In 1975, 25 per cent of the older population was below or near the poverty level, and a staggering number of older Americans are in need of nutritious meals and other basic services, such as transportation, home health aid, chore assistance, information and referral and legal services. Many are not taking advan-tage of the existing programs because of confus-ing Federal, state and local bureaucratic regula-tions and red tape. Our attempts to help our senior citizens lead more dignified and inde-pendent lives are fraught with fragmentation and duplication, which contribute even more to the indignity and dependency they suffer.

July 24/The Washington Post, 7-27:(A)26.

James S. Coleman
Professor of sociology, University of Chicago

3

... the value system that used to hold fami-lies together has been turned upside down. Now the husband and wife typically put their own individual interests first, their joint goals second, and any family interests beyond the couple, third. That is a reverse order from the traditional ranking that placed family concerns first and individual goals last. Because the fun-damental reversal of priorities leads to more divorce and parental neglect, it has serious im-plications for stability of the family. Of all the changes these young adults are bringing into society, I think this breakdown of the family is going to prove to be the most powerful, the most destructive and the most enduring.

Interview/U.S. News & World Report, 3-27:62.

Drew S. Days III
Assistant Attorney General, Civil Rights Division, Department of Justice of the United States

4

The name of the game is "getting ours and to hell with everybody else." We're not really concerned about the system; we're not con-cerned with those children who are in the cen-

(DREW S. DAYS III)

ter city who go to schools that are 90 and 100 years old—we just don't care about them. That's the great American way. If you've got enough money to move into a certain community or if you happen to be of a certain race and you're not going to have your home firebombed when you move there, then you've lucked out. You've really made it, from the American standpoint. And anybody who wants to tamper with that is going to find you very resistant.

Los Angeles Times, 6-22:(1)17.

Marian Wright Edelman
Director, Children's Defense Fund

1

Children's needs are being shortchanged in America because they do not vote. Their families often lack the confidence, information, access and resources to affect policies crucial to their children's lives . . . If a child is not white, or is white but not middle-class, does not speak English, is poor, needs special help with seeing, hearing, learning, adjusting, growing up, is pregnant or married at age 15, is not smart enough or is too smart, then in too many places officials and institutions exclude, discriminate against, neglect or even abuse them, frequently with impunity . . . We must make it clear to the Carter Administration and Federal, state and local elected officials, that rhetoric and symbolic actions are no substitute for programs and money. What we need in this Administration is someone to say children are as important as energy.

Washington, April 13/
Los Angeles Times, 4-14:(4)1.

Milton Friedman
Senior research fellow, Hoover
Institution, Stanford University;
Former professor of economics,
University of Chicago

2

[People] say they are depending on Social Security for retirement. They are, but it is not correct to suppose that Social Security is an insurance program in which each person is paying for his own retirement. He is not. It is a system of taxes where you are taxing some people, the young, in order to provide pensions to other people, the old. There is a little relationship between what people pay and what they receive, but that relationship is very loose. And, consequently, I have long been in favor of shifting a large part of the financing of Social Security to the general fund, to the general tax fund, in order to make it clear that, to the extent to which those payments are really welfare payments rather than insurance payments, they should be funded out of the general revenue.

TV-radio interview/"Meet the Press,"
National Broadcasting Company, 11-12.

Daniel R. Glickman
United States Representative, D-Kansas

3

[On the recent Social Security tax increase] : No issue has hit me harder. The reaction is unbelievable. A generation gap is developing. The young who have to pay these taxes see 30 years of high taxes and no guarantee of getting all or part of it back. And the old who are getting the benefits don't think they are getting enough.

U.S. News & World Report, 1-30:25.

Barry M. Goldwater
United States Senator, R-Arizona

4

My personal opinion is that Social Security has failed, and we would be better off in this country if we pledged to every person who has ever paid a dime into the Social Security fund that that money would be returned, and then forget about the whole [Social Security] thing. There does not seem to me to be any way to have what we call Social Security and avoid the politics every two years of having the House feel that it must make additions to the Social Security payments, regardless of whether the money is there.

Before the Senate, Washington/
The Wall Street Journal, 1-10:18.

Patricia Roberts Harris
*Secretary of Housing and Urban
Development of the United States*

1

[On the Administration's $9.5-billion housing budget] : This is a lean budget. It is a budget without a single milligram of fat. It is a budget for the long-distance runner and not the sprinter. It is a budget which, if trimmed, will prevent progress and, if added to, will throw into confusion the fine tuning that has been done.

*Before Senate Banking Committee, Washington,
March 6/The Washington Post, 3-7:(D)7.*

2

We've never liked the poor. The poor are a whip. They make us uncomfortable—especially in an affluent country. So there must be something terribly wrong with the poor. But that's not new in American society. It's at the base of the Puritan concept that the rich are the elect of God and the poor somehow are inferior. So there is, underneath, a very supportive American spirit that makes it possible for us comfortably to reject the poor, unless there is somebody there reminding the society that maybe the poor are not poor because they are stupid and evil and mean-spirited. Maybe they are poor either because they cannot cope, in which case we have to make some policy decisions about what we do with people who can't cope, or because they have been deliberately crippled by the society, as is the case of blacks in this society, or because they are temporarily unlucky, which is the case with a number of people who are poor. Until people are forced to identify the nature of the problem of poverty, they can go back to our old puritanical approach to this and say, "Well, they're poor because they're lazy."

Interview/Los Angeles Times, 5-24:(1)20.

Richard G. Hatcher
Mayor of Gary, Indiana

3

I confess that I see little hope for substantial reduction in welfare and other human-services fraud, error and abuse. I would like to have such hope. I am more than willing to join those who wish to exhort us all to be honest, to condemn carelessness and crime, cupidity and stupidity.

*San Francisco Examiner & Chronicle,
12-24:(This World)2.*

Carl Holman
President, National Urban Coalition

4

I work with businessmen and when I ask them to find jobs for young blacks, they say, "No, we cannot afford to as long as there is a pool of better-qualified whites to draw from." And I say, "Well, what are we to do?" And they say, "Nationalize welfare" . . . I find that it costs more to finance all those [Federal] programs than it would to provide jobs. What we are spending we are spending negatively. It seems to me that here in America we are running out of the creativity we used to have.

Interview/The New York Times, 2-26:(1)28.

Benjamin L. Hooks
*Executive director, National
Association for the Advancement of
Colored People*

5

There's a great lie abroad that black people don't want to work. I have an idea. You [whites] give us the jobs and we'll give you the welfare—and see how you like that for a while.

Before state Governors/Time, 3-13:67.

6

It is the best of times because today we have more than 1 million blacks enrolled in colleges; yet it is the worst of times because hundreds of thousands of young people, black and white, are finishing school functionally illiterate . . . It is the best of times because we are told that today more than 25 per cent of black families have achieved mythical middle-class income standards; yet it is the worst of times because 30 per cent of black families are below the officially defined poverty level . . . It is the best of times because we now have some forward movement in hiring practices all over the nation in police and fire departments and other public

WHAT THEY SAID IN 1978

(BENJAMIN L. HOOKS)

agencies; yet it is the worst of times because fiscal belt-tightening, Proposition 13 [California's property-tax-cut measure] and other tax revolts around the nation knock out the last hired, and reduce the delivery of human and essential services to minority and poor people.

At NAACP convention, Portland, Ore./
Los Angeles Times, 7-11:(1)18.

1

Inflation makes people mean, vicious and selfish. It draws them inward. People worry about "Can I eat? Can I buy a second car? Can I send my own child to school?" They stop worrying about the black child down the street. Black people are the draftees of the inflation fight. Poor people don't make the decision to put a voluntary ceiling on wages. If they're lucky enough to have a job, they won't be making the money they need to survive.

Providence, R.I., Nov. 10/
The New York Times, 11-12:(1)22.

Jesse L. Jackson
Civil-rights leader; President, PUSH
(People United to Save Humanity)

2

I've never been poor. We just didn't have any money . . . But we never perceived ourselves as poor. We would never *concede* to poverty. I guess I took my first bath in a bathtub when I was around 12. We just had cold water and you had to heat it up. Except at that time, you know, everybody was like that. But no one was allowed to develop a complex about the ghetto. In fact, I didn't hear the word "ghetto" until I was a senior in college. We didn't call it the ghetto. We called it our neighborhood, or community.

Interview, Washington/
The Washington Post, 3-14:(B)2.

Howard Jarvis
Co-author of California property-tax
limitation measure (Proposition 13)

3

I think welfare is a narcotic in this country. It will eventually destroy the country. To put welfare in the property tax is absolutely an abortion. A lot of people in this country are paying for welfare through property taxes when they don't have enough food to live on in their house. It should be that a guy can go home, shut the front door and tell the rest of the world to go to hell. Freedom is the name of the game.

Interview, Washington, June 19/
The Washington Post, 6-20:(B)4.

Donald M. Kaplan
Director, Office of Economic Research,
Federal Home Loan Bank Board

4

An impression has been created in the minds of many that some new type of Federal subsidy program might be necessary to make home-ownership once more affordable to the average American family. An alternative point of view is that, although homeownership affordability for median-income families has declined somewhat in recent years, no special governmental action, in the form of some type of new middle-income-oriented housing subsidy program, is needed. The serious housing problem that exists in this country lies with lower-income groups, and here the problem is probably more one of income than of housing.

At conference sponsored by Federal Home Loan Bank
of San Francisco/San Francisco
Examiner & Chronicle, 1-8:(TC)8.

Donald S. MacNaughton
Chairman, Prudential Insurance Company

5

It would be especially inflationary if Congress took the course of financing part of Social Security through general revenues. The same people pay both taxes. To camouflage the facts of life by taking general revenues to pay Social Security benefits would be a mistake, because we would no longer see what the increases of benefits are costing the nation . . . Most people don't understand Social Security. It transfers goods and services from those working today to those no longer working, or to their dependents. By automatically increasing benefits for non-workers, there has been an attempt to keep

(DONALD S. MACNAUGHTON)

their standard of living on an even keel or even to improve it. But that has to be financed by today's workers, and that means that their standard of living is going down. That cannot go on forever.

Interview, Newark, N.J./
The New York Times, 3-24:(D)2.

1

It was not coincidental that the major expansion in social programs came in the 1950s and 1960s—a time when business enjoyed dramatic improvements in productivity. These productivity improvements permitted redistribution of income without major political resistance, because the increased rates of output permitted increases in taxes, an improvement in the living standards of workers and a reasonable rate of return on capital for investors. We should face squarely the fundamental long-term question of whether business can continue to absorb the escalating burden of these programs and still show the productivity improvement required to continue the historical trend of a rising standard of living for all Americans. At the present time, it is difficult to be optimistic on this score. There seems to be little inclination to contain future [social-] benefit and tax increases.

Nation's Business, April:28.

Margaret Mead
Anthropologist

2

In the '50s, we made too many people get married. So we made a lot of bad marriages. We isolated the families in the suburbs and we made them have too many children. We don't need everybody married and we don't need bad marriages.

At University of Rhode Island, Jan. 28/
The New York Times, 1-30:(A)10.

Daniel P. Moynihan
United States Senator, D-New York

3

[On New York City's welfare burden]: If a middle-class family moves from New York to

Houston, its real income is increased by one-third. If a welfare family moves from New York to Houston, its income is reduced by one-third. Whilst this situation persists, our problems will persist. The number of people on welfare in New York City is somewhat larger than the number of people who live in New Mexico.

Before Senate Banking Committee, Washington/
The New York Times, 6-19:(B)2.

Graciela Olivarez
Director, Community Services
Administration of the United States

4

We need more than an Environmental Protection Agency to protect the snail-darter and environmental-impact statements to prevent pollution. We need *human*-impact statements to prevent further injury to the poor ... Poverty is injustice. I don't mean that in the old bleeding-heart-liberal sense. I mean poor people work like hell, and they are kept poor, they stay poor and the system keeps them poor ... This Administration is rediscovering poverty, and, as we do, we find it tangled in a web of laws which defies resolution.

At University of Notre Dame Law School
commencement/The Washington Post, 6-9:(A)18.

Ronald Reagan
Former Governor of California (R)

5

I've said repeatedly that we should be going out into the ethnic and blue-collar community. Not because they're somehow different or set apart, but because they're Americans as we're Americans, and they have the same hopes and dreams that we do ... I believe black Americans want what every other kind of American wants: a crack at a decent job, a home, safety in the streets, and a good education for our children—and the best way to have those things is for government to get out of the way while the rest of us make a bigger pie so that everybody can have a bigger slice.

At seminar sponsored by Citizens for the
Republic, Atlanta/
The Christian Science Monitor, 1-24:3.

WHAT THEY SAID IN 1978

Sheila C. Ribordy
Assistant professor of psychology,
DePaul University

1

Child abuse occurs when a society condones unlimited parental power over children. It occurs when we do not support the one-parent family. It occurs when we do not legislate money and support for day-care centers. It occurs when we allow violence in the media. I have been down the road of treatment—and I will continue to go down that road—but that is not the answer.

The Center Magazine, March-April: 75.

Arthur M. Schlesinger, Jr.
Historian; Professor of humanities,
City University of New York

2

It's been a hell of a long time since any American politician made a great thing about the condition of the poor and the powerless. But there is an inherent cyclical rhythm in our politics. You go through periods of [a] high degree of activism and commitment that exhaust the country; then you have a period of acquiescence and passivity and cynicism. In due course, the dam will break again and sometime in the '80s we will have another period of forward motion.

Interview, Los Angeles/
Los Angeles Times, 9-20:(4)1.

Charles L. Schultze
Chairman, Council of Economic
Advisers to President of the United
States Jimmy Carter

3

Last year the Congress . . . substantially raised Social Security taxes—absolutely necessary to preserve the financial soundness of that system. The President [Carter], in turn proposed a moderate, well-circumscribed way of using some general revenues for doing this. The Congress rejected it. For 40 years we have used payroll taxes. Now—in haste, and with a number of different proposals for doing it floating around—it seems to me is not the time, in a jerrybuilt way, to make substantial funda-

mental changes in the Social Security financing system as part of an economic stimulus program. On the other hand, it is clear that over time we will want to look at, take a new look at the financing of the Social Security System in terms of its long-running consequences, the possibility of using general revenues, but in a careful orderly way, not in a hasty, hurly-burly way in an attempt to reverse a decision that was only recently made.

TV-radio interview/"Meet the Press,"
National Broadcasting Company, 3-5.

William C. Simpson
Executive vice president,
Royal-Globe Insurance Companies

4

The [U.S.] Department of Housing and Urban Development, in a recent report, was extremely critical of the property-casualty insurance business for alleged redlining practices and its failure to satisfy the insurance needs of inner-city businesses and residents. Yet, only a week later, the General Accounting Office issued a report that was critical of property-casualty companies for providing insurance in inner-city areas in amounts exceeding property market values, thus providing an incentive for arson for profit.

Nation's Business, November: 110.

George Steinbrenner
Owner, New York "Yankees"
baseball club

5

I'll tell you when I really bristle. I'll be sitting at some board meeting, and I'll hear some big-shot say, "Look at those people"—and you'll know exactly which people he's talking about—"all they want is their unemployment checks." Well, let me tell you something. I've been to the South Bronx; how many of those big-shots have been to the South Bronx? You gonna tell me that's all that guy wants in life? No way . . . If he had the opportunity that I had, God knows he might be a better man than all of us.

Interview/The New York Times Magazine, 4-9:44.

Steve Suitts
Executive director,
Southern Regional Conference

1

What is happening in the South is increasingly frightful. People forget that the South is more urban than rural today and that most of the people leaving the rural areas in the South for cities like Atlanta are poor, uneducated blacks who are unequipped with job skills. The same unemployment rates that exist for blacks and other racial minorities in Detroit or Chicago or New York exist in Atlanta and New Orleans. Four out of 10 young blacks in Atlanta are unemployed. You go down to the corner of Walton and Fairlie and see folks who have nothing to do but stand there all day.

Los Angeles Times, 11-20:(1)28.

Margaret Thatcher
Member of British Parliament;
Leader, British Conservative Party

2

You cannot have national welfare before someone has created national wealth.

Time, 9-11:61.

Al Ullman
United States Representative, D-Oregon

3

[Opposing a plan to roll back Social Security tax increases and, instead, pay for the retirement system with general Treasury revenue] : I think we are not only making a mistake, but a disastrous mistake. Each dollar we take from general revenue to pay for Social Security is another dollar added to the Federal deficit. We don't have enough income tax to pay for the daily operation of the government.

Los Angeles Times, 4-6:(1)9.

Transportation

Brock Adams
Secretary of Transportation
of the United States

1

[Saying Amtrak will have to cut much of its system because of costs]: We're at the danger point, where the entire system could break down if we don't cut back. Several Congressmen and Senators are not happy with the plan because they would lose their favorite trains. But Congress handed me this political hot potato, and I'm trying to avoid getting third-degree burns. Congress is either going to have to accept a plan that saves millions of dollars, or it's going to have to dredge up more Federal money to keep everybody's pet train running.

To reporters, Washington, May 8/
Los Angeles Times, 5-9:(1)1.

2

We have to face up to the fact that the automobile is no longer a good means of urban transportation . . . If we're going to unclog and de-smog our cities, then we must shift from an urban highway philosophy to an urban transit policy.

At urban-development meeting,
Washington/Los Angeles Times, 6-27:(1)2.

Frank Borman
Chairman and president, Eastern Airlines

3

As quasi-utilities essentially in business to provide a public service, we [airlines] have to expect some [government] restrictions. However, I favor reform of the present regulations. We should have greater control over our ticket prices, meaning the basic freedom to price our product within a given limit. I am unalterably opposed to free market entry because, as quasi-utilities, we could be destroyed. The competitive nature of the industry could be de-stroyed. Free market entry would leave us open to skimming. Small outfits with two or three planes could fly heavily used routes in the winter, then go elsewhere to fly heavily used routes in the summer. Under present regulations, the regular airlines take care of these routes the year around. We serve them in-season and off-season, regardless of whether they are heavily traveled or not. Of course, the money we earn on the revenue-producing routes helps make up for whatever we might lose on the low-revenue routes.

Interview, Miami/
Nation's Business, September:67.

Jimmy Carter
President of the United States

4

[On the Senate's approval of a bill to reduce government regulation of the airline industry]: This is an important step in the fight against inflation. Many carriers have already begun to reduce fares in expectation of this amendment. This bill guarantees that the trend toward lower fares continues and broadens to benefit more passengers, and it will put an end to a form of government regulation of business.

April 19/Los Angeles Herald Examiner, 4-20:(A)11.

Joan Claybrook
Administrator, National Highway
Traffic Safety Administration
of the United States

5

I don't think the automobile industry has much credibility with the American public [regarding car safety] from what I can tell. And I know that's frustrating to the auto manufacturers. But I think it has a lot to do with their crying wolf a number of times . . . and their generally negative posture toward doing things which the public really cares about. I would

(JOAN CLAYBROOK)

like to see them discuss something other than style and whiz-bang and color. The manufacturers have said for years that safety doesn't sell. But they've never tried it, really.

Interview, Washington/
The Christian Science Monitor, 4-3:12.

1

Our kind of review of safety standards and compliance with them and the defect-investigation work serves another function besides protecting the public on the highways today in any one car. It serves the function of having the manufacturers give a priority, an attention, to the critical issues that are raised about the safety of their vehicles ... You see, recalls cost a lot of money. They [the manufacturers] don't want to be faced with large recalls. So there's a huge economic incentive in the auto companies if we are properly enforcing the law.

Interview/San Francisco Examiner & Chronicle,
9-24:(This World)44.

Harwood Cochrane
Chairman, Overnite Transportation
Company

2

We cannot operate without government regulation—that is, the regulation of the trucking industry by the Interstate Commerce Commission. If nothing else, we need the ICC to protect us from each other or even from ourselves. For example, there are 35 carriers operating between Baltimore and Atlanta. Without the ICC, you might come up with 35 different scales of rates for the same commodity. This would be chaotic. Shippers would find it most difficult in dealing with the carriers. Also, you might find a situation where a carrier has just gone deeply in debt, buying new buildings and new trucks. To maintain a high level of traffic, he would have to bid low to make sure he could meet his payments. With many, it would be a desperate situation.

Interview, Richmond, Va./
Nation's Business, July:42.

Ben Davis
Personal Representative to the
Secretary of Transportation of the
United States

3

Since the late 1960s, highway fatalities were increasing at a rate of about 500 a year. They reached 55,000-plus in 1973. Once the 55-mph speed-limit law was put into effect—the first year, 1974—the fatalities immediately dropped by 10,000. Since then, yearly fatalities have been about 9,000 lower than the 1973 level. Therefore, for four years the law has saved over 36,000 lives. There's additional proof: The Christmas-New Year holiday period is historically the time when most accidents occur. But since the 55 limit was imposed, there have been a hundred fewer fatalities each holiday season. And there have been 60 per cent fewer paralyzing spinal-column injuries because the accidents have been less severe. Now, all of these things suggest to me that this particular law has provided the traveling public with advantages that just weren't there before we had the law.

Interview/U.S. News & World Report, 3-20:50.

John P. Fishwick
President, Norfolk & Western Railway

4

The historic pattern of nationalization [of railroads] is, first, government subsidies to commuter lines, then a takeover of the passenger service—like Amtrak has already done—and most recently a takeover of the unprofitable branch lines. Conrail is resulting in a gradual nationalization ... [The problem] is that the railroad industry started out as a monopoly, and people still consider it as a monopoly despite the fact that a hell of a lot of business has moved off the railroads and onto barges and highways. Since railroads are still considered monopolies, they are not permitted to quit. The true strength of the free-enterprise system is the ability to quit. Many corporations have found that, if they cannot compete, the only way they can survive is to withdraw from the market.

The Dallas Times Herald, 8-27:(M)1.

211

WHAT THEY SAID IN 1978

Arthur Imperatore
President, APA Transport Corporation

1

[On possible deregulation of the trucking industry]: The sweeping reforms being discussed in some quarters would bring chaos to the industry. The lawmakers must realize that we aren't the airline industry. With airlines you were building a market. Deregulation of the trucking industry won't produce one more pound of freight. I think we have [to] be guided by the principle of "If it ain't broke, don't fix it" ... Our company handles freight in 6,000 towns a day. Some of the locations are profitable; many of them are not. If rates were not set jointly, it would be very easy for unskilled operators to move into the better markets and skim the profit. That would drive many marginal operators out of business and in the end competition would be reduced instead of strengthened. You must keep in mind that rate bureaus provide other valuable services to the carriers. They make traffic surveys and keep large amounts of data that help us determine our costs. Rate bureaus also offer stability. Because of them, our profits are not as sensitive to snow storms, labor stoppages, recessions and the like ... One myth that needs to be dispelled forever is the belief that there's no rate competition in the United States. There's a tremendous competitive atmosphere and literally thousands of rates. The ICC allows carriers to institute commodity rates for certain volumes or for certain methods of packaging or loading. These rates, in turn, affect the levels of general rates. There's also great concern in this industry about losing business to other modes and about pricing ourselves out of the market.
Interview, North Bergen, N.J., Nov. 7/
The New York Times, 11-8:(D)2.

Edward G. Jordan
Chairman, Consolidated Rail
Corporation (Conrail)

2

If the problem [with Conrail] is our own inefficiency as managers, then change us. But if it is, as I believe, our inability to get the right price for the services we perform, then we'd

better get to the root of that ... We're asking ourselves what services we should offer and what should be paid for them. If the public doesn't want to pay for the service, then the decision will be made. We should advance this railroad into the marketplace, rather than regulate it from Washington.
Interview/U.S. News & World Report, 11-20:62,63.

Alfred E. Kahn
Chairman, Civil Aeronautics Board of
the United States

3

The nation's economic system provides all sorts of services without [Federal] governmental licensing or restrictions. TV repairmen, dentists, lawyers, automobile salesmen—all offer services that are growing and thriving without governmental intervention. So why do we need government controls on the airline industry? Why should the CAB still act in the role of the *paterfamilias* to those who want to invest their money in this industry? Why shouldn't the market system work in such a way that, if the service is economic, it will pay somebody to invest his money in it? Look at the commuter airlines. Hundreds of these small carriers are successfully providing service to cities all over the country without much Federal interference. On the whole, these companies give better service than the regulated carriers.
Interview/U.S. News & World Report, 3-6:47.

4

[Saying the current trend toward airline mergers can be traced to the companies' search for security now that the CAB has relaxed many regulation protections enjoyed in the past]: It seems clear to me that if you have companies that have been living under a security blanket for 40 years, or with a pacifier for 40 years, and the government threatens to take them away, they're going to look for other security blankets.
News conference, New Orleans, Sept. 22/
The Washington Post, 9-23:(D)11.

(ALFRED E. KAHN)

1

Two functions are at the heart of the CAB, and I want to eliminate them both. First is to regulate entry into the airline industry. But if you want to be an auto mechanic, retail hearing aids or manufacture chemicals, there's no government agency that says you can't do it. The second essential function is price-fixing. But we don't do that in the economy at large. What all this means is that I want to eliminate the CAB... I am not an "abolish government" man. We've had 45 years of government interventions, and in many cases they've been important, and they've worked. But there are areas in which government is trying to protect existing interests, and airlines are an outstanding example. This is where government intervention should disappear. I want the CAB to be the first government agency to commit *hara-kiri.*

Interview/People, 10-2:71.

2

[The practice of the CAB choosing a particular airline to fly a certain route is like] looking terribly hard for a real but elusive black cat in a very dark room. The problem is that there is no cat there. The more clearly we describe the delicate gossamer of our decisions on the selection of carriers, the more transparent it becomes that there is nothing there—not even gossamer. The Board is simply not equipped to make a rational selection of carriers. It is not equipped to plan the optimum future structure and growth of this dynamic industry, to select for each market the ideal price, the ideal supplier, the ideal aircraft. No board is.

Before American Bar Association/
The Washington Post, 10-29:(F)6.

Edward M. Kennedy
United States Senator, D-Massachusetts

3

[Favoring less regulation of the airline industry]: It is clear beyond doubt that the aviation regulatory scheme devised in the Depression to protect an infant industry has resulted in higher fares, less services ... and generally less competition than the public deserves and has a right to expect.

The Dallas Times Herald, 4-20:(A)1.

James L. Kerrigan
Chairman, Greyhound (bus) Lines

4

No other transportation system can do what we [bus lines] do. Trains serve only 500 points; airlines, only 700 airports [while buses serve about 14,000 communities]. Trains carry 18 million passengers a year; planes, 209 million; but buses carry 340 million.

U.S. News & World Report, 1-30:59.

J. Kevin Murphy
President, Trailways Bus Lines

5

For too long, the legitimate interests of the nation's 350 million annual bus passengers—a group which comprises the poor, the old, the minorities—have been callously disregarded by a national transportation policy which heavily subsidizes the profligacy of Amtrak and the luxury of the airlines, while doing nothing to provide safe and comfortable bus facilities ... For too long, the concerns of the bus passengers have met with indifference on the part of the industry's giant—I speak of Greyhound Bus Lines—which, instead of forcefully representing its customers' interest, seems content to issue hollow denials of what everyone else can see plain as day—that bus terminals are dilapidated relics that have no place in the 20th century ... But we at Trailways refuse to stop with painting such a bleak picture. Much can be done if we have but energy, vision and nerve ... Now, imagine yourself as a bus passenger ... 10 years in the future. You arrive at a spacious, clean, safe facility called a Ground Transportation Center. Inside are not only terminals for all the bus lines, but also connections for limousines to the area's airports and stands for taxi-cabs. Down the long promenades, you can find shops, restaurants, perhaps a hotel. Commuters, travelers, shoppers are all accommodated comfortably and safely inside its spacious facilities. Outside, there is a parklike buffer zone, proper-

WHAT THEY SAID IN 1978

(J. KEVIN MURPHY)

ly policed and protected. We at Trailways already have plans for such facilities. We have met with business, labor, social and political leaders in all parts of this country to form creative partnerships which will transform "Downtown U.S.A." For the future of bus travel is bound up with the future of our downtown areas.

Before New York Rotary Club,
Feb. 2/Vital Speeches, 8-1:626.

John J. O'Donnell
President, United States Air Line
Pilots Association

1

We'll have [aircraft] collisions all over the place [if something isn't done to sort out the aerial traffic jams]. As long as we depend on the pilot to look out the window and see another plane, we're going to have accidents.

Before Congressional committee/
U.S. News & World Report, 10-9:45.

Richard Page
Administrator, Urban Mass Transportation
Administration of the United States

2

If there is to be any progress [in urban mass transit], it must involve a willingness to innovate and try new solutions ... I believe in the future of our cities, and I believe that providing convenient, effective and economical transit is an important part of an effective strategy to strengthen and revitalize them. Our problems with inflation, and the stiff competition that pits transit against other essential services in vying for a share of available tax resources, demand that we keep striving for new and more cost-effective solutions.

At Advanced Transit Association
International Conference, Indianapolis,
April 26/The Dallas Morning News, 4-27:(A)23.

Mike Parkhurst
President, Independent Truckers Association

3

[Disagreeing with the theory that the 55-mile-per-hour speed limit has decreased acci-

dent fatalities] : ... 55 per cent of all highway deaths involve a drinking driver; 69.3 per cent of all highway deaths and 82 per cent of all personal injuries occur within 25 miles of a victim's home. To me, these statistics mean that the primary reason people get into accidents is because their attention is diverted from the task of driving, not because they are disobeying the speed-limit signs, which are monotonous in the first place. If it is so important for the government to save lives, then why doesn't it attack the primary cause of the accidents: the drunk, ignorant or inattentive driver? Why put so much emphasis on a national speed limit?

Interview/U.S. News & World Report, 3-20:50.

Derry Pearce
President, International Federation of
Airline Pilots Associations

4

[On airliner hijacking] : The only lasting solution to the problem is to bring world pressure to bear on these states that continue to harbor hijackers. Civil aviation will be troubled until potential hijackers are convinced that there is no haven for them anywhere.

Interview, Hong Kong/
Los Angeles Times, 1-25:(1)16.

Michael Pertschuk
Chairman, Federal Trade Commission

5

[Saying the government should rate cars for repairs] : If the consumer knows not only the [price] but the average repair cost for a car, he's going to have another important factor to take into account in deciding whether to buy that car. The only widely known piece of hard information [now available to consumers is the EPA gasoline mileage ratings] ... Shouldn't other basic information concerning equally important matters—reliability, durability—also be made available? [Such a system] would provide a powerful stimulus to manufacturers to design and build better cars.

Before Senate Consumer Subcommittee, Washington,
March 22/Los Angeles Times, 3-23:(1)29.

Urban Affairs

Roger C. Altman
Assistant Secretary of the
Treasury of the United States

1

[On Cleveland's financial crisis]: Our judgment is that the Cleveland fiscal crisis can be solved on the state and local level, and therefore that Federal financial or fiscal assistance is not needed ... The principle to follow here is that the first responsibility for the city is clearly through the state, and only if the state exhausts its resources would it be appropriate for a Federal role.

Washington, Dec. 18/
The New York Times, 12-19:(A)9.

Barbara Blum
Deputy Administrator, Environmental
Protection Agency of the United States

2

The talents and energies of environmentalism must be mobilized to help cities to once again become the magnet and the stage for all that is best about being human ... Urban people need desperately to gain control over their destiny. They have had enough of other people planning for them. We need not depend upon technological tragedy to inform us when, every day, citizens are assessing their technologies with their eyes—it's ugly; with their ears—it's too noisy; with their noses—it stinks; and, above all, with their common-sense gut feelings and intuition—somehow this just doesn't make sense ... Environmental groups, long used to fighting for wilderness areas, national parks and other grand designs such as Gateway East in New York and Gateway West here in the Bay Area, need to focus their thinking about recreation on the urban reality and the wishes of inner-city residents. Greenlining and other modest water-reclamation recreation projects may be all that is possible in some cities. But

small parks can accomplish miracles in muting sound, lowering air pollution and providing new recreational opportunities.

Before Sierra Club board of
directors, Berkeley, Calif., May 6/
San Francisco Examiner & Chronicle, 5-7:(A)4.

Edmund G. Brown, Jr.
Governor of California (D)

3

... corporate America depends on the regulatory power of Washington, and if that regulatory power was used not just for profit and to prop up existing privilege but to renew the cities of America, they'd be renewed; and they won't be renewed until power is used for that purpose ... If people were told they can't have any more mergers, they can't have any more banks, they can't have any more secret little deals until they start going to where the people are, they'd go there. And they're not going to go there one minute before the government tells them that.

Before National Urban League, Los Angeles,
Aug. 8/Los Angeles Times, 8-9:(1)3.

Jimmy Carter
President of the United States

4

The deterioration of urban life in the United States is one of the most complex and deeply rooted problems we face. The Federal government has the clear duty to lead the effort to reverse that deterioration ... The gravest flaw in past Federal policy was not that we failed to spend money. It was that too many of the programs were ineffective, and too many that did work had their benefits canceled out by other Federal and state activities.

Before Governors, Mayors and
members of Congress, Washington,
March 27/Los Angeles Times, 3-28:(1)1.

215

WHAT THEY SAID IN 1978

(JIMMY CARTER)

1

[On signing legislation providing Federal guarantees for New York City bonds]: Those who thought that the United States was going to stand by while its greatest city went under were wrong. The bill that I will sign today represents a mutual concern and a spirit of cooperation . . . Let there be no mistake about what this bill does. It is not a handout; New York has asked for no handout and has received none. Nor is it a Band-Aid or a temporary approach that simply postpones an inevitable problem. Instead, through long-term loan guarantees, the bill opens up enough breathing space for New Yorkers to complete the difficult task of restoring yourself to financial and economic self-sufficiency. This bill is in the national interest. It's designed to put behind us a danger that would create problems for all our cities and for the financial markets of the nation and the world. If New York keeps its commitment—and I'm sure it will—then this bill will not cost the American taxpayers one cent. It will give this great city the security and the time it needs to bring its budget into balance permanently.

At signing of the legislation, New York, Aug. 8/The New York Times, 8-9:(B)2.

2

Plainly, the future of our cities is at stake in our fight against inflation. I don't need to tell you how inflation affects your cities. You see it every week on purchasing invoices, utility bills, higher salaries, all constantly increasing budget costs. Inflation eats into your maintenance and capital funds; and with restricted budgets your streets, buildings and parks fall into greater disrepair. In other words, inflation jeopardizes the economic progress we have made since the recession of 1974-1975—including the fragile recovery of our troubled cities.

Before National League of Cities, St. Louis, Nov. 27/The New York Times, 11-28:(A)16.

3

I'm conversant with the problems of the cities. I don't think any Administration has ever had a closer consultative relationship with the Mayors than our own has had. In the evolution of our urban policy earlier this year the Mayors were full partners in the process, along with Governors and other local officials . . . The revenue-sharing legislation is a multi-year authorization and we support the carrying-out of the revenue-sharing at its present level until this present law expires. I can't foreclose the possibility that it might be modified in the future. My own attitude has always been that, with a given amount for revenue-sharing, a greater portion of it should go to the cities and local governments than to the states.

News conference, Washington, Dec. 12/The New York Times, 12-13:(A)20.

Margaret Hance
Mayor of Phoenix

4

We used to be concerned about accepting any Federal funds, but with the state of the game today, there is no way that we could provide for our airport expansion and some of the major freeway portions coming through our town. [But] we must resist those programs in which we lose our ability to run our own cities.

U.S. News & World Report, 4-10:24.

Louis Harris
Public-opinion analyst

5

The image of the large city that emerges from our data is that of an economic, cultural-intellectual and recreational service center. The city's image today as a place to live and raise children is overwhelmingly negative . . . The much maligned cities of America turn out to be not simply indispensable but are the central pivot for many activities. Of all the occasions that suburban residents go to a movie, 53 per cent of the time they go not to a suburban movie house but instead to the city. When suburbanites buy furniture or a major appliance, 46 per cent of the time they go to the nearest city. Of all the times when suburban dwellers go to a doctor, a majority of the time, 52 per cent, they go to a doctor in the city. And when those in the suburbs visit friends,

(LOUIS HARRIS)

fully 47 per cent of the time do not visit in the suburbs, but go to the cities to see them.

March 23/Los Angeles Times, 3-24:(1)30.

Patricia Roberts Harris
Secretary of Housing and Urban Development of the United States

1

We have as a major concern of the urban policy making cities desirable places in which to live and work. We don't know at this moment how many of those people who are currently leaving the cities are leaving because the cities have been required to reduce services, because there is not adequate housing in the cities, because they have been deprived of a choice of living in the cities by the deterioration that is there. What we want to do is equalize the competitive positions of cities as the city competes with suburbs and rural areas for populations that want new housing, more space. I have the feeling that, as cities are made more attractive, more and more people will choose to remain in the cities, and more and more people will choose to come to the city to live.

TV-radio interview/"Meet the Press," National Broadcasting Company, 4-2.

Philip Johnson
Architect

2

Urban renewal, as this country knew it, once was what I always called "urban removal." That's all it was. The policy was an attempt to push problems of the inner city a bit further away to make it more profitable to erect skyscrapers. I don't think that approach will be used again, for it's been discredited for some time. But the policy was typical of the modern period of architecture. They just tore down the centers of our cities, and in some cases they're still leveled. Look at St. Louis; they tore down the middle of that city, and it's still completely empty. And take the South Bronx, which also has sociological problems; what's been done there is dreadful.

Interview/U.S. News & World Report, 6-5:75.

Vernon E. Jordan, Jr.
President, National Urban League

3

Revitalization of our cities is a crisis situation. Funds committed by the [President] Carter urban policy do not begin to be what is needed to solve the problem ... The heart of any urban policy must be jobs. Everything flows from jobs if the city is to be rehabilitated, stabilized and revitalized.

Before Urban League of Eastern Massachusetts, Boston/The Christian Science Monitor, 4-17:5.

Edward M. Kennedy
United States Senator, D-Massachusetts

4

[Calling for the cutting of red tape in dealing with urban applications for Federal aid]: The time has come for the Federal government to give greater breathing room to the Mayors and let them do their jobs. If we can deregulate the airlines ... we can also deregulate the Mayors so that they can serve the people of our cities.

At United States Conference of Mayors, Atlanta, June 19/The Washington Post, 6-20:(A)3.

Edward I. Koch
Mayor of New York

5

I do not exaggerate when I say that New York is unique in the history of human kindness. New York is not a problem. New York is a stroke of genius. From its earliest days, this city has been a lifeboat for the homeless, a larder for the hungry, a living library for the intellectually starved, a refuge not only for the oppressed but also for the creative. New York is and has been the most open city in the world, and that is its greatness and that is why in large part it faces monumental problems today ... Without question, this city has made mistakes. But our mistakes have been those of the heart. In my Administration, I intend to bring the heart and the head together.

Inauguration address, New York, Jan. 1/The New York Times, 1-2:13.

WHAT THEY SAID IN 1978

(EDWARD I. KOCH)

1

As long as I am Mayor of the city of New York, the city will make every effort to see that the dollars it spends are spent wisely and well. The citizens of my city are tired of the waste, mismanagement and abuse that have for too long been endemic in certain social programs, however well-intentioned, and in governmental operations generally. I intend to see that municipal government is administered fairly and openly, that inefficiency and corruption are rooted out, that city budgetary practices conform to the highest standards, and that services are rendered to our residents at the lowest possible cost in tax dollars. This I have pledged and, to the best of my ability, this I will do.

Before Senate Banking Committee, Washington, June 6/The New York Times, 6-7:(B)4.

2

... over the long run, the cost to the Federal government of not helping [New York] will be greater than the cost of helping. If the city does not undertake needed rehabilitation, it will decay and slowly die, becoming a ward of the state and Federal governments. This, I submit, is a strong argument why the cost of the guarantee program to the Federal government will be small and the reward great—among them the rehabilitation of the largest city in the United States.

Before Senate Banking Committee, Washington, June 6/The New York Times, 6-7:(B)4.

Dennis J. Kucinich
Mayor of Cleveland

3

[Calling for an income-tax increase to alleviate the city's perilous financial position] : Unless this tax increase is approved by the people, we will be short millions of dollars each month next year. The city will be so deeply in debt that I will be forced to cut services to such a drastic level that everyone living and working in Cleveland will suffer. There is no service area which will not be touched: waste collection, police and fire protection, snow removal,

health, recreation and others will all be cut back to levels which would be unacceptable, not only to myself but to you, the people of Cleveland.

Broadcast address to the city, Dec. 12/Los Angeles Times, 12-13:(1)1.

R. Robert Linowes
President, Metropolitan Washington Board of Trade

4

... in recent times, businessmen have taken a serious and sincere interest in the future of the cities. They have realized that the future of the cities is closely interwoven with the future of our country ... I believe that businessmen have come to realize that a city, by its very nature, requires an intricate number of partnerships if it is to survive. But those partnerships must not be just with all the groups that make up the public and the private sectors of our society. Economic development benefits the whole community, and so the whole community must be involved.

Before National Council for Urban Economic Development/The Washington Post, 12-1:(A)18.

Henry W. Maier
Mayor of Milwaukee

5

[On the causes for the erosion of population and the tax and industrial bases of cities] : The FHA and the Veterans Administration helped to build the suburbs and lure our middle class by providing attractive mortage-interest and insurance rates during the 1950s. Then Federal housing-subsidy programs were developed with a bias toward new housing construction in the suburbs and against rehabilitation of older housing in the cities. Federal tax incentives in the form of accelerated depreciation schedules and investment tax credits gave business and industry reasons to leave the older cities for greener pastures in the suburbs. These tax breaks made it advantageous for more businesses and industries to build new one-story and more technologically advanced facilities on open land outside the cities, rather than rehabi-

(HENRY W. MAIER)

litate and expand older multi-story factory
buildings in the city.

*At symposium on the exodus of
industry from cities, Milwaukee,
May 25/The New York Times, 5-26:(A)12.*

John Portman
Urban architect

1

The cities have gone down so far, and crime
has become such a major topic for so many
years, that the perceptions in the minds of
people are that cities are unsafe. And really it is
more a perception than a reality because here in
Atlanta, for instance, only 6 per cent of the
crime is committed in the central city. However, the perception in the minds of the people
would probably be more like 70 per cent.

Los Angeles Times, 11-20:(1)28.

William Proxmire
United States Senator, D-Wisconsin

2

[Arguing against the Federal government
providing long-term Federal guarantees to New
York to help that city in its fiscal crisis] : First,
[guarantees] would keep the Federal government running New York City for 19 more
years; I think we should get out of our involvement and stop being constantly pulled into
local matters. Second, long-term guarantees
would remove the pressure on the city and keep
it from making the tough decisions needed to
get the city back on a balanced budget and
back into the credit markets; it would allow the
city to borrow and spend today and put off
paying for years to come, which is what got
New York in trouble to begin with. Third, there
is no reason to believe, and no strong evidence
to support, the notion that one shot of long-
term guarantees would solve the problem forever and get New York City out of its involvement with the Federal government, any more
than the "one-shot" seasonal loans did; we run
the risk of turning New York City into a "guarantee junkie"—coming back and back, every
four years, rather than every three. Finally,

giving long-term guarantees to New York City
would set a terrible precedent; it would invite
other cities across the country to spend freely
and be fiscally irresponsible the way New York
was before 1975, because they would know
they could always come to Uncle Sam for a
long-term bailout.

*Before Senate Banking Committee, Washington,
June 6/The New York Times, 6-7:(B)4.*

David Rockefeller
Chairman, Chase Manhattan Bank

3

Some argue that "enough is enough," that
the city [New York] should go into bankruptcy [rather than receive Federal aid] , that
the risks have been grossly overstated in the
first place. I would say ... that no one can
really predict with precision what bankruptcy
would entail. I personally believe, however, that
the national market for municipal securities
would be seriously disrupted. I also have deep
concerns as to how this nation's largest city and
its nearly 8 million citizens would be governed
under Chapter IX. Further, I wonder what the
rest of the world would think of a political
system that allowed its largest city to go into
bankruptcy. In short, the risks are most clearly
not minimal. I would describe them as grave.

*Before Senate Banking Committee, Washington,
June 12/The New York Times, 6-13:(D)16.*

Gerald N. Springer
Mayor of Cincinnati

4

Those of us who represent cities have become Federal junkies, where every two months
we trek off to Washington and ask for hand-
outs. There is a philosophical motive behind
Federal tax retention. We in local government
are the ones most accountable to the public.
Why send our dollar to Washington and have it
come back worth 55 cents, and with all sorts of
strings attached?

*To reporters at National League of Cities
convention/Los Angeles Times, 12-3:(1)27.*

WHAT THEY SAID IN 1978

George Wendel
Director, Center for Urban
Programs, St. Louis University

1

The problem of today for cities like St. Louis is a process of class-skimming. Even middle-class blacks are leaving—5,000 to 7,000 a year—to make money in the suburbs ... We're being left with an increasingly dependent class in the city: older whites and younger, but poorer, blacks.

The Christian Science Monitor, 8-25:12.

PART TWO

International Affairs

Idi Amin
President of Uganda

1

I am not against [U.S.] President Carter and I love the Americans for their straightforward and frank policy in Africa ... Uganda will never change its friendly attitude toward the Americans. President Carter—whom I love like a brother—is misinformed about Uganda. If he comes to Uganda he would know what is happening in the country. We have not violated human rights in Uganda. But when we are attacked, we are forced to defend our sovereignty.
Radio Address, March 25/
The Dallas Times Herald, 3-26:(A)5.

Christiaan Barnard
South African surgeon

2

Whatever else I am, I'm a patriot. Every time I go overseas I come back and think, "Thank God I can live in South Africa." If people demonstrate against apartheid, I'm with them. But if I see them demonstrating against South Africa, I can't join them. It's fashionable these days to hammer this country.
Interview/People, 4-17:38.

Gerald J. Bender
Visiting assistant professor of political science, University of California, San Diego; Authority on Africa

3

The principal actors in the superpower competition in Africa today are the five permanent members of the [UN] Security Council: the United States, the Soviet Union, China, France and Britain. They are using all available means. There are no absolute angels, and no absolute devils. I think most African governments know that. The only thing that has changed recently is the great increase in military armaments, military advisers, even foreign military troops such as the French and the Cubans. I think that the military emphasis will pass and that the new emphasis will be on economic aid. That certainly would be a lot more salubrious for Africans.
Panel discussion/World Issues, Oct.-Nov.:4.

Pieter W. Botha
Prime Minister of South Africa

4

We must set ourselves certain goals: First, the maintenance and development of orderly government. Secondly, at all times to uphold honest public administration and effective government. Thirdly, to apply a positive policy to improve the relations between the different population communities, taking into account the inalienable right of self-determination of all peoples. I believe we have enough common ground in this country to work together to make it one of the most wonderful countries in the world.
Inaugural address, Cape Town, Sept. 28/
Los Angeles Herald Examiner, 9-28:(A)4.

5

While we [in South Africa] do not think we can fight the whole world, I want to give those who think they can chase us around this assurance: Don't underestimate our [whites] determination to stay in this country. Don't underestimate our will to safeguard South Africa and the integrity of its borders. Don't underestimate our will to keep this an orderly community of nations.
Pretoria, Sept. 30/
The Dallas Times Herald, 10-1:(A)5.

6

The United Nations decided to proclaim SWAPO as the sole representative of the peoples of South-West Africa. We say we can only determine who the leaders of the peoples

(PIETER W. BOTHA)

of South-West Africa are if you have a proper election. SWAPO was invited to take part in that election. They preferred not to take part, because they are not interested in elections. They are interested in foisting their own ideas at the point of a gun on the majority of the people of South-West Africa.

TV-radio interview, Pretoria/"Meet the Press,"
National Broadcasting Company, 11-19.

Leonid I. Brezhnev
President of the Soviet Union; General
Secretary, Soviet Communist Party

1

[Criticizing recent Western intervention to stop an attack on Zaire's Shaba province from Angola]: There are political circles that are evidently trying to mar the process of de-tente . . . and to return, if not to the cold war, then at least to a lukewarm war. This direction is taken through such actions as the bloody intervention of NATO member states in Zaire. These circles have tried to mask the cynical character of this interference, to divert attention by a propaganda campaign about a fabricated "Soviet" and, at other times, "Cuban" participation in the events.

At political rally, Prague, Czechoslovakia,
May 31/The New York Times, 6-1:(A)1.

Zbigniew Brzezinski
Assistant to President of the United
States Jimmy Carter for National
Security Affairs

2

The [conflict] between Somalia and Ethiopia should be resolved on a regional basis, involving the African countries themselves, and with respect for the principle of territorial integrity and non-intervention from abroad. Just as a Soviet/Cuban intervention is now developing, it can also be reversed—and it should be. I am sure most African countries do not want foreign intervention in Africa. I think the Soviets know our views on this subject.

Interview/U.S. News & World Report, 2-13:31.

3

The invasion of Katanga, or Shaba, [in Zaire] from Angola could not have taken place without the full knowledge of the Angolan government. It could not have taken place without the invading parties having been armed and trained by the Cubans and indeed perhaps also the East Germans; and we have sufficient evidence to be quite confident in our conclusion that Cuba shares the political and the moral responsibility for the invasion, indeed even for the outrages that were associated with it . . . We are talking about responsibility, responsibility for something which should not have taken place, which is a violation of territorial integrity, which in fact is a belligerent act. We believe that the evidence we have sustains the proposition—more than that, sustains the conclusion—that the Cuban government and in some measure the Soviet government bear the responsibility for this transgression, and this is a serious matter. This is a matter which is not conducive to international stability nor to international accommodation.

TV-radio interview/"Meet the Press,"
National Broadcasting Company, 5-28.

Robert C. Byrd
United States Senator, D-West Virginia

4

The continued involvement of the Soviet Union, directly or through the activities of her ally Cuba, in the internal affairs and conflicts of several sub-Saharan African nations, indicates that the Soviet Union has not swerved from its commitment to foment chaos wherever it believes it can benefit.

Before Delta Council, Cleveland, Miss., May 30/
The New York Times, 5-31:(A)14.

James Callaghan
Prime Minister of the United Kingdom

5

The West has much more to offer Africans than simply to treat them as pawns on the chessboard. The countries of Africa know this. They can recognize, without anyone lecturing them, the new imperialism that comes from the East. Our record since decolonization will bear

(JAMES CALLAGHAN)

examination. Despite the fainthearted, I believe that our approach will stand the test of time better than military adventurism or a new imperialism.

Accepting Hubert H. Humphrey International Award
from National Committee for American Foreign
Policy, New York/The New York Times, 7-2:(1)3.

Frank C. Carlucci
Deputy Director of Central Intelligence
of the United States

1

The degree of Soviet and Cuban military activity in sub-Saharan Africa is unprecedented. We are witnessing the most determined campaign to expand foreign influence in this troubled region since it was carved up by the European powers in the late 19th century.

Before Senate Armed Services Intelligence
Subcommittee, Washington, April 10/
U.S. News & World Report, 4-24:52.

Jimmy Carter
President of the United States

2

[On the conflict in the Horn of Africa]: We have three hopes there that we trust and certainly hope that the Soviets will honor. One is a Somalian withdrawal from the territories which they occupy in eastern Ethiopia in the Ogaden area. Secondly, a removal from Ethiopia of Cuban and Soviet troops. Third, a lessening of the tensions that exist between those countries and an honoring of the sometimes arbitrarily drawn international boundaries in Africa. And we would hope that the OAU ... would become more successful in their efforts to resolve this dispute in a peaceful way. But at this time, Somalia is the invading nation. We have refused to send any weapons into that area or to permit third countries who bought weapons from us to transfer them into that area. And I think our policy is completely accurate.

News conference, Washington, March 2/
The New York Times, 3-3:(A)10.

3

In the name of justice, we ... believe that South African society should and can be transformed progressively and peacefully, with assured respect for the rights of all. We have made it clear to South Africa that the nature of our relations will depend on whether there is progress toward full political participation for all her people in every aspect of the social and economic life of the nation and an end to discrimination based on race or ethnic origin. We stand firm in that message ... I believe we should therefore combine our determination to support the rights of the oppressed in South Africa with a willingness to hold out our hands to the white minority if they decide to transform their society and to do away with the crippling burdens of past injustices.

Lagos, Nigeria, April 1/
San Francisco Examiner & Chronicle, 4-2:(A)18.

4

[On alleged Cuban involvement in the Katangan raid on Zaire's Shaba province from Angola]: We have never accused the Cuban troops of being part of the invading force, but there is no doubt about the fact that the Cubans have a heavy—even dominant—position in Angola, that they were involved in training the Katangans who did invade Zaire. There is no doubt that the Cubans knew about it, encouraged it and were responsible for their training; [and the weapons used were] the same the Cubans use and which are supplied by the Soviet Union.

Washington, May 29/
The New York Times, 5-31:(A)1.

5

Our [NATO] alliance centers on Europe, but our vigilance cannot be limited to the continent. In recent years, expanding Soviet power has increasingly penetrated beyond the North Atlantic area. As I speak today, the activities of the Soviet Union and Cuba in Africa are preventing individual nations from charting their own course. As members of the world's greatest alliance, we cannot be indifferent to these events—because of what they mean for Africa

WHAT THEY SAID IN 1978

(JIMMY CARTER)

and because of their effect on the long-term interests of the alliance. I welcome the efforts of individual NATO allies to work for peace in Africa, and to support nations and peoples in need—most recently in Zaire.

At NATO meeting, Washington, May 30/
Los Angeles Times, 5-31:(1)1.

1

In Africa, we and our African friends want to see a continent that is free of the dominance of outside powers, free of the bitterness of racial injustice, free of conflict and free of the burdens of poverty and hunger and disease . . . The persistent and increasing military involvement of the Soviet Union and Cuba in Africa could deny this hopeful vision. We are deeply concerned about the threat to regional peace and to the autonomy of countries within which these foreign troops seem permanently to be stationed.

Before graduating class, U.S. Naval Academy,
June 7/The New York Times, 6-8:(A)22.

2

What we're trying to do is to end the bloodshed in Rhodesia. We've not caused the bloodshed; we've not caused a war. We have put forward publicly, without any secrecy about it, along with the British, to the front-line [African] Presidents, to the Patriotic Front, to the Smith regime, our proposals that there be all-parties conferences where people that are in dispute can get together and talk and try to work out a means by which free and democratic elections can be held in Rhodesia so that anyone who is qualified can run for office, and let the people of Rhodesia decide what kind of government they want. This is a proposal that [Rhodesian Prime Minister Ian] Smith and his regime have not been willing to accept. But this is what we've proposed. If the parties in dispute prefer a different proposal and agree upon it, we would have no objection to that . . . As I say, we are not wedded to a particular plan, although I think the Anglo-American plan—so-called—has been accepted in its basic elements.

So we're doing the best we can to end the bloodshed and to bring peace, without any tendency to force people to come to a certain place or to force people even to accept the elements of the settlement that we think are best.

News conference, Oct. 10/
U.S. News & World Report, 10-23:42.

Fidel Castro
Premier of Cuba

3

Imperialism and its reactionary allies madly demand the immediate withdrawal of Cuban combatants in Ethiopia. Anyone can understand that this also means the immediate initiation of new acts of aggression. We, as a matter of principle, emphatically refuse to discuss with the United States this point or any other point concerning Cuba's solidarity with the just struggles of the peoples of Africa. Yankee imperialism questions the right of Ethiopia to defend its territorial integrity and its unity against Eritrean secessionists. [But] the United States itself had a bitter historic experience with secessionism, [and] a very pacifist man, noble and of high stature, Lincoln, was forced to resort to arms to prevent it.

Introducing Ethiopian leader Mengistu Haile
Mariam at rally, Havana, Cuba, April 26/
The Washington Post, 4-28:(A)24.

4

[Denying charges that his country was involved in the recent attacks in Zaire's Shaba province]: Everything will be known sooner or later. History will prove some day that we were telling the truth and that the charges against us were really false . . . [The lie told against Cuba] is not a half lie. It is an absolute, total, complete lie. It is not a small lie; it is a big lie. It is not a negligible lie; it is an important lie.

Interview, Havana, June 13/
The Washington Post, 6-14:(A)18.

5

[On whether Africa will become Cuba's Vietnam]: I see no risk of that anywhere. In Vietnam, the United States was supporting a

(FIDEL CASTRO)

corrupted government. We cooperate, actually, with progressive, popular governments which receive the support of the masses of the people, and have supported them—not regarding their internal problems, but rather we cooperate in their defense against foreign aggression.

Broadcast interview/Los Angeles Times, 6-18:(1)5.

1

[On his country's involvement in Africa]: We are not a military power. We have no nuclear weapons, no navy, no strategic forces. We are just a small country whose most important raw material is its spirit, the willingness of our people to sacrifice and demonstrate solidarity with other peoples. In the current cases mentioned most often, Angola and Ethiopia, we have prevented two historic crimes: the occupation of Angola by South Africa and the disintegration of the Ethiopian state as a result of foreign aggression.

Interview/Time, 6-26:31.

Raul Castro
Armed Forces Minister of Cuba

2

[On his country's military role in Africa]: Thousands of Cubans are at this moment far away from the Fatherland, fulfilling their duty of helping other peoples and other countries that struggle against colonialism or confront with heroism the aggression of imperialism and the reactionary forces. Let us extend to them the emotional tribute of our admiration.

Oriente Province, Cuba, March 11/
The Dallas Times Herald, 3-12:(A)4.

Jeremiah Chirau
Leader, Zimbabwe (Rhodesia) United
People's Organization

3

It will be a sad day and a disaster for the country if something is going to happen and we lose the whites. On this I want to speak very strongly. This country was built by two groups, whites and blacks. The white man brought his skills and his money, and the black man

brought his labor. Together, over 90 years, we have built this nation. Still, today, black cannot do without white, and white cannot do without black.

Interview, Salisbury/
The New York Times, 2-23:(A)4.

Frank Church
United States Senator, D-Idaho

4

I don't believe in a demon theory of history. If the President's [Carter] policy is actually postulated on the premise that the Russians should stop what they are doing in Africa and elsewhere, then it is doomed to failure . . . [The U.S. should let] the Cubans and the Russians make their own mistakes in Africa without duplicating them.

To reporters, Washington, June 8/
The New York Times, 6-9:(A)3.

Rowan Cronje
Minister of Manpower, Health and
Social Affairs of Rhodesia

5

The Western world insists on painting us with the same [racial] brush as South Africa. We are developing the Africans here. For every white millionaire there are five black millionaires. And you have to remember that 80 years ago, when the whites arrived, the African didn't know the wheel. He didn't even wear clothes. I wouldn't exchange our blacks for any in Africa. Since 1962, no trade union can legally have racial privileges. There is not a single exclusively white trade union here. Wages are not, by law, based on race. The government's policy is a "rate for the job," a specific rate for a specific job without regard to race.

Interview/San Francisco Examiner & Chronicle,
2-12:(This World)45.

Donald B. Easum
United States Ambassador to Nigeria

6

African heads of state used to plead with [then-] President Nixon and [then-Secretary of State Henry] Kissinger to show real [U.S.] attention to the affairs of Africa, and our indif-

WHAT THEY SAID IN 1978

ference was very obvious. Kissinger kept saying, "How can you have an African policy when there are 50 different countries there?" He continually refused to see African ambassadors in Washington, except to occasionally receive the whole African diplomatic corps as a group, which the Africans saw as very demeaning.

Interview, Lagos, Nigeria/
Los Angeles Times, 3-31:(1)7.

Gerald R. Ford
Former President of the United States

1

[Backing the plan for black majority rule in Rhodesia worked out last month by the Salisbury government and moderate black leaders]: I strongly support the internal settlement. They have undertaken a process to transfer minority rule to majority rule, with the protection of the rights of the minority. They have, in effect, provided for open and free elections, which is what we want in this country. I believe that's a big step forward, and it will give stability and I think democracy to the six million blacks in Rhodesia, and at the same time protect the rights of the 250,000 whites.

Television interview, New York, April 24/
The New York Times, 4-27:(A)8.

2

[Criticizing the U.S. Carter Administration's cool attitude toward the Rhodesian government's plan for transition to black majority rule, as opposed to the black nationalist guerrillas who are trying to take over by force]: How [the Carter Administration] can support a group that wants to take over that country by bullets rather than ballots is beyond my comprehension.

Before lawyers and businessmen, Dallas, May 3/
The Dallas Times Herald, 5-4:(A)10.

E. J. (Jake) Garn
United States Senator, R-Utah

3

Lifting [U.S. economic] sanctions [against Rhodesia] will help transition government work toward black majority rule by December 31, when a new government is scheduled to take over the country. The transition government is pro-West and anti-Communist and deserves our support in working toward an internal settlement ... For years, British and American representatives have indicated that the economic boycott would be lifted if the Rhodesians accepted majority rule. They've promised to do just that, and now the [U.S. Carter] Administration has added a new condition—that Marxist terrorist leaders must be a part of any negotiated settlement. [Guerrilla leaders Joshua Nkomo and Robert Mugabe] believe that power grows out of the barrel of a gun. They have no vision for the type of government Rhodesia ought to have, but they would like personal power. They refuse to participate in the internal settlement because they know they couldn't win support in free elections.

/**

Valery Giscard d'Estaing
President of France

4

[On his country's military involvement in Africa in response to Soviet intervention on that continent]: We have long believed that economic and social development, to which we have been contributing in an important way, is the way toward assuring peace [in Africa]. Now we must face the fact that this peace is being increasingly threatened. It is henceforth peace itself that is the primary condition for progress in Africa.

May/Los Angeles Times, 6-6:(1)1.

Barry M. Goldwater
United States Senator, R-Arizona

5

Within 100 years or so, Africa, because of its resources, will become the dominant continent in the world. The Soviets are pouring billions in there and winning because of our lack of guts. Starting with Angola, we have backed down. We're giving South Africa a bad time. South Africa can live without the U.S., but we can't live without them. It's of strategic importance to us, and sits on top of two-thirds of the

(BARRY M. GOLDWATER)

world's gold. They could use that gold politically some day. [Secretary Juanita] Kreps at Commerce signs orders embargoing shipments to
South Africa of anything which can be used
for military or police purposes. Commerce
urges U.S. firms to get out. Our Embassy in
Pretoria insults them. Our Ambassador didn't
show up for a concert sponsored by the South
African Broadcasting Corporation honoring our
Bicentennial.

Interview/San Francisco Examiner & Chronicle,
5-7:(Sunday Punch)3.

Andrei A. Gromyko
Foreign Minister of the Soviet Union

1

[On U.S. President Carter's criticism of
Soviet involvement in Africa] : The information
which the President has at his disposal is not
correct—that is our assessment ... We have no
intention of grabbing either the whole of Africa
or its parts. We don't need it.

To reporters, Washington, May 27/
The Washington Post, 6-4:(A)17.

Louis de Guiringaud
Foreign Minister of France

2

We see Cuban forces—regular forces—and
large bodies of Soviet military advisers active in
Africa—in Angola, in the Horn of Africa, in
Mozambique—and we see the hand of the Cubans in many of the destabilizing tensions which
we have to face in Africa ... We are not defending in Africa a regime, or a man, anywhere.
We are trying to help this continent maintain
stability, [because the resources and attention]
spent on prevention of destabilization are lost
to development, and we think Africa has better
things to do than to fight.

Interview, Washington, May 29/
The Washington Post, 5-30:(A)1.

Sayeed Haji
Director, Somali National News Agency

3

[Criticizing U.S. failure to aid his country in
its current conflict with Ethiopia] : The Rus-

sians proved their might [in backing Ethiopia].
People are saying that if you are not with the
Russians, you are finished. The Russians act,
the Americans just talk. We have an old Somali
saying: "If you are fighting and one man holds
your arms while another man beats you, who is
your worse enemy?"

The New York Times, 3-23:(A)11.

S. I. Hayakawa
United States Senator, R-California

4

I think we [the U.S.] would have an influence if we tell the people in Rhodesia that
we will back them if they, like ourselves, try to
create an interracial government with visible
steps toward real racial equality in the future.
As it is, the United States is so frightened of the
disapproval of the so-called front-line states—
those miserably weak, economically fragile
front-line states which put on a big front, backed up by Russian weaponry, but have no inner
strength—that we don't dare do anything. And
we're peculiarly paralyzed by our own fears.

Interview/U.S. News & World Report, 10-30:32.

Jesse A. Helms
United States Senator, R-North Carolina

5

[Calling for an end to the U.S. trade embargo against Rhodesia] : As everyone knows—
everyone, apparently, except the [U.S.] State
Department—the principal leaders of Rhodesia,
representing both the white populations and at
least 80 per cent of the black populations,
signed an agreement on March 3, 1978, thereby
initiating a transitional government to full
majority rule by December 31, 1978. Despite
certain inevitable tensions, that transitional government has been functioning fairly smoothly.
Few would assert that the parties concerned
have failed to make a good-faith effort to see
that the internal settlement works, and that it
leads to peace and prosperity for all residents of
Rhodesia, black and white ... If there are to be
truly free elections, and if the elections are
going to be held in an atmosphere of peace and
emotional stability, it is imperative that sanctions be dropped immediately ... The carefully

WHAT THEY SAID IN 1978

(JESSE A. HELMS)

crafted plan of the internal settlement . . . is reasonable, humane and just to all parties. It is based upon traditional Western concepts of equity and justice. It was proposed in good faith. It should be given a chance.

Before the Senate, Washington/
Los Angeles Herald Examiner, 7-9:(E)4.

Benjamin L. Hooks
Executive director, National
Association for the Advancement of
Colored People

1

There is a legitimate difference of opinion among civil-rights organizations in this country [the U.S.], and some are convinced that it would hurt blacks in South Africa if American corporations pulled out. Our previous position was that corporations should not put more money into South Africa and that they should try to influence the country to change its [racial] policies. We also felt that in the United States we should resort to selective buying as a form of protest. But our task force on Africa has determined that the majority of black leaders in that country would prefer that we come to a showdown with South Africa and that economic sanctions are the best method of pressure. We have become convinced that the South African government won't be responsive to pleas from other governments or American corporations doing business there. So we think American corporations should pull out.

At NAACP convention, Portland, Ore., July 3/
The New York Times, 7-4:6.

Byron R. Hove
Former Minister of Justice of Rhodesia

2

[On he, a black, being ousted as Justice Minister by the biracial interim Rhodesian government]: What [Prime Minister Ian] Smith envisages is a situation in which the civil service, the police, the judiciary, the army and all the state apparatus remain in the hands of white people. In other words, he believes in the substance of power remaining in white hands, with the shadow of authority passing to blacks. That is his "majority rule."

The Christian Science Monitor, 5-1:36.

Huang Hua
Foreign Minister of the People's
Republic of (mainland) China

3

[Zaire] can count on the support of the Chinese . . . in their just struggle [against] Soviet-Cuban-backed mercenaries . . . Under the leadership of President Mobutu [Sese Seko], the Zairian people and army have waged a just struggle against the invasion by the Soviet-Cuban-hired mercenaries in the Shaba region, and for the defense of national independence, state unity and territorial integrity.

To reporters, Kinshasa, Zaire, June 7/
Los Angeles Herald Examiner, 6-8:(A)4.

Paulo Jorge
Foreign Minister of Angola

4

The Cubans are in my country for the simple reason that we have two bad neighbors—Zaire and South Africa—and Cuba will send us as many people as we need and they will stay until the work is finished, but I can't even guess when that will be . . . America responds with silence when thousands of French troops intervene in Africa, but we hear this hysterical scream when we invite the Cubans in . . . If we were involved [in the rebel raid on Zaire's Shaba province last month]—the Angolans and the Cubans—we wouldn't have stopped at Kolwezi. We would have pushed all the way to Kinshasa.

Interview, United Nations, New York, June 6/
Los Angeles Times, 6-7:(1)7.

Kenneth Kaunda
President of Zambia

5

[Saying the U.S. should reject the internal agreement made by Rhodesian Prime Minister Ian Smith and black leaders to solve the racial problem in that country, and instead push for the rival British-American plan which calls for the inclusion of black guerrillas in the settle-

(KENNETH KAUNDA)

ment] : If you Americans want to be useful in averting the racial and ideological conflagration which Zambia has been expressing anxieties about since 1966, then you must take over the initiative [from the British]. [The Americans] have the capacity, they have the ability, and I think now they have a man [President Carter] determined to implement human rights the world over . . . Either you use the Anglo-American initiative to help bring genuine peace to Zimbabwe [Rhodesia] or you go ahead and support the internal settlement and bring hell here to everybody in southern Africa.

Interview, Lusaka, Zambia, March 8/
The Washington Post, 3-9:(A)20.

1

I am not sure there is a single Cuban [soldier] on the African continent who has not been invited by some member of the continent. So long as this is the case, it is not easy to condemn their presence. Sisters and brothers, let us deal with the cause rather than the effect when we deal with these very serious matters of life and death.

Washington, May 17/Los Angeles Times, 5-18:(1)6.

Henry A. Kissinger
Former Secretary of State of the
United States

2

. . . We have an obligation to try to remove the legitimate causes of unrest and instability in Africa. Of course, the U.S. must stand for majority rule . . . At the same time, let us take care not to turn majority rule into a device by which those who could not win an election try to force their way into office by the threat of force. Majority rule must not become the slogan of those who have already rejected a multiparty system and already announced that they want to create a one-party state. And majority rule must include protection for minority rights. If the black and white communities cannot live together under the rule of law, we will

see a race war of tremendous proportions develop. We cannot want to encourage this.

Before International Radio and Television
Society, New York/San Francisco
Examiner & Chronicle, 5-7:(B)7.

3

[If the Cubans are involved in the Eritrean conflict,] we must hold the Soviet Union responsible. Ultimately they placed the Cubans there . . . I think the Soviet Union must be told that it has to choose between negotiations with us or an imperial policy in Africa. It cannot have both . . . Up to this point, I have agreed with the [U.S. Carter] Administration that SALT should not be linked with what has happened so far. But in light of what has happened recently in Afghanistan—where the Communists have taken over, [and in light of] what now appears to be occurring in Zaire [the invasion of Shaba province from Angola] . . . I think we ought to review the whole negotiations—all of our negotiations with the Soviets.

Television commentary, May 15/
The Washington Post, 5-17:(A)18.

4

I am not saying we [the U.S.] should have endorsed the internal settlement as the only solution in Rhodesia, but it seems to me that we are putting ourselves in the wrong position if we give no encouragement whatever to people who are trying to govern on the basis of the vote, and support totally those whose primary claim is that they have the guns, and guns moreover supplied by the Soviet Union and trained by the Cubans. This, in effect, is saying that anybody who is equipped by the Soviets and trained by the Cubans can have a veto, if we make the argument that there can be no solution until they are satisfied. Our weight objectively has been on the side of the so-called Patriotic Front, on the so-called radical forces which will make a bi-racial solution in Rhodesia extremely difficult, if not impossible, and therefore may make a solution of the South African problems very difficult, if not impossible . . . I think [guerrilla leader] Joshua Nkomo is an authentic leader of Rhodesian

WHAT THEY SAID IN 1978

(HENRY A. KISSINGER)

independence and should be part of a governmental structure, but it makes a great deal of difference whether Joshua Nkomo joins the government structure that is based on a balance of forces within Rhodesia, or whether he joins a governmental structure that has fought its way into Rhodesia, armed by the Soviets, trained by the Cubans, and who will then, if he is to prevail, have to fight his fellow leader in the Patriotic Front in a civil war in which both sides are armed by the Russians.

TV-radio interview/"Meet the Press," National Broadcasting Company, 9-24.

1

[On U.S. policy toward South Africa]: It should have three objectives: 1) to make South African institutions more compatible with widely accepted norms of human dignity; 2) to do so without a racial war; 3) to achieve this within a period of time that is relevant to the aspirations of the [black] majority. It can be done only by giving the white minority a sense that we understand the dramatic challenge change will bring. It must have a sense that the beginning of its adaptation is not the beginning of its total collapse. It requires an understanding that a policy of confrontation with South Africa is tantamount to a policy of fomenting race war.

Interview, New York/Newsweek, 12-11:62.

Pieter G. Koornhof
Minister for Black Affairs of South Africa

2

[In the future, South African blacks will have] complete human rights, participation in political decision-making, all of those things that have been demanded for so long ... We're on the verge of a completely new era in this country. I sincerely believe that if we have cooperation and the blessing of God Almighty, miracles can be performed. In fact, where human relations between black and white are concerned, the sky's the limit.

Interview, Pretoria, Nov. 30/ The New York Times, 12-1:(A)9.

Ngqondi L. Masimini
Minister-at-Large of Transkei

3

[On the world's lack of recognition of his country, which declared and was granted independence from South Africa in 1976]: Maybe we were too peaceful. Perhaps if we had killed some whites we would have gotten a lot of world publicity and everybody would recognize us now. Violence is the only thing that seems to get any attention. But we are not that way. We got our independence peacefully, and we want to stay that way.

Interview, Washington/ Los Angeles Times, 6-4:(1)28.

Paul N. McCloskey, Jr.
United States Representative, R-California

4

I feel sadness because I can't see any way that the South African government is going to change its policy [of separate development of the races]. Frustration, because I can see no way that my own government can assist South Africa unless there is a change in South Africa's policy. And fear, because it seems inevitable that there will be a collision between the aspirations of black people and an intransigent government.

To reporters, Johannesburg, Nov. 25/ San Francisco Examiner & Chronicle, 11-26:(A)22.

George S. McGovern
United States Senator, D-South Dakota

5

[On Cuban involvement in Africa]: I think one unfortunate aspect of this is that we are raising the wrong question about the Cuban involvement and what challenge it poses for American interests and what to do about it. I feel Africa is not fundamental to American interests and that we can't do much about it anyway.

Interview, June 10/ The New York Times, 6-11:(1)6.

6

I would certainly not want to say that there are not some positive features about the [Rho-

(GEORGE S. MCGOVERN)

desian] internal settlement. The ending of racial discrimination—even though this has not been implemented—is to be welcomed. However, the fact is that under the Salisbury agreement, for at least 10 years, one third of Rhodesia's Parliamentary seats will be reserved for that 1/20 of the population which is white. Many blacks find this unacceptable. It is not for us [the U.S.], however, to decide this question. It is for the people of Rhodesia to decide. Our aim is to help give them a chance to do so in free and fair elections, held in peaceful circumstances ... The U.S. should continue to play the role it is playing now: trying to bring the parties to the negotiating table so that a peaceful and enduring transition to majority rule can be arranged. This isn't easy, but the alternatives are worse. If we are to continue to play this role, then we will have to remain an honest broker in the dispute and refrain from choosing sides.

Interview/U.S. News & World Report, 10-30:32.

Mobutu Sese Seko
President of Zaire

1

[On the French troops that helped his country during an attack by rebels from neighboring Angola]: [French President Valery] Giscard d'Estaing is the European chief of state who best understands the problems of Africa. In the West's total abandonment [of Africa] to the Russians and Cubans, only France has shown a willingness to take up the challenge—but France does not have the means to do it alone.

News conference, Paris, May 25/
Los Angeles Herald Examiner, 5-26:(A)14.

Abdullahi Hassen Mohamoud
Secretary general, Western Somali
Liberation Front

2

[On Somalia's conflict with Ethiopia over the Ogaden region]: What did the Ogaden war accomplish? First, remember that this war has been going on for years. The international press focused on it for only nine months. And what

did we do? We defeated the Ethiopians. They were saved from total destruction only by the Warsaw Pact nations, and now we are fighting those nations, too ... And while the United States sat idly by with folded hands, we have showed the world that Russians are imperialists and not progressive people. They do not support liberation movements for the sake of movements themselves but only for their own interests. Our struggle may take many years. We can wait until the time is right. The Russians and Cubans will not be there forever, and in the end we will demoralize the Ethiopians until they are forced to declare our independence.

Interview, Mogadishu, Somalia/
Los Angeles Times, 6-7:(1-A)10.

Richard M. Moose
Assistant Secretary for African Affairs,
Department of State of the United States

3

There's a tragic choice [for the U.S. in Rhodesia] . I can understand those people who look at this situation and say, "Here is [Rhodesian Prime Minister Ian] Smith"—whose history and track record perhaps they don't understand— "offering genuine majority rule. Here are those moderate [black] leaders on the inside who are willing to join with him. Here are these people on the outside whom we see as Communists"— because they are taking Soviet aid. "So let's cast our lot with the Salisbury talkers, because, after all, they represent moderation, stability and respect for white rights." The trouble with that argument is that at the end of the road we will have a situation in which Smith and the internal nationalists are on one side, supported by the South Africans and ourselves, and on the other side are the rest of the African countries, and most of the ex-colonial world, supported by the Russians and Cubans. It would be a dreadful conflict.

Time, 4-17:30.

4

It's in economic development and trade where we [the U.S.] can do the most for the Africans. After the problems of liberation and the problems of regional stability, the big over-

WHAT THEY SAID IN 1978

riding problem is poverty, starvation, aspirations and so forth. And here our technology, our markets, give us a great ability to respond to real African needs.

Interview/The Christian Science Monitor, 6-5:38.

Robert Mugabe
Rhodesian black nationalist leader

1

Our principle about negotiations [on black majority rule in Rhodesia] is that their product should be equal to the product of the battlefield. If the British propose an arrangement of a nature that would cheat us of a victory that we would achieve by continuing our [guerrilla war against the white government] ... this of course would not be acceptable.

Rome, Feb. 11/The Dallas Times Herald, 2-12:(A)7.

2

[Saying his Patriotic Front must have large representation in an interim Rhodesian government in transition to black majority rule]: The Patriotic Front must have [a] predominant role in that council. The army must be our army—pure and simple. Our forces must constitute the police force. We are predominant just now in the country, militarily. Our military gains must translate themselves at the stage of achievement of political power in some form of that power.

April 16/Los Angeles Times, 4-17:(1)4.

Karega Muhati
Professor of linguistics,
University of Nairobi (Kenya)

3

[On the multitude of languages spoken in African countries]: As an instrument of nation-building, language is a potentially powerful unifying force. It serves as a major object and symbol of attachment by bridging immediate loyalties with transcendent ones. This, of course, is only true if all the different people within the nation accept the language. If each of the ethnic groups remains a separate linguistic entity and if there is no common language

among all the people, we cannot hope to build a single and homogeneous nation.

Los Angeles Times, 1-11:(1)1.

Cornelius P. Mulder
Minister of Information of South Africa

4

For many years, U.S. representatives all over the world have said quite bluntly that there should be a one-man, one-vote election [in Rhodesia] leading to majority rule. Well, that's exactly what Rhodesia's so-called internal settlement is all about. There is to be a one-man, one-vote election. The majority party or parties will select the Prime Minister. They will rule. But now the British and Americans refuse to accept this reality even though it's what you've been advocating all along. And why? Because the radicals of the Patriotic Front refuse to participate in the election. So the U.S. and Britain want the radicals—in the minority—to be given the right to veto the majority. The reason the radicals won't participate is that they know they can't win an election. They don't want an election; they want control. That's why they have to keep on using military means. And if they succeed, we will have a repeat of what happened in Angola: a minority group backed by outsiders to take charge over the majority.

Interview/U.S. News & World Report, 8-21:33.

Abel Muzorewa
Rhodesian black nationalist leader

5

[On whether it would be undesirable for a large proportion of whites to leave Rhodesia after a black government is established]: I think so, judging from what we have seen elsewhere in Africa. Today you go to Zambia or Mozambique and you find people queuing for bread and for meal, for salt at 4 a.m. And by the time you are almost at the door, it's no longer there. I'm saying that if independence means just a flag and people are starving, people become poorer than they were under colonialism, I'm saying it's worthless. We will do everything to prevent that, and if it means to keep

(ABEL MUZOREWA)

some whites in positions for a limited period of time, that's what we'll do.

Interview, Salisbury/
The New York Times, 5-7:(4)5.

Tertius Myburgh
Editor, "Sunday Times" (South Africa)

1

I can no longer say South Africa has a free press—a paper has been closed and an editor thrown in jail. All South African newspapers now live under the threat of being shut down and seeing their editors jailed, if the Minister of Justice sees fit. No charges need be brought, no trial held, no conviction obtained in a court of law.

San Francisco Examiner & Chronicle, 4-9:(A)18.

Agostinho Neto
President of Angola

2

It is the U.S. that will have to decide when it wants to establish relations [with Angola]. But they will have to take us as we are, the way we are. We are not going to change because of relations with the United States ... The U.S. is a big power and we are just being born. At this moment, we hope that the U.S. wants to establish good relations. We have no reservations. It all depends on the United States.

News conference, Khartoum, Sudan, July 21/
Los Angeles Herald Examiner, 7-22:(A)4.

3

We [in Angola] are not going to be so radical ... We are not going to attempt, as some comrades do, to get rid of the private sector ... The private enterprise of farmers, small-businessmen, masons and carpenters is an important facet of production which we need in the country.

Time, 12-25:42.

Gaafar al-Nimeiry
President of Sudan

4

The big powers made our continent a battleground and our people the cannon fodder for their wars. I do fear that our continent will go the same path that Asia has taken for 20 years of war and destruction.

At Organization of African
Unity summit meeting, Khartoum,
July 18/Los Angeles Times, 7-19:(1)10.

Joshua Nkomo
Leader, Zimbabwe (Rhodesian) African
People's Union

5

[Criticizing Rhodesian Prime Minister Ian Smith's plan for black majority rule]: What Smith has conceded is not majority rule, but one-man, one-vote for the election of 72 powerless seats in Parliament, 72 [black] dummies with no power ... We are not giving our lives for a constitution that is going to entrench the position of the black man and the position of the white man. We are fighting for a non-racial state. This alone disqualifies the whole [Smith] thing. We cannot be party to a document that entrenches discrimination.

News conference, Lusaka, Zambia, Feb. 17/
The Washington Post, 2-18:(A)12.

6

[On his guerrilla movement's acceptance of aid from the Soviet Union]: We grew up under British influence, but we didn't get indoctrinated ... Why does the West believe because we are getting assistance from the Soviet Union we will be indoctrinated? ... Nobody imposes their will on us. The West couldn't, so why should the Russians?

Interview, Lusaka, Zambia/Newsweek, 3-13:45.

7

[On his struggle to oust Rhodesian Prime Minister Ian Smith's government]: Like all the generals, I have been at the front but not fighting. I wish I was young. I wish the time was different. I wish this had happened when I was young. But I have to do the planning; I can't fight. I wasn't interested in being the President or the liberation leader when this all started. I have come to be associated with the problems of the struggle. I am not preoccupied with power.

Interview, Washington/
The Washington Post, 6-20:(B)7.

WHAT THEY SAID IN 1978

Julius K. Nyerere
President of Tanzania

1

[Defending Soviet and Cuban involvement in Africa against criticism by the U.S.]: If the only objective of the United States is the defense of capitalism and the fight against the Soviet Union, then we can't cooperate. There was a voice that was very helpful that was coming from Washington. Let that be the voice that Africa hears, not the hysterical voices talking about Africa being taken over by Cubans.

News conference, Dar es Salaam, June 8/
Los Angeles Times, 6-9:(1)5.

2

It is the height of arrogance for anyone [outside of Africa] to talk of establishing a pan-African force to defend Africa. It is quite obvious, moreover, that those who have put forward this idea, and those who seek to initiate such a force, are not interested in the freedom of Africa. They are interested in the domination of Africa.

To the diplomatic corps, Dar es Salaam, Tanzania,
June 8/The Washington Post, 6-9:(A)27.

3

[On Ugandan President Idi Amin]: There is this obnoxious tendency in Africa that if Amin had been white, so many resolutions condemning his genocide would have been passed by the Organization of African Unity. Blackness has become a certificate to kill with impunity.

At ceremony marking Tanzania's 17th year of
independence, Dec. 9/
The Dallas Times Herald, 12-10:(A)11.

Olusegun Obasanjo
Head of Government of Nigeria

4

To the Soviets and their friends I should like to say that, having been invited to Africa in order to assist in the liberation struggle and consolidation of national independence, they should not overstay their welcome. Africa is not about to throw off one colonial yoke for another ... The longer we continue to be spoon-fed by other powers, the longer we delay our indigenous capacity to learn and improve from one level to another. The Soviets should therefore see it to be in their interest not to seek to perpetually maintain their presence in Africa even after the purpose for which they were invited has been achieved.

Before Organization of African Unity, Khartoum,
Sudan, July 18/
The Christian Science Monitor, 7-21:11.

5

No African country is about to embrace Communism any more than we are willing to embrace capitalism. To the extent that any African can be considered by the West to have "gone Communist," it was as a direct result of the failure of Western policies.

Los Angeles Times, 7-22:(1)8.

6

We must all embark on the greatest care and economy in expenditure by all public institutions, and a return to sanity in the interests of the national economy. The nation must cut its coat according to its cloth.

Los Angeles Times, 11-26:(1)14.

Harry F. Oppenheimer
Chairman, Anglo-American
Corporation (South Africa)

7

Those who seek to bring about change in South Africa's racial attitudes and policies by cutting us off from the capital markets of the world should understand clearly that in practice, if not intent, they are aiming at change by violence. It would be naive in the extreme to suppose that by isolating South Africa economically it would be possible to bring about a change of mind or heart in our governing party; nor could anything be more absurd than to expect that a rapid change-over to majority rule based on one-man, one-vote—which is apparently what many of our liberal critics aim at— would be likely to boost the confidence of foreign investors. That confidence may be at low ebb but it is certainly far higher than in any of the black-ruled countries of Africa.

At International Monetary Conference,
Mexico City/The Christian Science Monitor, 11-1:23.

David Owen
Foreign Secretary of the United Kingdom

1

It is legitimate for us to ask what is the purpose of Soviet and Cuban involvement in Africa. As I have frequently pointed out, while the Russians give a great deal of military aid, there is very little real transfer of the resources which the African states so desperately need. While the United States' budget for military aid is equivalent to about 24 per cent of their total aid budget, Soviet military assistance is between 60 and 70 per cent of theirs . . . The overriding requirement is for sovereign African states to be able and be willing to solve their own problems, preferably through the Organization of African Unity. This is the only means of avoiding East-West rivalry and confrontation in the area. If detente is to survive, as it must do if we are to survive, it is essential that East and West should not be drawn into local conflicts on opposing sides. The main contribution that we in the West can make is to help create conditions in which there can be no call for massive infusions of foreign troops. This applies with particular force to Namibia and Rhodesia. The easiest way to lose the battle of ideology, which continues despite detente, would be for us in the West to espouse the lost cause of white minority rule and so assume the role of racist reactionaries in which others' propaganda would wish to cast us.

April 5/The Washington Post, 4-14:(A)16.

Alan Paton
South African author

2

When the time came for the colonial powers to get out [of Africa] they all went back where they came from and that was Europe. [But] the Afrikaner [of South Africa] has no link with Europe any more and he hasn't had for a couple of centuries. He always makes the plea, "I am a man of Africa." But he never adds that not only is he a man of Africa but he treated the other men of Africa in a way that won't bear scrutiny. But it's true: He's got nowhere to go, and that's why he would rather destroy himself than capitulate.

Interview/The Christian Science Monitor, 1-17:27.

Ronald Reagan
Former Governor of California (R)

3

[On Russian influence and intervention in Africa]: If the Soviets are successful—and it looks more and more as if they will be—then the entire Horn of Africa will be under their influence, if not their control . . . [And] whatever we may think of South Africa's internal [racial] policies, control of its mineral riches and its strategic position are the Soviet Union's ultimate goal in Africa.

At Conservative Political Action Conference, Washington, March 17/ Los Angeles Times, 3-18:(1)17.

Carlos Rafael Rodriguez
Vice Premier and Foreign Minister of Cuba

4

[Denying Cuban involvement in the rebel invasion of Zaire from Angola]: I can reiterate before the [General] Assembly that Cuba has had no direct or indirect participation in the events of Shaba, that not only were no Cubans present in that action but that, furthermore, Cuba has not supplied arms for it nor has it given training to the attacking force. Neither does Cuba have any political relations with the organization which assumes the responsibility for those actions.

At United Nations, New York, May 30/ Los Angeles Times, 5-31:(1)13.

Mohammed Siad Barre
President of Somalia

5

The Soviets are creating trouble everywhere in Africa to neutralize Western actions and reactions. Yet [U.S. President] Carter has now accepted the Soviet line on Ethiopia. We can only conclude that he must have made a deal with Moscow, or at least reached a tacit understanding. Otherwise, how can you explain that Russia is allowed to commit unprecedented criminal acts? Russia is outmaneuvering America. Soviet leaders have convinced the Carter Administration not to react to the biggest Soviet airlift in history—bigger than the October

WHAT THEY SAID IN 1978

(MOHAMMED SIAD BARRE)

[Arab-Israeli] war, bigger than Angola. They have moved to Ethiopia highly sophisticated equipment that the Ethiopians cannot possibly use themselves. At first the Cubans convinced [U.S. UN] Ambassador Andrew Young they were just sending a few doctors. Now their regular forces are in place. Moscow has hoodwinked you . . . Today the target of Soviet military might is Somalia. Tomorrow it will be another country in the region, and so on until the design is completed . . . If you [the U.S.] cannot see how your vital interests are affected, then we can only conclude you have decided to surrender to Soviet hegemony. But if that is the case, you should be honest enough to tell us so.

Interview, Mogadishu/Newsweek, 2-13:47.

Ndabaningi Sithole
Rhodesian black nationalist leader

1

[Rhodesian black guerrilla leaders Robert] Mugabe and [Joshua] Nkomo represent a different philosophy altogether [from the current black-white transition government]. They say they want all power handed over to them or to their party. But we [in the transition government] say no power should be handed over to any particular political party or to any particular political leader, but that power should be handed over to the people, so that the people themselves through the exercise of a one-man, one-vote may choose leaders of their own choice.

TV-radio interview, Washington/"Meet the Press,"
National Broadcasting Company, 10-8.

Richard L. Sklar
Professor of political science,
University of California, Los
Angeles; Authority on Africa

2

What is interesting about Nigeria is that, after this terrible conflict [the civil war] —so tragic in the loss of human life—the Nigerians themselves are now re-establishing free governmental institutions on a constitutional basis. The Nigerians are setting an example to coun-

tries throughout the world of the kind of government people create when they have the opportunity to do it by themselves, and democratically. The Nigerian constitutional committee and the provision that its report must be submitted to a constituent assembly are really a landmark in constitutional history. The committee provides for democratic representative government on the basis of full political liberties for the people. Those liberties include party competition without prejudice to any form of social or economic organization. This development reflects no British influence. If anything, it derives from the *Federalist Papers* of our own country [the U.S.] 200 years ago . . . Apart from the liberation of southern Africa, that is the single most significant thing happening in Africa today—the restoration of free institutions and constitutional government in Nigeria. And yet few people talk about it, or know about it.

Panel discussion/World Issues, Oct.-Nov.:4.

Ian Smith
Prime Minister of Rhodesia

3

[On the U.S. and Britain's negative opinions about the black-majority-rule agreement negotiated with moderate black leaders in his country]: It is incomprehensible to me. We are offering them a genuine settlement to produce a democratic system which will truly reflect what they've always asked for, majority rule, but they seem to be turning their back on this toward a solution which will end up with a dictatorship in Rhodesia, a Marxist dictatorship . . . An agreement in which 72 per cent of the people [in Parliament] are going to be black Rhodesians can hardly put us in a position where we are going to have something over which the white man will be in control. This is absolutely nonsensical, I would have thought patently so, to anybody who takes the trouble to study the agreement we have made.

Interview, Salisbury, Feb. 23/
The New York Times, 2-24:(A)1,8.

4

We have accepted majority rule for a future government. The majority of people in Rho-

(IAN SMITH)

desia are black people. This is what the world has asked us to do. The main criticism over the years has been that we would not accept this. Well, now we've accepted it. Our philosophy is to try to make this evolution while maintaining the confidence of the white man, to try to get him staying here and making a contribution, particularly in the economic sphere. We are trying to produce something different here in Rhodesia—a country which will stand on its own feet, perhaps unique in Africa, where the white man will continue to make a contribution, to work with the black. We can work together. This is the whole philosophy.

Interview/Time, 3-6:47.

1

For a long time there has been trouble and argument in our country because the white people believed in a qualified franchise and the black people wanted majority rule. Unfortunately, the trouble grew and it got worse, until there was war and the people were killing one another. What made things worse was that the Communist countries decided they wanted to come into African countries ... For this reason, the big countries of the free world became concerned about the possibility of Communist expansion here. Therefore they told me the time had come when I had to settle the dispute and stop the fighting. This is [the] reason which made my government and me change our minds. We changed; we accepted this thing called majority rule in order to help the free world bring peace to our country.

Mrewa, Rhodesia, May 10/
The Washington Post, 5-11:(A)31.

2

This is a period of transition [in Rhodesia], phasing out white government and moving to majority rule. But going overnight to 100 per cent black government with no white representation would upset the balance of the country. That would destroy white confidence; the country would lose their know-how, expertise and capital. The whites would probably leave.

What we want is a solution that contributes white expertise to the entry of the black man into a new experiment in government which he knows nothing about. We believe 85 per cent of black Rhodesians support this cautious approach, and if we can hold elections, we'll prove it.

Interview, Victoria Falls, Rhodesia/
U.S. News & World Report, 6-5:44.

3

... I believe it is incorrect to say that previously I was a racist or that my policies were racist. I have always believed in certain standards for the qualification for the franchise; yes, a kind of "meritocracy," if you wish, as opposed to pure democracy. But we have never had racialism as a basis of our policies in our country. We have in the main had voters' roles, which were open to black as well as white.

TV-radio interview, Washington/"Meet the Press,"
National Broadcasting Company, 10-8.

4

I think some people who have analyzed me—and I'm talking about people who are close to me, who have known me for a long time—say that they are satisfied that I am not a racist and there is no racialism as such in my system. I am a paternalist. I believe in training people and bringing them up correctly when they are young, in disciplining them. When I say somebody is not fit to do this, that or the other thing, it is not because of the color of his skin. It's because of his—call it what you like—education, behavior, right civilization. Black people who associate with me come to my home and sit down and have meals with me the same as white people. I sit with them in my government now. I believe it is a misconception to say that I am a racialist. I believe in standards.

Interview, Los Angeles/
Los Angeles Times, 10-22:(4)1.

5

What they [the U.S.] have got to do, I believe, is to face up to their responsibility in trying to keep Rhodesia as part of the free world and make sure that it doesn't find itself in the hands of Marxist terrorists. We don't

(IAN SMITH)

want American weapons or troops—we want people to get off our backs and give us a clear run. We have been pulled down; we have been held back; we have been tripped up. Leave us alone. At the moment, the free world is trying to destroy a small bastion of Western democracy, virtually siding with the Russians and the Cubans to pull us down.

Interview, Salisbury/
U.S. News & World Report, 12-18:38.

Leo Tindemans
Prime Minister of Belgium

1

Countries like the Soviet Union, East Germany and Cuba have no compunction about pooling resources to exploit tribal grievances against legitimate governments [in Africa]. These covert operations then acquire respectability through the very clever and simple device of creating a "national liberation front," which they then supply with advisers and weaponry. And any country that stands in the way is dismissed as retrograde and reactionary, or imperialist and neocolonialist. Democratic governments such as ours are then, in turn, paralyzed by this barrage of made-in-Moscow cliches, and the temptation is strong not to get involved in anything controversial.

Interview, Brussels/Newsweek, 6-19:50.

Cyrus R. Vance
Secretary of State of the United States

2

[Saying the U.S. seeks a more normal relationship with Marxist Angola]: We are convinced that an affirmative approach to African aspirations and problems is also the most effective response to Soviet and Cuban activities there. Any other strategy would weaken Africa by dividing it. And it would weaken us by letting others set our policies for us.

Washington, June 20/
Los Angeles Times, 6-21:(1)1.

3

With respect to Rhodesia, we have developed a proposal, in partnership with the British government and with the encouragement of African governments in the region, that would facilitate a rapid and peaceful transition to majority rule. The plan provides for bringing together the external [black] nationalists, who have formed the Patriotic Front, with [Prime Minister] Ian Smith and the black leaders who have joined him in an "internal settlement." It also calls for free elections, an impartial Administration during the election period and a constitution protecting the rights of all citizens—white and black. Concessions toward peace have been made by all parties in this gathering conflict. However, neither side can create a new nation, with a decent chance for a peaceful and prosperous future, without the participation of the other. And each now rejects the other's claim to predominance during the critical election period. It is our hope that we can help to bring them together, either to work out power-sharing arrangements among themselves, or to agree on a neutral solution such as the one we have proposed.

Before United States Jaycees, Atlantic City,
N.J., June 20/The New York Times, 6-21:(A)6.

4

The recent introduction of large quantities of Soviet arms and thousands of Cuban troops in certain parts of Africa raises serious concerns. The size and duration of their military presence jeopardizes the independence of African states. It creates concern on the part of African nations that outside weapons and troops will be used to determine the outcome of any dispute on the continent. And it renders more difficult the efforts of Africans to resolve these disputes through peaceful means. Our strategy is based upon an affirmative and constructive approach to African issues—helping African nations meet their pressing human and economic needs, strengthening their ability to defend themselves, building closer ties throughout Africa, and assisting African nations to resolve their conflicts peacefully.

Before House International Relations Committee,
Washington/The Christian Science Monitor, 6-30:23.

John Vorster
Prime Minister of South Africa

1

[On the "internal settlement" in Rhodesia which provides for one-man, one-vote]: How successful it will be in practice will depend, on the one hand, on the good faith with which the parties adhere to and implement it in practice, and, on the other hand, whether they are allowed by so-called "public opinion" as well as African and world organizations and countries, neighboring and far away, to arrange and determine their own affairs according to their own wishes. Time alone can give the answer to this.

Cape Town, South Africa, March 3/
The Washington Post, 3-4: (A) 12.

2

The American black is a black American. You have divested him of his African personality. He hasn't got a language or culture or tradition of his own. He is a descendant of a slave. The South African black man isn't the descendant of a slave. He is a member of a proud tribal nation in his own right, with his own language, culture and tradition; his own land—the land his forefathers occupied when they originally came from Central Africa ... We not only didn't take the black man's homelands from him but we added to his homelands and it cost millions and millions to do so. By refusing to acknowledge the multinational situation in South Africa, you look upon the black people as one because they have black skin. You refuse to accept that the Swazis are as different from the Vendas as the Italian is from the Swede. Therefore, our policy is that the blacks in southern Africa must govern themselves in their own homelands. They can become completely sovereign independent states and be a black African nation just as we are a white African nation.

Interview, Cape Town/
Los Angeles Herald Examiner, 3-5: (A) 14.

3

[Saying U.S. criticism of human rights in his country is inconsistent with U.S. policy else-where in Africa]: There are ever so many African countries whose domestic policies are also very, very different from that of the United States ... that have dictatorships, no press freedom or freedom of any kind, and apparently the U.S. government cooperates with these countries and has no quarrel with them. Nigeria is a case in point. But South Africa is condemned. So you can draw your own conclusion ... It certainly is a very selective morality if there are any moral principles involved ... [U.S. Secretary of State Cyrus] Vance said, in the case of the Philippines, that American security interests demanded that you overlook certain things. Well, that blows the whole bottom out of your whole policy, if your policy is such a high moral one.

Interview, Cape Town/
The Washington Post, 4-21: (A) 23.

Peter Wiles
Professor of Russian studies,
London School of Economics and
Political Science

4

[On how America should deal with Soviet and Cuban involvement in Africa]: Number 1, the U.S. Air Force should shoot down Cuban transport planes heading for Africa. Number 2, the U.S. should send in forces [to Africa] itself, like the French have. Number 3, the U.S. should pay Morocco so that the Moroccans will fight in Africa for the Americans. If you don't like numbers one, two and three—which I would expect Americans would not—then try numbers four and five. Number 4, instantly cancel all export credits for the Soviet Union. And Number 5, ban all exports of foodstuffs and machinery to the U.S.S.R.

Interview/Nesweek, 6-12: 41.

Donald Woods
Self-exiled former South African
newspaper editor

5

The real South Africa is the entire nation of 25 million, and the victims of apartheid are all 25 million of them. It has to be acknowledged that race prejudice exists in many parts of the

(DONALD WOODS)

world, but the unique affront which apartheid represents to all mankind is the fact that it is only in South Africa that racism is institutionalized through actual state law. For many years, and for a variety of reasons, the Western powers have resisted implementing effective punitive measures against the government of South Africa. But the time has now come for the West to reassess its past attitudes ... As mankind progresses, so the family of man draws closer together. And just as a member of any family might have to be chastised for his own good and in consequence be drawn closer into the body of the family, so today I believe that the rulers of my country have to face the concerted chastisement of the united family of man if they are to be brought peacefully into its brotherhood. Whether this can be done in time to prevent large-scale violence in South Africa now depends on the West.

*Before United Nations Security Council, New York/
The Christian Science Monitor, 2-2:27.*

Andrew Young
*United States Ambassador/Permanent
Representative to the United Nations*

1

[Saying all groups, including the Patriotic Front guerrillas, should be represented in Rhodesian elections]: We don't need to close out our options by choosing sides among the black organizations. Our policy is free elections, as provided for by the British-American plan for Rhodesia. But I still think that you can't have a lasting settlement without the participation of the people who are doing the fighting.

Interview, Feb. 26/The New York Times, 2-27:(A)10.

2

When I spoke about Cubans being a stabilizing force in Angola, there was no fighting going on in Angola; they were basically doing technical assistance ... [But] when they began the search-and-destroy missions in southern Angola and when they used military means to try to resolve a conflict of Angolans themselves, I had no hesitation to condemn that military role. The same thing is true in the Horn of Africa. When the first Cubans went into Ethio-

pia, they were medical personnel. I couldn't condemn the presence of medical personnel anywhere in the world where people are sick and in need of healing ... I wouldn't even condemn [Cuban Premier Fidel] Castro's going to try to negotiate between [President Mohammed] Siad Barre in Somalia and [President] Mengistu [Haile Mariam] in Ethiopia. I wish he had stuck with the negotiations. If he had stuck with the negotiations and been successful, I certainly would not have condemned a successful Communist effort at pacifying a situation that has been traditionally violent for centuries. When they instead, though, resorted to tanks and air power and the slaughter of people in order to settle a conflict, I have no hesitation to condemn that violence.

*TV-radio interview/"Meet the Press,"
National Broadcasting Company, 3-12.*

3

There is no doubt that Cuba perceives itself as an Afro-Latin nation. I don't believe that Cuba is in Africa because it was ordered there by the Russians. I believe Cuba is in Africa because it really has shared a sense of colonial oppression and domination.

Interview/Newsweek, 3-13:40.

4

If, in fact, there is a massive uprising and racial upheaval in southern Africa, the great danger perhaps is not that it will go Communist—because I don't think Africa will ever go Communist—but the great danger is that there will be a period of chaos. [If racial warfare erupts,] the thin veneer of educated leadership, that for the most part has been produced over 100 years by Christian missionaries from the United States and Europe, will be killed off—and you end up with a Uganda-like situation, where a formerly prosperous and highly educated African elite were destroyed, allowing that country to sink back into a level of tribalism and savagery that makes it impossible for us to have any kind of political or economic dealings with them.

*Before University of Georgia law students and
faculty, April 29/San Francisco Examiner &
Chronicle, 4-30:(A)18.*

(ANDREW YOUNG)

1

[On U.S. policy in Africa] : ... people are trying to paint our policy as either/or: either an interventionist policy or an accommodation of Communism in Africa. Really, it's neither. Our interests in Africa are a combination of economic interests and our human-rights interests. Many people are not aware of our definite economic interests. Eight out of 13 raw materials on which our economy depends, including cobalt, uranium, copper and chrome, are found primarily in southern Africa. I think we have an interest in preventing anyone else from dominating Africa, but I put that Number 3, after our concern for human rights and economic interests.

Interview, United Nations, New York, June 8/
Los Angeles Herald Examiner, 6-9:(A)6.

2

We [the U.S.] have more influence in Africa right now than in the recent past—including in Angola. The Angolans are presently cooperating with us. They see that it's in their interest to have a peaceful settlement in Namibia. They are protecting our economic interest in Angola with Cuban troops, and they are supplying the United States with almost $1-billion worth of oil a year. Now, they're not doing us any favor; they need the billion dollars to keep their country going. Even the Cuban presence in Angola has not threatened any material United States interest at this point, nor has it minimized U.S. influence in Angola. It has created a kind of psychological impotence among some people in this country [the U.S.]. If we're panicky about Cubans, and if we think that Cubans are 10 feet tall—that they are supermen and that they are going to sweep the African continent—we're in trouble. If we realize that Cubans bleed and die, and have the same kind of racial tensions and problems with language and culture that everybody else has—including the Russians—then we can keep a perspective about what's going on.

Interview/U.S. News & World Report, 6-12:24.

3

It drives my Nigerian friends up the wall when I say this, but Nigeria isn't free. It doesn't feed itself; and, until it does, it can't escape being dependent on someone. A nation that doesn't feed itself can't be really free.

Los Angeles Times, 11-27:(1)18.

The Americas

James B. Allen
United States Senator, D-Alabama

1

[On the proposed treaties which would gradually turn over control of the Panama Canal to Panama]: No amount of Band-Aid amendments can correct the basic faults embodied in any plan which gives control of the Canal to Panama at any time. No amount of words in no amount of amendments can ever provide to us the same needed guarantees as are provided by actual possession ... If we give up physical control, this country will still, sooner or later, find itself at the mercy of some petty dictator who decides, probably with the backing of the Soviet Union, to cause difficulties for the United States in using this vital strategic waterway.

Before House Merchant Marine and
Fisheries Committee, Washington,
Jan. 17/The Washington Post, 1-18:(A)16.

Nicky Barletta
Member of the ruling
junta of Panama

2

[On the pending new treaties with the U.S. which would gradually turn over control of the Panama Canal to his country]: What we are seeing today is Panama ready to take hold of her destiny. Panama has a piece of geography that is important to almost every country in the world. If we could use this location to help develop and grow, to make this a viable, vibrant, working, dynamic small society because of her geography, because of the Canal, it could be our claim to universality ... I never thought that we would get the Panama Canal tomorrow. We had to adapt to a middle-of-the-road, workable solution. But I have felt for many years that this is a crucial issue. Getting the Canal meant putting together our identity as a people, consolidating our development potential. Now

we live in a very special time and Panama is consolidating things. Many people just don't see them ... We are always aware that the 1903 treaty was unfair to us, that it was signed by some Frenchman in turmoil, in a speedy fashion, and we were faced with a *fait accompli.* And yet the Panamanians have always been friendly with Americans. But I don't think the U.S. ever was really aware of Panama. We were 74th on the U.S. priority totem pole. We wanted to make the Canal a priority issue.

Interview, Panama City/
The Washington Post, 3-9:(B)19.

Lloyd M. Bentsen
United States Senator, D-Texas

3

[Supporting the proposed treaties which would gradually turn over control of the Panama Canal to Panama]: ... I have become concerned about the potential consequences of [U.S.] Senate failure to approve the treaties. Those who will most rejoice at any Senate rejection of the treaties will be the leftist elements in Latin America and the Caribbean, the Castros of our hemisphere. I do not believe the Canal will be easy to sabotage, but I do believe Senate rejection of the treaties would give leftist elements in Latin America an issue they could exploit to their advantage. I do not dismiss lightly the possibility that Panama might turn to the Soviet Union and Cuba to build a new sea-level canal if the treaties are rejected.

News conference, Washington, Jan. 19/
The Dallas Times Herald, 1-20:(A)15.

Zbigniew Brzezinski
Assistant to President of the
United States Jimmy Carter for
National Security Affairs

4

I believe we have made a significant breakthrough in our relations with Latin America.

(ZBIGNIEW BRZEZINSKI)

We have abandoned the notion, which has been followed by almost every Administration since FDR's, of propounding a single slogan for the diversified region. Instead, we're pursuing a policy which is on the one hand more bilateral and on the other hand more related to global issues, thereby generating a more mature set of relationships with individual Latin American countries. By tackling what seemed like a hopeless task—the Panama Canal treaties—we have redressed a historical wrong, and we have opened up opportunities for a new relationship.

Interview/Time, 5-29:18.

William F. Buckley, Jr.
Political columnist;
Editor, "National Review"

1

Keeping [the Panama Canal] would incline people to believe we [the U.S.] have an appetite for colonialism. We should be big enough to grant a little people what we ourselves fought for 200 years ago.

San Francisco Examiner &
Chronicle, 1-22:(This World)2.

Robert C. Byrd
United States Senator,
D-West Virginia

2

[On the proposed treaties which would gradually turn over control of the Panama Canal to Panama]: The basic question to be considered is whether these treaties are in the best interest of the United States. I believe that the weight of the evidence argues convincingly that they are. It is particularly important for our relations with Latin America and should open a new era of mutual trust and cooperation in inter-American relations. Given the history of the Canal and the principles of our country, the treaties are in our interest, and ratification is the right step to take.

News conference, Washington, Jan. 13/
Los Angeles Times, 1-14:(1)8.

3

[Supporting the proposed treaties which would gradually turn over control of the Panama Canal to Panama]: While taking justifiable pride in the role the United States played in constructing and operating the Canal, we must also try to understand the pride and aspirations of the Panamanians. It is their nation which is bisected by the Canal Zone . . . Rejection of the treaties [by the U.S. Senate] would give extremists, right and left, the motivation to stir up trouble. It would give them all the ammunition they need.

Before Senate Foreign Relations, Washington,
Jan. 26/Los Angeles Times, 1-27:(1)5.

4

It is obvious that [Cuban Premier Fidel] Castro, having failed spectacularly in his efforts to set Latin America ablaze with his brand of revolution, has turned his attention to Africa. He is apparently more interested in the pursuit of violent revolution and subversion than in ties with the United States. I suggest that we recall our envoy in Havana for consultations, and think seriously about closing our operations there entirely until Fidel Castro demonstrates that he is willing to abide by the world rule of law and join the civilized world. If he so demonstrates, then we could respond in kind.

Before Delta Council, Cleveland, Miss.,
May 30/The Dallas Times Herald, 5-31:(A)24.

Jimmy Carter
President of the United States

5

[Supporting the proposed treaties which would gradually turn over control of the Panama Canal to Panama]: The most important reason, the only reason, to ratify the treaties is that they are in the highest national interest of the United States and will strengthen our position in the world. Our security interest will be stronger; our trade opportunities will be improved. We will demonstrate that as a large and powerful country we are able to deal fairly and honorably with a proud but smaller sovereign nation. We will honor our commitment to those engaged in world commerce that the Panama

WHAT THEY SAID IN 1978

(JIMMY CARTER)

Canal will be open and available for use by their ships at a reasonable and competitive cost, both now and in the future.

Broadcast address to the nation, Washington, Feb. 1/The New York Times, 2-2:(A)14.

1

There are some differences of opinion between ourselves and Brazil which have been very highly publicized. But in the long scale of things, both in the past history and the future, the major factors which bind us in harmony with Brazil far transcend, are much more important, than the differences that have been published between our approach to human rights, for instance, and the subject of non-proliferation of nuclear weapons. But our commitment to Brazil is as a friend, our need for Brazil as a partner and a friend has always been the case and is presently very important to us and will always be that important in the future.

News conference, Brasilia, Brazil, March 30/The New York Times, 3-31:(A)12.

2

[Cuban Premier Fidel] Castro has thousands of political prisoners in jail. I don't think that our relationships with Cuba are going to improve any further unless he shows in tangible form he is committed both to peace and the enhancement of human rights... [Cuba] would like to have the image of a non-aligned country. But that is obviously and absolutely a ridiculous claim because there is no other country that acts in harmony with and under the domination of the Soviets any more than the Cubans. They are completely aligned with the Soviets, and where most of the non-aligned countries seek peace and peaceful settlements of disputes, the Cubans are at the forefront of the cutting edge of providing military forces in areas of Africa, for instance, [and] wherever they possibly can find an opening.

Interview, Washington, May 12/ The Washington Post, 5-15:(A)7.

3

It's a joke to call Cuba non-aligned. They have military alliances with the Soviet Union; they act at the Soviet Union's direction; they're economically dependent upon the Soviet Union; they act as a surrogate for the Soviet Union.

News conference, Chicago, May 25/ U.S. News and World Report, 6-12:20.

4

[Addressing American residents of the Canal Zone on the recent ratification of treaties providing for the gradual turning over of control of the Panama Canal to Panama]: You know, as I do, that a great deal will change as a result of these treaties. A few of you will be leaving the only place on earth you have ever called home. That is a hard and painful thing to do. The adjustments and uncertainties that you now face will not be easy. I understand that. I understand, too, why you love this place. Seventy-five years ago, Americans came here as builders. In quiet ways, often unrecognized, often unappreciated, we have been builders ever since. For all the rest of your lives, every one of you can be proud... to have been part of this Canal, proud of what you have built and protected and loved... You have brought credit to yourselves and your country by operating the Canal efficiently, honestly and honorably for the benefit of all nations. The time when this was America's job alone is now coming to an end. The treaties reflect that time, and in so doing they help guarantee that the rest of the world will recognize our essential fairness and decency as a people.

Fort Clayton, Canal Zone, June 17/Los Angeles Times, 6-18:(1)1; The Washington Post, 6-18:(A)26.

Frank Church
United States Senator, D-Idaho

5

[Supporting the proposed treaties which would gradually turn over control of the Panama Canal to Panama]: It just isn't any longer possible for one country to maintain a colony

(FRANK CHURCH)

in another against the wishes of its inhabitants. A vote against this treaty is a vain attempt to preserve the past ... a sentimental journey back to the time of Teddy Roosevelt, the big stick and the great white fleet.

*Before the Senate, Washington, April 18/
The Dallas Times Herald, 4-19:(A)1.*

1

[On the rebellion against Nicaragua's President Anastasio Somoza]: [Somoza faces] a national mutiny in which almost every sector of the country has united against a dynasty which has plundered the country for nearly half a century. The question is not whether Somoza falls, but when. The longer Somoza resists the will of his people and uses his armed guard to quell resistance, the more likely it is that another [Cuban Premier Fidel] Castro-type revolutionary government will eventually emerge.

*Before the Senate, Washington,
Sept. 22/The Washington Post, 9-23:(A)9.*

William Sloane Coffin
*Senior minister,
Riverside Church, New York*

2

I wish [U.S. President Carter] had made the Panama Canal into a little more of a religious issue, saying I think we should do unto others as we would have them do unto us, and asking, You know to whom the Panama Canal belongs? It says in the Bible that the sea is His. He made it and His hands prepared the dry land. That sea belongs to God. Nobody owns anything in the secondary sense and the question of use is much more important than the question of ownership. So the really important thing about the Panama Canal is how we can use it. Can we use it for the betterment of all humankind, which probably means we should have international ownership. That would be a better solution. You see, you can bring a religious perspective to bear on the Panama Canal.

*Interview, New York/
The Christian Science Monitor, 1-5:14.*

Rafael Cordova (Rivas)
*Leader, Democratic Liberal
Union of Nicaragua (opposition
to President Anastasio Somoza)*

3

This country is ready for a general insurrection [against Somoza] ... The people are tired, and they are showing it now more than ever before ... All [Somoza] has is violence. He has lost all popular support, and the armed threat of his National Guard is about all he has left.

Interview/Newsweek, 9-11:46.

4

Don't let Somoza fool you. We are not Communists. We are not Marxists. We are not pro-Havana. Far from it. Many of us are conservatives. Many of us are moderates. And all of us back democracy as you know it in the U.S. Somoza can't say that.

The Christian Science Monitor, 10-2:13.

William G. Davis
Premier of Ontario, Canada

5

There is one fact of life which must be understood about Canada in North America. A French-speaking island [Quebec] in an English-speaking ocean has survived for several centuries, perhaps in defiance of all logic and reason, and will in my judgment continue and with sensible nourishment will flourish in our Confederation. Times change, and predictions about the future are notoriously unreliable, but assimilation is not a route that any reasonable Canadian would contemplate; and, indeed, I think if it ever came about we would all be poorer for it. Much of what makes Canada distinctive would cease to exist. More directly, it won't happen. So really, the great issue of public policy for Canadians is how do we ensure that two of the world's great cultures live together, under one roof, and in mutual respect and harmony? Soothsayers and doomsayers aside, I refuse to countenance the idea that Canadians have to consider, among themselves, a separated existence or that this so-called choice is a viable or sensible alternative to the

WHAT THEY SAID IN 1978

(WILLIAM G. DAVIS)

history we have shared for so long. Quebec is at the heartland of North America, and will forever remain there.

At Bucknell University, Lewisburg, Pa., March 10/Vital Speeches, 6-1:501.

Joao Baptista de Oliveira Figueiredo
President-designate of Brazil

1

[On his country's recent denunciation of its military accord with the U.S.]: We are no longer little boys to have our ears pulled. The time of economic and market dependence, and everything else that obliged us to an automatic alignment, is gone. The picture today is another one: We create alternatives.

The New York Times, 1-7:2.

Ruben Franco
Public Information
Secretary of Argentina

2

[On his government's abolishment of two decrees that limited press freedom]: No extremism or totalitarianism accepts or tolerates press freedom. This attitude shows clearly the way we are following. The abolition of these measures is a clear demonstration of the military government's confidence in Argentine journalism and in the foreign correspondents who carry out their tasks in the country, in the full knowledge they will not be cheated.

Buenos Aires, June 5/
The New York Times, 6-6:(A)8.

S. I. Hayakawa
United States Senator, R-California

3

The greatest objection to the Panama Canal treaties [which would gradually turn over control of the Canal to Panama] is the charge that the "giveaway" is a revelation of American weakness—of the decay of national pride and national purpose. I have tried to argue that the new arrangements regarding the Canal show the strength and self-confidence of a great nation that is willing to change an old and unequal

treaty. But how can I maintain this position . . . when there is nothing in our foreign policy that shows anything but silence or timid acquiescence in the face of determined Communist aggression?

Reading his letter to President Carter, at news conference, Washington, April 14/ Los Angeles Times, 4-15:(1)1.

Rene Levesque
Premier of Quebec, Canada

4

[On more future self-government for Quebec in relation to Canada]: Canadian democracy and Quebec democracy are strong enough to go through a democratic process of change. Constitutions are never written for eternity, even though we think of them that way. In the case of Britain and the [American] colonies, when the time came, the time came. It wasn't written anywhere, but that's the way it should be.

Interview/Time, 2-13:36.

Jose Lopez (Portillo)
President of Mexico

5

In times like these it is ridiculous, or at least naive, to proclaim victory, and dangerous to preach resignation . . . [But] our political stability has remained intact, and on that basis— despite the apocalyptic moanings and catastrophic laments we hear, despite the demagogic ravings and extremist rantings from those who exported capital or transferred their solidarity to other systems—we shall continue to act and to build our country in accordance with the values and principles that unite us. We are not sinking, nor are we in a state of collapse.

State of the Nation address/ San Francisco Examiner & Chronicle, 1-8:(C)9.

6

[On U.S. efforts to curtail Mexicans coming to work in the United States illegally]: Our compatriots continue their painful exodus northward and now they go not only to be exploited but to be rejected. Now the doors are closed and they cannot work despite the fact that at the end of World War II, and after,

248

(JOSE LOPEZ [PORTILLO])

many Mexicans went to the United States to contribute to its progress.

At University of Peking (China), Oct. 25/
The Dallas Times Herald, 10-27:(A)5.

Peter Lougheed
Premier of Alberta, Canada

1

[Saying disputes between provinces and the Federal government over control of energy resources show the strength of Canadian unity]: I think it's a natural part of the tensions within a Federal state when you have provinces who control the resources and have primary jurisdiction in numbers of areas. Regional positions are very important to us. A too-centralized Federal government is not in the best interest of Canada. We have balanced ... the centralization attitude that permeates from Ottawa, and from Toronto and Montreal to some extent, to the benefit of the regions of Canada. And so the control of resources in strong provincial governments, in my view, makes Canada a stronger and more unified country.

Los Angeles Times, 10-15:(1)13.

Claude Morin
Minister of Intergovernmental
Affairs of Quebec, Canada

2

[Seeing the future of Quebec as being a sovereign entity maintaining economic association with Canada]: The only comparison is with Europe of the future. We want to be what the European Common Market hopes to be in 10 or 15 years. Quebec and Europe are heading toward the same place from different directions.

Interview/Los Angeles Times, 12-25:(1)9.

Daniel P. Moynihan
United States Senator, D-New York

3

[On the proposed treaties which would gradually turn over control of the Panama Canal to Panama]: We have a long and good relation with the decent people of Panama. We trust each other. You cannot live together in close

relation as long as we have done without knowing whether we are worthy of mutual trust. This trust is incorporated in these treaties—not in what is not there but, rather, in what is there. Our negotiators never could have raised with any other country in the world the dense mixture of American and Panamanian rights in the Canal Zone that these treaties incorporate, except that our relations with this other nation, this small but important nation, are so good and so sound. Why exacerbate it? Why make Panama the object for expressions of fears which should be confronted on their own? If there are people in this body—and I hope there are—who are fearful of the U.S. position in the world, fearful of the positions of the free nations in the world, concerned for freedom, let us confront that. Let us not sublimate it by imposing upon Panama—friendly, proven, trustworthy Panama—conditions which are inappropriate to a republic.

Before the Senate, Washington,
April 13/The Washington Post, 4-16:(B)7.

Daniel Ortega (Saavedra)
Founder and member of the
national directorate, Sandanista
organization (opposition to
Nicaraguan President Anastasio Somoza)

4

It's a shame that the United States doesn't understand this revolution [against Somoza], because that was so much a part of their own history. They can say whatever they want about us, but the truth is found in deeds. We are, and have always been, for one very calculated goal—the fall of the Somoza dictatorship. We want the installation of a popular, democratic government that responds to the people's needs, that gives the people work, that gives land to the peasants, and health services.

Interview/
The Washington Post, 10-16:(A)20.

Eden Pastora
Leader, Sandanistas (opposition to
Nicaraguan President Anastasio Somoza)

5

Somoza has spent millions of dollars stolen from the people for a publicity campaign based

WHAT THEY SAID IN 1978

on the idea: Somoza or Communism. This is absolutely false. Our organization is ideologically pluralistic and nationalist. We have said a thousand times that our revolution will be democratic. We are not hot-heads . . . We don't want to be anyone's satellite. We don't want Communist dogma. We will recognize the leaders of the [present] opposition coalition, and Nicaragua can be pacified. The businessmen, like everybody else, can play an important and positive role.

Interview/Newsweek, 11-27:55.

Carlos Andres Perez
President of Venezuela

1

[Addressing U.S. President Carter about the U.S. Senate's deliberations on ratification of the treaties which would gradually transfer control of the Panama Canal to Panama]: You come to Latin America at a time when all of our people are directing their eyes and their ears toward the Congress of the United States, toward this great debate which the Senate has at present which will decide the fate of the relations between South America and North America. Each word pronounced there is of enormous importance, and it will have a very deep impact on Latin America.

Caracas, March 28/
Los Angeles Times, 3-29:(1)16.

Augusto Pinochet (Ugarte)
President of Chile

2

[On his authoritarian government]: I think that many times hard and strong authority is necessary because that strong and hard authority allows democracy later. It allows people to develop within an atmosphere of freedom without the anguish of fearing what will happen to them. That is why I say: [The recent plebiscite giving the government a vote of confidence] allowed Chile and the government to continue with plans to recover an authoritarian democracy.

Interview/The New York Times, 1-9:(A)12.

3

[Saying he is lifting the state of siege that has been in effect since 1973]: This is not a threat, but I am testing how the people will behave. The reality is that we are living [in] a tranquil period and there is support for the government . . . I believe that this backing permits me to lift the state of siege and maintain only a state of emergency.

Santiago, March 9/The New York Times, 3-10:(A)6.

Christopher Plummer
Canadian-born actor

4

Unfortunately, there are many Canadians who think you're a little bit of a traitor for having left. I've actually been called a second-class citizen—in print—simply because I went away to make a slight name for myself. What people here don't realize is it's impossible to make a name for yourself in Canada *unless* you leave. There's something about this country that never really allows you to become a star. Except, perhaps, if you're a hockey player.

Interview, Toronto/San Francisco
Examiner & Chronicle, 1-29:(Datebook)16.

Alfred A. Rattray
Jamaican Ambassador to the United States

5

. . . the strategies for development by the government of Jamaica aim, firstly, at converting our society from one which is merely a carryover of the slavery and colonial era to one which truly reflects the ambitions and aspirations of the people of an independent Jamaica. They are based upon creating the conditions where every citizen of Jamaica can feel that he is a first-class citizen of his own country. They are based upon replacing a system of elitism by one that is based upon equality of opportunity and upon recognition of the intrinsic worth of the individual. They are based upon the determination to develop the resources of the country for the benefit of the nation as a whole. They are based upon the belief that having regard to all the circumstances and to our needs, both the private and the public sectors have the right and the responsibility to con-

(ALFRED A. RATTRAY)

tribute toward, and participate in, the development of the country. They are based upon the recognition of the need for investment from the private sector and the determination to create the conditions which facilitate that investment. They are based upon the determination that each citizen must be made to feel the urge to contribute to his country and that this patriotic urge will not take hold until the citizen is convinced, not only that he belongs to his country, but also that his country can and will belong to him.

At Pan American Union Building,
Washington, Feb. 21/Vital Speeches, 4-15:400.

Ronald Reagan
Former Governor of California (R)

1

[Arguing against U.S. ratification of proposed treaties which would gradually turn over control of the Panama Canal to Panama] : Ratification of the new treaty would immediately cancel [the original Hay-Bunau-Varilla Treaty] of 1903. The Canal Zone would cease to exist. We [the U.S.] would simply be a foreign power with property in Panama. There would be nothing to prevent the government of Panama from expropriating our property and nationalizing the Canal, as they have already nationalized the transit company and the power system. International law permits expropriation by governments of foreign-owned property within their borders. But the United Nations Charter, which supersedes all other treaties, prohibits a member nation from using armed force to prevent such expropriation. This rules out the practice of *force majeure,* the idea that because we have the size and strength, we could just move [to protect the Canal] ... The second treaty, which comes into effect in the year 2000, when Panama has become the sole owner and operator of the Canal, promises complete neutrality for all users. This treaty is so ambiguous in its wording as to be virtually meaningless. Nowhere in this second treaty, or the accompanying protocol, is the word "guaranty" used. "Guaranty" is a word of art. It carries the

assurance that there is a guarantor. Our negotiators had capable lawyers advising them. The [omission] could not have been an oversight. "Guaranty" must have been left out, at Panama's insistence, with full knowledge of the consequences.

Television debate, Jan. 15/
The Washington Post, 1-24:(A)17.

Carolos Rafael Rodriguez
Vice Premier and
Foreign Minister of Cuba

2

Compared to what my generation and [Premier] Fidel's [Castro] knew, life [in Cuba] nowadays is easy, and this easiness may bring about a certain weakness. We don't believe in solving this problem with a cultural revolution, parading people around with dunce caps on their heads. We believe that internationalist tasks help the revolution because they are important in the political character-building and moral mobilization of our youth.

Time, 7-10:36.

Carlos Romero (Barcelo)
Governor of Puerto Rico

3

Should the day come when the people of Puerto Rico were to find themselves oppressed by the United States, it would not be necessary for a totalitarian adversary of the United States to bring the matter to the attention of this committee; I can assure you that the freedom-loving people of Puerto Rico would virtually lay siege to this building in their clamor for redress of grievances. And I should emphatically add that I myself would not hesitate to stand at the forefront of such a movement. Yet I remain fully confident that no such action will ever be necessary. Because, for all its occasional faults, the government of the United States has by and large conducted itself with grace and with fairness in its relationship with the American citizens of Puerto Rico. And I have every reason to believe that it will continue to do so.

Before United Nations Committee on
Decolonization, New York/
The Christian Science Monitor, 10-4:23.

WHAT THEY SAID IN 1978

Anastasio Somoza (Debayle)
President of Nicaragua

1

[On the opposition to his regime]: All those people said they wanted me to get out. But I looked around and said, who is ready to take the cake? Certainly not the [opposition] Conservative Party; they only drew 45,000 votes in the last municipal election. What about the clandestine Sandinista National Liberation Front? I don't know them, but they have maybe 1,000 to 2,000 activists. Could they handle it? No. Now, what about the Liberal Party? . . . they elected me. When I finished that analysis—bingo. That was it. I figured I better stay right where I am until my term of office expires in 1981.

Interview, Managua/
Los Angeles Times, 7-29:(1)15.

2

I know what it costs to be in power. I know what it means to give power to people who are not organized. The opposition here is not organized. Nobody is organized except the *Guardia Nacional* and the Liberal Party. If I allow somebody else to be President, nobody [will] get this state together. So I say, let's go to the regularly scheduled elections [in 1981] and I will hand it over to whoever wins. I am not chickening out. I am just being darned honest with the Nicaraguans.

Interview, Managua/
Newsweek, 10-23:69.

Herman E. Talmadge
United States Senator, D-Georgia

3

[Supporting proposed treaties which would gradually turn over control of the Panama Canal to Panama]: Determined guerrillas, operating from jungles more dense than those of Vietnam, could keep the Canal closed more than it is open. Military experts estimate that it could require as many as 100,000 U.S. troops to stand guard over the Canal. We cannot operate the Panama Canal at the point of a bayonet.

The Christian Science Monitor, 3-17:38.

Omar Torrijos (Herrera)
Head of Government of Panama

4

[On the U.S. Senate's ratification of treaties which will gradually turn over control of the Panama Canal to his country]: For us, this is a moment of great emotion. I feel proud that my mission is completed. I did not want to leave this problem to future generations, obliging them to live through the moments of shame that I have lived through.

Broadcast address to the nation, Panama City,
April 18/Los Angeles Times, 4-19:(1)1.

5

[On his statement that he would have destroyed the Panama Canal if the U.S. Senate failed to ratify the treaties giving his country gradual control of the Canal]: Yes, I spoke seriously. It was a decision very painful, but there was no other alternative to take . . . because [failure of the treaties] would have left us without any hope of coexisting peacefully and harmoniously with the United States . . . In 1968, all the officers of the National Guard swore jointly with all the cadres of the Panamanian youth that this situation of colonization of the Republic of Panama would be eliminated either via negotiation or via liberation . . . [But since the treaties have been ratified,] never before was the future of the Canal so secure as now, because those same forces that were disposed to take the Canal, to destroy it—we're now placing all this force to the benefit of securing the Canal.

Television interview, Panama City/ABC "Evening
News," American Broadcasting Company, 4-19.

Peter M. Towe
Canadian Ambassador to the United States

6

I think if the Quebecers had the will to secede [from Canada], there would be no doubt about their success. The fact is there is not in the province of Quebec any will at all to separate from Canada. The vast majority of Quebecers recognize that they are Canadians.

News conference, Dallas, Texas,
Sept. 13/The Dallas Times Herald, 9-14:(C)5.

Pierre Elliott Trudeau
Prime Minister of Canada

1

[On the possibility of independence for Quebec province]: There is a growing realization among all Canadians that we would surely be a foolishly self-destructive society if we allowed our country to be fractured because of our inability to imagine with generosity a solution to the problem of a Federal state composed of different regions and founded on the recognition of two languages. I am confident that the people of Quebec, when the choice is fairly put, will reject an ethno-centric nationalism in favor of a renewed and more productive relationship with their fellow Canadians.

Before Economic Club, New York,
March 22/The Washington Post, 3-23:(D)11.

2

Foreign investment will always be welcome in Canada, yet there is one very important provision. We hope it will be not only to the benefit of the foreign investor but also to the benefit of the Canadian people.... we have reached a stage now when we can become a little more choosy.

Before Economic Club, New York, March 22/
Los Angeles Herald Examiner, 3-23:(A)4.

3

Canada is the only country in the world—the only independent country in the world—which doesn't have its own constitution, written in Canada, for Canadians, by Canadians; the only country which, in a legal sense, is still a colony, because it still has to go to another country [Britain] in order to change its basic law.

Before provincial Premiers/
Los Angeles Times, 12-3:(8)1.

4

[On the tensions between English- and French-speaking Canadians]: We may be relatively poor in arms and battle equipment, but we [Canadians] are well supplied with all kinds of potentially explosive feelings. And because we are one of the world's most peaceful peoples, we are too easily inclined to close our eyes to the seeds of violence within us.

New Year's message/
Los Angeles Herald Examiner, 12-31:(A)4.

Cyrus R. Vance
Secretary of State of the United States

5

[Supporting the proposed treaties which would gradually turn over control of the Panama Canal to Panama]: These treaties represent an America that is looking to the future. They are entered into by an America that is confident of its strength and prepared to act as a responsible world power ... The treaties require no payments from the U.S. Treasury to Panama, either now or at any time in the future ... [As for defense rights,] the United States has the right to take any action we decide is necessary—including the use of troops—to meet threats or aggression directed either against the Canal or against the passage of any ship. We can defend and protect the Canal, before and after the year 2000 [when Panama would have full control]. [The agreements] separate out what is important to us—that is, continued use of the Canal.

At Morris Harvey College, Jan. 11/
The Dallas Times Herald, 1-12:(A)6.

Charles Wilson
United States Representative, D-Texas

6

I don't care if [Nicaraguan President Anastasio] Somoza himself stays in power. But I do care if his party does. Because if it doesn't, the vacuum will be filled by the Communists—I don't think there is any question. Nicaragua is the largest country in Central America. If it becomes Communist, Guatemala and El Salvador will fall within a year, and then we will have four Cubas instead of one.

Interview, Mexico/
The Dallas Times Herald, 12-2:(A)19.

Elmo R. Zumwalt, Jr.
Admiral (Ret.) and former Chief of
Operations, United States Navy

7

[Supporting the proposed treaties which would gradually turn over control of the Pana-

WHAT THEY SAID IN 1978

(ELMO R. ZUMWALT, JR.)

ma Canal to Panama]: [In the event of war,] we must be able to deploy ships from one ocean to the other. . . . the best security, the best certainty, the likeliest probability of being able to use the Canal is to have a friendly regime in support of the operation rather than a hostile regime. Those of us who have had to deal with insurgencies, as I did in Vietnam, can tell you that it is impossible to defend that Canal, as all the Joint Chiefs have agreed, against a hostile insurgency, and that the odds are greatly increased that that insurgency would occur if the United States fails to ratify these treaties.

Television interview, Jan. 15/
The Washington Post, 1-24:(A)17.

Georgi A. Arbatov
Director, Soviet Institute of U.S.A.
and Canadian Affairs

1

It is not our policy to try to spoil our relations with countries that improve their relations with [mainland] China. But if it's done on an anti-Soviet basis, it can affect our relations. The pursuit of rather short-term gains could lay the cornerstone of an absolutely new set of international relationships that would make nobody happy. There are several possibilities. One, which I hope will not materialize, is for China to become some sort of a military ally to the West, even an informal ally. Then the whole situation would look different to us. We would have to reanalyze our relationship with the West. If such an axis is built on an anti-Soviet basis, then there is no place for detente, even in a narrow sense.

Interview/The New York Times, 11-13:(A)7.

Zulfikar Ali Bhutto
Former Prime Minister of Pakistan

2

In my time [as Prime Minister], there was a Parliament in existence. There was democracy in existence. Speeches criticizing me were made in Parliament. Those conditions can never be compared to conditions under martial law [such as now exist in Pakistan]. You may say: "This man is a very vain man, a boastful man." But don't you see the void in the country [now]? There is no direction. The balance of power has shifted so much, and is shifting so fast, that the subcontinent is in a new political crisis of a great magnitude.

Appealing his death sentence before Supreme Court,
Rawalpindi, Dec. 18/
The Washington Post, 12-19:(A)20.

Harold Brown
Secretary of Defense of the United
States

3

We [the U.S.] are and will remain a major force in the Pacific. It cannot be otherwise. We cannot be strong in Europe and weak in Asia. Indeed, our strength in Asia supports our strength in Europe, and vice versa. They are two sides of a coin . . . If we don't give Asia its due—if we don't maintain the necessary military forces, as well as enough political and military strength, in the region to hedge against uncertainties—the favorable political balance we now find in Asia could deteriorate rapidly.

Before Los Angeles World Affairs Council,
Beverly Hills, Calif., Feb. 20/
The New York Times, 2-21:7.

4

[On the South Korea-U.S. Congress influence-buying scandal]: We condemn such actions as a serious misinterpretation of our governmental processes and of the mores of the American people. At the same time, we must not let the Tongsun Park affair obscure our basic national interests in Korea. To look at Korea solely in terms of this scandal without regard to our security interests and responsibilities would endanger not only South Korea and its people, but the stability of northeast Asia and the security of this country as well . . . Neither the Soviets nor the Chinese should have any doubts that we would meet North Korean aggression with overwhelming force.

Before House International Relations Committee,
Washington, Feb. 22/
The New York Times, 2-23:(A)10.

5

Human rights does affect our interactions with lots of countries, all of them, but not all in

(HAROLD BROWN)

exactly the same way. We certainly continue to be concerned about possible violations of human rights in the Philippines, and are going to continue to do what we can to improve, and encourage the government there to improve, the human-rights situation, as we do elsewhere. That's not a bar to continuing our base-rights negotiations, because the security of the Pacific area is important to the human rights of the people in the Pacific area. The two really have to go forward—our two efforts have to continue to go forward at the same time, even when there are frictions created.

News conference, Honolulu/
The New York Times, 2-23:(A)13.

1

I will argue that a SALT agreement puts us in a better position than no SALT agreement. We'll make the argument that a more predictable and stable situation will be achieved with SALT than without. I will not claim the earth for it . . . I'm disappointed that the Soviet arms build-up has not slowed down, and I would hope an arms-limitation agreement would have that effect. I worry quite a lot about their strategic capabilities, where they're spending two and a half times as much as we are, and their continued build-up in Europe. I'm less worried about, say, their activities in space, the capabilities of their Navy which, although continuing to grow, are not bigger than ours. It's when they have a capability greater than ours—and continue to increase them—that I wonder what is in their minds.

Interview, Washington, Dec. 28/
The New York Times, 1-3('79):(A)11.

Zbigniew Brzezinski
Assistant to President of the
United States Jimmy Carter for
National Security Affairs

2

[The U.S. approaches relations with mainland China] with three fundamental beliefs, [which are] that friendship between the United States and the People's Republic of China is

vital and beneficial to world peace; that a secure and strong China is in America's interest; that a powerful, confident and globally engaged United States is in China's interest.

Peking, May/The New York Times, 6-25:(1)7.

3

A [mainland] China that is increasingly modern, increasingly capable of dealing with its large number of people, increasingly a factor in stability both in its region and in the world as a whole—a China that is strong and secure—that is a China we would like to see. We do not see cooperation among China, the U.S., Western Europe and Japan as a hostile design against the Soviets. In different ways and on different issues, this same cooperation should also involve the Soviet Union. We see no fundamental incompatibility between a better relationship with China and a better relationship with the Soviet Union.

Interview/Time, 12-25:19.

Ellsworth Bunker
United States Ambassador-at-Large

4

[On U.S. involvement in the Vietnam war]: To try to fight limited war for limited objectives with limited resources, and, by inference, limited in time, because we are an impatient people, against an adversary whose objectives are unlimited and who has the means or is given the means to wage unrestricted warfare—this is not a viable policy.

Interview, Washington/
The New York Times, 5-16:2.

Jimmy Carter
President of the United States

5

In the diversity of languages, religions, political opinions and racial and cultural groups, India is comparable to the continent of Europe, which has a population about the same size as India's. Yet India has forged her vast mosaic of humanity into a single nation that has weathered many challenges to survival both as a nation and as a democracy. This is surely one of the

(JIMMY CARTER)

greatest political achievements of this or any century.

Before Parliament, New Delhi/
The Christian Science Monitor, 1-6:35.

1

We have had a defense pact with the South Koreans ever since 1954. We intend to honor all the elements of that defense treaty. We are committed to the security of South Korea. We would like to have the differences between them and North Korea resolved in a friendly and mutually constructive fashion.

Interview, Washington, Jan. 13/
The Washington Post, 1-15:(A)10.

2

America cannot avoid the responsibility to speak out in condemnation of the Cambodian government, the worst violator of human rights in the world today. [Refugees have] recounted abuses that include mass killings, inhuman treatment of the supporters of the previous government ... the total suppression of recognized political and religious freedoms, as well as deprivation of food and health care ... It is an obligation of every member of the international community to protest the policies of this or any nation which cruelly and systematically violates the right of its people to enjoy life and basic human dignities.

April 21*/The Washington Post, 4-22:(A)20.

3

On January 1, 1979, our two governments [the U.S. and mainland China] will implement full normalization of diplomatic relations. As a nation of gifted people who comprise one-fourth of the population of the earth, China plays an important role in world affairs—a role that can only grow more important in the years ahead. We do not undertake this important step for transient tactical or expedient reasons. In recognizing that the government of the People's Republic is the single government of China, we are recognizing simple reality. But far more is

involved in this decision than a recognition of reality ... Normalization—and the expanded commercial and cultural relations it will bring with it—will contribute to the well-being of our own nation, and will enhance stability in Asia. These more positive relations with China can beneficially affect the world in which we and our children will live ... I have paid special attention to insuring that normalization of relations between the United States and the People's Republic will not jeopardize the well-being of the people of Taiwan. The people of the United States will maintain our current commercial, cultural and other relations with Taiwan through non-governmental means. Many other countries are already successfully doing so. These decisions and actions open a new and important chapter in world affairs.

Broadcast address to the nation, Washington,
Dec. 15/The New York Times, 12-16:8.

4

[On his decision to establish full diplomatic relations with mainland China and withdraw recognition from Taiwan]: My reports from Taiwan, in the last day or few hours, have been that they studied the agreement with the People's Republic, that their original concerns have been substantially alleviated, and I don't think the people of Taiwan are any more concerned about future peace than they were before ... My Constitutional responsibility in establishing relationships with foreign countries is clear and cannot be successfully challenged in court ... As of the first of January, we will have relations with and acknowledge the nationhood of China. And Taiwan will no longer be a nation, in the view of our own country.

Television interview, Washington, Dec. 19/
The Dallas Times Herald, 12-20:(A)11.

5

[Saying that, despite the U.S. decision to establish full diplomatic relations with mainland China and withdraw recognition from Taiwan, the U.S. expects there to be no military confrontation between Peking and Taipei]: [For Peking] to violate that understanding with us would be to wipe out all the benefits to

WHAT THEY SAID IN 1978

(JIMMY CARTER)

them and to Asia of peace and their new relationship with us. But I don't want to speculate under what circumstances we might take military action, because I think it is absolutely an unnecessary speculation because the people of China want peace. They want good relationships with us and, of course, Taiwan is so strong and will stay strong.

Television interview, Washington, Dec. 19/
Los Angeles Times, 12-20:(1)9.

Chhang Song
Former Minister of Information of Cambodia

1

. . . Cambodia today [under the Communists] is a land where these signposts appear: There are no cities; urban dwellers have been driven like animals into the countryside, where they live and toil seven days a week in guarded village concentration camps. More than one million persons have been systematically slaughtered for the crime of having a relationship, however remote, with the old regime, while another million persons appear to have perished from disease and starvation. Organized religion has been destroyed and relegated to the dustbin. Schools and universities have been torn down. The economy has been reduced to the lowest level of subsistence agriculture, and the national currency has been abolished. Thus love, joy, beauty and hope—those precious qualities of human existence—have been banished from my country where, for many Cambodians, death comes as a welcome release from terrible toil and suffering . . . This, I submit, is a holocaust. What we are witnessing in my homeland is the eradication of the ancient and proud Khmer civilization—a horrendous crime that has too long been ignored by the so-called civilized world.

News conference, Washington/
Los Angeles Times, 5-12:(2)7.

Chiang Ching-kuo
President of Nationalist China

2

[On the U.S. decision to establish full diplomatic relations with mainland China and with-draw recognition from Taiwan]: The Chinese Communists are on the verge of collapse at this moment. The United States' establishment of relations with the Communists is to help save a bandit regime that massacres millions and millions of compatriots. Therefore, America is the biggest sinner in history.

San Francisco Examiner & Chronicle,
12-24:(This World)2.

3

[Criticizing the U.S. decision to establish full diplomatic relations with mainland China and withdraw recognition from Taiwan]: We must endure humiliation, take up our heavy duties and carry out our long-term struggle with the strongest fortitude and the most enduring patience. We must undertake careful review, think things out soberly and design our countermeasures with special calm and prudence to advance and carry out our policy and reach our goal . . . [The Nationalist Chinese government] is the sole legal government representing the people of the whole nation [of China]. The mainland is the territory of the Republic of [Nationalist] China, and the government of the Republic of China will never abandon its sovereignty there . . . [The Communist regime on the mainland] obviously cannot represent China, not to say the Chinese people. In time to come, we shall never enter into negotiations with the Chinese Communists. We shall carry out our struggle against the Communists and for national recovery to a successful conclusion.

Taipei, Taiwan, Dec. 24/
Los Angeles Times, 12-25:(1)4.

Frank Church
United States Senator, D-Idaho

4

[Approving U.S. President Carter's decision to establish full diplomatic relations with mainland China]: President Carter has cut the Gordian Knot. His decision to recognize China finally brings American policy into line with Asian realities. It also opens the gates to a peaceful trade of potentially great value to American agriculture and industry.

Dec. 15/Los Angeles Times, 12-16:(1)29.

William E. Colby
*Former Director of Central Intelligence
of the United States*

1

I think South Vietnam ... had essentially won the guerrilla war [during the Vietnam conflict] but still had to face the military threat from the North. I think they could have faced that with American supplies on a continuing basis and you would not have had a defeat in South Vietnam, but you would not have had perfect peace either ... At a time in which the South Vietnamese were under massive attack, the Congress of the United States decided not to give any more American logistical support. That kind of a change of attitude from our side almost foredoomed the eventual fall of South Vietnam.

*News conference, New York, May 15/
The Dallas Times Herald, 5-16:(A)9.*

Patricia M. Derian
*Assistant Secretary for Human Rights,
Department of State of the United States*

2

[On the restriction of civil liberties in Thailand, the Philippines, Singapore and Indonesia]: These people explain the lack of due process in terms of crisis and emergencies. In many cases, the crisis or emergency is 10 or more years old. All the countries are either under martial law or under some sort of emergency status, and civil liberties are heavily restricted, always in the name of a higher good: a threat to national security. Once a country has declared itself imperiled, it becomes very hard to figure out how to stop being imperiled. It is truly a case of the difficulty of how to dismount.

*Interview, Bangkok, Thailand/
The New York Times, 1-18:(A)3.*

Morarji R. Desai
Prime Minister of India

3

[On his country and Vietnam]: Though our methods were different, our goals were and are the same—not just liberation from a foreign yoke, but a life of dignity for our people. And,

beyond our national frontier, abolishing exploitation of nation by nation and of racial arrogance, and the construction of human society permeated by the spirit of interdependence and shared objectives.

New Delhi, Feb. 24/The New York Times, 2-26:(1)3.

4

[On U.S.-Indian relations]: Genuine friendship makes light of passing irritations and misunderstandings, as they are not allowed to affect the shared long-term objectives of our countries. I shall continue to have faith in this friendship.

*At National Press Club, Washington, June 14/
The New York Times, 6-15:(A)2.*

5

I am not pro-Western, not pro-Eastern, not pro-anybody. I am pro-everybody. Why should I be pro-anybody? That is what I made clear to them in Moscow, and also to [U.S. President] Carter when he was here in January. We are equally friends to all. Friendship with you [the U.S.] should not be at the cost of friendship with someone else. I think this is now understood in Moscow as well as in Washington. There is complete understanding: I understand them, and they understand me.

*Interview, New Delhi/
U.S. News & World Report, 6-19:30.*

Takeo Fukuda
Prime Minister of Japan

6

After the U.S. withdrawal from Vietnam, Asian countries thought the United States might lose interest in Asia and, as a result, felt uneasy. There were many countries like that ... Now such apprehensions have diminished. ... world peace cannot be ensured through stability in just Europe and the United States. Only with prosperity and stability in Asia can there be stability in the world.

*Interview, Tokyo, April 26/
Los Angeles Times, 4-27:(1)10,11.*

7

This is a period of global togetherness, of global shared responsibility. Japan has forsworn

259

WHAT THEY SAID IN 1978

(TAKEO FUKUDA)

military power, so our contribution [to world peace and security] cannot be one of force. Therefore it has to be economic, a question of money. I have already pledged to double our economic aid in five years, and more recently in three years.

Interview, Tokyo/
The Christian Science Monitor, 7-10:6.

1

In our century of modernization, we Japanese have weathered numerous periods of fluctuation. Although the international environment has at times favored Japan, this has been possible basically because of the emphasis on education, diligence, rich creativity and other outstanding qualities fostered in the Japanese people in the home, at school and in society. I am convinced that it is here that we Japanese should again seek the source of a new vitality in this contemporary age of change. I am confident that the creative qualities and brave disposition of our people are a national strength capable of weathering any change and of ensuring bright prospects for the future of Japan.

Before the Diet (Parliament), Tokyo/
The Christian Science Monitor, 11-17:17.

Indira Gandhi
Member of Indian Parliament; Former
Prime Minister of India

2

[On attempts to remove her from Parliament on charges she harassed officials while she was Prime Minister in 1975]: Every man, woman and child in India knows that if the drama of a kind of impeachment of a former Prime Minister is enacted, its sole purpose is not to solve any national problem, but to silence a voice which they find inconvenient . . . If the government believes that by sending me to prison or banishing me from this House the voice of protest against their wrong policies will be silenced, they are woefully mistaken. If the Janata Party thinks that acts of persecution and victimization can destroy the ideals for which I stand, it is cherishing false dreams.

Before Parliament, New Delhi, Dec. 13/
The New York Times, 12-14:(A)6.

Robert F. Goheen
United States Ambassador to India

3

. . . whether you look at it in geopolitical terms, in military terms or in economic terms, India and Pakistan really aren't competitors any more. India is clear and away the pre-eminent nation on the subcontinent. So that game we [the U.S.] played for many years—of trying to balance one off against the other—that's a dead game. And that was a terrific cause of friction between India and ourselves.

The New York Times, 12-31:(1)12.

Barry M. Goldwater
United States Senator, R-Arizona

4

[Criticizing U.S. President Carter's decision to establish full diplomatic relations with mainland China and withdraw recognition from Taiwan]: President Carter's decision on China represents one of the most cowardly acts by any President in the history of the country. The action stabs in the back the nation of Taiwan, one of the most faithful, trustworthy and valuable friends our country has ever had.

Dec. 15/Los Angeles Herald Examiner, 12-16:(A)4.

5

[Criticizing U.S. President Carter's decision to recognize mainland China and withdraw recognition from Taiwan]: In other words, he is saying that Taiwan has no right to exist in a two-China world. He is saying Taiwan is merely a rebel province of the mainland. One wonders whether, on some future date, he will tell us that West Germany has no right to exist outside of Communist Germany, or whether South Korea has no right to exist outside of Communist Korea. If the American people had been allowed to speak through the voice of their elected representatives in the Congress, I know a wave of outrage would have swept the country.

Television broadcast, Dec. 23/
The Washington Post, 12-24:(A)6.

Herman Guerrero
Mariana Islands Senator

6

[On the Marianas becoming a U.S. commonwealth]: This is our big day. We were occupied

(HERMAN GUERRERO)

by the Spanish, Germans and Japanese. But it was the Americans who displayed the type of government we wanted. The rights of the individual and the protection of those rights is what makes the United States so attractive to us.

San Francisco Examiner & Chronicle,
1-15:(This World)8.

S. I. Hayakawa
United States Senator, R-California

1

[Japanese legislators] are concerned almost solely with agricultural producers ... and their profits, [but think] very little about the consumer. The price of food in Japan is outrageous. It shocks me that there is no political party in Japan with a sense of political opportunism to grasp the idea of cheaper food for everybody and ride to power and lick the [ruling] Liberal Democratic Party.

Tokyo, Nov. 17/Los Angeles Times, 11-18:(1)7.

2

[Criticizing U.S. President Carter's decision to establish full diplomatic relations with mainland China]: We've given diplomatic recognition to perhaps the world's greatest concentration camp.

Dec. 15/Los Angeles Times, 12-16:(1)28.

Phan Hien
Vice Foreign Minister of Vietnam

3

Even if the U.S. Congress rejects the reconstruction aid [to Vietnam], we look forward to establishing full diplomatic ties ... The elements in the U.S. Congress opposed to aid for Vietnam will not always be around. America has been known to alter her course. What is important now is that both our countries get along well together ... In the past, the United States brought weapons and destroyed our cities. But these are now things of the past and we are ready to resume talks with them.

News conference, Tokyo, July 10/
Los Angeles Times, 7-11:(1)10.

Richard C. Holbrooke
Assistant Secretary for East Asia
and Pacific Affairs, Department of
State of the United States

4

From the standpoint of security, the strategic balance that exists today [in Asia] between the four most powerful countries in the region—[mainland] China, Japan, the Soviet Union and the United States—is clearly in our nation's interests. Although important differences remain with Peking, it is fair to say that the United States, China and Japan share an interest in maintaining that stability—a significant and hopeful change from the pattern of the past half century in which the United States' Far Eastern policy constantly required us to choose, in effect, between China and Japan.

Hawaii, June 16/The New York Times, 6-25:(1)7.

5

A striking new fact about Asia today is that the primary sources of tension and conflict are now almost entirely between Asian Communist states—the Sino-Soviet rivalry, the mounting hostility between [mainland] China and Vietnam, and the war between Vietnam and Cambodia. These conflicts follow age-old geopolitical, ethnic and historical patterns of rivalry and hatred. Indeed, it seems fair to say that nationalism has triumphed over ideology in much of Asia. What we used to call the East-versus-West struggle now seems more accurately described as an East-versus-East rivalry.

Before Boston World Affairs Council/
The Christian Science Monitor, 12-20:23.

Hua Kuo-feng
Chairman, Communist Party of China

6

U.S. imperialism occupies South Korea and pursues a policy of dividing Korea ... We maintain that the Democratic People's Republic of [North] Korea is the sole legitimate sovereign Korean state. We do not recognize the South Korean authorities. The reunification of Korea is the common desire of all the people.

At rally, Pyongyang, North Korea, May 7/
The New York Times, 5-8:(A)9.

WHAT THEY SAID IN 1978

(HUA KUO-FENG)

1

The Soviet revisionists are not abandoning their ambition to subjugate China and they are our chief and most dangerous enemy. We must maintain a high degree of mental preparedness against war. Our army must speed the improvement of its weapons and equipment and raise its tactical and technical level. At the same time, we must realize the primary question is who has the guns and at whom they are pointed.

San Francisco Examiner & Chronicle, 6-4:(A)2.

2

In the past few years, the Gang of Four wrought havoc with the economy and the aftermath of this continued to show itself in some areas in the first quarter of last year . . . Low productivity, poor quality of products, high production costs, low profits and slow turnover of funds—these can be found in most of our enterprises. . . . only when we are fully aware of the problems created by our low standards of management and inept managerial work can we sum up experience and lessons in earnest, study and master advanced science and technology and advanced methods of management . . . Many of our comrades are scarcely aware of what has been going on abroad. By comparing our position with that of advanced levels in other countries, it will be seen that our levels are still very low. China should learn everything that is advanced from other countries. Theory, politics, economics, management, science and technology all need to be studied and the general education level raised.

The Christian Science Monitor, 7-27:9.

Henry M. Jackson
United States Senator, D-Washington

3

I detected a new spirit in [mainland] China. The Chinese people and their leaders are determined to build a strong and modern nation, and to maintain their own security and territorial integrity. They are also playing an important role in the struggle for stability in key areas of tension around the world. Despite this reality, the United States has not been giving sufficient priority to [its] relationship with the People's Republic of China. Our leadership has been preoccupied with other issues . . . We share with China a common interest in key strategic issues. The lack of normalized relations makes working together on these common interests more difficult, and we should seek to resolve . . . the outstanding issues that stand in the way of full normalization.

Feb. 22/The Washington Post, 2-26:(D)6.

Shin Kanemaru
Director, Defense Agency of Japan

4

Japan cannot defend itself alone. That is why relations with the United States must be strengthened. To raise the level of trust between our two countries, Japan must make its own efforts for more self-reliance in defense and, at the same time, consider the burden of the United States in maintaining troops here. Without waiting to be asked by the United States, we should act to alleviate that burden by whatever amount is possible.

To reporters, Tokyo/
Los Angeles Times, 6-14:(1-A)1.

Kim Dae-jung
Leader of the opposition to South Korean President Park Chung Hee

5

[On his being released from prison after being held as a political prisoner]: At this moment of my coming home from prison, I, as before, firmly believe that the longer the present dictatorial system continues, the more ruin we may be forced to meet in the near future.

News conference, Seoul, Dec. 27/
Los Angeles Herald Examiner, 12-27:(A)4.

Kim Il Sung
President of North Korea

6

In order to reunify the country independently by peaceful means, the interference of the United States and all other outside forces must be categorically rejected. If the United States abandons its wrong stand to divide our

(KIM IL SUNG)

country into "two Koreas" and assumes the right attitude to bring about Korean reunification, we will start talks with it at any time and settle all necessary problems.

At celebration of 30th anniversary of founding
of North Korea, Sept. 9/
The Dallas Times Herald, 9-10:(A)4.

Henry A. Kissinger
Former Secretary of State of the
United States

1

[On his dealings with Japan while he was in the Nixon Administration]: It isn't true that I didn't like Japan or that I didn't pay attention to the importance of Japan ... [but] it is true that I did not understand the nature of Japanese culture very well, and I did not understand the extraordinarily subtle and polite way Japanese communicate. It took me many years to learn it ... At the beginning of any [U.S.] Administration—and this includes the [Nixon] Administration—there is not a full understanding of the intricate way in which Japan is governed. We tend to think that in Japan decisions are made as they are made here, by one or two individuals who have the power to order others to do what they want. It took me a long time to understand that in Japan decisions are made by consensus ... and you must give the Japanese government enough of an opportunity to work with all the important groups [which make up the consensus]. It is conceivable to me that [the Carter] Administration, being at the beginning of its term, may have to go through the same learning experience we did. And I hope that the Japanese, being an ancient people, will have patience with their friends as we go through this process.

Television interview/
The Wall Street Journal, 5-2:20.

2

I believe that the independence and independent foreign policy of [mainland] China is a major American interest, and the prevention of military pressures on China is also a major American interest ... I believe that the strengthening of the defensive capability of China is not against the American interest, and indeed is in the American interest. What I do not think we should do is use China for tactical purposes. The Chinese quarrel with the Soviet Union has its own motives and follows its own logic and does not need any encouragement from us.

News conference, West Berlin, Dec. 3/
The Dallas Times Herald, 12-4:(A)4.

3

[On how U.S.-Soviet relations will be affected by the recent U.S. decision to establish full diplomatic relations with mainland China]: On the whole, I have always believed that good relations with Peking make for good relations with Moscow, and vice versa. And so I think that, on the whole, it will help in our relations rather than hurt.

Television interview, Dec. 15/
U.S. News & World Report, 12-25:12.

Li Hsien-nien
Vice Premier of the People's
Republic of (mainland) China

4

The superpower [Soviet Union] that styles itself the natural ally of the Third World, and uses "support to national liberation" and "friendship and cooperation" as a cover, is trying by every means to barge into the South Pacific region. Against this, the countries in the region are on the alert. A united anti-hegemonist struggle in this region has steadily developed.

At dinner honoring the Fijian Prime Minister,
Peking, June 11/The New York Times, 6-12:(A)14.

Raul S. Manglapus
Former Foreign Minister of the
Philippines

5

... the love-hate relationship between Americans and Filipinos appears to have produced in the American soul a unique sense of insecurity about the Philippines. The United States should know that it is the United States

WHAT THEY SAID IN 1978

that has [Filipino President Ferdinand] Marcos over a barrel, not the other way. It is the United States that commands the options on the [military] bases, not Marcos, who needs them badly for his political image, and who recognizes that his own neighbors, even Peking, are not anxious to see those bases go. Yet when Marcos begins to rattle his rented sword, the United States appears to tremble. The United States sits down with Marcos, negotiates with him, tries to appease him with assurances of continued military aid. The catchword is stability. But ... the lesson elsewhere, in Greece, in Portugal, in Spain, in India, and now in the Caribbean—namely, that stability is not in one man or woman but in the people—appears yet to be applied to U.S. policy in the Philippines. And so, like Somoza [in Nicaragua], as Louis of France before him, Marcos plays his ultimate ace. He warns: *Apres mois, le deluge!* And his warning is heeded by enough men of influence so that a paralysis of policy is induced in fear of the specter of chaos.

The Washington Post, 10-11:(A)24.

Mike Mansfield
United States Ambassador to Japan

1

[On U.S.-Japanese trade relations]: The greatest danger for both countries ... lies in the widely held belief in the United States of an economic imbalance or [lack of American] opportunity in our bilateral trade. Japan's remaining import restrictions, its rising exports and problems American manufacturers have in selling their products here have brought about the serious situation in [the U.S.] Congress ... No politician can ignore the plight of constituents who have been thrown out of work because of competition from abroad ... If Americans have the same access into your market that you have in ours and still cannot compete successfully or balance our bilateral trade, then the blame for the imbalance will fall squarely upon the United States, its manufacturers and its exporters. But as long as unfair restrictions continue to exist, then Japan will

continue to be partially blamed—fairly or unfairly—for our trade imbalance ... Now the time has come to demonstrate your complete and open commitment to free trade by allowing others access to your market.

Before Japanese economic organizations, Osaka, Japan, April 5/Los Angeles Times, 4-5:(3)19.

2

The emphasis [by the U.S. Carter Administration] has been on NATO and the West, and not enough on the Pacific and East Asia, though I think it is changing for the better. We are trying to get Asia and Japan off the back burner and on to the front burner. I think we are gradually getting them there. I think this place is far more important than Western Europe in the future. You've got everything out here, including the world's next big oil fields off the East Asian coast.

Interview/The Wall Street Journal, 5-9:20.

3

[On U.S.-Japanese relations]: If I have anything to say about it, our relations are going to remain good—and get better. Strategically and militarily, our relationship is excellent now. Economically, there are some problems ... But I think we will find, on a comparative basis, the Japanese probably will be the most cooperative and accommodating of any of the countries we trade with. Both in Tokyo and Washington, we have to recognize that, to a large extent, Japan is dependent on the U.S., and we are dependent on Japan. And a large part of the world is dependent on both of us. It is very important that we maintain an honest perspective and a sense of balance and understanding in our mutual relationship.

Interview, Tokyo/ U.S. News & World Report, 10-23:42.

Mao Tun
Mainland-Chinese author; President, All-China Union of Writers

4

We hear people in some foreign countries talking about liberalization [in mainland China]. I think this is the wrong way to put it,

(MAO TUN)

to use the term "liberalization" about things in China. In other words, we have many, many people who are free to air their views; but if some people want to oppose socialism, to speak for our enemies, to spread bourgeois ideas—this means they are speaking for the enemy and there will be restrictions on them ... There are six political criteria in connection with this, so within the limits of the six political criteria, people can freely air their views and write whatever they want. Only anti-socialist ideas or views cannot be allowed—or sometimes they can be, but only as negative examples to educate people and enhance their ability to distinguish between "fragrant flowers and poisonous weeds."

Interview, Peking/
Los Angeles Times, 5-24:(6)5.

Ferdinand E. Marcos
President of the Philippines

1

There are no political prisoners in the Philippines. Those who are under detention are facing charges for commission of crimes punishable under specific laws in our revised criminal code. Nobody has been imprisoned ... because of his political beliefs ... We fought for human rights long before the United States brought our attention to it. You must remember that we fought American troops in 1898 because we believed you were violating our human rights. From that day on ... our adherence to the principle of human rights has been unwavering.

Addressing U.S. Vice President Walter Mondale
at news conference, Manila, May 3/
Los Angeles Times, 5-4:(1)1,20.

2

A weak government is not a safeguard but a menace to national security and human rights. While I am as anxious as anyone else about the lifting of martial law, prudence advises me not to speculate as to when we could finally do it ... With respect to the opposition, we have taken initiatives to remove the irritants that have strained their participation in our political

life. We shall strive to be one nation in which one would be free to disagree with another without undermining national unity.

At opening of National Assembly, Manila,
June 12/The Washington Post, 6-13:(A)16.

George S. McGovern
United States Senator, D-South Dakota

3

[Calling for international military action against the Cambodian government, which he says is committing murder against its citizens]: Do we turn away because of the bitter mistakes we made for so long in Vietnam, which helped to unleash the savagery of Cambodia? Do we turn away because Cambodia is small and weak? Do we turn away because Cambodians are Orientals far from our shores? I hate needless and ill-conceived military ventures. That is why I opposed our military intervention against Ho Chi Minh's popularly based revolution for independence in Vietnam. But to hate a needless and foolish intervention that served no good purpose does not give us the excuse to do nothing in the face of mass murder in another time and place and under vastly differing circumstances.

Before the Senate, Washington, Aug. 25/
The Washington Post, 8-26:(A)8.

George Meany
President, American Federation of
Labor-Congress of Industrial
Organizations

4

[On U.S. President Carter's decision to establish full diplomatic relations with mainland China and withdraw recognition from Taiwan]: [President Carter has] renounced [his] principle [of human rights] by extending diplomatic recognition to ... one of the world's most repressive violators of human rights. At the same time, President Carter undermined the credibility of the United States in its relations with other countries by unilaterally abrogating the U.S. treaty with the Republic of [Nationalist] China on Taiwan. Other nations may well now wonder whether the United States can be relied upon to fulfill its

WHAT THEY SAID IN 1978

treaty obligations and for how long . . . We can understand—although not approve of—the applause from the business community, which is in search of quick profits no matter what the cost in human rights. What we cannot understand, however, is how this President, who made human rights a world issue, could so suddenly and callously reject the human-rights concerns of both those enslaved on mainland China and those on Taiwan who fear such enslavement.

Washington, Dec. 20/
The Washington Post, 12-21:(A)3.

Walter F. Mondale
Vice President of the United States

1

The [problem of refugees from Vietnam, Laos and Cambodia] is a product of the most pressing and tragic human-rights problems in the world today. I believe there is no more profound test of our government's commitment to human rights than the way we deal with these people.

Bangkok, Thailand, May 5/
The Washington Post, 5-6:(A)14.

Masayoshi Ohira
Prime Minister-elect of Japan

2

Japan considers the U.S. economy as open and free. The Japanese economy is free, but it is not open. I would like to see the Japanese government encourage more openness. The United States needs Japan, but Japan needs the United States even more. The negotiations over our trade problems have to be successful, and I will see to that. It is going to be one of the most important issues confronting my Administration.

Interview, Tokyo, Dec. 4/
The Dallas Times Herald, 12-5:(D)5.

3

[On his becoming Prime Minister]: I am, as it were, like a fluorescent lamp, and it will take a little time before I light up.

San Francisco Examiner & Chronicle,
12-10:(This World)2.

4

[Mainland] China, the Soviet Union and the U.S. are our neighbors. As time goes on, there will be a natural increase in mutual understanding of positions and exchanges. There will be no emphasis in relations with one at the expense of the others.

Interview/Time, 12-11:58.

David Owen
Foreign Secretary of the
United Kingdom

5

[Approving the U.S. decision to establish full diplomatic relations with mainland China]: I do not accept that war is inevitable, as the Chinese think, between themselves and the Soviet Union. I think if we help the atmosphere of detente between the Soviet Union and China we will be doing a service to peace and, in that sense, good relations between the United States and China are beneficial.

London, Dec. 16/
The Washington Post, 12-17:(A)9.

Pol Pot
Prime Minister of Cambodia

6

The Kampuchea [Cambodia]-Vietnam conflict is not an ordinary border conflict. It is the carrying out of the strategy of Vietnam for its "Indochina Federation" and of the Soviet strategy in Southeast Asia, Asia and the world . . . Absolutely we refuse to be the satellite of Vietnam.

Interview, Phnom Penh/
The Washington Post, 12-31:(A)18.

James R. Schlesinger
Secretary of Energy of the
United States

7

[Mainland] China has visibly come to a turn in the road. The emphasis is whole-heartedly on economic progress. There is no longer emphasis on ideological differences. They have found ideological niceties don't produce any goods.

News conference, Tokyo, Nov. 7/
The Dallas Times Herald, 11-8:(B)12.

James C. H. Shen
Nationalist Chinese Ambassador to the
United States

1

[Upon closing Taiwan's embassy in Washington as U.S. recognition of mainland China and withdrawal of recognition from Taiwan is about to take [effect]: We didn't think it would end this way. With our effort, our hard work, we thought we had earned the right to live in the way we want to live without being made part of a bargain.

Washington, Dec. 29/
The New York Times, 12-30:2.

Charan Singh
Home Minister of India

2

[On his country's proposed preventive-detention powers]: To some, any law providing for preventive detention is objectionable as a matter of ideology. Those charged with the responsibility of governance, however, cannot allow themselves the luxury of mere adherence to theories. The country rightly expects the government to safeguard its security, to maintain law and order, and not to allow democracy to be butchered in the name of democracy itself.

The New York Times, 1-2:6.

S. Nihal Singh
Editor, "The Statesman,"
Calcutta/New Delhi

3

When it comes to nuclear energy, the problem is the new American law, under which, in 18 months or two years, a country that does not pledge to institute what are called safeguards will not be entitled to receive American uranium or nuclear supplies. We in India feel that this is unfair, in the sense that it is denying us something which is essential—specifically, the power program in western India. We are short of power already. On the general subject of disarmament, what the argument of the superpowers and the other nuclear powers really boils down to is: "We know how to deal

with these things, but it's too dangerous for you."

Interview, New York/
Atlas World Press Review, September:30.

John K. Singlaub
Major General, United States Army
(Ret.); Former Chief of Staff,
U.S. forces in Korea

4

[Saying South Korea is important to U.S. security]: Like it or not, we do a tremendous amount of business with the Pacific Basin. A Communist government in Seoul would have ramifications for all our other allies in the Pacific—primarily Japan. But South Korea is also important from a psychological standpoint. It is the product of the U.S. capitalistic system. Where once there was poverty, there now is a stable, flourishing government and people. We and the democratic countries should point with pride to Korea. If ever there was a phoenix, Korea is it.

Interview/People, 7-10:26.

Richard Stone
United States Senator, D-Florida

5

[On U.S. President Carter's decision to establish full diplomatic relations with mainland China and withdraw recognition from Taiwan]: It is a slap in the face to our staunch friend and ally, the Republic of China on Taiwan ... Who will be our ally if we are so willing to dump our allies?

U.S. News & World Report, 12-25:13.

Noor Mohammad Taraki
Prime Minister of Afghanistan

6

[On his new government]: The intelligentsia is the main force of the country and every effort will be made to attract them. But we want to re-educate them in such a manner that they should think about the people, and not, as previously, just about themselves—to have a good house and a nice car, and yet other people die of hunger.

News conference, Kabul, May 6/
The New York Times, 5-7:(1)9.

WHAT THEY SAID IN 1978

Teng Hsiao-ping
Vice Premier of the People's
Republic of (mainland) China

1

[On the new friendship treaty between his country and Japan]: This treaty builds a base for stable, friendly, neighborly relations between the two countries. By developing exchanges in political, economic, cultural, scientific and technological and in all other fields, even broader development of China-Japan relations will occur and unmistakably exert positive influence on the maintenance of peace and security in the Asian and Pacific regions.

At treaty ceremony, Tokyo, Oct. 23/
Los Angeles Times, 10-23:(1)1.

2

In 1972, through the Shanghai communique between the United States and China and through normalization of Chinese-Japanese relations, we produced the conditions for obtaining external assistance. However, we wasted four years. The chaos created by the Gang of Four delayed our start. Unless we got rid of the Gang of Four, we could not adjust our views and accept external aid. China has now reached the point where we can get the help of those with experience, and bring in funds and technology of foreign countries. On this point the whole Party and the masses agree.

Interview, Peking, Nov. 26/
The New York Times, 11-27:(A)9.

3

[On the expression of dissenting views in his country via posters on "democracy wall" in Peking]: If the masses feel some anger, we must let them express it.

Time, 12-11:46.

Ross Terrill
Research fellow in East Asian
studies, Harvard University

4

I don't think the [mainland] Chinese will formally renounce the use of force [against Taiwan]. That would contradict their position that the issue is a domestic Chinese affair. At the same time, we [in the U.S.] have to ask ourselves: Are we interested in the substance or the shadow? The substance is for the U.S. to have an ongoing link with Taiwan. The shadow, it seems to me, is the status of Taiwan as the Republic of China. There's no question that the Nationalists on Taiwan have been replaced as the de facto government of China by the Communists in Peking. But since Peking is more interested in the shadow than in the substance, in my judgment, we can get a reasonable deal . . . The U.S. could preserve non-governmental ties with Taiwan, including trade and cultural links and an unofficial office of some kind in Taipei. Normalizing with the U.S. would help lock Peking into its pro-West foreign-policy line—including accepting the status quo on Taiwan. It would be politically disastrous for Peking to disturb its friendship with Japan, with the U.S. and with Southeast Asian countries—the cornerstone of its foreign policy today—by attacking Taiwan. Moreover, Peking couldn't take Taiwan without a major fight—one that would damage mainland interests. And the Communists couldn't be sure that the United States wouldn't spring back—treaty or no treaty—and use its superior force to prevent a take-over of the island.

Interview/U.S. News & World Report, 9-4:31.

John G. Tower
United States Senator, R-Texas

5

I believe that it is in the national interests of the United States to normalize relations with Peking. However, I don't believe that we should abrogate our treaty commitments with Nationalist China, nor abandon our diplomatic recognition of Nationalist China. I don't believe that we have to. In the final analysis, the primary interest of Red China is assurances that we will demonstrate some will and backbone and capability in dealing with the Soviet Union.

Interview/The Dallas Times Herald, 11-5:(K)6.

Y. S. Tsiang
Foreign Minister of Nationalist China

6

[On the U.S. decision to establish full diplomatic relations with mainland China and with-

(Y. S. TSIANG)

draw recognition from Taiwan] : We strongly oppose this decision, which we believe is wrong, and which has most seriously impaired the rights and interests of this country. Although [U.S.] President Carter's decision is so far-reaching, we were advised of it only seven hours before it was made public. This is not the way for a leading world power to treat a long-standing ally, and it has aroused indignation among the Chinese people both at home and abroad.

Taipei, Taiwan, Dec. 28/
The Washington Post, 12-29:(A)1.

Nobuhiko Ushiba
Minister for External Economic
Affairs of Japan
1

When it was revealed that [the U.S. wanted major trade concessions from Japan], there were two rather strong reactions: 1) that we've got to do something quickly to meet some of the legitimate American demands, and 2) a degree of resentment that Japan was suddenly hit by such a hard request from the United States . . . Whether those kinds of pressures are always necessary to have Japan change her policy, well, I must say, it is *not* necessary . . . But I must admit our reaction was rather slow and, to that extent, rather regrettable.

Interview, Tokyo/Newsweek, 1-9:32.

Dmitri F. Ustinov
Minister of Defense of the Soviet Union
2

A serious danger for the cause of peace and socialism is presented by the policy of the Peking leaders. Pursuing great power, chauvinism and hegemonistic aims, they team up with the most reactionary forces of imperialism and inflict damage to the revolutionary and national-liberation movements . . . In these conditions, conducting firmly and consistently the policy of peace, the Soviet Union, together with fraternal socialist countries, gives a reso-

lute rebuff to the aggressive intrigues of imperialism and its flunkies.

At celebration of 61st anniversary of
Bolshevik Revolution, Moscow, Nov. 7/
The Dallas Times Herald, 11-8:(A)15.

Cyrus R. Vance
Secretary of State of the United States
3

I think that the normalization of relationships with the Peoples' Republic of China is a very major, indeed, an historic step, which will move us toward peace, greater stability in the region, will improve relationships bilaterally between our two nations. It will also promote increased trade between our country and that country, and it is part of an overall program which the United States has been carrying on during the Carter Administration of trying to move toward peace by dealing with specific situations such as the Middle East, where we have come in and tried to help the parties, move them closer together, in such things as we have done in moving forward and carrying out our obligations which have been going on for a number of years in trying to resolve the Panama Canal situation. A situation arose here [with China] where the conditions which were necessary for us to be able to go forward and normalize relationships were accepted by the action which the government of the Peoples' Republic of China has taken. We accepted and seized that opportunity, and I think that the result is going to be a very positive one for the region, for the United States, its people and for the people of Taiwan because we are insisting that, insofar as the people of Taiwan are concerned, normal relationships on an unofficial basis in cultural, trade and other matters will be maintained. We have expressed very clearly our deep concern that the welfare of the people of Taiwan be protected and that the transition be a peaceful transition, and that the Taiwan solution be a peaceful solution. This has not been contradicted by the People's Republic of China. In addition, we made it clear that we would continue in the period of post-normalization to supply a limited number of defensive weapons to the people of Taiwan, and we will continue

WHAT THEY SAID IN 1978

(CYRUS R. VANCE)

to do so. And of great importance is the fact that we insisted that the treaty, which will be terminated, will be terminated in accordance with its terms and not terminated immediately, as the Chinese—the Peoples' Republic of China—would have liked it to become.

TV-radio interview/"Meet the Press,"
National Broadcasting Company, 12-17.

John W. Vessey, Jr.
General, United States Army;
Commander, U.S. forces in Korea

1

Every indication we have is that North Korea is building an armed force oriented offensively toward attacking South Korea. That is its one reason for existence. It's far and beyond what is needed for defense. It's what keeps them buying and adding to their inventory in great numbers, and the arms the North Koreans are buying are not defensive weapons. I don't believe even [North Korean President] Kim Il Sung wants to start a war just for the sake of starting a war. But he's dedicated to unifying the peninsula on his terms, and he'd like to do it politically, but he's going to do it under the threat of an attack. Every evidence that we've seen is that he is preparing for an attack. When the time is right—if that's the only way to do it—I would guess that he would invade.

Interview, Seoul/Los Angeles Times, 5-28:(4)4.

Wang Tung-hsing
Vice Chairman,
Communist Party of China

2

The Chinese government and people resolutely support the Kampuchean [Cambodian] people's just struggle in defense of their independence, sovereignty and territorial integrity. Our friendship will tower majestically and last forever, like the Great Wall [of China] and the Angkor Wat.

At banquet, Phnom Penh, Cambodia, Nov. 6/
Los Angeles Times, 11-7:(1)1.

Lester L. Wolff
United States Representative, D-New York

3

[Saying the U.S. expects the Philippines to share the cost of maintaining American military there]: If there is mutual need, then there has to be mutual payment of the costs for these bases . . . We are not pulling out of Asia, nor are we using power to enforce our position. We are a Pacific nation and we are joining in a mutual effort for the security of this part of the world.

News conference, Manila, Jan. 7/
The Washington Post, 1-8:(A)12.

Leonard Woodcock
Chief, United States liaison office
in Peking, mainland China

4

[On mainland China's refusal to disavow the use of force against Taiwan]: When you ask a sovereign government whether they are prepared to disavow the use of force against one of their own provinces, what do you expect them to say? Even if there is no thought of using force, they can't say that, either on the record or off the record. [Nonetheless,] the American people will demand [when considering improved relations with mainland China] some assurances on Taiwan. How that will be done I don't even want to speculate.

Interview, Hong Kong, Jan. 7/
The Washington Post, 1-8:(A)9.

5

The greatest threat of another world war is in the northeast Pacific, probably on the Korean peninsula, [and the danger cannot be abated] until we take the step for a full and normal relationship between the world's most populous power [mainland China] and the world's mightiest power [the U.S.].

At legislative conference of United Automobile
Workers of America, Washington, Feb. 1/
The Washington Post, 2-2:(A)1.

Yeh Chien-ying
*Vice Chairman, Communist Party of
China*

1

[The new Chinese Constitution] makes fairly big changes in the articles concerning organs of state and state personnel and sets strict and necessary demands on them. The most essential of these is to maintain contact with the masses . . . It is necessary to have complete faith in them, respect their sense of responsibility to the revolution, care for and protect their socialist enthusiasm and initiative, share their feelings and sentiments and earnestly heed their criticism and complaints, particularly their criticism of leading bodies and leading cadres. All well-meant criticism from the grass-roots and masses should be warmly encouraged. The people's right to expose the evil-doers and evil deeds in state organs should be fully guaranteed.

*Before National People's Congress, Peking/
The Washington Post, 3-2:(A)20.*

Yun Yat
*Minister for Culture, Education and
Information of Cambodia*

2

Buddhism [in Cambodia] in the past was an instrument of exploitation and oppression of the ruling classes. They themselves did not believe in it. The influence of this religion began to weaken with the development of the liberation movement and the revolution. It is no longer a problem in Cambodia.

*To Yugoslav journalists, Phnom Penh, Cambodia/
San Francisco Examiner & Chronicale, 3-12:(A)21.*

Europe

Giulio Andreotti
Premier of Italy

1

It seems to me that the Italian Communists' anti-Stalinism is a conviction, not just a tactic. On the other hand, we can't forget that where Communists are in power elsewhere . . . liberties do not exist. So while we may have some trust in the evolution of Communism, we should also be very cautious, in view of history.

Television interview/
The Dallas Times Herald, 1-13:(B)8.

Raymond Aron
Professor of sociology,
College de France

2

The reality of the Soviet Union is a paradox. It presents a failure in ideology. Nobody believes any more in Marxist-Leninism in the Western world, and the ideological attraction has almost disappeared—even in France and the Communist Party of Italy. As for the Soviet economic system, nobody believes it is efficient. There is only one field in which the Soviet Union is successful: the projection of its military power throughout the world. The specter for the world is no longer Marxist-Leninism, but the Soviet Army. This has enabled the Soviet Union to reach the status of a real global power at a time when the United States gives the impression of losing its will . . . But the Russians are prudent and they know that, in spite of everything, the United States is enormously powerful if it decides to be. The majority of Europeans don't believe that the Russians will take the risk of direct military aggression.

Interview/U.S. News & World Report, 11-27:67.

Evangelos Averoff
Minister of Defense of Greece

3

Taking into consideration the state of mind of the Turks today, I really can't see what kind of a settlement could be reached [in Cyprus]. The Greek-Cypriots are not disposed to accept anything even approaching the actual Turkish proposals [which involve a return by Turkish-Cypriots of about 1 per cent of captured Greek-Cypriot land]. The positions are so far apart that I can't see how a solution could be reached. I'm afraid we shall live a long time under the present conditions. [A solution should in theory] be simple because it should be a matter of the Turks keeping a part of the land that is reasonably close to their portion of the population, which is absolutely moral, and of having a constitution for a state which now has a small minority and a big majority in two unequal communities. This is not complicated if we are going to solve things by principles of equity rather than strength.

Interview, Athens/
The Washington Post, 4-26:(A)18.

Raymond Barre
Premier of France

4

[On the forthcoming national elections]: I would conclude that even though the Communist Party is strong in France, the French will never allow it to come to power. French dogmatism finds its limits in common sense. The French want a free society, democratic pluralism, greater social justice, a continued effort for a better quality of life. They don't want a society that is collectivist, planned, bureaucratic, that locks them into a political, social and economic iron collar. I don't believe in the success of the [left's] Common Program, because I think its inspiration is profoundly

(RAYMOND BARRE)

contrary to the deep aspirations of the French. What I hope is that they realize it before and not after the elections. Because after the elections the damage will be considerable. And when the damage is done we'll have to live with the consequences—and, believe me, it's easier to go downhill than uphill.

Interview/Time, 3-6:32.

Leonid I. Brezhnev
President of the Soviet Union;
Chairman, Soviet Communist Party

1

We are prepared at any time ... to sign an agreement on the [mutual] reduction of the level of forces and armaments in Central Europe by 5, 10, 20, if you like even by 50 per cent. The Soviet Union has no intention of attacking any state in the West, East, North or South. The Soviet Union has no intention of "conquering" Western Europe.

Interview/The New York Times, 5-3:(A)8.

2

There are peaceful skies over Europe for the fourth decade now. History, it seems, never has had such a long period of peace to the peoples of our continent. And people must be aware that this is largely and decisively due to the fact that half of Europe now lives under socialist conditions. Peace in Europe is largely a result of our common efforts and of the concerted foreign policy of the Warsaw Treaty member-countries.

Before Czechoslovak Communist
Party representatives, Prague,
May 31/Vital Speeches, 6-15:518.

3

... we see no way of cooling down those in the U.S. opposed to good relations [with the Soviet Union]. They are in favor of crossing out all good things achieved; they want to whip up an arms race; they have absurd concoctions about a so-called "Soviet military threat." You have seen the losses of the Soviet people during [World War II]. Twenty million were lost in

defense of Soviet ideals. We have not labored to rebuild our country in order to have another war. All we do today and all our plans relate to grandiose and peaceful construction. We need no land because we have enough. We do not need to conquer the U.S. or Europe even if we could.We do not want to unleash a nuclear war because we are not crazy. What we want is lasting peace with all countries.

To visiting U.S. Senators, Moscow,
Nov. 17/The Washington Post, 11-18:(A)12.

Lawrence Caldwell
Professor of political
science, Occidental College

4

The Soviets' behavior reflects the complexity of politics in the Kremlin. Even though [President] Leonid Brezhnev has committed a great deal of his personal prestige to detente and is indisputably in command of the Soviet political environment, and even at a time when the detente relationship was at its relative best, the Soviets chose to engage in ... clearly opportunistic actions. This underlines the fact that there are bureaucratic pressures in Moscow, there are views in the Kremlin that are relatively more conservative than those of Brezhnev's, views relatively less committed to detente than Brezhnev is. Every leader in the Kremlin has a divided mind on these questions, and when the opportunities arise to reassert the revolutionary strand of Soviet foreign policy, there is always a temptation to do so.

Discussion at Center for the Study of
Democratic Institutions, Santa Barbara,
Calif./World Issues, April-May:10.

James Callaghan
Prime Minister of the United Kingdom

5

[The Soviets] do not appear to understand the deep concern of public opinion at some of their present policies, notably in Africa, in the steady build-up of their military power and in the disregard of human rights to which they subscribed at Helsinki. The Soviet leadership must realize that these developments affect the

WHAT THEY SAID IN 1978

(JAMES CALLAGHAN)

climate of public opinion and make further progress toward detente very difficult.

Before miners, Nottingham, England,
June 10/The Washington Post, 6-11:(A)30.

1

[Saying he will not call new national elections this fall]: Let's have a look at the great domestic issues and ask ourselves whether a general election now would make things any better this winter. Would a general election make it easier to stop inflation going up? Would it improve unemployment this winter? Would a general election solve the problem of how to deal with pay increases? Would it improve productivity? No ... The government must and will continue to carry out policies which are consistent, determined and do not chop and change, the policies which brought about the present recovery in our fortunes.

TV-radio address to the nation, London,
Sept. 7/Los Angeles Times, 9-8:(1)9.

2

It is the government's inescapable responsibility to keep down inflation—not against any individual but in the interest of the whole of the people of this country. It is necessary that the government should know we accept that responsibility. We shall not seek to avoid it and no one can relieve us of it. If yesterday's decision [by the Labor Party not to limit wage increases to 5 per cent as Callaghan had suggested] resulted in a weakening of the impact that pay policy has had on inflation, and inflation starts to move up, then the government will take offsetting action to keep inflation down through monetary and fiscal measures. ... we are ready to encourage wage settlements that include genuine productivity deals and that, therefore, give higher earnings which at the same time reduce and do not increase wage costs. I have seen it argued that this may leave companies with higher profits. Where that happens, then it is their responsibility to keep their plant and equipment up to date by new investments, and, if their profit is

still high, then they can reduce inflation by cutting their prices.

At Labor Party conference, Blackpool, England,
Oct. 3/Los Angeles Times, 10-4:(1)6.

3

We have every right to assert that Britain would be a much cruder, more unjust, more selfish society if Tory values were to prevail. In and out of office, they are the consistent champions of privilege and of the strong and of the wealthy.

At Labor Party conference, Blackpool, England,
Oct. 3/The Christian Science Monitor, 10-4:9.

Jimmy Carter
President of the United States

4

The commitment of the American government and people to the security of Europe is absolute. There should be no doubt that we will maintain in Europe whatever forces are needed to meet that commitment.

Paris/U.S. News & World Report, 1-16:25.

5

There has been an ominous inclination on the part of the Soviet Union to use its military power—to intervene in local conflicts with advisers, with equipment and willful logistical support and encouragement for the mercenaries from other Communist countries, as we can observe today in Africa ... We are prepared ... to cooperate with the Soviet Union toward common social, scientific and economic goals. But if they fail to demonstrate restraint in missile programs and other force levels and in the projection of Soviet or proxy forces into other lands and continents, then popular support in the United States for such cooperation will erode.

At Wake Forest University, March 17/
Los Angeles Times, 3-18:(1)16.

6

[On NATO]: History records no other alliance that has successfully brought together so many different nations for so long, without the firing of a single shot in anger. Ours is a defen-

(JIMMY CARTER)

sive alliance. No nation need fear aggression from us. But neither should any nation ever doubt our will to deter and defeat aggression against us. The North Atlantic Alliance is a union of peoples moved by a desire to secure a safe future for our children—in liberty and freedom. Our Alliance is unique because each of our 15 democratic nations shares a common heritage of human values, the rule of law and faith in the courage and spirit of free men and women. The military strength and common political purpose of the North Atlantic Alliance has led us to cooperate in a thousand individual efforts, rightly conferring upon us the name of "community." And it has given us the self-confidence and strength of will to seek improved relations with our potential adversaries.

At NATO conference, Washington,
May 30/The New York Times, 5-31:(A)14.

1

[On the Soviet Union] : The abuse of human rights in their own country, in violation of the agreement which was reached at Helsinki, has earned them the condemnation of people everywhere who love freedom. By their actions they have demonstrated that the Soviet system cannot tolerate freely expressed ideas or notions of loyal opposition and the free movement of people. The Soviet Union attempts to export a totalitarian and repressive form of government resulting in a closed society . . . Outside their tightly controlled bloc, the Soviet Union has difficult political relations with other nations. Their cultural bonds with others are few and frayed. Their form of government is becoming increasingly unattractive to other nations so that even Marxist-Leninist groups no longer look on the Soviet Union as a model to be imitated.

Annapolis, Md., June 7/
Newsweek, 6-19:43.

2

The most immediate and urgent foreign-policy decision to be made by the current legis-

lative session is in lifting the [U.S.] arms embargo against Turkey. The points the Congress intended to underscore three years ago, when the embargo was imposed [in response to Turkey's invasion of Cyprus], have all been made. But now the embargo is not contributing to a settlement of the Cyprus dispute, nor is it helping to improve our relationship with our allies, Turkey and Greece. It's driven a wedge between those two countries and has weakened the cohesiveness and the readiness of NATO . . . I'm asking the Congress to support me in enacting the full program which, in addition to removing the embargo against arms sales to Turkey, provides for military sales credit to both Turkey and to Greece; provides for economic aid to Turkey; and provides further funds for relief and rehabilitation for refugees in Cyprus. Both Greece and Turkey are valuable friends and allies of our own. Lifting the embargo is essential to our hopes for peace and stability in the eastern region of the Mediterranean.

News conference, Washington, June 14/
The New York Times, 6-15:(A)18.

3

[On the conviction and prison sentence in Russia of Soviet dissident Anatoly Shcharansky] : [The Shcharansky verdict was] saddest of all for the Soviet people . . . who yearn like all others for peace and liberty, who have seen their own government pledge two years ago to respect those human rights and desires, and who now have seen that pledge broken once again. The struggle for human liberties is long and difficult, but it will be won. There is no power on earth that can long delay its progress.

At City Hall, Bonn, West Germany,
July 14/The Washington Post, 7-15:(A)1.

4

. . . we don't want to see Communism increase; we want to do everything we can to prevent its growth. At the same time, we have to recognize that Eurocommunism is not a monolithic structure completely dominated or incapsulated within the Soviet Union itself. I think that gives us some additional hope that even Communism itself in the Western democ-

WHAT THEY SAID IN 1978

racies might have some beneficial aspects of democratic principles in which we believe so deeply.

Berlin/Los Angeles Times, 7-19:(1)14.

1

Every member of NATO ... [is] deeply interested in removing the [U.S. arms embargo] against Turkey [imposed after Turkey invaded Cyprus]. This embargo was imposed, I think rightly, three years ago. The results that were expected have not been realized; it has not resulted in any progress being made in resolving the Cyprus dispute or restoring the human rights of the Greek Cypriots, who have indeed suffered and who suffer today. It's driven a wedge between Turkey and the rest of the NATO countries, between Greece and NATO, between Turkey and Greece, between us and Turkey ... I believe [that lifting the embargo] will, in the long run, benefit Greece as well. It's a very important subject, the most important foreign-affairs subject that the Congress will consider the rest of this session.

*News conference, Washington, July 20/
The New York Times, 7-21:(A)6.*

Nicolae Ceausescu
President of Romania

2

[On his recent attendance at a Warsaw Pact meeting in Moscow]: We are an independent Romania and we will always remain an independent Romania. I signed no piece of paper committing Romania or its armed forces to any course of action that is not approved by the nation as a whole.

*Before Romanian Communist Party
Central Committee, Bucharest,
Nov. 29/The New York Times, 11-30:(A)10.*

Prince Charles
Prince of Wales

3

[On the British Commonwealth]: Any association of states, freely entered into, which comprises almost a quarter of the world's pop-

ulation and contains a multitude of races, creeds and cultures, and which can contribute toward the destruction of artificial barriers between peoples, must surely be worth preserving.

The Christian Science Monitor, 6-12:(B)2.

Jacques Chirac
*Leader, Gaullist Party of
France; Former Premier of France*

4

The tradition of Gaullism has led us not to worry about whether a necessary decision should be considered as coming from the [political] left or the right. All great decisions taken by [the late President Charles] de Gaulle entirely escaped this classification, and many of them figure with honor among the great schemes of a government of the left.

Los Angeles Times, 3-8:(1)17.

Milorad M. Drachkovitch
*Senior fellow and archivist,
Hoover Institution, Stanford University*

5

... there is something at the very core of the Soviet system which the holders of power in the Soviet Union are not willing to abandon at any price, namely, the monopoly of political power and the claim of ideological orthodoxy. The regime may pursue different policies in many fields, and make practical accommodations whenever it deems it necessary or expedient. But all its most authoritative spokesmen insist invariably that, while the peaceful coexistence between different political and social systems is desirable, there is one domain which excludes such a coexistence, namely, the ideological domain. Marxist-Leninist ideology is the source of the Communist regime's legitimacy, and if that source of legitimacy becomes threatened or contaminated, the entire party, state and socio-economic structure becomes imperiled. Here, then, is why the regime is not willing to tolerate the dissidents, or to engage in a free ideological confrontation with them, because in doing so it would admit that other schools of thought, or movements the latter could trigger, could be considered as legitimate

(MILORAD M. DRACHKOVITCH)

contenders for truth and public allegiance. But in that case, the science of Marxism-Leninism would be undermined and the exclusivist rule of the Party jeopardized.

Before Commonwealth Club, San Francisco, Aug. 18/Vital Speeches, 10-1:764.

Bulent Ecevit
Prime Minister of Turkey

1

[On his country's difficulties with Western countries since Turkey's invasion of Cyprus in 1974, such as arms embargoes]: This sad experience has proved the disadvantages of relying for our national security solely on one source. Our government is therefore giving priority to the development of a new national-security concept, suiting Turkey's interests and conditions. This concept will take into consideration the national security and independence of Turkey while bearing in mind the importance of our membership with the (NATO) Alliance. The government will readjust its foreign policy in accordance with the national-defense policy. It will try to promote mutual trust with the countries in this area and [to ensure] that Turkey's contributions to the Alliance should not be the source of concern and mistrust to other regional countries . . . Within or outside the Alliance, our government will refrain from any action that could damage this principle.

Before Parliament, Ankara, Jan. 12/ The Christian Science Monitor, 1-13:15.

2

As long as Turkey's position in NATO and vis-a-vis her relations with the United States are sort of suspended, uncertain, it is not always possible for us to engage ourselves in certain policies and attitudes. Defense matters, particularly in Turkey's geopolitical position, are inevitably linked with international relations in general. So the continuation of the [U.S. arms embargo against Turkey], and our problems with the Alliance, sometimes may make it difficult for us to follow the same line of policies or attitudes that our allies may see fit to in

certain cases, although in general our policy lines may and should converge.

Interview, Washington, May 29/ The New York Times, 5-30:(A)6.

3

[On the just-signed friendship pact between his country and the Soviet Union]: The whole document is proof and pledge that two neighboring countries have no aggressive intentions, respect their independence, territory, different regimes and way of life. During our relations and talks in Moscow, the Soviet leadership has acted out of the correct understanding that we are both members of different alliances.

Moscow, June 23/ The Washington Post, 6-24:(A)19.

Klaus Engelen
United States correspondent,
"Handelsblatt," Dusseldorf
(West Germany)

4

One of Germany's big disappointments is weak American leadership. No other European country is so reliable a U.S. ally and yet dependent on the U.S. as Germany. It is probably fortunate that in the past five to 10 years Germany matured from a son-father relationship with the U.S. to a partnership. Having experienced the [U.S. President] Nixon years, then Ford, and now the many Carter shocks, Germany has begun to feel it has to rely more on European coordination.

Panel discussion, Warrenton, Va./ Atlas World Press Review, November:26.

Melih Esenbel
Turkish Ambassador
to the United States

5

[Calling for an end to the U.S. arms embargo against Turkey, imposed in 1975 after Turkey used U.S. arms in its invasion of Cyprus]: Our position is clear. The question of Cyprus is a separate question; it has been there for some time; it should be solved within its own conditions. But as long as this kind of "linkage" continues, there is, I believe, no hope for bring-

WHAT THEY SAID IN 1978

(MELIH ESENBEL)

ing out a solution ... One side [Greece] only focuses its attention on keeping pressure on Turkey and doesn't want to *give* on Cyprus or try to sit at the table and make an effort to reach a compromise. So the solution to Cyprus starts with lifting the embargo and undoing the linkage which has been established, unfortunately, by this country's [the U.S.'] Congress.

Before Women's National Democratic Club, Washington, May 4/The Washington Post, 5-5:(A)17.

Edward Gierek
First Secretary,
Communist Party of Poland

1

We have no intention of changing our friendship with the Soviet Union; it is an alliance based on friendship and natural reasons of defense. But this doesn't place any restraints on our moving closer to the U.S. As a matter of fact, we have better relations with America today than ever before.

Interview, Warsaw/
U.S. News & World Report, 1-9:15.

Francoise Giroud
Former Secretary of
State for the Condition of
Women, and former Secretary of
State for Culture, of France

2

[On the 1978 French elections]: The Communists worked so hard to lose the election, they succeeded. This was a conscious plan. They told the voters three or four years ago that rising unemployment and inflation were problems they could solve if they were in control of the government. Then they found that the Socialist Party was becoming stronger and stronger, and they would have had to share the power, so they deliberately tried to lose the election. The left is in bad shape now. The Socialists represent one French voter of every four, and that's not enough. The split with the Communists will continue. So maybe we are condemned to a rightist government.

Interview, New York/
Atlas World Press Review, October:36.

Valery Giscard d'Estaing
President of France

3

It has always seemed to me that two alternatives command the fate of France. Sometimes when she takes herself in hand she is a brave, willing, efficient country, able to face up to the worst and go far. Sometimes when she lets herself go, she becomes a country which slithers toward the easy way out, toward confusion, egoism and disorder.

Los Angeles Times, 3-8:(1)17.

4

I am addressing myself to those who voted for the opposition [in the recent elections]. It was your right. But you should know that for the President of the republic, those who voted Socialist or Communist are as French as anyone else—equal members of a national community ... It is time to achieve what I might call reasonable cohabitation.

Broadcast address to the
nation/Time, 4-3:34,37.

5

The threat overshadowing Europe does not come from the accumulation and sophistication of nuclear weapons alone. It also stems from the presence on our continent of enormous arsenals of conventional weapons, and the disparity between them ... The visible inequality in conventional weapons constitutes a block to nuclear-arms reductions.

At United Nations special session on disarmament,
New York, May 25/The Washington Post, 5-26:(A)31.

Nicolai Glushkov
Chairman, State Committee for
Prices of the Soviet Union

6

With the exception of the war years, there has never been any inflation in the Soviet Union, nor does it exist today ... In the U.S.S.R., prices on essential commodities and services are invariably and deliberately kept at a low level, while prices on non-essential ones are mobile, either rising or falling. When changing them, we proceed primarily from the premise

(NICOLAI GLUSHKOV)

that the increased prices on some goods should be balanced by lowered prices on others. For instance, this year the rise of prices on coffee, gasoline, jewelry and some other commodities are balanced by the lowering of prices on some fabrics, garments and footwear, and black-and-white television sets and refrigerators. [Therefore,] the price index in the Soviet Union remains unchanged and that's the main thing.

Interview/The Dallas Times Herald, 3-21:(D)10.

Alexander M. Haig, Jr.
General, United States Army;
Supreme Allied Commander/Europe

1

There has never been a question in my mind about the absolute imperative of the continuing Western guarantee for the viability of West Berlin. Indeed, were we to suggest otherwise, I think we would profoundly shake the whole essence of the Atlantic community relationship.

TV-radio interview/"Meet the Press,"
National Broadcasting Company, 4-23.

2

We frequently hear on this [U.S.] side of the Atlantic that we [the U.S.] are paying all the [European defense] bills and, "How long are we going to carry our European allies on our backs?" I think statistics do not confirm this imbalance, if you will, in burden-sharing. In fact, today 90 per cent of my ground forces come from the European nations; 75 per cent of my air and 80 per cent of my naval forces. In the last five years, the United States' contributions to NATO defenses have declined by 20 per cent. European contributions have increased 13 per cent. This past year, as a result of President Carter's initiative at the London summit, the nations have agreed to a 3 per cent increase in spending in real terms for the coming five years, and our assessments . . . are that most of the European nations will meet or exceed this goal, and I am quite encouraged about it.

TV-radio interview/"Meet the Press,"
National Broadcasting Company, 4-23.

3

In an interdependent, shrinking world, NATO must understand there can be no NATO security if it continues to ignore the implications of events occurring outside its geographic confine—just as the United States learned in two conflicts that there could be no American security without Western European security. Now, how we deal with this challenge collectively in the context of the Atlantic Community is a political question. Whether we work through a modified NATO or some other multilateral forum is less important than the reality that we collectively face up to these challenges outside NATO's traditional area of geographic concern and concert together more effectively to meet them.

Interview/U.S. News & World Report, 6-5:21.

W. Averell Harriman
Former United States
Ambassador to the Soviet Union

4

I know the Soviet Union very well. I've dealt with it. I know it well for a foreigner and I want to say this of the Soviet people: No people in the world are more anxious to have peace and less anxious to have war come. It is my very strong impression of [Soviet leader Leonid] Brezhnev that the last thing in the world he has in mind is to start a first strike.

At United Nations special session on disarmament,
New York, June 21/The New York Times, 6-22:(A)8.

Edward Heath
Former Prime Minister
of the United Kingdom

5

To achieve success, the Conservative Party will need to show that it is broadly based. The British people are moderate and fair-minded. After the last four-and-a-half years [of Labor Party rule], they want to see a government which reflects this attitude. This is the tradition of the Conservative governments in which I have served under Churchill, Eden, Macmillan and Home. It was the purpose of the government over which I presided.

The New York Times, 7-10:(A)3.

WHAT THEY SAID IN 1978

Huang Hua
Foreign Minister of the People's
Republic of (mainland) China

1

The Soviet Union is increasing its military threat to Western Europe, striving to expand its influence in the Middle East and carrying out a series of military adventures in Africa. Facts show that this superpower, flaunting the label of socialism, is more aggressive and adventurous than the other superpower [the U.S.]. It is the most dangerous source of a new world war and is sure to be its chief instigator.

At United Nations special session on disarmament,
New York, May 29/The New York Times, 5-30:(A)1.

Hasan Esat Isik
Minister of Defense of Turkey

2

[On the U.S. arms embargo against Turkey imposed after the 1974 Turkish invasion of Cyprus]: If the embargo is not lifted, it does not mean we will withdraw from the [NATO] Alliance, but we will not be as enthusiastic a member ... We will commit less of our armed forces to the Alliance and more to our own needs ... We will close down the American bases in Turkey for good.

Interview, Ankara/
The New York Times, 4-28:(A)5.

David C. Jones
General, United States Air Force;
Chairman, Joint Chiefs of Staff

3

... the Soviets are a superpower only in the military sense. They're not an economic superpower. They have very little impact on the world economic situation. Japan and Western Europe have more economic impact. The Soviets really are not a superpower from a political standpoint. Even though there's a lot of Communism in the world, it's a diverse Communism, not just a Soviet brand. Technologically, they're certainly not a superpower. They're a superpower in one aspect only: military capability. What we're trying to do in our negotiations with the Soviet Union is to reduce

the decibel count of the military competition and shift the competition into other areas.

Interview/U.S. News & World Report, 10-30:51.

Janos Kadar
First Secretary,
Communist Party of Hungary

4

[On the Soviet troops stationed in his country] : ... there are also thousands of foreign troops in the Federal Republic of [West] Germany; and nobody has any doubt about the authority and political independence of the Federal Republic or that it makes its own politics as an authentic entity. Why have such doubts about us? We, too, represent a solid political power. The Soviet troops are here in relation to the international context, just as the American troops in the Federal Republic of Germany. There is no internal political connotation whatsoever to be found in the presence today of Russian troops in Hungry.

Interview, Budapest/
The New York Times, 6-10:6.

Urho Kekkonen
President of Finland

5

Finland has had her third consecutive year of zero growth and record unemployment. Particularly in times of economic difficulty such as these, people have often stressed how important economic and commercial cooperation with the socialist countries and with the Soviet Union in particular is to us. This is quite right. When the possibilities of exporting to the West decrease, trade with those countries whose economies are less susceptible to business cycles becomes all the more important. ... the Soviet Union's share of our total foreign trade has since the beginning of the 1950s averaged some 15 per cent per five-year period. Throughout the post-World War II period, the Soviet Union has continuously figured among Finland's foremost trading partners. Over the past three years, the Soviet Union has risen to be Finland's most important trading partner, with almost one-fifth of our total foreign trade. We have every reason to believe that this leap is not

(URHO KEKKONEN)

a temporary one but indicates a permanent increase in economic cooperation with our Eastern neighbor.

On 30th anniversary of Finnish-Soviet Treaty of Friendship, Cooperation and Mutual Assistance/The Christian Science Monitor, 6-19:23.

John Killick
Permament British representative on the North Atlantic Council

1

These days, the Soviet Union is acknowledged to be a superpower. But it is an extremely deformed superpower whose military strength is its sole attribute. The appeal of Soviet ideology, its political influence in the world these days, derives essentially from its military support of liberation movements and possibly from the implicit military threat that it poses to neighboring countries that are weak and small. In the economic field, the Soviet Union is demonstrably unsuccessful at home. And in the field of proper economic aid—the granting of which I would welcome, as I think all our Western leaders would—we repeatedly challenge the Soviet Union to match what we are doing in helping the developing countries.

Interview, Center for the Study of Democratic Institutions, Santa Barbara, Calif./World Issues, Dec.-Jan.:5.

Henry A. Kissinger
Former Secretary of State of the United States

2

If you compare the performance of Communism wherever you go around the world, if there is a free system and a Communist system competing, the free system invariably has done more for its people. And yet, it is precisely in the free countries of Western Europe that Communism is now finding adherents. One has to say this is a moral problem and not a material problem for which one has to look for an explanation and factors that go beyond, far beyond, a material condition.

Television interview/ The Dallas Times Herald, 1-13:(B)1.

Wim Kok
President, Dutch Federation of National Trade Unions

3

[On the European economic situation]: In my father's time, there was the depression; the battlelines were clearly drawn. After the war, there was a consensus; everybody wanted to work together to put our countries on their feet again. Then, in the '60s, growth was so rapid that many people, even in labor, were optimistic that there would be enough prosperity for everybody. Today, we have entered a completely new and uncertain era. It is difficult to find anybody who believes that Europe can return to a prolonged period of high economic growth. People are even wondering whether Europe can maintain its industrial leadership and competitiveness.

Interview, Amsterdam/ The New York Times, 7-2:(3)5.

Spyros Kyprianou
President of Cyprus

4

[On the Greek-Turkish dispute over Cyprus]: We have made the concession of accepting the idea of a truly federated state ... But they [the Turkish-Cypriot leaders] are thinking in terms of two separate states ... of partition ... where the central government is a ghost government. The very concept is objectionable to us, so there is no point in negotiating. The Turkish proposals amount to legalizing the results of the (1974 Turkish) invasion [of Cyprus]. It is something we shall never accept.

Interview, Nicosia, April 27/ The Washington Post, 4-28:(A)21.

5

[Calling for the demilitarization of Cyprus]: No Turkish troops, no Greek troops, no Cypriot troops. Only a small, mixed police force, composed of Greek Cypriots and Turkish Cypriots in proportion to the population ratio, under the guidance, the control, the supervision for as long as necessary of an international United Nations police force.

Interview, Washington, June 8/ The New York Times, 6-9:(A)9.

WHAT THEY SAID IN 1978

Jack Lynch
Prime Minister of Ireland

1

I wish to appeal again to Irish people abroad, especially in the United States, who might not be fully aware of the atrocities committed [by the IRA] in the name of Irish patriotism and who might be induced to contribute to organizations which provide the raw materials for . . . bombings and killings. If those who contribute believe that their money goes to support widows and orphans, let me make it clear that it goes to *make* widows and orphans. They are not helping to fulfill the aspirations of the Irish people but to destroy them.

At Fianna Fail Party conference, Dublin/
The Christian Science Monitor, 2-21:11.

Georges Marchais
Secretary general,
Communist Party of France

2

[On the left's failure to win a majority in the just-completed French national elections]: It's a fact—the majority keeps its majority. The balance of power in France is about what it was before, equally divided. But now those who want change will be conscious of the force they have in this country, and the Communist Party will continue its struggle at the side of those who fight to impose their demands for redress of grievances.

New conference, Paris, March 20/
The New York Times, 3-20:(A)5.

Georges-Henri Martin
Editor-in-chief,
"Tribune de Geneve," Geneva

3

While the Swiss Confederacy was being formed, a very interesting agreement existed. As far back as five or six centuries ago, when a new state would join, it would make two commitments. The first was that in the case of a dispute among old members it promised to act as a mediator. The second was that, if mediation failed and there was a civil war, as a new member it would remain neutral. So, long before neutrality was practiced with respect to

foreign states and policies, the concept of neutrality had been developed as the cornerstone of domestic consensus and compromise. Now Swiss neutrality in foreign matters means the Swiss don't have to feud over problems that divide the rest of the world.

Interview, New York/
Atlas World Press Review, August:22.

Mihajlo Mihajlov
Yugoslav writer

4

There is full freedom in Yugoslavia as far as artistic expression is concerned. With one exception: You cannot be realistic about today's life in Yugoslavia.

At Waldorf School, Garden City, N.Y.,
June 6/The New York Times, 6-11:(1)14.

Francois Mitterrand
Leader, Socialist Party of France

5

[On left-right political relations in France]: It is in the higher interest of the country that beyond our disagreements . . . there should be new rules and new customs in what might be called the daily practice of democracy. Of course, it is not a question of reversing our roles. It is for the majority [currently the government of Valery Giscard d'Estaing] to govern. It is for the opposition to exercise its rights to criticize and to propose opposition [such as the Socialists currently] to criticize and to propose. But it is for both to respect what they represent together . . . the national community.

Paris, March 28/
The Washington Post, 3-29:(A)16.

Margaret Murray
Paris correspondent,
"U.S. News & World Report"

6

I think the Europeans—at least the French— feel that the Americans may make concessions to the Russians which will prejudice Europe's safety. They fear that the [U.S. President] Carter Administration is looking at things from a purely American point of view, with not

EUROPE

(MARGARET MURRAY)

much concern for the free world's interdependence. And people over here still look to America—the most powerful democracy—to defend, if need be, the rest of the free world.

Round-table discussion, Paris/
U.S. News & World Report, 2-13:60.

Oliver Napier
Leader, Alliance Party of
Northern Ireland

1

There is a new mood emerging in this province after all the horror, the violence, the destruction and the hatreds of the last eight years. It is a mood of cold anger against the paramilitary organizations which have bombed and murdered in the name of Ireland or of Ulster. But this mood also has its warmth. There is a growing realization that most Catholics and most Protestants are decent, peace-loving and honorable people . . . that we have more in common with each other than anything that divides us . . . that we can indeed live in peace, and, more than that, we can work in peace and together rebuild the structures of our shattered province. The old political tribal groupings are beginning to break away at the edges. The political dinosaurs are beginning to go the way of their primeval predecessors.

At Alliance Party conference/
The Christian Science Monitor, 5-4:14.

Olof Palme
Former Prime Minister of Sweden

2

[On the Administration of Prime Minister Thorbjorn Falldin, which was victorious over Palme's party in the 1976 election]: If there would be an election today, we'd win. The people demand stability and coherence and they're not getting it. We'd [have had] difficulties, too, with the economy. But we'd have handled it differently. The tax cuts they made increased liquidity and that pushed up inflation. They let investment fall away. They've been unable to handle the energy issue. We couldn't have helped but do a better job.

The New York Times, 3-25:2.

Andreas Papandreou
Leader, Panhellenic
Socialist Movement of Greece

3

I don't believe that socialism should be imposed from above. That requires the dictatorship of the party and inhibits individual freedom. I believe in a decentralized socialism which offers people the opportunity to determine their own fate and the power to do so . . . I am against Greece being a member of NATO or the Warsaw Pact or the Common Market because it means being subservient to a center of power outside Greece . . . If we are exposed to real danger, we could and should arm ourselves with nuclear weapons. And I can assure you we can get them.

Interview, Athens/
The New York Times, 4-12:(A)2.

Jody Powell
Press Secretary to President of
the United States Jimmy Carter

4

[On the political trials of dissidents in the Soviet Union]: It's our view that this sort of repressive action, which strikes at the conscience of the entire world, is a defeat not for those who work for human rights and human dignity, but a defeat and a sign of weakness on the part of those very forces of oppression and injustice which we protest . . . If such actions are designed to put an end to those who seek increased human rights within the Soviet Union, they will not do that. If they are meant to stop this [U.S.] President or others in this country from speaking out on human rights, they will not do that. If they are meant to bury the issue of human rights in the international community, they will not do that. In effect, they will not bury it, but most likely raise it higher.

To reporters, Washington, July 10/
The Washington Post, 7-11:(A)7.

Donald W. Riegle, Jr.
United States Senator, D-Michigan

5

[On the political trials of dissidents in the Soviet Union]: I cannot imagine a SALT treaty

WHAT THEY SAID IN 1978

(DONALD W. RIEGLE, JR.)

I could support with a nation that terrorizes its own people. I am ashamed of the conduct of the Soviet government and I must urge my own government to do nothing that would give aid and comfort to a Soviet regime that would devour its own people. What sick and twisted bureaucratic midgets demand and carry out these fraudulent trials? The dead heroes of Russian history would be sickened and ashamed to see their state become a monster, one so empty and paranoid that it cannot stand the threat posed by the dissenting voice of a single individual.

Before the Senate, Washington,
July 11/Los Angeles Times, 7-12:(1)14.

Manfred Rommel
Mayor of Stuttgart, West Germany

1

West Germany should be faithful to its friends. Its target should be maintaining peace. It should not try to play a leading world role. German history is too much for us. The shadow is too great. I belong to the generation of burned children and I am not so sure of our capabilities.

San Francisco Examiner &
Chronicle, 2-12:(This World)2.

Kenneth Rush
Former United States Ambassador to
France and to West Germany

2

[Criticizing the U.S. arms embargo against Turkey resulting from that country's invasion and occupation of Cyprus in 1974]: The arms embargo has not helped Greece. It has not helped restore Greek forces to the North Atlantic Treaty Alliance command. It has not helped Turkey. It has not helped either the Greek or Turkish communities on Cyprus. It has not helped restore good relations between these national elements. It has not helped U.S. relations with anyone ... The arms embargo has weakened the Alliance militarily, seriously impairing the effectiveness of the Turkish armed forces and resulting in the suspension of U.S. base rights in Turkey. The choice is simple: either we lift the embargo, enhancing NATO security by strengthening Turkey militarily and politically, improving chances for a settlement of the Cyprus issue, and bringing about improvement in Greek-Turkish relations, and helping to maintain Turkey as a factor of stability in the Middle East; or we continue to risk our own security interests in these respects.

Before House International
Relations Committee, Washington,
April 25/The Dallas Times Herald, 4-26:(A)22.

Dean Rusk
Professor of international
law, University of Georgia;
Former Secretary of State
of the United States

3

I think our friends in Europe have relied too long on the United States' carrying the major political burdens of important issues. For example, on the neutron bomb, before President Carter made his decision to postpone the decision on the neutron bomb, I am not aware that any member of NATO stepped up publicly and said: "Yes, we want the neutron bomb, and, if you make it, we want it in our country." They were letting Mr. Carter take the whole burden of the political problems of moving ahead on the neutron bomb. They have to do better than that.

TV-radio interview/"Meet the Press,"
National Broadcasting Company, 4-30.

Aarne Saarinen
Chairman, Communist Party of Finland

4

We have our own identity, but that doesn't mean we are opposed to other Communist parties. Our Party maintains active relations with all parties of the international Communist movement except those of China and Albania. In Western Europe we have many common problems and many similarities, but also many differences. There are many models of socialism, and each party must choose its own.

Interview, Helsinki/
Los Angeles Times, 1-25:(1)15.

Helmut Schmidt
Chancellor of West Germany

1

By comparison to all other important industrial states, the Federal Republic [West Germany] has far and away the lowest interest rates. Our discount rate of three per cent compares to 6.5 per cent in the United States. All of this means that the Federal government and the central bank have done all that is possible domestically to create the conditions for a further strengthening of our economy, for the reduction of unemployment and for the maintenance of our international competitiveness. [But] that requires a strong and stable [U.S.] dollar.

Before Parliament, Bonn, Jan. 19/
The Washington Post, 1-20:(B)7.

2

Let me state frankly that I have always been doubtful about political leaders who promote visions. We have in this century seen at least two periods of, shall we say, visionism in German leaders—Kaiser Wilhelm II, and the second one much worse. Both lead to catastrophic results. I do believe in solid, step-by-step progress in economic and international fields. I think we have shown we were able to establish a rather solid, stable democratic process in this country and a well-accepted and very dependable social order. I'm not a visionary and I'm skeptical of all the visionaries. The Germans have an enormous capability for idealism and for the perversion of idealism.

Interview, Bon, April 19/
The Washington Post, 4-20:(A)17.

3

Today's Germans are mostly innocent [of the Nazi horrors perpetrated on Jews during World War II]. More than two-thirds of them were either born after the war or were children during the war. Yet we have to carry the political inheritance of the guilty and draw the consequences. That is our responsibility. But we ask those Jews in the world and our neighbors not to measure our second German democracy by the handful of mistaken extremists and ter-

rorists who, as in other countries, cannot be changed.

At synagogue, Cologne, West Germany,
Nov. 9/The Washington Post, 11-10:(A)29.

Mohammed Siad Barre
President of Somalia

4

[The Soviets want to] take over, one way or another, the [Persian] Gulf states with their petroleum energy and win on this. [Then] they plan to dictate to European countries what they want because they have cut their supply lines, waterways and raw materials. Then, with the help of their forces at the front, they plan to cut off the United States. Of course, when the West loses its supplies of raw materials, I do not think it will cope long. It would have to accept the conditions of the Soviet Union.

Interview, Mogadishu, Somalia,
July 2/The New York Times, 7-3:3.

Mario Soares
Prime Minister of Portugal

5

In contrast with other European countries, we do not have social agitation; we have no terrorism; we have total tranquility in the country. People say that I am too optimistic, that I see things through rose-colored glasses. But the truth is the truth. I tell you that I wander about the streets, undisturbed, completely alone. People greet me, say things to me, not always altogether agreeable things. I ask you—what other European head of government can afford himself that luxury?

Interview, Lisbon/The New York Times, 5-27:3.

Margaret Thatcher
Member of British Parliament;
Leader, British Conservative Party

6

I believe that we shall succeed in maintaining and securing our traditional tolerance and fairness in this country only if we cut the number of [non-white] immigrants coming in now.

Harrogate, England, Feb. 12/
The Christian Science Monitor, 2-14:5.

WHAT THEY SAID IN 1978

(MARGARET THATCHER)

1

[On immigration to Britain from such places as India and Pakistan]: People [in Britain] are really rather afraid that this country might be swamped by people of a different culture. And, you know, the British character has done so much for democracy, for law, and done so much throughout the world, that if there is any fear that it might be swamped, people are going to react and be rather hostile to those coming in.

Television interview/Time, 2-20:35.

Malcolm Toon
*United States Ambassador
to the Soviet Union*

2

... the age of the [Soviet] Politburo doesn't have much impact on our relations. What does bother me is the fact that most of the members are so inaccessible. If I, as American Ambassador, am to understand these people and their attitudes and aspirations, then I have to see them occasionally. I have met with [Soviet President Leonid] Brezhnev several times, and I appreciate this; but it's equally important to have access to his senior colleagues as well—particularly those who might reach the top ... They tell me it's because it's not their custom [to have such meetings]. I respond that if this is the case, then the time has come to change their pattern of behavior, because otherwise it's difficult to bring about this mutual understanding in which we both profess an interest.

*Interview, Moscow/
U.S. News & World Report, 1-9:28.*

Dmitri F. Ustinov
*Minister of Defense
of the Soviet Union*

3

The Soviet people have never rattled arms and are not going to do so. At the same time, let no one take our love of peace for weakness and let no one try to scare us with new types of lethal weapons. It seems in place to recall here that to try to scare us is a senseless and hopeless thing. Our economy, science and technology can ensure the development of any arms on which our adversaries may try to place reliance.

*Before Soviet armed-forces leaders, Moscow,
Feb. 22/The Dallas Times Herald, 2-23:(A)5.*

Cyrus R. Vance
*Secretary of State
of the United States*

4

[Urging Congress to end the U.S. arms embargo against Turkey, which was initiated after Turkey's 1974 invasion of Cyprus]: The time has come to look forward rather than back. Continued maintenance of the embargo would be harmful to U.S. security concerns, harmful to NATO, harmful to our bilateral relations with Turkey and harmful to our role as a potential contributor to a Cyprus settlement.

*Before House International
Relations Committee, Washington,
April 6/The Washington Post, 4-7:(A)3.*

5

The Soviets are very tough negotiators. They strike a very hard bargain. They have very clearly in their minds what their self-interests are, and they will doggedly pursue those interests. Negotiating with the Soviet Union is a sometimes frustrating experience, but at the end of the road, when you reach an agreement, they stick to their bargains. In the past, where we've reached an agreement with them in which other parties are involved and one of their friends moved away from the bargain we had reached, I brought this to the attention of the Soviets and, within hours, in the middle of the night, they corrected that situation, saying, "our reputation is behind that agreement; this is unacceptable," and the situation is straightened out by the next morning.

Interview, Washington/Time, 4-24:21.

6

[On the political trials of dissidents in the Soviet Union]: They are being tried for asserting fundamental human rights—to speak out and to petition and criticize their government—rights guaranteed in international agreements

(CYRUS R. VANCE)

entered into by their government. These trials, with their lack of due process, violate fundamental principles of justice. I reflect the deepest feelings and values of the American people when I deplore these events.

Washington, July 8/
The Dallas Times Herald, 7-9:(A)10.

Harold Wilson
Former Prime Minister
of the United Kingdom

1

You could disrupt the whole of NATO if one country in a strategic position—look at Italy which is very vulnerable now—were to go Eurocommunist or, worse still, fully Communist.

Television interview, Singapore/
The Washington Post, 1-16:(A)2.

2

The arrival to the scene of Eurocommunism is the latest and most subtle of threats. It demands that this generation must face the problems of today with the same vigilance of the past against the Communists and their more frontal attack. Simply because the threat we now face is subtle, it does not mean it is less real or less dangerous.

At University of Singapore/
The Wall Street Journal, 1-27:8.

Andrew Young
United States Ambassador/Permanent
Representative to the United Nations

3

The over-all trend in Soviet society is toward protest among Soviet citizens ... People are bored with bureaucracy. People spend most of their time in hobbles. They are frustrated with red tape and a lack of consumer goods. The protest in the Soviet Union is not just from Jewish citizens. Next, I would say protest will come from Siberian technocrats. They are now showing signs of freedom ... not unlike the free-wheeling style of the American frontier.

Interview, Geneva/
The Christian Science Monitor, 7-14:7.

4

[On the political trials of dissidents in the Soviet Union, despite U.S. criticism of the human-rights situation in that country]: Oh, it's certainly a challenge, a gesture of independence on their [the Soviet government's] part. But that will not prevent them from pursuing the SALT negotiations. And then, one doesn't know what can happen to the dissidents. After all, in our [U.S.] prisons, too, there are hundreds—perhaps even thousands—of people whom I would call political prisoners. Ten years ago, I myself was tried in Atlanta for having organized a protest movement. And three years later, I was a Georgia Representative. It's true that things do not change that quickly in the Soviet Union, but they do change.

Interview/U.S. News & World Report, 7-24:56.

The Middle East

James Abourezk
United States Senator,
D-South Dakota

1

I have always thought that the foreign-policy attributes of the [U.S.] Administration and the Congress, so far as the Middle East is concerned, have tilted too much toward one side. In this case it has been tilted toward Israel, and they have done so, I think, in detriment to the American national interest, and I strongly oppose that. I think that no ethnic lobby should have that kind of control over American policy, and the Israeli lobby in this instance has had overwhelming and almost total control over American foreign policy in the Middle East . . . Israel is America's client state. We provide money out of the [U.S.] Treasury; we provide political support for Israel. That is the only thing that keeps Israel as obstinate and as intransigent as they are in the Middle East, and that is what keeps things boiling in the Middle East. If we should ever decide to use our leverage on Israel and withhold or condition our support in return for Israel making an over-all peace settlement—unless we are willing to do that, I submit we have not gone far enough.

TV-radio interview/"Meet the Press,"
National Broadcasting Company, 8-6.

Fouad Ajami
Assistant professor of
politics, Princeton University

2

When it is in the West, the machinery of the West makes sense. It emerges from a larger social and political order. But imported, the same machinery poses serious problems. The narrow streets of most Middle Eastern capitals are as inhospitable to the machines of the West as are the hearts and habits of men.

San Francisco Examiner &
Chronicle, 12–31: (This World)2.

Ghazi A. Algosaibi
Minister of Industry and
Electricity of Saudi Arabia

3

Saudi Arabians always considered the economies of the Western countries. It is our belief that any or all of our oil [-price] policies really are designed with the well-being of the world at large. We like to think that this is a somewhat altruistic position. But it is also in our national interest because we believe the consequences of harming the Western economies cannot help, but hurt, our economy.

Los Angeles Herald Examiner, 5-16:(A)1.

Yasir Arafat
Chairman, Palestine
Liberation Organization

4

You [the U.S.] are controlled by the blackmail of the Israeli lobby in the United States. The American Administration has retreated back completely [from its support for Palestinian self-determination]. You are supplying your naughty baby, your spoiled baby, Israel, with everything from *Phantom* [fighter planes] to flowers. You are not neutral, because of your spoiled baby.

Television interview, Beirut,
Lebanon/"Issues and Answers,"
American Broadcasting Company, 4-2.

5

Would you believe that Israel, which scares all the Arab states around it, is afraid of the Palestinian resistance movement? This state, armed to the teeth, including nuclear weapons? Assume that a Palestinian state has been founded. Would you believe that a state which is going to start from zero for the establishment of its institutions, its economy, culture, social problems—would such a state be able to form

(YASIR ARAFAT)

any serious threat against Israel? . . . Assuming that the fear exists, why are the Israelis refusing to withdraw from the Sinai despite the fact that [Egyptian] President Sadat has gone to Israel and offered a peace treaty, and there are no commandos in the Sinai? Which do you think will endanger peace more: having the Palestinians as they are, deprived of their national rights, their human rights, scattered here and there, having ill treatment everywhere, or having the Palestinians settle as normal civilians with their national pride restored and with a flag of their own? . . . We have to differentiate between a state and revolution. Now we are a revolution. But once we become a state, we'll be taking a different form and different restrictions and a different outlook. From the president of that state to a small citizen, everyone will be very keen and careful and worried about the safety of his establishment and the institutions. In addition to that fact, a guerrilla war could never emerge from a small young state just coming into existence. And with such a state's abilities, and with the balance of power, it's crazy to think of waging a classical war against the huge power of Israel. The blah-blah about fear is nothing but justification for the permanent Zionist strategy of expansion . . .

Interview, Beirut, Lebanon,
May 1/The New York Times, 5-2:8.

Hafez al-Assad
President of Syria

1

[Criticizing Egyptian President Anwar Sadat's unprecedented trip to Israel last year] : . . . he went to Israel, which meant the recognition of Israel. He went to occupied Jerusalem, which meant the recognition of Jerusalem as the unified capital of Israel. He broke Arab solidarity and dealt separately and alone with affairs that concern the whole region, which he had no right to do. And he destroyed efforts for peace which were on the way to being fruitful. By doing all of this, he gave up the process of peace and shifted to capitulation. He weakened the Arab stand and acted against

the desires and aspirations of the Arab masses. These are some of the most important meanings of Sadat's visit. When he came to see me before going to Israel, I warned he would get nothing out of it.

Interview, Damascus/Newsweek, 1-16:41.

2

In general, it is unreasonable for anyone, American or otherwise, to expect us to be satisfied with all this huge American military aid to Israel, which includes the most modern weapons and equipment. It is this aid that enables Israel to continue its arrogance and perpetuate its occupation of our lands, and so it is this aid that prevents the achievement of peace in the area.

Interview, Damascus/
The New York Times, 3-14:16.

3

[Criticizing the framework for peace negotiated between Egyptian President Anwar Sadat and Israeli Prime Minister Menachem Begin at Camp David, Md.] : It is very possible that in the future Sadat and Begin are going to prepare a military operation against Syria. We must plan for the future and be faithful to our cause . . . He [Sadat] turned his back on the Arab and forgot his own pledges. Yesterday I planned the October [1975] war with Sadat. But [today] he deserted us and we are alone in the trenches. He makes peace with the enemy and [now] we are his enemies.

Before Arab Steadfastness Front, Damascus,
Sept. 20/Los Angeles Times, 9-21:(1)1.

Shlomo Avineri
Professor of political science,
Hebrew University, Jerusalem

4

The main reason for the difficulties we are having now in the Middle East peace-making process has to do with the approach taken by the [U.S.] Carter Administration. Before Carter came to power, the American Administration was convinced that the only way the Middle East crisis could be resolved was by a piecemeal approach. When you try to approach some of

WHAT THEY SAID IN 1978

(SHLOMO AVINERI)

the easier issues first, we reach limited agreements and then, one step by another step, we go to more complicated issues ... The basic philosophy behind it being that the gaps between the Israeli position and even the most moderate Arab position is so great that you can't really bridge it in one move, in one conference, in one dramatic summit meeting ... President Carter's approach is a very different one, not only to Mideast problems, but generally to global problems. He prefers to use the comprehensive approach, which means that you try to confront all the issues at one time with all participants. To use Middle East jargon, President Carter was committed immediately after coming to power to convene a Geneva peace conference with all participants including the Soviet Union during 1977. This was asking too much, and I think one of the reasons that we are in trouble now in the Middle East has to do with this approach.

Interview/
Los Angeles Herald Examiner, 4-28:(A)1.

George W. Ball
Former Under Secretary of
State of the United States

1

... we must necessarily exercise a judgment as to what is in the interest of all concerned, including particularly the United States, when we look at the problems in the Middle East ... How do we spend our resources? Do we spend our resources to encourage, for example, a military occupation of 1,250,000 Arabs [by Israel] in the West Bank and Gaza Strip, which has already gone on for 10 years, which can only in the end lead to more and more trouble, to terrorism, continuation, intensification of terrorism and ultimately to war? It seems to me, therefore, we have to face a question. It isn't a matter of putting pressure on Israel; it is a matter of making up our own mind as to whether we are spending our resources in the most useful way ... The idea of a reasonably balanced distribution of arms in the Middle East is one that we have pursued for years and

years, and I think it would be a very great mistake for the Israelis to have the sense that they are so superior that they need not do anything toward settlement. I think they have got to recognize that their only hope in the long run is not to remain a ward of the United States, but to bring about a peace which is their only real hope for security, because otherwise they are simply moving into a situation which, at the end of the road, is going to be catastrophic for them as well as for everybody else.

TV-radio interview/"Meet the Press,"
National Broadcasting Company, 4-30.

Menachem Begin
Prime Minister of Israel

2

[Arguing against the establishing of an independent Palestinian state]: ... self-determination does not mean the right to independence by fractions of nations. For instance, there are 6 million Mexicans in Texas and New Mexico who speak a different language and are part of the Mexican nation. Does that give them a right to create an independent state on U.S. territory? Nobody would make such a suggestion. The French give us advice about self-determination, but they don't give it to the Corsicans. The Iraqis don't give it to the Kurds. The Palestinian Arabs are 1 per cent of the great Arab nation, whose self-determination is expressed in the existence of 21 sovereign states. It is hypocrisy and misuse of the term "self-determination" to say that it should apply to 1 per cent of the people. The fair arrangement for the Palestinian Arabs is to have autonomy which will not threaten the security of the Palestinian Jews. This is the only fair and positive solution. There is no other.

Interview, Jerusalem/Newsweek, 1-16:40.

3

... peace cannot be established with the redivision of Jerusalem, the capital city not only of the state of Israel but traditionally and culturally of the Jewish people since the days of King David. And why should it be redivisioned? London and Paris are one city; Moscow and Washington are one city; Cairo and Damascus

(MENACHEM BEGIN)

are one city. Can anyone envisage barbed wire dividing this city? Just impossible, inconceivable.

At dinner for participants in
Egypt-Israeli peace talks, Jerusalem,
Jan. 17/The New York Times, 1-19:(A)12.

1

We have never asked anybody to recognize our right to exist. We exist, our dear Egyptian friends, without your recognition, for 3,700 years. Our right to exist was given by the God of Abraham, Isaac and Jacob. We never asked your President or your government to recognize our right to exist. What we expect from you is to recognize our right to our land.

At luncheon, Jerusalem, Jan. 19/
The New York Times, 1-20:(A)6.

2

[On Israeli control of the West Bank and Gaza]: Just think what could happen with an independent Palestinian state on our borders in the hands of radicals belonging to the so-called Palestine Liberation Organization. Our enemy would command the mountains west of the Jordan River looking down on us and be supplied with Soviet artillery. The flight from Odessa [U.S.S.R.] is two hours. All of our cities along the Mediterranean would be within the range of conventional artillery—every man, woman and child. The distance between the hills and the sea is nine miles at its closest point. As for the Gaza Strip, a look at the map will show that it is a pistol aimed at our country ... The people in these regions [now] have never known more self-rule and autonomy than what we're offering in all their centuries under Turkish rule, British rule, Egyptian rule and Jordanian rule. They will be able to freely elect an administrative council, with all departments of regional government under their control except defense and public order. Any other form of autonomy would mean a Palestinian state. And we believe that if Israel did relinquish these territories, the PLO would take them over in 24 hours. Therefore, we are suggesting autonomy to the Palestinian Arabs and security to

the Palestinian Jews. This is the most decent proposal ever made.

Interview, Jerusalem/
U.S. News & World Report, 2-6:34.

3

[On his country's strikes at Palestinian guerrilla bases in Lebanon in retaliation for a recent PLO raid in Israel]: Our army was not sent into southern Lebanon to stay there. We want an arrangement in which all those places from which the murderers were ejected shall not return there. Southern Lebanon will not serve as a base for future attacks against Israel ... What we want is simple security, so our citizens can live and work in peace. We do hope there will be an arrangement so southern Lebanon will not in the future be a base for intolerable attacks on Israel.

News conference, Jerusalem,
March 15/The New York Times, 3-16:(A)16.

4

... Israel is still the only country in the world against which there is a written document [the PLO charter] to the effect that it must disappear. There is no country, either large or small, or even the smallest, against which there is such a document demanding, saying publicly, that country should not exist, should be wiped off the map. And behind those people who carry out also the abominable acts to prove that they mean it, there is an alignment of many Arab states, armed to the teeth by the Soviet Union, and sometimes getting modern weapons from the West. This is the decisive problem we face, which is called, sometimes, security. I would like to reaffirm what security means to us. It means the preservation of the lives of our elderly people, of our women and our children—the lives which are threatened daily—so that to make sure that the future generations, as ours, will live in a free and independent country. This is the great issue we face, or continue to face.

Washington, March 22/
The New York Times, 3-23:(A)16.

5

... we don't want even one American soldier to fight our battles or to lose his life. We

WHAT THEY SAID IN 1978

are a small nation. We have a wonderful, serene young generation. We can sustain our independence. From time to time we need some tools—that is true. Greater nations ask for tools. We are entitled to receive them mainly because on the other side there are the often unlimited stores of Soviet weapons given to our enemies. But let no American soldier die for Israel. This is our principle, the standard.

At National Press Club, Washington,
March 23/The New York Times, 3-24:(A)10.

1

[On his country's settlements in the West Bank, Gaza and the Sinai peninsula]: The settlement of Jews in the land of Israel is absolute and in accord with international law. Settlement is a positive act and constitutes no obstacle whatsoever to the [Arab-Israeli] peacemaking process.

Before the Knesset [Parliament], Jerusalem,
March 29/Los Angeles Times, 3-30:(1)16.

2

Demilitarization in the Sinai is a practical proposal. It is a desert; it can be checked. [But] any idea of demilitarization of part of the populated land [of the West Bank and Gaza] under foreign sovereignty would be a hoax because you can keep a gun in every garage. This is not a theoretical assumption; we have had experience from the past. And let us not forget the so-called PLO. If we should relinquish control of security and public order in Judea and Samaria and the Gaza Strip, the PLO would take over in no time and nothing would prevent them from doing so. This is the reality of the Middle East.

Interview, Jerusalem, April 4/
The Washington Post, 4-6:(A)18.

3

[On the framework for Middle East peace just worked out by Egyptian President Anwar Sadat, U.S. President Jimmy Carter and himself at Camp David, Md.]: The Camp David Conference should be renamed. It was the Jimmy Car-

ter conference. Mr. President [Carter], you took an initiative, most imaginative in our time, and brought President Sadat and myself and our colleagues and friends together in one group, which in itself was a great achievement. But the President [Carter] took a great risk on himself . . . a great show of courage.

At the announcement of the
agreement, Washington, Sept. 17/
Los Angeles Times, 9-18:(1)8.

4

[On the framework for peace he reached with Egyptian President Anwar Sadat at Camp David, Md.]: We bring you from Camp David a peace agreement of security and honor . . . Yes, we really have an agreement and the foundation for peace . . . Can we tell you today, citizens of Israel, that we have brought peace? Not yet. We still have to overcome hard days ahead—tests and trials and problems. But a firm basis has been laid for a peace treaty between us and Egypt, and, in its wake, between us and other neighbors. Soon we will be able to sign a peace treaty and to bring the message that not only this generation but coming generations, too, shall live in our country [with] peace, honor . . .

At Ben-Gurion Airport, Tel Aviv,
Sept. 22/The Washington Post, 9-23:(A)1.

5

If Egypt leaves the cycle of wars [by signing a separate peace agreement with Israel], Syria cannot attack us because it means suicide, and Jordan cannot start up because King Hussein will lose his crown. The vicious cycle of wars will be broken.

Before the Knesset [Parliament], Jerusalem,
Sept. 28/Los Angeles Times, 9-28:(1)1.

6

In peace, the Middle East, the ancient cradle of civilization, will become invigorated and transformed. Throughout its lands there will be freedom of movement of people, of ideas, of goods. Cooperation and development in agriculture will make the deserts blossom. Industry will bring the promise of a better life. Sources of water will be developed and the almost year-

(MENACHEM BEGIN)

long sunshine will yet be harnessed for the common needs of all the nations. Yes, indeed, the Middle East, being at the crossroads of the world, will become a peaceful center of international communication between East and West, north and south—a center of human advancement in every sphere of creative endeavor. This and more is what peace will bring to our region.

Accepting Nobel Peace Prize, Oslo, Norway,
Dec. 10/The New York Times, 12-11:(A)12.

1

[On the continued difficulties in working out a peace treaty between his country and Egypt]: ... there is no reason to blame Israel as if it caused the postponement of the signing of the peace treaty. The truth is the opposite. We were ready to sign the peace treaty without official interpretations, without digressing from the Camp David accords; and the responsibility for not signing the treaty, as far as we know, falls on Egypt.

Before his governing coalition, Dec. 18/
The Dallas Times Herald, 12-19:(A)3.

Eliahu Ben Elissar
Director General, Office of Israeli
Prime Minister Menachem Begin

2

We don't believe very much in [big-power security] guarantees. As Prime Minister Begin puts it, there is no guarantee to guarantee a guarantee. World history has witnessed a lot of guarantors and guarantees which were fine maybe when the guarantees were granted, but sometimes didn't prove to be efficient. We will prefer a comprehensive settlement between the nations—between Israel and Egypt and then Israel and Jordan and Syria, I hope. I don't think that we have big problems with Lebanon. With the Soviet Union and the United States playing the role of co-chairmen at the Geneva conference, okay. But as guarantors, I wouldn't accord too much place to this.

Interview/
Los Angeles Herald-Examiner, 3-14:(A)2.

Lloyd N. Bentsen
United States Senator, D-Texas

3

[Supporting U.S. plans to sell warplanes to Saudi Arabia]: For the past five years, Saudi Arabia has been a force of moderation within OPEC on the question of oil prices. The Saudis have steadfastly resisted efforts by some of our friends, Venezuela and Iran in particular, to raise oil prices even higher. In the process, they have been branded the lackeys of the United States. To discourage the sale would do incalculable damage to Saudi-American relations.

Before the Senate, Washington, May 15/
The New York Times, 5-16:12.

Leonid I. Brezhnev
President of the Soviet
Union; General Secretary,
Soviet Communist Party

4

[Criticizing the recent framework for peace worked out between Egypt and Israel at Camp David, Md.]: The road of separate talks and concessions to the aggressor does not bring peace any closer. It only further aggravates the situation in the Middle East. There will be no reliable peace until the causes of the Arab-Israeli conflict are removed, until the consequences of Israeli aggression are eliminated. [The] organizers of separate deals ... act as if there were no other Arab countries in the Middle East besides Egypt, whose leader [President Anwar Sadat] obediently bows to American-Israeli dictation. The Arabs, however, are no submissive pawns in a game but the makers of their own destiny. No one will succeed in ensuring a firm settlement of the conflict without them, for them and contrary to their legitimate rights and interests.

At dinner honoring Syrian
President Hafez Assad, Moscow,
Oct. 5/Los Angeles Times, 10-6:(1)10.

Harold Brown
Secretary of Defense
of the United States

5

[On U.S. arms sales to the Middle East]: The situation in the Middle East is dangerous

WHAT THEY SAID IN 1978

and difficult, and not selling arms would not make it any less so ... [Our arms-sales policy] is to maintain mutual trust and to maintain their [Middle East countries'] perceived security needs. Arms sales by themselves are not going to bring a peaceful and stable and lasting settlement of the issues in the Middle East. They are helpful only insofar as they give the nations involved a sense of sufficient security so that they are willing and able to negotiate toward a peace settlement.

News conference, Washington,
March 10/The Washington Post, 3-11:4.

Zbigniew Brzezinski
Assistant to President of the
United States Jimmy Carter for
National Security Affairs

1

[Arguing against division of Jerusalem into an Israeli and an Arab sector] : A city undivided means a city not partitioned, not partitioned physically, but a city in which, perhaps, arrangements can be contrived that are responsive to the religious and political sensitivities of the parties concerned ... As we all know, this is an issue which is not just strategical-political. It's a deeply emotional religious issue. But, with good-will, I think we will find a solution whereby the city is undivided, accessible to all—with proper arrangements, not only for the religious, but for the political sensitivities of all parties concerned.

TV-radio interview/"Face the Nation,"
Columbia Broadcasting System, 1-8.

2

There is one thing which has to be stressed. The American interest in Iran is a vital one. Iran represents strategically, both in an economic and political sense, a vital cog in the collective Western economic and political system. Therefore, we have a considerable stake in the peaceful management of Iranian modernization. The Iranians are a people with a 2,500-year-old tradition of statecraft. If they are not interfered with from abroad, if their internal difficulties

[the current anti-Shah unrest] , which are real, are not artificially fanned by ideological or religious fanatics, I don't have any doubt that they will manage their problems. If they do not, however, there is no doubt that this will have far-reaching consequences for the stability of the Persian Gulf, and the United States would be very directly and seriously affected.

Interview/
The New York Times Magazine, 12-31:10.

Jimmy Carter
President of the United States

3

We believe that there are certain principles, fundamentally, which must be observed before a just and a comprehensive [Arab-Israeli] peace can be achieved. First, true peace must be based on normal relations among the parties to the peace; peace means more than just an end to belligerency. Second, there must be withdrawal by Israel from [Arab] territories occupied in 1967 and agreement on secure and recognized borders for all parties in the context of normal and peaceful relations in accordance with United Nations Resolutions 242 and 338. And third, there must be a resolution of the Palestinian problem in all its aspects. The problem must recognize the legitimate rights of the Palestinian people and enable the Palestinians to participate in the determination of their own future.

Aswan, Egypt, Jan. 4/
The New York Times, 1-5:(A)4.

4

I have never thought, and do not think, that it is advisable for us, for the Middle Eastern countries or for the world to have an independent Palestinian nation located between Israel and Jordan ... I think there would be a concentrated influence, perhaps, exerted there by some of the more radical other leaders of the world, and I think that a Palestinian entity or homeland ought to be tied in, at the least, in a very strong federation or confederation with Jordan.

San Francisco Examiner &
Chronicle, 1-15:(This World)16.

(JIMMY CARTER)

1

[On the U.S. role as mediator between the Arabs and Israelis]: It is a very discouraging and frustrating thing to be the intermediary or the messenger boy between a group of leaders in the Middle East who won't even speak to each other. And when you carry a message from one to the other, the one who receives it doesn't like it and blames the adverse message partially on the messenger.

Before newspaper editors,
Washington, February 10/
U.S. News & World Report, 2-27:22.

2

[On his plan to sell warplanes to Egypt and Saudi Arabia, as well as to Israel]: ... we are honoring—completely—the commitments made to Israel in the fall of 1975, concerning an adherence on our part to the adequate defense capabilities of Israel, including advanced aircraft like the F-15 and the F-16 ... In the fall of 1975, commitments were also made to the Saudi Arabians to provide them with advanced aircraft to replace their present lightning planes, which are becoming obsolete ... And so the sale of the F-15s to Saudi Arabia is consistent with the commitment also made in the fall of 1975, and repeatedly reconfirmed. The sale of the F-5Es—a much less capable airplane, by the way—to the Egyptians is, I think, a very legitimate proposal because the Egyptians, in effect, have severed their supply of weapons that used to come from the Soviet Union and have cast their lot with us—which is a very favorable development, one of the most profound developments of all. I have no apology at all to make for this proposal. It maintains the military balance that exists in the Middle East. I can say without any doubt that the superior capabilities of the Israeli Air Force, compared to their neighbors, is maintained, and at the same time it reconfirms our own relationship with the moderate Arab leaders and nations for the future to insure that peace can be—and will be—maintained in the Middle East.

News conference, Washington, March 9/
The New York Times, 3-10:(D)12.

3

... the United Nations Resolution 242 was passed about 10 years ago. Since then, it has been endorsed with no equivocation by our own country, by the entire international community, by the Israeli government and by the Arab countries who border on Israel. It calls for the withdrawal of Israel from territories occupied in the 1967 war. It calls for the restoration of the security of Israel behind recognized and defensible borders, and this has been the basis on which all of our efforts since I've been in office, and also my predecessors' efforts, have been based. For any nation now to reject the application of 242 to the occupied territories, including the West Bank, the Sinai, the Golan Heights, would be a very serious blow to the prospects of peace in the Middle East.

News conference, Washington, March 9/
The New York Times, 3-10:(D)12.

4

My belief is that a permanent settlement [of the Arab-Israeli conflict] will not include an independent Palestinian nation on the West Bank. My belief is that a permanent settlement will not call for complete withdrawal of Israel from occupied [Arab] territories. My belief is that a permanent settlement will be based substantially upon the home-rule proposal that [Israeli] Prime Minister Begin has put forward.

Interview/The New York Times, 5-1:(A)4.

5

For 30 years we have stood at the side of the proud and independent nation of Israel. I can say without reservation, as the President of the United States of America, that we will continue to do so not just for another 30 years, but forever.

Washington, May 1/
Los Angeles Times, 5-2:(1)16.

6

From time to time we have our transient differences with the leaders of Israel, as we do with the leaders of other countries. [But the U.S.] will never waver from our deep friendship and partnership with Israel, our total absolute

WHAT THEY SAID IN 1978

(JIMMY CARTER)

commitment to Israel's security. The establishment of the nation of Israel is a fulfillment of Biblical prophecy. In Jewish tradition, 30 years stands for the age of strength, and Israel, thank God, is strong.

At White House celebration of
Israel's 30th anniversary, Washington,
May 1/The New York Times, 5-2:9.

1

[Announcing a framework for Middle East peace just worked out by Israeli Prime Minister Menachem Begin, Egyptian President Anwar Sadat and himself at Camp David, Md.]: When we first arrived at Camp David, the first thing upon which we agreed was to ask the people of the world to pray that our negotiations were successful. Those prayers have been answered far beyond any expectations ... The questions that have brought warfare and bitterness to the Mideast for the last 30 years will not be settled overnight. [But] we should all recognize the substantial achievements that have been made.

Broadcast address to the nation, Washington,
Sept. 17/Los Angeles Times, 9-18:(1)1.

2

[On the framework for peace just agreed to by Egyptian President Anwar Sadat and Israeli Prime Minister Menachem Begin at Camp David, Md.]: None of us should underestimate the historic importance of what has been done. This is the first time that an Arab and an Israeli leader have signed a comprehensive framework for peace. It contains the seeds of a time when the Middle East, with all its vast potential, may be a land of human richness of fulfillment, rather than of bitterness and conflict ... For the last 30 years, through four wars, the people of this troubled region have paid a terrible price in suffering and division and hatred and bloodshed. No two nations have suffered more than Israel and Egypt. But the dangers and the costs of conflict in this region and for our nation have been great as well. We have long-standing friendships among the nations there and peoples of the region, and profound moral

commitments which are deeply rooted in our values as a people. For many years, the Middle East has been a textbook for pessimism, a demonstration that diplomatic ingenuity was no match for intractable human conflicts. Today we are privileged to see the chance for one of the rare bright moments in human history—a chance that may open the way to peace.

Before joint session of Congress in
House of Representatives, Washington,
Sept. 18/Los Angeles Times, 9-19:(1)20.

3

[On the current treaty disagreements between Israel and Egypt following the recent successful meetings at Camp David, Md.]: ... I think it would be obvious that both sides want peace and I think that is the main hope that we have in spite of these differences. When you balance the enormous benefits of peace, compared with the horrible consequences of failure, and then look at the tiny differences that exist between them now on wording, language, linkage, schedules, hill tops, valleys, security outposts, these things are really miniscule in comparison with the advantages of peace.

Nov. 16/The Washington Post, 11-22:(A)18.

4

[On the anti-Shah unrest in Iran]: ... I think the Shah understands the situation in Iran very clearly and the reasons for some of the problems that he's experienced recently. He has moved forcefully and aggressively in changing some of the ancient religious customs of Iran, for instance, and some of the more conservative or traditional religious leaders deplore this change substantially. Others of the Iranian citizens who are in the middle class who have a new propriety brought about by enhanced oil prices and extra income coming into the country, I think, feel that they ought to have a greater share of the voice in determining their affairs of Iran. Others believe that the democratization of Iran ought to proceed more quickly. The Shah, as you know, has offered the opposition groups a place in a coalition government. They have rejected that offer and demand more complete removal from the Shah

(JIMMY CARTER)

of his authority. We trust the Shah to maintain stability in Iran, to continue with the democratization process and also to continue with the progressive change in the Iranian social and economic structure. But I don't think neither I nor any other national leader could ever claim that we have never made a mistake or have never misunderstood the attitudes of our people. We have confidence in the Shah. We support him and his efforts to change Iran in a constructive way, moving toward democracy and social progress. And we have confidence in the Iranian people to make the ultimate judgments about their own government. We do not have any intention of interfering in the internal affairs of Iran, and we do not approve any other nation interfering in the internal affairs of Iran.

News conference, Washington, Nov. 30/
The New York Times, 12-1:(A)22.

Frank Church
United States Senator, D-Idaho

1

[Arguing against the U.S. selling warplanes to Saudi Arabia]: We should not be selling $5-billion worth of airplanes into the Middle East at this time. Why don't we give peace a chance? If we would just withhold the sale of all these planes ... at this time and get the [Arab-Israeli] parties back to the negotiating table and see some momentum toward peace, that would greatly change the whole picture.

Washington/San Francisco
Examiner & Chronicle, 5-14:(This World)22.

Alan Cranston
United States Senator, D-California

2

I am not supporting any aspect of the proposed arms sale [by the U.S. to various Middle Eastern countries]. My position is based on the principle of what will keep the peace. If we continue to give arms to combatants, no peace is possible.

San Francisco Examiner &
Chronicle, 5-21:(This World)7.

Moshe Dayan
Foreign Minister of Israel

3

If [Egyptian] President Sadat really insists on Israel's withdrawing from all of the Arab territories and that Israel would accept the right for the Palestinians for self-determination—which would be eventually a Palestinian state—and if he calls for Israel to withdraw all the settlements and the Israeli forces and to give back East Jerusalem, then I don't think this is a peace plan. I don't think it will ever be accepted by Israel.

TV-radio interview/"Meet the Press,"
National Broadcasting Company, 2-12.

4

[Egyptian] President [Anwar] Sadat is sincere and I think he wants peace. But the problem is that he cannot make a separate peace with us. He asks us for concessions, but suppose we were to agree to everything that he asks—would President Sadat make peace? President Sadat cannot make a separate peace without Jordan. So what are we to negotiate? Supposing that you find a house and want to buy it and the other party says "yes." Why, you go ahead and buy it if the terms are right. But a problem arises if the other man says that he just has to get the approval of his mother-in-law or something—and he's not sure that he can sell. In that case, you just have to pack in the negotiations until the situation becomes clear. The house is not available. That's the point.

Interview, en route to Miami, Fla./
The New York Times, 2-18:3.

5

[Criticizing U.S. President Carter's "package" plan of selling warplanes to Israel, Egypt and Saudi Arabia]: 1) We oppose jet sales to the Saudis and the Egyptians at this time because we think it is dangerous. 2) We resent the concept of a package deal. We think the provision of selling arms to Israel should be conducted on its merits and not within any package. 3) If because of this view we shall be punished because we oppose the system of the package deal and the arms sale to Egypt and

WHAT THEY SAID IN 1978

(MOSHE DAYAN)

Saudi Arabia and should not get the planes, we should accept the punishment but shall not change our position about it.

To reporters, Washington,
April 27/Los Angeles Times, 4-28:(1)1.

1

When you people [the U.S.] say that we should stay out of your business about sending jet planes to Saudi Arabia, I do agree that as far as you are concerned it is your business. But these are killing machines; they are not washing machines. And who are they going to use these killing machines against?

TV-radio interview/"Issues and Answers,"
American Broadcasting Company, 4-30.

2

We [Israelis] do not regard ourselves as foreigners in [the West Bank and Gaza] areas. The Israeli settlements in Judea, Samaria and the Gaza district are there as of right. It is inconceivable to us that Jews should be prohibited from settling and living in Judea and Samaria [the West Bank), which are the heart of our homeland.

At United Nations, New York, Oct. 9/
Los Angeles Times, 10-10:(1)13.

3

In the final analysis, Israel cannot be forced to accept what it is not willing to accept [in a peace treaty with Egypt]. There may be [American] pressures—public-opinion pressures, perhaps also economic pressures. But if Israel will stand up to these pressures, firmly and united, it will not only have a chance—but it may be assured—that what it will not wish to do, it cannot be forced to do.

Jerusalem, Dec. 15/
The Washington Post, 12-16:(A)16.

Simcha Dinitz
Israeli Ambassador
to the United States

4

[On Israeli-U.S. relations] : Our special relationship rests on a community of interests in

the strategic field. We are both in the same camp fighting totalitarianism and dark forces. Unless the American people are told this by their President, then in time Israel will become a moral burden [to America] rather than a strategic or political asset. The weakening of the state of Israel can occur ... by breaking the spirit of Israel through political criticism and through intimidation and recrimination. And an Israel with a broken spirit is an Israel that cannot live beyond its meager physical dimensions.

Before Council of Presidents of Major
American Jewish Organizations, New York,
Dec. 18/Los Angeles Times, 12-19:(1)22.

Thomas F. Eagleton
United States Senator, D-Missouri

5

[Supporting U.S. plans to sell warplanes to Saudi Arabia] : It would be catastrophe [if the Saudi oil reserves fell under a hostile power]. Better that we provide a means for the Saudis to defend that vital resource themselves than face the possibility of some day being forced to commit our own military forces. That's the hard choice we face.

Before the Senate, Washington,
May 15/The New York Times, 5-16:12.

Abba Eban
Member of Israeli Knesset
(Parliament); Former Foreign
Minister of Israel

6

[Supporting autonomy for the Palestinians in the West Bank] : Let each side dream its dreams, and we shall see in a few years who is right and who is wrong. It will be up to the Palestinian Arabs to dispel our fears that any separation [of the West Bank from Israel] would be hostile to our security. I assume the Israeli government knows that autonomy carries certain risks, and that it will not stop there but develop further. But you cannot have peace without risks.

Interview/Time, 3-6:37.

7

[On Egyptian President Anwar Sadat's unprecedented trip to Israel last year] : I think

(ABBA EBAN)

that the Sadat voyage in a sense vindicates our foreign policy. We said that if we were patient, tenacious, strong, they would have to reconcile themselves to our resistance. Sadat's visit was a tribute to our strength, not to our weakness. And having come to that point, the question is, how do you ratify this victory? There is a chance that this opportunity might be squandered. I am quite certain that unless there is some very inspired mediation by a third party, it will be squandered; and the third party can only be the United States, because that is the will of Egypt and of Israel.

Interview/
Los Angeles Herald Examiner, 6-10:(A)9.

1

[On Egyptian President Anwar Sadat's stand that Israel must withdraw from East Jerusalem]: I suggest that he forget about that. If he means that Israel is going to give up East Jerusalem to some Arab government, then hell will freeze over before that happens. That's never going to happen in the whole of human history.

Interview, Jerusalem/
Los Angeles Herald Examiner, 7-9:(A)4.

Dariush Forohar
Leader in the National
Front (opposition to the
government of the Shah of Iran)

2

The country is facing a crisis because justification for the present ruling system has diminished. Therefore, I believe since the legality of the government comes from the people, there must be a referendum for the people to decide.
Los Angeles Times, 11-3:(1)8.

Andrei A. Gromyko
Foreign Minister
of the Soviet Union

3

It is not superfluous to mention ... that the Middle East region is in direct proximity to the borders of the Soviet Union and countries of the socialist community, and that the course of

events there is far from being a matter of indifference to us.
Aug. 30/U.S. News & World Report, 9-11:18.

4

[Criticizing the framework for peace worked out between Egypt and Israel at Camp David, Md.]: A radical and comprehensive settlement in the Middle East can be achieved only on the basis of joint effort by all the sides directly concerned. Separate deals at the expense of the Arabs have only sidetracked the solution of the problem. And such precisely is the nature of the understandings reached at the recent three-sided meeting at Camp David. If a realistic look is taken at things, no grounds can be found to believe that they, as claimed, bring closer the Middle East settlement. On the contrary, what this is all about is a new anti-Arab step making it difficult to achieve a just solution of this pressing problem.

At United Nations, New York, Sept. 26/
The Dallas Times Herald, 9-27:(A)5.

Mordechai Gur
General and Former
Chief of Staff, Israeli Army

5

[On the possibility of Arab-Israeli war diminishing as a result of an Israeli-Egyptian peace treaty]: We hear that by removing the Egyptians from the war cycle, the danger of war diminishes; [but] in 1972, after Egypt expelled the Russians, we also thought that the Egyptians had given up on the military option. The thesis, that the cycle of war has terminated, is a very dangerous thing ... Because if we give in to this festival [the recent Camp David accords], we will stand before a severe strategic situation. We mustn't let our minds freeze up when our neighbors still speak in terms of hatred. There are no tired soldiers. There are only tired leaders.

Newsweek, 11-6:68.

George Habash
Leader, Popular Front for
the Liberation of Palestine

6

We will continue to strike at Israeli targets, avoiding injury to third parties or groups not

WHAT THEY SAID IN 1978

directly aiding Zionism. We might hit a few U.S. targets, though, just to continuously remind the U.S. leadership of how our people suffer . . . We are against the idea of two states in Palestine, an Arab one and a Jewish one, because what would be the basis of a Jewish state? It could only be racist . . . That is why I, as a Christian, prefer a single state where Muslims, Christians and Jews live together.

Interview, Beirut, Lebanon/
The Christian Science Monitor, 3-27:9.

Chaim Herzog
Israeli Ambassador/Permanent
Representative to the United Nations

1

An independent, PLO-ruled Palestinian state would be a mortal danger to Israel, which we'd made quite clear, and would be a mortal danger to [Jordanian] King Hussein because they are committed not only to the destruction of Israel but to the destruction of the Hashemite regime in Jordan. Furthermore, they know as well as we do, and Saudi Arabia above all knows it, that the PLO, which is sponsored by the Soviet Union, would create a mini-state that would not be viable and would bring the Soviet Union right back into the area.

Interview, San Diego, Calif./
The San Diego Union, 3-12:(C)5.

2

I don't want to underestimate the importance of [Egyptian President Anwar] Sadat's visit [to Israel last year], but I'm not in the doldrums of pessimism today—just as I was not in the peaks of euphoria before. I think we have to take a more reasoned view of this whole situation. My own feeling is that we've entered into an irreversible process and that we will ultimately achieve a breakthrough. After all, the reason for the breakdown of the Sadat-Begin Egyptian talks was not because of recalcitrance or intransigence on the part of Israel—although that's the propaganda line being turned out against Israel today—but because we were on the verge of agreement with Sadat. He

got a fright. He suddenly found he was odd man out with no support from the Arab world, and he therefore realized that he would be in trouble. So he pulled back very rapidly and changed his course.

Interview, New York/"W":
a Fairchild publication, 3-31:4.

3

I can look back to the period when we [Israelis] were living behind the 1967 lines and remember again that for 19 years, from 1948 to 1967, Jordan and Egypt controlled the West Bank and Gaza and could have set up an independent Palestinian state if they wanted one. The truth is, they never wanted one and they don't want one today—and all they're saying about it is lip service.

San Francisco Examiner &
Chronicle, 4-16:(This World)2.

Eric Hoffer
American philosopher

4

One of my worries has been that there are no great leaders on this planet . . . Then suddenly here are two potential great leaders—[Israeli Prime Minister] Menachem Begin and [Egyptian President] Anwar Sadat. What is it about Israel—that little sliver of land—that produces so many remarkable people? Perhaps because their citizens live on the edge all the time. It must bring out the power.

Interview, San Francisco/People, 1-16:31.

Darius Homayoun
Minister of Information of Iran

5

Ten months ago we opened up freedom of the press in this country. Its purpose is to show where things are going wrong and to correct them . . . We think of the newspapers as a corrective channel between people and government. Basically, there are two kinds of opposition. There are dangerous opponents of the rule and the program of the Shah, of the monarchy

(DARIUS HOMAYOUN)

itself. We cannot give space to these subversive groups and their propaganda. [But there are also dissidents who challenge not the system itself but the way it operates.] These people are legitimate dissidents. They are free to expose their grievances and problems, and they are encouraged to come forward and do so, peaceably.

Interview, Teheran/
The Christian Science Monitor, 5-30:5.

Hussein I
King of Jordan

1

Security cannot be guaranteed unless there is a peace between partners giving both dignity, something lasting. In Jerusalem, for example, if there is Israeli sovereignty over-all in an open city, open to all people, that would lead to cooperation between Israelis and Arabs, in itself a security guarantee. If there is a link of some kind between the West Bank and Gaza, that would require cooperation between Israelis and Arabs, another guarantee. Removal of barriers, fruitful cooperation, these are the things that provide security, not some military installations which can be removed or may become obsolete.

Interview/Time, 1-30:38.

2

If all that happens is an Egyptian-Israeli peace treaty, and the rest of the Palestinian problem . . . is not solved, I feel that there would be upheavals in this area that might not be limited in terms of the threat . . . The majority of the Arab people will feel more and more that this important part of the world is not treated fairly . . . and there is no balance between Israel and the Arabs in terms of the way they are looked upon by our friends, particularly the United States [where the Israeli-Egyptian peace framework was recently agreed upon]. There is a feeling throughout this area that, after all, the Arab world is contributing to the rest of the world and in particular to the United States—in terms of energy production, in terms of stabilizing the world monetary

system—yet in reality there is an imbalance. I am not talking necessarily of another oil embargo, but I am saying that many eruptions could occur in this area and the future of the area could be in jeopardy.

Interview, Amman, Jordan/"Face the Nation,"
Columbia Broadcasting System, 10-1.

Ahmed Iskander
Minister of Information of Syria

3

Since 1973, all the positive phenomena for [Middle East] peace have come from the Arab side. But it has been misunderstood as a sign of collapse—a sign that the Arabs will accept Israel's refusal to withdraw [from occupied Arab lands] and her refusal to recognize Palestine identity. That is why Israel resists any real settlement.

The New York Times, 5-8:(A)19.

Harold Jacobs
President, Union of Orthodox
Jewish Congregations of America

4

Twice in the last 11 years, Israel's survival depended on the unwavering friendship and support of an American President. God forbid, if another such crisis were to confront us tomorrow, I and many of my colleagues could not confidently predict which side [current U.S. President] Jimmy Carter would support.

At UOJCA dinner, New York, May 21/
Los Angeles Herald Examiner, 5-22:(A)6.

Mohammed Ibrahim Kamel
Foreign Minister of Egypt

5

[On Israeli settlements in occupied Arab territory]: The decision of the Israeli settlements is really a very dangerous thing. The United States and all other countries have stated very clearly that establishing the settlements is an obstruction to peace. But even though we are now actually negotiating peace, the Israeli Cabinet has chosen this moment to confirm that they are obstructing peace by continuing with their settlements.

Cairo, Feb. 28/
The New York Times, 3-1:(A)9.

WHAT THEY SAID IN 1978

(MOHAMMED IBRAHIM KAMEL)

1

[On the U.S. approval of arms sales to his country as well as to Saudi Arabia and Israel]: We are very happy with this vote because, in the first place, it shows that all the confidence and trust we place in the United States is being reciprocated. It shows that the United States is playing an even-handed role. It encourages us to continue our peace efforts.

Cairo/San Francisco Examiner &
Chronicle, 5-21:(This World)7.

2

This approach of trying to find whether the Israeli proposal of self-rule and the Egyptian proposal for the West Bank and Gaza have common grounds will lead to nothing. The philosophy and objectives of both proposals are totally contradictory and opposite. The Israeli proposal of self-rule is based on the continued Israeli occupation of the West Bank. Our proposal is based on [UN Resolution] 242, and the starting point is withdrawal.... it is like saying that there is a resemblance between a cobra and a gazelle.

Interview/Time, 8-14:21.

Ruhollah Khomeini
Exiled leader of the opposition to
Mohammad Reza Pahlavi, Shah of Iran

3

The Shah [of Iran] did not gain power by universal consent of the people ... He's destroyed the economy and given away our natural resources, especially our oil, to the industrial powers. He's reduced agricultural production to provide a market for American goods. The Iranian armed forces have been subjected to foreign leadership. Freedom of expression and of the press have been destroyed. And his police have massacred thousands of Iranian people ... At the present, we are confronting the regime with only demonstrations, protests and strikes ... Obviously, if nothing works and the situation becomes intolerable for the people, we may consider giving permission for an armed popular struggle ... The symbol of

the struggle is the one who talks with the people ... That's why the Iranian people consider me a symbol. I talk their language, I listen to their needs, I cry for them.

Interview/Newsweek, 11-6:80.

4

Until the day an Islamic republic is installed in Iran, the struggle of our people will continue ... It is the absolute right of people to fight against this regime with whatever means they choose ... We hope that the armed forces will see that this movement is for the betterment of our brothers and sisters, and that the Shah is a traitor who has betrayed the nation ... [In Iran] the Americans have at least 45,000 military advisers, and the Iranian Army is totally under their control ... The relationship between the American government and our government that is now like that of a master and a servant should finally cease, and a healthy relationship would then replace it. [The U.S. supports the Shah] obviously to serve their own interests.

Interview, Pontchartrain, France,
Nov. 6/Los Angeles Times, 11-7:(1)8.

5

Our aims and goals are different from those of Communists and Marxists. Our movement is based on Islam and monotheism, and they are against both of them. Thus, there is no cooperation and compatibility between our movement and theirs. As for Russia, we are not concerned, because a nation is raised to take command of her own affairs.

Interview, Neuphle le Chateau,
France/Los Angeles Times, 12-13:(2)7.

Henry A. Kissinger
Former Secretary of
State of the United States

6

[On Israel's strikes at Palestinian guerrilla bases in Lebanon in retaliation for a recent PLO raid in Israel]: I think they had to strike back for two reasons. First, there has to be a resistance to terrorism in which innocent civilians are being used for political purposes on matters

(HENRY A. KISSINGER)

which they cannot possibly affect. Second, there have been too many attacks from this area against Israel itself, so that some sort of retaliation was inevitable ... I don't think [Israel] could [refrain from retaliating] and I don't think they should.

Interview, March 15/
Los Angeles Times, 3-16:(1)12.

1

[On the anti-Shah sentiment in Iran] : The Iranian situation is a tragedy for the West. The Shah is a leader who on every critical foreign-policy issue has been totally on the side of the West and who has been a stabilizing factor in every crisis in the area. Beyond formal documents, it was a very close coordination of our respective foreign policies. The Shah never interrupted the flow of oil to anybody for political reasons. His economic-development program was a great success. He moved his country from feudalism into the modern age. The Shah is paying the price of modernization: He is being attacked by those who think he moves too fast and by those for whom he is not moving fast enough ... In this context, our own [U.S.] answer [to the anti-Shah demonstrations] was not very strong. I don't think it came across as a ringing affirmation of a commitment to a country that is so vital to us or as a warning to the Soviets not to meddle in Iranian affairs. It almost sounded as if we were declaring Iran an area of neutrality.

Interview, New York/Newsweek, 12-11:56.

Teddy Kollek
Mayor of Jerusalem

2

[On Israel's strikes at Palestinian guerrilla bases in Lebanon in retaliation for a recent PLO raid in Israel] : An act of violence is being reacted to by another act of violence, but the country [Israel] has an obligation to protect its citizens and can't do less than that. I imagine with what a heavy heart people decided on this attempt to get at the source of the PLO ... People will see more urgency on both sides

now. Secondly, I believe both the Americans and [Egyptian] President [Anwar] Sadat will see why we can't risk a PLO state on the West Bank, why we couldn't possibly accept a Palestinian state which might suddenly be ruled by the PLO.

Interview, Los Angeles,
March 15/Los Angeles Times, 3-16:(1)10.

3

[On last year's unprecedented visit to Israel by Egyptian President Anwar Sadat] : I think that it was a tremendous affair because he went around as if he were in a dream. Finally, what we had hoped for, an Arab leader, came and said that "I recognize Israel and I come to your capital to say so." This was a great moment. I believe that the high feeling, both in Israel and in Egypt, was because you can't decide questions of the security of nations by declarations on television or radio or in the newspapers. We have been attacked four times by the Arabs. If we lose a war, it is the last war that we will lose because we can't afford to lose even [one] war and we must take care of our security. Therefore, this great appearance of President Sadat has to be followed by hard-nosed and difficult negotiations, not only by declarations on television. After all, what he has given us was important, but it was only [a] statement, even if he is the President of the Egyptian Republic.

Interview/
Los Angeles Herald Examiner, 3-25:(A)2.

4

Jerusalem must never be divided again ... I do what I can for the Arabs, and this is responsible for the relative peace and quiet in the city. It's their city, too. They have lived here for 1,300 years. My policy brought peaceful coexistence. Arabs and Jews live next to each other without fear. Three religions peaceful in one city. That's what it's all about. Jerusalem works.

People. 11-6:90.

Bruno Kreisky
Chancellor of Austria

5

[Saying Egyptian President Anwar Sadat did not receive a generous response from Israeli

WHAT THEY SAID IN 1978

(BRUNO KREISKY)

Prime Minister Menachem Begin when they met in Jerusalem last year]: He [Sadat] found himself dealing with political grocers like Begin, a little Polish lawyer from Warsaw or whatever he was. They are so alienated, they think in such a warped way, these eastern Jews, because they have never had political responsibilities.

Interview/The Washington Post, 9-4:(A)21.

George Meany
President, American Federation of Labor-Congress of Industrial Organizations

1

[Criticizing the U.S. plan to sell warplanes to Saudi Arabia and Egypt, as well as to Israel]: In submitting the arms package to the Congress, the [Carter] Administration said, in effect, that the security of Israel had become negotiable. I hope our government will help to keep Israel strong and free and that we will never again put Israel's national security interest on the bargaining table. Israel's right to exist in freedom must always be non-negotiable ... I don't pretend to have a magic formula to bring peace to the Middle East, but I do know that peace—real peace—will not come by lessening our support of Israel, by rewarding Arab inflexibility. So I would suggest to the Administration that the road to peace in the Middle East is not through arms sales to the Arabs. Peace will come when the Arab nations become aware that they cannot disrupt the "special relationship" between the United States and Israel, that this relationship will always operate to keep Israel strong and that there is simply no alternative to direct negotiations.

Before Zionist Organization of America, Washington, June 6/Los Angeles Times, 6-7:(1)31.

Golda Meir
Former Prime Minister of Israel

2

[Peace will come in the Middle East when the Arabs] will love their children more than they hate us. When peace does come, we will, perhaps—in time—be able to forgive the Arabs for killing our sons. But it will be more difficult

for us to forgive them for having forced us to kill their sons ... I'm grateful that I live in a country whose people have learned how to go on living in a sea of hatred without hating those who want to destroy them and without abandoning their own vision of peace. To have learned this is a great art, the prescription for which is not written anywhere. It is part of our way of life in Israel.

Interview/The Dallas Times Herald, 5-7:(E)6.

Walter F. Mondale
Vice President of the United States

3

Of all American security assistance proposed in next year's budget, 42 per cent of our supporting assistance and 48 per cent of military sales credits and 56 per cent of all military grants are distributed to a single nation, the nation of Israel. And repayment on half of those credits, which total $1-billion, is systematically waived by the United States. That's a benefit enjoyed by no other nation on earth. And that military assistance to Israel will continue regardless of any negotiating differences. It will continue not as a lever to force accommodation, but as a fundamental commitment to the strength and survival of a free democracy. It will never be used as a form of pressure against Israel. And it will always reflect a special relationship—which will always remain special.

Before American Jewish Committee, New York, May 18/ The New York Times, 5-19:(A)5.

4

We are convinced that without eventual withdrawal [by Israel from occupied Arab lands] on all fronts, to boundaries agreed upon in negotiations and safeguarded by effective security arrangements, there can be no lasting peace. Only Israel can be the final judge of its security needs. Only the parties can draw the final boundary lines. But if there is to be peace, the implicit bargain of UN Resolution 242 must be fulfilled ... Resolution 242 is an equation. On the one hand, it recognizes the right of every state in the area to live in peace within

(WALTER F. MONDALE)

secure and recognized borders free from threats or acts of force. The United States believes such a peace must include binding commitments to normal relations. In return, Israel would withdraw from territories occupied in the 1967 war. But the principles of 242 cannot be viewed in isolation. They cannot be applied selectively. Together they form a fair, balanced formula and the best basis for negotiating a peace between Israel and all her neighbors.

At dinner in his honor, Jerusalem,
July 2/The New York Times, 7-3:3.

Daniel P. Moynihan
United States Senator, D-New York

1

[On Israel's strikes at Palestinian guerrilla bases in Lebanon in retaliation for a recent PLO raid in Israel]: There has been no government in southern Lebanon for about three years now and the Israelis are responding in a situation where, if they didn't, no one else would. What's going on there [the actions of the guerrillas] has been illegal, but no one [is] in a position to enforce anything. The world is steadily getting an idea what the PLO is all about. It's unthinkable that they should be given the status of an independent state—a totalitarian, Marxist, terrorist group. To strengthen the PLO is to weaken peace in the Middle East.

To newsmen, March 15/
The New York Times, 3-16:(A)17.

2

[Criticizing U.S. plans to sell warplanes to Saudi Arabia]: It happens that the foreign and domestic well-being of the United States—the world's foremost democracy, which claims to be the world's most powerful country—is in fact increasingly dependent upon the decisions taken by the royal family of Saudi Arabia. Five years ago, we could not live with Saudi foreign policy; today we cannot live without it. Is this not the measure of our position in the world, and what has become of that position in the world in that period?

Before the Senate, Washington,
May 15/The New York Times, 5-16:12.

Dennis Mullin
Middle East correspondent,
"U.S. News & World Report"

3

Egypt and Israel will both need massive amounts of American support to develop and enforce any kind of peace agreement. There is no way the Egyptian economy can be repaired without a major international effort that will involve the U.S. and its allies in providing financing and technology. The Israelis will also require massive economic aid. This means that there will be a dramatic increase in America's role in the Middle East—economically and, as a consequence, politically. In a sense, the U.S., by proxy, would be assuring the security of every country in the area.

Interview, Jerusalem/
U.S. News & World Report, 10-2:28.

Mohammad Reza Pahlavi
Shah of Iran

4

[On foreign criticism of his country's arms purchases]: We have probably seven times the airspace of West Germany. Just tell me how many planes West Germany and NATO have and compare it to our airspace. Why is it that you white people, you European[s] or American[s] . . . you can afford to have that number of planes and guns and tanks for that number of kilometers or miles? Why should we have less than you?

Interview, Teheran/
The Washington Post, 3-13:(A)22.

5

Nobody can overthrow me. I have the support of 700,000 troops, all the workers and most of the people. Wherever I go, there are fantastic demonstrations of support. I have the power, and the opposition cannot be compared in strength with the government in any way. However, we shall always have some people who are dissatisfied, who carry out attacks on television-relay stations, banks and even schools. The alliance between the radicals on both the left and the right will continue.

Interview, Teheran/
U.S. News & World Report, 6-26:37.

WHAT THEY SAID IN 1978

1

[Reacting to the current anti-Shah dissent in his country]: I promise that the past mistakes and illegalities, cruelty and corruption will not be repeated... The government of Iran in future will be based on the Constitution, social justice, and freedom from injustice, corruption and oppression... Your revolutionary message has been heard. I am aware of everything you have given your lives for.

Broadcast address to the nation, Teheran,
Nov. 6/The Christian Science Monitor, 11-20:16.

2

[On the anti-Shah turmoil in his country]: If only I could find out what they want. They accuse me of not being religious. But, as anyone who knows me can testify, that's entirely wrong. I'm even something of a mystic. They simply want more and more salary increases. They are now demanding anything that goes through their heads, as if anything and everything were possible. No. There must be something else, but what? Freedom? They have it today and they would have had it even without these events. The record of the last 30 years should make them all think again. Everything has changed in Iran, but what will remain of these changes under the demagogues?

Interview, Teheran/Newsweek, 11-13:81.

Shimon Peres
Member of Israeli Knesset
(Parliament); Chairman,
Labor Party of Israel

3

[Supporting ratification of the framework for peace worked out between Egypt and Israel at Camp David, Md.]: A price must be paid for peace. A bad agreement is better than failure. If the agreement failed [to be ratified by the Knesset], the chance for peace would be put off for future generations. Israel would bear the blame for this and would be forced into isolation by the other nations of the world, including the United States.

At Labor Party meeting, Sept. 25/
Los Angeles Herald Examiner, 9-26:(A)4.

4

[Addressing Israeli Prime Minister Menachem Begin and criticizing parts of the recent peace framework worked out by Begin and Egyptian President Anwar Sadat at Camp David, Md.]: Whatever you say about there being no referendum and no state [in Israeli-occupied Palestinian areas], you have sown the seed of a Palestinian state and the Palestinians will get it. You won't be able to stop it. This is your greatest mistake.

Knesset debate, Jerusalem, Sept. 25/
The Christian Science Monitor, 9-26:4.

Muammar el-Qaddafi
Chief of State of Libya

5

[On criticism of Arab terrorism in the conflict with Israel]: We want to redefine terrorism. We say that American fleets in our waters are terrorism. When the Americans refuse wheat to starving people, that is terrorism. A Palestinian expelled from his home [by the Israelis] is able to say that is terrorism. Ask the people involved—if they feel they are being terrorized, they are. Actually, by supporting Israel, it is the Americans who are the terrorists.

Interview, Tripoli, Libya/
Los Angeles Times, 10-20:(2)7.

Yitzhak Rabin
Former Prime Minister of Israel

6

[On the peace negotiations between Egyptian President Anwar Sadat and Israeli Prime Minister Menachem Begin]: Sadat and Begin remind me of the musical *Annie Get Your Gun*—"anything you can do I can do better." It's a competition to see who will have more time on the American networks and space in the magazines and newspapers. Sometimes I ask myself, are they really serious, or is this a competition between actors?

Interview/Time, 3-6:37.

7

[On the framework for peace worked out between Egyptian President Anwar Sadat and Israeli Prime Minister Menachem Begin at Camp

(YITZHAK RABIN)

David, Md.]: Begin is the only Israeli leader who could have signed such an agreement, since he doesn't have a Begin in opposition to his Cabinet.

Time, 10-2:16.

Anwar el-Sadat
President of Egypt

1

I do not agree to the presence of a single Jewish settlement on my land. Let them destroy them. Neither do I allow a single Israeli civilian or soldier to remain. This is something I have categorically stated and we are finished with it.

Interview/The New York Times, 1-8:(1)13.

2

[Israeli Prime Minister Menachem] Begin gave me nothing [in the recent Arab-Israeli peace negotiations]. It was I who gave him everything. I gave him security and legitimacy and got nothing in return. It is not my divine mission to pamper the Israelis, talk about them and their sufferings and justify their mistakes without reaching a solution which, in any event, will serve them more than it will serve us.

*Interview/ San Francisco
Examiner & Chronicle, 1-15:(A)24.*

3

I spoke to the Israelis with an open mind and an open heart. I called on every man and woman in Israel to tell their children that what has passed is the end of war, the end of pain; and what is coming is the beginning of a new life, the life of love, prosperity, freedom and peace ... We embarked on negotiations. I broke those negotiations after it was proven beyond a shadow of a doubt that the Israeli negotiators ... were all planning to exploit time, exploit our admission of the importance of Israel's security ... The Israelis wanted to attain the results of peace—normal relations—while continuing to occupy the [conquered Arab] land, before we had even made a peace agreement.

*Before People's Assembly, Cairo/San Francisco
Examiner & Chronicle, 1-29:(This World)14.*

4

Peace cannot be built when a country treads on the land and sovereignty of another ... When the Israeli Foreign Minister says we can sit and negotiate and go halfway, I answer: Halfway is, for us, to lose our land and our sovereignty. No!

Time, 1-30:35.

5

We want to put an end to wars and bloodshed [in the Middle East]. We want every people to be free and secure within its own land. We want to create a new Middle East where nations, including the Palestinians, live together in harmony and fraternity. We want to purge all souls of prejudice and hatred. And, God willing, we shall overcome.

*Washington, Feb. 3/
Los Angeles Herald Examiner, 2-4:(A)1.*

6

It has been suggested that the establishment of any Palestinian entity, even when accompanied by all guarantees, means the destruction of Israel. This is a fallacy. A Palestinian state, linked with Jordan, will be a positive force of stability and normalcy in the area. Without it, the structure of peace will remain vulnerable. Any peace treaty could collapse so long as the Palestinians are left frustrated and unsatisfied. In short, that would be an open invitation to renewed violence and unrest. The conflict would be like a volcano in dormant state, which might erupt at any moment. Is this what we are working for?

*Before National Press Club, Washington,
Feb. 6/The Washington Post, 2-7:(A)8.*

7

When I went to Jerusalem [last year], it was the impossible mission that went far beyond the wildest of dreams. No one can belittle the dimensions of this historic act today or tomorrow. You have described it as an act of courage and vision. To me, it was, and still is, an article of faith, faith in mankind and in the future. Some are suggesting, in hindsight, that I should have bargained with the Israelis, or perhaps

WHAT THEY SAID IN 1978

with the United States, before taking this gigantic step. But they are missing the point. I did not go to Jerusalem to strike a deal, but to make peace; I did not go to win an argument, but to reassure the minds and hearts of millions of Israelis and Arabs. If some were unable to grasp the great significance of such a unique step, the fault is only theirs . . . I must tell you in all candor, however, that events of the past few weeks have caused us some concern. The Israeli government has chosen to go back into the vicious circle of arguing over every single word or comma. They are resorting, again, to the old tactics and worn-out ideas. One gets the impression that there is a deliberate attempt to erase the impact of the historic initiative and divest it of its driving spirit. This is most dangerous and no one stands to gain of such a development . . . I would like to make it crystal clear that we remain committed to the cause of peace. I am determined to give it every possible chance. Despite all difficulties, we will persevere. To us, the pursuit of peace is a strategic goal which we pursue with determination.

Before National Press Club, Washington,
Feb. 6/The New York Times, 2-7:4.

1

I shall never oppose the United States' sending a plane and a tank to every Israeli man and woman. But let them use them inside their borders to feel secure, not to claim others' land. I have nothing against the special relationship between the U.S. and Israel.

Interview/Time, 2-13:9.

2

[On the recent PLO raid in Israel] : I condemn it. This is part of the vicious circle that I've done my best during my last visit to Jerusalem to break. And I thought at one time that I broke it. But the response of the other side [Israel] was not at the responsible level of my action. Let me repeat: Let us break this vicious circle of action and reaction because it will lead to nothing. I am against anything done against the civilians . . . I wonder really what is the

result of such acts. I'm sorry to say that we shall enter the vicious circle again if we do not heed and lose no time at all toward a peaceful settlement. If all the confrontation states reach settlements with Israel [but] the Palestinian question is not settled, we shall not establish peace. I think this has been proved lately by what has happened. Let us try to overcome the sadness of this incident [by working] toward the establishment of peace in the area.

To newsmen, March 14/
The New York Times, 3-15:(A)12.

3

No one can agree to what [Israeli Prime Minister Menachem] Begin is saying. He wants peace, land and sovereignty—everything. My initiative was an attempt to jump over the psychological barriers. My visit to Jerusalem [last year] said, "We recognize you; we are asking for normal relations and open borders; we want to be good neighbors." But look at the result. We agreed to direct negotiations and normal relations. Mr. Begin gives us nothing at all and says Judea and Samaria belong to Israel . . . Begin's proposal is to legalize the occupation, while we ask that the land be liberated. Let me be frank. The desperate state of the Palestinians is pushing them to fanaticism. Begin's hard line damages everything and pushes them to desperation.

Interview, Cairo/Time, 4-10:28.

4

If Israel, as it has said for 30 years, is really for peace, there is only one obstacle to peace— [Israeli Prime Minister Menachem] Begin. Peace can be established within hours. The Prime Minister thinks he can have peace, recognition and, above all, [Arab] land, but we tell him "no." Peace, yes. Guarantees for both sides, yes. Neighborly coexistence, yes. Recognition, yes. But land, no. Sovereignty [of Israel over Arab land], no. No and a thousand times no.

Before Arab Socialist Union, Cairo,
July 22/The New York Times, 7-23:(1)4.

5

[Criticizing the PLO and other Arabs for rejecting the framework for peace he worked

(ANWAR EL-SADAT)

out with Israel at Camp David, Md.] : . . . until today, they [the PLO] live in strife . . . and painful fighting among themselves. I do not think they should oppose the comprehensive settlement that Egypt is working for unless they have a better solution that we do not know about. Egypt is trying to save the situation from stagnation and from the vicious circle of PLO differences . . . At Camp David we have shattered stagnation without spilling one drop of blood. Why is it that some of them [in the Arab world] want this stagnation to return?

Before People's Assembly (Parliament),
Cairo, Oct. 2/Los Angeles Times, 10-3:(1)18.

1

Today we are approaching the conclusion of a peace treaty [with Israel] which will restore our full sovereignty over our land [in the Sinai], guarantee all the rights of the Palestinian people, help destroy the barriers of suspicion and bitterness, and safeguard man's right to enjoy life free of fear and the constant threat of destruction . . . To this giant of a man, a man of principles and ethics, to [U.S.] President Carter, I present my heart-felt greetings and the deepest gratitude in the name of the people of Egypt and all who struggle for love and peace as well as in my own name. Today we are building peace amidst conspiracies hatched and engineered by a superpower, the Soviet Union. The Soviet Union is using all its potential and all its agents to destroy the peace edifice.

Before Egyptian Parliament, Cairo,
Nov. 4/The Dallas Times Herald, 11-5:(A)4.

2

[On the continued difficulties in working out a peace treaty between his country and Israel] : It was in [Israeli Prime Minister Menachem] Begin's interests that we return to the state of no war, no peace [that existed before Sadat's visit to Jerusalem last year]. That would have been the most suitable situation for him to achieve his goals. [Begin faced a] terrible struggle [with himself after the Sadat visit, because peace was incompatible with Begin's

desire of] a greater Israel from the Nile to the Euphrates.

Interview, Dec. 25/
The Washington Post, 12-26:(A)1.

Mamdouh Salem
Prime Minister of Egypt

3

[Egyptian] President [Anwar] Sadat may, indeed, break with the PLO leadership in general and with [PLO leader Yasir] Arafat personally. The entire Palestinian movement is torn by factional quarrels. But anti-Palestinian feeling among Egyptians does not mean that Egypt will abandon the Palestinian cause. It remains the heart of the entire Mideast conflict.

Before Parliament, Cairo, Feb. 27/
The Christian Science Monitor, 2-28:4.

Moshe Samir
Member of Israeli
Knesset (Parliament)

4

[Criticizing Prime Minister Menachem Begin's agreement with Egyptian President Anwar Sadat on a framework for peace at the recent meeting in Camp David, Md.] : I no longer believe you [Begin], or in your leadership, or in your intentions. You have knowingly misled me and the nation. Your so-called peace agreements are a rejection of Zionism and will lead to the destruction of the Jewish state.

Before the Knesset, Jerusalem,
Sept. 28/Los Angeles Times, 9-28:(1)1.

Karim Sanjaby
Leader, National Front of Iran

5

[On the large demonstration in Teheran against the Shah] : Millions showed by this great demonstration their firm decision to end the regime of dictatorship, despotism and corruption. This great tide, despite threats and plots, demonstrates the justice of our cause.

Dec. 10/Los Angeles Times, 12-11:(1)1.

WHAT THEY SAID IN 1978

Harold Saunders
Assistant Secretary for Near
Eastern Affairs, Department of
State of the United States

1

The economies of [the Middle Eastern countries] have suffered from a common disruption: the diversion of resources and the impediment to growth that are consequences of the Arab-Israeli conflict. At this moment, as the countries of the Middle East contemplate their futures and attitudes toward the peace process, it is of utmost importance that the United States continue to display its readiness to assist them in meeting their economic-development goals.

Before Senate Foreign Relations
subcommittee, Washington, April 25/
The Washington Post, 4-26:(A)6.

Saad Shazli
Former Egyptian Ambassador to
Portugal; Former Chief of Staff,
Egyptian military forces

2

One of [Egyptian President Anwar] Sadat's big mistakes was to substitute the Soviet Union with the United States. We must find a super-power who is willing to give us weapons parity or superiority with Israel, and Washington has made it clear that it won't do this ... The Americans say we can't use their weapons against Israel, while the only condition set by the Soviet Union was that their arms not be used to destroy Israel but only to free our occupied lands ... Our main armament is still Soviet, and for the last several years we've received no spare parts. I don't think there will be another war soon because Israel is sitting on all the land it wants and we're too weak to challenge her.

Interview, Lisbon, Portugal,
June 21/Los Angeles Times, 6-22:(1)14.

Yitzak Unna
Israeli Ambassador to South Africa

3

[On the good relations between his country and South Africa] : We [Israelis] are not bless-ed with an abundance of friends. Some friends, in moments of need, turn out to be fair-weather friends and tend to leave us in the lurch. South Africa has never wavered in her attitude toward Israel.

The Washington Post, 2-8:(A)17.

Cyrus R. Vance
Secretary of State
of the United States

4

[On the U.S. plan to sell warplanes to Egypt and Saudi Arabia, as well as to Israel] : Our commitment to Israel's security has been and remains firm. Israel must have full confidence in its ability to assure its own defense. [But] Egypt, too, must have reasonable assurance of its ability to defend itself if it is to continue the peace negotiations with confidence. We believe we have a basic interest in responding to Egypt's legitimate needs. Saudi Arabia is of immense importance in promoting a course of moderation in the Middle East, with respect to peace-making and other regional initiatives, and more broadly in world affairs, as in petroleum and financial policy. The Saudi government has a legitimate requirement to modernize its very limited air defenses. We believe their request is reasonable and in our interest to fulfill.

Los Angeles Herald Examiner, 2-15:(A)4.

Lowell P. Weicker, Jr.
United States Senator,
R-Connecticut

5

[U.S. President Carter's National Security Affairs adviser Zbigniew Brzezinski's view] requires that the U.S. disengage from its historic alliance with Israel, [since] the vision of a world order always seems to require that certain groups be trimmed off in the interests of neatness. Mr. Brzezinski has said this world-order process in the Middle East must be a zig-zag effort because supporters of Israel in America will object to it. And the supporters of Israel in America, according to Brzezinski, are American Jews. It must follow, in his view, that if this vision of a new world order is thwarted, in the present cockpit of world conflict, it will

(LOWELL P. WEICKER, JR.)

be because of American Jews and because of Israel. We know from history that time and again, when national leaders ran into difficulties, they found it convenient to blame their problems on the Jews. And we know what were the results. If there is a meaningful distinction between those historical proclivities and the signals which Brzezinski is sending today, I don't know what it is. I can tell you that, if I were President and I had a national security adviser who singled out American Jews as an impediment to my policies, I would have his resignation before sundown and his reputation for breakfast.

Before American Israel Public Affairs Committee, Washington, May 8/The New York Times, 5-29:(A)6.

Ezer Weizman
Minister of Defense of Israel

1

[Criticizing the proposed U.S. sale of warplanes to Egypt and Saudi Arabia] : In the last three months, the Egyptians made serious mistakes in their conduct of the peace negotiations [with Israel] ; we may also have made some mistakes. But the recent arms deal is the American contribution to this series of mistakes ... In Egypt today, the Russians are out and the Americans are in. In the Middle East it is customary for whoever comes in to come mounted either on a tank or a plane.

Interview, Feb. 17/ The Washington Post, 2-18:(A)11.

2

For [Egyptian] President [Anwar] Sadat to come to Israel [last year] was something magnificent. But as a result of this euphoria, he expected that anything that he said or wished must be done. I told him seven weeks ago in Aswan ... "President Sadat, what you did by coming to Jerusalem I usually refer to as the equivalent of the act of the first man landing on the moon." He enjoyed this very much. But then I told him, "But, Mr. President, the first man on the moon came back to earth. The problem now is how can everyone return to earth and stop orbiting. I think you have to

realize, the Egyptians have to realize, that you cannot forget 30 years of misunderstanding, 30 years of hard battles."

Before businessmen and editors/Time, 4-10:30.

3

We've been fighting with them [the Egyptians] since we were youngsters. I've dropped bombs on them. Perhaps because we've been bleeding each other, we care more about finding out what makes the other tick. But they are all just human beings. Some are good, openhearted people and some are S.O.B.'s. We shall have to get used to being with each other, though. We'll have to overcome the results of our cultural and religious differences. For 30 years now, Israel has been hermetically sealed. We've had more in common with the British and the French than we have had with our neighbors in Egypt, or any of the other Arab countries.

Interview/The Washington Post, 10-15:(M)3.

James C. Wright, Jr.
United States Representative, D-Texas

4

Before [Egyptian President Anwar] Sadat made his move [his visit to Israel last year], most of us accepted the Israeli position in a manner that was uncritical and unquestioning. To some, it now looks like Israel is negotiating in less than good faith. There is real consternation.

U.S. News & World Report, 2-20:14.

Ahmed Zaki al-Yamani
Minister of Petroleum and Mineral Resources of Saudi Arabia

5

[On a proposed sale of military jets to his country by the U.S.]: We place great importance and significance on this transaction. We feel we badly need it. It's for our security. It is to defend Saudi Arabia. If we don't get it, then we will have a feeling you [the U.S.] are not concerned with our security and you don't appreciate our friendship.

Interview, Riyadh, Saudi Arabia, May 1/Los Angeles Times, 5-2:(1)16.

WHAT THEY SAID IN 1978

Andrew Young
United States Ambassador/Permanent Representative to the United Nations

1

[On Egyptian President Anwar Sadat's visit to Israel last year]: The Americans were so taken with the sincerity and courage of [Sadat's] peace initiative that he almost single-handedly balanced what had been an irrevocable 30-year commitment to Israel which did not consider what the Arab world wanted. [Sadat is] the most popular man in the United States, bar none, including [U.S.] President Carter, unfortunately.

Interview/The New York Times, 5-25:(C)2.

Clement J. Zablocki
United States Representative, D-Wisconsin

2

[Saying the U.S. should sell warplanes to Saudi Arabia]: ... the Saudis have been cooperative with the United States in keeping oil prices down. They have a right to say: "Well, now, if you are a friend, as we have been to you, demonstrate your friendship by selling the planes we need. We can buy them elsewhere, but we'd rather have them from you, even with some of the conditions that you have put on their use." Why shouldn't we sell these planes to Saudi Arabia to meet their defensive needs? ... Saudi Arabia has real security problems. First of all, it's a very large country with great oil wealth. She already has had problems with Iraq, which is getting modern warplanes from the Soviet Union. There are problems, too, with South Yemen, which also is supported by the Soviets. Another thing: Late last year a report was issued that stated that Iran is prepared to defend the oil fields of Saudi Arabia. No country that has any self-respect should have to depend on another country for defense and security of its borders ... If the Saudis do not buy the F-15s from the United States, they will buy the *Mirage* from France. I think it would be in Israel's interest if the Saudis buy planes from the United States, which can restrict their future misuse and transfer, and can even influence where these planes would be based.

Interview/U.S. News & World Report, 5-15:17.

Ardeshir Zahedi
Iranian Ambassador to the United States

3

[On a reason for the current anti-Shah turmoil in his country]: Think of all those boys and girls going to school in America, fresh from Iran. Here [in the U.S.] they see a heaven of democracy. Unique in industry. Unique in power. And they see the gap between America and home. Being young, loving your native Iran, having ambition, and seeing America, it makes you unhappy, disappointed, frustrated ... Whatever the frustrations in Iran, whatever is best for our country, we will do it. Iran has always been a bridge. The old silk route from China to Rome. The bridge of victory—as Churchill and Roosevelt called it in World War II—for lifeline supplies from the West to reach the Soviet Union. Over the centuries, invasions and conquests, and yet Iran is a nation. There is surprising tolerance among Iranians, and for all the ups and downs, still the love for their country will bring unity after all.

Interview, Washington/ The Washington Post, 11-10:(E)3.

The United Nations · War and Peace

Harry S. Ashmore
*Associate, Center for the Study of
Democratic Institutions*

1

I am unable to distinguish any wars I know anything about, including the one I was in, in terms of justice. The effort to make World War II a just war sort of appalls me. There is a new book in which somebody is again trying to make the distinction between bombing Dresden, which was "just," and dropping the bomb on Hiroshima, which was "unjust." This is a philosophical exercise that I simply have never been able to follow to a logical conclusion, either way.

*Panel discussion/
The Center Magazine, July-Aug.:39.*

Frank Barnaby
*Director, International Peace
Research Institute, Stockholm*

2

In our opinion, the probability of a nuclear war is increasing. The nuclear arms race is totally out of control. The politicians are not in control of their arsenals.

Stockholm/The Christian Science Monitor, 4-28:2.

Menachem Begin
Prime Minister of Israel

3

Peace is the beauty of life. It is sunshine. It is the smile of a child, the love of a mother, the joy of a father, the togetherness of a family. It is the advancement of man, the victory of a just cause, the triumph of truth. Peace is all of these and more and more.

*Accepting Nobel Peace Prize, Oslo, Norway,
Dec. 10/The New York Times, 12-11:(A)12.*

Leonid I. Brezhnev
*President of the Soviet Union;
Chairman, Soviet Communist Party*

4

During war, one gets used to danger, and, in good times, to prosperity. As long as one isn't sick, you get used to good health. For more than 30 years now, there is peace in Europe. That has never happened before. People have started to get used to peace as if it were something natural, as if detente isn't subject [to] too many trials.

*At state dinner in his honor, Bonn, West Germany,
May 4/The Washington Post, 5-5:(A)22.*

Abba Eban
*Member, Israeli Knesset (Parliament);
Former Foreign Minister of Israel*

5

I don't think that anybody should aspire to be esteemed at the UN. The UN represents international decadence at its highest pitch. It's a steamroller of what is called the Third World, the Communist world, and it has lost all of its unpredictability. The UN will do exactly what the Arabs want it to do. I don't know anybody in Israel who would include among the calculations of his policy the idea that it is important to be well considered at the UN. It is impossible. The UN is an organization that is financed by the free world for the benefit of the despoted world. That's a change that came both over its structure and its spirit.

Interview/Los Angeles Herald Examiner, 6-10:(A)9.

Takeo Fukuda
Prime Minister of Japan

6

World peace is maintained by a balance of power between East and West, between the socialist states and the free-enterprise states.

WHAT THEY SAID IN 1978

(TAKEO FUKUDA)

Although socialist countries have their economic troubles, too, it is the free world which is facing the most severe pinch. If economic troubles turn into political chaos, the strength of the free world would be damaged, thus disrupting the East-West balance and threatening the foundations of world peace.

To reporters, Tokyo, Feb. 15/
Los Angeles Times, 2-16:(3)12.

Barry M. Goldwater
United States Senator, R-Arizona

1

As presently constituted, [the United Nations] is a circus of the absurd. It has been completely politicized, oriented to the Communist viewpoint, and has adopted the double standard as its mode of operation. It is downright ludicrous that the United Nations operates under a charter so sanctimonious that it can be compared only with the Bible. There was a time when many people scaled down their expectations of an effective organization for world peace and suggested that the main value of the United Nations lay in the fact that it provided a forum for open discussion of the world's problems. But even this justification is no longer valid because too many nations actually refuse to speak because so many United Nations members would rather walk out than listen to disagreeable truth.

At Rand Afrikaans University, South Africa,
March 28/Vital Speeches, 5-15:456.

Huang Hua
Foreign Minister of the People's
Republic of (mainland) China

2

There are some people in the West today who are cowed by the Soviet military threat and are afraid of war, or who indulge in a false sense of security and deny the existence of a serious danger of war. Militarily, they seek a respite through compromises and concessions. They even dream of averting the danger threatening themselves by sacrificing the security of others. Politically, they seek peaceful cooperation to accommodate the Soviet hoax of "detente." Economically, they offer big loans and technical equipment to pacify the Soviet Union. Whether they do it knowingly or not, to pursue such policies of appeasement will only serve to camouflage and abet social imperialism's war preparations. Facts show that this superpower flaunting the label of socialism is more aggressive and adventurous than the other superpower [the U.S.]. It is the most dangerous source of a new world war and is sure to be its chief instigator.

At United Nations, New York, May 29/
Los Angeles Times, 5-30:(1)11.

David C. Jones
General, United States Air Force;
Chairman, Joint Chiefs of Staff

3

One of my worries is that we [in the U.S.] tend to "mirror image." We tend to examine a problem using our mores, our background and our values, and come to a conclusion, and then assume the Soviets come to the same conclusion. That's very dangerous. The Soviets may see the world much differently than we do. For example, in the strategic field, we in the U.S. regard strategic nuclear war as basically unthinkable. Soviet doctrine talks about it as being thinkable.

Interview/U.S. News & World Report, 10-30:52.

Edward M. Kennedy
United States Senator,
D-Massachusetts

4

The overriding priority of the United States must be the prevention of nuclear war and, therefore, the establishment of cooperative relations among the nuclear powers. Only by avoiding unparalleled destruction can we turn with confidence and hope to the great tasks of construction and social equity ahead of us.

San Francisco Examiner & Chronicle,
3-5:(This World)2.

Edgar F. Magnin
Rabbi, Wilshire Boulevard Temple,
Los Angeles

1

Even if you win a war, you lose. You lose something. You gain nothing in the long run, except that you still live. Billions of dollars go to waste blowing up property, blowing up human life. It's stupid, it's silly and it's worthless . . . People don't create wars. Governments create wars. The average man or woman doesn't want war, because he or she is the victim.

Interview/Los Angeles
Herald Examiner, 10-20:(A)1,10.

Mengistu Haile Mariam
Head of the Revolutionary Council
of Ethiopia

2

While gracing their cities with skyscrapers and fragrant and scented flowers, imperialists are callously experimenting with their weaponry on the oppressed peoples of the world. What more outrageous crimes could be committed by man against his fellow man?

Los Angeles Times, 3-5:(1)14.

Paul VI
Pope

3

Who today can measure the tragedy of the dangers that science and technology have turned against human life, that can dash the face of the earth? If a madman became chief of a nation that had these weapons, what would happen to humanity? We have already seen sad episodes that have produced scars that have yet to disappear. . . . the danger has grown immensely, with instruments refined by intelligence to kill and humiliate, to smash down and dominate. All of this is a colossal mistake.

Vatican City, June 21/
The Washington Post, 6-23:(A)30.

Helmut Schmidt
Chancellor of West Germany

4

What's important is to maintain an objective, psychologically credible countervailing power to deter would-be aggressors. I strongly believe in the balance of power. We should also try to reduce tensions, extinguish fires wherever possible, maintain the balance at lower levels to release new economic forces for the well-being of people instead of defense. To be credible, however, you must be decisive.

Interview, Hamburg,
Newsweek, 5-29:56.

John K. Singlaub
Major General, United States Army
(Ret.); Former Chief of Staff,
Army Forces Command

5

The men in the Kremlin are born-again Bolsheviks, not born-again Christians. The surest road to peace is unchallengeable strength; history proves that weakness is the road to war.

San Francisco Examiner & Chronicle,
7-23:(This World)2.

Sunao Sonoda
Foreign Minister of Japan

6

When thinking of the world's future, China operates on the premise that some day war is inevitable. We in Japan believe that we must do everything possible to avert war . . . Whether people call me a coward, whether they call me un-Japanese, I shall never tire of my search for peace, nor give up my feeling that war must be prevented at all costs, by whatever means.

Interview, Tokyo/
The Christian Science Monitor, 7-19:9.

PART THREE

General

The Arts

Edward Albee
Playwright

1

Around the time John Kennedy was elected President, something rather marvelous happened. We had an artistic and cultural explosion. Suddenly there was Genet, Beckett, Ionesco, Off-Broadway. Theatre departments on college campuses started to admit that there were playwrights who were still alive. The government began to realize that it had a responsibility to the arts. We saw the beginning of an education to the metaphor. It was an exciting time. But in the late 1960s, concurrent with a repressive Administration [in Washington], there came an intellectual retrenchment, feeling that we must ask the arts to comfort us, to lie to us, to become our servant.
Interview, Palo Alto, Calif./
Los Angeles Times, 10-15:(Calendar)6.

2

The condition of the arts in a commodity-oriented society is perilous. Television and film postulate that that which sells the greatest number of tickets is of the most merit. This hides under the notion that, in a democracy, the public must be given what it wants. But it just means that we'll give the public what it will most easily accept.
At University of California, Los Angeles,
Oct. 17/The Hollywood Reporter, 10-19:23.

Joseph Alsop
Former political columnist

3

[Patronage of the arts] has all but vanished. In the abnormal situation of the 20th century, almost all art is made for the market, without a patron's intervention. I cannot take time to explain how abnormal this is. There has in fact been nothing like it before in the world history of art.
Andrew W. Mellon Lecture, Washington, June 5/
The Washington Post, 6-6:(B)11.

Mikhail Baryshnikov
Ballet dancer

4

Art reaches people like a common language. I think that art, by its very nature, has a humanizing influence on situations, and this is good for the world ... I don't find audiences different anywhere in the world. If the dancing is good, audiences are always enthusiastic no matter where you are.
Interview/U.S. News & World Report, 4-24:54.

Saul Bellow
Author

5

There are very few poets and writers in the wealthy community. The universities are at fault; those that had the opportunity to educate the sons and daughters of the rich—they sent them back to their country clubs and their guilt-rich offices and their businesses, without having laid a hand on them. They taught them virtually nothing about poetry or art, and we live with the consequences. We live in a business society and a business struggle, and both the artists and laborers are part of the business struggle. Everything is business.
Interview/The Christian Science Monitor, 3-2:24.

Leonard Bernstein
Composer, Conductor

6

Artists ... are very sensitive to what goes on around them, and they are the first people to strike for freedom, because freedom is essential in artistic expression ... Therefore, the artist is

WHAT THEY SAID IN 1978

the first one to go out in the streets and march, the first one to sign a manifesto and to organize a protest. The artist is the first one to say, "I am a dissenter." And sometimes this leads the artist to dissent artistically and to make him go further than he would ordinarily, just to exercise his rebelliousness and to make the point that he is a free man.

Los Angeles Herald Examiner, 8-20: (F) 10.

Livingston Biddle, Jr.
Chairman, National Endowment for the Arts of the United States

1

Today, more than 50 per cent of the public takes part in some manner of cultural activity. Orchestras and opera companies have doubled in the past 10 years. Dance companies have increased seven times—from 10 to 70. As the arts increase in scope and meaning, they appeal more and more to diverse groups who didn't enjoy them a decade ago . . . People are finding that the arts enrich their lives. Wherever the arts touch lives, they increase awareness. They excite imagination. They open eyes and ears and minds to new perceptions. I think the arts can do more for the individual and his appreciation of life than any other aspect of our national life.

Interview/U.S. News & World Report, 3-20:59.

Robert Bishop
Director, Museum of American Folk Art, New York

2

I don't know anyone who collects [art] simply for money. They collect for love. They like to wake in the morning and see something that thrills them. Once you're bitten, it's all over.

Time, 2-13:51.

Winton M. Blount
Chairman, Blount, Inc.; Former Postmaster General of the United States

3

. . . it is arguable whether a high quality of life is a necessity for society as, say, capital or the law. But I would place art in the category

of law, and capital and freedom and opportunity as a fundamental requirement for maintaining any society fit for the human spirit. I do not think it is a coincidence that those societies which we remember as having an important influence on the course of civilization have always been receptive to an encouraging of art and the artist, and not just the graphic arts. I mean art to include theatre, poetry, architecture and music as well. From the amphitheatres of Athens, where any citizen might go to see and hear the works of the great Greek playwrights, to the concerts and plays in Central Park, we see the good society verifying those things which are of value to itself by making art available to its citizens.

At "Business in the Arts Awards" ceremony, Los Angeles, June 15/ Vital Speeches, 8-15:666.

J. Carter Brown
Director, National Gallery of Art, Washington

4

It is shocking to realize how many Americans are visually illiterate—ignorant about paintings, sculpture and other visual arts that are so important to our culture. People get into universities without having the first clue as to how to use their eyes critically and without grasping the cultural significance of what constitutes our common heritage. Some study of the visual arts should be as much a part of the core curriculum in elementary and secondary schools as the verbal arts and other basics. Museums can be helpful in that—and some already are. They are interpreting art to the public, providing educational programs and cooperating with public schools. But we still have a long way to go.

Interview/U.S. News & World Report, 11-20:96.

Jimmy Carter
President of the United States

5

In an open society, like our own, the relationship between government and art must necessarily be a delicate one. We have no ministry of culture in this country and I hope we never will. We have no "official art" in this

(JIMMY CARTER)

country and I pray we never will. It can never be government's role to define exactly what is true, good or beautiful. Instead, government must limit itself to nourishing the ground in which art and the love of art can grow.

At opening of East Wing of National Gallery
of Art, Washington, June 1/
The Dallas Times Herald, 6-2:(A)7.

Schuyler Chapin
Dean, School of Arts, Columbia
University; Former general manager,
Metropolitan Opera, New York

1

We're in a tremendously exciting period of artistic flowering in this country, a maturity of the American spirit after 201 years. And in this disagreeable, plastic, middle-echelon world, we're increasingly going to need the strength of spirit that comes from the arts.

Interview, New York/
The Dallas Times Herald, 5-16:(B)5.

Van Cliburn
Pianist

2

All the great strides we have made in the arts in this country [the U.S.] have been largely due to private enterprise and the personal initiative of philanthropic people who have a burning desire to share the strength and comfort of the divine mystery of great art with as many people as possible. The quest for beauty and spiritual consolation is deeply inherent in all of us. The increase in interest in the arts and attendance will be spurred on as people have more time to think and meditate, and thus want to do something with their leisure time that is both constructive and soul-satisfying. Great art is not only nourishing—it is totally compelling.

Interview/U.S. News & World Report, 12-4:75.

Agnes de Mille
Choreographer

3

[On the average American's attitude toward the arts] : It has been terrible because it comes

right from our earliest history, the beginning history when we were living very hard lives—the lives of pioneers, deprived in every sense. We had to learn what was useful and what was good and what was necessary, and we valued what was useful above all else. If a thing wasn't useful to us in a practical way, it had no use, no value. A man who just played the fiddle or wrote poetry was considered a time-waster, and the community would just indulge him by permitting it. But gradually, as we became more comfortable and richer, we found a need for some of the arts. We had them. We had artists, but we didn't trust them. We're very insolent. We're colonists still in our own view of ourselves. I think it's true even in Hollywood, at least it was in the days that I worked here. "If he came from England, he was much better"— not necessarily, of course.

Interview, Los Angeles/
Los Angeles Herald Examiner, 6-20:(A)17.

Bob Dylan
Singer, Songwriter

4

The myth of the starving artist *is* a myth. The big bankers and prominent young ladies who buy art started it. They just want to keep the artist under their thumb. Who says an artist can't have any money? Look at Picasso. The starving artist is usually starving for those around him to starve. You don't have to starve to be a good artist. You just have to have love, insight and a strong point of view. And you have to fight off depravity. Uncompromising, that's what makes a good artist. It doesn't matter if he has money or not. Look at Matisse; he was a banker. Anyway, there are other things that constitute wealth and poverty besides money.

Interview/Playboy, March:90.

Paul H. Elicker
President, SCM Corporation

5

. . . as far as I can see, corporate sponsorship [of the arts], rather than restraining freedom, has had the effect of *furthering* freedom in the arts. There seems to be a much greater balance among all the influences on art than has ever

WHAT THEY SAID IN 1978

(PAUL H. ELICKER)

existed at any prior time in history. The arts are no longer dependent on any one sector for sole support; they can look to government, to private individuals, to foundations—and now to corporations—for support. In a very real sense, corporate sponsorship has helped to emancipate art from the drawing-rooms of the very rich and powerful. A much broader constituency is now being served.

At Arts and Business Council Encore Awards luncheon, New York, Oct. 24/ Vital Speeches, 12-15:149.

Bernard L. Faber
Executive director, Center for Study of Public Policy in the Arts

1

We tend to see the arts as a very pure and pristine kind of concern.... we think art shouldn't be sullied by practical concerns and political considerations. It's one of those myths that surround the arts.

The Washington Post Magazine, 7-30:10.

Joseph Farrell
Vice chairman, Louis Harris Associates (public-opinion analysts); Vice chairman, National Research Center of the Arts

2

[In a survey,] around 40 per cent of those who said the arts were very important never go to the theatre and 75 per cent never go to a classical-music event. A large number said they'd never been exposed to the arts as children, while the frequent goers all had been exposed. It's that gap that's involved. It's the name of the game. We've got to get quality arts to more people.

Panel discussion sponsored by Club 100, Los Angeles, Jan. 18/ Los Angeles Times, 1-20:(4)14.

Robert Fitzpatrick
President, California Institute of the Arts

3

Money is the name of the game at private school. It tears my heart out to know that some qualified students can't attend CalArts because they lack funds. It hurts deeply to realize a Renoir, a Rodin or a Stravinsky might be standing outside the gates, kept out by high costs. But, unlike a medical institution, whose alumni can help, a school of the arts doesn't turn out many money-making graduates ... The cost crisis is just a little worse in a place like this because families are less than delighted with their kids' future prospects. I mean, what's in store for a child pursuing the creative arts? When parents come to visit and ask questions, I tell them frankly, "Look, after a four-year superb education at CalArts, your offspring is probably going to be on governmental or parental food stamps for at least two years." This is the nature of what it means to be an artist in our society.

Interview/Los Angeles Times, 4-23:(Home)53.

Thomas P. F. Hoving
Former director, Metropolitan Museum of Art, New York

4

The great sources [of art] are drying up. Art is not around to be acquired the way it was a decade or two ago, and it's going to get worse. There are ways of collecting now that are not linked to full ownership. I would go after the larger institutions in the United States and impress upon them their obligations to make loans of certain things on a rotating basis. These ways of acquiring are going to have to be initiated in this era when one can't just go into a gallery and say, "How many Matisses do you have, 20? I'll take one."

Dallas/The Dallas Times Herald, 2-21:(B)6.

Peter C. Marzio
Director-designate, Corcoran Gallery of Art, Washington

5

In my opinion, a museum fails if it does not interest the scholarly community. We are also the one museum in town where local artists should exhibit. We'll show student work. And we're a museum of modern art. These missions must be balanced. First we must raise money. It's a chicken-and-egg problem. You can't do

(PETER C. MARZIO)

anything if you don't have money, and if you don't do anything you can't raise dough.

The Washington Post, 5-10:(B)3.

Rollo May
Psychologist, Author

1

Real creativity is very close to psychosis. Creative people are often the most disturbed. They feel compelled to write, paint, compose music and so forth. The goal must always be to help them channel their energy and drive into artistry, but never to thwart their neurotic tendencies, because that can mean an end to creativity. Now, what's the distinction between channeling and thwarting? The artist's function is to look at the chaos of the world and present it in an esthetically clear form or style. I know what I'm talking about, because I write books and paint pictures. I'm very much a believer in chaos as a necessary ingredient.

Interview/Los Angeles Times, 6-25:(Home)28.

James McCracken
Opera Singer

2

Sadly, there is a terrible financial crisis for the arts [in the U.S.] at the same time that audiences are growing so fast. There just aren't as many rich people around who are willing to support the arts, and it's going to take some big government subsidies to make up the deficits. Some opera enthusiasts are against government help because they are afraid of government interference. But I've always said: "Let's try it." It's better to have people telling you how to do it than no opera at all.

Interview/U.S. News & World Report, 1-23:57.

Joan Mondale
Honorary Chairman, Federal Council on the Arts and Humanities

3

I think it's a tragic mistake the way state and local boards of education have cut out arts education in the schools. In part, this reflects the back-to-basics movement and the anti-tax mood in the country. Schools have said, "Well, the arts are a frill. We don't need them. Slice." The Federal government somehow is going to have to provide financial assistance for arts education. Children aren't automatons who do nothing but read, write, add and subtract. They're human beings, and the arts help them to express their feelings, to think, to create, to use their imagination. When we don't develop these skills in our children, they grow up as incomplete people. That's the paradox in our country today. There are incredibly large audiences for the arts. And then the school board cuts out any training or perception or sensitivity or experience on the part of the schoolchildren.

Interview/U.S. News & World Report, 10-23:72.

I. M. Pei
Architect

4

It is not an individual act, architecture. You have to consider your client. Only out of that can you produce great architecture. You can't work in the abstract.

Interview/The Washington Post, 5-14:(F)15.

Nelson A. Rockefeller
Former Vice President of the United States

5

.... I like modern art better than representational art, because in representational art the subject is so powerful that the appreciation becomes intellectual. You know the subject and lose track of the art, because the subject dominates. But in abstract or semi-abstract art you see something different every time, depending on your mood ... I'm embarrassed to say that this is not a conscious process or a very intellectual process. It's an emotional one. I can go through the most difficult political or business problems, government problems, and then lose myself in looking at paintings, looking at books or sculpture, and just cut it off.

*Interview, New York/
The Christian Science Monitor, 4-26:17.*

WHAT THEY SAID IN 1978

Herbert Ross
Motion-picture and stage director

1

As our times grow more depressed and troubling, I strongly feel a need for formal structure, for values, for centuries-old good attitudes that our culture and civilization have bequeathed us. In music, ballet and other arts, I feel the explosion of *avant-gardism* drawing to an inevitable conclusion. We'll see more of a classical tradition.

Interview, New York/
The Christian Science Monitor, 1-30:15.

Herbert Schmertz
Vice president for public affairs,
Mobil Oil Corporation

2

I think financial support of the arts is in transition. We've gone through a period where it was basically private philanthropy that did it. I think that is finished. The arts are in a state of flux, trying to find new sources of financial support. I would hope that what will emerge is a wide diversity of financial sources, so that nobody has to rely ... on any particular source. I think it's important that the public support the arts through admissions or contributions. The foundations should be helping; labor unions should also be doing it; corporations and government also in some fashion ... I think we have an arts explosion in this country, and we're going to see much wider citizen's participation, foundation participation, government participation and, I am sure, corporate participation. But let me say that corporate participation is really citizens' participation in the sense that we are spending shareholders' money on this.

Interview, New York/
The Christian Science Monitor, 4-3:26.

Saul Steinberg
Artist, Cartoonist

3

I enjoy selling the rights of reproduction. In that way I consider myself to be doing the work of a poet who prints the words but keeps the manuscript. I kept most of my original drawings. I believe every artist in the world would like to sell only the rights of reproduction. Except for the ones who make giant paintings—they are very happy to get rid of them. And sculptors—there is nothing more tragic than the unsuccessful sculptor, faced constantly by his large, reproachful objects.

Interview/Time, 4-17:96.

4

The doodle is the brooding of the hand.

Time, 10-16:88.

Rufino Tamayo
Painter

5

I will not paint the raised fist. I will not be a demagogue. I was against the political in art from the very beginning ... I have joined none of the art groups that have formed in my country [Mexico]. All of them attempt to build some sort of "Mexican School." I don't believe in that. Art is universal. We can only add to art the accent that was given us in the place where we were born. The subject matter of a painting is of small importance.

Interview/The Washington Post, 10-6:(D)5.

Richard Thomas
Actor

6

The talk about censoring television shows worries me. Once in a while you hear people say they would like to have a newspaper that only prints good news. But that's unrealistic. That sort of newspaper wouldn't last long. The same thing is true in the arts. Art isn't art that represents only the rosy side of life.

Interview/U.S. News & World Report, 2-13:87.

Elie Abel
Dean, School of Journalism,
Columbia University

1

Where news is concerned, the essential complaint of Third World intellectuals and government officials boils down to these: That the peoples of the developing countries are forced to see the world, including their own regions, through foreign eyes, those eyes belonging to staff reporters for the major Western news agencies—AP, UPI, Agence France-Press and Reuter. That much of the output they receive is superficial or irrelevant or marred by ethnocentric bias. That the big four agencies are treating news as a commodity, rather than as a social good. That indigenous cultures and value systems tend to be undermined by the unceasing flow of alien perceptions. And finally, that the achievements of Third World countries in developing their own resources and skills get short shrift from agency reporters who are captives of their traditional news formula—that, for example, a *coup d'etat* or an earthquake is bigger news than the dedication in the same country of a new dam or a clinic or a fertilizer factory.

At United Nations Association seminar, New York/
The Christian Science Monitor, 10-25:22.

Roone Arledge
President, American Broadcasting
Company News

2

[On broadcast news anchor people] : They're indispensable. They're the glue that holds a newscast together. They are the front page that tells people what news show it is they're watching. They provide familiarity. And, presumably, they are also your best reporters. There's no question that they become stars and that people tune in to watch news stars the same

way they do other kinds of celebrities. I think if we can change the role of the anchor people so that they do less reading and more reporting, that would be desirable.

Interview/U.S. News & World Report, 11-20:54.

Ben H. Bagdikian
Professor of journalism,
University of California, Berkeley;
Former editor, "The Washington Post"

3

The small number of private corporations that are increasingly gaining control over our mass media do not have government powers, but they are too small a group of fallible human beings to have such unified control. Even if they should be philosopher-saints in their wisdom, this country was founded on the theory that no small group, even philosopher-saints, should have so much power over public information and discourse.

At conference on media concentration, Washington/
The Christian Science Monitor, 12-18:4.

Griffin B. Bell
Attorney General of the United States

4

I fully understand that the press plays an important role in our society. The press, together with the Congress and public opinion, make up our society's system of official accountability. They are the means by which policy is examined and explained. In Great Britain, a principal instrument of accountability is the question hour in the House of Commons, in which the government is examined, often to its discomfort, on matters of policy or conduct. Press conferences fill much the same role in the United States. Since the days of the first President, press and government have been wary and sometimes hostile adversaries. No one with any pretention to serious understanding of this

WHAT THEY SAID IN 1978

(GRIFFIN B. BELL)

complex political process would wish that to change.

Before American Society of Newspaper Editors,
Washington/Los Angeles
Herald Examiner, 4-23:(E)1.

1

. . . applying the usual rules regarding [police] searches to the media poses a particular threat to the independence and function of a free press in a democratic society. Those who gather and disseminate information to the public must rely heavily on persons both within and without government to disclose instances of wrongdoing, inefficiency or neglect of duty. At the heart of the newsgathering function is the sensitive, fragile relationship between a reporter and his or her source. That relationship could be seriously jeopardized by the fear that the reporter's solemn pledge of confidentiality will be negated by a police search of the reporter's files. The interest of the media in this regard is not unlike that we in law enforcement have as it concerns our informants and sources. The danger is not diminished merely because the power to search may be invoked only on rare occasions by the law-enforcement officials, since the potential exercise of that power alone may chill sources on which the media and the public at large depend.

The Washington Post, 12-17:(D)6.

Benjamin C. Bradlee
Executive editor, "The Washington
Post"

2

[On the recent Supreme Court ruling upholding unannounced searches of news-media offices for evidence in criminal investigations by police with search warrants]: How the [Court] majority can conclude that the threat and the fact of police searches of newspaper offices doesn't strike freedom of the press a crippling blow is beyond understanding. The "Pentagon Papers" could never have been published. The police would have entered newspaper offices and seized them before news-

papers could bring the facts to the people. If this decision were in force during Watergate, it requires no stretch of the imagination to see police in these offices on a fishing expedition for Messrs. Nixon, Mitchell, Haldeman, Ehrlichman and company. The requirement of a warrant is no real protection, for the government can always find a judge to issue a warrant. It's just plain awful.

May 31/The Washington Post, 6-1:(A)7.

David Brinkley
News commentator, National
Broadcasting Company

3

Why doesn't TV devote more air time to the news and do it more thoroughly? Because the local affiliated stations will not give us the air time, and by law we cannot force them. Why doesn't TV do more news documentaries on serious subjects? We do a fair number of them, simply because we think we ought to, and we don't do more because nobody looks at them . . . We can put on a documentary about the gross national product, but we cannot force anyone to look at it. And most of them won't . . . Many nights there is next to nothing [to report] . . . People have the illusion that all over the world all kinds of sensational events are happening all the time. The fact is that over most of the world, most of the time, nothing is happening.

At University of Southern California, March 13/
The Hollywood Reporter, 3-14:4.

John Chancellor
News commentator, National
Broadcasting Company

4

[On his being an anchorman rather than a field man]: I'll tell you what I miss. I miss getting out, covering stories. I originally wanted to be an anchorman because I figured my legs were gone. I had been running for a long time, and I didn't want to end up at age 60 as the guy in the rain outside the Foreign Ministry at 2 in the morning. The other side of that is I want to get back to reporting.

Interview/Los Angeles Times, 1-3:(4)11.

Connie Chung
News commentator, KNXT, Los Angeles;
Former news correspondent, Columbia
Broadcasting System Television

1

There is a great demand for there to be strong personalities in TV [news broadcasting]. No one can deny this is a little bit of show business; anyone denying it is kidding themselves. Big names in news are personalities. The key is that many local anchors are just personalities; they don't have news backgrounds. I am opposed to this. I'm against someone being just a pretty face.

Interview, Los Angeles/
Daily Variety, 2-9:17.

Walter Cronkite
News commentator, Columbia
Broadcasting System

2

[Saying most of today's television newscasters do not have experience working on newspapers]: . . . it seems to be better to have had that newspaper training. So many today never have had a chance to learn how to organize a story beyond the second paragraph. If you don't know how to organize a story down to the 23rd paragraph, how can you know enough to be able to distill it down to the two paragraphs you're going to have on the air? The most frightening thing of all is that there's a whole new set of ambitions. Going through communications schools and out into the broadcasting world, they have the objective of being stars. They view journalism as a ladder to personal glorification.

Interview, Beverly Hills, Calif./
San Francisco Examiner & Chronicle,
3-5:(Datebook)38.

3

. . . TV today is doing things on a daily basis which are as hard-hitting as some of the things that [the late broadcast news reporter Edward R.] Murrow is properly praised for. Reporters today hit harder, ask tougher questions, do investigative reporting which is not even called that any more. If there is any problem with the young journalists today it is that they're all steamed up to do investigative reporting, and there's not very much to investigate—at least on the scale they would like. They don't have enough crises to live with. If news coverage seems to be softer, it is not only because of intent in some cases; it is often because the news itself may be softer.

Interview, New York/
The Christian Science Monitor, 3-24:21.

4

We [at CBS] have been a leader in good, solid, ethical journalism. We have eschewed the show-business aspects as much as possible. We've hired solid news people rather than "show people." We have remained absolutely free of influence, either political or commercial. All these things have given us a reputation for solidity, honesty and integrity. I'm lucky enough to be the front-man for that . . . I'm critical of many local newscasts—not all of them, by any means. I'm critical of the attempt to turn them into show business, to hire the attractive performer rather than the good reporter, writer or editor. And asking them to "relate" with the other members of the "cast" demeans the news and uses up time which they should not have.

Interview/Los Angeles Herald Examiner, 10-15:(A)1.

Lester Crystal
President, National Broadcasting
System News

5

The informality in the news started at a network level when [broadcasters] Chet Huntley and David Brinkley said "Good night" to each other and talked to each other in the convention and election programs. But that was information delivered in an informal style. The trouble with [many of today's] "happy talk" [news shows] is that it's inanity or lack of information delivered in an informal style. It is silly talk, not happy talk.

Interview/U.S. News & World Report, 11-20:54.

WHAT THEY SAID IN 1978

Allen Drury
Author; Former journalist

1

In my books I've suggested the press is not necessarily without flaws. I've knocked it for irresponsibility. I've observed it can't be reformed from the outside but must initiate its own reforms from within, aiming always at bringing balance, perspective, honesty, fairness toward those with whom it doesn't agree.

Interview, Tiburon, Calif./
Los Angeles Times, 5-28:(Home)40.

James E. Duffy
President, American Broadcasting
Company Television Network

2

[Saying broadcast and print journalism serve to build interest in each other]: You see this perhaps most clearly in the big stories of our time. Watergate, for example, was a print story, the work of investigative journalism. But it took television to bring the story home with impact to the mass of American people, not only in television news coverage but especially in the televised hearings of the Senate Select Committee and the House Judiciary Committee. On the other hand, the tragedy of the Vietnam war came across first in the visual form on television, the precondition for the hard-hitting analyses and commentary of the print media.

Before Audit Bureau of Circulation, Los Angeles,
Nov. 8/Los Angeles Times, 11-9:(4)25.

Betty Cole Dukert
Producer, "Meet the Press," National
Broadcasting Company Television

3

To be a good television journalist you also need to be an excellent reporter. Although you may have [only] 30 seconds or a minute and a half to deliver, unless your judgment is good and your selection wise, your superficiality will come through. To be brief sometimes is harder than to be more lengthy.

Interview/Los Angeles Herald Examiner, 12-28:(A)12.

Myron A. Farber
Reporter, "The New York Times."

4

[On his refusal to turn over story material from his files as ordered by a judge in a murder trial]: If I give up my file, I will have undermined my professional integrity and diminished the credibility of my colleagues. And, most important, I will have given notice that the nation's premier newspaper is no longer available to those men and women who would seek it out—or those who would respond to it—to talk freely and without fear . . . I did not join my profession to cloak myself in the First Amendment or to flaunt it. But I cannot cast aside my obligations as a reporter simply because they are being contested. The inevitable result of my compliance with this order would be my conversion as an investigative agent for the parties in this case.

San Francisco Examiner & Chronicle,
7-30:(This World)8.

Clay Felker
President and editor,
"Esquire" magazine

5

Two things are responsible for the magazine comeback. First, there is a strategic change in what magazines do. The magazines that overlapped television died—magazines like *The Saturday Evening Post* and *Life*. *Life* had still pictures, television had moving pictures; same thing with *Look*. Television was simply a more dynamic, visual media. *The Saturday Evening Post* and *Colliers* couldn't exist because their basis was the short story, and television does the short story better. What television doesn't do, that print can do, is provide in-depth reporting.

Interview/Los Angeles Herald Examiner, 2-27:(A)2.

Jerry W. Friedheim
Executive vice president, American
Newspaper Publishers Association

6

Every day, newspapers are involved in gathering information and reporting to the

(JERRY W. FRIEDHEIM)

people concerning the operation of government—including the police, the prosecutors and the courts. Much of this information comes from confidential sources—people who would not or could not publicly provide this information about alleged abuses or outright criminality. This flow of information—vital if the press is to fulfill its watchdog function for the public—could slow to a trickle if newspapers can no longer guarantee confidentiality ... Similarly, the investigatory spirit of a newspaper itself may be sapped in some instances. It would be regrettable but understandable for a reporter to be reluctant to pursue leads if he knew that perhaps the target of his story, or the target's friends, could obtain a warrant and uncover all of the reporter's information and sources.

Before Senate Constitution Subcommittee,
Washington, July 13/Vital Speeches, 9-15:722.

Fred W. Friendly
Professor of journalism, Columbia
University; Former president,
Columbia Broadcasting System News

1

Many local [TV] news directors are so frightened of ratings that they pursue the worst values, because in the short term that's where the audiences are. They trivialize the news, making the weather more important than Mideast events or the SALT negotiations.

U.S. News & World Report, 11-20:51.

Henry Geller
Administrator, National Telecommunications
and Information Administration of the
United States

2

[On the broadcast Fairness Doctrine]: It's very troublesome on an issue-by-issue basis. In trying to insure fairness, the FCC has to cull out everything in the subject before it makes a determination of "reasonable" fairness. But the FCC can't act evenly. The broadcaster doesn't know if he's been fair or not until the FCC tells him one way or the other. The FCC makes the

determination—and the FCC is the government. That's no good. I wouldn't scrap the Fairness Doctrine, but would like to see it used differently. Instead of applying it case-by-case, I'd look for over-all patterns, at stations, of malice or flagrant disregard for truth. When the FCC finds such a pattern, it could tell the broadcaster he's not of good character and, therefore, not entitled to keep his license.

Interview, Washington/
The New York Times, 7-18:(C)17.

Ellen Goodman
Newspaper columnist

3

I'm very aware that my column wraps up fish the next day. But that doesn't bother me. I'm writing for the moment. When you start thinking you're writing for posterity, you're less a journalist and more a pedant.

Interview, Brookline, Mass./
TWA Ambassador, March:36.

Paul Harvey
News commentator, American
Broadcasting Company

4

... I have a tremendous amount of respect for the freedom that I have [as a newscaster]. I don't abuse it. But I realize that a lot of Paul Harveys might be a scary proposition for the networks—the idea of one man out in the hinterlands, going virtually unchecked. I don't know if the opportunity exists for others to do what I've been doing. The network news as it stands now is a corporate product. I suppose it has to be. But with cable television coming on strong, with no one knowing its potential, maybe we will get back to the individual, the one man out there pounding a typewriter. I hope so.

Interview, Los Angeles/
Los Angeles Times, 10-8:(Calendar)3.

Tomoo Hirooka
Chairman, "Asahi Shimbun," Tokyo

5

[On his newspaper's huge circulation]: We need competition. It's good for Japanese journalism and Japan. Our democracy is still new and weak. If a dictator like the military in the 1930s ever showed up again, one good newspaper might be easy to handle. But if there are many, then the people and their freedoms are stronger.

Interview, Tokyo/
The New York Times, 3-19:(3)3.

Jesse L. Jackson
President, Operation PUSH (People
United to Save Humanity)

1

The media is a primary transmitter of folkways, mores and values, and thus, with that tremendous increase in power, its responsibility must be comparable ... From purely a point of view of inner-city black children, the media tends to project us as less intelligent than we are; it projects us as less hard-working than we work; it projects us as more violent than we are, and as being less universal than we are. In part, that is because the mass media—even though it has the power of appraisal—of 40,000 daily journalists, less than 1,700 are black. Of 1,769 daily newspapers, only five have blacks in executive positions. And so the mass media, which assumes the role to appraise and judge the entire society, must radically make some adjustments.

TV-radio interview/"Meet the Press,"
National Broadcasting Company, 5-21.

Hamilton Jordan
Assistant to President of the
United States Jimmy Carter

2

I can't remember five times since I've known Jimmy Carter where he has displayed any anger with a newspaper or magazine article. There are things he reads that he likes and some that he does not like, but he has developed a very mature and realistic attitude about the press. That attitude is that, by and large, the press is responsible. There are some people in the press who do an excellent job, some who do a poor job, and most of them are somewhere in the

middle. But I would discount all this stuff about some kind of paranoia or siege mentality [about the press] at the White House.

Interview, Washington/
U.S. News & World Report, 5-22:24.

Joseph Kraft
Political columnist

3

I can write about anything I want. The range that is open to you lends some enchantment to the job and gives you a sense of freedom. I get up in the morning and I like what I have to do. I'm interested in understanding new things. In that sense, I suppose I'm almost juvenile or adolescent. But for journalists, I think that's necessary.

Interview, Washington/
"W": a Fairchild publication, 10-13:5.

Philip B. Kurland
Professor of law,
University of Chicago

4

[Saying newsmen do not have the Constitutional right to keep their information and sources confidential when, for example, they are demanded in a court of law]: I feel that way for two reasons: One, because the Supreme Court has said there is no such right. Reporters can live in a dream world and say, "We know what the Constitution says, and the Supreme Court doesn't." But, as the law exists today, the press doesn't have that right. Second, because the right of freedom of speech and press is given to everybody, not just the institutional press. The use of the word "press" at the time it was put into the First Amendment did not denote newspapers or magazines but anybody who was engaged in the printed rather than the spoken word. So there's no reason to say there's a greater privilege for the institutional press than for the individual who seeks to publish his views ... Not long ago, the press maintained that even the President of the United States can't be a judge in his own case. The same holds true for the press. Reporters have to obey the law like everyone else.

Interview/U.S. News & World Report, 10-9:71.

Jack C. Landau
Director, Reporters Committee for
Freedom of the Press

1

The First Amendment to the Constitution says that the press is supposed to be immune from government. By requiring reporters to disclose sources, government hampers the press from collecting information. If you can't collect it, you can't publish it. This is clearly contrary to the First Amendment. While the press has always made this First Amendment argument very strongly, it seems to me there's also First Amendment argument relating to freedom of association. A reporter should be free to circulate through the community. He should be free to talk with people and to have those people have the assurance that their identities aren't going to be disclosed . . . We are not putting ourselves above the law any more than a major law firm is putting itself above the law when it asserts its attorney-client privilege. The lawyers say, "We have to have a confidentiality privilege or else we can't do our job." The press says, "We have to have a confidentiality privilege or we can't do our jobs." If you want to look at the social impact, the lawyer is protecting only a single individual. But in a case like Watergate, the reporters may be protecting thousands, maybe millions, of individuals.

Interview/U.S. News & World Report, 10-9:71.

William Leonard
Executive vice president, and
president-designate, Columbia
Broadcasting System News

2

I come down on the side of those who believe that we have an obligation to report what's out there and what's important by the standards of trained journalists, whether or not it is what people "want." News is what's important and what's interesting, and we need some combination of the two. It's obvious that you're not doing a very good job if everybody turns you off. On the other hand, you may be doing a dreadful job if everybody turns you on simply to satisfy their preconceptions or their amusement.

Interview/U.S. News & World Report, 11-20:53.

John V. Lindsay
Commentator, American Broadcasting
Company; Former Mayor of New York

3

I'd prefer not to see any journalist join any political administration. It's fraught with danger. An administration only wants loyalists—believe me, I know—and no matter how professional the guy is when he goes back to reporting, he's going to have a credibility problem—a public perception of continuing partisan loyalty.

Los Angeles Times, 2-28:(1)3.

Leonard H. Marks
Secretary-treasurer, World Press
Freedom Committee

4

. . . some Third World countries candidly admit that they cannot afford the luxury of a free world press. Their developing society and institutions are too fragile to stand the criticism of Western-style journalists and the second-guessing of commentators and columnists which is a fixture on the American scene. Instead, they regard the journalist as a servant of society with a responsibility to carry out the programs of the government and to promote its objectives. For this role there is a new phrase—developmental journalism . . . The world benefits when there is a multiplicity of news sources and differing views. It is the choice of viewpoints which is a most valuable right of a free society. But regrettably, some Third World countries are not content with creating a news agency as a supplemental source of information. Instead, they have decided that it will be the *exclusive* source, inside the country and throughout the world. In that way, there will be no "bad news." The world will only be told what the governmental spokesmen want to reveal—sometimes true, sometimes fiction.

Before World Press Institute, St. Paul,
Minn., May 11/Vital Speeches, 8-15:651.

Robert Maynard
Chairman, Institute for Journalism
Education

5

[Urging newspapers to hire more minority-group reporters] : Ten years after the death of

WHAT THEY SAID IN 1978

(ROBERT MAYNARD)

[civil-rights leader Martin Luther] King, at the end of this long, sorrowful decade, the American press still has a long, long way to go. When will we see editorials urging this industry to move forward and stand for equality? . . . There is an awful lot that people don't know about our communities unless they come from them . . . We are asking that neighborhoods be accurately portrayed. Where there is crime, report crime. Where there is hunger, report hunger. But where there is health, report health. We believe that can only happen if newsrooms in America reflect the population of America.

At National Conference on Minorities and the News, April 7/The Washington Post, 4-8: (A) 14.

Ali Moertopo
Minister of Information of Indonesia

1

As democratic countries, we value press freedom as a precious principle. We uphold this principle to encourage the expression of fresh and creative ideas which are of vital importance to our progress and development. The exercise of this freedom, however, should take place in a manner which does not, in any way, jeopardize the preservation of stability without which no development can have a chance of success. In other words, the freedom we enjoy should be coupled in its application with a sense of responsibility toward the improvement of law and order, toward the general well-being of the people, and toward the effective implementation of democratic processes.

At Conference of the Coordination Committee, Press Agencies Pool of the Non-aligned Countries, Jakarta, Indonesia, April 3/ Time, 8-21: Special-Section.

Walter F. Mondale
Vice President of the United States

2

[On the recent Supreme Court ruling upholding unannounced searches of news-media offices for evidence in criminal investigations by police with search warrants] : The fears expressed by journalists include the risk of un-

announced police invasions of the newsroom. They include serious questions shared by newspeople about their ability to guard the identity of sources. They include questions among reporters that their notes could become the subject of official hunting expeditions, searches that would stifle the courageous activism of the press, as well as intimidating those who talk to journalists. Perhaps the greatest danger is that these fears, in and of themselves, could have what could be called a chilling effect on the energy, ingenuity and independence you [in the press] always brought to your profession. That is a risk which no free nation can accept. It imposes a challenge for all of us—for those who make the law, for those who enforce it, for those who report it, and for every citizen who relies upon the wisdom and fairness of that process.

Before Washington chapter, Sigma Delta Chi/ The Christian Science Monitor, 7-11:23.

Bill Monroe
Executive producer and moderator, "Meet the Press," National Broadcasting Company

3

I believe that the present apparatus of broadcast regulation cheats the broadcast journalist of the independence promised by the First Amendment and so cheats the American people of the vigor and diversity they're entitled to from all of our nation's media . . . The very existence of the FCC, with its compulsion to sanitize the airwaves of the unequal, the unfair and the impure—the very existence of this Federal control commission discourages the idea of assigning keen, thoughtful people to say what they want to say . . . Democracy needs not only the meat and potatoes of fact and information. It also needs the vitamins and minerals of argument and debate.

Before Radio-Television News Directors Association, Atlanta/ Los Angeles Times, 9-26: (4) 13.

Rupert Murdoch
Australian/American newspaper publisher

4

I think when all of us are so inclined to be detractive of the United States, we should re-

(RUPERT MURDOCH)

member the most important thing: It remains the freest country, with the freest press. Although it might not be the most readable press in the world, it is the most responsible. No case can be made that the great freedoms that are enjoyed there lead to any expansion of irresponsibility.

*At luncheon for International Press Institute,
Canberra, Australia, March 8/
The Dallas Times Herald, 3-9:(A)5.*

Ralph Nader
Lawyer; Consumer advocate

1

Newspapers are a privileged and lucrative industry. The only way to ensure that they become more accountable to the people they serve is through active appraisal by the public. No other industry has explicit Constitutional protection against government regulation of their product, and no other industry has a local monopoly in 97½ per cent of the towns they operate in without any form of public review. It is clear that some sort of reader feedback to newspapers is needed. Most editors recognize this need in principle, but it is up to the consumers if newspapers are to make meeting it a reality.

*News conference, Washington, April 9/
The Christian Science Monitor, 4-10:2.*

Allen H. Neuharth
*Chairman, Gannett Company;
President, American Newspaper
Publishers Association*

2

I believe the only judges of the quality of a newspaper are the people who read them, not on the campus of Columbia University . . . or anywhere else, but in their communities. We start with quality products for the communities we serve and that leads to greater profits; there is no other way to do it.

The Christian Science Monitor, 4-4:17.

3

The United States is on the threshold of an imperial judiciary that would be every bit as destructive as was the imperial Presidency. An imperial judiciary would bend the First Amendment to make the press the servant of the courts and of law-enforcement agencies [by forcing journalists to divulge their sources], rather than a servant of the public. It is society's right to know the facts, not just the journalist's right to publish them, that is at stake.

*San Francisco Examiner & Chronicle,
10-1:(This World)2.*

John B. Oakes
*Former editorial-page editor,
"The New York Times"*

4

What essentially worries critics of the growing concentration of power in the news industry in the hands of relatively few communications companies—publicly and privately held—is that the more concentrated power becomes, the more likely it is to move the focus of print journalism away from its original goals and purposes into becoming a mere money-machine, as has happened in the television industry. It is this potential threat that inevitably colors the public perception of the press as an independent institution. That perception is further altered—and not for the good—when the press lobbies for special privileges and exemptions from, for example, the anti-trust laws—as it did in connection with the Failing Newspaper Act a few years ago—and from the child-labor laws a good many years before that. To use the battle cry of "Freedom of the Press" as a shield on every possible occasion for special economic benefits is to debase the currency of freedom whose integrity we desperately need to preserve.

*At Washington Journalism Center, May 17/
Vital Speeches, 7-15:590.*

Jody Powell
*Press Secretary to President of the
United States Jimmy Carter*

5

[Saying he might leave his post before President Carter leaves office]: I think that probably there comes a time when a Press Secre-

WHAT THEY SAID IN 1978

(JODY POWELL)

tary is not worth much any more. He's got too many scars and too few ideas and he's worn out his welcome with the press, and it's time for the President to bring in somebody new without all those cans tied to his tail.

Interview/Los Angeles Times, 12-5:(1)2.

William Proxmire
United States Senator, D-Wisconsin

1

[Advocating repeal of the Fairness Doctrine and the equal-time rule which apply to broadcasters]: Other means of mass communication—newspapers, magazines, pamphlets, books and motion pictures—have kept their free-press rights. But not broadcasting. This would be a grave omission under any circumstances. But broadcasting—radio and television—is the preferred source of news for 76 per cent of the American people. Yet, because of governmental controls like the Fairness Doctrine and the equal-time rule, broadcasters are second-class citizens when it comes to First Amendment rights. It is not necessary to "deny freedom" in order to "gain fairness." In actual operation, the Fairness Doctrine has not stimulated the free expression of diverse ideas. Rather, it has had the opposite effect. It has promoted the "sameness" of ideas. Stations avoid the airing of controversial issues because they fear a challenge to their license renewal, or expensive litigation resulting from a fairness complaint.

Before Senate Communications Subcommittee,
Washington, June 7/The Hollywood Reporter, 6-7:19.

2

News is a very important part of the job of being a Senator. It's a means of communicating with other members, of letting them know your viewpoint. Nobody reads the *Congressional Record* or transcripts of committee hearings. If you're going to have an effect on your colleagues, the newspaper can do it. I often find out what someone's position is on some issue by reading about it in the newspaper. Communication is of the greatest importance. The

media reaches millions of people. You can have the most logical viewpoint, reasoned and well thought out; but if no one hears about it, you're not going to have much effect.

Los Angeles Times, 10-1:(1)2.

Harry Reasoner
News commentator, American
Broadcasting Company

3

[Saying he's looking forward to moving to CBS, where he will be involved in feature reports rather than anchoring the daily news]: The general feeling in this craft or racket, or whatever it is, is that the anchor guy gets the money and the field guys get the fun—by that I mean all sorts of professional satisfaction. The anchor job is satisfying, too—because there are only a few of you, because of the profound responsibility it carries—but it can also get to be a five-day-a-week grind. Field work frequently involves stretches of 20-hour days, but afterward you don't have to go into the office just because it's Thursday.

Interview, New York/
San Francisco Examiner & Chronicle,
7-9:(Datebook)28.

George E. Reedy
Professor of journalism, Marquette
University; Former Press Secretary
to the President of the United States
(Lyndon B. Johnson)

4

There are two different world views—the press's and the politician's. And the psychology of a politician is the psychology of a warrior. They think the press is a battleground.

Newsweek, 4-17:22.

5

Any time a President gets into political trouble, he will have a bad relationship with the press. To people in the White House, the press comes to symbolize a President's troubles. They are a group of outsiders who ask a lot of nasty questions.

U.S. News & World Report, 8-7:29.

A. M. Rosenthal
Executive editor, "The New York Times"

1

[On the libel charges brought against two American reporters by the Soviet Union]: If Soviet state organizations—and in the Soviet Union all organizations are state organizations—follow a policy of dragging reporters into court when they don't like their reporting, it would become impossible for them to work. It also is quite plain that if the Soviet Union embarks upon a policy of harassment of American foreign correspondents, in time neither Soviet nor American correspondents would be able to work fruitfully in each other's country . . . We do not expect the Soviet Union to like everything our correspondents report. We do think they should be allowed to report without attempts at legal or political intimidation, just as Soviet correspondents are allowed to work in this country. We think this is a particularly serious incident in its implications for the future, and we hope and trust that Soviet officials will give careful study to all its potential for damage.

June 28/The New York Times, 6-29: (A)12.

James N. Rosse
Economist, Stanford University

2

The thing that mainly needs to be done is to get the [newspaper] industry to think of itself as a vigorous competitor rather than a sacred cow. Vigorous and effective management is more likely to preserve newspaper competition than all of the public policy we are likely to conceive.

At conference on media concentration, Washington/ The Christian Science Monitor, 12-18:4.

Vermont Royster
Political columnist, "The Wall Street Journal"

3

[On today's detailed television coverage of Presidential appearances and statements]: . . . I'm not persuaded, I fear, that all is for the better. President [Franklin] Roosevelt could, and often did, just think out loud without fear

that every word was put indelibly upon the record. The President could, and sometimes did, misstate himself at first expression, as everyone may do in casual conversation, and then on second thought rephrase his remarks. [But] the modern President has no such latitude. He must live in constant fear of the slip-of-the-tongue. A misstated name can be an embarrassment. Awkward phraseology on some matter of public import is beyond recall or correction. One consequence is that Presidents today try to say no more at a press conference than what might be put as well in a carefully drafted statement. The President has thus lost an opportunity to be frank and open. The press has lost an opportunity to share his thought processes, which, without being the stuff of tomorrow's headlines, nonetheless could help them do a better job of informing their readers and listeners.

Upon receiving Fourth Estate Award from National Press Club, Washington/ The Washington Post, 12-25: (A)19.

Richard S. Salant
President, Columbia Broadcasting System News

4

[Criticizing newscasters who also do commercials]: Being a salesman and being a journalist are simply incompatible. At CBS, no one reads commercials or endorses products. And when I leave, if anyone has the notion to change that policy, I don't think we would have any journalists left—and good for them. That's why they're so good.

Los Angeles Times, 10-29: (Calendar)92.

Mihailo Saranovic
Editor-in-chief, Tanjug (Yugoslav News Agency)

5

Any kind of information that any [news] agency in the world intends to publish must satisfy certain criteria. Above all, it must be accurate and factual, acceptable in regard to style, content and form, have topical significance and value in every country and region; be true, attractive, objective, balanced and timely.

WHAT THEY SAID IN 1978

(MIHAILO SARANOVIC)

It must promote cooperation and should not constitute political propaganda or reflect one-sided views or biases. It should create good will among people instead of stressing differences. It must be properly sourced, authentic, complete and meet the needs of readers in every region. Finally, the information must be precise for its dissemination to be facilitated, must not be written in bad taste, be blatantly abusive, or constitute contempt of court.

At United Nations Association seminar, New York/
The Christian Science Monitor, 10-25:22.

Ernie Schultz
President, Radio and Television News
Directors Association

1

[On the Supreme Court's ruling permitting police with warrants to search newspaper and broadcast newsrooms for material relevant to a crime]: The possibility of abuse is tremendous, up to and including shutting down the entire operation. In many cities and towns it could become open season on journalists, and I call on my fellow journalists to make plans now to carefully document and widely publicize any such use of search warrants.

Daily Variety, 6-6:9.

Eric Sevareid
Former news commentator, Columbia
Broadcasting System

2

Publishers and editors have fought courage-ously, sometimes heroically, for the freedom of the printed press, and thank God you and your predecessors did so. [But] only slowly and reluctantly have many publishers and editors come to accept that the notion of the divisibil-ity, the dilutability of the First Amendment simply because of technological change in the transmission of information and ideas is an absurd and dangerous notion. I am quite aware that a good many broadcast owners and mana-gers were slow themselves. They thought, origi-nally, that they were just in the advertising business and found, often to their discomfort,

that they had become co-trustees of the First Amendment. Those who still won't face that ought to be out of the broadcasting business.

At United Press International luncheon/
The New York Times, 5-9:39.

James N. Sites
Senior vice president, National
Association of Manufacturers; Former
Special Assistant to the Secretary
for Public Affairs, Department of the
Treasury of the United States

3

After seeing the inside working of that enormous Colossus on the Potomac, and even though I suffered many trying moments at the hands of many reporters as a government infor-mation man, I came to have great respect for the adversary relationship that exists between the Washington press and the Federal govern-ment ... And I came to believe that the nation is fortunate indeed to have the constant threat of exposure by the press hanging over the heads of our government representatives, as well as over all others who exercise power and influ-ence in whatever field. "How will it look on the front pages?" sums it all up. Indeed, without this threat of exposure exercised by a free press, what kind of society would we have then?

Before Akron Forum, Akron, Ohio, Jan. 26/
Vital Speeches, 3-1:293.

Liz Smith
Newspaper columnist

4

What is gossip but unsubstantiated rumor? People are universally interested in gossip. I think gossip is just news running ahead of itself in red satin dress. As much as I detested Walter Winchell, there was some truth in his saying, "Today's gossip is tomorrow's headline." We have certainly seen that proved a lot—although I don't believe where there is smoke there is necessarily fire.

Interview, Dallas/
The Dallas Times Herald, 8-3:(E)10.

Alexander I. Solzhenitsyn
Exiled Soviet author

1

[Criticizing the Western press] : "Everyone is entitled to know everything" [is a] false slogan, characteristic of a false era. People also have the right not to know, and it is a much more valuable one. The right not to have their divine souls stuffed with gossip, nonsense, vain talk. A person who works and leads a meaningful life does not need this excessive burdening flow of information . . . Hastiness and superficiality are the psychic disease of the 20th century, and more than anywhere else this disease is reflected in the press . . . The press has become the greatest power in Western countries, more powerful than the legislature, the executive and the judiciary. One would like to ask: By what law has it been elected, and to whom is it responsible?

*At Harvard University commencement, June 8/
Los Angeles Times, 6-9:(1)12; Newsweek, 6-19:43.*

Robert S. Strauss
*Special Representative for Trade
Negotiations of, and Adviser on
Inflation to, President of the United
States Jimmy Carter*

2

I don't orchestrate the press. People who have problems with reporters are those who try to orchestrate them. I like the press. Sure the press is prejudiced and biased. They are, but in my behalf.

*Interview, Washington/
U.S. News & World Report, 8-7:16.*

Morris K. Udall
*United States Representative,
D-Arizona*

3

What I fear is that the way this spiral of acquisitions and mergers [in the media] is going, in 15 years or so from now we'll end up with 3 or 6, or 8 or 9 very large communications conglomerates that are feeding you your newspaper news, that are owning your television stations, giving you your books and news

magazines, and hit you from clear across the spectrum of communications.

The Christian Science Monitor, 4-4:17.

Barbara Walters
*News commentator, American
Broadcasting Company*

4

I had never wanted to be just an anchor [on a newscast]. That's a safe, easy job. To read from a teleprompter is not hard. You know you don't have to create anything, because you come in every night, and it's written for you. You can rewrite if you want to—but if not, you can walk into the office at 4 o'clock, and it's there. What I do now is create spots to do—special reports, reporter's notebooks, interviews—and that's much tougher. But it's far more satisfying for me.

*Interview, New York/
The Christian Science Monitor, 10-26:(B)2.*

William C. Westmoreland
*General (Ret.) and former Chief of
Staff, United States Army; Former
Allied Commander in Vietnam*

5

Few realized that the Vietnam war was the first war ever fought without some sort of official [news] censorship. This situation thrust upon the news media a responsibility unto itself—one never experienced heretofore. As an institution, in my opinion, it failed the test . . . If the media can create a defeat of our armies on the battlefields [such as when it falsely characterized the 1968 Tet offensive as a victory for North Vietnam], they can also eventually defeat the viability of our system. In that regard, it may be later than we think.

*At Accuracy in Media conference,
April 22/The Washington Post, 4-23:(A)28.*

Clay T. Whitehead
*Former Director, Federal Office of
Telecommunications Policy*

6

The news media have always had this great preoccupation with fairness. What's fair in

WHAT THEY SAID IN 1978

(CLAY T. WHITEHEAD)

covering a story really depends on the reporter's point of view. Pretty much the same people work for ABC News, CBS News, NBC News. They tend to have a pretty homogeneous view of the world, kind of a romantic view. It's almost inevitable that they're going to be slightly liberal.

Interview/Los Angeles Herald Examiner, 2-6:(C)2.

Brian Aldriss
Chairman, committee of management,
British Society of Authors

1

[On whether writers should be unionized in order to have strength in dealing with publishers] : Lord Byron was thought to be showing bad form when he accepted payment for his poems. Not long ago, any thought of authors receiving royalties or employing literary agents was laughable. May Webb stormed into Bedford Square and slapped Jonathan Cape's face because he would not send her money against hypothetical royalties. Nowadays, writers' actions need to be more sustained, if less dramatic, for us to make an impression.

The New York Times, 12-10:(1)7.

Kingsley Amis
Author, Poet

2

... I'm pessimistic about English verse in general, because I can't take seriously any verse that has no form—that is, verse which, when read aloud, seems to be prose, with, if you like, conscientious pauses every now and then to show when the lines come to an end. And when verse in general stops rhyming and scanning, then light verse is going to do that, too. And that means a very large part of its function has disappeared. Because light verse depends to a great extent on metrical skill and ingenuity. You must have the capacity to discover or invent elaborate and difficult rhymes and to handle difficult verse-forms with apparent ease—that's to say, after a lot of false starts and mistakes. And unless and until some sort of form comes back—and I don't mean, for example, syllable-counting, because that's a purely mathematical concept which has nothing to do with how the verse runs—unless some form comes back I can't see that any serious light verse will go on being written. Limericks will last, I imagine, as long as the language lasts, and

there will be epigrams and squibs and such. But the idea of somebody like Calverley or Gilbert arising today is impossible.

Interview, London/
The New York Times Book Review, 6-25:45.

Herbert S. Bailey, Jr.
Director, Princeton University Press

3

Books have functions beyond the conveyance of information, just as the human mind is much more than an organ for the storage of useful facts. Books have the qualities of the minds that produced them—reason, emotion, interpretation, values, imagination, hope and a multitude of other attributes . . . We think of books written in loneliness and passion, read in solitude, mind meeting mind. That is the ideal of the book, the conveyor of experience and thought and even wisdom . . . Books are the collective memory of mankind.

Bowker Memorial Lecture/
Great Falls (Mont.) Tribune, 1-25:3.

Saul Bellow
Author

4

It's very hard for [young writers today] because, if a young man or woman wants to make a career as a writer, they'll soon find that the world has brought the people of talent into institutions or into universities or into the mass media. There doesn't seem to be any middle ground. There's no independent literary culture. Whatever existed once has been swallowed up. The very *avant-garde* magazines in which we used to publish are gone. The universities and their editors have all become professors, and it's very sad that there is scarcely a trace of life for writers outside the institutions. I think we've failed badly in this respect.

Interview/
The Christian Science Monitor, 3-2:24.

WHAT THEY SAID IN 1978

Daniel J. Boorstin
Librarian of Congress
of the United States

1

[On the Library of Congress]: Many of Europe's national libraries grew out of aristocratic or royal collections. In this country, however, from the beginning, our national library has been shaped by the needs of the people as expressed by their elected representatives, and by the nation's libraries and institutions of learning ... It has advantages. For one thing, it imposes the therapy of action on the world of scholarship. When a member of Congress wants an answer to a question for a committee hearing or debate on the floor, he can't wait until the next summer vacation. He has to have it tomorrow. Scholars tend to follow a more leisurely pace—and so do most scholarly libraries. Furthermore, Congress is proud of our library, and takes an active interest in the Library of Congress, since in their daily work they benefit from the extent and completeness of the national collections.

Interview/
U.S. News & World Report, 5-15:57.

2

It is no accident that books are sacred to civilization. They open the past to us. A book is magical; it transcends time and space.

Interview, Washington/
The Christian Science Monitor, 7-27:(B)9.

Jimmy Breslin
Author

3

The Number 1 reason anyone writes, any professional, is to pay the bills. This isn't the Lawn Tennis Association, where you play just for the thrill of it.

Interview/"W":
a Fairchild publication, 6-23:2.

John Brooks
President, Authors Guild of America

4

A big-book syndrome has developed, with furious competition among a few combined giants for a few surefire winners. Books are degraded to the status of a commodity, and those of merit are being squeezed out of sight by the conglomerate-hyped and packaged bestsellers.

At Federal Trade Commission-sponsored
symposium on conglomeration in the
book business, Washington, Dec. 15/
The New York Times, 12-17:(1)100.

William F. Buckley, Jr.
Author; Editor, "National Review"

5

... I don't deny that I write fast. I have so many compensating disabilities, like reading slowly. I think what makes people write novels fast is a combination of things: Number 1, impatience. And Number 2, sort of a lingering question about whether or not you have the basic skills to bring off a novel. And if that disturbs you deeply enough, as it always has me, it causes you, I think, to speed up the tempo of a book so that you don't indulge yourself in the kind of appoggiatura that you would go in for if you were absolutely confident of your skills.

Interview, New York/
The New York Times Book Review, 5-14:13.

Stan Corwin
President, Pinnacle Books, publishers

6

"Literature," unfortunately, is no longer selling. I remind myself that what you're aiming for is more or less a "Laverne & Shirley" American mentality. This seems to be the level people want to read. I doubt that Marcel Proust would be palatable in a commercial way if he were writing today. Although I consider myself a very literary person and wish, as a "responsible publisher," that I published great quality literature, I'm afraid that there is a bottom-line necessity to publish "what they want out there."

Interview, Los Angeles/
Los Angeles Herald Examiner, 9-13:(A)11.

Malcolm Cowley
Author; Editor, The Viking Press

7

American authors are more self-conscious than the British, a little more preoccupied with

(MALCOLM COWLEY)

what the critics will say. If their first book has been well received, that is often deadly, because the author feels that his second book has to be better in some way. He gets stage fright, otherwise known as writer's block, and the book is never finished. [Ernest] Hemingway thought that the real thing that killed [F. Scott] Fitzgerald as a writer was the wonderful review of *The Great Gatsby* written by Gilbert Seldes. That destroyed him, according to Hemingway. After that, Fitzgerald took nine years to finish another novel. Actually, the writer's problem is one of self-esteem. He thinks: Is this worthy of the picture I form of my own talent? Fitzgerald paid a great deal of attention to this, and almost all American writers do.

Interview, New York/
The New York Times Book Review, 4-30:18.

1

[On the affinity between writing and drinking]: I don't know that writers as a class drink more heavily than actors, advertising men, painters, one type of salesman, or any other maniacs who want to be brilliant and self-assured.

Time, 9-11:61.

Allen Drury
Author

2

... I've been criticized at times for not having red-hot sex scenes. Well, I read a great deal, and I'm not especially moved by an author's labored description of what has become in fiction a stereotyped process of gasping, groaning and grunting. I just assume most adults know what it's all about, without my telling them. Maybe I'll lose more readers by saying it, but what turns me on is the challenge of developing insights to humanity in high places, and then following a strict discipline of writing the story.

Interview, Tiburon, Calif./
Los Angeles Times, 5-28:(Home)40.

Richard Eberhart
Poet

3

... I think the state of poetry in America is vigorous and healthy and exciting and very fine.

And I think that compared with when I was starting to write in the 1930s—back then you could almost count the poets on your two hands, and the poet was an extreme individual, he was a very strange or odd kind of person. There didn't seem to be any corporate sense. Now I have a feeling that when there are hundreds, if not thousands, of young people writing from the age of 15 to the age of 35, that they all take power from each other and they give power to each other and they don't have a sense of the loneliness of the writer so much as when I was there, nor the harshness of it.

Interview, Hanover, N.H./
The New York Times Book Review, 1-1:20.

Harlan Ellison
Author

4

If my work alarms people and shocks people, that is as I intended. I don't write to lull people, to soothe people, to convince them that what they have always believed is true. I write to alarm them and to stir up the soup. I'm a troublemaker. That's what I think a writer should do. That, I think, is the obligation of the writer—to be as dangerous, to be as alarming and to be as painful as possible to himself as well as to his readers.

Interview/
Los Angeles Herald Examiner, 5-30-(A)15.

Howard Fast
Author

5

There's practically unlimited freedom in putting a story on paper for the first time. I can take it in any direction. But once the words are all in place, and I begin to labor over it, tightening, editing, restructuring, traveling the dark and mysterious route called rewriting, it becomes a vastly annoying experience, a bleak and dreary time.

Interview, Los Angeles/
Los Angeles Times, 2-26:(Home)35.

Ernest J. Gaines
Author

6

The job of any writer is to write truly about what he knows and feels. But I do think—and

WHAT THEY SAID IN 1978

(ERNEST J. GAINES)

I've been criticized for saying so—that too many blacks have been writing to tell whites all about "the problems," instead of writing something that all people, including their own, could find interesting, could enjoy. And in so many cases, they leave out the humanity of their characters. Black writers have to do more than work out their anger on paper. I like pride in people; I try to show the strength of black people; but I was criticized when I was writing *(The Autobiography of) Miss Jane Pittman* because blacks were expected to write novels of protest; it was your duty as a black writer. I stuck to my guns and wrote what was true to me. And if you read that book you'll see that there *is* protest in it. Every novel has its own protests—if you're not commenting on the human condition then what are you doing but playing with words, shuffling paper?

Interview, San Francisco/
The New York Times Book Review, 6-11:44.

Erwin A. Glikes
Publisher, general adult books,
Harper & Row, publishers

1

Television is not satisfying to many Americans. It cannot feed that part of their spirit that searches for meaning. Good books can do this, and the challenge for publishers is to find and encourage good writing and good thinking.

U.S. News & World Report, 6-5:57.

Herman Gollob
Editor-in-chief, Atheneum Publishers

2

There is one kind of fiction that is disappearing—the non-friction novel that gives off no sparks, that is self-conscious, competent, tedious. But the rest of the list [today] has unprecedented vitality and variety. If you can get Judith Krantz's *Scruples* and John Irving's *The World According to Garp* on the same bestseller list, you have a thriving democratic literature.

Time, 10-30:127.

Graham Greene
Author

3

A novelist can easily unself himself. He can write as a woman or a child. The opinions in my novels are not mine; they are the opinions of my characters. Readers are very stupid about this. I do not take people straight from real life in my novels. A novel is not a work of travel or autobiography. Even these are re-creations. I shall never write my own reminiscences because I have a poor memory. Real people are crowded out by imaginary ones; that is why I have to stare at them so long. There has once or twice been a little straight reporting in my novels—there was some in *The Quiet American*—but no real people. Real people would wreck the design. The characters in my novels are an amalgam of bits of real people; one takes the isolated traits from many; they are fused by the heat of the unconscious. Real people are too limiting.

Interview, Vence, France/
The New York Times Magazine, 2-26:41.

Pete Hamill
Author, Journalist

4

A good columnist is like a good sketch artist, like Daumier, for example; but it takes fiction to get inside someone's head. You can't go there in journalism, even though I know a number of guys—and some of them are friends of mine—have tried . . . There ought to be more reporting in novels. The great novelists of the past were also great reporters—Dickens and Balzac, for example. Today there are a lot of novelists who seem to be writing to be reviewed, not read.

Interview, Dallas/
The Dallas Times Herald, 1-5:(D)8.

Michael Harper
Poet; Nominee for
National Book Award

5

I guess I have a few thousand readers. Some would say that's enough. I'd like to have more. Readership is important. But I'm more concerned with expressing poetic themes. Poets

(MICHAEL HARPER)

shouldn't be too concerned with audiences. The worry brutalizes them.

Interview, Washington/
The Washington Post, 3-9:(B)4.

Charlton Heston
Actor

1

[About putting together the daily journal of his life he has been working on for 20 years]: It's taught me one thing: never to trust a memoir or a biography again . . . I discovered that the way you remember things just isn't the way they were. Which now makes me suspect the whole of recorded history, for almost everything we know was written down a long time after the event. Maybe George Bernard Shaw was right when he said history was bunk. Since I started this, I've been reading other actors' memoirs. Sometimes they'll write about a film I was involved in. And almost invariably I find myself saying, "Now wait a minute, that wasn't how it was." My own memories of, say, *Ben Hur* are that it was a happy experience. But it wasn't, judging by the journal. Not at all. It was an endurance test, a nightmare. Ten months' hard work. But now I remember it through a golden haze.

Interview/Los Angeles Times, 5-25:(4)17.

Eugene Ionesco
Playwright

2

I was not cut out to be a literary critic or a writer of novels. Maybe because there are many contradictions in me. In theatre, contradictions are indispensable, while in an essay or a novel you can have just one idea. But in a play, people present ideas that are opposite. Theatre is a coexistence of contradictions. You cannot write novels or essays when there are contradictions inside you.

Interview, Los Angeles/
Los Angeles Herald Examiner, 10-1:(F)8.

John Jakes
Author

3

How does it feel to be rich and famous? It's fun. And it has its funny side. You know, I had written 55 books, and paid my dues as a professional, and then when the Kent Family series hit, the neighbors back in Ohio would say, "Oh, how does it feel to have your first book published?" So I'd kind of grit my teeth and say, "Oh, it's wonderful." Until you get highly successful and highly visible, there's a certain per cent of the reading public that's never heard of you . . .

Interview/San Francisco
Examiner & Chronicle,
5-28:(Datebook)32.

Erica Jong
Author

4

For centuries, women have had to keep a sort of good-girl, ladylike image. Therefore, when women wrote books, they left out many things that were parts of their lives. They left out sex, incestuous urges, fantasies, feelings of anger toward men, toward children, their mothers and so forth. So we have in women's writing a kind of off-balanced picture of a woman's life. Now that there are beginning to be changes in the stereotypes of what a woman is or can be, we will see a lot of writing in which, suddenly, female anger, female sexuality will surface. That, in fact, has happened and I think that that's a very needed thing. Women should have absolutely the full range of emotion in their writing that men have. But naturally, in this period of writing the adjustment, of writing the balance, there are going to be exploitation books written by women just as exploitation books have always been written by men. And there will be women who say, "Erica Jong was successful because she put in a lot of sex. I'm going to put in a lot of sex and be successful, too." This is only to be expected, and it doesn't denigrate the women's movement or the need for female authors to deal with the whole spectrum of life. It doesn't denigrate anything. It just means that there will always be a lot of crap published as well as good stuff. Nobody ought to be surprised about that.

Interview/
Los Angeles Herald Examiner, 8-14:(A)1.

WHAT THEY SAID IN 1978

Garson Kanin
Author, Playwright

1

Writing is so much a part of my routine that when I don't do it ... I'm no good at all. It comes down to the actual act of writing. If you're writing something you want to convey, and if you're writing well and not to order, it's a release. There are thousands of causes for stress, and one antidote to stress is self-expression. That's what happens to me every day. My thoughts get off my chest, down my sleeve and onto my pad.

Interview, New York/
Publishers Weekly, 1-23:277.

Elia Kazan
Author

2

The only reaction [to my writing] I cannot bear is no reaction at all. Truthfully, I've really failed if nobody gets mad at what I write. You know, when I affront someone, I get a certain amount of pleasure.

Interview/
The Dallas Times Herald, 7-30:(K)5.

Alfred Kazin
Author

3

When a writer talks about his work, he's talking about a love affair.

Interview, Stanford University/
San Francisco Examiner &
Chronicle, 7-16:(Scene)4.

Winthrop Knowlton
President, Harper & Row, publishers

4

... book publishers have for a long time been viewed as gentle, slightly foolish, isolated folk—dreamers, readers, frustrated writers. And the industry has long been considered cottage, that is to say, small, casually managed, benignly inefficient—a gathering of muddlers doing harm to no one except possibly to authors, for whom the compelling methaphor—the obverse of Mussolini's ability to get the trains running on time—is our inability to get books into the stores on time. But now a new mythology is emerging, not to displace the old but appar-

ently to coexist with it. According to this vision, we publishers have become managerial and systems-happy, remote and rapacious, aligned with or embraced by "a new breed of corporate manipulators" or "corporate carnivores," in the words of Archibald MacLeish. So on the one hand, we are bumbling and a little silly; on the other, crass and a little venal. I think we have an identity crisis on our hands.

At Association of American Publishers
meeting, White Sulphur Springs, W.V./
Los Angeles Times, 5-28:(Book Review)3.

Stanley Kunitz
Poet

5

Poetry is a discipline, an art form, not a spontaneous overflow of your immediate feelings. It doesn't depend on a big audience. We're not competing with punk rock. It's essentially a rather secret and intimate art.

News conference, Washington, March 6/
The Washington Post, 3-7:(C)11.

Louis L'Amour
Author

6

If you write a book set in the past about something that happened east of the Mississippi, it's a "historical novel." If you write about something that took place west of the Mississippi, it's a "Western"—and somehow regarded as a lesser work. I write historical novels about the frontier.

Interview/
The Dallas Times Herald, 2-19:(F)1.

Irving Lazar
Literary and theatrical agent

7

Publishing today is show biz. You walk into Random House or Knopf or Simon & Schuster and they look like movie moguls; they don't look like publishers. I mean, they're doing million-dollar deals.

The Washington Post, 5-6:(B)6.

Ernest Lehman
Author, Screenwriter

8

[Comparing writing for films and writing novels]: Some films have a kind of power you

(ERNEST LEHMAN)

can't find anywhere else . . . But the novel gives you more freedom to be expansive, to get inside the characters and their thoughts and feelings. The writer has more chance to digress, to reveal what he thinks and feels and believes about humanity, life, the world. The characters can ruminate without holding up the movie and getting the audience restless. In this sense, the novel is a more powerful tool for expressing ideas. Screenplays are more constricted. You don't waste time writing things that can't be photographed. There are no interior monologues, just action and dialogue. Anything more than that is merely a luxury, or a kind of note to the director.

Interview, New York/
The Christian Science Monitor, 1-26:21.

Tom Lipscomb
President, Times Books

1

Books have become a new form of journalism. It was only five years ago that we found out—in a book—that the German intelligence was right in ascertaining that the "Lusitania" was in fact carrying arms. The simple fact is that more people read the front page than the book reviews. The publishing business realizes that. Books are getting more like long news stories. It's like giving a reporter $20,000 and saying, "Track that story down and turn it in when you've got it nailed solid."

The Washington Post, 5-6:(B)6.

John D. MacDonald
Author

2

The best therapy in the world [for a writer] is to drop what you're working on and read everybody else's stuff. Pretty soon you find some stuff that causes you to say, "Oh, Jesus, I can do a lot better than that."

Interview, Sarasota, Fla./
The Dallas Times Herald, 1-29:(F)4.

Shirley MacLaine
Actress, Author

3

It only seems natural for me to write—both fiction and non-fiction. I happen to be an ac-

tress, but if you asked what I am, that isn't what I'd answer, because I'm several other things, too. I guess what I really am is a communicator. As such, writing is a natural, necessary part of my every-day existence. To feel ink squishing out of a pen onto paper isn't just a frill for me; it's a prerequisite for fulfilling myself.

Interview/
Los Angeles Herald Examiner, 7-30:(F)10.

Archibald MacLeish
Poet, Playwright

4

I refer to the contemporary practice by which certain corporations, having no connection with literature, no knowledge of literature, no interest in it, have acquired publishing houses—not to enter publishing, but to diversify their investments. These are the conglomerates, corporate carnivores conceived by a new breed of corporate manipulators who believe that if the greatest possible number of ways of making money can be crowded into a single corporate fist, the old dream which eluded the manipulators of the 1920s, the dream of permanent prosperity, can be achieved.

Upon accepting the National
Medal for Literature, New York,
April 6/The New York Times, 4-7:(C)22.

William Manchester
Author

5

I tend to escape into the past. My study is in the Wesleyan University library building, and sometimes I wander into the stacks and pick up a bound volume of, say, *The London Times* from the early 1800s, and just lose myself in reading about historical events in the actual newspaper accounts of the time. I try to carry this sense of actuality, the small details that give the reader the sense of being right at the scene of events, into my historical writing. Essentially, it's a technique of fiction—like characterization, silent transition, so forth—that a number of excellent writers are now applying to non-fiction. I'm criticized sometimes for including a lot of so-called trivia in my work, but

WHAT THEY SAID IN 1978

(WILLIAM MANCHESTER)

that's the kind of detail I use deliberately to place the reader at the scene. Strangely, writers of fiction are praised for using detail that way . . .

Interview/Los Angeles Times, 10-2:(4)4.

Larry McMurtry
Author

1

The vital attraction of writing novels is the curiosity of what your imagination will lead to if you work it to its maximum extent. People are often led to believe that novelists do not have an imagination. And I'm often asked if my characters and stories are taken from my friends and experiences. I don't think I could write a story about a friend. The thrill of writing is in invention and not reporting . . . casting your experiences in places you have never gone and never can go.

Denton, Texas/
The Dallas Times Herald, 10-15:(G)5.

John McPhee
Writer

2

I recall after one of my profiles ran in *The New Yorker,* somebody got hold of me on Nassau Street and said, "What a miserable puff piece that was! Aren't you ashamed? How could you over-praise that man? What are you, his flack?" He chewed me out from Hulit's shoe store to the Five-and-Ten. I felt miserable. That night I went to a party and met someone who had read the same profile and said, "That was the most malevolent, gratuitous attack on anyone I have ever read. How could you cut up this poor man with such a barbarous satire?" In each case I was hurt. Adding the two together, however, I was extremely pleased.

Interview, Princeton, N.J./
The Christian Science Monitor, 8-31:(B)7.

Scott Meredith
Literary agent

3

[Bookstores] all want the hot authors even if they do have return rights on the books they take from publishers. If a bookstore puts 10 books on the shelf by a hot author, they know they will probably be sold. If it is an unknown author, they may have to go to the trouble of returning the books. Everybody wants to concentrate on the big guns. That is not only bad for the beginning, unknown writer, but for the middle-level writer as well. It is now more difficult for middle-level authors, who may have steady, if not big, sales . . . Agents now, for the most part, do the discovering of young writers. It is not altruistic at all; it is survival. It is very short-sighted not to develop new authors. What is going to happen when the big guns die off or quit writing?

Interview, New York/
The Dallas Times Herald, 5-3:(F)3.

James A. Michener
Author

4

I've been called an "epic" writer. But I've always worked in a smaller area. Just off to one side. I've always underestimated the time it is going to take to finish something. But I often stop. And I feel no pangs about it. I've abandoned some projects. I've always been a free-lancer and in the beginning—I started to write when I was 40—I never had any option but to work hard. Now I feel no pressure to produce. I can take it easy. I want to have that time. Yes. I do enjoy the production once, as a French philosopher put it, the "work of art is released."

Interview, St. Michael's, Md./
Los Angeles Herald Examiner, 8-1:(B)6.

Henry Miller
Author

5

My books are all autobiographical. I can't write about other things. Is it vanity? Maybe, but I don't think so. It's just that I think my life was so interesting, why should I go to outside material? Anyway, I would take off—exaggerate—many times. That's what a writer is: a fabulator. He loves words, the language, and he loves to embroider. So I never feel guilty

(HENRY MILLER)

about any inaccuracies. They were done with a good heart.

Interview, Pacific Palisades, Calif./
The Dallas Times Herald, 3-5:(D)19.

1

I've written about 60 books, and only part of them have dealt with obscenity. It was because of my obsession for telling the truth that I fell into this. It was never with the idea of shocking. I don't consider myself as having written pornography. I wrote obscenity, which is pure. But the other thing, pornography, is impure. It's like a caricature of the real thing.

Interview/People, 8-21:62.

Alberto Moravia
Author

2

I don't believe in the single work but in the entire *oeuvre*. Every true writer is like a bird; he repeats the same song, the same theme, all his life. For me, this theme has always been revolt.

Interview/
Atlas World Press Review, September:59.

Octavio Paz
Poet

3

When I write prose, it is for moral, political, intellectual reasons; there is something that needs to be said, and nobody else is saying it. I want to communicate ideas, to be accepted and understood. When I am writing a poem, it is to make something, an object or organism that will be whole and living, something that will have a life of its own, independent of me. You don't care, with a poem, whether you are popular or unpopular. The important point is that the thing is made and that it is good.

Interview/
The Washington Post, 9-30:(D)11.

Harold Robbins
Author

4

Walk into any airport in the world and look at the book racks. I don't care if you recognize the language. It may be Turkish, or Arabic or what have you. The thing you can read is the name Harold Robbins. I go around the world. Like Coca-Cola.

Interview, Dallas/
The Dallas Times Herald, 1-29:(E)1.

5

What made Dickens? What made Dumas? Dickens was considered a two-penny writer because he was delivering pages of installments of his books and stories to the daily paper, for his daily bread. The serious critics of his day did not consider Charles Dickens as a literary writer, yet we do today. Alexandre Dumas and his son went through the same thing in France. I say that critics do not make literature. Writers make literature.

Interview/Book Digest, April:22.

Harold Roth
President, Grosset &
Dunlap, publishers

6

[On former President Richard Nixon's newly published memoirs]: There are people who feel that the publication of a book by Richard Nixon, a man who lives under the shadow of suspicion, is a totally inappropriate act. I find it difficult to understand such sentiments. It is incredible that anyone could suggest that a book not be published. If we abridge the freedom of any one writer or publisher, we effectively abridge the freedom of all.

News conference, Atlanta, May 27/
The New York Times, 5-28:(1)16.

Francoise Sagan
Author

7

[Saying she disapproves of the public invasion of a writer's privacy today]: Before, it was a matter of writing in a dark room by yourself. No one cared if you were a good citizen, if you liked to go to bed with men, women or dogs, whether you were of the right or the left. A writer should write with just a candle and many phantasms. Now he has to go on stage under a

WHAT THEY SAID IN 1978

spotlight and say, "Hello, my name is so-and-so, I like asparagus, and I'm for the left."

Interview, Paris/
Los Angeles Herald Examiner, 12-25:(B)1.

Max Shulman
Author

1

Sinclair Lewis said when he was teaching my creative-writing class: "You guys want to be writers? What are you doing here? Go to work in a grocery store, meet people. You'll never learn a damned thing in a classroom."

Interview, Los Angeles/
Los Angeles Times, 4-28:(4)22.

Isaac Bashevis Singer
Author

2

. . . I don't think I'm so popular. All I would say is that, in the languages into which I am translated, there are people who are interested. A writer, like a woman, never knows why people like him or why people dislike him. We never know . . . The guess is that there is always a kinship between souls. Souls are either close to one another or far from one another. There are people who, when they read me, they like what I say. And there's nothing else I can tell you.

Interview/
The New York Times Book Review, 7-23:1.

3

I need three conditions to write a story. One condition is I have to have a plot. I don't believe that you can write a story without ; story—in other words, just sit down and write ; slice of life, hoping against hope that it will come out right; it happens once in a while, but most of the time if you don't have a plan there won't be a story. The second condition is: I must have a desire to write the story—or a passion to write it; I must get up with an appetite to do this story. And the third condition: I must have the illusion that I am the only one who can write such a story.

Interview/
Los Angeles Herald Examiner, 10-22:(F)9.

4

Novels have never been a major force in society. They're actually a way of entertaining people. The only difference between good and bad novels is that cheap literature entertains cheap people, and good literature entertains better people . . . If ever [humanity's] situation is going to be improved, no novel will do it, and no poetry and no story. It will be done by scientists, by technology, maybe by some good politicians. Literature stirs the mind, but it does not direct it.

Interview/
U.S. News & World Report, 11-6:60.

5

When I was young, I used to read books and I never really looked at who was the author. I didn't care. What's the difference? When I was a boy of 12, I read Tolstoy. But I didn't know it was Tolstoy. I was interested in the story, not the author. A real reader, especially a young reader, never cares too much about the author. He wants to read the book and he enjoys it. When people begin to be less interested in art, they become more interested in the artist.

Interview/
The New York Times Magazine, 11-26:26.

6

The storyteller of our time, as in any other time, must be an entertainer of the spirit in the full sense of [the] word, not just a preacher of social and political ideals. There is no paradise for bored readers and no excuse for tedious literature that does not intrigue the reader, uplift his spirit, give him the joy and escape that true art always grants. Nevertheless, it is also true that the serious writer of our time must be deeply concerned about the problems of his generation . . . In their despair, a number of those who no longer have confidence in the leadership of our society look up to the writer, the master of words. They hope against hope that the man of talent and sensitivity can perhaps rescue civilization. Maybe there is a spark of the prophet in the artist after all.

Nobel lecture before Swedish Academy,
Stockholm, Dec. 8/The New York Times, 12-9:4.

Richard Snyder
*President, Simon &
Schuster, publishers*

1

When I was growing up, Scribner's [in New York] was the most wonderful bookstore in the world. It carried books published by people who had private incomes. It was a carriage-trade book shop. All of a sudden, chains developed in the United States. Books began appearing in drugstores and supermarkets. For the person intimidated by Scribner's, it became very natural for him to buy a book. The chains were reaching out. The supermarkets were geared to quick turnover and high velocity. Some people look on the big chains like B. Dalton or Waldenbooks as negative because they think that some of the "good" books are not getting through. On the contrary, I think it's better for people to read anything than not read at all . . . The number of people who read in this country [the U.S.] is stunningly low . . . Is publishing an act of commerce or isn't it? Those who say it's literature have private incomes.

*Interview, New York/
The Christian Science Monitor, 6-1:17.*

Tom Tryon
Author, Actor

2

[Saying he prefers writing books to acting] : This is much more satisfying. Granted, it's lonely, but I prefer it to the politicking and endless petty details of working on a film set. An actor can't help being aware he's a puppet—not only of the director, but the original work's author, the author of the screenplay, the editor, the other actors and the producers . . . So much time spent on a set or location is sitting around waiting for the next scene to be set up. As a writer, I waste hardly any of my working time; I put it to maximum use, and, when I have a good day, I know it's a hundred per cent my own doing.

*Interview/
Los Angeles Herald Examiner, 7-30:(F)10.*

Barbara Tuchman
Author, Historian

3

As I read [in doing research for a new book], the structure begins to appear and I file

my notes by chapter. I'm attached to the narrative form, to cause and effect and sequence rather than category. I don't file things by category. Narrative is the spine of what I do because that's the way life is lived; it isn't lived in categories. The principle is "today and tomorrow and the next day"—that's the bloodstream of history.

*Interview, Cos Cob, Conn./
The Wall Street Journal, 9-28:22.*

4

I get into the condition where I work, work, work—I feel an intense compulsion to finish. I try to tell myself, "You've shown how history can be written as literature—people buy it, enjoy it—why push?" But it doesn't work. I can't work at a leisurely pace because the engine runs down. Work—creative work—makes you feel doubly alive. When I'm resting, I don't feel as alive as when I'm working and feeling miserable.

*Interview, New York/
"W": a Fairchild publication, 10-13:45.*

Leon Uris
Author

5

You are subjecting yourself to tough things as a writer. It erodes a person. That's why the casualty rate is so high. You fear the exhaustion of your reserve, the collapse of your ambition, involuntary retirement by your readers. The psychic drain is enormous.

*Interview, Baltimore/
The Washington Post, 5-2:(B)3.*

Mario Vargas (Llosa)
Peruvian author

6

[On the political aspect of Latin American writers] : . . . traditionally, literature in Latin America has been an outlet for information as well as a whole body of social criticism that could never have been offered in other ways, because of rigid censorship and repression in countries with no free press or free political life. Where there were no congresses and no political parties functioning freely because of the dictatorial systems, literature has often

WHAT THEY SAID IN 1978

(MARIO VARGAS [LLOSA])

been the only forum in which some countries' real problems could be expressed. That situation has given the writer a certain political presence. In back of the demand for the writer to be politicized, however, there is a certain contempt for literature itself. The notion that literature must justify its existence by extraliterary motives, that it must be a didactic instrument for political and social instruction, can only be held by those who think that literature has no purpose of its own. But I believe that each person reading a poem or a novel or seeing a play feels pleasure, discovers a way to know himself better, as well as a stimulus for living, and doesn't ask literature to justify itself with religious, philosophical or political reasons.

Interview, New York/
The New York Times Book Review, 4-9:32.

Gore Vidal
Author

1

... every major [American] review of my book[s] is of me as a figure. Often they've not even read it, and I can tell. I am serene and anodyne about it. You want reviews—go to Italy and England, where the critics are reasonably disinterested, and thus healthier.

Interview, Los Angeles/
Los Angeles Times, 4-30:(Book Review)3.

2

Each writer is born with a repertory company in his head. Shakespeare has perhaps 20 players, and Tennessee Williams has about five, and Samuel Beckett one—and perhaps a clone of that one. I have 10 or so, and that's a lot. As you get older, you become more skillful at casting them.

The Dallas Times Herald, 6-18:(K)9.

Irving Wallace
Author

3

[Living in] Los Angeles is very good for a writer because it is 3,000 miles away from his editors and publishers. Friends of mine in New York like to run up to their editors all the time; but I would find that upsetting. There is a

tendency to see those people too often. I don't want them to know what I'm writing and I don't want to know what they think until I'm done. Writing is a fragile thing. Also, I think there is more of a mystique when you don't show up in New York. You're treated better. Familiarity breeds contempt—or at least low advances.

Los Angeles Herald Examiner, 8-13:(F)6.

Jerome Weidman
Author

4

I am not one of those people who say that they can learn something even from bad reviews. It's a funny thing that the writer has about reviewers, and it has to do with your own emotions and with selling books. I am crazy about favorable reviews even if they're written by Jack the Ripper, and I hate a bad review, even if it comes from Edmund Wilson. It's a psychic blow, no matter how thick a writer's skin is.

Interview/
The New York Times Book Review, 5-28:14.

Eudora Welty
Author

5

I think the novel can do about anything it wishes to, but I don't think it can stand still. I don't think it can be static, and I don't think that it can get along without finding a line of communication that is indelible, something that has always been there in human emotions. I don't think you can write about something that is not felt. If a novel does not *connect* with us, it's lost.

Interview/
The New York Times Book Review, 5-7:42.

Tennessee Williams
Playwright

6

... there are many mysteries about writing which are incommunicable. It's not a profession you can talk about easily. I have found talk about my writing far too private, far more intimate than writing about love affairs, for example.

Interview, Kiawah Island, S.C./
Los Angeles Times, 7-9:(Calendar)62.

Medicine and Health

Christiaan Barnard
South African surgeon

1

America is too scientific in its medical training. You train good scientists, but not good doctors. Students must learn they are treating a patient, not a disease. I learned it working in general practice as a young man. I would drive 60 miles in the middle of the night. I knew the problems in my patients' families. I think any doctor, whatever he specializes in, should have that experience.

Interview, Beverly Hills, Calif./
"W": a Fairchild publication, 5-12:14.

2

Abortion isn't a medical problem at all. It's a moral problem. Abortion is killing a life, and life begins at conception. At that moment, all the ingredients of a human being are there. Women argue they can do whatever they want with their own bodies. But they're destroying another body, not theirs. If a woman requests an abortion on medical grounds, that is one thing. But simple abortion on request, no.

Interview, Beverly Hills, Calif./
"W": a Fairchild publication, 5-12:14.

3

Life means different things to different people. To a particular individual, life means something if it is worth it for him to be alive . . . My concept of medicine is for doctors to give their patients a good life, and death is part of life. If we cannot give them life, let us give them a good death.

Nairobi, Kenya, May 17/
Los Angeles Times, 5-18:(3)13.

Leslie M. Bodnar
Coordinator of sports medicine,
University of Notre Dame

4

[On malpractice suits]: This matter of litigation involving the medical profession has increased by leaps and bounds in the last few years, creating near panic reaction on the part of physicians. The medical profession has been seriously hurt not only in the pocketbook, but, even worse, in the matter of reputation of individuals and the profession. We have been given clay feet as we were lowered from our marble pedestal.

At American Medical Association convention,
St. Louis, June 17/
The Dallas Times Herald, 6-18:(A)10.

Walter Bortz
Physician, Stanford University
Medical School

5

The solution [to increased longevity] is in celebrating old age. Our idea of who we're to be when we're 85 is just so grim. And if there is no value to it, then why seek it? . . . Nobody dies of old age. You die of a disease. You die because you wear out at one critical point. The rest of your body is fine, but the chain is only as good as its weakest link . . . If I could convince you that to be 85 is really an exciting opportunity and that you will be valuable to yourself and others, then you would give up smoking, you'd run three times a week, you'd lose weight. And you'd live longer. But we don't want to be 85. That's not so much a conscious decision as it is a kind of abandonment [of the body], and, because of it, we wear out prematurely.

Panel discussion sponsored by American Medical
Association, Las Vegas, Nev./
Los Angeles Times, 12-11:(2)4.

WHAT THEY SAID IN 1978

Peter G. Bourne
*Special Assistant to President of the
United States Jimmy Carter for
Health Issues*

1

In the past, many people were misled into believing that national health insurance would result in a radical change that would allow ill persons no flexibility in choosing the type of medical care they wanted or that would promote one health-care-delivery system to the exclusion of all others. They also envisioned it as creating a horrible bureaucratic tangle. Terms like "socialized medicine" were coined to frighten people into opposing programs before they really understood the benefits that would be provided. National health programs in England, Canada, Germany and other countries have been criticized—but not one has considered reverting to their old system, and the public in those countries seems overwhelmingly satisfied with the improvement in the over-all quality of their health that the programs have produced. We have tried to benefit from their experience and to avoid some potential pitfalls by designing a pluralistic approach that builds on the strengths of the existing private and public systems. We certainly do not feel that a state-run system such as exists in England is appropriate in this country. We simply want to spread the excellent care now available in the U.S. only for those who can afford it to a broader segment of the population without doing anything to damage the good system that already operates.

*Interview, Washington/
U.S. News & World Report, 4-17:76.*

Peter G. Bourne
*Former Special Assistant to President of
the United States Jimmy Carter for
Health Issues*

2

There's a real problem in the gravitation to the use of drugs, including alcohol. I'm very concerned about the very high use of marijuana by young people of this country—45 million people have tried it, 11 million are regular users. One out of 10 high-school students smokes marijuana every day. . . . if it comes to a question of are you for or against marijuana, one must be against. Not using drugs is clearly vastly better than using drugs.

*Interview, Washington/
Los Angeles Herald Examiner, 9-21:(A)2.*

3

[Saying the war against cocaine use is lost] : It is unrealistic to think that we're going to wipe it out. I don't think we need a massive law-enforcement crackdown. We can't enforce the drug laws that we have on the books now. So I don't think the interests of the American people would be served by having more stringent laws. I think at the same time legalizing it or even decriminalizing it would compound the problem. We would have more people using it. We would have more problems. I think at the moment we have kind of a standoff. And my personal belief is that the current standoff probably isn't too bad from a policy standpoint.

*Television interview, Oct. 9/
Los Angeles Herald Examiner, 10-10:(A)7.*

Michael D. Bromberg
*Executive director, Federation of
American Hospitals*

4

[Suggesting there is too much emphasis on cost containment in health care] : Twelve years ago, with Medicare and Medicaid, the Number 1 policy was access to medical care for more Americans. The policy was extremely successful, to the point where the budget could no longer contain it. So they turned their policy 180 degrees. We don't disagree with the general policy of controlling costs. But there should be a balance between access and quality of health care on one hand and cost on the other, not just one priority.

The New York Times, 5-7:(1)69.

Robert N. Butler
Director, National Institute on Aging

5

The concept of a hospice—a place dedicated to providing comfort, support and dignity for

(ROBERT N. BUTLER)

those who are dying—is an idea whose time has come. Although a hospice can offer great comfort and service, it need not necessarily be a specific, separate place such as a facility principally devoted to the care of dying. "Hospice" is really an attitude that could be utilized by our hospitals and nursing homes ... While care in the final days need not be directed toward curing a specific disease, it is not just custodial care. We cannot afford to have our super-specialists abandoning their patients when they have done all they can medically. We must retrain our physicians so that they are able to treat not only diseases, but people as well. We must provide counseling for hospital staff, the dying person and the family.

The Washington Post, 2-7:(A)16.

Joseph A. Califano, Jr.
Secretary of Health, Education and Welfare of the United States

1

We need a nation-wide, comprehensive health-insurance system, but I don't believe we can move to it until we change the nature of the medical system in this country. The reason for the inflationary spiral is that there is essentially no competition for health care. There is no incentive to hold down costs or to be efficient. None of the ingenious competition that makes our industrial system work so well operates in the health industry—which is the third-biggest in the country, behind agriculture and construction.

Interview, Washington/
U.S. News & World Report, 1-9:43.

2

... the Surgeon General and I have an obligation to educate the public—and particularly children and teenagers—to the dangers of smoking before they get hooked. People have a right, within obvious limits, to eat or drink or smoke whatever they like. But if you have a product like cigarettes that results in the premature death of thousands of people every year and adds billions to our national health bill,

then people ought to be alerted to that fact. We plan to announce a campaign early this year that will employ some very sophisticated advertising, telling people that smoking, by every statistical measure we have, is slow-motion suicide.

Interview, Washington/
U.S. News & World Report, 1-9:44.

3

[On his national anti-smoking campaign]: Teen-agers often start without the benefit of a fully informed perspective. Cigarette advertising portrays smoking as attractive and mature ... All we can do is provide information about the other side. It's one of the most significant things we can do in this country in the area of public health ... Contrary to those who charge that our efforts are somehow an intrusion on individual liberties, I must underscore that our primary goal is to provide information and conduct research that will enhance, not reduce, personal choice. If citizens are given all the facts from government or other sources and they still do not wish to give up a personal habit, then, except for protecting the rights of non-smokers, I think government can properly do no more.

Before House public-health subcommittee/
The Washington Post, 3-7:(A)3.

4

If we do not have national health insurance in this country, we will have the most incredible health-cost inflation. The American people will pay more for health care without a national health-insurance plan than with it. Indeed, health-care costs allowed to run wild the way they are running now [will] hit more than $300-billion in 1983 [and] make hamburger [out of recent meat-price increases).

TV-radio interview/"Issues and Answers,"
American Broadcasting Company, 7-2.

5

There's no single thing that Americans can do that will better improve their health, their longevity, reduce cancer, reduce heart disease, reduce emphysema, than quit smoking. Take

WHAT THEY SAID IN 1978

(JOSEPH A. CALIFANO, JR.)

the Social Security disability program alone. It is costing the American people $15-billion this year in disability payments, and $1-billion of those payments are attributable to cigarette smoking, to heart disease, cancer and respiratory diseases, like emphysema and chronic bronchitis, caused by cigarette smoking... Last year the budget for the Office of Smoking and Health was $900,000. The budget that I've asked for will be roughly $6-million in fiscal 1979 and I expect to get that from the Congress. That's an increase of more than six times. A lot of that money will be targeted on teenagers. I think the reason we've had the severe reaction from the Tobacco Institute and tobacco companies is because we're now targeting on the same audience that they're targeted on.

Interview, Washington, July 12/
The Dallas Times Herald 7-13:(A)13.

1

... the greatest life-saving breakthroughs of this century have been breakthroughs in preventive, not curative, medicine: vaccines to eliminate diseases, from smallpox to polio, pure water and pure food. So successful have preventive public-health measures been in this country, the pattern of crippling and killing diseases has shifted. At the turn of the century, the big killers and cripplers were infectious diseases. Today, the big killers and cripplers are related to environment and life-style: heart disease, cancer, stroke and accidents. Yet our health policies and health budgets are focused almost obsessively on treatment, not prevention. The Federal government will spend $48-billion on health care this year; of that amount, fully 96 per cent is aimed at treatment; only four per cent—less than $2-billion—is earmarked for programs to prevent disease or promote health.

Before American Federation of Labor-Congress of
Industrial Organizations, Washington, Sept. 11/
Vital Speeches, 10-1:739.

2

If the full consequences of occupational exposures [to carcinogens] in the present and the

recent past are taken into account, estimates of at least 20 per cent appear ... reasonable and may even be conservative. This means that at least 20 per cent of all cancer in the United States, and perhaps more, may be work-related.

At AFL-CIO conference on occupational safety
and health, Washington, Sept. 11/
Los Angeles Herald Examiner, 9-12:(A)5.

3

[On government involvement and aid in handling the problem of teen-age pregnancy]: The role of government must necessarily be limited when we approach a problem that deals with private lives and behavior. But when the social costs and consequences of a problem are so great, we must not fail to take what steps we can ... Whatever our opinions about adult morality and sexual standards, it is sad to contemplate the specter ... of children becoming parents while they are still children. Our society today is one in which personal self-discipline is more necessary than ever—and less popular than ever.

Congressional testimony/
The Christian Science Monitor, 9-13:7.

Jimmy Carter
President of the United States

4

Doctors care very seriously about their patients. But you have doctors organized into the American Medical Association, and they're interested in protecting the interests not of patients but of doctors. And they've been the major obstacle to the progress in our country to having a better health-care system in years gone by.

At town-hall meeting, Spokane, Wash., May 5/
The Dallas Times Herald, 5-6:(A)1.

5

As I am deeply interested in the small farmers of this nation, as I am deeply committed, and permanently, to a fine tobacco loan program, obviously I am also interested in the health of America. And I would say that the tobacco industry, the tobacco farmers, the Federal government, all citizens ought to have

(JIMMY CARTER)

an accurate and enlightened education program and research program to make the smoking of tobacco even more safe than it is today.

Wilson, N.C., Aug. 5/
San Francisco Examiner & Chronicle, 8-6:(A)1.

1

. . . those who own and operate many of our hospitals are the very ones who decide whether a patient should be admitted or not, who decide how long they stay, who decide what treatment they shall get, who decide how much to charge for that treatment. Because of this extraordinary monopoly over a certain aspect that is crucial to every American's life, the cost of hospital care is increasing at twice the rate of inflation in our country.

Before United Steelworkers of America,
Atlantic City, N.J., Sept. 20/
The Washington Post, 9-21:(A)2.

Denton Cooley
Surgeon

2

The average physician in this country is overworked, under-paid, over-insured and over-sued. Many are practicing defensive medicine and have become disenchanted because of the overkill by the press regarding the mistakes of the few.

Interview, Houston/
"W": a Fairchild publication, 9-15:10.

James C. Corman
United States Representative,
D-California

3

People who have reasonably good private insurance coverage, group policies, have pretty fair access [to health care]. But many people are driven into bankruptcy because they have to provide the total amount of dollars needed for their health care. If they paid into a compulsory [health-] insurance system all the time, and the payments reflected their ability to pay, the costs would be manageable and service would be available when they need it. That ought to be universal.

Interview/The New York Times, 7-23:(4)3.

Philip M. Crane
United States Representative, R-Illinois

4

I don't think the magnitude of the real problems in our health-care system warrant throwing out the baby with the bath water—which in my judgment is what you would do if you went to a comprehensive government compulsory health-care scheme. The examples of the Post Office and Amtrak strongly suggest that government really does not do anything very well. And I think, further, one must recognize that there are certain liabilities involved in politicizing such a thing as the provision of health care. In Great Britain three years ago, one of the complaints recurrently heard from people in the health-care field was that the politicians found it infinitely more attractive to spend public money on low-cost subsidized housing or mass-transit systems or highways or whatever, than they did on health care. And I think the reason for this is because . . . the average person doesn't give a great deal of thought to health care until either he is sick himself or has a close member of the family who is sick. And thus, in Great Britain, they have managed to hold the percentage of gross national product spent on health care to about 5.6 per cent. To preserve the fiction that they are guaranteeing free health care to one and all over there, they have been forced, on the one hand, to ration the service with 600,000 to 700,000 people on the waiting list for surgery, and secondly, to cut back on the quality, particularly in some of the more exotic areas.

Interview/The New York Times, 7-23:(4)3.

Michael Crichton
Physician, Author

5

I think we can all agree that American medicine, the way it is now, is not successful. But there's no evidence that the government can run anything. If you like the Post Office, you'll like socialized medicine.

Time, 2-20:91.

WHAT THEY SAID IN 1978

George Crile, Jr.
Surgeon; Emeritus consultant in surgery, Cleveland Clinic

1

[Saying hospital surgeons should all be salaried so that they do not depend on performing operations in order to be paid, which leads to much unnecessary surgery]: The government ought to say that no hospital can accept Medicare or Medicaid patients if it appoints any more surgeons to its staff except on a salaried basis. If the government did that, over 10, 15, 20 years, all the surgeons in the country would be salaried. There is nothing degrading about being paid a salary.

Interview/
Los Angeles Herald Examiner, 11-9:(A)1.

Robert L. DuPont
Former Director, National Institute on Drug Abuse

2

Ten years ago, only 1 in 20 American college students had tried marijuana. Today, 11 out of 20 have tried the drug, and 2 out of 20 are using it every day. Probably 15 per cent of the auto accidents in this country today are associated with marijuana intoxication . . . So far, we have only seen the tip of the iceberg. We're going to see more evidence of the harmful consequences of marijuana use on health, social activities, family living and work performance as time goes by. Those people going around today emphasizing the benignness of marijuana are going to have a tough time with their consciences . . . One of the most distressing facts to me has been the difficulty communicating the risks of marijuana use. Probably no issue was more frustrating to me in five years as Director of the National Institute on Drug Abuse. I have supported throughout that time the decriminalization of the personal possession of marijuana—the substitution of a non-criminal fine for the user of small quantities of the drug. By that means, we establish that marijuana use is prohibited behavior, but we do not use the criminal law and arrest records and tie up the courts to discourage it. That substitution of a fine for the current criminal penalty is perceived by 90 per cent of the public as being soft on pot. But,

actually, I am very deeply concerned about the rising levels of marijuana in this society. Too many people conclude that, because we have increasing levels of marijuana use, we will inevitably move toward legalization. I do not believe this is the way of the future. I can foresee the time when young and old will hold attitudes toward recreational drug use which are similar to those now held toward herbicides, pesticides and food additives—that they are unhealthy and should not be used.

Interview/U.S. News & World Report, 8-7:30,31.

Albert A. Gore, Jr.
United States Representative, D-Tennessee

3

[Saying the Blue Shield health-insurance system may be dominated too much by physicians]: Whenever a supplier of a service controls how much the largest group of consumers is willing to pay, the cost of providing the service will go up and up and up. [Information indicates] that the medical professional retains effective control of Blue Shield policies. If this is true, it should surprise no one that medical bills have been rising much faster than the overall rate of inflation.

At House Oversight and Investigations
Subcommittee hearing, Washington, March 21/
The Washington Post, 3-22:(A)10.

Lester Grinspoon
Psychiatrist, Harvard University Medical School

4

[On revelations of the use of illegal drugs by members of the White House staff]: If there were no use of marijuana and cocaine in a group of young people with the kind of educational and social background White House people have, that would characterize them as rather unusual in the United States today . . . I certainly can see that young people in the White House might find it [cocaine] attractive. It gives a sense of confidence to people who work hard, who burn the midnight oil. It helps them work under pressure. If you take away the White House aspect and just think of people

(LESTER GRINSPOON)

in their situation—very savvy, well-educated people working under lots of pressure—then you would expect to find people who would find cocaine attractive.

Interview, Boston/The New York Times, 7-22:7.

John W. Hanley
Chairman and president, Monsanto Company

1

In the chemical industry, all responsible companies are working overtime to search out and remedy any potential health hazards to employees or consumers that might be associated with chemical substances that can be toxic to humans. Our concern is being expressed not simply by claims that we are "doing our best," but by committing millions of dollars to the testing of our products for any and all potential harmful effects ... Study after study has confirmed that less than five per cent of all cancers result from workplace exposure. Of course, even that percentage is unacceptable, and industry is working hard toward the goal of eliminating those incidences altogether.

At City Club, Cleveland, April 14/
Vital Speeches, 6-15:536.

Howard H. Hiatt
Dean, Harvard University School of Public Health

2

Many current practices in medicine and surgery have not been evaluated. Radical mastectomy remains the most commonly practiced procedure for breast cancer, though there is no persuasive evidence that it is better than a simpler treatment. Tonsillectomies are being done less frequently, but one can still seriously question the need for close to a million a year. Last year over 80,000 Americans had coronary surgery at cost in excess of $1-billion. High costs make it necessary for us to set priorities, and we need more Federal support for the needed evaluation. The cost of not undertaking such research will be greater than undertaking it.

News conference, Washington/
The Washington Post, 5-19:(A)16.

Sheppard Kellam
Director, Social Psychiatry Study Center, University of Chicago

3

There are four levels of care in the health delivery system. The first is the epidemiological levels, that is, the occurrence of disorder and suffering in a population. The second is the outpatient-clinic level, either the traditional outpatient office or other types of outpatient health-care facilities. The third is the hospital, possibly backed up by the fourth level, the academic and scientific institutions. The rationing of resources within or across these levels of care will be sophisticated to the degree to which the functions and needs of those levels are understood. For example, communities often insist on participating at the epidemiological level; so, the allocation of resources has to take into account the aspirations, values and epidemiological characteristics of the community. There is a political collective-bargaining process that is appropriate to that level.

Panel discussion/
The Center Magazine, Sept.-Oct.:27.

Donald Kennedy
Commissioner of Food and Drugs of the United States

4

I believe the drug law, as now written, contributes to a kind of "mental set." We seem to have a national belief that there is a drug for every affliction. Physicians as well as patients are too often victimized by a kind of chemical ceremony in which no visit to a physician is complete without ending in a written prescription. The law should articulate clearly the standards for new-drug approval—safety and efficacy—in a way that can be clearly understood by our whole society. It needs to be conveyed that no drug is safe in the absolute sense, and no drug is safe in all applications. It needs to be made clear that some drugs, like amphetamines, are useful in very limited clinical applications but may be socially outrageously damaging in actual use. The definition of safety needs to be broadened to encompass the public health in its societal sense.

Before Consumer Federation of America,
Washington, Jan. 19/Vital Speeches, 3-1:314.

357

WHAT THEY SAID IN 1978

(DONALD KENNEDY)

1

... there is a growing realization on the part of the American people that individual habits, together with the artificial environment we have constructed for ourselves, are the primary determinants of health outcomes. Increasingly, "wars" on specific diseases are resulting in the startling discovery that: "We have met the enemy and he is us." This, initially, strikes many as profoundly discouraging; for it places the responsibility upon the individual, rather than the physician or the health establishment, and a great many of us would prefer to exchange money for better health rather than to exchange our habits for better health. After all, the basic American attitude toward the world is that if you want something you do not start a war to get it, or foment revolution, or establish colonies—instead, you *buy* it. And now we are told that you can't buy better health. That may sound like bad news; but it is also infinitely encouraging to know that we are not, like Job, always the agonized and bewildered recipient of injury disconnected from fault or identifiable individual responsibility, and that, while it is our ballgame, we have a chance to play. And that, in the long run, is good news.

At Third Annual Conference on Health Issues, Washington, May 23/Vital Speeches, 8-1:617.

Edward M. Kennedy
United States Senator, D-Massachusetts

2

The current non-system of medical care [in the U.S.] is a failure. If left unchecked, that failure will become a disaster—a disaster that will destroy Federal and state budgets, seriously injure the economy, cause countless human tragedies and, in my opinion, create a citizens' revolt that will pale the current concern over taxes ... Some who espoused [the right to health care] want to condition it—to condition it on many things over which the health-care system has no control—the general state of the economy, the size of the budget deficit, the presence or absence of major strikes, or oil

embargoes. But human rights are not conditional. And a commitment to conditional human rights is no commitment at all.

Before National Governors' Association, Boston, Aug. 28/Los Angeles Herald Examiner, 8-28:(A)6.

Horace R. Kornegay
President, Tobacco Institute

3

[Criticizing U.S. HEW Secretary Joseph Califano's anti-smoking campaign]: Secretary Califano recommends such things as heavy-handed anti-smoking propaganda, regulations to prohibit smoking in public places and regressive tax measures. Of the many proposals he has made, at least half represent the intrusion of government into individual freedom of choice.

Los Angeles Times, 2-16:(1)17.

Patrick J. Leahy
United States Senator, D-Vermont

4

Does it make sense to ban carcinogenic chemicals [such as food additives] which are a thousand times less deadly than tobacco, but not ban tobacco? And conversely, does it make sense not to allow people to make their own choice about chemical carcinogens when we allow them to choose to smoke cigarettes?

At Senate committee hearing on nitrites, Washington/Los Angeles Times, 9-24:(1)15.

William Masters
Sex therapist

5

I am totally, bitterly opposed to sex with a client. If any psychotherapist convinces the client he has the best of all worlds and winds up in bed with a client, he should never be sued for malpractice, he should be sued for statutory rape.

San Francisco Examiner & Chronicle, 10-8:(This World)2.

George S. McGovern
United States Senator, D-South Dakota

6

I have a suspicion that we're losing the war on cancer because of mistaken priorities and

(GEORGE S. MCGOVERN)

misallocation of funds. There has been no lack of funds—it's almost $1-billion a year ... On the one hand, we worry about saccharin, parts per billion of nitrosamines in nitrite-cured meats and possible mutagens in fired hamburger. On the other, we have a National Cancer Institute which spends only 1 per cent of its budget on the diet-cancer relationship when approximately one-half of all cancers may be diet-related.

At Senate Nutrition Subcommittee hearing,
Washington, June 13/
The New York Times, 6-14:(A)21.

Walter J. McNerney
President, National Blue Cross
Association

1

In cities like Baltimore, Washington, Cincinnati, Kansas City, Minneapolis and Los Angeles, there is an over-abundance of hospital beds, and patients pay for the unused capacity. Though in some other areas there aren't enough, Blue Cross has called for a moratorium on hospital construction until it can be clearly demonstrated that the unit is needed by a community. One of the most poignant pleas is: "We need a hospital." What politician has the guts to say no?

Interview, Chicago/People, 7-17:78.

Robert Mendelsohn
Assistant director, Michael Reese
Hospital, Chicago

2

I suggest that we should do whatever we can to encourage patients to distrust their physicians, to regard members of the medical profession the same as they would other professionals; that is, with suspicion. Ten or 20 years ago, the common advice was, "Ask your doctor." Today, the advice should be, "Question your doctor; challenge your doctor; do not believe him." You may not be able to get people to give up automobiles, but you can try to persuade them to reject allopathic medical care. Until we begin to discredit the physician and

modern scientific medicine, there will be no opportunity to place the other health items on the agenda in a serious and comprehensive way.

Panel discussion/
The Center Magazine, Sept.-Oct.:31.

Roy W. Menninger
President, Menninger Foundation

3

I estimate that 80 per cent of the complaints people take to their doctors—colds, upset stomach, back pains, loss of appetite, insomnia, fatigue—are not physical ills as much as they are psychosomatic reactions to problems of living. Moreover, emotional tensions and anxieties contribute directly to the increasing incidence of serious illnesses. As people try to cope with new life-styles, they often end up smoking, eating poorly, turning to alcohol or drugs, and failing to exercise properly. Thus, although we have conquered such dreaded diseases as smallpox and polio, we are seeing more heart problems, cancer, accidents, strokes and lung disease—problems that can frequently be related to life-styles. In many ways, modern America has become a much unhealthier place in which to live.

Interview/U.S. News & World Report, 5-1:80.

Gabe Mirkin
Teacher of sports medicine,
University of Maryland

4

A person's mood is helped significantly by exercise. There are many physicians who prescribe exercise for those people who don't feel very good about themselves. Exercise is effective as a tranquilizer. Tests have shown that a 15-minute walk can have a more tranquilizing effect than the most-used tranquilizers on the market today. It has been demonstrated that people who exercise suffer less from anxiety and are able to work harder. Lack of physical fitness is often associated with decreased performance at work or in school ... Exercise also helps you sleep at night.

Interview/U.S. News & World Report, 12-4:58.

WHAT THEY SAID IN 1978

Muriel Nellis
National Director, National Institute
on Drug Abuse report on over-medication

1

Without doubt, the most critical health problem with women today is the indiscriminate over-prescription and over-use of legal and prescription drugs. There are about 20 million women in the U.S. with a drug-abuse and alcohol problem—more than twice the number of men ... Most of these drugs are usually taken in combination—uppers, downers and alcohol. The extent of the problem is readily seen by the fact that, in 1975, a study showed some 229 million prescriptions were made out for mood-altering drugs—amphetamines, tranquilizers, sedatives. That year, 80 per cent of *all* prescriptions for amphetamines went to women. More than two-thirds of all the other drugs also went to women.

TWA Ambassador, October:48,49.

Barbara Nichols
President, American Nurses Association

2

[Advocating entrance requirements for the nursing profession]: ... every study and every discussion brings us to one conclusion: We are the only part of the health professional team that demands less than a baccalaureate degree for entrance into practice. If we are to raise the standards of our profession, we must be prepared educationally ... The entrance issue has been debated since 1903, largely because nurses themselves cannot agree on criteria for entrance. If we are going to survive as a profession, we must have basic entry rules. It will not be easy and there are many people in the health professions who hope that we fail ... [Nurses are] the most undervalued, underestimated, under-utilized, underpaid profession in the world. Neither doctors nor hospital administrators can mold our profession. We must do that ourselves.

At luncheon, Dallas/
The Dallas Times Herald, 11-15:(F)1.

David Reuben
Physician, Author

3

There's nothing ... as lacking in nutrition as breakfast cereal. One of the largest-selling cereals is 88 per cent refined sugar and flour. I like the commercial that says, if you eat their cereal, a banana and a glass of milk, you'll have a nutritious breakfast. If you eat the banana, drink the milk, throw away the cereal and eat the carton, you'll be better off.

Interview/San Francisco Examiner & Chronicle,
11-5:(This World)49.

Julius Richmond
Surgeon General of the United States

4

I would stress the need to pursue not only biological research, but behavioral research as well, since we now recognize that factors involved in the development of human disease and in its prevention are being shown more and more to be related to personal life-style at least as much as to fundamental biological processes. But we are a long way from understanding, for example, the behavioral factors that cause some individuals to start smoking, some to become habituated to cigarettes, and some never to start.

At meeting of National Heart, Lung and Blood
Institute and American Heart Association,
Washington/Los Angeles Times, 2-19:(4)5.

5

There is no known safe level of smoking of any cigarette of any type. While some cigarettes are less hazardous than others, there is no data anywhere in the large body of scientific evidence on the dangers of smoking that holds out any hope that there is such a thing as a safe cigarette or a safe level of smoking.

Aug. 10/Los Angeles Herald Examiner, 8-11:(A)10.

Jonas Robitscher
Fellow, American
Psychiatric Association

6

Anybody who wants the services of a psychiatrist should be entitled to seek them. But perhaps we make it too easy for people to get psychiatric care. Insurance reimbursement is sometimes too readily available. Many people end up spending more time in a psychiatrist's office than is essential. It may sound callous, but in a free economy where people have to

(JONAS ROBITSCHER)

pay for psychiatric care out of their own pockets, the fact that such care is expensive can be a way of differentiating between those who really want and need treatment and those who might like it but don't think it's too important to them.

Interview/U.S. News & World Report, 2-27:42.

Benjamin S. Rosenthal
United States Representative, D-New York
1

There are today at least 284 food categories that are exempt from listing some of their ingredients. The Food and Drug Administration has established "standards of identity" for such foods. There are certain ingredients which these foods must contain but need not label. There are other ingredients which they *may* contain and need not label. And there are still more ingredients which they may contain and *must* label ... As a result, tens of millions of people—at least one in four Americans—who, for various reasons, must know what is in the food they eat, are left in the dark. Allergy specialists estimate that over seven million Americans suffer from allergy reactions to food ingredients such as milk, eggs, nuts and monosodium glutamate. Another 23 million people have heart conditions and must avoid saturated fats, sodium and caffeine. There are over four million diabetics and kidney patients who must restrict their intake of sugar and/or salt ... Yet, according to [a] GAO study, 45 per cent of standardized foods are allowed to contain, unlabeled, at least one ingredient that must be avoided by one of those groups of Americans.

Before House Health and Environment Subcommittee, Washington/The Washington Post, 7-23:(C)6.

C. H. William Ruhe
Senior vice president for scientific affairs, American Medical Association
2

[On U.S. President Carter's criticism of the AMA as being too concerned with doctors' interests and being an obstacle to medical progress] : [His remarks] are a disservice to the 200,000 physicians and medical-student members of the American Medical Association ... The Association has a long record of accomplishment in scientific activities, medical education and the delivery of medical services. The President's comments simply do not reflect the historical record.

Chicago, May 5/
The Dallas Times Herald, 5-6:(A)1.

Jack C. Schoenholtz
Chairman, cost review committee,
National Association of Private
Psychiatric Hospitals
3

Government regulation has imposed a new set of problems on the health-care industry. It now costs a general hospital about $35 per patient-stay to comply with government regulations, according to the Michigan Hospital Association. The Task Force on Regulation of the Hospital Association of New York State finds that 164 different regulatory agencies have one kind of jurisdiction or another over hospitals. Twenty-five separate agencies are involved in just reviewing admitting procedures; 33 profess to protect patients' "rights"; and another 31 are supposed to oversee patient safety. And remember, health care is considered to be one of our newer regulated industries. It would seem that we are destined, as time goes on, to give less of ourselves to our patients and more of ourselves to the regulators.

Before National Association of Private
Psychiatric Hospitals, Hawaii/
The Wall Street Journal, 1-25:18.

W. Leonard Weyl
Clinical assistant professor of
surgery, Georgetown University;
Former president, Medical Society
of Virginia
4

I would say this—maybe a little bit with tongue in cheek, but I mean it: Our American [hospital] patients could learn something from the Russians as far as creature comforts are concerned. They could learn to get along with a little less "conspicuous consumption" when they're sick. The people over there [in Russia] manage to get treatment on a fairly primitive

WHAT THEY SAID IN 1978

basis. We don't have to get that primitive, but, on the other hand, some of the frills we have added to our hospitals and other facilities shouldn't be standard. If you want to have the frills, you should have to pay extra for it and know it. Our general insurance system and the government-supported health-care system shouldn't have to pay for the frills. We should provide basic "Volkswagen care" for all Americans through insurance and public aid. Those who want "Cadillac care" should buy the extra frills.

Interview/U.S. News & World Report, 11-20:66.

Theodore H. White
Author; Political historian

1

I'm pro-abortion. No legislature should tell a woman what to do with her body. And I'm no baby-killer. But up until six months, it's nobody's goddamn business what she does.

Interview, New York/
"W": a Fairchild publication, 9-15:41.

Sidney M. Wolfe
Director, Public Citizen Health
Research Group

2

I think, when all is said and done, the answer to the cancer epidemic we are now facing is not going to be in curing it. If it is ever going to go away, it is going to be by preventing it. The major known causes of cancer, emanating from corporations in the form of cigarettes, asbestos, estrogens in the form of drugs, are preventable. Until we change our priorities and prevent them, we are never going to be able to eliminate or even reduce significantly the cancer problem.

TV-radio interview, New York/"Meet the Press,"
National Broadcasting Company, 6-25.

The Performing Arts

MOTION PICTURES

Edward Albee
Playwright

1

I have an interesting arrangement with Hollywood. They commission me to write screenplays. They pay me handsomely and then they don't film them. It's invisible work.

Interview/The New York Times, 5-23:(C)4.

Irwin Allen
Producer, Director

2

I have a simple belief. As long as there are people, there are going to be calamities. As long as there are people, there is going to be a marketplace for disaster movies. I see no reason to believe that marketplace has dried up, as some have said. I think it is greater than ever. I also think that has to do with human nature. You never see a car wreck that doesn't attract a crowd. Or a fire. People are attracted to calamities. I'm not going to play psychiatrist and try to go into the reasons for that. But it does exist. And when you present a gigantic calamity people can watch from a comfortable seat in a lovely theatre, you are going to have an audience.

Interview/The Dallas Times Herald, 7-18:(B)4.

Woody Allen
Actor, Director, Writer

3

I keep trying to progress. The trap in film-making and in comic work in general is to find out what works and stay with it. The Marx Brothers made the same movie over and over again. Chaplin took risks and failed, but even the failure I find interesting to see over and over again. It's good *not* to find the form. If

you're not failing now and again, it's a sign you're playing it safe.

*Interview, New York/
Los Angeles Times, 1-29:(Calendar)1.*

4

The problem with people who do comedy is that it's tough for us to be taken seriously; but you can't let that prevent you from trying to do serious things. The object is not just to make people laugh and leave it at that. You can go deeper—make them laugh and *feel* and remember. Some things can be expressed in a funny way. But I'd hate to think I could only make amusing films. I'm too much a fan of serious films. Everybody says comedy is harder to do. That's become a truism by now, but it's wrong. Comedy is not harder. The hardest thing to do is good work, whatever it is.

*Interview, New York/
Los Angeles Times, 1-29:(Calendar)36.*

5

[On the Academy Awards]: I don't believe in competition for artistic achievement. I think it is impossible to say that one actress gave a better performance than another actress at certain levels. Once you get to a certain level of achievement I don't think that it is constructive. What I have seen of all of the awards, including the Academy Awards, there are large studios spending large amounts of money trying to influence members of the Academy to vote, taking ads out and campaigning so that the awards that are supposed to be based on the merits of the artistic achievement is frequently not what happens. I personally disagree with so many people that win awards in all fields, including the Academy Awards, that I make it none of my business. I feel that certain people

WHAT THEY SAID IN 1978

that deserve recognition don't ever get it. I don't really want to lend myself to that.

Interview, New York/
Los Angeles Herald Examiner, 4-3:(A)1.

Robert Altman
Producer, Director

1

It would be better not to discuss my [film] ideas at all, because articulating them destroys the natural, impressionistic arena where they come from: Then I *know* the idea consciously, and if enough of that piles up, it's like becoming an adult; your naivete gets destroyed. But to avoid that would mean becoming a hermit and losing the very references you deal with. It's all life and death; the growth process. You have to go with films the way you feel them, without fussing about what people will say. It's not so bad. There's no abyss out there—or else it's *all* abyss.

Interview, New York/
The Christian Science Monitor, 11-17:(B)21.

Lindsay Anderson
British director

2

As an economic fact, the American cinema has dominated British screen since the beginning of film. The relative failure of British cinema is due to factors other than economic—Britain has a class-divided tradition that has militated against the development of a popular medium. I feel I'm representing a nonexistent film tradition.

At symposium sponsored by United
Nations Educational, Scientific and
Cultural Organization, Beverly Hills,
Calif., Aug. 15/Los Angeles Times, 8-17:(4)1.

Michelangelo Antonioni
Director

3

[On watching his movies on television]: I feel like a father toward my old films. You bring children into the world, then they grow up and go off on their own. From time to time

you get together, but it isn't always a pleasure to see them again.

Time, 2-27:47.

Samuel Z. Arkoff
Chairman and president,
American International Pictures

4

The [motion-picture] market has changed . . . sharply within the last two years. TV has broadened its own boundaries, for one thing; it can do almost anything now that theatrical films can do. [TV] has stuff that's loaded with sexy and suggestive material, stuff that would be R-rated material in a movie. So we have to make something that is not on TV. Either the subject has to be something special or the way you do it or the size, the stars, the special effects, something.

Interview/Los Angeles Times, 8-25:(1)26.

Jerry Belson
Screenwriter

5

The writer getting more power [over final scripts] seems like an idea whose time has come. But I think you have to win power with talent. Those who have made it have made their splash somewhere else—like with books—and returned to films with the room to ask for control. I read 100 good reviews of *Smile* that never mentioned my name.

Los Angeles Herald Examiner, 3-17:(B)10.

Ingmar Bergman
Director

6

Somewhere, a long time ago, I wrote that the theatre was my wife and the movies my mistress. I wouldn't say the same thing today. If I had to choose between the film and the theatre, I would certainly choose the theatre. Movies are an obsession; the theatre, on the other hand, is an agreeable *metier* which one pursues with tranquil joy. You spend four or five hours a day rehearsing with actors, and if a scene doesn't come off, well, then it'll work tomorrow or next week. There is always plenty of time. But when I am shooting a film and I

(INGMAR BERGMAN)

manage to turn in three good minutes of film a day, then I'd best be satisfied. Movies are totally absorbing; they demand your total concentration and energy and strength. The time factor is always threatening, always hanging over you. You must always finish quickly. Film is incredibly demanding; it requires a permanent mobilizing of all your strength.

Interview, Munich/
The New York Times, 1-22:(2)1.

1

I can't stop myself from believing that I am employing an instrument which is so refined that it makes it possible for us to shed light on the human soul, to reveal it the more brutally and thereby add to our knowledge new dimensions of the "real."

San Francisco Examiner &
Chronicle, 1-29:(This World)2.

Ingrid Bergman
Actress

2

Everyone in the movies wants to work, and it's difficult to say no to a promising script. But I've always been happy I didn't have to grab any old project just for the money. I turned down a lot of work in Hollywood, and now I'm glad, because when all the old movies are shown on TV, I don't have to be embarrassed . . . I remember when I went to Alaska once to entertain American soldiers, and a movie of mine was being shown up there! I stopped and thought, what a responsibility—these movies go out everywhere in the world. I must never do anything I'd be ashamed of, or that my children would be embarrassed about. Now, with every script I read, I'm thinking, would my children like it? Is this all right to show them?

Interview, New York/
The Christian Science Monitor, 11-6:18.

Tony Bill
Producer

3

The question I ask myself is whether a serious person can remain active in the movie business. This industry is eating itself alive. There are so few films being made that you've got to wonder whether lightning can strike often enough to keep you going. With all the incredible dealing between studios, stars, distributors and theatres, dear old Hollywood is being vaporized into a steam cloud of money.

Interview/The New York Times, 2-12:(2)15.

Jacqueline Bisset
Actress

4

Great parts are easier to play because they carry you through. It's very difficult to play a role that doesn't have impact or a clear-cut attitude . . . If a part calls for circles under your eyes and requires you to fall apart, people will say "what a fine actress she is," just doing histrionics. Audiences react to hysterical roles, grubby characters, alcoholics, neurotics and prostitutes and the insane. Actresses get Academy Awards for playing those flashy roles. They aren't half as difficult as the roles that hold a picture together without flash, because you don't have a fixed attitude to get into . . . They don't give awards for those roles.

Interview/The Dallas Times Herald, 5-14:(D)11.

Karen Black
Actress

5

There are enormous amounts of money pouring into movies and they're the opposite of what people want to be done. Look, people liked *Rocky* because it was hopeful, not because it was a boxing movie. But producers will go out and make more boxing movies based on the *Rocky* success. Films are not dealing with people any more.

Interview, New York/
Los Angeles Herald Examiner, 3-4:(B)6.

Ray Bradbury
Science-fiction writer

6

I won't say a word against *Star Wars*. For a science-fiction writer, it would be like attacking the Pope! It's like a religion. You take a poke at any successful film that people are madly in

WHAT THEY SAID IN 1978

(RAY BRADBURY)

love with, and it's like hitting at their husband or girl-friend. I've seen it twice, and I enjoyed it more the second time around. I was curious to see what makes it work, and it's the same reason as ever—people love the unusual. They love to have their minds expanded into other worlds, areas of excitement and possibility that takes them out of their own orbit.

Interview, Beverly Hills,
Calif./San Francisco Examiner &
Chronicle, 1-15:(Datebook)18.

Marlon Brando
Actor

1

Nobody is more impressed by movie stars than other movie stars. You see it every time a bunch of actors get together at a party. There's always a phony heartiness in their greetings to each other, and then they engage in furtive eye-work and start sizing each other up, hoping they are on the skids career-wise, but telling each other their last picture was great.

Interview/
Los Angeles Herald Examiner, 6-20:(A)2.

2

My dream, as far as making movies is concerned, is to do a film where I receive no billing and there's no advance publicity nor critical reviews. Then the audience would go in, see the film and be pleasantly surprised and evaluate my performance without having been told what to think by reviews or how to react by publicity and propaganda. It's a pipe-dream, of course, but those are the ideal circumstances for my making a movie, and someday I may choose not to film any more unless I can have those circumstances guaranteed in my contract.

Interview, Los Angeles/San Francisco
Examiner & Chronicle, 12-10:(Datebook)17.

Marshall Brickman
Screenwriter

3

... collaborating [as he did with Woody Allen on *Annie Hall*] is definitely more fun than writing alone. You get gratification at the

moment—a laugh, some kind of feedback. Also, you're more honest. Not that you lie to yourself when you write alone; but, if you have to defend your idea to another human, you often see it for the stupid idea it is, rather than waiting nine months for the audience to tell you.

Interview, New York/
The Christian Science Monitor, 8-3:(B)10.

Mel Brooks
Actor, Director, Writer

4

... comedy has a long life. Just pick up a paper. What's playing? What's always being revived? Your comedies. Sometimes I wish I could open a university for young comedy writers and directors, because it's not enough if it's only Woody [Allen] or me coming along with a new picture every 18 months or so. Where comedy is concerned, less is not more. More is more, and less is less.

Interview, New York/
The Washington Post, 2-5:(F)8.

5

You don't make a picture just for the smarties. That's no good. You want all the people. You want a potato-salad picture. You know what I mean by a potato-salad picture? You're in the deli and there's this guy with a little piece of potato salad stuck in the corner of his mouth, and he's talking about your picture to his cronies. He's saying, all the time with the potato salad hanging, "You gotta see this Mel Brooks pitcha. You'll laugh so hard you'll pish yourself." What you don't want is this: Someone with a monacle says, "This is *tres interessant.*" Right away you know you're in trouble. Only Truffaut, Lelouch and their uncle Bernie will go.

Interview, New York/
The Dallas Times Herald, 2-20:(B)5.

Ellen Burstyn
Actress

6

Acting to me is problem-solving. If I know how to do a part going in, there's nowhere to

(ELLEN BURSTYN)

go. Everything is sent my way; but I only want what artistically presents a problem. Acting should be solving the unsolved.

Interview/Los Angeles Times, 12-27:(4)8.

James Caan
Actor

1

Nothing seems to hold my interest for long—except acting. There has to be fun in the work, I guess, to attract the kid in me. So I get lost in the character for two or three months. You know, it's like when you were a kid—after you left the theatre, you were Humphrey Bogart for a week.

Interview/Los Angeles
Herald Examiner, 1-1:(California Living)9.

Allan Carr
Producer; Theatrical manager

2

The star system has never gone away. Without stars, there is no Hollywood. Anyone that says that is not true is crazy, because stars are what people pay to see. Certainly, occasionally a story with unknowns works. They are unknowns until the picture comes out. Then they all become stars from their work. People are interested in looking at interesting people on the screen.

Interview/
Los Angeles Herald Examiner, 4-2:(A)9.

John Cassavetes
Actor

3

An actor, even more than a writer, is at the mercy of a good piece of writing. If the material is good, an actor gets nervous that he won't fulfill it. And if it's bad, he gets nervous about being able to make anything of it. I have always liked my work, although I do get bored once in a while, with the long waiting around. It is not always a glossy, beautiful profession. Sometimes it is demanding, hard work with no glamour at all. The most difficult thing is realizing you're a person speaking for others not able to express themselves as easily. It's very hard to keep track of yourself.

Interview, Bern, Switzerland/
San Francisco Examiner &
Chronicle, 6-11:(Datebook)22.

Richard Crenna
Actor

4

No actor ever does completely [grow up]. Can you imagine a grown person hooked for life on a game of charades, acting out fantasies and masquerades?

Interview, Los Angeles/
Los Angeles Times, 7-9:(Home)27.

Michael Crichton
Director, Screenwriter

5

To be effective, a director must be the person with the most detailed image of the finished film. What happens on any production is that everyone comes in with his own idea. The actors are making *their* movie; the camerman is making *his* movie; the designer is making *his* movie. You're obliged not to be confused by all this input, not to forget what you had in mind. When you fail to control or resolve all those influences, the picture is going to be screwed up in some way. It will be unsteady. The tone will wobble.

Interview/The Washington Post, 2-26:(F)7.

6

In some circles, the word "entertainment" is pejorative. But this is a genuinely frivolous attitude. If only "art films" were made, eventually there would be no funds to make any films at all. It's nice that [Michelangelo] Antonioni makes his pictures, and Universal makes *Earthquake*. There's a spectrum. I believe the greatest challenge is to express ideas so you find the largest possible audience. Some people think a work must somehow be bad if there's a large audience, but that's idiotic. If you do your work because you want to communicate with people, how can you say you don't want to communicate with as many people as possible? Look at Woody Allen—he's become a more

WHAT THEY SAID IN 1978

(MICHAEL CRICHTON)

widely appealing creative personality, and *Annie Hall* is not only his most popular movie, it's his best.

Interview, New York/
The Christian Science Monitor, 6-26:22.

1

There's always a certain tension between the director and the screenwriter on a movie. It's a tension that I hate. When I'm writing, I'm convinced that the screwball director will never get my idea across; and when I'm directing, the writer always seems to give me a half-finished piece of stuff. You can tell why Woody Allen began to direct his own films when you see *What's New, Pussycat?* It's the only Allen film that didn't get the jokes across—and that's because the director obviously didn't understand the jokes.

Interview/"W":
a Fairchild publication, 11-24:2.

George Cukor
Director

2

... when a director deals with actors, it must be a collaboration. The worst thing a director can do is kiss an actor's butt. I run a lighthearted set, but when the camera turns, *I'm* in charge, because—as I explain to them—I'm the only one who can see what is going to go on the screen. It's in my head, so I surprise them by never looking through the camera. This sometimes leads to complications when you have an accomplished actor with great individuality, say, a John Barrymore. With him, I had to know when to speak and when to shut up—and not to be intimidated. So I choose my actors well and get to know the quirks of their personalities—and, most of all, I share humor with them. That's how to effect the best collaborations. Then I keep my eyes open when they rehearse and perform, because you never know where the next stimulation comes from.

Interview, Los Angeles/
The New York Times, 4-30:(2)15.

3

To me, the director is the most important person on a film. He works on the script; he is in touch with actors, writers, the producer. He's in charge of the whole thing. It used to be you had the studio behind you, and they were wonderfully well-organized. Today it's so fragmented. One person goes out and gets the money. Somebody else gets the actors. Another finds the script. I'm no company boy, but there's no particular advantage to this new system. Now I read about these small independent production companies. They say they want to make meaningful pictures. There's a word for that—Bull. We *all* want to make good movies.

Interview, Los Angeles/
"W": a Fairchild publication, 5-12:26.

Bette Davis
Actress

4

The greatest compliment to a director is you don't realize he's directing. He should never be a star, but a mirror for the actor, the story.

Interview, New York/
"W": a Fairchild publication, 10-13:23.

Dino De Laurentiis
Producer

5

My philosophy is very simple. Making movies is a one-man operation. Somebody must take the responsibility, all of it. Forty-four years I've been in this business. I've made 600 pictures. And every time I do a picture where there are no problems, I arrive at the end with nothing on the screen. Where there are big problems, we have something up there.

Interview, Tahiti/San Francisco
Examiner & Chronicle, 9-17:(Datebook)20.

Bruce Dern
Actor

6

Hollywood is definitely an endurance contest. The movie business is the most competi-

(BRUCE DERN)

tive in the world. There are 32,000 members of the Actor's Guild, and only 1,400 making a living wage—that's $6,200 a year. To succeed you need staying power, and I'm an athlete training for the distance.

Interview, Los Angeles/
The Washington Post, 5-4:(B)1.

Barry Diller
Chairman, Paramount
Pictures Corporation

1

Pictures that make people feel good are especially effective [at the box-office] now because we haven't seen them for a long time. But serious pictures don't have to be unappealing. By December, the next good picture that burrows a foot below the surface will go through the roof at the box-office. We look for signs. We play witch-doctor. We project what will work from what has worked. But we don't really know anything.

Interview, Los Angeles/
The New York Times, 8-1:(C)3.

Kirk Douglas
Actor

2

I think, in a sense, that anyone dealing with the public has to have a moral conscience about what he does. An actor, because of his power as a star, can almost distort history. I feel that there is usually a point—very often a moral point—that pictures of mine are making. But I don't feel that that's the reason you do a picture. You make a movie to entertain. You make a movie to allow people to forget all their problems for a couple of hours.

Interview/U.S. News & World Report, 9-18:74.

Richard Dreyfuss
Actor

3

[As an actor,] I'm much more interested in imagination [than technique]. You can be "trained" to hell and gone, but if you don't have the imagination to conceive a perfor-

mance, you'll be technically trained to achieve mediocrity. You have to tell the truth, with as much attention to detail as you can. That's what makes [Marlon] Brando so amazing. It's not his technique—it's his imagination and his attention to detail. Brando sees a performance in his mind's eye, and then achieves more of that than any other actor I know.

Interview, Los Angeles/
Los Angeles Herald Examiner, 1-15:(E)1.

4

[On his winning an "Oscar" for best actor]: We [in the film industry] all spend most of our lives sitting at home, laughing [at the Academy Award presentations. But once nominated for an "Oscar"] you say, "Hey, wait a minute. I think I'm going to go to this tasteless, gaudy evening. Since I won, I think it's an absolutely perfect institution."

News conference, New York, April 4/
Los Angeles Herald Examiner, 4-5:(B)9.

Peter Falk
Actor

5

Actors care about two things: their kids, if they have any, and good parts.

Los Angeles Times, 3-11:(2)10.

Carl Foreman
Director, Producer, Screenwriter

6

I'll wake up at three or four in the morning, drenched in perspiration, so despondent I could cut my throat, enveloped in despair because I haven't been able to solve some story problem. But I've learned this much: If I can manage to live through the night, something good usually happens at daybreak. The expression, "dawn of a new day," is a terrible cliche, but it has special significance for me. It's the time when ideas begin to boom in my mind. Then I'll go to my typewriter and, with luck, solve all the problems that seemed impossible in the darkness a few hours earlier. To me, daybreak is absolute magic.

Interview/Los Angeles Times, 1-15:(Home)33.

WHAT THEY SAID IN 1978

John Frankenheimer
Director

1

I spent many years with David O. Selznick. If there is anything he taught me, it is the value of a powerful story clearly and dramatically told. That means a close collaborative effort between the very good writer, producer, cinematographer and director. I don't hold to the theory that film is a "director's medium," or anyone else's medium. I think it's important to get the best out of people. And, to do that, you have to let people know you trust them. Let them do their job. I always trust people until I find I can't.

Interview/Daily Variety, 4-20:17.

Larry Gelbart
Screenwriter, Playwright

2

[On writing comedy]: I know I can do it, but why can I do it? What is the mechanism that allows a person to express himself in a humorous way? Why does he or she look at the world through a totally different prescription? I can only think of it as a gift—one that's not asked for, that comes from no apparent source, but a gift which enriches your life forever.

Interview/Los Angeles Times, 7-16:(Home)28.

Lillian Gish
Actress

3

Some of the things that have happened to movies hurt my pride, like these little theatres where they show movies in places no bigger than this hotel room ... I remember when our pictures played in theatres with 3,000 seats. I believe in films so strongly that signs like these small theatres hurt. Films are the greatest force the world has ever had to move the hearts and minds of the world. And these small theatres are signs that we treat it like, well, like little entertainment.

Interview, Beverly Hills, Calif./
Los Angeles Times, 11-19:(Calendar)62.

Paul Michael Glaser
Actor

4

In this business, *the* bottom line is how well you get along with people. How much money you make, how many provisions you put in your contract don't add up to anything. Because at the end of the road, all you have are the friendships, the memories and what you went through together.

At Symposium for Actors and Actresses,
University of California, Los Angeles/
Los Angeles Times, 11-16:(4)29.

Marvin Goldman
President, National
Association of Theatre Owners

5

Lately you've been besieged by articles calling attention to some of the strange customs of the movie business. You've heard about kickbacks, quaint methods of accounting, actors suing distributors, agents suing actors, underreporting, overcharging. It reads like one of those plots that emanate from Hollywood. Tinseltown is fast becoming tarnished town in the public's perception. Some of the magic is rubbing away, revealing the seamy interior of the structure. It's like seeing a Hollywood set for the first time. The exterior is beautiful, true to scale, but the insides are wood, wire and completely exposed. And it's too bad that the public has to see this cancer in our core ... Besieged on all sides by this public exposure of the business' dirty linen, who can blame the average moviegoer and reader from looking on all of us as corrupt, money-hungry jackals feeding on one another for additional profit?

At ShoWest '78, Coronado, Calif.,
Feb. 12/Daily Variety, 2-13:14.

William Goldman
Screenwriter

6

I'm not in control of my scripts, nor do I wish to be. A contract [that gives writers final script authority] means spending a lot of time on the movie set, which to me is so boring. A movie is still a group endeavor. Sure there's a certain interest in screenwriters today, but it's predicated on the money. There's a shortage of competent writers ... It's all guesswork in movies anyway. If they knew what would work, they'd all be *Star Wars* ... I don't think [script control] will help [many] writers much.

(WILLIAM GOLDMAN)

For, you see, most people don't stay screen writers if they can help it. If they do, they go mad.

Los Angeles Herald Examiner, 3-17:(B)10.

1

There is a quote by Isherwood from, I believe, *Prater Violet,* that goes: "Once a movie is set in motion it cannot pause, it cannot apologize, it cannot retract anything, it cannot wait for you to understand it." A novel is different. The reader is basically alone with the book. He can put it down, skip, go back to something he's not sure of. The novel-writer can take side trips. Screenplays are structure. That's all they are. They are not art, they are carpentry.

Interview, New York/
The New York Times, 11-12:(2)24.

Charlton Heston
Actor

2

[On acting]: it isn't fun, like playing tennis or drawing or going riding with my daughter. People say it must have been fun to make *The Ten Commandments.* It wasn't fun. It's bloody hard, hard work. The days are long, and you drink failure like coffee every day, realizing that you have not done what you wanted to do. But it's your life. I couldn't do anything else. It's not fun to act. It can be rewarding and challenging and satisfying and all those things, but it's not fun.

Interview/
The Dallas Times Herald, 12-20:(E)11.

William Holden
Actor

3

[On film music]: You can get a lot of help from the man who scores the picture and puts in an oboe or a flute at just the right moment. Music can make all the difference. In *Picnic,* Kim Novak and I were just doing a little dance together, but when Morris Stoloff scored the number, it became a love duet. And in *Love Is a Many Splendored Thing,* every time Jennifer Jones looked to the hill for her lover's return

and the theme music played, you felt like crying.

Interview, Los Angeles/
The Dallas Times Herald, 1-22:(I)5.

4

An actor must make his character believable to the audience, not just to himself. If not, how can he get across the feeling of what he believes? It's a very fragile area to be in. You have to create a false innocence in your character. The actor, of course, has read the third act. He knows how the story ends. But the character he plays must never convey for a moment that he knows what is going to happen. The actor has to block it off.

Interview/
The Dallas Times Herald, 5-8:(E)5.

5

A great deal of what would have been great Hollywood story-telling is done now on the basis of a lower common denominator [caused by television]. We are accepting lower standards, and I resent that. There was always a discipline in those [old] days and that meant good morale in the studios. Today in the film business there's a tremendous amount of indiscretion because of a lack of discipline.

Cannes, France/
The Dallas Times Herald, 5-31:(A)2.

Rock Hudson
Actor

6

I'd love to play more villains. I'd even welcome the opportunity to play the antihero roles that are being done these days. There must be a reason . . . I haven't been offered villain parts. Maybe it's because no one thought [I] could play them with conviction. I imagine personal appearance has something to do with it. A sinister appearance gives an actor a better chance to play a heavy than one who doesn't look menacing. But sinister facial characteristics certainly aren't mandatory. Ernest Borgnine and Charlie Bronson started out as villains and eventually wound up playing good guys. Sometimes it's to everyone's advantage for an actor to play against his type. It adds an unexpected

WHAT THEY SAID IN 1978

(ROCK HUDSON)

dimension to the story ... Strangely enough, heroes are more difficult to play than heavies because they require greater restraint. But they aren't half as much fun. Playing straight leading men is boring, boring, boring. I'd dearly love to play some heavies, just for the change.

Interview/The New York Times, 1-11:21.

John Huston
Director

1

What makes a fine actor? That great power of perception followed by presentation. I don't believe any amount of application and study can enhance a relatively small amount of talent. When you have great talent, it blazes.

Interview, Los Angeles/
The Hollywood Reporter, 5-5:27.

Glenda Jackson
Actress

2

Acting as a profession provides the fulfillment of never being fulfilled. You're never as good as you'd like to be ...

Interview/
Los Angeles Herald Examiner, 5-3:(A)2.

3

I think the great hurdle of the moment is that few writers are able to get over the idea that women are only concerned with their emotions or other people's emotions. The idea, for example, of a woman as a captain of industry, or as someone who makes decisions, or someone whose life is okay emotionally and has other strands to it, is something that is not being considered by writers. Women in films are always caught up in the emotional aspect of everything. They're either causing a man a lot of trouble or giving him the greatest happiness he's ever known. But in both cases, the women are merely an adjunct. They don't exist in their own right.

Interview, Los Angeles/
The Dallas Times Herald, 6-30:(E)3.

4

English actors are vastly overrated. I don't understand it. American actors have this terrible inferiority complex. They don't believe they can do certain things. They don't believe they can do Shakespeare, which is rubbish. Their negative attitude toward their own work is not borne out by what I see in films and television. I mean, consider the appalling stuff that is the daily diet of most actors in America, and yet they can still make it interesting. That's true ability.

Interview, Los Angeles/
The Dallas Times Herald, 6-30:(E)3.

Norman Jewison
Producer, Director

5

[On film critics]: A full theatre is far more important than what someone writes about the film that's playing there. In an empty theatre, a film is not alive.

At Los Angeles International Film
Exposition, April 30/Daily Variety, 5-2:2.

Gene Kelly
Actor, Dancer

6

[On the musicals he did over the years at MGM]: I could not have done those pictures without the great studio system. It would have taken too long. By the time you wheel and deal and get financing today, you're practically an old man. The big studios gave you a base from which to work. It seems to me that there is a certain kind of insecurity in the performing arts today ... In my generation, a star was one who had a certain longevity. We just didn't feel like stars until we had 20 years of work. The system worked. Fred Astaire is still a star. So is Cary Grant. And Jimmy Cagney could come out of retirement and fill a theatre anytime.

Interview, Beverly Hills,
Calif./San Francisco Examiner &
Chronicle, 3-12:(Datebook)29.

Deborah Kerr
Actress

7

... the old, old Hollywood—oh, the luxury of it all. It was like this enormous private club.

(DEBORAH KERR)

There were limousines and special dressing-rooms. You were constantly being carted around. But in another way it was like going to a new boarding school. On the first day you were taken to see the new headmaster—who was Mr. L. B. Mayer.

Interview, Washington/
The Washington Post, 8-28:(B)3.

1

[On sexual explicitness in today's films] : I think there's been a tremendous loss of what we used to call romance. You're almost considered square if you use the word "romance." And certainly [its absence] has resulted in a loss of values . . . The coarsening of life through the medium of the movies and television has certainly left some sleazy dregs behind.

Interview, Washington/
The Christian Science Monitor, 9-28:(B)15.

Jennings Lang
Producer

2

I've certainly had my share [of flops]. But I'm a percentage player . . . I always welcomed taking chances. I start out with the premise that "you can't win 'em all" and then, knowing I'm going to lose some, I try to win at least 51 per cent of the time. It's okay to be rebellious, as I've been all my life. It's okay to be flamboyant and assert my independence. It's great to find an attention-grabbing incident. But ultimately the audience has to be pleased. That's the one indispensable key to showmanship.

Interview, Beverly Hills, Calif./
Los Angeles Times, 2-19:(Home)25.

Norman Lear
Writer, Producer

3

[Saying he is leaving television to return to motion pictures] : The excitement of television is that you can have a good idea on the first of September and it can be broadcast to 40 million people in mid-November. Now, in that process is the crunch of getting it out—getting it

cast, getting it written, getting it made well. The excitement of a theatrical film is that you can get an idea and then, in the writing, make love to it for three months. You can film it slowly, making sure you have everything you want over a period of eight or 10 weeks. Then you can rewrite it wherever you want to in the editing and again make love to that material for anywhere from three months to a year. You can finish it, hone it, get it as complete as you'd like it.

Interview, Los Angeles, March 1/
Los Angeles Times, 3-2:(4)1.

Claude Lelouch
Director

4

Cinema is made of tricks. It's nothing but tricks. Yet, as in all the other arts, the tricks mustn't be seen. Tricks are necessary. We have to tell the life of a man, or some other large subject, in two hours. So one must be like a magician: If you don't see the trick, he's fantastic. In most of today's films, including mine, you see them. In the most *successful* films, you don't. Sometimes I don't see a trick for the first 10 minutes, and then it's like I'm not watching a film at all. Then for one second I see the trick, and that's the end of it—I detach myself from the film.

Interview, New York/
The Christian Science Monitor, 8-7:22.

Jack Lemmon
Actor

5

Various roles demand different approaches and uses of your technique and present a different problem. Often, the ability to make a performance seem extremely simple is the most difficult thing to do of all, and very often critics and the public will overlook some of an actor's finest work because he was successful in making his scene non-"actory" and simple.

Interview, Beverly Hills, Calif./
The Christian Science Monitor, 4-6:27.

WHAT THEY SAID IN 1978

Sergio Leone
Italian producer

1

[In Italy] it is impossible to become the real producer that existed once upon a time in America—the one who starts with a good idea, has a script written by good writers, calls in a leading director, casts the best actors and actresses, and in the end takes full responsibility for better or for worse. In Italy, at the smallest level, every director is really the author; he has to invent everything himself. So as a producer, either I impose my will on the director and we have a catastrophe, or I withdraw into myself and leave the director to his idiotic devices. That is why in the last two films I produced, I used the name "Rafran" and not Sergio Leone.

Interview, Europe, Italy/
The Dallas Times Herald, 12-14:(B)1.

Richard Lester
Director

2

Film-making is anguish of the worst kind. It is a day-by-day ordeal, even under the best of circumstances with the best cast, crew and script. I live and work on nervous energy. I try to produce a sense of exuberance so it will be passed on to others. If I sat down, so would other people. So I haven't sat down for the last 60 days. I have to keep the crew going, sometimes by hitting myself over the head with a blatter.

Interview, Alamosa, Colo./ San Francisco
Examiner & Chronicle, 6-25:(Datebook)19.

Joshua Logan
Director

3

... the fact that *Paint Your Wagon* became the biggest hit of my career makes me think God hasn't been very fair. That film wasn't even good, much less the best thing I've ever done. When we were making it, everyone at Paramount was sure it would be a smash, and I kept thinking: Poor things—won't somebody tell them? I thought it was the biggest bungle I'd ever been concerned with. And yet it turned out to be my biggest success. Isn't that awful!

Interview, Los Angeles/
The Dallas Times Herald, 10-16:(B)5.

Shirley MacLaine
Actress

4

I'm getting a lot of scripts with women starring together, but they're things like caper pictures. Instead of the guys going in and stealing the diamond, the girls do it. It's horrifying—what they're doing is putting all us women back into the Paul Newman-Robert Redford buddy syndrome. They're starring the women together now, just like they starred the men together for five years. But they still can't figure out what to do with adult men and adult women on the screen. And starting a serious discussion about feminism in Hollywood is still the quickest way to empty a room out there. Frankly, I think they're making a big mistake. But that'll change as soon as a picture about women cleans up and shows them there's money to be made. Really, that's Hollywood's only criterion.

Interview, New York/
The New York Times, 1-22:(1)40.

Louis Malle
Director

5

I must say that basically I hate to make decisions. Since directing a picture means making decisions every 10 seconds, there's an obvious contradiction. That may account for my reputation as a disorderly director. I think of the script as a rough blueprint and like to change things as the shooting proceeds. This caused some problems since . . . crews like to be well prepared and have everything in order. That's fine, but my definition of a good technician is one who's well prepared—but also prepared to change everything in five minutes.

Interview, Washington/
The Washington Post, 4-30:(L)7.

Rouben Mamoulian
Director

6

The best award is when you find your films have held up. Time is the best critic.

Interview, Beverly Hills, Calif./
Los Angeles Herald Examiner, 5-14:(F)11.

Henry Mancini
Composer, Conductor

1

[On writing music for motion pictures]: I no longer worry about whether a film is going to be a success or not. Not any more. I must be getting mellow in my old age. Films are like streetcars; they keep coming and going. You do what you can; you do your best on every film. That's all you can be concerned about.

Interview, Hawaii/ San Francisco
Examiner & Chronicle, 8-30:(Datebook)21.

James Mason
Actor

2

Most of the distribution companies, like Paramount and MGM, are now headed by agents. When they get into trouble, or fail to come through with a hit picture, they get demoted and go back to their agencies, and some other agents are elevated to take their place. I find the situation funny and very sad at the same time. It means that the conglomerate men, who have all the money but are complete amateurs in film-making, either have to go by rule of thumb, which means following the latest trend, or do what these agents instruct them. Unfortunately, what the agents tell them can often be a series of set-ups devised by the agents for their own good.

Interview, London/
"W": a Fairchild publication, 9-15:24.

Marsha Mason
Actress

3

I go to a cocktail party and I hear producers talk about "Barbra" ... Everybody knows they're talking about Streisand. There is something identifiable about her in each picture, no matter what part she plays. Her personality stands by itself. I'm not quite sure what that kind of "an established personality" means for an actress. It's a very peculiar dichotomy. On the one hand, you are supposed to be able to portray a character very realistically—be a fine actress. On the other hand, you are supposed to have this quality of being recognizable as yourself no matter what role you play. I think that's a very old-fashioned concept. I'd much rather have people walk up to me and say, "I didn't realize that you're the one who played in *Blume in Love.*"

Interview, Los Angeles/
Los Angeles Times, 5-5:(Fashion-78)4.

Walter Matthau
Actor

4

I was better on stage. In movies, I don't have much control and I don't really know what I'm doing. I just depend on the director, and when things really get rough I just remember what Kim Novak told me: She said to just speak softer and softer until they are forced to listen. It's true. When you're screaming on the screen, people tend to want to run out and buy popcorn.

Interview, New York/San Francisco Examiner &
Chronicle, 4-9:(Datebook)17.

Paul Mazursky
Producer, Director, Writer

5

There are two kinds of movies—movies made out of passion and movies made to make money. They're both authentic, but the pictures I've loved were made out of passion.

Newsweek, 3-13:75.

6

I make films to be seen in a theatre. The human experience is a group experience. That is the way films should be experienced. Whatever is to come in the way of TV, taping machines and the like, I hope motion-picture theatres will always be with us. The audience experience is important. I know I personally prefer seeing a movie with an audience.

Interview, Dallas/
The Dallas Times Herald, 4-18:(B)8.

Roddy McDowall
Actor

7

[On actors]: The Hollywood myth is a myth. It's to do with a need for royalty, for

WHAT THEY SAID IN 1978

(RODDY McDOWALL)

deification. But if you see yourself as a myth, you cannot exist. You're living a pose. You're the author of your own foolishness.

Interview/Los Angeles Times, 11-15:(4)1.

Daniel Melnick
Executive in charge of world-wide production, Columbia Pictures

1

If I don't have a profitable group of pictures, I'm going to get fired. This is a no-win job. Regardless of how good you are and how careful, luck enters in and eventually your luck will run out. The difficulty we all face is that the industry is polarized between enormous hits and total washouts. There aren't many films in the comfortable middle.

Interview/The New York Times, 2-12:(2)15.

Daniel Melnick
President, Columbia Pictures

2

Historically, some studios *permit* you to make a film. Some studios *defy* you to make a film. I'd like to see Columbia *help* you to make a film by stimulation, by inspiration and by some cash at the right time.

*Interview, Los Angeles, June 1/
The New York Times, 6-2:(D)3.*

3

Genuine artistic conviction is a good reason for making a film, but it isn't the only reason. It's well for a studio head to remember that sentimental drama, broad comedy and rough action have been the commercial mainstays of show business for 4,000 years.

June 1/Daily Variety, 6-2:8.

Robert Mitchum
Actor

4

When I first went to work, I'd go into casting offices and they'd say, "What's he do?" Or, "Did you ever think about getting your nose fixed or changing your name?" Then later, not too much later, they'd say, "We need a Mitchum type." I'd say, "What exactly is that?" I turned out to be the only one, which ensured

my longevity. As long as you're not dependent on youthful beauty and display versatility, you've got far greater opportunities.

*Interview, Los Angeles/
The New York Times, 4-9:(2)17.*

Paul Newman
Actor

5

[On whether he has any bitterness about never having won an Academy Award]: Oh, maybe 20 years ago there would have been. But now I'm a little mellower. So, no, no bitterness. It doesn't bother me. Besides, all you have to do is remember that the stars of the two biggest box-office films of all time were two robots and a shark. That gives an actor something to think about, doesn't it? . . . it's a very whimsical business.

*Interview, New York/
The Dallas Times Herald, 11-5:(H)3.*

Leonard Nimoy
Actor

6

. . . given a challenging script, a three-dimensional part, an actor then has a clear shot at making a rainbow flight . . . Not just an acting job, but a mystical or spiritual adventure. To stand in another person's shoes, to see as he sees, to hear as he hears, to know what he knows, to do all this with a sense of control, a mastering of the dramatic moment. To do it with a well-written part—this is the supreme moment. It's a merging of all the hopes, fantasies, talent, opportunity and work of a lifetime, focused into a performance. If an actor has never traveled that journey, life is still an unfulfilled dream. But I've been there. I've touched the rainbow, and it's like flying my plane along the edge of sunrise, somewhere between sea and sky. I just can't imagine a more beautiful experience.

Interview/Los Angeles Times, 4-16:(Home)75.

David Niven
Actor

7

[On acting]: At best, we're playing children's games. We get up in the morning, put on

376

THE PERFORMING ARTS—MOTION PICTURES

funny clothes, and show off in front of the grown-ups. And we get paid for it, which, I suppose, is why everybody wants to work in the movies.

Interview, Rhodes, Greece/San Francisco Examiner & Chronicle, 6-25:(Datebook)41.

1

Where work is concerned, I ask four questions—in this order: Where is it going to be made? Who is going to be in it? How much am I going to be paid? If the answers are satisfactory, I then ask what it is all about. If I like the sound of that, I read the script.

Interview, London/ The Dallas Times Herald, 10-23:(B)6.

Rudolf Nureyev
Ballet dancer

2

[On his acting in the film *Valentino*]: . . . I would have regretted not having taken the opportunity. But I do find that one has an extraordinary sense of void after doing a film. It is as if this great machine has rolled over you and left you behind, or under the wheels. It's very different from ballet; the theatre, with a live audience, is always somehow a source of regeneration, no matter how the performance went.

Interview, Washington/ The Washington Post, 8-6:(H)5.

Laurence Olivier
Actor

3

I am an actor because that is all I am qualified to do. I shall go on acting until a couple more illnesses cause me to drop. And then I shall write that dreaded book.

Interview, Vienna/ Los Angeles Times, 2-26:(Calendar)33.

Geraldine Page
Actress

4

If you make good, interesting films about human experience that people can share, it

doesn't matter what the "going thing" is . . . [But] the people who plan films and make them go along shoals, like fish, [are] always startled when something does well that isn't popular at the moment. The people who put projects together want to be comfortable; they don't want trouble. Then they're disappointed when the products they've assembled with all the comfortable elements put people to sleep. Or they don't care, so long as they make money, get a tax refund. It takes some doing to get to the volatile moments.

Interview, New York/ Los Angeles Times, 9-3:(Calendar)27.

Nicola Pagett
Actress

5

I want to be a good actress—but, even more important, I want to be a good liver. I suppose whatever I really am comes out on the screen somehow. If I develop as a human being, then my acting will inevitably get better—they are all tied up together. If I sell out, then my acting will be sellout-acting. And that's what the audience picks up. There are so many ways to sell out in acting—prestige, power, success, ego trips. I watch myself very carefully.

Interview/The Christian Science Monitor, 3-16:33.

Gregory Peck
Actor

6

[On questionable accounting practices in the film industry]: There's no doubt that there has been some fast bookkeeping going on . . . A clean-up is due, and, like a minor-league Watergate, it took the press to bring it about. The trouble with actors is that they are too busy acting. Many are not good businesspeople. All the tycoons and producers are; they are bound to come out on top in any deal. I think there will be a reform of the fast bookkeeping and more personal audits, but an actor will never be able to protect himself in Bangkok.

Los Angeles Herald Examiner, 2-15:(A)2.

7

What's wrong with Hollywood today is that these studios are appendages of giant corpora-

WHAT THEY SAID IN 1978

tions, and the men who run them are cold-hearted accountants. They'd rather risk $12-million on a potential blockbuster than $400,000 on a fresh, creative, little, simple idea from a new director or a new director-writer. So those are the ground rules and there's no use kidding yourself. Those high-powered chaps in New York are not concerned about quality, just profit and loss. And the men they put in charge are disposable, like Kleenex. If the balance-sheet doesn't read well, throw the rascals out and get some new rascals in.

Interview, Los Angeles/
Los Angeles Times, 10-22:(Calendar)37.

Anthony Perkins
Actor

1

I've always believed you have only to look at the careers of stars who've sold out to see that an increase in luxury means a corresponding decrease in ability. So I deliberately shun the sybaritic life. I live modestly and I truly don't care when my next job comes along. Inordinate security is stifling for an actor's progress. Marlon Brando used to say he'd done his best work here before he was settled and when he didn't know anyone and was unhappy. Well, I don't say you should be unhappy in order to do good work—only that you shouldn't be comfortable or at ease ... I always remember something [director] Mike Nichols said when he was asked, "What if your next film is a flop? What will you do?" Mike thought for a moment and then answered, "But I'll still be me, won't I? I'll still have myself." It's a nice outlook. I've made it my own ...

Interview, Los Angeles/
Los Angeles Times, 4-27:(4)16.

Jon Peters
Producer

2

... when I was a kid I was a very big liar. If I wanted something, I just said I had it—I created my own reality wherever I was. That can come in very handy in a business [motion pictures]

where you sometimes have to say, "Give me red curtains and a yellow sun and make the roof move up and down and vibrate as she walks in."

Interview, New York/
The New York Times, 1-29:(2)17.

Frank Price
President, Columbia Pictures
Productions

3

Television has had a substantial impact on film audiences. It has made them more sophisticated about films, more choosy about what they want to see. They are more visually oriented today. Films have to be better, more entertaining, with something very special, to attract an audience today. The only place they can get the total experience of a film is in a theatre, with a big screen and Dolby [high-fidelity] sound. They're not going to get it from TV.

Interview/Los Angeles Times, 8-25:(1)26.

Mario Puzo
Author, Screenwriter

4

[The film industry] is the most crooked business that I've ever had any experience with. You can get a better shake in Vegas than you can get in Hollywood. [For those who are going to write for films,] make sure you get a gross, not a net, percentage of the profits. If you can't get gross, try and get as much money as you can up front. But the best way is to go in with a mask and a gun.

Time, 8-28:72.

Robert Redford
Actor

5

Overnight success is the single most difficult thing that an actor must learn to overcome. At that point, an actor is very easily tempted to become dependent on that peaked moment of fame and glamour. If you ever get totally dependent on one thing, you're in bad shape. Maybe one of the reasons why I've had a relatively happy life is that I've always had several things to dedicate myself to. The British actors have a certain advantage over Americans in the

(ROBERT REDFORD)

diversity of their work. But they don't have a choice because there's not enough money to go around in England. An actor might have to go from working on the stage to working in the dockyards. I wonder if British performers would have the same emotional problems that American performers have if they had the same temptations that go with Hollywood money.

Interview, New York/
"W": a Fairchild publication, 5-12:27.

Burt Reynolds
Actor, Director

1

I think I'm an actor's director. I love actors. And I don't mean that to sound like a stupid thing coming from an actor. I realize how terribly personal acting is, how difficult it is. And I also realize and know some actors have to be coerced, some have to be kissed, some have to be driven, some have to be spoiled, some have to be yelled at, and you can't treat them all the same.

Interview, Los Angeles/
The New York Times, 1-15:(2)12.

2

I told someone recently that I was a star in spite of my movies. I didn't mean that they were necessarily bad movies. I meant that if I'd listened to those who wrote about them I'd have quit the business long ago. But the fact is most of them made money, despite what people said. Look at the reviews for *Smokey [and the Bandit)*. And look what happened to it [its box-office success]. As I said on a TV show not long ago, it must be very disheartening for a critic to say a film is a piece of junk and then have it go on to make millions of dollars.

Interview/Los Angeles Times, 5-7:(Calendar)33.

Herbert Ross
Director

3

I don't believe in politicizing films and I don't believe in propaganda in terms of dialec-

tics, but I do think that . . . just as the films of the past decade reflected social conditions, in a strange way even the shallowest of movies are more revealing about our thinking process and our historic process than any other form, because they capture on film the way people dressed, ate, talked, sat. That's what film history has begun to discover about the movies of the '30s and '40s. They're a permanent record of the way people lived in a certain historical period.

Interview, New York/San Francisco Examiner &
Chronicle, 1-15:(Datebook)15.

4

As you get older and more experienced, you begin to understand that film should never be effortful. Many young directors with enormous talent continually wrench you out of the picture, to remind you that they're making it. But the real artist should be as self-effacing as possible. The whole point of art is not to let the audience in on the effort.

Interview, New York/The Christian
Science Monitor, 1-30:15.

5

It is the humanity in a film that makes it live. To me, plot is subservient to developing human qualities in a character. Even with Woody Allen or Neil Simon, I approach comedy as drama and get the characters' attitudes right; then the laughs fall into place. The more human, the more an audience cares.

Interview, Los Angeles/
The New York Times Magazine, 11-12:17.

Mort Sahl
Writer, Humorist

6

If you brought in *Gone With the Wind* now, it would be rewritten to please the National Organization for Women so that Rhett Butler would be thrown down the stairs by Scarlett. The ethic in the motion-picture industry, which is largely underwritten by liberals, is: "I'm not a prisoner of the machismo culture, as my father was. I'm therefore proud to say I'm

WHAT THEY SAID IN 1978

(MORT SAHL)

ashamed to be a man." That's kind of the current retreat.

News conference, Washington/
The Christian Science Monitor, 11-16:(B)38.

Robert Shaw
Actor

1

I'm in the ironic position of someone who achieved commercial success rather late in life after spending years on the stage and in making quality films that no one went to see. Being 51 years old and having 10 children . . . creates the economic necessity that forces me into all those big-budget movies in which I often don't say a single realistic line. I can't say that I enjoy working as an actor the way I used to, but at the same time I can see the way things are going, and I know that it's better to be at the top of the heap than at bottom. I have no intention of having to make television commercials when I'm old. Money in the bank means freedom of choice, and if someone wants to pay me $1-million to make a film, I'll make it.

Interview, Palm Springs, Calif./
The New York Times, 3-24:(C)8.

2

I fell into a trap, and now I'm getting out. I wanted to be a Film Star, and appear in Big Pictures. Having done that, I found I couldn't escape. I was like a slave in a galley ship. The result was I became a haunted man, taking the money and running, speaking lines in scripts I'd have been ashamed to have written . . . I wanted to beat the game. I just couldn't accept the fact that I was getting less than half what Paul Newman got. Being a competitive man, I resented that deeply. So I went after the big money. Which meant being in big pictures. I convinced myself that with my responsibilities and my tendency to give money away like a punch-drunk boxer, I had to earn a lot of the stuff. But after a while you get sick of being in blockbusters. Ask any actor. There's no satisfaction in them.

Interview, Palm Springs, Calif./
Los Angeles Times, 4-4:(1)20.

Sidney Sheldon
Author; Former screenwriter

3

When you write movies, you have a hundred collaborators. The actor says he can't say your lines. Everybody's got ideas. You can't describe a character as short and stocky because they may want a tall, thin star instead. But when I was doing it, I didn't mind it; I loved it. It was the way it was. The same with television. Everybody knew what you couldn't do. But that was all right, too. It was the way it was. The way it was was also very comfortable, and quite insulated. I remember once, in Europe, hearing about someone who was making $1,000 a week, and I heard myself saying, "Is that *all*?" and I thought, "Wow, you really do get insular in Hollywood."

Interview, Los Angeles/
Los Angeles Times, 3-19:(Calendar)40.

Simone Signoret
Actress

4

I know actors with "method," a more technical approach. But the older I get, I'm less and less conscious with my brain and my intelligence—if I have any. I approach [a] character with no analysis, no rationalization. I don't want to know how it happens. Before I play a new woman, there are plenty of things that happen to me in a mysterious way. I'm too afraid of letting the mystery get away by talking about it.

Interview, Paris/
The New York Times, 3-19:(2)22.

Stirling Silliphant
Screenwriter

5

I have written 35 motion pictures, and out of that group there are not four or five I like. Each one you had to compromise, to condense. In movies, you literally cannot write scenes unless you're Woody Allen or Paul Mazursky. *Charly* was the last film I wrote in which I felt I could really develop a scene. If you're a professional top-rated writer, which I am, you're expected to play the game according to their

(STIRLING SILLIPHANT)

rules. It denies you the kind of writing you really want to do . . .

Interview/Los Angeles Times, 10-27:(4)15.

John Simon
Film Critic

1

Film criticism is really the most peculiar kind of criticism there is. It is a world of its own. It is very much more violent than the worlds of most other kinds of criticism. It is more internecine. It is more bloodthirsty. It is more megalomaniacal. And it is also more diverse. There is more flagrant disagreement in film criticism than there is in almost any kind of criticism . . . Film is the only criticism in which you have to be all brows at once—you have to be high, middle and low and there's no getting out of it. That is a very unhealthy state of affairs, obviously. It creates values that are so undefined, so amorphous, so self-contradictory that it confuses the whole issue. If you are reading an attack by a serious critic on a serious bad film such as *3 Women* and then you read an attack by that same serious critic on a film like—what's silly enough—let's say *The Fury*, it confuses the issue terribly. To an impressionable reader, somehow *The Fury* and *3 Women* become interchangeable.

At Los Angeles International Film Exposition, April 22/Los Angeles Times, 4-24:(4)9.

Sylvester Stallone
Actor, Director

2

Actors are a walking, throbbing mass of unhealed scar tissue by the time they get anywhere. That's why they ask for millions. Because of all they took on the way up. Vengeance is theirs . . . I mean, in the past I've had things said to me you wouldn't believe. On *Farewell, My Lovely* an executive walked within five feet of me and said, "Can't we get the other guy?" "No," they said, "he's out of town." "So we're stuck with *him*?" the executive said—meaning me. "Yeah," they said. It destroyed me. So when I was directing *Paradise*

Alley I told every actor on set, no matter how small the part, "You're the greatest, the best. That's why I hired you . . ."

Interview/Los Angeles Times, 10-29:(Calendar)37.

3

No matter how successful you become in this business and how much money you earn, someone will always be trying to cut you down and make you seem like an avaricious hog . . .

Los Angeles Times, 11-9:(4)18.

Rod Steiger
Actor

4

You dream of pictures like *The Pawnbroker, In the Heat of the Night* or *Across the Bridge,* but they aren't being made. This is the age of humanized comic strips—Popeye, Dick Tracy, Superman. Ten years ago I would have bet my house that no top star would appear in movies like those, but I guess a $2.5-million fee can be very persuasive. Special effects have become more important than relationships and conflicts between human beings. The equipment gets more elaborate but the thought behind it gets smaller.

Interview/The New York Times, 4-28:(C)6.

5

. . . the basic problem of the actor never changes. He worries about getting a job. He gets the job, then he worries about doing the job. He worries about how the job will be received, and then he worries if he'll ever get another job. There is something very masochistic in it all . . . I have faith in myself—and faith is what you need a lot of in this business, because it's one of the roughest, dirtiest businesses in the world. Faith is saying to yourself, "I think I can do it—and I think I can do it better than most people." Coupled to my faith is a fear of failure, and a will to challenge myself. When all these elements come together, and they hit talent, you really see something special.

Interview, Los Angeles/Los Angeles Herald Examiner, 5-7:(F)11.

6

. . . an actor is one who creates different human beings, different lives. Actors try to

WHAT THEY SAID IN 1978

(ROD STEIGER)

communicate through themselves, to discover something in front of an audience. There's a beauty about this. With all the dirtiness and viciousness of show business, and the odds against success, actors try to offer a memory, a moment of happiness ... [The actor] tries to bring life to its highest level, to explore life and exchange ideas. His ambition is not to become a television star, but to explore life more fully through the traditions of the theatre and film. The best thing an artist can leave behind is a constructive and warm memory, a moment or two you can't forget.

Interview, New York/
The Christian Science Monitor, 6-30:14.

1

When people ask me what I'm doing, I always say I'm looking for a job. That's what all actors are doing, whether they live in poverty or in Bel-Air. We're all looking for parts that excite us. And a part is like a woman; either it turns you on or it doesn't. There's no halfway. If you take a part you only half like, it's like sleeping with a woman you only half love ...

Los Angeles Times, 8-29:(4)6.

James Stewart
Actor

2

I'm glad I was here at the peak [of Hollywood]. That's gone, but the movies are still special. Giving hope, telling about noble things, that's tremendously important. Somebody's got to tell every young man and woman growing up in today's world that the whole thing's worth pursuing. There's no reason to throw in the sponge. *It's a Wonderful Life* was saying that people aren't born to be failures. The quiet, the persevering, they've got a chance. The ability to say this kind of thing is something the movies had to do on their own. Nobody's duplicated it yet. Nobody's improved on their power to impart universal emotions, and let people know they're not alone.

Interview/Los Angeles Times, 12-7:(4)27.

Lee Strasberg
Artistic director, Actors Studio

3

When I make movies, I just enjoy myself. It's not really working. I don't argue with myself. I don't talk back to myself. Acting in movies is a vacation, and for me it confirms everything about acting that I've been teaching all those years. The problem with movies is the cuts. Any actor with any background will relate one scene to another, but then certain things will be cut out. It's a problem.

Interview/The New York Times, 2-17:(C)2.

Richard Thomas
Actor

4

It's hard to find originality in films today. Almost every commercially successful new film is based on a movie that was successful six months before—or a remake of something made 30 years ago. So it is hard to find film-makers who will take a chance on an original idea ... I hope more films eventually will try new themes, because that is the only way this art will expand.

Interview/U.S. News & World Report, 2-13:87.

Francois Truffaut
Director

5

It is always a moral question how to finish a film, because it must respect two laws—the law of life and the law of spectacle. Life by definition goes downhill, into decrepitude, illness, death. But spectacle by definition keeps going up. It is triumphant. So you have the dual laws of the exultation and the *verite.* You try to respect both, but how? It's very difficult to find the point between—the happy ending that respects the *verite,* let's say. I always give myself that problem to solve, and it is never easy.

Interview, Los Angeles/
Los Angeles Times, 1-1:(Calendar)24.

6

I believe that color has done the cinema almost as much harm as has TV. We must struggle against too-great realism, otherwise

(FRANCOIS TRUFFAUT)

there is no art. When a film is in color, filmed in the street with sun and shade and dialogues drowned out by the noise of Mopeds, this is no longer cinema. Now ugliness dominates. Eight of 10 films are as boring to watch as a traffic jam.

Interview/San Francisco Examiner & Chronicle, 6-11:(Datebook)25.

Jack Valenti
President, Motion Picture Association of America

1

[On current news coverage of alleged corruption in the film industry]: We are under attack because of allegations which emerge from contractual misunderstandings and just plain difference of opinion, not deliberate mischief. It is an outrageous twist of truth to smear the entire American movie industry . . . Much of what has been written in the press is what I would call family quarrelling. However else it may be described, by no stretch of the imagination can it be called wholesale cheating and corruption. The fiscal disagreements that exist between film-makers and distribution companies, differences of opinion over arithmetic and what should and should not be charged to a film's budget and distribution costs, and the arguments between theatre owners and distribution have been going on for over 40 years without front-page attention. Edmund Burke once said that one cannot indict an entire society. Yet that is precisely what is happening to the entire film industry. Is this the price we must pay because our industry is so glamorous and newsworthy? Everyone is eager to read about Hollywood, and thus, suddenly we find ourselves in a publicity spotlight whose glare is not justified. Movie industry disagreements, so common in our marketplace, have become greatly magnified. The same arguments in other industries would draw little notice. We are not perfect. What group is? The essence of my outrage is that a few problems and misdeeds are allowed to blot and scar the integrity of the entire film industry.

Daily Variety, 2-9:14.

[On the MPAA rating system]: From the outset, the purpose of the rating system was to provide advance information to enable parents to make judgments on movies they wanted their children to see or not to see. Basic to the program was and is the responsibility of the parent to make the decision. The rating board doesn't rate for quality or the lack of it—that role is left to the movie critic and the audience . . . I would hope it's fair to say that today the screen has never been more free from the standpoint of the film-maker's right to create any story he wants to tell. At the same time, the public is better advised in advance by the ratings about the content of films than ever before, and parents can be confident their children are restricted in viewing certain films. No other entertainment communications medium turns away business at the box-office to fulfill its pledge to the public.

Interview/TWA Ambassador, April:15.

3

In Hollywood today, talent is king. Talent—that mysterious, sourceless human chemistry that no physicist or laboratory scientist has been able accurately to dissect or duplicate. It is this enigmatic alchemy of talent that has produced the spacious reach of the American movie, endowing it with a quality of imagination and excellence far beyond the wildest imaginings of a generation ago. Alongside the introduction of new young talent has been the advance of technology in new cameras, fast film and special effects . . . But with all the experience and creative instinct of the wisest of film-makers, no one can forecast the value of a film to an audience . . . Not until the film opens in a darkened theatre and sparks fly up between the screen and the audience can one truly say "this film is right." Excellence is a fragile substance . . . It can shatter at the slightest mistake; and even the film-maker, no matter how sprinkled with genius, may be unaware of the cracking of his creation. That is really what makes film-making such a fascinating enterprise.

Before Midwest Research Institute, April 25/ The Washington Post, 5-31:(A)14.

WHAT THEY SAID IN 1978

(JACK VALENTI)

1

The biggest thing the [MPAA] rating system has done is keep the government out of our business. In 1968, the Supreme Court handed down two decisions that made it perfectly legal for states or localities to organize their own rating systems. None has caught on since we began a rating system, and the threat lessens every year ... The thing that makes our system good is that it's flexible. It bends with the times. If it hadn't, it would have cracked by now. It's a canopy under which a film-maker can make his story.

Interview/The Washington Post, 11-26:(H)3.

Gore Vidal
Author

2

... I don't see myself doing any more screenplays. No. The ship has sailed. There is just no point in doing it other than money. That's entirely a director's game, and the director is often the weakest link in any movie. The strongest and most important aspect of the film is always the script. However, we live in an era in which the director is the *auteur du cinema.* He thinks he owns the creative artist, and he must always get the script away from the writer as quickly as possible and claim it for his own.

Interview/
Los Angeles Herald Examiner, 4-30:(A)8.

Jon Voight
Actor

3

A series of films I chose to make didn't do very well at the box-office and, as a result, I wasn't offered a lot of good things, and what I was offered I turned down. One of the basic problems in the film industry and in our culture is this commercialization of everything. It's power perpetuating itself, and it's the motto, "Money Is Right." Hollywood is a tough system to survive in and I don't like it very much.

Interview, Chicago/San Francisco Examiner &
Chronicle, 4-30:(Datebook)25.

Joseph Wambaugh
Author, Screenwriter

4

[On his Dramatists Guild contract which provides that his scripts cannot be altered without his approval]: What frustrated me in the past is that most people I dealt with don't read; about 90 per cent of the people in Hollywood have forgotten that it all begins with the printed word. They haven't a clue about plot and character and dialogue. Hollywood functions on the shotgun approach: If you shoot enough shells, you bring down a duck or two. In this age of the *auteur,* the director can take a good script and make a good movie. Or a mediocre movie. Or wreck it. But he can't take a bad script and make it good. The time for the Hollywood writer to come into his own is now.

Interview, San Marino, Calif./
The Hollywood Reporter, 5-11:12.

Henry Winkler
Actor

5

I'm 32 years old, so actually I'm a neophyte as an actor. I mean, I know that I must grow. I consider acting to be very much like being a brain surgeon: When you're 55, you finally get it all together.

Interview, New York/
Los Angeles Herald Examiner, 3-28:(B)6.

Michael Winner
Director

6

Obviously, I'd like every critic to love me. I'd like *everybody* to love me. But I'm also a realist, and that's not going to happen. Throughout the world there are a number of people who appreciate what one is doing, and a number who don't. I'd like the balance to change, numerically. But I don't fall into tears about it. I can only do what I think is honorable. I will fail, because every director makes films that don't come up to his dream. But at least one goes in with serious intent, and takes the results.

Interview, New York/
The Christian Science Monitor, 5-24:17.

Shelley Winters
Actress

1

Making movies used to be more fun ... I don't know what happened to the fun, or even why it went away, but today's actors are altogether too serious on a soundstage. They all act like accountants.

Interview, Los Angeles/
Los Angeles Herald Examiner, 1-10:(B)1.

Frank Yablans
Producer; Former president,
Paramount Pictures Corporation

2

Studios are making fewer films because costs are rising. It's an inescapable economic problem. It may cost more to promote a film than make it. When you make a film for $2-million, you've actually made a $6-million film, considering the costs of mass advertising, exploitation and distribution. The so-called small film tends to suffer because it costs the same to sell a $10-million production as the $2-million production. All the same, that extra production cost had better show up on the screen. Of course, it's become very difficult to lose money on a presentable film these days because film companies have so many ancillary sources of income—television, records, paperback books. When home video systems become widespread, they'll create an enormous additional market and almost certainly lead to an increase in production.

Interview, New York/
The Washington Post, 3-19:(F)6.

Susannah York
Actress

3

Acting is about discovery. Acting *is* discovery. That's what is so exciting about this business—I'm constantly exploring new areas, changing direction, moving into a different stream. Perhaps I haven't been given some roles because I've always insisted on not doing the same thing twice running. Hollywood hates that. But the way I see myself is like someone with many facets—it's where the spotlight falls that shines on which part is showing. I don't know any other way to be ...

Interview, London/San Francisco Examiner &
Chronicle, 7-23:(Datebook)27.

Franco Zeffirelli
Director

4

[On directing a film]: You never think, "This is going to be a work of art," because no matter how pompous your style is, in the end, cinema is not a museum. Cinema is the story *of* living people *for* living people.

Interview, Beverly Hills, Calif./
The Washington Post, 5-14:(H)3.

385

MUSIC

Paul Anka
Singer, Songwriter

1

I don't really know if pop music has progressed since the 1950s. It seems to have gotten lost a few years ago and has begun to fall apart. "Punk" never took hold and disco music is really catering to one type of listener. Bruce Springsteen, behind the big hype, and Bob Seeger are really doing a 1970s version of 1950s music . . . I'm never going to be in the vanguard of way-out sounds. The music of the Rolling Stones is dying fast. But my kind of music is the solid, people's kind of music, and it'll be around for a long time.

Interview, Carmel, Calif./
The Christian Science Monitor, 8-25:19.

Count Basie
Musician, Bandleader

2

We Americans continue to initiate new musical eras for the rest of the world, just as we've done in the past. There's been ragtime, jazz and, now, rock—but to me they've all really been the same thing. The only difference is that we, as musicians, dress up the music in various ways. I like rock music and find it interesting. In many ways, arrangements for rock groups are more complicated than for the big bands or orchestras. I wish our band could include rock as part of our repertoire, but it's really not our sound. I like the new songs coming along. Some say the words may be too suggestive, but I really think that it's the way people take the lyrics. The public is accepting an awful lot of things today, and perhaps some people aren't getting the real meaning of the words.

Interview/
U.S. News & World Report, 4-3:77.

Tony Bennett
Singer

3

I don't care how long it's [rock music] been going on; I can't help but think it's still a big fad that will kind of fade away because it's not really based on terrific music . . . The new kids really like good jazz. The generation before, it was strictly rock and they wouldn't adhere to anything else. Whereas now, the young kids are coming up saying, "Hey, wait a minute. There's a big world out there. Let's find out all about it." So they're getting back to a kind of more normal way to listen to music . . . I like a lot of rock music. My own personal thing is that I dislike the anger in any music, whether it's "acid rock" or this new craze, "punk rock."

Interview, Las Vegas, Nev./
The Dallas Times Herald, 1-10:(B)5.

Irving Berlin
Songwriter

4

[On his 90th birthday]: Oh, yes, I'm still writing songs. But things have changed. You don't just write a song, as I used to and others used to in the old days, and then put it out and have song pluggers go to work on it. Unless you're doing a show or a movie, there's no market, no need for it. I have them if I ever get around to doing another show, which I hope to. But it's very tough for me to make that kind of decision, because I'm not like Oscar Hammerstein used to be. You remember he took a full page ad in *Variety* after *Oklahoma!* opened and was such a smash—he listed about seven or eight of his flops and he said, "I did it before and I can do it again." Which is wonderful. But you get scared. Once I make a commitment, then I have to go through with it. Then it's a question of how you feel—with the auditions and rehearsals that you have to go through. It's not

(IRVING BERLIN)

just a matter of feeling good one day or the next day, but if you have a bad night's sleep—and I've been a bad sleeper all my life—then you say, "Why the hell did I take this on?"

Interview/The New York Times, 5-10:25.

Leonard Bernstein
Composer, Conductor

1

The whole point of composing . . . is not to find one chord or one note you love. It is only when they progress to another chord or note that you have something. The mind, where all this creativity takes place, is an immensely complicated circuitry of electronic threads, all of which are connected at a certain point and are informational. But, every once in a while, there is something like a short circuit; two of them will cross, touch, and set off something called an idea. This is the most exciting moment that can happen in an artist's life . . . I am grateful for that gift, for those moments, just as I can be terribly depressed by the moments in-between when nothing happens. But . . . eventually those two strands will come together, a spark will fly, and I'll be off, sailing, my ego gone. I won't know my name. I won't know what time it is. Then, I'm a composer.

Los Angeles Herald Examiner, 8-20:(F)10.

Anthony Bliss
Executive director, Metropolitan Opera, New York

2

Inflation lies ahead, and there is no way to produce grand opera at bargain-basement prices. Opera is the most expensive of the performing arts. There is no way to achieve quality without heavy costs, and no way to do it within costs that can be put upon the general public. I hope to enable the Met to survive until substantial government money is available.

The New York Times, 2-12:(2)1.

Karl Boehm
Conductor

3

Composers so often come to me with a score and I ask them, "What kind of form is your

music in?" They usually say, "I don't need to have a form." Well, you might as well put a child at the piano and have him bang out notes at random. To me, form is everything in music.

Interview, New York/
Los Angeles Herald Examiner, 3-21:(B)4.

Pierre Boulez
Director, Institut de Recherche et Coordination Acoustique-Musique, Paris; Former musical director, New York Philharmonic Orchestra

4

I am certain that you cannot express new ideas with old material. History shows that constantly. When we look for new composers, we look for those who have a new thought corresponding to a new material. But beyond that, you have to make people conscious of the fact that there is not an "experimental music" and a "normal music"—it's all the same thing.

The New York Times, 6-4:(2)15.

Jose Carreras
Opera singer

5

To be a tenor today, one must be a combination of things. One must have musical intelligence, a good physical appearance and, hopefully, a charismatic stage presence. Above all, one must be an expressive singer and actor. In a way, the voice need not even be the most important thing. Of course, the voice counts for a lot, but to conjure a vivid characterization—*that's* what's vital! That's far more desirable than coming on stage as Mr. Carreras or Mr. X. Of course, when all these qualities are wedded to a great voice, then one is in the presence of an exceptional artist.

Interview, New York/
The New York Times, 2-26:(4)23.

Schuyler Chapin
Dean, School of Arts, Columbia University; Former general manager, Metropolitan Opera, New York

6

In the long run, I don't think an opera house can be run by committee. It's the nature of the business that the impresario should have the final

WHAT THEY SAID IN 1978

(SCHUYLER CHAPIN)

word. The U.S. government is complicated, but we haven't thrown away the President.

Interview, New York/
The Dallas Times Herald, 5-16:(B)5.

Ray Charles
Singer

1

Your voice actually depends on how you're feeling, how much sleep you've had and so on, and when I get out on-stage I need to know what I can make my voice do under the worst conditions. So I just keep constantly fooling with my voice. It's like it's a house I'm keeping up. You know, you don't just build a house and do nothing else to it. You're always washing the windows, painting, adding a room. Because anything that you don't use, I think I heard somebody say, you lose.

Interview, Cleveland/
The Dallas Times Herald, 2-12:(E)1.

Van Cliburn
Pianist

2

If a young person enters the classical [music] field solely to seek monetary reward, he is in the wrong profession. If rewards come to him along the way, he must be extremely grateful but not allow himself to become complacent with expectation. Otherwise, he is certainly not properly motivated. No one should be in the classical field unless he or she is totally dedicated to music and art and would never consider any other kind of life endeavor. To be an artist is a sublime vocation. Along with obvious love for your work, you have to be prepared for tremendous self-discipline and sacrifice as a classical artist. As a result, an artist gains a perspective on life which enables him to perceive more clearly humanity as it operates on the three life levels: body, mind and spirit.

Interview/U.S. News & World Report, 12-4:75.

Aaron Copland
Composer, Conductor

3

Conducting is a real sport. You can never guarantee what the results are going to be, so

there's always an element of chance. That keeps it exciting. Even the same orchestra playing the same piece twice never plays it exactly the same way. Then there's always the risk you take in sport—that somebody will play it better, or conduct it better.

Interview, Washington/
"W": a Fairchild publication, 11-10:42.

Mac Davis
Singer, Songwriter

4

Even if nobody listened to the stuff, I'd be a songwriter, because music is my therapy, my $50-an-hour psychiatrist. I can be lonesome, tired, angry—you name the feeling. If I held it inside me, I'd have all kinds of serious problems. But I take my guitar and let it all out. Some philosopher once wrote, "Without music life would be miserable." I'd say it even stronger—without music there would be no life at all.

Interview, Los Angeles/
Los Angeles Times, 4-2:(Home)33.

Edo de Waart
Music director, San Francisco
Symphony Orchestra

5

[On conducting]: You must shut off your head and analytical and observing strengths while you perform, and that is difficult because those parts of you are what you're using during rehearsal. You must not get tangled up in the details you were seeking in the rehearsals. I must just let go. It's not for nothing that [Herbert von] Karajan closes his eyes when he conducts. You see a wind player waiting until the second he is to play before he puts his instrument to the mouth and, if you register that fact, how can the free flow of music come [from the conductor]? The time is here for me to stop being a teacher all the time. That was the one weakness in [Georg] Szell. At night he couldn't let go. He was still checking the things he told them to do. You lose concentration because of it. You have to find the middle ground between being listener and doing it, but

(EDO DE WAART)

no longer being hurt by some players not coming in right. You have to have a relaxed awareness.

Interview/San Francisco Examiner & Chronicle,
11-26:(This World)58.

Bob Dylan
Singer, Songwriter

1

Music is my first love. But in writing songs I've learned as much from Cezanne as I have from Woody Guthrie. I feel I have a lot in common with the visual side of it, because the songs I write are basically songs of realism. To play upon the realism and draw the abstraction out of the realism is what I do.

Interview, Santa Monica, Calif./
The New York Times, 1-8:(2)1.

2

Being a musician means—depending on how far you go—getting to the depths of where you are at. And most any musician would try anything to get to those depths, because playing music is an immediate thing—as opposed to putting paint on a canvas, which is a calculated thing. Your spirit flies when you are playing music. So, with music, you tend to look deeper and deeper inside yourself to find the music.

Interview/Playboy, March:69.

Billy Eckstine
Singer

3

I think it is very evident that romantic ballads are back in favor—even with the kids. We are seeing more sensible love songs being written and becoming popular . . . rather than protest songs—and I welcome that. I think people come to a club to be entertained, not be hit over the head by stuff that was on the 7 o'clock news . . . I was brought up in this business with the idea it was your responsibility to entertain an audience. And that you did that with a certain deportment. Look at some of these rock musicians. They come out with their behinds hanging out of their pants. Who wants to pay

$10 to see someone who shows up on stage without any socks and dirty feet?

Interview, Dallas/
The Dallas Times Herald, 3-10:(E)1.

Dizzy Gillespie
Jazz musician

4

There is some [racial] prejudice in jazz, and some of it's reverse prejudice. But that's natural, you see, because jazz *is* our [blacks'] music. That doesn't mean that Stan Getz can't play or that Bunny Berigan can't play. But your playing is so much a part of you that your early life has to come out in your music. Every now and then you hear a teety-teety-teety from a trumpet-player and you know it's a white musician. But music is music—you're dealing with the same notes.

Interview, Englewood, N.J./
The New York Times Magazine, 6-25:60.

Carlo Maria Giulini
Musical director, Los Angeles
Philharmonic Orchestra

5

The problems of the audience are everywhere . . . But it belongs to us to make each time an event. We must create that atmosphere of mystery and greatness. If they sleep, we must wake them up. I cannot accept routine, not for the audience, not for the musicians. We must get through that tremendous curtain to the people on the other side, until that curtain no longer exists. We must be like the sea—coming and going, giving and receiving.

Interview, Los Angeles/
Los Angeles Herald Examiner, 10-20:(B)6.

Benny Goodman
Musician, Band leader

6

Popular music, in my estimation, has possibly deteriorated. All the music you listen to on the radio is the same: one-dimensional. On the road, I walk into a store and usually they will have the top 10 records all over the place. And the way they play most records! The decibels are so high that the songs come screaming at

WHAT THEY SAID IN 1978

(BENNY GOODMAN)

you. My records—and, I presume, many others—by comparison sound as if they are coming from way off in the distance. I liked some of the Beatles' songs, and we did a couple of them at our Carnegie Hall concert this year. But I am not very much for rock, and if rock fans don't want to come and see me, it's all right. I think there will always be that kind of audience that wants to listen to me.

Interview/U.S. News & World Report, 8-14:54.

Arlo Guthrie
Folk singer; Songwriter

1

I think it's better to give you a definition of what I *don't* think is folk music in order to understand what I think can be folk music. I don't think that a guy who's standing up there playing the most boring song you ever heard on an acoustic guitar or blowing his guts out on a harmonica is necessarily folk music. It can look like folk music, it can sound like it, it can have all the images of what people image-wise consider to be folk music; but if folks don't like it, there's no way it's going to be folk music. So I think what people like, the songs people whistle, the things they think about—I don't care how they're played: a symphony orchestra, the Mormon Tabernacle Choir can sing folk songs as far as I'm concerned—things that are a part of our culture, that stay a part of it, that's folk music.

Interview, New York/
The Dallas Times Herald, 8-6:(H)4.

Marilyn Horne
Opera singer

2

Coloratura singing, to this day, is still enormously difficult. I don't dare sing any *fiora* without calculating the last breath, the amount required to negotiate a single passage, the grade at which I release the breath ... Models have always been important to me. In *bel canto* it was Ponselle for *cantilena,* and Callas for dramatic recitative, along with the wonderful teachers I've had such as William Vennard and

Lotte Lehmann. Beyond that, it's instinctive first and intellectual only afterwards.

Interview, Glendale, Calif./
Los Angeles Herald Examiner, 8-4:(B)7.

Vladimir Horowitz
Pianist

3

For me, the intellect is always the guide but not the goal of the performance. Three things have to be coordinated and no one must stick out. Not too much intellect, because it can become scholastic. Not too much heart, because it can become schmaltz. Not too much technique, because you become a mechanic. Always there should be a little mistake here and there—I am for it. The people who don't do mistakes are cold like ice.

San Francisco Examiner & Chronicle,
1-15:(This World)2.

4

I must tell you I take terrible risks. Because my playing is very clear, when I make a mistake you hear it. If you want me to play only the notes without any specific color dynamics, I will never make one mistake. Never be afraid to dare. And never imitate. Play without asking advice.

Newsweek, 1-23:63.

5

Singing is the key to everything in music. All my life I have tried to make a percussive instrument sing. It is the most important challenge for the pianist, to achieve that singing tone.

Interview, Beverly Hills, Calif./
Los Angeles Times, 2-12:(Calendar)67.

Harry James
Musician, Bandleader

6

There's only two kinds of music. If you like it, it's good. If you don't like it, it's bad.

Albany, N.Y./Los Angeles Times, 7-6:(1)2.

Quincy Jones
Composer

7

There's a lot of good music around now, but I haven't heard much lately that's new in the

(QUINCY JONES)

sense that [Charlie] Parker was new. Recording techniques are what's different now. The velocity of the world's life-style has pushed everything way ahead. Everything is faster . . . [But] we're all dealing with the same 12 notes. We still have the same problems Beethoven had.

Interview/Los Angeles Herald Examiner,
10-22:(Sound)8.

Rafael Kubelik
Conductor

1

[In opera, a "mature performance" is one in which] everyone knows what he or she is doing, what the tempo is, what the producer wants done. Whether one likes the result or not is something else, but the performance is molded, a unit. The producer's job is to bring out the Verdi Otello in Verdi's *Otello,* the Rossini Otello in Rossini's *Otello,* the Shakespeare Otello in Shakespeare. He must use the means of the 20th century, of course—you can't go back to candlelight—but you can't have a mixture of styles. And the conductor must agree with the stage man about every aspect of the production, or else quit, as I have done on occasion. Why waste each other's time and end up fighting in public, at rehearsals? The conductor must not be a *prima donna* about all this or put himself in a selfish dictatorial position. But he must not compromise. It is foolish to simply pay attention to the orchestra and settle for precision there. There is no such thing as perfection, but one can demand a matured performance, a combination of fantasy, talent and precision.

Interview, New York/
The New York Times, 1-22:(2)16.

James Levine
Music director and principal conductor,
Metropolitan Opera, New York

2

A [guest] conductor must have at least two months to give us in order to rehearse a production and lead a series of eight or 10 performances. The big guns all have permanent posi-

tions and commitments that won't permit them to come here. I have the same problem if La Scala asks me to conduct. I simply can't be away from the Met for such an extensive period. Most critics of the Met don't seem to realize how this delicate jigsaw puzzle shifts. It's as if people thought there was a floor in this building filled with drawers and inside the drawers are all the singers and conductors. All you have to do is decide what opera you want to do, open the drawer and pull them out. What you actually find, if you haven't planned everything well in advance, is a note saying that this particular artist is performing in Vienna just when you'd like him here.

Interview, New York/
The New York Times, 2-12:(2)35.

3

There was a time in musical history when you had conductors like Toscanini, Klemperer, Furtwangler, Walter, De Sabata—these men, whether you like all of them or not, had certain things you don't see much of now. They stayed in one place; they had a commitment to developing one organization, not flitting all over. The paradox is that we now have more technically competent orchestras than ever before, musical education is generally improved, but the general state of conducting today is nowhere near what it used to be. The administrative work can be tiring—but you can achieve so much better work than you can when you're just going from orchestra to orchestra. You can't do your best work when you just spring full-blown onto the podium. It's not like what you achieve when you're used to working with the same men, when your rapport is so good you can work on subtleties, not just over-all shape.

Interview, New York/
"W": a Fairchild publication, 2-17:8.

Lorin Maazel
Musical director, Cleveland Orchestra

4

What's needed in the conducting field is a series of preparatory steps that can be defined: academic studies, music school, an internship

WHAT THEY SAID IN 1978

(LORIN MAAZEL)

with a major orchestra and major conductor—unfortunately, they don't always come together—and then a period with a pre-professional orchestra ... They [potential conductors] must have perfect pitch. To conduct contemporary music without perfect pitch is well-nigh impossible. And they have to have mastered an instrument ... I think it's a gross imposition on the public to be told that an artist who has achieved a reputation as a virtuoso should suddenly be taken seriously as a conductor. If you were to ask these soloists-turned-conductors to read an E-flat clarinet line, or for memorization of "Le Sacre du Printemps," they'd be weeded out in a hurry.

Interview/The New York Times, 2-17:(C)14.

Johnny Mathis
Singer

1

Sometimes I'll meet people who say, "Hey, your routine is too quiet and humdrum. You're supposed to be a star." Well, I try to keep from laughing. You see, they want glamour and fantasy. But they're confusing the songs with my life. I don't deal in glamour and fantasy, just in reality. Talk to any serious singer, and you'll find the same structure of reality ... To me, the whole concept of stardom is hilarious. All I've ever wanted to be is a good singer. That's the driving force in my existence. The public taste can be very fickle. I've been very lucky, but I've seen lots of entertainers flash onto the horizon, then disappear. When it happens, they get terribly depressed, maybe suicidal. The only way to protect oneself is to feel secure in terms of reality. Practice hard, build a solid foundation for your craft, and don't worry about the fame, glamour or stardom. This, in the long run, is the sensible way to approach life.

Interview, Los Angeles/
Los Angeles Times, 10-29:(Home)18.

James McCracken
Opera singer

2

The Met[ropolitan Opera] has always been in trouble with covers [substitutes] and always

will be until they develop their own minor league. One night last month when I arrived to sing *Tannhauser,* they asked me if I would sing Manrico on the following evening. At the next *Tannhauser* performance they wanted me to do Canio a day later. Now, I would like to help out all I can, but that's asking too much from anyone's vocal chords. There's got to be a way, perhaps a tie-in with university music schools or America's smaller opera companies, a means of developing young singers who will be ready to come in and do the job. Professional ball teams have the right idea: If there's any quarterback potential out there, you can be sure it will be found, nourished and trained.

Interview/The New York Times, 2-12:(2)35.

Mehli Mehta
Director, American Youth Symphony
Orchestra

3

A musician is not a shoemaker. He cannot produce quality performances on that same time basis. He cannot play five or six concerts a week, make do with minimum rehearsals and be traveling in buses ... and so on. His playing will not remain superior with that kind of exhausting schedule. Yet that is what the current system demands. And what stimulates it? Audiences that give automatic standing ovations, deserved or not. Audiences that do not discern between the perfunctory and the special. More people attend concerts today than ever before, and never have they been less discriminating. Quite commonly I look around the hall and spot the same couples sitting in their fine orchestra seats, a man here and there snoring. I know their patronage is necessary, too. But an orchestra needs more than the financial support to thrive. It needs active interest and alert listeners. Otherwise, caring ceases on both sides of the stage.

Interview, Los Angeles/
Los Angeles Herald Examiner, 2-26:(E)1.

Zubin Mehta
Musical director, Los Angeles Philharmonic
Orchestra; Musical director-designate,
New York Philharmonic Orchestra

4

I was a very ambitious young man. I'm not ambitious any more. The fact that I know I can

(ZUBIN MEHTA)

conduct anywhere in the world takes care of ambition. I will do the best job I can in New York and hope it is appreciated. More than that, I can't say. Conductors aren't like baseball managers. Thank God we don't have a league where we go up and down in standing.

Interview, Los Angeles/
Los Angeles Times, 4-30:(Calendar)115.

Zubin Mehta
Musical director, New York
Philharmonic Orchestra

1

Inexperienced conductors hear something wrong and have trouble putting it right. I've learned to diagnose quickly and find an instant cure. There's no time to lose. The patient can die on the table.

Newsweek, 12-18:74.

Robert Merrill
Opera singer

2

One reason singers often end up such unhappy people is that opera is the toughest of all the arts. The stress is enormous . . . After retirement, some singers lead very sad lives. For years they are lionized, and then you lose your voice and you are forgotten. I was in Dallas when Lily Pons died—that dear lady. She had moved to Dallas after her career ended. She was an old person and she had no one. Her fans had long since forgotten her. There was an auction sale and people came in off the streets who had probably never heard an opera in their lives and grabbed up some of her precious things. It made me sick to see it.

Interview/The Washington Post, 10-28:(B)7.

Leslie Parnas
Cellist

3

. . . one can no longer separate political convictions from art. I feel deeply that music can express a profound feeling of freedom, and I feel no government can successfully suppress freedom of expression in one area and not feel the effects in another. Therefore, when I play

music, it is not only an example of *emotional* freedom, but it is also a message for peace and for the right of each individual to express himself.

Interview, Leningrad, U.S.S.R./
The New York Times, 7-2:(2)16.

Dolly Parton
Country-music singer

4

Country music is simple stories told in simple ways. I think it's music with a lot of class. It just talks about everyday problems, everyday situations, and I don't think you have to be from the country to relate to it, either . . . I don't care where you're from, we all have the same feelings inside. We hurt, we cry, we laugh, we know jealousy, we know love. We're all made up of the same things. Look at Hank Williams—he was considered the "country-est" of all country people, and his songs are taken now and just redone with different instruments. And they are classic songs, and that's the heart of country. It's just getting to the heart of people.

Interview, Columbia, Md./
The Christian Science Monitor, 9-7:(B)3.

Mstislav Rostropovich
Cellist; Musical director, National
Symphony Orchestra, Washington

5

[On his being a cellist and a conductor]: I get great pleasure in switching back and forth. After doing the one, I'm always glad to get back to the other. Contact with orchestras, with different types of sound, and tackling larger musical forms, like symphonies, is very helpful for my cello playing. And because of my experience as a player, it works the other way, too. I know precisely what I can get from a string section and I think the players trust me, too.

Interview/Los Angeles Times, 7-9:(Calendar)73.

Andres Segovia
Guitarist

6

. . . the career of the composer is opposite to the career of the artist, who is always on the go.

WHAT THEY SAID IN 1978

(ANDRES SEGOVIA)

For instance, the composer has to remain in one place. He has to write and wait and decide, and think again and rearrange—all that is part of the composition. And the artist is all to the contrary. First, he has to play the work of the other men. He has to play here and there and the other place—traveling, speaking with people, etc. A quite different life. But I have met many musicians who have committed the sin of composing.

Interview/Los Angeles Herald Examiner, 4-15:(A)1.

1

I have put my life in the making of four tasks. First, to redeem the guitar from frivolous amusements. Second, to create a repertoire of good music for the guitar. Third, to go everywhere and attract a public that is fond of good music. Fourth, to influence the directors of conservatories that the guitar may be taught at the same level of dignity as the piano, cello, voice and so on.

Interview, New York/
The Dallas Times Herald, 5-7:(K)8.

Beverly Sills
Opera singer

2

[Saying she will retire as a singer in 1980 to become co-director of the New York City Opera] : In 1980 I will be 51. I have no operas left that I want to sing. I have sung in every opera house I wanted to sing in, and by the time the next year or so is over, I will have recorded everything I ever dreamed of. My voice has served me very well, and I would like to be able to put it to bed, so that it can go quietly and with pride.

Time, 1-23:82.

Georg Solti
Musical director, Chicago Symphony Orchestra

3

I think that talent is about half of it, and you can't create that. The other half of leader-ship is work, grit development, sacrifice and all that. And this business of leadership is no laughing matter. We are woefully short on giants both in statecraft and in artcraft . . . And the same is true in music—literally this decline of the West. In his way [conductor Lorin] Maazel is right about conductors. Just think back to 1920 or 1930 when I can name you 25 giants, all performing at the same time. I won't bore you with a list, but just think about Toscanini, Walter, Krauss, Furtwangler, Richard Strauss and so on. We don't have it today.

Interview, Washington, May 13/
The Washington Post, 5-15:(B)13.

Bruce Springsteen
Rock singer

4

You've got to always remember rock 'n' roll's never about giving up. For me—for a lot of kids—it was a totally positive force . . . not optimistic all the time, but positive. It was never—never—about surrender.

Interview/Time, 8-7:73.

Janos Starker
Cellist

5

I conducted, I conduct, I will conduct—but I don't consider myself a conductor. I consider that any highly trained musician, of which I am one, should be capable of conducting the major part of the literature—but that doesn't make him a conductor. The unfortunate thing is that too many instrumentalists who are successful, like myself, get anxious to wield the baton, and that they consider themselves conductors. It's even worse that the audiences consider them conductors. And cellists are very well known for this inner desire, which they display unfortunately in public too frequently. [Why?] Well, one of the reasons is that where the cellist sits there's a peculiar acoustical phenomenon that the principal cellist hears all the things that the conductor doesn't, so he considers himself a

(JANOS STARKER)

better conductor because he hears more than the conductor. The other thing is that he plays the bass line, which is the structural part of the music, so that it gives him seemingly an understanding of the composition structurally better than, let's say, the clarinet players get. And also the fact that the cellists play less notes than the violins so they are not as busy. And then one of the elements is that, because they are less busy, they always give the eye to the ladies, hopefully a rich lady in the audience who eventually will marry them and sponsor their conductorial ambitions.

Interview, Dallas/
The Dallas Times Herald, 9-28:(E)7.

Virgil Thomson
Composer

1

Music in any generation is not what the public thinks of it but what the musicians make of it. The lay public has no responsibility at all toward music. It is under no obligation to like it, to protect it, encourage it, quarrel with it, or consume it. Musicians can cater to public taste, cooperate with it, raise it or lower it; and lay encouragement can stimulate them to great and disinterested achievement. But always the music of any time is the music that the musicians of that time make. Musicians, in other words, own music, because music owns them.

Before graduates of Mannes College of Music,
New York/Los Angeles Herald Examiner, 7-3:(B)6.

Mel Torme
Singer

2

I think jazz is very much of a viable entity within the so-called firmament of show biz. It's selling far better than you would expect on record. And I think that it's evidenced in jazz concerts and concerts that I've played for jazz festivals. . . . there's obviously a large audience for jazz, and I do believe that from the standpoint of popular mass sales it could be even bigger. It's just that the heads of the disc jockeys are into rock, and the pendulum, as it always has done, is almost certain to swing at least to center, if not all the way back to where people are listening to more sophisticated music. [And] jazz is sophisticated.

Interview/Los Angeles Herald Examiner, 7-7:(A)19.

Pete Townshend
Rock musician; Member of The Who

3

I still believe in the power of rock. To me, it was always a way to inspire people and to make them aware of what was going on. I tried to produce pieces of music that people could not only listen to but identify with. The ultimate goal was to make it appear by example that all problems can be transcended by people coming together with optimism, joy and aggression. That was the idealism I always attached to rock. [But] I've come to realize that we've also got to judge rock by the end product—the human beings. If what we do is burn ourselves up and end up in a swimming pool suffering from over-sedation, then rock's no answer to anything.

Interview, Beverly Hills, Calif./
Los Angeles Times, 8-20:(Calendar)70.

THE STAGE

Edward Albee
Playwright

1

I'd like to think that every community in America had a theatre that did adventurous work. Used properly, the regional theatres are the closest thing we have to a national theatre. Unfortunately, too many of them are being used by the commercial theatre as try-out houses. There are some exceedingly greedy people in regional theatre, doing plays only in hopes of catching the brass ring in New York.

Interview, Palo Alto, Calif./
Los Angeles Times, 10-15:(Calendar)6.

Donald Albery
London theatre-owner

2

[On charges that Americans and other tourists, who now make up the majority of theatregoers in London, bring down the standards of British theatre]: I know Americans and I cannot accept they are a different lot of people from people of the same intelligence in this country. I think they help maintain the standard ... It's my considered belief that it has been the tourists, particularly the American tourists, that have supported the more serious theatre and has allowed us to have more than drawing-room comedies. The two-by-twos who come from America are very interested in the "real" theatre—far more than the British theatregoer.

Interview, London/The New York Times, 2-28:35.

Victor Borge
Entertainer, Musician

3

For me, the two most exciting moments in the theatre are when the curtain goes up—and

this, when the clapping and cheering have stopped and all the commotion is done; when the house is cleared and the theatre is dark and empty. It's two worlds. Two different worlds. It reminds me of a time when I was living in California. It must have been 1942. This voice came over the radio giving the war report. So many men dead, so many wounded. Towns lost, won. And then, Jascha Heifetz came on and played a Beethoven sonata. One world, and then another.

Interview, Boston/
Los Angeles Times, 10-29:(Calendar)59.

Oleg Briansky
Ballet dancer; Choreographer

4

[On the growth of ballet's audience]: In 1965 it was, say, a million people who were interested. Now it's more like 17 million. In Saratoga, where I have my school, people used to go just to get some culture. Then they started to like it. And they began to see different productions of the same ballet, and to compare protagonists, and to develop a taste. Dance used to be just for connoisseurs. Now the Broadway theatres are full of it!

Interview, New York/
The Christian Science Monitor, 3-15:33.

Michael Caine
Actor

5

Despite television, there will always be an audience for live theatre ... There will always be theatre fanatics—the people who pack the galleries on a first night. It is absolutely essential for actors to work in the theatre before they go into movies or TV. There is no substi-

(MICHAEL CAINE)

tute for the contact between performers and a live audience.

Interview/U.S. News & World Report, 1-9:66.

Joseph Chaikin
Director

1

The challenge now, in terms of producing a piece for the public, is that audiences are so televisionized these days that our job in theatre is to find ways to give fresh expression to certain things that are contaminated, to produce work to which audiences can refer emotionally but through something other than that diminished, recycled experience.

Interview, San Francisco/San Francisco Examiner & Chronicle, 5-28:(Datebook)23.

Alfred de Liagre, Jr.
Producer

2

It's distressed me enormously, the direction in which the theatre has been going in the last 10 years. I have been very upset over the preoccupation with obscenity and sexual deviation. I've grown weary of seeing actors trail their genitals across the footlights, and this is one of the reasons why I haven't produced in the last few years. You've got to remember that in my golden era I produced plays by Philip Barry, Terence Rattigan, Robert Sherwood, Archibald MacLeish and Benn Levy. They were all play craftsmen, but play craftsmanship has gone out of fashion. Playwrights today don't care very much about telling a story that has a beginning, a middle and an end. It's become a mood thing, and so many of them have gone into the same kind of abstract impressionism that you find in painting and sculpture.

*Interview, Boston/
The New York Times, 2-26:(2)6.*

Phyllis Diller
Comedienne

3

Being a successful comedienne is almost impossible. There is so much negativity against any woman who dares to make fun of anything.

That goes way back in history, when women were pictured as madonnas. It's the old double standard. Women are supposed to be that virginal object. It's just a picture, but of course men will not give it up. So you have the whole world of men ready to shoot you full of arrows. Male critics still knock me for my mother-in-law jokes. It takes a strong trust to get you through that. It's fine for men to tell jokes about their obnoxious wives. But turn that around, and the big ninnies will yell help.

*Interview, Philadelphia/
The Dallas Times Herald, 8-2:(G)6.*

Kirk Douglas
Actor

4

There's something that most actors in movies miss, and that is the contact with live audiences. I'd like to go back to the theatre and do a play that excited me. When you finish a day after performing in a play. you're exhilarated. You're keyed up because it's complete: with a beginning, a middle and an end. You have the immediate contact with the audience, and a fresh one every night. You take your curtain call, and you feel good!

Interview/U.S. News & World Report, 9-18:74.

Alvin Epstein
Artistic director, Guthrie Theatre, Minneapolis

5

In Minneapolis, people can concentrate much more on their work. There's no place to breed the sort of scattered hysteria that's in New York. There, it's easy to think you're an actor for 10 years without acting, because you're going out to readings, to plays, to films, you're talking theatre all the time. Here, you're an actor or you're not.

Interview/"W": a Fairchild publication, 3-31:2.

Eliot Feld
Dancer, Choreographer

6

At first, the relationship I have with the dancers is a romance. Then it becomes a marriage, with the constant battle of egos and

WHAT THEY SAID IN 1978

(ELIOT FELD)

needs. Aside from that, I'm terribly insecure when choreographing. I doubt the validity of everything and get impatient to see what is developing. That puts a severe pressure on the dancers who don't really get any help from me until I've finished the piece.

Interview, Los Angeles/
Los Angeles Herald Examiner, 1-3:(B)1.

Henry Fonda
Actor

1

To me, it's indulging myself to go back to the theatre. The rewards of acting are there. Not anything so simple as playing to a live audience. The first time you do a runthrough of a play is unforgettable. With a movie, you start tomorrow on Stage 11 with scenes 88 and 89. You do the scenes before lunch and that's your performance. You never get a chance to do them again. You've never played the role from beginning to end. You never feel you've created it.

Interview, Los Angeles, Feb. 28/
The New York Times, 3-3:(C)8.

2

[On acting in the theatre] : I like to make it a new play every night, because if it becomes mechanical, then it ain't fair. You owe it to an audience; they should get the play they heard about, and they deserve to enjoy it like it was the first night. And besides, that's where the fun of it all lies. If it ever stops being fun, I'll go back to my garden and my bees and my painting.

Interview/Time, 10-9:118.

Bob Fosse
Director, Choreographer

3

I like to work with dancers who are not just *technical* people. They have to be able to act, so it's not just a step they're dancing but an emotion. On the other hand, I don't have time for what some people think of as artistic temperament. Rehearsals are hard enough without

having personality problems. As soon as people give me everything *they've* got, I can give them everything *I've* got.

Interview, Boston/The New York Times, 3-26:(2)4.

Max Frisch
Playwright

4

I have become bored with theatre. No matter how well it is done, you always come out saying nothing more than that was good theatre, but still theatre. If you see really good cinema, you feel that it is a piece of life.

Interview, Kusnacht, Switzerland/
The New York Times Book Review, 3-19:37.

Rex Harrison
Actor

5

[On the differences between British and American audiences] : Even though we have the *Concorde* [SST] going in three hours, it doesn't really change the mentality of the two countries all that much. The good thing about American audiences is that they go to the theatre for an event, and in actual fact it makes them a little more lively in feeling. The British audiences go to the theatre as a part of their lives and they're not so demonstrative . . . but they're very intelligent and they will accept anything!

Interview, Boston/
The Christian Science Monitor, 12-1:(B)2.

Florence Henderson
Actress, Singer

6

. . . I really love a live audience. It's the most frightening, but I think it's really what performing is all about. You really aren't performing unless you have an audience, and it's amazing how much the audience affects your performance. They are so much a part of it. You send the energy out and they send it back to you, and it's a very chemical thing that happens, a very electric thing . . .

Interview, Beverly Hills,
Calif./San Francisco Examiner &
Chronicle, 10-22:(Datebook)17.

Geoffrey Holder
Director

1

Doing a show is a bit like cooking. It's not a chore. You've got guests coming and you know what you want to give them. You throw in a bit of this and that, a herb or two, a little rosemary, thyme, garlic, and then you marinate it overnight. Let it go right through the veins, and there it is. A show is the same.

Sky (Delta Air Lines magazine), March:37.

John Houseman
Actor, Producer

2

As far as I am concerned, the New York theatre is sick. I am much more interested in regional and repertory theatre. They are finally getting around to doing new plays and, when many of these new plays finally appear in New York, everybody [there], including [producer] Joe Papp, is so proud of these wonderful new plays they claim to have discovered.

Interview, New York/
The Christian Science Monitor, 9-18:18.

Eugene Ionesco
Playwright

3

From the start ... I've always had to battle against the critics. When *The Bald Soprano* first came out, for example, the *Le Monde* reviewer said it was worth a "shrug of the shoulders." When *The Chairs* was produced, he said it was very bad, not living up to the brilliance of *The Bald Soprano.* When *Amedee* arrived, he called it terrible and wondered what had happened to the fine author of *The Chairs.*

Interview/San Francisco Examiner & Chronicle,
3-12:(Datebook)20.

4

Eventually, I think theatre will attract only a minority of people, not an elite, but an artistic minority who want to see real people, not people on a screen. The trend is toward smaller theatres ... That is how it can continue. And I would like to add that there is no need to be upset because there are people who don't like

theatre. There is no theatre for everyone. There is no music for everyone. There is no painting for everyone.

Interview, Los Angeles/
Los Angeles Herald Examiner, 10-1:(F)8.

James Earl Jones
Actor

5

I would like to spend my life doing subtle characters on film and full-out characters in the theatre. The simpler the character, the better in the theatre. The opposite is true in films. Film is more mental than theatre. It's oblique and suggestive and depends more on imagery than on action and words ...

Interview/Los Angeles Herald Examiner, 5-3:(A)2.

Deborah Kerr
Actress

6

Very often I've been trying to describe feelings about doing a scene—I'm talking now about the stage or theatre—and I've likened us [actors] to race horses. We really are like a stable of thoroughbreds who are twitching, twittering, nostrils flaring, can't wait to get into the starting gate, you know. But nervy to the degree that if you flick a little piece of white paper alongside them, why, they've reared up, thrown for a loop, unseated their rider. You know, we're very like race horses.

Interview, Washington/
The Christian Science Monitor, 9-28:(B)13.

Eartha Kitt
Entertainer

7

... I love working in front of the public. The public is your greatest director. A director never can tell you how to be a character. Only the public can tell you. Therefore, you have to have 1,550 antennae all over your body, nervous centers covering you everywhere all the time. The theatre to me is also a form of educating you as a person. The theatre has given me the greatest education anyone could have. Not in any scientific way—I'm not saying I can take an atom and split it. But to be able

399

WHAT THEY SAID IN 1978

to be sensitive, to be able to have all of your pores open at all times and never to be afraid of some feeling touching you—that's what makes an artist and the kind of human being we'd like to be.

Interview, Chicago/
The Dallas Times Herald, 11-5:(H)10.

Jack Lemmon
Actor

1

If I read one more article about an actor who has been primarily involved in films, who then decides to do a play and starts talking [about how] now he can breathe, and the greatness of theatre as opposed to film, I'm going to vomit. Why didn't he do more of it, if that is true? I love film and I love the stage and they are radically different in their appeals.

Interview/Los Angeles Herald Examiner, 9-18:(A)1.

2

[On the regimen of doing a stage play] : You don't do anything else. Up late, go to the gym, a deli sandwich at 6, a 20-minute nap, feet up listening to music, then I'm ready for the show. But once in a blue moon you reach somebody—and your whole career is worth it.

Interview, New York/
Los Angeles Times, 11-26:(Calendar)5.

David Mamet
Playwright

3

Theatre people are seen as interesting but not constructive creatures. In contrast, people automatically treat doctors as laudable. There are probably as many charaltans in the medical profession as there are in theatre. People in the theatre are always told to make themselves clear. But nobody says to a doctor, "What do you mean? Make yourself clear, bozo!" Who questions doctors, lawyers and stockbrokers? Which is not to knock them. They have to make a buck, too.

Interview, New York/The New York Times, 1-15:(2)4.

Marcel Marceau
Mime

4

[On why he chose mime]: When I was a child, great film actors like [Charles] Chaplin made me laugh and cry and expressed their feelings to the whole world without speaking a word. I said why not recreate this in the theatre? And, of course, with mime it's very difficult because not only do you not have any sets or characters, you also have to make an invisible world visible without one word. This is really pure creation. There is also a great tradition of mime in France, stemming from the 19th century, the Romantic period. Pierrot, Columbine, Harlequin, all the characters who come from the *Commedia dell-arte,* have influenced the modern theatre. I decided that there was no reason why this art which was once admired by the Greeks and Romans should not exist in the present, especially in such a visual time as ours—a time of electronics, the poster, the movies. The eye has become a fantastic medium.

Interview/Atlas World Press Review, August:27.

E. G. Marshall
Actor

5

[Saying he never reads reviews]: I really don't. They have nothing to do with my performance. They cannot help me in any way. It's the director's job to read reviews and come and tell me if he thinks I'm doing something wrong. But I can't possibly read a critic. He is writing for the theater-goers. I've seen performances damaged when an actor reads reviews in which he is damned or over-praised.

Interview, Bedford, N.Y./
The New York Times, 6-4:(2)4.

Walter Matthau
Actor

6

There are few very good stage actors, but there are a lot more good movie actors. Part of what makes them good is the director, the cameraman, the editor ... On stage, you can only be naturalistic as opposed to realistic, be-

(WALTER MATTHAU)

cause otherwise you won't be heard in the second row. On stage, it's different timing. You say a line and wait for a laugh. The audience is half your play. In a movie, you can't wait for laughs. It may be 11 in the morning in Evansville, Indiana, and 16 people are in the theatre. Your timing is way off if you wait for laughs.

Interview, New York/
The New York Times, 3-26:(2)17.

Burgess Meredith
Actor

1

[Comparing Broadway today with its earlier years] : Broadway! Oh, my God! But in one way it's better, I suppose–more experimental with all the off-Broadway stuff. Even this, though, is being stifled by rising costs. Broadway itself is overwhelmed with today's production costs. I'm much more interested in regional theatre–grass-roots stuff. And anyway, I don't think Broadway competes as well with movies as it used to.

Interview, New York/San Francisco
Examiner & Chronicle, 4-16:(Datebook)26.

Rita Moreno
Entertainer

2

It costs a lot of money up-front to put on a nightclub act. What is scary is all of the out-of-pocket expenses. There are the myriad arrangers you have to pay. I have three dancers, a producer and a conductor on the payroll. You do all of this in the hope you will have a successful act–in the sense a lot of people will want you. Think of the horror of doing all of that and then getting rotten reviews. That would be crushing–not only financially but on the personal side. You have to put it on the line. You expose yourself that way and people say they don't like what you are. That would be horrible.

Interview, Dallas/
The Dallas Times Herald, 12-5:(C)4.

Peter O'Toole
Actor

3

I'd rather do than talk; I'd rather act than discuss. In North America actors have to talk about the play, analyze it. There is a passion in the 20th century for analysis. Everything has to be analyzed. Why? Why? Everything has to be wholly quantified and measured; God, the whole dissection of things–body, soul, mind, words! My passion is language. The most satisfying thing for me is having worked with fine writers–John Osborne, Samuel Beckett and Robert Bolt. Give me literature, not meditating and brooding. You're better off spending your money on Shakespeare than a psychiatrist, yes indeed.

Interview, Chicago/
The Washington Post, 11-12:(G)12.

4

I was taught many years ago . . . that if your feet are all right on stage, the rest of you will be. [I was told,] "Pay more attention to your shoes than you would to any other single thing you wear." You find a comfortable stance, with your feet like this [planted on the floor]. A lot of people when they stand, they're sort of hunched, they're pressing the ground very lightly. Now I'm pressing very firmly. When I can *feel* the ground, feel the territory, feel the stage, I can stoop, do anything. Then there's the other rule, which is never to stand when you can sit; never to sit when you can lie down.

Interview, Washington/
The Christian Science Monitor, 12-21:(B)19.

Irene Papas
Actress

5

[Comparing acting in *Iphigenia* on the stage and in the film] : You're naked out there on the stage. You have no pockets. You cannot have a cup of coffee, as you could when we were shooting [the film]. I had to get out of the play. You can't act tragedy every night at 7:30 and four times on the weekends!

Interview, Los Angeles/
Los Angeles Times, 3-22:(4)13.

WHAT THEY SAID IN 1978

Joseph Papp
Producer, New York Shakespeare Festival

1

I'm against any type of [U.S.] national theatre in principle. Our country is simply too large. It takes years to create a national theatre, and its formation must evolve out of experience, practice and its own impulses. It cannot be done by fiat. The danger of a single national theatre is the tendency to become monolithic. It's like having one major company, which is the same as establishing a monopoly. Rather, the U.S. should consider a loose grouping or federation of regional theatres, including the Spanish, black and Oriental theatres. In this way, we wouldn't wipe out the diversity of theatre that exists in this country today.

Interview/
U.S. News & World Report, 5-1:84.

2

I guess everybody feels that if they have a show that's going to be a big popular success, they'd like to see it get to the place where it can make the most money [Broadway]. But there's no way you can plan for success. I have as many notions as anybody else would have, but I have no idea what will be successful in a commercial sense.

Interview, New York/
Los Angeles Times, 12-10:(Calendar)86.

Tony Randall
Actor

3

I love my career, but there are many things I wish I had done. A man with a gift has a mission. When he has the theatrical training, the voice, knows the literature and has a historical perspective, he should bring all of these things to the great roles. I've never done that. I've always gone after the buck. I may turn straight one of these days and join a repertory company and do all the parts I should have done.

Interview, Atlanta/
The Dallas Times Herald, 8-4:(F)1.

John Reed
Principal comedian, D'Oyly Carte
Opera, London

4

People always ask me how I keep fresh, repeating the same roles nightly for months. The secret is caring. I really care about each performance, and I'm nervous—you know, not hysterical, but apprehensive—before every one. I want to give what I've got to give and I'm haunted by a desire to please, hoping to be better each time . . . I think, "Oh, dear, to disappoint somebody!" It really worries me.

Interview, Los Angeles/Los Angeles Times, 6-13:(4)1.

Ralph Richardson
Actor

5

[On being in a long-running play] : You've got to perform in the role hundreds of times. In keeping it fresh one can become a large, madly humming, demented refrigerator. You go mad.

Time, 8-21:75.

Tom Stoppard
Playwright

6

[On writing plays compared with writing novels] : The advantage of a novel is that it stays the way you left it, and that's also the disadvantage. In live theatre, you can't really control what happens to your stuff, because it wouldn't be any good if the performers weren't making their own contribution. It balances out. But it is alarming. If you have something running for quite a while and you visit it from time to time, you can hit a dud night and get thoroughly depressed at what you've written. Or you can go there terribly worried about how it's holding up and have a terrific night when it works beautifully.

Interview, Washington/
The Washington Post, 8-29:(D)9.

Lee Strasberg
Artistic director, Actors Studio

7

A theatre must have three essential elements—of which the building itself is the least

(LEE STRASBERG)

important. It must have some *idea* which will make people want to be part of it. Otherwise, these people will not come back. Why should they? They won't get paid as much; the productions are haphazard; their reputations are being used as "box-office." Next comes a—how shall I put it?—a technical approach, the training of a company in the problems of ensemble theatre; the building of a company which has some kind of artistic unity that makes it want to be together and that can share a common enthusiasm for the play. And, finally, there is the leadership: the people who represent it and—especially for the actors—represent an integrity of approach which will make them want to be part of it. Otherwise, the pressures of the other competing forms—movies and television—are just too great to resist.

Interview, Los Angeles/
Los Angeles Times, 6-25:(Calendar)58.

1

The time for regional theatre is gone. I dislike mentioning a "national theatre" [for the U.S.], but I think it is necessary. Our country is too big for a national theatre such as Britain has—one theatre—but there could be five, six, eight theatres around the country. Each year now, the government gives something like $200-million for the arts. I think it is pumped down the drain. What good does it do for the National Arts Foundation, or whatever, to give such-and-such a sum to a regional theatre for this year or for next year? There's no long-range creative approach . . . There also is an effort to divide the money up on a geographic basis. That doesn't really help much. We should put our money and our best people into one effort.

Interview/The Dallas Times Herald, 7-25:(B)7.

Gwen Verdon
Dancer

2

There have been moments when I have danced in rehearsal studio that have been far better than anything I've ever done publicly. It

all comes together sometimes. There's so much stress when you're on stage. It's so hard to have that kind of real, complete abandon, where you'll take chances. On stage, you're always just slightly cautious, knowing you've got to do it just right. I mean, you owe it to all those people sitting out there to give them your best, and that's what you do.

Interview/San Francisco Examiner & Chronicle,
6-25:(Datebook)15.

Edward Villella
Ballet dancer

3

America's biggest contribution to ballet is style. In Europe, you'll find massive productions of romantic ballets. At the outset, in this country, we did not have the dancers with years and years of experience. Nor did we have the funds to build huge sets with lots of costumes or to finance big orchestras. Without financial assets, we had to do something else in this country. So we became very oriented to the 20th century. Using classic beginnings as a foundation, we developed a neoclassic or American style. The American style of ballet represents a clear, sharp attack—very precise movements.

Interview/U.S. News & World Report, 7-17:58.

Ken Waissman
Producer

4

One thing that annoys me about the theatre industry is when amateur producers who have the dollars move in and try to act like experts. It reflects on all of us because it lowers the success statistics and turns off investors.

Interview/"W": a Fairchild publication, 6-23:2.

Jack Weston
Actor

5

Hearing an audience scream at something you've done—how marvelous, what power you have. I swear to you . . . one night in Boston with *Cheaters,* I got a laugh that seemed like minutes, although probably it was only

WHAT THEY SAID IN 1978

(JACK WESTON)

seconds, and I almost cried. I get crazy when the laughs come. It's like Christmas Eve.

Interview, New York/
The New York Times, 1-20:(C)2.

Tennessee Williams
Playwright

1

Too many writers expect themselves to surpass the early work on which their reputations are still based. This early work is like a GREAT EEERRRUPTION of a volcano that's been buried in them for such a long time. When it's released, they create several plays that have a magnitude, almost like a bomb blast. That's what I call a blockbuster play. Ha! I'm no longer interested in blockbusters. I know that's where the money is. But I'm no longer interested.

Interview, Kiawah Island, S.C./
Los Angeles Times, 7-9:(Calendar)62.

TELEVISION AND RADIO

James A. Alcott
Publisher, "Harper's" magazine

1

The written word is no longer pre-eminent as a shaper of thought. It has been usurped by electronics. By the year 2001, the United States will be well on its way to becoming a post-literate society. Television started as an educational medium; it is now perceived as an entertainment medium, but it actually is an advertising medium.

San Francisco Examiner &
Chronicle, 4-2:(This World)2.

Steve Allen
Entertainer

2

Much of television is what I call junk food for the mind. Like junk food for the stomach, it's not terribly harmful in itself. It's just that it's empty, escapist—just something to pass the time. I don't see any hope in lifting the quality of commercial television. The people who run the networks are perfectly intelligent gentlemen—responsible citizens. They may personally prefer opera or a Leonard Bernstein concert, but if they put that sort of thing on against some detective thriller, they know what will happen to the ratings: They will go down.

Interview/U.S. News & World Report, 3-13:76.

James Arness
Actor

3

These [network] censors say you can hit so many guys, throw so many punches, fire X-number of shots—they count them. They base it on quantity of violence, not on the way it is handled. It's ridiculous. I don't think some of these censors are really qualified to judge, because they are not story people. It's not their

forte. They couldn't give you a valid judgment whether a certain act of violence is really necessary to tell a story or whether it is thrown in for shock value. You need violence in a Western. Without, it's a phony. How the hell can you win the West without having a little violence?

Interview, Los Angeles/
The New York Times, 2-12:(2)31.

James Brolin
Actor

4

I don't watch television much these days. I know how poorly it's manufactured. Directors become yes-men in series television or they get fired. The whole object is to hold down costs. When a network orders a television show, it tells the producer exactly how much it will pay, so the producer tries to widen his profit margin by doing everything as cheaply as possible. In movies, the profits are related to how many people go to see a picture and, since producers are usually optimistic, the sky's the limit on costs.

Interview, New York/
The New York Times, 7-21:(C)8.

Kitty Broman
Chairman, television
board of directors, National
Association of Broadcasters

5

[Opposing a ban on television commercials aimed at children]: Children get a lot of great things from television, and advertising is one way that some of these marvelous programs are paid for. I think only a small minority—although a vocal one—is concerned about TV commercials for children. According to a 1976

(KITTY BROMAN)

Roper study, 66 per cent of the parents surveyed said they could see nothing wrong with advertising on children's programs. I think television is damned for a lot of things that it shouldn't be damned for . . . I think that TV is being unfairly singled out if a product can't be advertised there but can be in a magazine, newspaper or on radio. I don't agree with the argument that television is such a powerful medium that it needs to be restricted more than a newspaper or magazine . . . I look at any restriction, no matter how limited, as unconstitutional. You don't have to let children watch television. Nobody says that you have to put a child in front of the television, turn it on and make the child sit there. You always have a choice.

Interview/
U.S. News & World Report, 1-16:47,48.

Tyrone Brown
Commissioner, Federal
Communications Commission

1

As a black American, I vividly recall my early experience when virtually all the people I saw on television were white. With Commission prodding, things have improved, but I for one would not want to rely solely on the altruism of broadcasters to air programming reflecting the world as it really is. My sons watch TV. I want them to grow up watching a more realistic representation of our diverse society than I did as a child.

At hearing on the Communications
Act, Washington, July 18/
The New York Times, 7-19:(C)22.

Carol Burnett
Entertainer

2

On most television variety shows the [performers] look as though they haven't even rehearsed. Why aren't the guests professional enough to learn their lines? We've always done our show cold-turkey, live on tape, without stopping even if someone blows his lines. Today, if someone has a hit record, the networks give him a variety show. They think they can make a singer funny by writing funny sketches for him. But it doesn't work that way. You have to pay your dues. I started out in summer stock; you got up at 7 a.m. and went to bed at 2 a.m., and did a different play each week.

Interview, Los Angeles/
The New York Times, 3-23:27.

Howard W. Cannon
United States Senator, D-Nevada

3

[On television programming]: We must recognize the growing disenchantment of many Americans not simply with the violence and vulgarity too often programmed for them today, but with the general banality of much of the fare they're offered every day. We have gone far beyond the point where the option of switching channels or turning off the set is sufficient. The medium is here to stay and it is a public medium from which the public has a right to at least good taste, if not some variety.

Before National Association of
Broadcasters, Las Vegas, Nev./
Los Angeles Times, 4-14:(4)26.

Dick Cavett
Television interviewer

4

[Supporting government financial assistance to public television]: We're [the U.S.] way behind other countries in the quality of our programming. Programs shown on public television here are on prime-time in England. Furthermore, I don't think the things we see on public TV should be there by the grace of the gargle manufacturers and the panty-hose spinners.

At New York State Senate panel hearing,
New York/The Dallas Times Herald, 3-5:(A)2.

Peggy Charren
President, Action for
Children's Television

5

Television ads for children are an inappropriate use of the public air waves. They exploit America's most vulnerable population. Because

(PEGGY CHARREN)

children are inexperienced and lack consumer sophistication, they deserve the highest standard of protection from the unconscionable, hard-sell commercials manufacturers now use on TV... The young child—the 2-to-8-year-old—mixes up the commercial message with a program's content. He cannot appreciate the commercial motives behind advertising or make discriminating choices. And even the older child who can recognize a misleading commercial is still gullible. Parents can tell him, "That toy's going to break when you get it home." Having had that experience with other toys, he will say, "Yes, I know—but I want it anyway." I want to make it clear that ACT doesn't think there shouldn't be any television commercials, but only that there shouldn't be any commercials specifically geared to children. The commercial should be directed to adults who have the experience and intelligence to know if, when and how a product should be used. You gear a candy-bar message to an adult who will know what place that candy bar should take in a balanced diet. You let the adult beware.

Interview/
U.S. News & World Report, 1-16:47.

James Coburn
Actor

1

[I have] great dissatisfaction for the amateurs in television—who want to make everything so bland. You'd think they'd be glad to do things that are different, exciting. But they don't. [TV is awash with] executives who just want power—just want to enjoy controlling things. But they don't know real power. Real power becomes manifest when the audiences get a feedback of impressions that are meaningful and uplifting.

Los Angeles Herald Examiner, 12-11:(A)2.

James E. Duffy
President, American Broadcasting Company Television Network

2

The chief beneficiary of competition is the viewer. Television has gone through its stages of

infancy and adolescence until now, in the 1970s, it has reached new levels of maturity. Quality is steadily improving, and there is more creativity and diversity of choice for the viewer than anywhere else in the world... Television is a business. There are always critics who are disturbed by this, who think that because TV is a business, it aims for a common denominator in taste and intellectual level in its programming in order to attract the largest possible audience and, therefore, the greater financial return. They would rather see TV used to upgrade tastes, to enrich and educate the people. I would argue that TV does both, or certainly tries to. The point here is that a basic choice was made long ago in this society to put faith in maximum freedom for individual initiative rather than entrusting everything to the government. It was thought that this would be more productive, more creative, more diversified, and more in tune with the real needs and wants of the people. I think without question it has proven to be so... I think it is useful to view the [TV] system as a whole and to appreciate it for what it is. American TV is a system which has worked—and is working—extremely well.

Before Greater Madison (Wis.) Chamber of Commerce/The Hollywood Reporter, 1-27:56.

3

[Criticizing efforts to limit or ban certain advertising on children's programs]: These proposals are directed only at television advertising. If a product can really be shown to be harmful to the health of children, it should be banned from the marketplace entirely, not just from the television screen... The idea of banning ads only on television has a kinship to the notion that dramatic episodes on television can be held to be the cause of criminal acts [in real life]. Both spring from the curious view that problems can be solved by tampering with the television system. This is a dangerous delusion.

Before Commonwealth Club, San Francisco,
Aug. 4/Los Angeles Times, 8-5:(2)12.

4

In the end, public opinion is the dominant force [in TV], but this... is a complicated

WHAT THEY SAID IN 1978

subject. Each component of the system tends to have its own interpretation of public opinion. These points of view may range from high-sounding notions of public interest to more pragmatic translations of public opinion into marketplace dollars. It is in this regard that the TV ratings are controversial. We have concern about the influence of ratings as much as anyone. But we should be clear about one thing: The ratings are indispensable. We must have a barometer of public acceptance and of popularity. We absolutely must have a means of quick feedback, just as every other form of communication does in one way or another. We cannot operate in a vacuum . . .

Before Boston chapter, National
Academy of Television Arts and
Sciences, Oct. 12/Variety, 10-18:255.

Ralph Edwards
Producer

1

Television has a voracious appetite [for programming]. But it isn't the appetite of a gourmet, but a glutton. This creates a kind of sheep-follow-sheep pattern, and this, in turn, numbs or nullifies creativity.

Interview/
Los Angeles Herald Examiner, 12-27:(A)1.

Vince Edwards
Actor

2

Before [his former TV series] *Ben Casey,* I'd done 24 pictures . . . and I was usually offered two or three pictures a year. But after *Casey* was off, I never got another offer. The *Casey* image was just too strong. I was up for the part of Sonny in *The Godfather* and I understand the director's decision not to use me. But I hope it's over now. *Ben Casey* was in black-and-white, so it's still running in only a few isolated markets. Free at last! . . . [But] listen, it was great being Ben Casey and I have no regrets about it. In those days, though, if you made a couple of hundred thousand a year, you were sensational—but when it was all over, unless

you lived frugally, you had to go out and hassle again. Nowadays these kids make a couple of hundred thousand in three shows. It's a different world. But they'd better keep in mind that, when it's over, it might be over.

Interview, New York/
The Christian Science Monitor, 8-11:11.

Harlan Ellison
Author

3

There is no art in television, none whatsoever. I've stopped writing [for] television. I've given it up and will not go back. As a television critic and as a writer working in the field for 15 years, I found my position about what I was writing, and the medium itself, becoming more and more radical. At first I thought, well, it is only the quality of the writing, and then perceived it was the regimented thinking television, in which life and reality must be denied because the hero has to come back next week.

Interview/
Los Angeles Herald Examiner, 5-30:(A)1.

Charles D. Ferris
Chairman, Federal
Communications Commission

4

The fact that I don't have a broadcasting background nor a common-carrier background nor a cable background or any kind of communications background is probably what President Carter found appealing. The fact that I didn't come in with a set of prejudgments, that I would have a capacity to look at things fresh and new, to make judgments, recommend a course of action based on fresh evaluation, I think he found appealing. I'm not a known quantity. They [the industry] don't know what my bottom line is, and I don't know what my bottom line is.

Interview, Washington/
The Christian Science Monitor, 1-26:26.

5

[Addressing broadcasters]: The demands on you to provide a public service and not simply to maximize profits are not the mere whims of

(CHARLES D. FERRIS)

Federal regulators. It is the mandate of the law that binds us both ... Today, too much [TV] programming is still the same from hour to hour and channel to channel, with only the names of the networks changed to protect the appearance of competition ... Today, the tyranny of Nielsen's numbers has strengthened its hold. The only places in our republic where points and point-spreads are given greater urgency than here in the casinos of Las Vegas are the corporate headquarters of the three networks in New York.

Before National Association of
Broadcasters, Las Vegas, Nev.,
April 12/Los Angeles Times, 4-13:(1)18.

1

I don't think any government should be dictating what the content of a specific [TV] program is. We can get involved in the percentages of programming and licensing; you know, that 15 per cent of a station's programming will be public affairs, as opposed to entertainment programming—but not what that 15 per cent, or that 85 per cent, should contain. However strong my personal feelings are, I don't think it's my job to impose my tastes on an industry and on 200 million people. The ones who prevent us from doing that are Thomas Jefferson and the others who wrote the Constitution and the first amendments. I think the First Amendment is very strict with respect to government dictating program content.

Interview, Washington/TV Guide, 7-15:8.

Sally Field
Actress

2

Because I came up through television I had a real no-no image where [feature] films were concerned. I was the all-American, syrupy, meaningless girl-next-door with no belly-button. Just about as bland as you can get. So finally I said to myself, "Fieldsy, get out [of TV] before you sink." And I did. I quit cold. And I had a hard time. No one would even consider me for films. I didn't even get to bang

on the door. Even when I was absolutely right for the part, they wouldn't consider me ... And it took a long time, almost three years, before I got the chance to show what I could do.

Interview, Los Angeles/
Los Angeles Times, 12-10:(Calendar)58.

Henry Fonda
Actor

3

... I think TV is getting better. That's not to say there's not a lot of garbage ... just as there is on the big screen and all the other media. But there are some brilliant things being done on TV. Not so much in the series, although I think *All in the Family* is one of the most brilliant things on TV. But some of the specials, like *Roots* and *Eleanor and Franklin* shows and *The Missiles of October* were brilliantly done. I'm impressed with shows of that caliber.

Interview, Los Angeles/
The Christian Science Monitor, 3-13:39.

Glenn Ford
Actor

4

[On the attitude of some actors when their series is cancelled]: An actor shouldn't pass judgment on a network. When you sign for a series you take your chances. When actors complain, I think that's childish. They make up the most ridiculous excuses: They were bored with the characters; they were tired of the series. Why don't they just say, "I'm sorry it's cancelled"? Who do they think they're kidding?

Interview, Los Angeles/San Francisco
Examiner & Chronicle, 8-13:(Datebook)40.

John Furia, Jr.
Former president,
Writers Guild of America

5

[On the exploitation of sex on TV]: The Writers Guild has been very vocal in opposition to censorship, and now we find ourselves in a peculiar position—we want the broadest possible expression on television, but the sex we have been forced to defend has not been

WHAT THEY SAID IN 1978

(JOHN FURIA, JR.)

healthy or constructive but leering and at the sophomoric level; instead of using sex in a good way, the networks have exploited it.

The Christian Science Monitor, 3-30:24.

Leonard Goldberg
Producer

1

When you enter television, you enter the ratings game. If you get high Nielsen ratings, you stay on the air; if you don't, you go off. You can try to change the rules, but I don't know many games where the rules have changed over the past 25 years. Within limits, Nielsen is accurate.

TV Guide, 6-24:6.

Lawrence K. Grossman
*President, Public
Broadcasting Service*

2

[Television] is a force at the center of our lives. It must in some way give people a sense of who they are, a sense of themselves. Do we dare rely on commercial television to do that for us? Commercial television says almost nothing of life as it really is and what we really are. What commercial television is, first and foremost, is a marvellous system for moving goods. Its product is the audience. Its content is merely the bait. If it is true, as William Blake wrote long before television, that "we become what we behold"—and I believe that it is true—then this nation cannot afford to allow public television to be merely an alternative [to commercial TV]. We need public television to stand as the model of excellence. It must stand up for the best our society has to offer in the areas our people should care about most: education, information, art and culture and creativity. Excellence must not be judged simply by size of audience. Leadership cannot come merely from the amount of money earned. We represent something better than that public television has the responsibility to reflect what we want our country to be, our society to be, our lives to be.

In that respect, public television in America is not just an alternative. It must inevitably become a primary force.

*At PBS programming conference,
Jan. 12/The Washington Post, 1-19:(A)24.*

3

Greed is in charge of TV; fear is what runs TV. The tense battle for survival in the executive suite. The struggle for corporate power dulls creativity, kills experimentation, makes everyone follow the leader. Fear makes TV what it is today. The viewers really control TV. They vote with their dials. The people are getting what they want. They can't be watching more than six hours per day, spending more time with TV than with anything else—if they don't like what they get. It's the people who control TV. My colleagues from commercial TV feel very comfortable with that explanation.

*Before Boston chapter, National
Academy of Television Arts and
Sciences, Oct. 12/Variety, 10-18:255.*

John Hawkesworth
British producer-writer

4

[Criticizing the U.S. television system]: At the heart of the matter is preparation [of programs]. Your system is frightening to anyone creative. You start with a thousand subjects which get whittled down to a few which they make pilots of, and you put all your heart into the pilot. Then you don't know 'till March or April whether or not the show is going on. And even then you don't know when it's going to end—so there is no security. And you've got writers being commissioned to write scripts in three weeks, directors hurriedly chosen, and in the end the whole thing is based on ratings. On Wednesday morning you decide whether to cut the thing or go on. Everybody gets into a state of utter jitters—they can't think. A series can never be planned as an entity as most of our [British] series are.

*Interview, London/
The Christian Science Monitor, 10-23:20.*

410

John Houseman
Actor

1

[On whether he has lowered his artistic sights by working on a weekly TV series] : I am in show business. I played two *Bionic Womans* and one *Six Million Dollar Man.* If you do that, you're not above anything. I am an actor. Obviously I do what is offered.

Interview, Los Angeles/TV Guide, 11-18:32.

Eugene Ionesco
Playwright

2

In theatre, there is a human presence. The absence of that presence is felt very much in television. The theatre is a very alive community in which the actors and the audience participate. A group of actors become friends. But in mass audiences people participate only in a very anonymous way, and people sit alone in front of a television.

Interview, Los Angeles/
Los Angeles Herald Examiner, 10-1:(F)8.

Barry Jogoda
Special Assistant to President of
the United States Jimmy Carter for
Media and Public Affairs

3

I think television in the '80s will be marked by what's called "narrowcasting"—quality television for small audiences of hundreds of thousands instead of millions and millions. So, instead of having to appeal to our lowest-common-denominator instincts, television will be able to appeal to the genuine interests of diverse audiences. Then you'll have channels for jazz, for cooking, for understanding the performing arts, and so on. I think that people in television will begin to think more like magazine editors think, aiming at narrow audiences rather than broader audiences. That's why I use the term "narrowcasting" instead of "broadcasting."

Interview/The Washington Post, 6-18:(G)5.

Gene F. Jankowski
President, Columbia Broadcasting
System Broadcast Group

4

[Saying TV creators should slow the pace of objectionable programming] : [Staying in step with what viewers want to see] in no way suggests a stultifying of creativity. Good taste and high ratings are not mutually exclusive . . . We are not asking for morality plays, for that is not the role of television. We are not asking for "messages" in every series, in every special, for that is also not the role of television. Television is to inform and to entertain, to make life more understandable and more pleasurable . . . We must not push our audience to some seemingly inelastic outer limit of quality and taste. Good judgment has to prevail, and we must continue to be dedicated to providing what we consider to be the best in television programming. I would venture to suggest that if there are taboos on subject matter for television presentation, there are few. Almost any subject may be treated, if it is handled tastefully and in the proper context.

Before Hollywood Radio and
Television Society, Beverly Hills,
Calif., Feb. 13/Daily Variety, 2-14:1,6.

5

It seems that hardly a day passes without television being blamed for illiteracy, for crime in the streets, for the common cold and for the corn blight. . . . we broadcasters are often looked upon as some sort of evil incarnate. To some degree, that's our fault for not telling our story—and telling it well . . . We have spent too little of our total communications effort in stressing the positive, in publicizing our accomplishments. We are often attacked in an unknowing way by people who are thinking of the past and ignoring the present. Many of them have not allowed the facts to interfere with a good argument.

At seminar sponsored by
Broadcasters Promotion Association,
St. Paul, Minn., June 8/Daily Variety,
6-9:1;The Hollywood Reporter, 6-9:3.

411

WHAT THEY SAID IN 1978

David Janssen
Actor

1

[I] question the validity of the difference between TV movies and feature films. There are few subjects that can't be handled just as well on TV as in a feature film these days. The success of long-form TV films has put a negative pressure on theatrical pictures. Producers are in the position of making films they hope will lure viewers away from their sets. Why should viewers gamble on paying a small fortune to go out and see a movie when quality TV films with top creative talent and distinguished authors can be seen at home?

Interview/
The Dallas Times Herald, 9-20:(D)5.

Nicholas Johnson
Chairman, National Citizens
Committee for Broadcasting;
Former Commissioner, Federal
Communications Commission

2

[Saying improvement of TV will come about from public pressure on the FCC, not on broadcasters]: We are dealing with a business. We've been too easy on the FCC. It's too much to expect the broadcasters to act out of moral or ethical responsibility. It's not enough for the FCC to issue statements or give speeches telling the broadcasters it would be nice for them to program for children, or not to advertise to children. If you've been around this town long enough, you know that's an official kiss-off. The broadcaster knows it. Their lawyers know it, and the FCC knows it. No one ever lost a license for violating an FCC speech.

At symposium sponsored by
Action for Children's Television,
Washington/Los Angeles Times, 5-4:(4)7.

3

[Criticizing the proposed government deregulation of broadcasting]: I see this bill as making the Teapot Dome scandal look like petty larceny. This bill overnight increases by billions of dollars the wealth of the single most powerful industry in human history . . . [Under

the bill, radio stations could] take all the agricultural service, the market reports and weather off of the air and there's nothing the farmers can do about it. They can take the early-morning education programs off the air and there's nothing the educators can do about it. They can wipe out all news and public affairs and there's nothing anybody can do about it . . . Every effort that we've made to really enhance competition in this industry has been vigorously and violently opposed by the broadcasting industry itself. The broadcasters don't have any more interest in marketplace competition than any other American industry does.

Interview, Washington, July 19/
The New York Times, 7-20:(C)21.

Bob Keeshan
Television's "Captain Kangaroo"

4

No matter what we [in TV] do in terms of quality, it's not going to work unless parents take an active role in selecting programs [for their children]. I think too many people who are involved with questions of children and television seek simple answers, and it's hardly a simple question. The answer isn't that if the industry provided more quality programming, there would be no problem. That's not true. The quality programming is there, and it's not watched. You can put quality programming on all day long, and without parental guidance children will still be watching soap operas, game shows and *The Little Rascals.*

Interview, New York/
Los Angeles Times, 10-31:(4)1.

John D. Kersey
Vice president, broadcast
standards and practices, American
Broadcasting Company Television

5

There is no idea, no concept, that is unacceptable to TV if it is handled with taste and judgment. TV is like a mirror reflecting on society. Things, people and society move in that mirror, and TV reflects those dynamics.

Interview/The Hollywood Reporter, 5-4:4.

Michael Landon
Actor

1

Why is there so much sex and violence in the movies and on television these days? Whose fault is it? If adults would take their children to theatres when G-rated films are playing, there would be nothing but G-rated films made. But they don't. It's the same with television. It's tough to make it with a family show. The networks don't arbitrarily put on sex and violence; they put on what the public apparently watches ... People complain [about TV] a lot, but what do they do about it? They should support the things they talk about, but they always seem to want to leave this to somebody else.

Interview/Nation's Business, August: 24.

Norman Lear
Writer, Producer

2

I have other friends, movie directors, who do a good picture, but it takes them 2½ years to make it, and then they say, "You know, this would have been great two years ago; it's just after its time." But in TV you can avoid that. That's the great joy of television—to read something in a newspaper and comment about it or reflect it eight weeks later on the air. That is incredible joy.

Interview, Los Angeles/
The Washington Post, 2-1: (B)11.

3

The tool that a creative individual has is his own belly. My belly is my slide rule and when it is a creative slide rule, it's the best one available, better than research. If something makes me laugh, I think that it will make you laugh ... All I know is going back to that slide rule in the belly—what interests me will interest you. What interests me happens to be issues of human value, whether they are political, social or sexual. If you care more about what you are watching and listening to, you will laugh harder or cry more. The more you care, the more you will respond in the way the show is asking you to respond. That is the way I behave when I am

a member of the audience, and I will always think that what I feel, you will feel.

Interview/
Los Angeles Herald Examiner, 2-23: (A)15.

4

There are huge frustrations in television. You deal with people who are trapped in a system that has made them tense and nervous. Everything about the system defeats creativity, innovation and quality.

Interview, Los Angeles/
The New York Times, 4-9: (2)31.

William Leonard
Executive vice president,
and president-designate,
Columbia Broadcasting System News

5

I have a crazy theory that television is an audio medium and that radio is a visual medium. I obviously don't mean that quite literally, but what I mean by that is that good radio, which depends on words, requires of the listener a whole range of visual images in his mind in order to be part of that radio broadcast. Television, with its pictures, is almost useless without good words to go with it. So I tend to want to emphasize the words on television and the images created on radio.

Interview/
U.S. News & World Report, 11-20: 53.

Eugene J. McCarthy
Former United States
Senator, D-Minnesota

6

The television networks operate between greed and fear. The problem is how you use a medium that's inherently totalitarian in a free society.

Interview/"W":
a Fairchild publication, 10-13: 12.

Arthur Miller
Playwright

7

I hope that before the century is through we'll take television more seriously. Right now, most TV writing is like writing for cartoons.

Interview/"W": a Fairchild publication, 3-3: 10.

WHAT THEY SAID IN 1978

Newton N. Minow
Chairman, Public Broadcasting Service

1

The worst thing [PBS] could do is to make the mistakes that commercial television makes, and that's to regard the TV audience as a bunch of dummies. We treat our audience with respect because we know that they are just as smart as, and smarter than, we are. The people who call us elitists are, in my opinion, the worst form of elitists because they think the American public is dumb. They think that somebody with a blue collar does not have a taste for good music or good drama or the discussion of controversial issues, or that kids don't deserve programs like *Sesame Street* and *Zoom.* I regard them as the worst form of intellectual snobs. Our audience research shows that the people who watch public television are a cross-section of America—every element of income, education and race ... The idea that we reach an elitist audience is a myth and I reject it.

Interview, Chicago/TV Guide, 11-4:8.

Mary Tyler Moore
Actress

2

[On why she voluntarily gave up her TV series after a seven-year run]: Playing Mary Richards was getting too easy. It wasn't creatively stimulating. It was comfortable and I could have very easily gone on the rest of my life playing that character. But that's not what an actress is about. You need challenges, fears, uncertainty, a certain amount of crying at night and wondering whether it's going to make it.

Interview, Los Angeles/San Francisco Examiner & Chronicle, 2-12:(Datebook)40.

3

I've learned some lessons. You cannot just do an interesting character. You've got to do a character with which people can empathize and sympathize. That's one of the rules for keeping going in television.

Interview, Los Angeles/ Los Angeles Times, 11-5:(Calendar)1.

Bill Moyers
Journalist

4

[On why he is leaving CBS to return to public television]: I am not a romantic about public television, nor do I harbor illusions about it. Public television is under-financed, inadequately organized and uncertain about its own role in our society. I do not regard it as paradise. What it offers is air time and mastery over my own material. CBS has the money but little air time [for public-affairs programming]; public television has the air time but little money. For a journalist, air time is what counts. To have impact as a journalist you must have regularity of access, variety of subject matter and autonomy over your own ideas of what journalism on television is about.

Interview, New York/ Los Angeles Times, 7-5:(4)1.

Robert E. Mulholland
President, National Broadcasting Company Television

5

Organized criticism of TV has itself become a growth industry. Never before have we experienced the kind of sophisticated professional public-relations and political tactics used by these groups. All across the political and social landscape, determined organizations seem to be on the march—and all in different directions. It's confusing, and especially confusing for the broadcaster. There are something like 250 groups actively dedicated to changing television so that it will reflect their particular positions. They range from the PTA to black militants, from the National Federation of Decency to defenders of gay rights, from the NOW organization defending abortion to the Right to Life movement opposing it. All these groups may be wide apart on their goals, but they are agreed on one thing: They want to do something about television. The modern pressure group is no longer content with the traditional ways, like testifying in hearings, license challenges, firing off press releases, organized mail campaigns, and so on. They are finding new muscle

(ROBERT E. MULHOLLAND)

through boycotts of networks and sponsors, proxy motions at shareholder meetings, "quality" indexes for judging programs. And, in most cases, these groups conduct their campaigns in ignorance of—or without concern for—the economics of TV, its operating realities, or the structure of a mass medium based on advertising, program suppliers, news responsibilities, affiliated stations and networks.

Before Boston chapter, National
Academy of Television Arts and
Sciences, Oct. 12/Variety, 10-18:255.

1

If you ask who's in charge of TV in the U.S., you might as well ask who's in charge of taste in the U.S. The answer is nobody and everybody. That's the way of a democracy, and broadcasters respect it. In the final analysis, the viewing public commands, and the broadcasters obey.

Before Boston chapter, National
Academy of Television Arts and
Sciences, Oct. 12/Variety, 10-18:255.

Laurence Olivier
Actor

2

. . . you have to be a damned sight slicker in television because you have only three or four days' shooting time. With a film you might have eight, 10, 12 weeks. The stage is different from either. It's all a question of the size of the canvas, isn't it? The stage is a much bigger canvas and must be filled in a bolder kind of way, usually. In television and film there's one fatal error an actor can make and that's to regard what he's doing as being a "performance." That is something you must never *think* about. For either of those media, you just *have* to think only that it is a series of rehearsals— the best one of which will be accepted. If you think of it as a "performance," it will come across like that. You'll look as if you *know* you're giving a performance. These media are

very close-scrutiny. They'll tell you what they see. You have to be dreadfully careful.

Interview/TV Guide, 10-21:16.

Frederick S. Pierce
President, American
Broadcasting Company Television

3

There are many things that television cannot do . . . or does not do as well as it should. But it sometimes seems to me we've lost sight of all the learning experiences television does bring into our homes. I'm not referring to such dramatic events as trips to the moon or visits to China, but to the daily knowledge television gives us about ourselves, our neighbors and our own hometowns. When we look in on the lives of other people, real and fictional, we have the opportunity to learn about ourselves. Television has made the world smaller because we have seen how other people live—not just the places where they live. This medium entertains, informs and bears witness, and in all three capacities it gives our children and us exposure to new experiences.

Before National Education
Association, Dallas/
The Christian Science Monitor, 7-18:23.

Frank Price
President, Universal Television

4

We bring unknown kids into television, they become big stars, and then they move upward into films. Maybe *that's* where our true prestige should be evaluated—the fact that the movie industry is feeding on *us*. Look at some of today's movie box-office hits—*Heroes* with Henry Winkler and Sally Field, *Saturday Night Fever* with John Travolta, *Semi-Tough* with Jill Clayburgh. All fresh out of television.

Interview/TV Guide, 4-8:8.

Tony Randall
Actor

5

The only thing you could do to save television now is start all over. You'd have to fire

415

WHAT THEY SAID IN 1978

everybody in a position of responsibility—that's how bad it is. I don't think I'll ever do another TV show. The network executives don't even look at them. [They] are usually attorneys. They'll tell you their kids love your show, but all they themselves watch is the ratings.

Baltimore/Variety, 5-31:63.

Lee Rich
President, Lorimar Productions

1

[Saying there is too much attention given to ratings and money at TV networks today] : I think what is happening is a tragedy for television producers. Television always was a business, but never like this. Now you find the president of RCA [parent company of NBC] talking to security analysts and pointing out what a rating point means in terms of profits; top executives at ABC and CBS talk about rating points in terms of dollars; and newspapers all over the country carry the Nielsen top 10 every week... The business has changed radically. The networks no longer give television shows time to mature. If a show doesn't make it in three or four weeks, if it gets low ratings, the show is cancelled. I don't think [the long-running] *The Waltons* could have made it in today's market.

Interview, New York/
The Dallas Times Herald, 12-26:(D)6.

James H. Rosenfield
President, Columbia
Broadcasting System Television

2

Children's programming has taken rather a beating from some quarters... One of the problems is that not too many of its critics seem to get around to watching this product. Another is that it isn't made for them, so they really aren't very good judges of it. We begin with a simple philosophy here. We don't think Saturday [morning] TV should be a sixth day of school. That's because the kids have to have fun or they won't watch it at all. At the same time, there is a responsibility to provide them

with materials of substance. What all three networks do is interweave useful information throughout their children's schedules on Saturdays...

Before Boston chapter, National
Academy of Television Arts and
Sciences, Oct. 12/Variety, 10-18:255.

Elton H. Rule
President, American
Broadcasting Companies

3

The FTC staff proposes that television advertising directed to young children be banned, as well as television advertising of sugar-coated cereals and similar products to older children. If the idea behind the FTC's proposals is to get children to eat less sugar, they are raising a question that goes beyond television advertising. Kids will still have a sweet tooth. The FTC won't change that. The targeted products will still be on the grocery shelves. That won't change. The sugar bowl and jelly jar will still be on the breakfast table. That won't change.

Before Hollywood Radio and
Television Society, April 6/
Los Angeles Herald Examiner, 4-7:(A)2.

Eric Sevareid
Former news commentator,
Columbia Broadcasting System

4

I do not believe TV is a serious danger to American newspapers or to American society, education or cultural standards. I do not believe the incessant cry of critics that TV is turning us into a passive, inert people, minds and bodies becoming mush. "Zombie" is the word. I have never met a zombie in my life, save some drunks and mental defectives. If those charges are right, then I do not understand the meaning of certain facts: that some 60 million newspapers are purchased every day in this country and read by perhaps twice that number, far more than the number of people listening to network news—at least—each day; that sales per capita of books, including children's books, hold right about where they were before TV

(ERIC SEVAREID)

came along; that many millions more young Americans are studying in colleges, millions more adult Americans are studying courses at home; that extra millions fill the sports arenas, the tennis courts, the jogging tracks, the hunting fields and fishing streams, the planes and ships as they travel the world. The alarmist intellectual critics of television show us precious little direct evidence of what they *think* TV is doing to the mass of people. They do not know ordinary people, or understand their resilience. Nor do they love them, this particular type of intellectual. They have *always* opposed anything new that was massive and popular—the first printing presses, even the typewriter, the silent films, the talking films, radio, television. They *cannot* approve the popular. That would cost them their sense of distinctiveness. As Eric Hoffer said once: "The businessman just wants your money. The military man just wants you to obey. But the intellectual wants your soul. He wants people to get down on their knees and love what they hate and hate what they love."

*At United Press International
luncheon/The New York Times, 5-9:39.*

Sidney Sheldon
*Author; Former television
producer-director-writer*

1

... I think there's room for everything [in TV]. There's an audience for *60 Minutes,* there's an audience for ballet, certainly for sports; and it's wonderful that each person can pick out what he likes. It's wonderful that there is something for everyone. People complain about television, and some of the complaints are justified because I think everything always should be better all the time. ... but people who complain now about television don't realize that 100 years ago kings would have given half their kingdoms to have a magic box like that in their palaces.

*Interview/
Los Angeles Herald Examiner, 8-2:(A)1.*

Fred Silverman
*President, National
Broadcasting Company*

2

[On those who criticize TV] : Their criticism may be exaggerated and may not fully recognize the positive contributions TV has made to American life. Yet there is a basis for criticism of the TV medium. It raises questions as to whether TV is doing all it can to realize its enormous potential. These are very complex questions, because the very strengths of a mass medium may also create some shortcomings in the nature of programming designed to engage so broad an audience. Those are the shortcomings we must constantly evaluate and correct. But certainly by understanding and stepping up to the complexities and criticisms, we will open the way to constructive action. [TV has] been a great influence for public good. It has operated as a transmission belt of national experience that has carried the country through times of crisis. It has helped unify the nation as a unique national communications medium. It has accelerated social change.

*Before NBC-TV affiliates, New York,
June 19/Daily Variety, 6-20:10.*

3

[The U.S.] is a diversified and sectional country, but the nearest thing to a national community is the television audience. Through television, that audience shares a common experience, in entertainment and sports as well as information programs. We provide a very precious resource to the public and to the nation. We must not squander that resource, and we must earn the trust of the public.

*Before NBC-TV affiliates, New York,
June 19/Los Angeles Times, 6-20:(4)1.*

4

If one [TV] network wins the season by a rating point or two, it's meaningless. The time has come to say the hell with increasing the ratings really for its own sake. As we consciously try to improve our quality, improved ratings automatically happen ... In the competitive frenzy for ratings, which I helped create, we

WHAT THEY SAID IN 1978

have virtually driven important programs such as news documentaries off all three networks. That trend must be reversed.

Before TV critics, Los Angeles,
June 23/San Francisco Examiner &
Chronicle, 6-25:(A)6.

1

[On his new job as NBC chief and his efforts to improve his company's TV ratings]: The thing about this business is that after you've done it, after you've become the leader, things get tenser. That's when it's really tense. The most fun I had at ABC was at the beginning, that first year, when everybody pitched in to make it work, and the ratings started getting better, and there was a wonderful atmosphere about it. Once you arrive at the point of leadership, you turn into a caretaker, a custodian. Then if, God forbid, the ratings should slip a tenth of a point, the guys in the sales department start screaming, and if the stock should fall a half a point, the people downstairs start screaming. I think that, in five or 10 years, the people who are at NBC now are going to look back on this period as the best time of their lives.

Interview, New York/
The Washington Post, 10-11:(B)11.

Tom Stoppard
Playwright

2

I have always been suspicious about writing for television because I miss the writer's ability to control the frame. On the stage, I have a total picture in my mind about how something is going to look. But when I write for television I'm completely at sea because I don't know whether, during the scene I'm writing, the viewer will be looking at my hero's left nostril or the four walls of the room. I write TV plays as though they were stage plays. You know the camera is just sitting there, and there are no instructions about how to use it. That's why I like to be around during the shooting to see

what is happening to my situations and dialogue in terms of the accompanying image.

Interview, London/
The New York Times, 4-23:(2)27.

Lee Strasberg
Artistic director, Actors Studio

3

Television can do everything that every other medium can do with no difference of the treatment of the material. The problem is that when actors do something for TV they think "it's only for television." We should be doing great American plays on television with our best actors, which means Paul Newman, Joanne Woodward, Al Pacino, Robert De Niro, Ellen Burstyn. They don't appear on television often, not because of the money, but because television is what it is ... Pay television can play an enormous part in breaking through this area in the future. If people paid for individual television shows, you would not need millions of people to watch. One million would be enough. The only other possibility is government subsidy in television in really large amounts, not in trickles like for the Public Broadcasting Service. And it should be handled like a dignified arts program, not like a poverty give-away.

Interview, New York/
The Christian Science Monitor, 6-23:18.

4

I think the caliber of acting on television settles for something that seems natural. I call it casual acting. Reality is always natural, but being natural isn't always reality.

Interview, Los Angeles/
The Dallas Times Herald, 6-25:(H)2.

David Susskind
Producer

5

I've grown up. I once idealized television. I thought [American] television could be much more of an illuminating beacon—informing, instructing, educating, taking the public by the hand and leading it—perhaps much more like the BBC. But American television was never that, could never be that, was not intended to

(DAVID SUSSKIND)

be that. I was a younger and more idealistic David Susskind. I am not a cynic today; I am simply pragmatic.

Interview/
The New York Times, 2-19:(2)31.

Richard Thomas
Actor

1

I found as a young actor that television offered a wonderful opportunity to work and learn at the same time. An actor has a chance on TV to make occasional appearances in many roles and become known without laying his whole career on the line—as you do sometimes if you're suddenly put into a major movie role before you've done much else. On TV, you don't feel that every time you open your mouth, your career hangs in the balance. The TV audience allows you an occasional mistake.

Interview/
U.S. News & World Report, 2-13:87.

Burr Tillstrom
Television puppeteer

2

Early TV was close to theatre. We thought of it as theatre. We modeled it after theatre. TV wasn't film then. It was live performances that were only incidentally caught by a camera. Television just isn't that way any longer. The only ones who do it that way now are the British. The British actors pause more; there are more silences. They allow you to know what the actors are thinking. Now it's so hard to have style in American television any longer. You only have style in theatre.

Interview, New York/
The New York Times, 3-3:(C)2.

Grant Tinker
Producer

3

People in our business react in an obvious way to ratings. If your shows are rating well, Nielsen is terrific. If they're not . . . you're

more likely to qualify your answers. I've spent 30 years of my life in television. And all those years I've been vitally affected by the Nielsen numbers. Quality shows go down the tubes because Nielsen says nobody is watching. I hate to think I've been living a lie all those years.

TV Guide, 6-24:6.

4

I don't want to sound self-righteous, but most of television right now is pretty unimportant. I liken television today to a radio. It's something humming in the corner. You don't really listen to it. It's sort of like Muzak. But I do think the public will soon tire of the nothingness that is the present programming . . . They'll only put up with it for so long.

Interview/
The Dallas Times Herald, 6-27:(D)5.

Abbott Washburn
Commissioner, Federal
Communications Commission

5

Today's outstanding children's television programs have distinctive characteristics. For example, they tend to have characters who care about others. Another characteristic, the children contribute their own creative talents and skills. Some of the best shows go out into the community. The better shows inform as well as entertain.

At symposium sponsored by National
Association of Broadcasters, Washington,
June 6/The Dallas Times Herald, 6-7:(A)16.

Theodore H. White
Author, Political historian

6

TV can be absolutely outrageous. It has done more to foul the minds of our children than the worst smoke in the air we breathe. On the other hand, it's done more to bring civil rights to black people. At its worst, it's the most despicable medium of communication developed by man; at its best, it's the noblest we've ever created, except, of course, for books.

Interview, New York/
"W": a Fairchild publication, 9-15:41.

Personal Profiles

Woody Allen
Actor, Director, Writer

1

The schlemiel image never did describe me. I've never been that. It's an appellation for the unimaginative to hang on me. The things I did on nightclub stages were fantasies or exaggerations from my own life—school, women, parents—which I set out in an amusing way. But you look up after a year and the press has created you: "Well, he's a small man at odds with mechanical objects who can't cope with his relationships with women." But all I was doing was what was funny; there's no conscious design to anything.

Interview/Newsweek, 4-24:63.

Fred Astaire
Actor, Dancer

2

If I had my choice of anything, I would have loved to have been good enough to be a professional golfer. I wasn't crazy about being a professional dancer except when it happened to me—and then I *had* to be crazy about it.

Interview, Beverly Hills, Calif./
Los Angeles Times, 3-24:(Fashion-78)10.

Alan Bates
Actor

3

Money and stardom don't motivate me. Mansions, yachts and big cars would weigh me down. I want freedom, not the imprisonment of fame.

San Francisco Examiner & Chronicle,
9-3:(Datebook)16.

Warren Beatty
Actor

4

My idea of freedom and independence is to live on top of a hill with clean air—no smog— and some good food vaguely in the area. The window is ajar, and there's a breeze that smells of geraniums or honeysuckle. And there's a room with a typewriter, where you go in for a few hours a day and tell your version of things. And you get a call from someone in a distant, dirty city who tells you that you can have more money and more time to write because people are so eager to read what you have to say. That's the fantasy of quitting. The other day I was thinking about quitting, and it was really attractive to me—for 15 or 20 minutes. But then you go out to a movie theatre and get this thrill when something good goes on the screen. And you want to raise your hand and say, "Wait a minute! Wait a minute! I want to make one of those!"

Interview/Time, 7-3:74.

Griffin B. Bell
Attorney General of the United States

5

[On the time he's spent as Attorney General] : I've used up 16 months of my life. I'm paying a price for the time I'm giving. I ask myself, "Am I helping the country?" If not, it's a bad bargain.

Interview/People, 5-22:49.

Yul Brynner
Actor

6

I've never cared to go into details about my background simply because I never thought it was anyone's business but my own. A writer once said to me, "I've got to have the facts about your existence." I said, "Why? The facts of my existence have nothing to do with the realities of my life."

Interview, New York/
Los Angeles Times, 7-9:(Calendar)54.

Carol Burnett
Entertainer

1

I know what I want out of my life. When I'm 80 years old, I want my kids to be calling me, saying: "Why don't you ever call any more?" That's what I want—to be a lively old lady. When I'm 80, I want them to be worrying about the old lady having too much fun.

Interview, Chicago/
The Dallas Times Herald, 10-3:(B)7.

Truman Capote
Author

2

I had to be successful and I had to be successful early. The thing about people like me is that we always knew what we were going to do. Many people spend half their lives not knowing. But I was a very special person and I had to have a very special life. I was not meant to work in an office or something, though I would have been successful at whatever I did. But I always knew that I wanted to be a writer and that I wanted to be rich and famous.

Los Angeles Herald Examiner, 7-9:(F)1.

James Coburn
Actor

3

I travel in a rarified atmosphere. I don't have a chance to touch down. When I get to New York—bang!—out of the plane and into the limo. Whoosh—I'm whisked to the 47th floor and—pshoo—when I come out I put on the shades and run down the street. I try to keep my life peaceful. So I generally travel alone and walk fast.

Interview/People, 5-29:76.

4

To tell the truth, work is my only reality. The rest of my life is total fantasy. The only time I really find sanity is on a movie, when my complete attention is directed to getting the work done. Once it's finished, I feel lost in this mad, crazy world.

Interview, Los Angeles/
The Dallas Times Herald, 10-1:(H)2.

Richard Crenna
Actor

5

... somewhere over the years, as I watched my fellow actors crowding each other and trying desperately to reach the top of the ladder, I stopped measuring success and failure on a vertical scale. The vertical measure is treacherous. Once you arrive at the top, there's nowhere to go but down. I call it a maturing process because I've begun to look at my life as a horizontal plane. All the experiences are projections, like the spokes of a wagon wheel. When a good acting part comes along and I'm lucky enough to get it, it becomes another spoke on the wheel. In the long run, it gives me a place to go and grow.

Interview, Los Angeles/
Los Angeles Times, 7-9:(Home)27.

James H. Doolittle
Aviator

6

I grew up in Nome, Alaska, and I was the smallest kid in school. Each youngster that came to town had to whip me before he could whip a bigger kid. I learned early how to take care of myself and learned the importance of keeping yourself in shape. So there's an advantage in being small. It's an incentive to tiny excellence.

Interview, Los Angeles/
Los Angeles Times, 4-16:(2)1.

Jane Fonda
Actress

7

I learned from the Vietnamese people that you have to assume that the changes you desire are not going to happen in your lifetime. For me, that has been the hardest thing to change in myself, because I have always felt, "I want it now."

San Francisco Examiner & Chronicle,
10-15:(This World)2.

Lynn Fontanne
Actress

8

[On her marriage to the late actor Alfred Lunt]: We usually played two people who were

WHAT THEY SAID IN 1978

very much in love. As we were sort of realistic actors, we became those two people. I had an affair with him, so to speak, and he with me.

Time, 5-8:65.

Carlo Maria Giulini
Musical director-designate, Los Angeles Philharmonic Orchestra

1

I always think I am a very small man. When I shave myself, I look in the mirror and see behind me Beethoven and Brahms.

Time, 4-3:63.

Cary Grant
Actor

2

My formula for living is quite simple. I get up in the morning and I go to bed at night. In-between times, I occupy myself as best I can.

Interview, Los Angeles/
Los Angeles Times, 6-11:(Calendar)39.

Patricia Roberts Harris
Secretary of Housing and Urban Development of the United States

3

I know I'm not arrogant, and that's something only I could know. Now, I am not shy about stating my convictions. But I'm also very quick to change my mind when it is proved I am wrong. When there is a difference in judgment between me and somebody else and there are no facts that change my judgment, then I will always rely on my own because I have found over the years that my judgment in that kind of situation is rarely wrong. Now, people who differ with me may consider that arrogance, but to me that's the quality of leadership.

The Dallas Times Herald, 2-12:(I)1.

John Huston
Motion-picture director

4

People keep asking me why I go on making films. It seems to me a silly question. Does a painter ever give up painting? Anyway, I need the money. I'm not rich. I've spent as I've gone along. Maybe that's the secret of my longevity in this business. I *have* to work. But I tell you, I've enjoyed every minute of it. I've had a hell of a good time. Better than a lot of other fat cats I know.

Interview, Puerto Vallarta, Mexico/
Los Angeles Times, 4-9:(Calendar)37.

Glenda Jackson
Actress

5

[As an actress,] I'm not worth anything myself. There are certain people—call them "stars" or "entertainers"—who just come on as themselves and are worth paying money to see. I always have to have a character to play, or some other person to hide behind. That's not to say I don't consider that I have something worthwhile in the work I do, but me as me is not particularly interesting.

Interview, Los Angeles/
The Dallas Times Herald, 6-30:(E)3.

Reggie Jackson
Baseball player, New York "Yankees"

6

It's uncomfortable being me. It's uncomfortable being recognized constantly. It's uncomfortable being considered something I'm not, an idol or a monster, something hated or loved.

Interview, Chicago, July 23/
The New York Times, 7-24:(C)6.

Elia Kazan
Motion-picture and stage director; Author

7

I believe in beauty a great deal. I think I'm an aesthetic. I enjoy nature and handsome people, acts of faith, gratitude, grace, generosity and all those human qualities. I like that in people.

Interview/
Los Angeles Herald Examiner, 8-4:(A)8.

Deborah Kerr
Actress

8

Basically, I'm a person who desires tranquility, because I don't function well in an atmo-

(DEBORAH KERR)

sphere of unrest. It makes me very nervous. I don't really work at it [tranquility]. But I like to exude it or make other people feel at ease, because I think that way we all get on much easier than if everybody has got little prickly thorns out all over them in defense against the unknown. They really don't know why they're being prickly. It's a defense form, you know. And I think if one can just step over that and say, "Don't wear a crown of thorns with me," if you extend a hand, people will look at it in amazement and take it.

Interview, Washington/
The Christian Science Monitor, 9-28:(B)14.

Eartha Kitt
Entertainer

1

I don't think there is anything I have done that I wish I hadn't done. Because I learn from everything I do. I'm in school every day. My diploma will be my tombstone.

Interview, Washington/
The Washington Post, 1-19:(B)13.

Jack Klugman
Actor

2

I don't have a love life. If the most desirable woman in the world were to desire me, I wouldn't have the energy. I'm a loner. I like a good meal, a good script and a good BM [bookmaker].

Interview/People, 3-13:88.

Sophia Loren
Actress

3

I'm a very authentic person. I always say what I feel. I like if people tell me I'm wrong. If people tell me I'm wrong I never get offended. Maybe because I never consider myself a star. To be capricious, a little dictator—I hate that, absolutely. I am one of the easiest people in the world to get along with.

Interview, Washington, June 19/
The Washington Post, 6-20:(B)7.

Lee Marvin
Actor

4

I used to work all the time. That was because I was unhappy. Now I'm not. Now I can sit around and watch the sunsets and read my books and enjoy my life. And you know one of the good things about getting older? You discover you're probably more interesting than most of the people you meet.

Interview, Los Angeles/
Los Angeles Times, 12-17:(Calendar)85.

Marcello Mastroianni
Actor

5

At the end of the war, when Mussolini fell, I was recruited by the Germans to draw military maps. I escaped and hid in Venice for more than a year. Often I think about those days, about the people who helped hide me. But I do not go back to see them. You know why? Because I do not want to see what happened to those friends, for I know they will mirror what has happened to me with the years. I, Marcello, need to keep my illusions.

Interview, Rome/
Los Angeles Times, 3-12:(Calendar)41.

6

When I was 11, I worked as an extra in a film ... They paid me one cent for one night ... Things like that gave me a small measure of practical wisdom, a capacity for judgment. They enriched me with a kind of elementary philosophy common to Mediterranean people. I learned not to be a snob. I detest vulgarity and brutality. I love civilized behavior. This bundle of dreams, rejections and small adventures that I accumulated in my childhood lives on in me and is part of my culture, which is only my experience of living.

Interview/San Francisco Examiner & Chronicle,
7-30:(Datebook)30.

Walter Matthau
Actor

7

I guess the reason I'm successful is because I'm interesting. I'm a good actor and I'm inter-

WHAT THEY SAID IN 1978

esting. And I think people constantly want to know what I'm going to do. Or what I'm going to say. And I'm unpredictable, too, because I myself don't know what I'm going to do next. There's a bit of insanity running through my life.

Interview, New York/San Francisco Examiner &
Chronicle, 4-9:(Datebook)17.

Robert Mitchum
Actor

1

Sometimes it seems I spend half my life trying to get a good night's sleep. Once I didn't get a proper night's rest for a year. Fifteen minutes in three days, once. That was when I was working at Lockheed in the '40s. I went to see the doctor. He said the reason I wasn't sleeping was because I knew when I woke up I'd have to go to work. And I hated it. "Blow your job or blow your mind," he said. So I blew my job.

Interview, Vienna/
The Dallas Times Herald, 10-17:(B)5.

Malcolm Muggeridge
British author; Former editor,
"Punch" magazine

2

The English have this extraordinary respect for longevity. The best example of this was Queen Victoria, a most unpleasant woman who achieved a sort of public affection simply by living to be an enormous age. I can't say I've cashed in on this as yet, but perhaps if I live a few more years . . .

San Francisco Examiner & Chronicle,
7-30:(This World)2.

Joe Namath
Actor; Former football player

3

The longest I've been able to live with a woman is five days. My nervous system is not geared to having somebody around all the time. There is a freedom within me—or perhaps it is a lack of responsibility—that controls me.

San Francisco Examiner & Chronicle,
6-4:(This World)2.

Alfredo Nobre da Costa
Prime Minister of Portugal

4

I consider myself completely inadequate [to be Prime Minister]. Every morning I first have to make an effort not to laugh at myself. Then I have to make an effort not to cry. Then I have to do the job.

Interview, Lisbon/
Los Angeles Times, 8-30:(1)5.

Peter O'Toole
Actor

5

[On whether he enjoys fame]: I never have. And I've never searched for it, and never been spurred by it. If anything, the contrary is the case. It's driven me into a deeper and deeper privacy. I'm a private man . . . [Fame] goes hand in hand with being able to do what I can do. There isn't one without the other. [But] I've wanted fame to be reserved for a performance, not for how I look or may not look within a [hotel] lobby.

Interview, Washington/
The Christian Science Monitor, 12-21:(B)19.

Dolly Parton
Singer

6

I'm a person that cares a great deal about other people. I care a great deal about my work. And I appreciate the talent I was born with . . . but I'm childlike in a lot of ways, to the point where I have good times. I take life serious, when it needs to be taken serious, but I can be as playful and mischievous as anyone else. And I like to pride myself on being reasonably smart when it comes to business—especially when it comes to business for me. . . . and that's what works for me. It might not work for someone else. But I *know* who I am. I know what I want, and I know how to go about getting it.

Interview, Columbia, Md./
The Christian Science Monitor, 9-7:(B)38.

Jon Peters
Motion-picture producer

7

. . . I was, for a long time, a very successful hairdresser. I walked into the beauty shop and

(JON PETERS)

people had respect for me. I'd do your hair and you would like me for it—I could give you something. Then, when I left that business and went into this one [films], all I read was that I was a pimp and a conniver and a nobody latching on to a star's wings. I would meet people, and they would look at me funny because they'd read all those things about me. It was a very painful time.

Interview, New York/
The New York Times, 1-29:(2)17.

William Proxmire
United States Senator, D-Wisconsin

1

... I'm much too competitive. Competition can be good, but it also can be overdone. I have to resist it. When I'm driving a car, and someone drives by, I have to fight hard not to try to catch up. When I'm running to work and some runner who is a little faster goes by, I do my best, no matter how hard it is, to try to stay up with him or pass him. Walking, even walking! Isn't that terrible?

Interview, Washington/
The Christian Science Monitor, 11-2:(B)3.

Lynn Redgrave
Actress

2

The real joy of acting to me has always meant attempting to play people quite unlike myself. Characters like myself don't really interest me a lot. I think I first wanted to act to escape from myself.

Interview/The New York Times, 6-18:(2)11.

Nelson A. Rockefeller
Former Vice President of the United States

3

I'm very grateful for the opportunities I've had in life, and I've had an exciting life, a wonderful, thrilling life with a whole range of interesting experiences, and am continuing to do so. Most people think that what I say sometimes is too simple and therefore it can't be true and there must be another motive or another reason. But I really am rather simple,

and I can get interested in anything that's creative.

Interview, New York/
The New York Times, 3-9:(B)6.

Samuel Rubin
Philanthropist; Founder, Faberge, Inc.
(perfumes)

4

I never gave my business more than half my time. So I went to concerts and museums while my competitors sat behind their desks. We [at Faberge] never sought the maximum capacity for volume. I live unlike [other] wealthy men. I have no car or chauffeur; I rent from Avis or Hertz. I have no yacht, no private plane. I don't go out to eat much; I don't trust restaurant kitchens. I enjoy conversations at home. I like worn shoes. I walk instead of taking expensive taxis.

Interview, Washington, Sept. 21/
The Washington Post, 9-23:(B)4.

Leon Spinks
Heavyweight boxing champion of the world

5

People can't take me being myself. I'm just a real, down-to-earth person and people can't accept that. They always hear the bad parts but they never see the good points about me. I'm just like them, trying to make a living and trying to be a man to make it in this world today. I'm living my life the best way I can. The ball rolls and the punches blow and that's the way life's going to be.

Interview/Los Angeles Times, 9-10:(3)14.

Sylvester Stallone
Actor

6

I try to remain happy Monday through Friday and then I go into an inconsolable depression on weekends. That way I get a nice balance.

Interview/People, 5-8:95.

Ringo Starr
Musician; Former member of the Beatles

7

People see me as a hell of a nice guy in a wicky-wacky, wonderful way. I was the clown,

WHAT THEY SAID IN 1978

(RINGO STARR)

the one with the funny name and played the drums. The image was created by other people. I was just doing what I was doing. People, especially the media, would say what I was. That image still carries on ... They still call me "boy." You see, I've never been a man. They always say, "He's one of the boys." We [the Beatles] were always "the boys." I'm nearly 38 and I'm still one of the boys. Which is good in one way and weird in another. I'm dying for the day they'll say, "Here's the man."

Interview, Beverly Hills, Calif./
The Dallas Times Herald, 4-26:(F)2.

Barbara Walters
News commentator, American
Broadcasting Company

1

My life is very special. I never have to worry about going to a party alone. I never have to worry about meeting a man. There's always someone new to meet because that's the world I live in and my reputation precedes me. For a long time, whenever I thought of marriage, I thought of doors closing, windows shutting. But I'm just beginning to think there could be a window opening. I'm not there yet, but at least I can see it. I can imagine how wonderful it would be.

Interview/The Dallas Times Herald, 5-21:(E)6.

John Wayne
Actor

2

What do I want to be remembered for? You mean besides pictures ...? I'd like to be remembered as a guy who learned how to get along with the average person, to be a little tolerant, understanding and forgiving ... I'll tell you what I'd like on my tombstone: my name, the years of my birth and death, then three short, simple Spanish words: *Feo, Fuerte y Formal.* They mean "ugly, strong and with human dignity."

Interview, Newport Beach, Calif./Parade, 10-22:5.

Ezer Weizman
Minister of Defense of Israel

3

I have always said exactly what I believed. Fortunately and unfortunately. Some people

say I could have gone further and earlier if I hadn't said what I thought ... I can understand the image of me which has developed over the years. I resent it, but I understand it. I do fly off the handle. And I do like to play. It's just that I'm not a boy any longer. Certain things I've done could have given the impression of being a playboy. It didn't just develop in the last two years. I've had a knack to drive a little faster than most people, to drink somewhat more than my next-door neighbor, to fly a bit lower than other pilots. But people have a tendency to judge me on my outward acts of behavior instead of their looking into my other achievements, like building the air force with the kind of spirit and morale it has. But I'm not sorry I did any of these things.

Interview/The Washington Post, 10-15:(M)2.

Raquel Welch
Actress

4

People are always surprised that I can talk and walk. They're always telling me, "Gee, I'm so surprised. I didn't know you could dance," they say. "I didn't know you could sing. And you write, and you have a very active sense of humor. Oh yes, and you're quite intelligent, too. You can read!" I always like to hear compliments. But I'm used to hearing them from a more patronizing level, maybe, than most people. I really have no illusions. Whatever kind of transition I'm able to make as an actress, I'll never be anything more than a sex symbol who somehow gained legitimacy.

Interview, London/
San Francisco Examiner & Chronicle,
9-10:(Datebook)24.

Orson Welles
Actor, Director

5

I began as a painter. I had no desire to be in the theatre ... I daydreamed theatrical figures. I regretted all my life not continuing. To this day I still think of myself as a failed artist.

Discussion sponsored by American Film Institute,
Los Angeles, Nov. 19/
Los Angeles Times, 11-24:(4)32.

Mortimer J. Adler
Author; Former professor of
philosophy, University of Chicago

1

. . . a good life does not consist of just having a good time. There are two kinds of desires, and two kinds of "goods" corresponding to them. On the one hand, we have acquired individual desires that each of us develops during the course of his lifetime. I may desire a speed-boat or an expensive sports car. Let us call these desires "wants." The things we want appear to be "good" to us because we want them. Whether they are really good for us is another question. In contrast to our acquired wants, we have certain natural *needs*. We need food, clothing, shelter, sleep, knowledge, love, honor, respect. These natural desires or needs are common to all human beings. They are built into our human nature. What Aristotle [says] is that the pursuit of happiness consists of trying to get all things that are really good for you, the things your nature *needs* in the course of a complete lifetime. The things you *want* may also be good but only if they don't interfere with what is really good for you. Take the classical case of the miser who says, "All I want is gold . . ." He calls himself happy because he has everything he wants. But Aristotle would say he's the most miserable of men because he has ended up having none of the real goods that he needs.

Interview,
New York/Book Digest, May:30.

Fred Astaire
Actor, Dancer

2

I've never been one to think about what I'm going to do next in life. What's the use of planning? You can't plan too far ahead because you don't know if it's going to be washed out by the rain. I don't say that with gloom. I think it's funny.

Interview, Beverly Hills, Calif./
Los Angeles Times, 3-24:(Fashion-78)10.

Lauren Bacall
Actress

3

What is very important in life is to do things that are really important to your own being. You must not spend life doing things other people expect you to do. Everyone has his own route. I've got one time around and I am not planning to waste it. Not to dismiss one's family, children, husbands or lovers, I really believe in work. One's life should be concentrated on work, and everything else should be fringe. Work is the most rewarding and lasting thing.

Interview, Paris/
"W": a Fairchild publication, 6-9:14.

Lucille Ball
Actress, Comedienne

4

Luck to me is . . . hard work—and realizing what is opportunity and what isn't. I think knowing what you can *not* do is more important than knowing what you *can* do.

The Dallas Times Herald, 12-31:(J)5.

Candice Bergen
Actress

5

I think maybe the longest marriage you can think of today is like a 10-year marriage, as a general thing. And I think that's really sad. But maybe with the way our lives are bombarded today, the way things are telescoping—maybe that's the best you can hope for. I mean, it's *such* a weird time to think about marriage. I mean, since we have been born there has been atomic weaponry, people landing on the moon,

WHAT THEY SAID IN 1978

sending out cassettes with "Johnny B. Goode" playing on them, global climates changing, transexual operations. I mean, if men aren't necessarily men and women, women . . . I mean, there is *nothing* reliable any more. But listen. Don't make this so people jump off their roofs and kill themselves. I mean, make it so there's a new set of realities. The old realities are not. The old realities are no more.

Interview, Washington/
The Washington Post, 3-15:(B)3.

Robert Blake
Actor

1

You can get a job, get an education, have good times, join the Pepsi generation, and never have to have a family. But what happens is you end up with a life that has no third act. The hardest job in the world is being a parent or a husband or a wife. But if you walk away from it, there's nothing left.

Interview, El Paso, Texas/
Los Angeles Times, 10-8:(Calendar)34.

Marlon Brando
Actor

2

There is no point at which one becomes old or loses one's youth, which is a very ethereal thing. No one can stay young, so isn't it healthier to try and develop a society in which aging is gently accepted and even revered, rather than perpetuate a society in which every wrinkle is a kiss of death? Why not give *everybody* something to look forward to, instead of filling them with fear and shame when they pass 30? This is an ugly masochistic facet of our society, but the media has been unwilling to give the masses a chance to discover that there's another way of thinking and feeling about growing older.

Interview, Los Angeles/
San Fransisco Examiner &
Chronicle, 12-10:(Datebook) 18.

Leonid I. Brezhnev
President of the Soviet Union; General
Secretary, Soviet Communist Party

3

Marxist-Leninist ideology now holds the vanguard positions in world public thought. Passions are raging around it, and different social movements are attracted to it. This is largely a result of the joint creative activity of our parties, a result of the influence of the vast practice of constructing a new world. Great prestige has been earned by socialist culture, which is profoundly humanistic in spirit and is inseparately connected with the best national traditions and is, at the same time, an innovatory, internationalist culture that reflects the creative genius of many nations and peoples.

Before Czechoslovak Communist Party representatives,
Prague, May 31/Vital Speeches, 6-15:518.

Yul Brynner
Actor

4

Like the gypsies, I live for today. It's the only thing that makes sense. If you think only the now exists, how closely you listen to everything, how carefully you choose your words, how much you treasure the moment . . .

Interview, New York/
Los Angeles Times, 7-9:(Calendar)54.

George Burns
Entertainer

5

Retire? That's ridiculous. What does it for you is to have something to get up for in the morning. Now, they say, you should retire at 70. When I was 70, I still had pimples.

Interview, New York/
The New York Times, 7-25:(C)1.

Ellen Burstyn
Actress

6

Sharing, as in marriage, is not a bad idea, if it's in harmony. But being unmarried isn't being bereft. To live as a single unit is one of the most

(ELLEN BURSTYN)

satisfying lessons you can learn in life. You confront your destiny without *leaning.*

Interview/Los Angeles Times, 12-27:(4)9.

Hugh L. Carey
Governor of New York (D)

1

A mentor long departed told me that the greatest gift in political life, in any life, is to view yourself objectively—at arm's length—to make an assessment of yourself. So whom do I rely on? I rely on myself.

The New York Times Magazine, 6-11:27.

Jimmy Carter
President of the United States

2

The experience of democracy is like the experience of life itself—always changing, infinite in its variety, sometimes turbulent, and all the more valuable for having been tested by adversity.

Before Indian Parliament, New Delhi, Jan. 2/
The Washington Post, 1-3:(A)1.

3

Our democratic order has come under challenge. There are those who question whether democratic values are appropriate for contemporary circumstances ... But we defend these values because they are right, and because there is no higher purpose for the state than to preserve these rights for its citizens.

Before French-American organizations, Paris,
Jan. 4/The Dallas Times Herald, 1-5:(A)12.

4

For most of human history, people have wished vainly that freedom—and the flowering of the human spirit which freedom nourishes—did not finally have to depend upon the force of arms. We, like our forebearers, live in a time when those who would destroy liberty are restrained less by their respect for freedom itself than by their knowledge that those who cherish freedom are strong.

At Wake Forest University, March 17/
The Washington Post, 3-18:(A)11.

5

As a young man and as President, I have learned some things about leadership. One is that the fear of failure is one of the greatest obstacles to progress. How timid we are when we challenge some obstacle or engage in some contest or set a high goal for ourselves. How timid we are that we might fail in the effort and perhaps be the subject of ridicule or criticism or scorn. It is always a mistake to try for universal approbation, universal approval, because if you fear making anyone mad, then you ultimately probe for the lowest common denominator of human achievement.

Before Future Farmers of America, Kansas City,
Nov. 9/The Washington Post, 11-10:(A)4.

Alex Comfort
Gerontologist

6

A lot of working men say, "When I'm retired I'm going to be able to do all the things I always wanted to do and finally be happy." Of course [he's wrong. He] goes fishing for two weeks and realizes he never wants to see another fish in his life. Then he finds that his friends are still working, that he's lost touch and that the boredom is making him lose his marbles.

San Francisco Examiner & Chronicle,
10-8:(This World)2.

Olivia de Havilland
Actress

7

People with ungovernable tempers should never marry; people who can't accept reality should never marry; people who don't enjoy responsibility should never marry. In fact, an awful lot of people should never marry.

Los Angeles Times, 11-2:(4)16.

John D. Dingell
United States Representative, D-Michigan

8

I hope for the best, anticipate the worst and take what comes along.

The Washington Post, 8-4:(A)4.

WHAT THEY SAID IN 1978

Will Durant
Author, Historian

1

Death is the greatest invention that life ever made. It allows new life to have room to operate.

Interview/Parade, 8-6:12.

Bob Dylan
Singer, Songwriter

2

Each man struggles within himself. That is where the fight is—one part of a man against the other part. That is the real struggle. No man can fight another like the man who fights himself. Who could be a stronger enemy? Who can do you more harm than yourself? It is true that a man is his own worst enemy, just as he is his own best friend. You can either do yourself in, or do yourself a favor. If you can deal with the enemy within, then no enemy without can stand a chance.

Interview, Los Angeles/
The Dallas Times Herald, 3-21:(B)5.

Mircea Eliade
Professor, University of Chicago
Divinity School

3

As long as there is the rhythm of day and night, winter and summer, man will continue to dream, to believe in being saved. The idea of being renewed is part of the cycle—you feel it every spring. I do not think that man will disappear, not even in an atomic holocaust. I always believe in the creativity of the human spirit.

Interview/People, 3-27:49.

Joan Fontaine
Actress

4

The main problem in marriage is that, for a man, sex is a hunger—like eating. If a man is hungry and can't get to a fancy French restaurant, he'll go to a hot-dog stand. For a woman, what's important is love and romance.

Interview/People, 11-20:55.

Abe Fortas
Lawyer; Former Associate Justice,
Supreme Court of the United States

5

The concept of individual freedom has exploded in the last 10 to 20 years, and individual freedom means a lot more than technical civil rights and the Bill of Rights. Now I think it means access to and entitlement to a basically decent standard of living; an environment that is agreeable, pleasant and enriching to individuals; and medical care and a lot of other things that were unimaginable, say, 30 years ago.

The New York Times, 12-3:(1)83.

John Frankenheimer
Motion-picture director

6

I believe that there's nothing a person can't do. It's the indomitability of the human spirit. I believe in heroes, but not in the classic sense. It's the person who hangs in there and really goes on in spite of all kinds of odds that really interests me.

Interview/Daily Variety, 4-20:17.

William Friedkin
Motion-picture director

7

People can be secure even in conflict. Some people's security comes from being in constant turmoil, either with themselves or with another person. We know of these legendary love/hate relationships that keep couples together fighting for 40 years. Why? For a lot of reasons. But one reason—the phrase really belongs to prisoners of war—when a prisoner of war is asked, "How did you learn to stand the torture?" the common answer is, "You learn to love the rope." And in a conflict between human beings, or in a self-conflict, or in trying to make a movie, you learn to love the rope.

Interview/
Los Angeles Herald Examiner, 12-23:(B)10.

Milton Friedman
*Senior research fellow, Hoover
Institution, Stanford University;
Former professor of economics,
University of Chicago*

1

A society which aims for equality before liberty will end up with neither equality nor liberty. But the society which aims first for liberty will end up not with equality but with a closer approach to equality than any other kind of system that's ever been developed.

*Lecture, Stanford University/
The Wall Street Journal, 6-7:20.*

Princess Grace
Princess of Monaco

2

Having a daughter is like riding a young horse over an unknown steeplechase course. You don't know when to pull up the reins, when to let the horse have its head . . . or what.

*San Francisco Examiner & Chronicle,
7-2:(This World)2.*

Frank E. Hedrick
President, Beech Aircraft Corporation

3

As I planned my life, I was very cautious not to set goals. When I talk to young people, I encourage them to do whatever they're doing better than anybody else did that particular job. That's the surest formula for success I know of.

*Interview, Wichita, Kan./
Los Angeles Herald Examiner, 7-21:(A)12.*

Eric Hoffer
Philosopher

4

The average intellectual contrasts authority and freedom. I say that freedom is *impossible* without authority. The absence of authority is anarchy—and anarchy is a thousand-headed tyrant.

Interview, San Francisco/People, 1-16:30.

5

The vigor of society right now is dependent upon the willingness of people to make an effort and to be honest in their work. The great secret of our time is this terrific negligence, you know. It just takes your breath away. Labor-faking has become a world phenomenon, you see, and we can no longer derive comfort from the fact that people refuse to work in Communist countries because, right now, people refuse to work in non-Communist countries, and the fateful fact of our time—I never tire of repeating it—is not the advancement of backward countries, but leveling down of advanced countries.

*Television interview, San Francisco/
"Eric Hoffer: The Crowded Life,"
Public Broadcasting Service, 2-5.*

Eugene Ionesco
Playwright

6

The new can only be created from traces of the past. The most minor mosaic is of much more interest to me than the currently fashionable revolt.

*Interview/San Francisco Examiner & Chronicle,
3-12:(Datebook)21.*

John Paul I
Pope

7

The danger for modern man is that he would reduce the earth to a desert, the person to an automaton, brotherly love to planned collectivization, often introducing death where God wishes life.

*San Francisco Examiner & Chronicle,
9-3:(This World)2.*

John Paul II
Pope

8

While respecting those who disagree, it is very difficult—even objectively and impartially—to countenance those who violate the sanctity of marriage or destroy life conceived in the womb. It is impossible to say that the principle of divorce or the principle of abortion help mankind and make life more humane, more filled with dignity, that they help make society better. The family carries with it the most fundamental values of mankind. Too often, those

431

WHAT THEY SAID IN 1978

values are crushed by socio-economic tendencies that prevail over Christian feeling and humanity. It is not enough to express doubt. These values must be sustained with tenacity and firmness, because to violate them is of incalculable damage to man and society. It [is] easy to destroy values, far more difficult to reconstruct them.

At Mass, Rome, Dec. 31/
The Dallas Times Herald, 1-1('79):(A)4.

Yousuf Karsh
Photographer

1

[On recognizing greatness in his many famous subjects]: Intuitively you sense that you are in its presence, but I cannot tell you how. At times, you can tell by someone's conversation and compassion. But not all great people are articulate or verbal enough to express it. Nevertheless, you feel that it's there. But I have found that great people do have some things in common. One is an immense belief in themselves and in their mission. They also have great determination as well as an ability to work hard. At the crucial moment of decision, they draw on their accumulated wisdom. But above all, they have integrity. I've also seen that great men are often lonely. This is understandable, because they have built such high standards for themselves that they often feel alone. But that same loneliness is part of their ability to create. Character, like a photograph, develops in darkness.

Interview, Ottawa, Canada/Parade, 12-3:6.

Deborah Kerr
Actress

2

[On what makes a successful marriage]: At the top of the list, I think, is a sense of humor. Not feeling competitive, acknowledging the other's attributes or whatever it is they do, but not trying to compete with them. And, of course, having a certain outlook on life that is the same, that you want, desire out of life, the same sort of things even if they're expressed in

a different way. I think a lot of marriages run into trouble where there's been no meeting of the minds. There's been a meeting of the bods, but not a meeting of the minds. And by that I don't mean you have to be an intellectual genius. But there is something; there's a great deal of understanding.

Interview, Washington/
The Christian Science Monitor, 9-28:(B)16.

Richard Leakey
Anthropologist

3

I don't think that we can destroy the earth. I think it would also be very difficult to destroy all forms of life. It would be a relatively easy matter, with the technology we now have, to destroy most forms of life which humans today identify as forms of life. I think the life at the bottom of the deep sea, some of the microorganisms in the soil, things of this type, would be extremely hard to destroy. I do not think we can destroy life or the world as a physical phenomenon, but we can surely destroy human life which, after all, is what we think of as the world.

Interview/Los Angeles Herald Examiner, 3-12:(A)12.

Claude Lelouch
Motion-picture director

4

Women today are just as feminine as they ever were. But they exhibit less of their femininity because it annoys them to show that side of their nature to men who seem more feminine than they are. The problem today is that while there are more and more "real women," there are fewer and fewer "real men."

Interview, New York/
Los Angeles Herald Examiner, 3-19:(E)8.

Claude Levi-Strauss
Anthropologist; Professor, College
de France

5

Western civilization may be said to be a superior society, but that statement does not extend universally. In some primitive societies—which I would prefer to call societies without

(CLAUDE LEVI-STRAUSS)

writing—man is not necessarily considered the ruler and master of life. There is a balance struck between man and his natural environment, a balance we have all but lost in the 20th century. We are just starting to get back what the primitives knew all along . . . The greatest threat to mankind is the family of man itself.

Interview, Baltimore/
The Washington Post, 2-24:(D)3.

Bernard-Henri Levy
Philosopher

1

My philosophy has always been a philosophy of resistance and revolt, in 1968 as now. What I discovered, however, was that Marxism, which I had long thought of as being a philosophy of revolt, was actually just the opposite. Marxism does not say to people, "you are always right to revolt or resist"—but on the contrary, to submit and obey. To fight against Communism means to fight against the most sophisticated form of order in the world today.

Interview, New York/The New York Times, 5-13:24.

Sophia Loren
Actress

2

I have never counted on my beauty. Never. I have never believed in it. There are so many beautiful people in this world, you can only rely on talent and feelings. How can you rely on beauty? Beauty is something that comes and goes. You have to really get down and scratch yourself for talent.

Interview, Washington, June 19/
The Washington Post, 6-20:(B)7.

Marcel Marceau
Mime

3

We [humans] are exactly like flowers. They decay and new flowers come out. They are different flowers, but they are flowers. Men and women die and other men and women come, and we are immortal because humanity will survive, even if the specific personality of some-

body is gone. What is incredible is that there has always been just one Mozart, one Beethoven, one Bach. It is fantastic that through one individual creator all men recognize their own life. This is why Mozart or da Vinci, all the great artists, the scientists—Einstein—they all live in us, and this is why for me they still live.

Interview/Atlas World Press Review, August:27.

Carlyle Marney
Theologian

4

A culture that offers unlimited access to possessions as the hallmark of freedom doesn't really care very much for the person. Our Anglo-Saxon ancestors must have been starved to have bred successfully in us such an incredible desire for more than we can eat, more than we can spend, more than we can wear.

Dallas/The Dallas Times Herald, 2-11:(C)4.

Marcello Mastroianni
Actor

5

Woman is the sun, an extraordinary creature, one that makes the imagination gallop. Woman is also the element of conflict. With whom do you argue? With a woman, of course. Not with a friend, because he accepted all your defects the moment he found you. Besides, woman is mother—have we forgotten?

Interview/Atlas World Press Review, August:50.

David McCullough
Author; Winner, National Book Award
for history

6

The arguments over the relevance of history are absurd and a waste of time. Of course history matters. Civilization is nothing without continuity. A nation that forgets its past can function no better than an individual with amnesia. The lessons of history are multitudinous, which in itself is a lesson. History, like humor, teaches tolerance. History, like travel, enlarges our experience. Times change; the world moves on. That, too, is among the largest of history's truths, and we ignore it at our peril.

Accepting the NBA National Book Award, New York,
April/Los Angeles Times, 4-23:(Book Review)3.

WHAT THEY SAID IN 1978

Rod McKuen
Poet, Songwriter

1

I've always said that it doesn't matter who you love or how you love, but *that* you love. If you're not in love or loving somebody, you're only half alive. I think it's my most important message.

The Dallas Times Herald, 5-4:(E)5.

Marshall McLuhan
Professor of English and director,
Center for Culture and Technology,
University of Toronto

2

In the year 1900, Max Planck produced this new quantum physics in which he pulled out all the connections, said there's no connection in matter. The same year, Picasso pulled out all the connections in space between art forms. The same year, Freud—that's 1900—Freud pulled out the connections between the conscious and the unconscious and began his dream analysis. In that year, all the connections were pulled out between all the things that had been joined before ... That is where modern man started—in 1900. Back into the most primitive kind of awareness. And this is where it's at.

Interview/Los Angeles Times, 3-12:(5)6.

Margaret Mead
Anthropologist

3

I think the most optimistic thing is that we are still here! We have attained the capacity to destroy the planet, and haven't done it. The longer we don't do it, the better chance we have.

The Washington Post, 2-28:(A)19.

Henry Miller
Author

4

... at heart I'm an anarchist. I'm agin everything. The whole damn civilization, to my mind, could blow up tomorrow and it would be all to the good.

Interview/People, 8-21:60.

Edmund S. Muskie
United States Senator, D-Maine

5

In any organization—a social club, the Boy Scouts, or the Senate—when a guy is ready to go out and do the dirty work, the legwork, it's a good case for advancement ... When anyone does that kind of job, it's convertible to power. Respect and leadership count whenever a member of a group steps forward and does something well.

TWA Ambassador, October:61.

David Niven
Actor

6

We have to face it. An awful lot of my age group has been called up already. So many chums have gone. Cooper, Gable, Bogart. To say nothing of men of my own vintage—Errol Flynn and Ty Power. But there's no way they're going to get me off. I just won't go. I'll kick and scream and make a terrible fuss. But I try not to think of myself as being any particular age ... No, the thing is just to press on and do the best you can for your weight and age. Rather like a horse. I can't stand men who try to look younger than they are, brushing their hair forward in a desperate attempt to look "with it." And a license should be required to do some of these modern dances—and nobody over 25 should get it.

Interview, London/
Los Angeles Times, 10-1:(Calendar)31.

Richard M. Nixon
Former President of the United States

7

A man is not finished when he is defeated. He is finished when he quits. My philosophy is that no matter how many times you are knocked down you get off that floor, even if you are bloody, battered and beaten, and just keep slugging—providing you have something to live for. If you have something you believe in, and worth fighting for, the greatest test is not when you are standing, but when you are down on that floor. You've got to get up and start banging again. When I study men and women leaders

(RICHARD M. NIXON)

in history, those I admire the most are those who have gone through adversity and come back. You've got to learn to survive a defeat. That's when you develop character.

Interview, New York/
The Dallas Times Herald, 12-10:(A)1.

Laurence Olivier
Actor

1

Living is strife and torment, disappointment and love and sacrifice, golden sunsets and black storms. I said that some time ago, and today I do not think I would ... add one word. I take a simple view of living. It is keep your eyes open and get on with it.

Interview, Vienna/
Los Angeles Times, 2-26:(Calendar)35.

Irene Papas
Actress

2

... I like to sit in a chair for eights hours and think. When I think, I'm working. Look at the philosophers. Thinking was their life. Activity is the result of a creation. Thinking *is* the creation.

Interview, Los Angeles/
"W": a Fairchild publication, 4-14:13.

Paul VI
Pope

3

A new society is not built by those who are only capable of machinating violence and destruction, but by those who work in generous dedication, some of them in silence or suffering, in favor of their neighbors.

Address to crowd, Vatican City/
The Washington Post, 3-23:(A)23.

George Plimpton
Author

4

Most people live out their fantasies like [Walter] Mitty did—dreaming. That's much more safe and in a way the most sensible. It

doesn't take as much time, it doesn't hurt as much and in many ways it is almost as vivid. I mean, you always see the touchdown pass in your mind. And, if it's incomplete, you can go back and throw it 100 times. You don't get that chance in real life.

Interview, Dallas/
The Dallas Times Herald, 12-15:(Sportsweek)2.

J. B. Priestley
Author, Playwright

5

... I'm thinking of writing one last piece called "Doing Nothing." It's not easy to do nothing. You have to spend an hour or two dictating letters. You have to read the newspapers and answer the telephone. It's almost as hard as writing, doing nothing. Only certain gifted individuals know how to do nothing.

Interview, Stratford-upon-Avon, England/
Los Angeles Herald Examiner, 2-26:(E)10.

William Rees-Mogg
Editor, "The Times," London

6

Freedom is not something which just happens to a community, nor is it something which is preserved by accident. It is not a privilege which is ever long retained by those who are idle, who lack responsibility, who lack self-discipline. Those who prefer state discipline to self-discipline lose their freedom in the end and usually before very long. How stands this ideal of the free society, with free men depending upon their own self-discipline to maintain which the community requires if it is to survive? It is still in existence. If it were not in existence we should not be here. But it is impossible to pretend that it exists with the same vigor and self-confidence as it did a generation, or two generations, ago. There are those who wish to erode it, who wish to make their attack upon it. There are those who do not share this ideal. But, I believe, more insidious are those who would in fact pay some sort of shrugging lip service to this ideal, but are not remotely prepared to pay the price which it involves.

Before Salt Lake Area Chamber of Commerce,
Salt Lake City, March 29/
Vital Speeches, 6-1:496.

WHAT THEY SAID IN 1978

Elliot L. Richardson
United States Ambassador-at-Large

1

The world can never become a true community until nation-states can agree to balance ideology and humanity and do so on such a grand scale that concern for the individual becomes a primary force in shaping national goals.

Before University of Florida graduates,
Gainesville, March 18/
San Francisco Examiner & Chronicle, 3-19:(B)9.

Carroll Rosenbloom
Owner, Los Angeles "Rams" football team

2

Anything in life that you can buy limits its value. The things you end up wanting most are always the things without a price.

Interview, Los Angeles/
The Washington Post, 12-30:(D)7.

Dean Rusk
Professor of international law,
University of Georgia; Former Secretary
of State of the United States

3

A leader is someone who is able to move us, stimulate us and inspire us as we join together in various groups throughout society to achieve common objectives. We find leaders in education, business, the professions, religion, politics, sports, in the military, and in almost every phase of our society . . . Persistence, determination and courage have a lot to do with the qualities of leadership that are needed in our free society. I say a free society because a democratic political system and a free-enterprise economic system depend to an extraordinary degree upon the element of confidence. And if that element of confidence disappears, then things begin to fall to pieces.

At Atlanta University, May 2/
Vital Speeches, 8-15:643.

Yves Saint Laurent
Fashion designer

4

When a woman loses her mystery, she is all finished forever. She has lost the most impor-

tant thing she had. It is rare to find a man of mystery. But each woman has something mysterious within. She may be young or old, plain or beautiful; she may be doing the same work for the same pay as a man. But she must not want to *be* like a man. She must appreciate the specialness of being a woman—the powerful mystery of that is what keeps her appeal alive. I do not think this is—how do you call it?—a regressive attitude I have toward women. It is simply a law of life. Women are in a totally different and much more mysterious universe than men.

Interview, New York/Los Angeles Times, 9-21:(4)1.

Walter Scheel
President of West Germany

5

The freedom of expression that is constitutive of democracy is basically nothing other than the freedom to philosophize. After all, every person, whether he knows it or not, has his "philosophy," his views on life, God and the world, family, state, job and so on. All this forms a "system" in every individual which to the critical eye of the philosopher may not always appear to be a brilliantly clear product of the intellect but, nonetheless, has its meaning in the life of the person holding such views and hence its own human and spiritual dignity. And the right of free speech allows him to voice that philosophy whenever he wishes—and to the Head of State, incidentally. It gives me pleasure to invite to my home precisely people who have been critical of me. We then learn from each other in discussion. Thus philosophers, too, ought really to be in favor of free speech in their own fundamental interest. But as far as I can see, that is not always the case. Some philosophers, as soon as they think they have found the truth, are quite ready to do away entirely with all other opinions, especially when they assume the form of full-grown philosophies.

At World Congress of Philosophy, Dusseldorf,
West Germany, Aug. 27/Vital Speeches, 11-15:71.

John Schlesinger
Motion-picture director

6

. . . most people are failures, aren't they? I've failed many times. I've never regarded any-

(JOHN SCHLESINGER)

thing I've done as perfect. I wish one could. I've had good strokes of luck, and some of the films have been okay. But I think failure is the norm, isn't it? In one's own eyes one is a failure, but you may appear a success to other people. I suspect that once you believe you're there, possibly you've had it. The only gain from success is confidence, to go on and try something different.

Interview, Stalybridge, England/
The New York Times, 7-9:(2)13.

Dick Shawn
Actor, Comedian

1

Any comic worth his salt is organic. You can't buy material because what you're buying is someone else's background. You have to buy your own childhood, your own frustrations, create your thing even if it doesn't get as many laughs as someone else's. The only way you sustain in this business is by making your own statement. The more intelligence and imagination you have, the more you'll present your particular background in a specific and honest way. Comedy is very logical. Humor is given us so we can see our problems in a clear light. Few people want to be serious about anything, but comedy relates to us all ... To be a comic you have to retain a childish part of you and that's why comics are indestructible. The Bob Hopes, Jimmy Durantes, Jack Bennys. The point of view is youthful. That's also why a comic never gets the girl. The minute she puts her hand on his knee he acts like a child. That's why Steve McQueen could never be a comic.

Interview, San Francisco/
Los Angeles Times, 3-9:(4)15.

Neil Simon
Playwright, Screenwriter

2

Being very successful and suddenly having your name in the paper and having made huge sums of money puts you in a place where people don't quite know how to deal with you. They say you're not quite the same person you were, and obviously you're not. For some strange reason, for a long time I kept trying to hold on to the person that I was, rejecting the changes that were coming over me. But I said, "Wait a minute. I *have* changed. I have been to some other places" ... There are new experiences that come with success. Suddenly walking down the street, having people turn to look at you robs you of your privacy. Already you are not the same person you were before. Especially for a writer—it is one of the things that I miss most.

Television interview, Los Angeles/"The Wit and
Wisdom of Neil Simon," KCET, Los Angeles, 8-3.

Isaac Bashevis Singer
Author

3

Basic human problems are eternal. Ten thousand years from now it will be just as difficult for a girl to find the right husband as it is now. And people will still get sick and die, and they will worry. And there might be still enmity amongst groups; they're not going to make peace and love one another forever. But many changes will take place. We will go to Paris in 5 minutes; but it won't help us. We'll still worry about being late and getting sick. We'll still feel that there is a crisis in our lives.

Interview/U.S. News & World Report, 11-6:61.

4

I would say that if a man understands men, he understands also women, and vice versa. I would not say there is a man who has a great understanding of man and no understanding of women. I don't believe in this. Either we understand everybody or nobody. Most people understand almost nobody, except themselves, their business and their little clan.

Interview/The New York Times Magazine, 11-26:32.

Yuri Solomin
Soviet actor

5

[On being a celebrity] : ... I must say that nobody ever died of popularity, and I'd be much more upset if I weren't popular ... [But] your life is disrupted and you feel all the time

(YURI SOLOMIN)

the eyes around you, as if someone were always following you ... Celebrity has its good side, too. Like "alcazam," it opens doors. Whenever I'm stopped by a policeman, I put my hands up and say "guilty," but the policeman says "drive on."

Interview, Moscow/
Los Angeles Herald Examiner, 3-13:(B)7.

Alexander I. Solzhenitsyn
Exiled Soviet author

1

Should someone ask me whether I would indicate the West, such as it is today, as a model for my country [the Soviet Union], frankly I would have to answer negatively ... Through intense suffering, our country has now achieved a spiritual development of such intensity that the Western system in its present state of spiritual exhaustion does not look attractive ... After the suffering of decades of violence and oppression, the human soul longs for things higher, warmer and purer than those offered by today's mass living habits, introduced by the revolting invasion of publicity, by TV stupor and by intolerable music.

At Harvard University commencement, June 8/
Los Angeles Times, 6-9:(1)1,12.

Leon Spinks
Heavyweight boxing champion of the world

2

I know a lot of people think I'm dumb. Well, at least I ain't no educated fool. To the kids in high school, I say stay in school and learn what you can. But learn about what's happening in your streets, too. I was talking to some college group in Burlington, Vermont, and some girl was using such big words that I thought she was cussing me out. But I told her that all the education in the world ain't worth nothing [un-] less you got some common sense. Really, the only thing school knowledge is good for is to keep people from taking advantage of you. Now when I hear a word I don't understand, I run to the dictionary. I'm learning to read the little sneaky stuff between the lines, which add up to big things.

Interview, Atlanta/Los Angeles Times, 6-28:(3)14.

David Steel
Leader, Liberal Party of Britain

3

A strong local community is the only place for the full development of the individual ... It is a tragic paradox that in our rush to modernize and rationalize, we have so often discarded the very basis of a civilized life. A lively community, with its own local school and health center, with good public transport facilities, with restored local buildings, with a local policeman on the local beat, with thriving local enterprises and a real sense of local identity— that's real civilization. And it wouldn't just be better in the countryside but in the rundown areas of our great cities, too.

At Liberal Assembly, Southport, England/
The Christian Science Monitor, 10-11:23.

Rod Steiger
Actor

4

I am amazed that 1,500 people in a theatre laugh and cry at the same time. They must somehow be related, regardless of their creeds and colors and so forth. There seems to be a family of mankind, after all. In fact, our behavior proves we're a family. Why else would we seek recognition or comfort or warmth from other people? Why else would the two of us talk to each other, each hoping we are understood and liked?

Interview, New York/
The Christian Science Monitor, 6-30:14.

Irving Stone
Author

5

I believe that work is good unto itself, that it is one of the two highest forms of human expression. Love and work or work and love: It seems to me they grow out of each other.

Interview, Beverly Hills, Calif./
Los Angeles Times, 7-14:(4)4.

Lewis Thomas
President, Memorial Sloan-Kettering
Cancer Center, New York

1

It is not so bad being ignorant if you are *totally* ignorant. The hard thing is knowing in some detail the reality of ignorance.

Before American Association for the Advancement of Science/The Washington Post, 6-30:(A)16.

Ernest van den Haag
Psychoanalyst and sociologist

2

[On the upsurge of violence in society] : I think we live in a society where people have far more freedom—or, if you wish, license—than they ever had: freedom from conformity to class and group mores. This is due partly to ideological changes, partly to great mobility that makes it very easy to escape the bounds of one's family or group. Moreover, people's lives are much less structured than before ... so anything goes. Yet, in exercising their freedom, they find that happiness has escaped them. The paradise they promised themselves has proved empty ... Look at the violence occurring in Italy and West Germany, where a few young people see absolutely nothing that gives meaning to their lives—so the meaning they found is to destroy society.

Interview/U.S. News & World Report, 12-11:25.

Gore Vidal
Author

3

Marriage is breaking up, and it's a good thing. Much of the illness of our times comes from it. You know, John meets Mary and they are supposed to remain sexually interested in one another for 65 years until John dies of a heart attack. People stray from this ideal, of course, but they feel guilty. That brings lots of money to psychiatrists, which is always a bad thing. As a science, I place psychiatry somewhere between tarot cards and astrology.

Interview, New York/
"W": a Fairchild publication, 4-14:8.

Guillermo Vilas
Tennis player

4

I think the best thing is when you wake up in the morning and see yourself in the mirror, you do not spit on yourself. That's the most important thing. You have to do what you feel like. If you are happy with yourself, that's it. I try not to spit on myself.

The Washington Post, 9-2:(D)1.

John Vorster
President, and former Prime Minister,
of South Africa

5

[Change exists] because nothing is static in this life ... But allow me one word from experience. While, on the one hand, there must be change, don't change just for the sake of change. Do not change without counting the cost and before you've answered the question where it is going to lead and exactly what the consequences will be. Once you've done that, then go ahead, regardless of the consequences.

Inaugural address as President, Pretoria, Oct. 10/
Los Angeles Herald Examiner, 10-11:(A)4.

Lina Wertmuller
Motion-picture director

6

Life is full of images today, from newspapers, magazines, television. We are never alone. This is a sensation of our life, for the past 70 years. And there is a danger in this. When you turn on your TV you see a terrible thing, like Vietnam or a factory that has exploded. And your skin loses its sensitivity—it's too much, too much! We feel nothing. There is a terrible earthquake in Turkey, and we say we don't know them, it's far away. It's like a machine-gun: image, image, image! At times I am afraid audiences will have no more sensibility to anything. I am afraid for human values.

Interview, New York/
The Christian Science Monitor, 4-26:25.

WHAT THEY SAID IN 1978

John Wooden
Former basketball coach, University of California, Los Angeles

1

My definition of success is peace of mind obtained through self-satisfaction by doing the best you can to be the best you are capable of.

At Orange Coast College/
Los Angeles Times, 12-1:(3)9.

C. Vann Woodward
Emeritus professor of American history, Yale University

2

Pessimism is borne out by what I know of history. Human affairs have not earned any right to expect the best. Where possible, people tend to make the wrong choice, and make a mess.

Interview, Washington, May 3/
Los Angeles Times, 5-4:(1)13.

Religion

Arie R. Brouwer
*General secretary, Reformed Church
in America*

1

There's more awareness than there has been
for some time of the religious dimension of
reality. Without that vision, society is in real
trouble and more and more people are realizing
it. I think there's more religion around than
there has been for quite a while ... In some
ways, [today's cults, charismatic groups and
novel movements are] a secular response to the
mysterious. It's all pretty religious, but it
doesn't care for organized religion. The churches generally have not found the way to channel
and nurture it.

Interview, New York/
The Dallas Times Herald, 7-22:(A)17.

Jimmy Carter
President of the United States

2

There is nothing wrong in bringing one's
religious life into the political arena, because
you can't divorce religious beliefs and public
service ... I have never detected or experienced
any conflict between God's will and my political duty. It is obvious that if I were to violate
one, I would violate the other.

Before National Conference of Baptist Men,
Atlanta, June 16/The New York Times, 6-17:1.

3

[On whether the U.S. government should
have taken steps against the San Francisco-
based People's Temple before the mass suicide-
murder of its members took place in Guyana]:
It's un-Constitutional for the government of
our country to investigate or to issue laws
against any group, no matter how much they
might depart from normal custom, which is
based on religious beliefs. The only exception is

when various substantive allegations that the
activities of those religious groups directly violate a Federal law ... I don't think that we
ought to have an overreaction because of the
Jonestown tragedy by injecting government into trying to control people's religious beliefs;
and I believe that we also don't need to deplore
on a nation-wide basis the fact that the Jonestown cult, so-called, was typical of America,
because it's not.

News conference, Washington, Nov. 30/
The New York Times, 12-1:(A)22.

Richard Delgado
Visiting professor of law,
University of California, Los Angeles

4

[On whether the government should intervene when religious cults may present dangers,
such as the recent mass suicide-murder of People's Temple members in Guyana]: I don't
favor government intervention in religion generally. But any organization that poses demon-
strable threats to an individual's physical or
psychological well-being, or to the family as
an institution, warrants government intervention. ... the government should intervene
wherever it finds extremely harmful, psychologically manipulative actions being used to facilitate conversion. Whether it finds this conduct
in mainstream churches or fringe cults is a matter of indifference to me. As a practical matter,
we're unlikely to find such conduct in mainstream churches. Most of them perceive very
strong differences between their own methods
and those of religious cults. They have labeled
the abuses of some cults as tantamount to spiritual Fascism, which no self-respecting religious
organization should utilize.

Interview/U.S. News & World Report, 12-11:29.

WHAT THEY SAID IN 1978

Mircea Eliade
Professor, University of Chicago
Divinity School

1

[Young people today] don't know anything about their religion, or at least they are not satisfied with their Christian, Judaic, Muslim, Hinduistic traditions. They want something new, and in America and Europe they are searching for this in yoga or Zen. The hippies living in the woods are looking for a ritual nudity, a kind of nostalgia for paradise. I believe in the creativity of some ot these movements.

Interview/People, 3-27:49.

Marc Galanter
Associate professor of psychiatry,
Albert Einstein College of Medicine,
New York

2

[On the recent mass suicide-murder of People's Temple members at Jonestown, Guyana]: In Guyana, it's evident that many members of that cult were divorced from the normal values around them—divorced both physically, because of their isolation, and psychologically. The influences on their behavior and their plans may have come almost exclusively from the word of the leadership. Because of that, in a crisis situation they were much more vulnerable to group hysterical reaction. And once that begins to sweep through a group, behaviors that are entirely unpredictable and unexpected may arise. So it isn't terribly surprising that such a group fell upon a bizarre and tragic solution to an overwhelming disruption in their perspective on what the world around them was about.

Interview/U.S. News & World Report, 12-4:29.

Langdon Gilkey
Professor of theology, University
of Chicago

3

[On the "cult" movement]: The theology of the cult is always dependent on a message of salvation not believed to be available in ordinary experience. They are sometimes radically separated from the world, going into their "em-

bassy." The world is a foreign continent and they, the ambassadors.

The New York Times, 11-28:(A)14.

Billy Graham
Evangelist

4

[On the death of Pope Paul VI]: Pope Paul presided over the Roman Catholic Church when it was going through one of the most critical periods in its history. In one sense, he witnessed a revolution within the Roman Catholic world that has developed for several decades. In another sense, he sought to give that revolution direction and guidance. I believe history may show he was one of the most significant Popes in modern times.

Aug. 6/Los Angeles Times, 8-7:(1)1.

John Paul I
Pope

5

[The church's first duty is] to spread the word, to proclaim the message, to announce its salvation which creates in a soul a restlessness to pursue truth and at the same time offer strength from above. If all the sons and daughters of the church would know how to be tireless missionaries of the gospel, a new flowering of holiness and renewal would spring up in this world that thirsts for love and for truth.

Vatican City, Aug. 27/
Los Angeles Times, 8-28:(1)10.

6

The danger for modern man is that he would reduce the earth to a desert, the person to an automation, brotherly love to planned collectivization. The church, admiringly yet lovingly protesting against such "achievements," intends, rather, to safeguard the world that thirsts for a life of love from dangers that would attack it.

Inaugural address to Cardinals/Time, 9-11:82.

John Paul II
Pope

7

We desire to make an effective contribution to the cause of permanent and prevailing peace,

(JOHN PAUL II)

of development, of international justice. We have no intention of political interference or of participation in the working out of temporal affairs.

Broadcast address, Vatican City, Oct. 17/
Los Angeles Times, 10-18:(1)1,8.

1

[On his being elected Pope and being Polish] : Only in the light of the faith is it possible to accept with spiritual tranquility and confidence the fact that, by virtue of your choice, it was my fate to become the vicar of Christ on earth and the visible head of the Church. Venerable brothers, it was an act of confidence and at the same time of great courage to call a non-Italian to be bishop of Rome. One cannot say anything more, but merely bow one's head before this decision of the sacred college.

Before College of Cardinals, Vatican City,
Oct. 18/Los Angeles Times, 10-19:(1)24.

2

[Upholding mandatory celibacy for priests] : Yes, we are in the world, but we are not world- ly. We must retain the sense of our unique vocation and this uniqueness must be express- ed, also, in our exterior clothing. Let us not be ashamed. Our priesthood must be clear and expressive. And if in the tradition of our church it is strictly associated with celibacy, it is be- cause of the Gospel clarity and expressiveness to which our Lord refers with his words on celibacy "for the kingdom of God."

Before priests, Vatican City, Nov. 9/
Los Angeles Herald Examiner, 11-9:(A)4.

3

[Reaffirming the church's opposition to divorce] : Christian marriage is essential and in- dissoluable. You must resist the pressures of the times and the worldly currents, sometimes erod- ing from within, that lead to the dissolution of Christian law and values.

Before Canadian bishops, Vatican City, Nov. 17/
The Dallas Times Herald, 11-18:(A)7.

Dean M. Kelley
Executive for religious and civil
liberty, National Council of Churches

4

[On whether government should intervene when religious cults may present dangers, such as the recent mass suicide-murder of People's Temple members in Jonestown, Guyana] : I'm upset by what happened in Jonestown. And I wish there were some way to prevent such situations from occurring—consistent with the [U.S.] Constitution. But I can't think of any. In many instances, the results of well-meaning measures of intervention have been just as dam- aging or dangerous as the lack of them. I give pre-eminence to religious liberty—to the pre- sumption that a person who joins a religious organization and adheres to it knows what he is doing and should not be prevented from his religious activity so long as no crime is being committed. If there are other rights or free- doms that conflict with that activity, I think the presumption has to lie with the right men- tioned in the Constitution: the free exercise of religion.

Interview/U.S. News & World Report, 12-11:29.

George A. Kelly
Director, Institute for Advanced
Studies in Catholic Doctrine,
St. John's University

5

. . . latter-day parish priests have in far too many instances not been good at their work, and bishops have done little to see that they were good or remained good. As a result, we have dying parishes all over the country—not because today's people are poorer or more diffi- cult to evangelize than they once were, but because bishops have not given their parishes top priority, and priests no longer worked as well or as hard as they once did doing the basic liturgical, evangelical, catechetical, social work of the parish. Vital parish life, and *ipso facto* parish renewal, means at base root bishops and priests committed to developing a sense of the eternal in their faithful, teaching effectively the significance of Christ and his doctrines, bringing

WHAT THEY SAID IN 1978

(GEORGE A. KELLY)

people to Mass and the Sacraments. Parishes which fail to do these basic things well are for all practical purposes dead to the essential meaning of Catholicity. If they remain dead, it will be for the reason that bishops and priests are dead to this basic work of the Catholic parish. Nor will parishes revive without living priests, who will again go about their rounds of apostolic chores working against powerful forces arrayed against them, as once their predecessors walked in the midst of cholera, fearless of dying because their people needed the Word, the Hand, the Presence, the Sacrament.

At National Conference of Catholic Charities, New Orleans, Sept. 16/Vital Speeches, 11-15:83.

Andrew Lester
Associate professor of psychology of religion, Southern Baptist Theological Seminary

1

Many males have unconsciously thought that ministry was asexual or neuter. Since all ministers have been male, they have rarely had to think otherwise. However, when they run into a female minister, they must encounter this largely unconscious assumption, and that can be threatening . . . Men have almost no experience relating to women in the role of minister, which creates problems concerning normal sexual attraction. Men are not surprised to find themselves sexually attracted to the females who teach their children, greet them in offices, pour their coffee or nurse them in hospitals; but to feel sexual attraction to someone who is a minister seems somewhat shameful, even sacrilegious. Some still believe that religious professionals—those closest to God—do not, or at least should not, have sexual thoughts and feelings. Therefore, to experience a minister as sexual and, furthermore, to be attracted to one, can be a disturbing experience.

At Consultation on Women in Church-Related Vocations, Nashville, Tenn./ The Washington Post, 10-6:(C)21.

Gillian Lindt
Professor of religion, Columbia University

2

Religious toleration in the judgment of the general public [in the U.S.] has only recently, and then often grudgingly, been extended to non-believers. Religious freedom has only in recent decades, and then by a very small minority, been accepted as implying a guarantee of freedom of conscience and practice . . .

At religious symposium, Newport, R.I./ The New York Times, 5-30:(A)8.

Timothy Manning
Roman Catholic Archbishop of Los Angeles

3

We cannot compromise fundamental principles simply to keep people in the church. The church can indeed show sympathy and compassion in many respects. But it cannot compromise on certain basic principles. Abortion, for instance, is clearly contradictory to the law of God. The church has called it an "unspeakable crime" and, therefore, there's no problem for one's attitude here. I also think the ordination of women is a closed issue, because the last Pope addressed himself to this in detail and indicated it quite clearly. [As for celibacy among priests,] I see no signs of any change in church practice here. Certainly not for those who are already priests. In some special cases—in some geographical areas—it might become feasible to ordain priests who are already married. But I don't think there would ever be permission for an ordained priest to then marry.

Interview, Vatican City, 9-2:(1)25.

4

An obvious deduction from the election of the last Pope [the late John Paul I] is the terrible burden of the papacy, the extraordinary strain on a Pope unschooled in the Roman offices. From conversations I have had, I think there is a trend now to seek more of a combination both of pastoral background, which is a dominant requirement, with schooling in the

444

(TIMOTHY MANNING)

Curia or diplomacy. Many in curial positions come from a rich background in pastoral work. That we did not analyze enough before.

Interview, Rome/
Los Angeles Times, 10-13:(1-B)1.

Martin E. Marty
Professor of the history of modern
Christianity, University of Chicago

1

No society before our own [the U.S.] confronted people with as much choice in religion as ours does and that colors religion very much. In a primitive society, nobody asks an adolescent, "Do you want to be initiated into the tribe?" You all are. In historic European societies, if you grew up in a Jewish home, Judaism was transmitted through the genes. If you grew up in a Catholic nation, you are automatically Catholic. If a king turned Protestant, you grew up Protestant. In America, every year there are more choices, more reason for confusion. Therefore, every year it is more startling to see the kinds of loyalties that do develop.

Interview/Los Angeles Herald Examiner, 3-23:(A)1.

2

[On independent, non-institutionalized religion]: Too many followers of "invisible religion" slide around in a world of infinite possibilities, where no one judges them and there are no hard choices to help them form their thoughts. In our times, it's not secularism but do-it-yourself religion that is the real enemy of the church.

U.S. News & World Report, 10-16:64.

Wallace Deen Muhammad
Spiritual leader of the Black Muslims

3

Unity of spirit cannot be achieved from a pulpit but only from the public, with human beings addressing human beings . . . We all have our favorite prayer-hall and places of interest. However, private interests and personal tastes are crippling burdens on the effort to unify the human spirit. The most effective way to serve God is still the method practiced by Christ Jesus and the Prophet Muhammad. They both were roving preachers. The role of the leadership is to serve families, homes and neighborhoods and nationalities, while resisting and never allowing itself to be localized and ethnicized.

Lecture, Atlanta, Sept. 10/
Los Angeles Times, 9-12:(1)13.

Vincent T. O'Keefe
Jesuit official; Former president,
Fordham University

4

[On Pope John Paul II's being from Poland, a Communist country]: As a first reaction, I would see a Communist government being pleased to have such a man as Pope, because its leaders could say: "We don't have to know how to deal with the Vatican now. The Pope knows how to deal with us." The risk of misunderstanding is lessened. Yet, I think there could also be a feeling of uneasiness—even alarm—because of a fear on the part of Communist regimes that the naming of a Polish Pope might arouse the hopes of the people for more freedom. On balance, I am inclined to feel that the church will be strengthened in its dealings with Communist governments, based on their recognition that the new Pope knows them far better than any other in their history, and therefore is better equipped to pursue the church's program of dialogue with them.

Interview, Rome/
U.S. News & World Report, 10-30:25.

Paul VI
Pope

5

Being a Christian today . . . requires a seriousness, a vigilance, a generosity, a dedication even more determined and lucid than in the past. The great social communication instruments [the mass media] . . . spread—not only slyly and hiddenly, but sometimes even in an open and virulent way—conceptions, orientations and ideologies that are not always in harmony with the demands of the message of the Gospel and the teaching of the church.

WHAT THEY SAID IN 1978

(PAUL VI)

Atheism, both theoretical and practical, is propagandized, as is indifference in the religious field. Criticism and irony are heaped on the Christian view of matrimony and of the family, which is considered outdated.

Before pilgrimage of workers and students,
Vatican City, May 27/
The Dallas Times Herald, 5-28:(A)7.

Bernard Rosensweig
President, Rabbinical Council of
America; Adjunct professor of
religious studies, Queens College,
Flushing, New York

1

[On reaching college students with religion] : One of the prime functions of college is to undo what people believe. It could be said colleges have a God-given right to make them godless. But, seriously, I think young people are reaching for something authentic at this time in their lives. They are cynical on the surface, but they want something genuine. The young people who enter cults are very sincere people, let me tell you. If they wind up in cults, we failed them. I'm not saying you will save them at the college age. But you must try harder. You must know how to listen.

Interview, Toronto/
The New York Times, 7-6:(A)17.

Alexander M. Schindler
President, Union of American
Hebrew Congregations

2

I want to reach a different audience entirely—the unchurched, the seekers after truth who require a religion which tolerates, nay, encourages, all questions; and especially I want to reach out to the alienated and the rootless who need the warmth and comfort of a people [the Jews] well-known for its close family ties and well-known, also, for its ancient and noble lineage ... Millions of Americans are searching for something ... Many of the seekers have fallen prey to mystical cults which literally enslave them. [But Judaism] offers

life, not death. It teaches free will, not surrender of body and soul to another human being [as do some cults] ... Judaism is a religion of hope and not of despair ... Judaism has an enormous amount of wisdom and experience to offer to the troubled world, and we Jews ought to be proud to speak about it frankly, freely and with dignity.

Before UAHC board of directors, Houston, Dec. 2/
The Washington Post, 12-3:(A)2.

Fulton J. Sheen
Roman Catholic Archbishop

3

[On evangelism] : The new approach is, people are ready to hear about Christ. The time is right to talk about sin, our Savior and redemption. The only way to win audiences is to tell people about the life and death of Christ. Every other approach is a waste.

At National Conference of Catholic Bishops,
Chicago, May 3/The New York Times, 5-4:(A)17.

Isaac Bashevis Singer
Author

4

... the Jewish people have been in exile for 2,000 years; they have lived in hundreds of countries, spoken hundreds of languages and still they kept their old language, Hebrew. They kept their Aramaic, later their Yiddish; they kept their books; they kept their faith. And, after 2,000 years, they are going back to Israel. This is such a unique case in human history that if it wouldn't have happened, no one would believe that it's possible. If someone would have written a fantasy about such people, the critics would call it a silly fantasy. This makes the history of the Jewish people terribly, terribly unique. This power of being a minority, a persecuted minority, and staying with one's culture for 2,000 years, denies all sociological theories.

Interview/The New York Times Magazine, 11-26:38.

5

... the power of religion, especially belief in revelation, is weaker today than it was in any other epoch in human history. More and more

(ISAAC BASHEVIS SINGER)

children grow up without faith in God, without belief in reward and punishment, in the immortality of the soul, and even in the validity of ethics.

Nobel lecture before Swedish Academy, Stockholm, Dec. 8/The New York Times, 12-9:4.

William Stringfellow
Lawyer; Lay theologian

1

The government has leverage on religious groups because of the tax-exemption privilege. Church leaders, eager for the church to be free to be the church, should ask for the removal of this privilege. If there were no tax privilege for religious groups, hucksters and people who are using religion as a cover for political movements would be discouraged.

The Dallas Times Herald, 12-9:(A)27.

Thomas Tschoepe
Roman Catholic Bishop of Dallas, Texas

2

[On the death of Pope Paul VI]: It doesn't make a bit of difference who the man is [who is Pope]; it's the office that matters. Whether the new Pope is a liberal or traditionalist, he is still the custodian of divine revelation. The only changes he can make are in things that stem from church law and not divine law . . . I don't foresee any great changes of any kind, no matter who the new Pope is. I think the media has overreacted to the importance of Pope Paul's death. I can't quite understand why there is so much publicity. I would like to know the reason why the death of a religious leader makes such an impact. I guess it is a good sign people are so interested in religion.

Interview/The Dallas Times Herald, 8-12:(A)14.

Gore Vidal
Author

3

Christianity was one of the greatest disasters ever to befall the West . . . As it is now decaying, we are in an interesting period. All sorts of new religions are beginning and the old religions are losing their force. I think that's probably a good thing. Certainly, this death cult should be eliminated as quickly as possible . . . [Christianity is] a nightmare and all the saints and martyrs, each murder, more hideous than the other. It's one of the ugliest religions man's mind has ever conceived. [D. H.] Lawrence said, why is it that we always emphasize, in these churches, the crucifixion and never the resurrection? It is always an obsession with pain and murder.

Interview/Los Angeles Herald Examiner, 4-30:(A)8.

Space · Science · Technology

Richard C. Atkinson
Director, National Science Foundation

1

Telling scientists to forget basic research and work on things of practical value is the great danger of our time ... If there had been a war on polio in the '20s or '30s, we'd have ended up engineering the most elegant and beautifully running iron lungs one could imagine.

Los Angeles Times, 7-19:(1-A)7.

Richard Berendzen
Provost, American University, Washington

2

Accumulating evidence during the last two decades has convinced many scientists, worldwide, that extraterrestrial life probably does exist, possibly in enormous abundance. It must be noted, however, that incontrovertible proof has yet to be found. To date, the evidence is strictly circumstantial, but it is highly suggestive and possibly compelling.

Before House Space Science Subcommittee, Washington/The Christian Science Monitor, 9-21:6.

Frank Borman
Chairman and president, Eastern Airlines

3

[On his flight in the *Apollo 8* spacecraft 10 years ago] : The greatest emotion I had ... was looking back [at] earth. It has a very lonely appearance. You can say what you like about future encounters of the third kind, but the facts of life are that there is not going to be any physical encounter of intelligent life [in the universe] in any of our lifetimes and probably ever in the history of earth. The facts of life are that we are, as Archibald MacLeish says, riders on the earth together. From the vantage point of space, you have appreciation of how precious is earth. If I was left with one sensation, it is the importance we have as human beings in general, and as Americans in particular, to take advantage of the freedom and dignity that has been bequeathed to us all.

Interview/San Francisco Examiner & Chronicle, 12-24:(A)7.

Paul R. Chernoff
Associate professor of mathematics, University of California, Berkeley

4

If theoretical science is fundamental, no science is more fundamental than mathematics. It is extraordinary that mathematical ideas, cultivated originally merely because they were beautiful, so often turn out to be useful—indeed essential—in understanding the physical world.

San Francisco Examiner & Chronicle, 12-32:(This World)2.

Robert A. Frosch
Administrator, National Aeronautics and Space Administration of the United States

5

The argument that high technology is a drain on the national economy is nonsense. I have never seen a good case made for it. On the other hand, if you take a look at those industries in the U.S. that have turned their backs on high-technology spending in the past 25 to 50 years, you are looking at some dying industries or industries that are in deep trouble. If you want to kill off an industry, just let the technology remain static for a few years.

Nation's Business, February:41.

Philip Handler
President, National Academy of Sciences

6

Scientific knowledge allows 50 million Americans to stay home, drink beer and watch the Academy Awards. It allows us to wipe out

(PHILIP HANDLER)

diseases like typhoid and pellagra. It allows us to say that 1978 is the year when the last person will ever have smallpox. But we haven't developed the social instincts to keep pace with our ability to develop technology. We haven't learned how to resolve conflict, either between nations or within nations. That's what keeps science from being the blessing it might be.

Interview, Washington/
"W": a Fairchild publication, 5-12:17.

R. Heath Larry
President, National Association of Manufacturers

1

I recognize science as an unending search for truth and knowledge. Because it is important that it continue in that role, I will put the case that scientists may ignore neither politics nor the market, except at considerable peril to themselves and to the remainder of society.

San Francisco Examiner & Chronicle,
10-22:(This World)2.

Hans M. Mark
Under Secretary of the Air Force of the United States

2

What will come from the technology of the 20th century? Our venture into space and our development of much better astronomical instruments has already revealed some important new mysteries. What are quasars and where does the enormous energy they emit come from? What is the true nature of neutron stars? What happens to matter under the unusual conditions that exist inside completely collapsed gravitational objects—the so-called "black holes"? A fuller investigation of all of these will, in my opinion, lead to the fulfillment of Albert Einstein's dream—namely, a unified field theory of all the forces that govern the universe. It is likely that from this theory there will emerge principles that rank in importance with the one formulated by Heisenberg in the 1920s. Finally, it is also likely that we will also learn more about the nature of life itself

through our venture in space. We have already seen that complex organic molecules can be created from simpler ones and that this process happens all over the universe. We have seen these molecules in interstellar clouds and we have also seen them in meteorites that clearly originated elsewhere in our solar system. Here, also, we are on the edge of important new discoveries. There can be little doubt that a deeper understanding of the nature of life will be the most intellectual revolution of all.

At National Space Club, Washington, March 10/
Vital Speeches, 5-1:444.

Frederik Pohl
Science-fiction writer

3

There's no doubt in my mind that we have the technology to do anything we want to do. If we wanted to feed the whole world and eliminate starvation, we could. If we wanted to conserve energy so fossil fuel would last another 500 years, we could. The trouble is that the institutional and political barriers may prove insurmountable.

San Francisco Examiner & Chronicle,
9-24:(This World)2.

W. F. Rockwell, Jr.
Chairman, Rockwell International

4

[There is a] growing number of politicians and social groups who, through lack of understanding or fear, have adopted a philosophy of rejecting advanced technology. I'm personally concerned that if we do not take steps to thwart this social myopia, America—once the home of a dynamic, energetic and vigorous people—will atrophy into a second-class industrial power where everyone wears a helmet and walks around in an air bag, afraid of the dark and with their eyes closed to the future. I'm concerned about this trend because, all too often in today's world, there are people who are too quick to turn their backs on the contributions that American technology has made to U.S. economic development.

Before American Textile Manufacturers
*Institute, San Francisco, March 17/***

449

WHAT THEY SAID IN 1978

Carl Sagan
Director,
Laboratory for Planetary Studies,
Cornell University

1

We live in an age dominated by science and technology. One way to realize this is to look at a list of imminent catastrophes facing the world [ranging from accidental nuclear war to destruction of the ozone layer], brought on by something so unimportant as a spray can which makes our underarms smell better . . . A prescription for suicide in a technological world is for the public not to be knowledgeable about developments in science and technology.

At Public Broadcasting Service annual meeting,
Dallas, June 26/
The Dallas Times Herald, 6-27:(B)6.

Lewis Thomas
President, Memorial Sloan-Kettering
Cancer Center, New York

2

The solidest piece of scientific truth I know of, the one thing about which I feel totally confident, is that we are profoundly ignorant about nature . . . It is, in its way, an illuminating piece of news. It would have amazed the brightest minds of the 18th-century enlightenment to be told by any of us how little we know, and how bewildering seems the way ahead. It is this sudden confrontation with the depth and scope of ignorance that represents the most significant contribution of 20th-century science to the human intellect.

Before American Association for the Advancement
of Science/The Washington Post, 6-30:(A)16.

Muhammad Ali
Former heavyweight boxing champion of the world

1

[On his losing the championship to Leon Spinks]: I amazed you when I won, and I amaze you when I lose. Everybody loses, but the real man goes on. Some lose mothers and fathers and wives. Some lose their legs or their jobs. You got to keep living, keep trying. I want to be the first man ever to win the title three times. Like MacArthur, I shall return!

Las Vegas, Nev./Newsweek, 2-27:89.

2

[On why he lost the championship to Leon Spinks last February]: Every time I picked up a newspaper I read about how this was a mismatch [with Spinks being an underdog]. So I'm out there running two miles, and I say to myself, "That's enough; why should I run five miles a day?" Well, you whup me again, when I run five miles and chop my trees, and you'll be the real champion.

News conference, New York, May 1/
The New York Times, 5-2:43.

George Allen
Football coach, Los Angeles "Rams"

3

[On the increase in low-scoring games]: It isn't the rules that are keeping the scoring down. It's the ball-control philosophy of so many coaches today. With ball control, you're eating up the clock—meaning the other side can't score—and you're not scoring yourself. We're face to face now with an elementary human principle: You can't help a man who doesn't want to be helped. You can't change the rules to encourage passing when your coach is philosophically opposed to passing.

At National Football League convention,
Palm Springs, Calif./Los Angeles Times, 3-14:(3)6.

4

The way professional football is structured today, everything is tied to winning the Super Bowl. You can win all your regular-season games, but if you lose in the playoffs or even the Super Bowl itself, you've had a lousy season. In fact, the two best teams don't always get to the Super Bowl. All it takes for that to happen is to have one bad day in the playoffs against an opponent that suddenly plays over its head or gets a couple of lucky breaks.

Interview, Los Angeles/
The Christian Science Monitor, 7-26:15.

George Allen
Former football coach, Los Angeles "Rams"

5

[On his being fired after the *Rams* lost two pre-season games following his return as *Rams* coach after coaching the Washington *Redskins* for seven years]: If we'd won one of those two exhibition games, this never would have happened. It's an unbelievable thing. Do you think I got a fair chance—two pre-season games? You give a rookie coach more than two games, and I'm not a rookie. I've always been a successful coach . . . All I know is that I did everything in my power; I did it the way it should be done; I did it my way . . . The only way I know how to coach is to work hard, to be totally dedicated. I don't spare myself, and I dreamed the same of everyone else.

Aug. 14/The Washington Post, 8-15:(D)1.

6

I like to think that the next job that I have will be with an organization where everybody will be committed to going to the Super Bowl. I'm talking about the entire organization—not just the players and the coaches. I'm talking about the business manager, the trainers, the doctors, the secretaries, the scouts, everybody.

WHAT THEY SAID IN 1978

(GEORGE ALLEN)

I'm talking about people who will work noon and night to achieve that goal and not think about the other person making $100 a month more than they are. So what? There's more in your life than just collecting a check and going home to drink a beer and watching television. You've got a chance in life to really achieve something. A job shouldn't be just a job.

Interview, Rancho Palos Verdes, Calif./
Los Angeles Times, 12-31:(3)3.

Sparky Anderson
Baseball manager, Cincinnati "Reds"

1

The game used to be played by guys with a one-year contract and a one-year option. Today, it seems, everybody has a three or four. So they don't have a financial incentive to keep putting out any more—and I think this has hurt every club in baseball, especially the good clubs . . . A little security goes a long way for a ballplayer. With a long-term contract he just isn't the same guy he used to be . . . Do you remember the old days, when August and September were the months when a lot of players came to life and started putting out? Everybody used to call this the "salary drive." Well, nobody is driving for next year's salary now. They're all signed up . . . I agree with [former player] Mickey Mantle that there was a different environment in baseball 10 years ago . . . He said that before the big money in baseball, the players' attitude was, what can I do for you? Now they ask: What can I do for myself? The money thing [large salaries] created a new kind of ballplayer. But I don't mind the money they make. It's the multiple-year contracts that have done the real harm. Ballplayers don't have to work any more.

Interview, Los Angeles/
Los Angeles Times, 9-20:(3)1.

Mario Andretti
Auto-racing driver

2

It's one thing being frustrated by mechanical failure, things beyond your control, but another to know that you're the one making mistakes. That's how I'll know it's time to retire. There comes a time in every human being's life when stamina, physical strength and reaction time will deteriorate. These are the times when some of the edge will disappear. I feel I can give more today than I ever have in my career. I don't know how long it will last but I hope that, when I detect my deterioration, I'll be man enough to accept that fact and get the hell out.

Interview/Los Angeles Times, 1-18:(3)9.

3

[Saying he prefers Formula-I racing to Indy cars]: I enjoy both types of racing, but the truth is I hate pit stops. I like flag-to-flag racing, and that's Grand Prix. At Indianapolis, or even in 200 miles at Ontario, too much depends on the pit stops, when they are made and how quick your crew gets you out. If you're lucky, in a USAC race you can pick up a lap. If you're unlucky, you lose one. In Formula-I, you go all the way. In racing against the caliber of competition you face at Indy or in a Grand Prix, you need to sort out your position and set up your passing points. Just when you've got a plan figured out at Indy, the yellow caution light comes on and you're called in for a pit stop. When you come back out, you're racing against a different group of drivers and the situation has completely changed. It is hard to develop a pattern, a feeling for the race, when you make as many as 11 pit stops in 500 miles.

Interview/Los Angeles Times, 3-23:(3)6.

4

My goal has been to win in every category of racing—to smoke them all where they least expect me to. I have won on 127 different kinds of track, clockwise and counterclockwise. I have experienced the passing of the engine from front to back. I have raced with the greats who have since retired, and in places that are now parking lots. So I'm an old fogy—but how many guys have done all that? . . . The danger I was imposing on myself at the early stages of my career is over. Back then, I had goals to achieve and didn't give a damn how I achieved them. I've outgrown that. There is none of this bullshit of a death wish. I know now that with my experience I could never make a fatal mis-

(MARIO ANDRETTI)

take—little ones, perhaps, but not a big one. The risks I take are calculated. You have a feel of the car, a feel where the edge is. If you don't disregard it, then you're okay.

Interview/People, 8-28:38.

Reubin Askew
Governor of Florida (D)

1

[Arguing against legalizing casino gambling in his state]: It is tempting to criticize gambling and gamblers on moral grounds—especially if you don't gamble yourself. But that would be a self-damaging strategy and one the proponents of casino gambling are hoping we will use. Rather, I would hope that people who gamble would take the time to consider thoughtfully this issue and decide to join with us. Because it's one thing to visit Las Vegas and go on a spree, and it's another thing entirely to drag Las Vegas home with you.

San Francisco Examiner & Chronicle,
10-15:(This World)35.

Red Auerbach
President, Boston "Celtics"
basketball team

2

Athletes no longer have that do-or-die attitude. It used to be that hungry athletes were in the majority. That's no longer the case. There are some, but not as many. They used to play to put food on the table for themselves and their families. Now everybody plays [out their] contract in order to become a free agent. Everybody wants to be a Catfish Hunter. The drive is gone and, believe me, it's a different ballgame.

Los Angeles Herald Examiner, 2-4:(C)3.

3

[Advocating a third referee in basketball games]: Having a third official would actually cut down on the number of fouls. It's like when you're out on the highway and you spot a police car. Because you know the law is nearby, you drive differently. It's human nature. Players would react the same way to a third official and you would also be returning more finesse to the game . . . It's the veteran referee

who knows how to control the game and who can sense an explosive situation is building—and move to stop it. That third official would certainly cut down on their [the officials'] running, which should prolong their careers.

Los Angeles Herald Examiner, 3-12:(D)12.

George Bamberger
Baseball manager, Milwaukee "Brewers"

4

Times are different. The kids [players] today . . . well, you can't yell at them. When I was a kid, they yelled at me and I accepted it. Today they go into a shell if you do that and so you have to do a lot more talking to them. That's what they mean by communicating. Some [managers] can communicate and some can't.

Interview, Milwaukee/
The Dallas Times Herald, 4-23:(C)3.

Sal Bando
Baseball player, Milwaukee "Brewers"

5

[On being a designated hitter]: I've learned to enjoy it because of the rest it provides. It enables you to give 100 per cent, mentally, to hitting. I'm a firm believer in, if that's what they ask you to do, go do it 100 per cent and learn to enjoy it.

Los Angeles Times, 7-13:(3)10.

Filbert Bayi
Track metric-mile record-holder

6

. . . to say that politics is not part of sports is not being realistic. When I run, I am more than a runner. I am a diplomat, an ambassador for my country [Tanzania] . . . The name of the nation is as much a part of competition as is my own name. Win or lose, the two are inseparable.

Interview/Los Angeles Times, 1-7:(3)1.

Johnny Bench
Baseball player, Cincinnati "Reds"

7

[On being a 30-year-old player]: I want to win, but there's the grind. There's so much responsibility for a catcher. I have to contribute on offense and work with the pitching, too. I've got a fine contract. I should play for five more

WHAT THEY SAID IN 1978

years. But then I ask myself if that's what I really want. My arm feels good. My legs will be all right. How long will I go on? How long can I go on? How long do I want to go on playing baseball? Is this what it's like to be 30?

Interview, Tampa, Fla./
The New York Times, 3-27:(C)5.

Bob Berry
Hockey coach, Los Angeles "Kings"

1

My coaching philosophy won't fill a book. Mainly, it's to be prepared for anything. There has to be discipline ... I believe in discipline and strong defense ... What I mean by good defense is not only having good defensemen. It means all six playing good defense at the same time ... We are a group ... A team ... But each player is an individual ... If a player needs a pat on the back, I'll be there to give it to him. I believe in pats on the back.

Interview/Los Angeles Times, 9-14:(3)3.

Paul Blair
Baseball player, New York "Yankees"

2

A mystique of history and heritage surrounds the New York *Yankees*. It's like the old days revived. We're loved and hated, but always in larger doses than any other team. We're the only team in any sport whose name and uniform and insignia are synonymous with their entire sport all over the world. When you're with another team, you have to accept it; but the *Yankees* mean baseball to more people than all the other teams combined. Heck, we draw standing-room-only in spring training.

Boston, June 21/The Washington Post, 6-22:(D)1.

Bob Briner
Executive director, Association of
Tennis Professionals

3

The sociology of international tennis is incredible. We are dealing with Arabs and Jews, South Africans and Eastern Europeans. We actually have Eastern Europeans who are closet members of the ATP, who have had to join

clandestinely. Tennis players are among the most apolitical of athletes. They may be patriotic, but politics seldom cross their minds. Tom Okker, perhaps the top Jewish player in the world, and Ismael el-Shafei of Egypt, have the same attorney. Ray Moore of South Africa and [black American player] Arthur Ashe work together within the ATP and are close personal friends.

Los Angeles Times, 10-2:(3)2.

Lou Brock
Baseball player, St. Louis "Cardinals"

4

I'd like to prove that age is a calendar coincidence and not a calamity. After all, I was 35 years old when I stole 118 bases in 153 games. You get older, you lose a few steps. So what do you do? It's still 90 feet from first base to second, but you don't have to race the clock to get there. It's me against three other guys: the pitcher, the catcher and the man making the tag. And the element of risk, the initiative, is still mine. I still have the advantage of the element of surprise. I'm the one who puts the sequence in motion, and I compensate for being slower by being smarter.

Interview, St. Petersburg, Fla./
Los Angeles Herald Examiner, 3-12:(D)2.

Paul Brown
General manager, Cincinnati "Bengals"
football team

5

[Criticizing bump-and-run defense, in which pass receivers can be knocked around before the ball is thrown]: There was nothing in the original intent of football to defend against pass offense by bumping receivers. It isn't just the decline in points that worries me. It's the decline in big plays. Because of the bump, you don't see many long passes any more. The receivers are held up so long the passer can't wait for them to come open. And to me, big plays—including big pass plays—are an integral part of the game.

At National Football League convention,
Palm Springs, Calif./Los Angeles Times, 3-14:(3)6.

Jimmy Carter
President of the United States

1

[On whether the national anthem is downgraded by its being played before almost every sports event]: I personally don't think that frequent playing of the national anthem downplays its importance. No matter how often I hear the national anthem, I'm always stirred within myself toward more intense feelings of patriotism and a realization of what our nation stands for. And I think for audiences at sports events to hear the national anthem played is good and not contrary to the influence that the national anthem has on all of us.

News conference, Washington, Dec. 12/
The New York Times, 12-13:(A)20.

Orlando Cepeda
Baseball manager, Juncos (Puerto Rico)
"Mules"; Former major-league player

2

[Baseball manager] Alvin Dark is a baseball genius, but he can't communicate with his players. That's why he gets fired every time. But [manager] Billy Martin—he feels like a ballplayer himself. That's why he's such a good manager. So many managers forget they were players themselves. To respect your ballplayers is the main thing. The problem of managing is human relations.

Interview, El Mango, Puerto Rico/
Los Angeles Times, 4-9:(3)14.

Wilt Chamberlain
Former basketball player

3

The players just don't have any respect for each other nowadays. How can guys go around sucker-punching other guys? I'll tell you why. Because they don't give a damn about each other. I think it all starts from the top. There aren't owners around today like when I started out in 1959. There aren't any Eddie Gottliebs or Danny Biasones, owners who really cared about the players and about each other. The owners now don't have any respect for the players or for each other. Everyone is trying to cut everyone else's throats. There's no camaraderie any longer. I bet if you gave a couple of owners a chance to take a punch at [owner] Jack Kent Cooke, they'd do it.

Interview, Los Angeles/
Los Angeles Herald Examiner, 1-4:(D)2.

Jimmy Connors
Tennis player

4

I was pretty young when I started doing well in tennis; and I was a little immature, and maybe I got branded early with a bad image. It's tough to change that. And the public only sees one side of me. I'm a different person on the tennis court, no doubt about it. The style I play, the things I do, the way I try for every ball and fly through the air and all that stuff—let's face it, I'm an animal. I give everything I've got every time I go out there, and I'm proud of that.

Interview/The Washington Post, 1-31:(D)5.

Howard Cosell
Sports commentator, American
Broadcasting Company

5

There are two professions that one can be hired at with little experience. One is prostitution. The other is sportscasting. Too frequently, they become the same.

Los Angeles Times, 11-6:(3)2.

Al Davis
General manager, Oakland "Raiders"
football team

6

Fear of losing has become the dominant philosophy in the [National Football] League. And no rules change is going to change a coach's basic approach. Take any walk of life—most people are just trying not to lose. It's become part of our culture.

San Francisco Examiner & Chronicle,
3-26:(This World)2.

Jack Dempsey
Former heavyweight boxing champion of
the world

7

[On the large amounts of money fighters make today]: A couple of top fighters may

WHAT THEY SAID IN 1978

make $2-million now, or whatever, but the business has suffered. If they offered it to me? I'd have to go for it, I guess. But it'll kill boxing.

Interview, New York/
The New York Times, 2-23:(D)15.

Dan Devine
Football coach, University of Notre Dame

1

[On the recruiting of college player-students]: The thing that bothers you and is kind of frustrating to any coach is that when the youngster comes in to visit and you talk with him and he's all goggle-eyed and excited and sold on Notre Dame, and then you visit him three months later after all this fussing, and now his sense of values has been distorted. And we, as coaches, did it to him. We're creating monsters out of some good kids. You used to be able to buy him a dinner and he appreciated a 10-ounce steak and he had never had a shrimp cocktail. Then, three months later, when you took him out he ordered two shrimp cocktails and a 16-ounce steak. Now, these kids come in with a distorted sense of values and they find out on the first day of classes that they aren't so cool after all. Their assignment isn't to read 10 pages but to read an entire book. You have to spoil them to get them and then unspoil them once they are yours.

Interview, South Bend, Ind./
The Washington Post, 11-3:(D)5.

Harry Edwards
Professor of sociology,
University of California

2

Football is the sport of the historical moment. It's the most violent collision sport that really involves strategy, speed and aggressiveness. The Super Bowl is the ultimate conclusion. They hard-sell you on it from July to January, and it's like plugging into the red, white and blue. It's a corporate blueprint for American society. Coming when it does, at the beginning of the new year, it's the ultimate religious spectacle.

The New York Times, 1-9:(C)12.

Julius Erving
Basketball player, Philadelphia "76ers"

3

When people tell me fans are cheated because they came to see me do this or that, I tell them that supposedly they are coming to see their team win. The role of a player should be results first, effects second. And that's a whole philosophy, too. I don't go in to dunk the ball or dribble behind my back for the effect of doing it. Those are skills that were developed in the course of trying to reach my potential as a player. My methods have created a reputation for myself because it has a certain effect on people watching the game. If they like it and they dig it—hey, that's cool. It's helped my market value to become a tremendous thing. But if they don't like me shooting a layup instead of dunking the ball, I realize they might boo—but that's not going to stop me from functioning.

Interview/The New York Times, 4-23:(5)5.

Chris Evert
Tennis player

4

Sometimes I look at myself and I wonder why I'm in the position I'm in. They talk about a "killer instinct." I've never looked across the court and hated my opponent. I love the feeling of winning and accomplishing something. But in terms of passion and killer instinct, I'm not up there with Billie Jean [King] or with Jimmy [Connors]. I'm more consistent, and maybe my consistency makes up for their flashes.

Interview/Los Angeles Times, 6-18:(3)5.

Ron Fairly
Baseball player, California "Angels"

5

When you earn the kind of money we [players] earn, doing what we do, how can baseball give you a mental problem? All my life, I've liked nothing better than playing baseball. In what other way could you make money having as much fun? So baseball doesn't give you mental problems. What happens is, we all have mental problems that we bring to the park. And when we do, our concentration is diluted and we get the feeling that the game is wearing us

(RON FAIRLY)

down. But the truth is, when 30,000 people are in the stands, we are doing what all 30,000 would love to be doing if they had the chance.

Los Angeles Herald Examiner, 1-12:(C)2.

1

[Saying pinch-hitters and designated hitters should be able to play until age 46 or 48]: What's to get tired from? This isn't like football or basketball. Even if you play 100 games in the outfield, you handle only six or eight balls a game. What can wear you out? It's hard to get physically tired in baseball, unless you pitch or catch. You only get mentally tired . . . Many of us couldn't run when we were 21. So guys like us pinch-hit and get on base—and they send in a rabbit to run for us.

TV Guide, 5-27:34.

2

When I started playing the game of baseball, it was survival. If you didn't play, and play well, you didn't go to another organization, you went to the minors. Now, if you don't play here, you'll play someplace else in the majors. There are 10 more teams, 250 more jobs. It's probably easier to get into the majors than at any other time. A lot of young players here really don't know that much about baseball. It amazes you how little some players know. They do things, but they don't know why they do them. It's not survival, like it used to be. You used to hate the other organization. You wouldn't even talk to the sonsabitches. If you walked by a guy at the batting cage and he said hi, you wouldn't even say hi back. Now everybody is friendly with everyone.

Interview/Los Angeles Times, 7-12:(3)10.

Rollie Fingers
Baseball pitcher, San Diego "Padres"

3

[A] big part of relief pitching is confidence. If you don't have it, you're not going to get many people out. Whenever we're in a jam, I always hope the call is for me when the telephone rings in the bullpen. I've also discovered that the learning process connected with pitching in the big leagues never stops.

Interview, San Diego/
The Christian Science Monitor, 8-1:18.

Charles O. Finley
Owner, Oakland "Athletics"
baseball club

4

[On baseball commissioner Bowie Kuhn]: The man is literally driving me out of baseball financially. I've been in it for 18 years and I'd love to stay in the game. But by not allowing me to sell [pitcher] Vida Blue, he's depriving me of keeping my ship afloat. I'd stand on top of the Sears Tower—the largest building in the world—waving a sign: "Fire Bowie!"

Chicago, Feb. 22/The Washington Post, 2-23:(D)3.

5

The defense [in baseball] is overshadowing the offense. And it's beginning to be felt. In football, 11 players go against 11. In basketball, 5 go against 5. And in hockey, 6 go against 6. But in baseball, 9 go against one. There's no balance to the game. There's too much pitcher . . . As I've told them before, the solution is the three-ball walk. It would boost attendance 20 per cent in the first year. I don't know why the game won't change. It changed before. In 1886, it was nine balls for a walk, five strikes for a strikeout.

Interview/Los Angeles Herald Examiner, 4-10:(D)2.

6

[On the current top performance by his club, which is made up mostly of unknown players who do not receive the ultra-high salaries of players at other clubs]: If some owners in baseball wish to go out and pay two, three, four, five, six hundred thousand a year for a player, that's their prerogative. But I'd certainly like to prove to them that it can be done the hard way. The way . . . we did it winning five straight divisions and three world championships. With hard work and blood and sacrifice. Finley's going to try to keep his ship afloat his way. I don't know how long it's going to last, but we're sure as hell going to try.

Interview, Chicago/
Los Angeles Times, 5-16:(3)1.

457

WHAT THEY SAID IN 1978

Jim Fregosi
Baseball manager, California "Angels"

1

I like to think that I'm close to my players, but I think they know that I'm the boss and I'm going to do whatever it takes to win a ballgame. Sometimes you have to hurt players' feelings because a lot of time players don't know what's best for them and the team, because every player in the big leagues has a great deal of pride in himself, and to be a good player you have to have that pride. Now, what I try to do is keep the player with pride in himself and magnify that pride in the team. I think if you get that feeling, the players go about the game with a winning attitude.

Interview/Los Angeles Herald Examiner, 7-19:(A)11.

Roman Gabriel
Football player, Los Angeles "Rams"

2

Since (*Rams* coach] George [Allen] started playing guys in their middle 30s, a lot of smart teams in every league are doing it. In baseball, Willie McCovey and several others are 39 or 40. There's a 50-year-old hockey player out there someplace. Pro football players today go on and on. It used to be that the cutoff age was around 30. Just when a lot of guys were just hitting their stride, their coaches thought they ought to retire. George has proved that life begins at 30 in sports.

Interview/The Dallas Times Herald, 4-23:(C)7.

Joe Garagiola
Sports commentator, National Broadcasting Company

3

[Saying you need perseverence to root for the Chicago *Cubs* baseball club] : One thing you learn as a *Cubs* fan: When you bought your ticket, you could bank on seeing the bottom of the ninth.

The Christian Science Monitor, 10-10:26.

E. J. (Jake) Garn
United States Senator, R-Utah

4

I've always felt that the Olympics should reflect the ideals of brotherhood and true competition. In view of the dissident trials and indications that the Soviets intend to bar certain nations and news organizations from the Games, I don't think Moscow is an appropriate site for the Olympics . . . It appears that there is little hope that the 1980 Olympics would be free from political discrimination and harassment by the Soviet government. It's an honor for any nation to host the Games, and the Soviets have shown that they do not deserve that honor.

/**

Tom Harmon
Sportscaster; Former football player, University of Michigan

5

[On his 1940 win of the Heisman Trophy] : Nothing can touch it. Its critics can't cut it down. It stands apart from all the rest as the single outstanding award in sports, and those of us who have won it are set apart as heroes beyond anything we ever dreamed possible. No other group has given greater performances. No other award could mean more to an athlete.

Los Angeles Times, 11-16:(3)3.

Elvin Hayes
Basketball player, Washington "Bullets"

6

Athletes are nothing but shy, spoiled babies—and I am one of them. Athletes do things to make people think they're really tough. We're really kids. There are so many similarities. You look at a baby and an athlete . . . take something away and they both pout . . . I think most girls like athletes because athletes are like babies; they need to be reassured. An athlete will give his life to hear "Way to go." That's why it's hard to leave sports.

Interview/Los Angeles Times, 6-8:(3)2.

Billy Herman
Former baseball second-baseman and member, Baseball Hall of Fame

7

A lot of good infielders who can play first, shortstop and third can't play second, and that's because it's an awkward position. Half

(BILLY HERMAN)

your throws are behind you. You have to throw sideways and backhanded instead of overhand. You have to throw with runners coming at you from behind. You have to be a little unorthodox.

Los Angeles Times, 6-20:(3)2.

Whitey Herzog
Baseball manager, Kansas City "Royals"

1

The rules are changed now. There's not any way to build a team today. It's just how much money you want to spend. You could be the world champions, and somebody else makes a key acquisition or two and you're through.

Interview, Clearwater, Fla./
The Christian Science Monitor, 3-20:40.

Lou Holtz
Football coach, University of Arkansas

2

The man who complains about the way the ball bounces is likely the one who dropped it.

Los Angeles Times, 12-13:(3)2.

3

A lifetime contract for a coach means if you're ahead in the third quarter and moving the ball, they can't fire you.

The New York Times, 12-17:(5)13.

Reggie Jackson
Baseball player, New York "Yankees"

4

It's been very difficult for me here in the east. On the west coast I'm projected as a hell of a nice guy. They give a lot of background on my situation, how I stick up for people and how I contribute to orphanages and do things for under-privileged people. But, on the east coast, it's "Reggie Jackson with the $3-million; he's unhappy, he complains"—things of that nature ... I'm projected as something that's horrible, and it's very, very uncomfortable. I try to give of myself and do things for people, and to be spit at and thrown at and cursed at is a very uncomfortable thing. ... it's hard to play when somebody says you're no good or

somebody says you can't do this or you can't do that or you're a lousy person or you're greedy or egotistical. Those things are tough and unfair. I'm human. I've played my butt off for 10 years. I'm not a loafer. I'm not a jerk. I'm a baseball player. That's what I want to do. I don't want to get famous. If I deserve it with my bat, give me credit. If I don't, leave me be.

Interview, New York/
The Dallas Times Herald, 8-27:(C)3.

Bruce Jenner
Olympic decathlon champion

5

What does a fellow compete for, anyway? A gold medal? No; 95 per cent of it is fulfillment. I've interviewed a lot of players going into the Super Bowl. "If you win," you say to him, "it's a $15,000 bonus." They don't care about that. The money is nothing. They're football players; they want to win. The decathlon was a constant challenge. If I ran 100 meters in 11.2, I felt sure I could do it in 11.1. If I broadjumped 21 feet, I was positive I could do 22.

Interview, New York/
The New York Times, 6-20:(B)14.

Darrell Johnson
Baseball manager, Seattle "Mariners"

6

Probably the biggest thing a manager has to learn with young pitchers is patience. You can't rush them and you can't do it for them. It's also better in the long run if you don't yank them at the first sign of trouble. Otherwise, they never learn what it takes to work themselves out of a jam, and often you mess up their confidence. Oh, if a kid obviously hasn't got it on a particular day and is getting pounded, I'm going to my bullpen. He's also going to come out if he gets into trouble late in a game in which we're leading. At that point, I want somebody in there who can get us the win. But in most situations with men on base, my young pitchers are going to get the chance to help themselves.

Interview, Tempe, Ariz./
The Christian Science Monitor, 3-27:19.

WHAT THEY SAID IN 1978

Al Kaline
Former baseball player, Detroit "Tigers"

1

I'm worried about the game. I'll tell you what's really going to hurt baseball in the long run: all the money that is being paid out in front [to players]. Five or six or 10 years down the road, some of these teams will be in hock for eight, 10 and 12 million dollars to players who may not even be on the field, and the teams still have to pay off the salaries. I'm worried about teams going under. There are a lot of teams that are very, very close to that now ... The players are jumping from one team to another so fast that the fans don't really have a chance to associate with an individual today. A kid growing up may not be able to have an idol any more. To be very honest with you, I have to look at a scorecard now just to see who is playing with what team. It's as if all of a sudden the dollar has taken over the loyalty of players to teams. I'm talking about teams that have been good to you over the years ... The teams that are winning are going to keep getting more and more players for more and more money and, consequently, will always be winners unless the present system is drastically changed. The teams that are losing are never going to be able to catch up.

Interview, Los Angeles/
San Francisco Examiner & Chronicle, 12-10:(C)5.

Billie Jean King
Tennis player

2

I like [to play]. I don't have to; I never did. Nobody makes you play. *You* make you play. I think it's mostly, for me, a striving for perfection. People think of me as being real competitive, but I think I'm more of a perfectionist. I still relate it to being as perfect as possible. There's probably only two or three times a year when you hit a shot and you say, "Wow—all those years—all right!" That one shot when everything was right, from your head to your fingers.

Interview, New York/
The New York Times, 1-9:(C)3.

3

I remember when there was no women's pro tour, when the Wimbledon final didn't get as much publicity as our first-round matches will this week. And that was just 10 years ago. It's a downright luxury to play tennis in times like these. We've waited years to have depth and balance in our fields, and I'm certainly not going to complain now because the good, young players beat me once in a while.

Interview/Los Angeles Times, 1-10:(3)4.

Bowie Kuhn
Commissioner of Baseball

4

I am not very happy when I see stars like Luis Tiant and Tommy John signed by the world champion New York *Yankees.* The *Yankees* are fully within their legal rights, but this trend fulfills a prophecy some of us made that the star free agents would tend to sign with the best teams. It's inevitable that this process will lead to a group of elite teams controlling the sport. Already, five teams have signed 53 per cent of the free agents during the first three years of the new system.

At baseball business convention, Orlando, Fla.,
Dec. 4/The New York Times, 12-5:(B)15.

Tom Lasorda
Baseball manager, Los Angeles "Dodgers"

5

It's been said you shouldn't hug your players. I've been reading the rule book for years and I have yet to find a clause that reads you can't hug your players. It also has been said that a manager shouldn't eat with his players, or go visit them in their homes. I do both. We are told, too, to be sparing in our praise so that the players will feel we're sincere. I praise everyone. Like my pop said, show me a law in the United States that says I can't tell everyone he's great.

Interview, Vero Beach, Fla./
Los Angeles Herald Examiner, 3-2:(D)2.

(TOM LASORDA)

1

When I took this job, they asked me if I was worried replacing a man [Walter Alston] who'd had it 23 years. I told them no; I was worried for the guy who'd have to replace *me*. I'm the greatest American optimist since General Custer. I try things they say won't work in the majors. Rah-rah stuff. Being close to my players. Hugging them. They say all players are becoming businessmen, but I managed these guys, some back at Ogden, when they were playing for $500 a month.

Interview, Vero Beach, Fla./
The New York Times, 3-20:(C)3.

2

There is nothing [a manager] can do about games that have been lost. All he can do with talk is try to control the way players react to the losses. If he can encourage them enough, he can stabilize the situation. By that, I mean he can prevent them from blaming each other, blaming the manager, blaming the ownership and throwing the situation into chaos. If a good team stays calm, it eventually will right itself.

Interview/Los Angeles Herald-Examiner, 6-15:(D)2.

Niki Lauda
Auto-racing driver

3

An accident is frightening. Together with the fear you have to begin with, the logic of the accident tells you there's something to be frightened of. But I'm staying in racing because, to me, the positive aspects outweigh the negative ... The problem after a big accident is the mental approach. Let's say I stay home three months and I'm completely fit. Then I start racing and it takes me two years to get over the problem mentally. The quicker you get back in, the better you go in the end.

Interview/Los Angeles Times, 4-1:(3)1.

Abe Lemons
Basketball coach, University of Texas

4

I don't understand why coaches think they're failures unless they win the national championship. There's only one every year, like the Heisman Trophy. They don't understand that there's a hell of a lot more to life than a basketball game.

The Dallas Times Herald, 2-24:(C)1.

5

All I do is coach and put my players on the floor. If they win, fine. If they lose, it's their fault.

The Christian Science Monitor, 5-8:27.

Skip Lockwood
Baseball pitcher, New York "Mets"

6

What makes players unhappy? Envy or jealousy? Well, maybe; but if you go through your whole life comparing yourself to other people, you're in trouble. There's always a guy with more money, a bigger car, a better house. It's gotten to be a problem now because salaries are out in the open; they're published. But once, they were private—the clubs didn't want players to know about salaries. Now guys wonder: Is Willie Montanez worth $350,000 a year to the *Mets*? Is he more valuable than Jerry Koosman. On the *Yankees*, Graig Nettles may get half what Reggie Jackson gets, though he's been there longer. A guy may feel, why should he make it when we've been working our backs off for years?

Interview, St. Petersburg, Fla./
The New York Times, 3-5:(5)5.

Davey Lopes
Baseball player, Los Angeles "Dodgers"

7

On a team that has the talent we have, I think a player's main job ... is to help keep everybody going. I'll give you an example. If a good hitter isn't hitting, he tends to get frustrated. He wants to isolate himself and brood. But that just makes things worse, and pretty soon he's doing other things wrong, too. Maybe he starts having trouble in the field. So I think a player's main responsibility—every big-league player's—is to help keep that from happening to anybody. You've got to get his mind off his troubles and on to other things ... You keep

(DAVEY LOPES)

things as loose as possible in the clubhouse. The laughing and joking we do there, the needling, the horseplay, make us look like a bunch of kids; but there's a dead-serious reason for it. We're putting away the pressures of outside life. We're dealing with the pressures of baseball. The way humans are built, they can't laugh and worry at the same time. If a few laughs have cleared the worry out of your mind before you go out to hit a baseball, you concentrate better.

Interview/Los Angeles Times, 5-9:(3)8.

Ron Luciano
Baseball umpire, American League

1

The umpires have kept this game honest for 100 years. We're the only segment of the game that has never been touched by scandal. We've got to be too dumb to cheat. We must have integrity, because we sure don't have a normal family life. We certainly aren't properly paid. We have no health care, no job security, no tenure. Our pension plan is a joke. We take more abuse than any living group of humans, and can't give back any. If we're fired without notice, our only recourse is to appeal to the league president. And he's the guy that fires you. That's got to be un-Constitutional. If you ask for one day off in a seven-month season, they try to make you feel three inches tall. If you call in sick, you're hounded and ostracized by the brass. Umpires must be the healthiest people on earth, because none of us ever gets sick.

Interview, Baltimore/
The Dallas Times Herald, 9-13:(E)1.

Lee MacPhail
President, American (baseball) League

2

In every sporting endeavor that is measurable by a clock—which baseball isn't, of course—the performances are superior with each succeeding generation. So why shouldn't baseball players be as good or better than their dads?

The Dallas Times Herald, 10-22:(B)2.

Bill Madlock
Baseball player, San Francisco "Giants"

3

A surgeon may be making less per year than I am now, but he's going to be a surgeon a heck of a lot longer than I'm going to be a baseball player. A doctor's career might span 40 years, while a baseball player is lucky to last five or 10. Too, people in radio, television and movies make more than most baseball players, and we're all in the same type of business, entertainment. Basketball players make more than baseball players. And a tennis player can make as much as $200,000 for winning just one tournament.

Interview, Phoenix, Ariz./
Los Angeles Herald Examiner, 4-2:(D)18.

Mickey Mantle
Former baseball player, New York "Yankees"

4

People talk about all the money the ballplayers make today. I don't think it's that much out of line. When I played with the *Yankees,* I made $100,000 a year the last few years, and I could buy a Cadillac for $5,000. Now the players make $300,000 a year, and a Cadillac costs $15,000. Everything is relative. Besides, ballplayers are better businessmen today.

Interview, Ft. Lauderdale, Fla./
Los Angeles Times, 2-28:(3)7.

John Mariucci
Coach, United States hockey team at world hockey championships, Prague

5

[On the poor showing of U.S. teams at past championships]: Don't blame the coach. There's nothing a coach can do for a team if he doesn't have the mules. Either you've got them or you haven't ... Everybody else puts together their teams with the best they can find. The Canadians have their pick of 200 players from the teams eliminated from the Stanley Cup. I can call on maybe 15 guys. So we wind up with college kids, amateurs, minor leaguers. I telephoned maybe 85 guys and asked them to join our team, some of them classy players.

(JOHN MARIUCCI)

Almost all of them had some excuse: The house burned down, I'm getting married, my father is sick, I'm tired. The trouble is that we've got 20 players on the United States team and each and every one of them went to college. The point is that college kids have lots of other things to think about besides hockey. For the Canadians, hockey is a way of life, just as it is for the Europeans.
Interview, Prague/The New York Times, 5-8:(C)11.

Mike Marshall
Baseball pitcher, Minnesota "Twins"

1

I feel there's something wrong with people who boo. They are negative, insecure people. My minor degree is psychology, so I know a little about this. In baseball, I see beauty and artistic, acrobatic movement. Human movement is beautiful to watch. It's a combination of ballet and chess. They should enjoy it, regardless of whether their team wins or not.
Interview, Bloomington, Minn./ Los Angeles Times, 7-2:(3)18.

Billy Martin
Baseball manager, New York "Yankees"

2

I think I control myself a lot better than people give me credit for. I'm a patient person. My temper has not been a detriment; it's been an asset. It can be a good force if you use *it* and it doesn't use *you*. I used to use it on *me* as a player. I was tougher on Billy Martin than anybody.
The New York Times, 6-5:(C)5.

3

[On his feuding with player Reggie Jackson]: I've always said I could manage Adolf Hitler, Benito Mussolini and Hirohito. That doesn't mean I'd like them, but I'd manage them.
Interview/Los Angeles Times, 8-1:(3)4.

Harvey Martin
Football player, Dallas "Cowboys"

4

Fans like roughhouse football. I like to think we're gladiators in the Roman Colosseum. Fans

don't pay to see pretty football. They want to see somebody hit. The guys who give them that are the ones they remember.
Interview/Los Angeles Times, 9-15:(3)1.

Eddie Mathews
Baseball scout, Milwaukee "Brewers";
Former player

5

The one thing I'm proudest of is that every time I played, I gave the best I had. I don't think the players today do that. And I don't think they're as happy as we were. I feel sorry for them. Every day you read about how they don't like the way the uniform fits, or their locker is too close to the shower. For the money they make, I don't think the production or attitude is there.
New York/Los Angeles Times, 1-20:(3)1.

Marshall McLuhan
Professor of English and director,
Center for Culture and Technology,
University of Toronto

6

Football itself is the biggest dramatization of American business ever invented. You have your scoreboards, your individual and team statistics, your steady gains and your emergency board meetings in your huddle. The nature of the aggressions and calculations is pure business.
The New York Times, 1-9:(C)12.

Hal McRae
Baseball player, Kansas City "Royals"

7

[On being a designated hitter]: I've been successful at it, and I'm getting to the age where it's a good thing to do. But I'd like to play some; I'd like to play [outfield] 40, 50 games a year. A lot of people say DHing will prolong your career, but I think you get old faster when you're not playing. Your career is your legs, and when you don't use them, they go faster.
Los Angeles Times, 7-13:(3)10.

WHAT THEY SAID IN 1978

Walt Michaels
Football coach, New York "Jets"

1

Statistics are like loose women. Once you get them, they let you do what you want with them.

Los Angeles Times, 12-22:(3)2.

Marvin Miller
Executive director, Major League Baseball Players Association

2

[On whether players should be able to renegotiate long-term contracts during the run of the contract] : If you're speaking legally, we all know the answer: If you have a contract, you don't have to change it. But the other aspect involves philosophy and good business sense. The peculiar nature of what happened in baseball the last two years created a two-tier structure. On one tier, you have free agents and players whose abilities are comparable—the clubs have moved their salaries up near the free-agent market level to keep them happy. On the other tier, you have players who were not raised. The club has a right not to open their contracts but, in reality, it might do so. For example, you have four top pitchers on one team and three can become free agents. To keep them, the club offers contracts several times higher than their previous ones. But the fourth pitcher still has several years to go on his contract, and he'll be earning one-third of their pay. Legally, the club doesn't have to do a thing. But if you create an inequity, you have to make a judgment. You've got a player at less than the going rate, but he's got feelings, too.

The New York Times, 3-5:(5)5.

Red Miller
Football coach, Denver "Broncos"

3

The one thing football can't be—for anybody who wants to succeed in football—is an ego trip. I ask [the players] to alter their ego a bit and think about what's good for the team. The best kind of football player is one who can tell himself, "I'm the greatest," and mean it, and at the same time be a 100 per cent team

man. When you have an athlete who has both great confidence in his own ability and a realization that he can't do it alone, you've got a football player.

Interview, New Orleans/
Los Angeles Times, 1-11:(3)8.

Doug Moe
Basketball coach, San Antonio "Spurs"

4

The problem is that the NBA has stationed its best referee in the middle of the court and assigned its other officials to areas nearer the basket where the traffic is heavier. Consequently, the weaker officials are now involved with more calls that can affect the outcome of a game than the head man. I just think the emphasis is in the wrong place.

Interview/The Christian Science Monitor, 11-1:9.

Thurman Munson
Baseball catcher, New York "Yankees"

5

What is a catcher anyway but a guy with a lot of confidence and brass who likes to run things? I'm aggressive because there is no way a man can be a top catcher and not be aggressive. It goes with the position. Basically, I have to think that every ballgame is my ballgame and that I have the right to run it. Since I play almost every game, I know opposing hitters a lot better than most pitchers. That's why I don't want anyone, including the manager, calling pitches for me from the bench.

Interview/The Christian Science Monitor,10-18:6.

Joe Namath
Former football player

6

I don't think I'll ever return to football as a coach. I think I could coach, but from what I've seen of other coaches, such as Weeb Ewbank with the *Jets* and Chuck Knox with the *Rams,* it takes up too many hours to do it right. And if I was going to do it, I'd want to do it right.

Interview, Ft. Lauderdale, Fla./
Los Angeles Herald Examiner, 1-25:(D)3.

Ilie Nastase
Tennis player

1

I do not like women linesmen because they make bad calls and because they do not belong where they are. They are useless because they can be intimidated. I yell and stare at them all the time. I tell you to look at pro football and tell me if you see any women among the officials out on the field. Of course you do not, because the football people are too smart for that and so are the baseball people. I wonder when the tennis people are going to get smart. I wonder when tennis is going to get rid of women linesmen.

Interview, Palm Springs, Calif./
The Christian Science Monitor, 3-6:25.

Graig Nettles
Baseball player, New York "Yankees"

2

I don't think there's any loyalty in baseball at all. It's become such a transient business. If you knew you were going to be with a team 10 years, then you could be loyal to a tradition. But when you know they can get rid of you tomorrow ... They've got to put a stop to some of it [free agency]. It's all right if there are a few who have bona fide gripes, like it was intended for. But when so many are just testing the market to see how much money they're worth ...

Interview, Ft. Lauderdale, Fla./
Los Angeles Times, 3-23:(3)8.

Jack Nicklaus
Golfer

3

I do not like to lose. It's as simple as that. Pride is probably my greatest motivation, because I just refuse to get beat, I can't stand to get beat, and I hate to have somebody come along and beat me. But I don't mind losing if a guy plays better than I do. I get beat a lot. That's one nice thing about golf—it's a humbling game. Golf is the only sport where, if you win 20 per cent of the time, you're the best. In other sports you must win as much as 90 per cent of the time to be the absolute best.

The New York Times, 7-23:(5)2.

Lawrence F. O'Brien
Commissioner, National Basketball Association

4

... I don't enjoy the game as commissioner nearly as much as I did before [becoming commissioner]. When I had season tickets to the *Knicks,* I'd see former commissioner Walter Kennedy sitting through a game, stony-faced and expressionless, and I'd wonder why. Now, when I go to a game, I sit there stony-faced and expressionless and think, "I wonder what's gonna come out of this game and be on my desk in the morning." I listen to the fans screaming around me about the officiating, as I used to do my own screaming. So I'd have to tell you that's the unfortunate fallout from this job. I'm not enjoying the game nearly as much as I used to ... I can go to a football game, a hockey game, a baseball game, you name it, and enjoy it. I'll have to wait until I retire from the NBA before I start enjoying professional basketball again.

Interview, New York/Flightime (Continental
Airlines magazine), December:49.

Bruce Ogilvie
Sports psychologist

5

The professional athlete is in a unique high-stress situation. His ego is on the line on every pitch. In no other area of life is one's ego before the world continuously when he goes to work each day. The salary of an athlete doesn't protect him from the public's demand for perfection. Very often, in fact, the larger the salary the larger the stress.

Los Angeles Times, 4-20:(3)10.

Amos Otis
Baseball player, Kansas City "Royals"

6

Hitting is concentration, confidence, knowing yourself and being able to take advantage of those times when the pitcher makes a mistake against you. I get on base by making good contact with the ball, but whenever I hit a home run I'm as surprised as everybody else.

Interview/The Christian Science Monitor, 10-3:18.

WHAT THEY SAID IN 1978

Danny Ozark
Baseball manager, Philadelphia
"Phillies"

1

As a manager, your chief concern going into the playoffs is to have everyone healthy. Although you never mind winning with less than your best, you certainly hate to lose that way. But I can tell you this—breaks often have a lot to do with who wins, and sometimes baseball's two best teams don't always make the World Series.

Interview/The Christian Science Monitor, 9-1:11.

Arnold Palmer
Golfer

2

You can't compare tournaments from one year to another. You can't even compare tournaments from one day to the next. The greens change every day—even during the day—and every time you change pin placements you alter the character of the hole.

Oakmont, Pa./Los Angeles Times, 8-3:(3)7

3

In my mind, I attack the course the same way I did 20 years ago, but I don't attack it physically the same way because I'm not 28 years old. I keep remembering what my father told me when I started playing golf—that 90 per cent of golf is played from the shoulders up.

Interview, Latrobe, Pa./
Los Angeles Times, 8-4:(3)12.

Jack Patera
Football coach, Seattle "Seahawks"

4

Football is basically a low-scoring game—like hockey. Suppose the *Rams* win 28-14. That sounds impressive, but what really happened is that the *Rams* won 4-2. The genius we should really be honoring this week is the guy who first realized, years ago, that six points should be awarded for one touchdown.

At National Football League convention, Palm
Springs, Calif./Los Angeles Times, 3-14:(3)6.

Joe Paterno
Football coach, Pennsylvania State
University

5

Our definition of a winner is a guy who does the best he can. Of course, we work hard to win every game. Winning is the most fun, but it isn't everything. It isn't life or death. The main thing is the *effort* to be great—the striving to achieve.

Interview, State College, Pa./
Los Angeles Times, 11-3:(3)10.

Gaylord Perry
Baseball pitcher, San Diego "Padres"

6

. . . on certain days everything works, and on other days nothing works. But most of the time you're going to get one or two pitches that you can make work, so it's a good idea to be able to throw several kinds of pitches well. Over the years, I have learned not to fool around with a pitch if it isn't doing what I want it to do. I immediately switch to something else and, if it works, I stay with it. I probably pitch as much with my body as I do with my arm, and that makes things a lot easier for me physically. The trouble with baseball is that it is not played the year 'round. In order to make a living, the poor guys like myself have to go back and work on the farm in the wintertime to make ends meet. I mean, all that farming can tire a man.

Interview, San Diego/
The Christian Science Monitor, 9-28:12.

Richard Petty
Auto-racing driver

7

If you never drove a 500-mile race, especially in really hot weather, you can't appreciate how punishing racing can be. It's like being cooped up in a blast furnace. You're in that car for four or five hours at 140 to 150 degrees, and there's nobody to help out.

The Christian Science Monitor, 8-10:16.

Gary Player
Golfer

8

If you took a man like [boxer] Muhammad Ali and put him in Timbuktu or Atlanta or on

(GARY PLAYER)

the moon, he's still going to be a great boxer. And I feel that if a man is going to be a great golfer, he's got to be able to play under all types of conditions. It helps you to play under all kinds of conditions, in front of different kinds of people. It improves your golf and it teaches you to accept adversity.

New Orleans, April 26/
The New York Times, 4-27:69.

George Plimpton
Author

1

There's sort of a universal wish among us all to be the great American sports hero. Thurber once said that 95 per cent of the male population puts themselves to sleep striking out the lineup of the New York *Yankees*. It's the great daydream, an idea that you never quite give up. Always, somewhere in the back of your mind, you believe that [baseball-great manager] Casey Stengel will give you a call.

Interview, Dallas/
The Dallas Times Herald, 12-15:(Sportsweek)2.

Richie Powers
Referee, National Basketball
Association

2

[Arguing against the NBA rule outlawing the zone defense]: I've been fighting against this rule over the years because it's difficult to enforce and it's easily circumvented by coaches when they choose. Let the referees go back to what is normal—calling fouls and violations and out-of-bounds. But the [NBA] rules committee and the board of governors feel that this [the zone] is like a cancer, and if they ever let it into the league it would destroy professional basketball. That rule [banning the zone] has become untenable because of the way the game has progressed. The reason they outlawed the zone defense was because it slowed down the offense. They put the rule in to speed up the game, but the 24-second clock takes care of that. It [the zone] adds a dimension to the game and makes the coach coach ... I think it

makes it more intriguing for a team to come down and concentrate on what defense a team might be throwing at it at a certain time, instead of all the time badgering and baiting and castigating a referee. I think it's an idea whose time has come.

Interview/Los Angeles Herald Examiner, 3-7:(D)5.

Homer Rice
Football coach, Cincinnati "Bengals"

3

You can motivate [players] by fear. And you can motivate by reward. But both of those methods are only temporary. The only lasting thing is self-motivation. You have to have it within yourself.

The Washington Post, 10-29:(D)5.

Mickey Rivers
Baseball player, New York "Yankees"

4

Basically, the only difference between me and most leadoff hitters is that I always go up there intending to swing. I walked only 18 times last year in more than 550 at-bats, so you know I'm not looking for the base-on-balls ... I can't tell you why one man hits better under pressure than another, because I don't think you can reduce hitting to a formula. But I can tell you this: The best hitters do their thinking before they get to the plate. After that, they hit by reading; and they don't just make contact, they drive the ball.

Interview, Anaheim, Calif./
The Christian Science Monitor, 7-5:13.

Frank Robinson
Baseball player, Baltimore "Orioles";
Former manager and player,
Cleveland "Indians"

5

[On his recent experience as both manager and player]: As a manager, I found that I had to be much more patient than as a player. As a player I was only responsible for myself, but as a manager I was responsible for 25 others. Managing and playing at the same time is tough, but it can be done. Every time I'd go up to hit, I felt as if the players were saying, "Now let's

467

WHAT THEY SAID IN 1978

(FRANK ROBINSON)

see what he can do," and actually I think that helped me. When I'd get a hit, I could sense them saying to themselves, "Wow, he did it, and if he can do it, why can't we?" In that sense, I think it helped.

Interview, Miami/Los Angeles Times, 3-5:(3)10.

1

[On close final scores]: Close doesn't count in baseball. Close only counts in horseshoes and grenades.

Time, 7-31:73.

Pepper Rodgers
Football coach, Georgia Institute of Technology

2

Winning's fun, but coaching's no fun because it's not really a game. It's a business.

San Francisco Examiner & Chronicle, 9-10:(C)1.

Art Rooney
Owner, Pittsburgh "Steelers" football team

3

[On less prosperous days as a team owner]: The biggest thrill wasn't winning on Sunday, but meeting the payroll on Monday.

Los Angeles Times, 11-6:(3)2.

Pete Rose
Baseball player, Cincinnati "Reds"

4

I got 3,000 hits in 15 years, one month and one week, and that's the fastest anybody ever got so many hits. And I'm not over the hill at 37. I've never been a fast runner or good thrower, but my legs and arms are my strongest things. I'm strange.

The New York Times, 7-30:(5)9.

5

I don't think any player ever gets tired when he's hitting [well]. The ball looks bigger than usual and the fielders seem spaced way out. When you're *not* hitting, the ball looks smaller and it seems like even the umpires have gloves and you can't find a hole.

Interview, Cincinnati/Los Angeles Times, 8-11:(3)1.

Pete Rozelle
Commissioner, National Football League

6

[On the increase in low-scoring games]: I think it's important that, after careful thought, we made some [rules] changes this year to help the offense. The basic problem is that the bigger, faster men playing defense these days have in effect created a smaller field than we used to have.

At National Football League convention, Palm Springs, Calif./
Los Angeles Times, 3-14:(3)6.

7

[On injuries to quarterbacks]: We thought recent changes liberalizing the rules about holding and preventing bumps of receivers going beyond five yards of the line of scrimmage would help the quarterbacks, and they have. Still, we have had a number of quarterbacks injured. There has been talk about padding the outside of helmets. That is a simplistic answer that is not valid. As an example, it has been said that a soft outer padding would reduce injuries from blows by helmets. Experimentation has shown the opposite. It creates a friction, so that a blow which otherwise might glance off a smooth helmet does not with outer padding. And the wearer of the padded helmet would receive more serious neck and spine injuries.

The Washington Post, 10-17:(D)6.

Sam Rutigliano
Football coach, Cleveland "Browns"

8

[On extra-close losses]: It's like a heart attack. You can survive them, but there is always scar tissue.

San Francisco Examiner & Chronicle, 11-26:(C)1.

Leo J. Ryan
United States Representative, D-California

9

Nothing that commands world-wide attention, as the Olympics does, is unpolitical. The mere fact that our own youngsters—the finest we have—are there is political, because the rest

(LEO J. RYAN)

of the world forms an opinion from seeing them. That's political—and terribly important to me. Like every country, large or small, we seek to influence world public opinion. We want the world to think well of us. And God knows we spend enough time and effort and money and everything else in other areas of government doing the same thing. I think it's important to do at the Olympics, too. Our own youngsters are our own best ambassadors and advertisement.

Interview/U.S. News & World Report, 8-28:33.

Tex Schramm
President, Dallas "Cowboys"
football team

1

[On the increase in low-scoring games]: Maybe it's just the weaker teams that aren't scoring. Maybe there are fewer imaginative coaches than there used to be. You can't take a figure like average points scored and say it proves anything. You can't correlate points and excitement. A football game played with great skill isn't necessarily dull—regardless of the amount of scoring. The fan watches both sides of the line of scrimmage. He likes to see defensive specialists. I haven't had one letter this year complaining about low-scoring offenses.

At National Football League convention,
Palm Springs, Calif./
Los Angeles Times, 3-14:(3)6.

2

In football, intangibles like communication, team spirit and togetherness are everything. But in baseball they don't appear to mean that much. It has always seemed to me that baseball is a team sport made up of individual performances. The success of the Oakland *A's* a few years back and the *Yankees* last year seemed to indicate you don't need togetherness and communication to win baseball games. I've never heard [*A's* manager] Dick Williams described as a great communicator. Who does [*Yankee* manager] Billy Martin communicate with? If you have the talent in baseball, it evidently doesn't matter if they like each other.

Los Angeles Times, 4-20:(3)10.

...the [college] draft is working better than ever these days... Speaking broadly and generally, I think two main forces have been at work. First, more NFL clubs are being run by good football men—trained professionals—than ever before. Second, the draft is being held in late April or May now, instead of February. With a later draft there is more time to grade the available college players accurately. And nobody runs any business better than a professional.

Interview/Los Angeles Times, 12-15:(3)10.

Tom Seaver
Baseball pitcher, Cincinnati "Reds"

4

Pitching is part mental and part physical, but I don't think most people have any idea about the relationship between the two. All most of them see out on the mound is a man looking down at his catcher and then throwing the ball. But a pitcher's body is so important to him that he should never abuse it. I've always worked hard to stay in shape between seasons and between starts. If it's meant running extra laps to build up my legs or not eating something fattening or not going somewhere because my sleep was more important, then I've always done what's best for my body.

Interview, Los Angeles/
The Christian Science Monitor, 4-26:11.

Don Shula
Football coach, Miami "Dolphins"

5

If it comes to where the richest [sports] clubs can buy up the top talent, like, say, the *Yankees* in baseball, what's the satisfaction of having a bunch of superstars thrown in your lap and winning with them?

The Christian Science Monitor, 10-6:15.

Reggie Smith
Baseball player, Los Angeles "Dodgers"

6

When I think of the $100,000 ballplayer, I think in terms of Willie Mays, Mickey Mantle, Sandy Koufax, Bob Gibson and Don Drysdale.

WHAT THEY SAID IN 1978

(REGGIE SMITH)

I also think of Joe Morgan. These people did it all. They had to work up slowly to that $100,000 figure, the symbol of a very special ballplayer. But look around the two leagues today and see who is rolling in superstar money. They got there not for performance, but because of lucky timing. Salaries used to set the great players apart from the others. But they don't any more.... too many players today, both white and black, have climbed the salary scale so fast that they cheapen the art of playing baseball. They aren't far enough advanced as players to warrant the pay they get.

Interview, Vero Beach, Fla./
Los Angeles Herald-Examiner, 3-13:(D)2.

George Steinbrenner
Owner, New York "Yankees"
baseball club

1

I'm not against superstars getting super contracts. Not as long as some rock-music guy makes $200,000 for going on the stage and babbling for thirty minutes, and me paying $25 for a ticket so my kid can go. If I'm dumb enough to pay it and the kid is dumb enough to go see it, more power to him. But some guys [in baseball] are getting super salaries when they're just good players, not super. We're going to have to get on that.

At Associated Press sports editors meeting,
Dallas/The Dallas Times Herald, 6-1:(F)1.

2

[On his club's poor performance this season despite winning the World Series last year]: The mark of a champion is not winning the championship; it's how you defend the championship. We're playing awful.

July 12/The New York Times, 7-13:(B)5.

Don Sutton
Baseball pitcher, Los Angeles "Dodgers"

3

Whenever I pitch during the regular season, it's work. To me it's a routine thing, like going

to the office or walking into a factory. You have a job to do and you go out and try to do it. But the playoffs, the World Series and things like the All-Star game are just plain fun. Let me put it this way: Suppose you were an actor and made a regular appearance every day in a TV soap opera. Of course you'd enjoy it, but after a while it would become routine. Then suppose somebody in the television producing business comes to you and says: "Hey, we'd like you to host a two-hour special for us in prime time and we also want you to be the featured performer." Now, that I could get excited about if I were an actor; and that's exactly the way I feel when I'm asked to start a playoff of a World Series game.

Interview/Los Angeles Times, 10-6:(8)5,8.

Barry Switzer
Football coach, University of
Oklahoma

4

I've always said that if I had my way, I'd like to be undefeated and unimpressive.

San Francisco Examiner & Chronicle, 10-22:(C)1.

Billy Talbert
Former Davis Cup captain

5

[On why many of today's tennis players behave badly]: It's the modern generation. The money. The pressure ... What tennis needs is strong administration. It is being allowed to run amok with no governing hand. Tennis needs a czar.

The New York Times, 3-5:(5)7.

Fran Tarkenton
Football player, Minnesota "Vikings"

6

You show me a quarterback, and I'll show you a critic of that quarterback. You show me anybody who has done something in this world, and I'll show you a critic of that person. The best way not to be criticized is to go in a closet and never come out. I don't like to be criticized. I'd like for everybody to love me and respect me and I think I'm a great player, but that's not quite possible ... People are always

(FRAN TARKENTON)

taking shots at you. They second-guess you. One week they call you the greatest and the next week some jerk says you're not what you used to be or you can't play any more or you can't run or you never could run or never could throw. I think that's the biggest enemy of a quarterback . . . the extreme highs and lows of how you are appraised.

Interview, Tucson, Ariz./
Los Angeles Times, 12-29:(3)1.

Jack Tatum
Football player, Oakland "Raiders"

1

Ever since I started playing football—eighth or ninth grades—they [the coaches] always told me, "Hit 'em hard, punish 'em." It's the way it's taught. A lot of guys we have to run into, like tight ends, outweigh us by 30-40 pounds. You have to be tough. I'm not trying to hurt people in a game. I'm just trying to take away their confidence . . . That's what it comes down to. You have to beat your opponent both physically and mentally. Not everyone is going to take that kind of punishment for four quarters.

Interview, Cincinnati, Ohio/
Los Angeles Times, 11-18:(3)1.

Joe Torre
Baseball manager, New York "Mets"

2

I was one of the architects of the free-agent system. But, frankly, I did not foresee all this conflict over renegotiating contracts. I felt every player should have his day—this one shot at being a free agent. Since then, the loyalty factor is not as great as it was. Guys change uniforms all the time now. I feel a player who has signed a multiyear contract has a right to ask to renegotiate his contract—but only to ask. Are the players ruining baseball? I hope not. I think it's just a settling-down phase.

Interview, St. Petersburg, Fla./
The New York Times, 3-5:(5)5.

Wes Unseld
Basketball player,
Washington "Bullets"

3

I've always had this theory that winning teams consist of a lot of different people who are somehow able to blend their styles effectively. Like, each man plays a particular role, only in such a way that the team becomes greater than its parts. For example, if you've got three players who are great scorers but only one of them is exceptional on defense, I think the answer is obvious. It's the defensive player who makes the adjustment for the good of the team. There is just no other logical way to go.

Interview, Los Angeles/
The Christian Science Monitor, 1-30:22.

Al Unser
Auto-racing driver

4

In our business, reflexes have to be sharp. We're running 220 miles per hour on the straights. The experience thing comes into it later on. You become trackwise after years of racing. The more you see, the better you become. You're better equipped to make the right decision at the right time. You have to know the difference between what's going to bite you and what isn't. We all get bit once in a while. We all crash and all have accidents. As for when to retire, that's a hard question to answer. How much desire a driver has can be important. When I'm not competitive, though, I'll know inside myself when it's time to quit. And I won't like it.

Interview/Los Angeles Times, 1-18:(3)10.

Rogie Vachon
Hockey player, Los Angeles "Kings"

5

[On the reported $600,000-per-season contract offered him by the New York *Rangers*]: Right now I'm rated among the top two goaltenders in the National Hockey League, along with Ken Dryden, and I feel I have to be paid as one of the top two goaltenders. Look at what baseball players are signing for now. Some free agents are signing for $2-million and $2.5-

(ROGIE VACHON)

million. I know a contract like mine probably is going to hurt hockey in the long run and it's all going to have to stop some day, but it's not the players' fault. It's the fault of management. They're willing to give us that kind of money, and the players would be crazy not to take it. Speaking for all the players, I know we probably would play for half of what we're getting now and still be happy.

Interview/Los Angeles Times, 6-25:(3)7.

Bill Veeck
President, Chicago "White Sox"
baseball club

1

I've never argued that promotion can do much if you aren't winning. That isn't the psychology of the fan. The fans identify with the home team. When the home team wins, they feel they win, too. They get away from the galling losses of life. When the home team gets beat, they get negative identification—the same rich, fulfilling experience they get when they're three months late with payments to the Friendly Finance Company. What I do say is promotion, plus a winning team, breaks attendance records. So I have fireworks and special nights, and any fan who calls the office can get me. I answer my own phone. But first I need a team that plays competitively.

Interview, Sarasota, Fla./
The New York Times, 4-3:(C)3.

El Viti
Spanish matador

2

[On his profession]: I was born and grew up in the country. I like animals; I like bulls. I respect them. I like to measure myself against them, to know everything about myself through them—my soul, my courage, my fear. The bull as a mirror pleases me above everything else ... I do not believe the bullfight will disappear. It is very closely linked to our heritage. Furthermore, it creates emotions and passions that are becoming more and more rare in modern society. The bullfight speaks to what is

instinctive in us. It is one of our cultural assets. I hope we will never lose it.

Atlas World Press Review, October:63.

Darrell Waltrip
Auto-racing driver

3

Getting older in racing is definitely a virtue. The older you get, the longer you're in it and the more you realize what it takes to win. You see guys 42, 45 years old racing and winning. I think my generation is going to be more alert, live longer than the generations past. So you feasibly could have a race driver reach retirement age, 65, and still running strong.

Interview/Los Angeles Times, 1-18:(3)10.

Earl Weaver
Baseball manager, Baltimore "Orioles"

4

There is only one legitimate trick to pinch-hitting, and that's knowing the pitcher's best pitch when the count is 3-and-2. All the rest is a crapshoot.

TV Guide, 5-27:34.

5

Nobody likes to hear it, because it's dull. But the reason you win or lose is darn near always the same ... pitching. You look invincible when you're winning, because pitching complements everything else. You look horsefeathers when you're going bad, because bad pitching magnifies every weakness.

Interview, Baltimore/
Los Angeles Times, 6-16:(3)1.

Jerry West
Basketball coach, Los Angeles "Lakers"

6

... some [players] now have a crutch when they aren't doing well. They say, "I've got a four-year contract and they can't cut me." I'd like to see players paid on an incentive basis based on the team's performance as well as individual performance. Then you'd have guys working hard every night, not every third night.

Interview/Los Angeles Herald Examiner, 2-22:(A)2.

(JERRY WEST)

1

A lot of players—some of them great players—simply do not seem to be able to make a crucial play for you. Most players can't cope with being failures, so when they're in a situation where they have to put their professional reputations on the line, it's easier to let someone else take the shot that will decide the game.

The Dallas Times Herald, 4-23:(C)8.

Bud Wilkinson
Football coach, St. Louis "Cardinals"

2

Football isn't overly fun to practice. Most football players never get to handle the ball—so this is a game in which winning is the enjoyment. In other sports, everyone handles the ball. Practice isn't a grind for baseball and basketball players because there's always a ball for them to hit or catch or throw in a hoop. But football is practiced in the dirt. Although football players can keep their spirits up for a while in a good organization, there comes a time down the road when, if you don't win, you lose morale. I think this might be one reason there's so much emphasis on winning in football.

The Dallas Times Herald, 9-8:(C)2.

3

Football, truly, is a team game, whereas baseball isn't. The batter either hits the ball or he doesn't; it goes into the record book that way. And if he hits it to the shortstop, he makes a perfect throw and the first baseman drops it, that's the first-baseman's error. Clearly defined. But in football, to throw the ball at all, the line has to do a good job of protecting the passer. Now the receiver is open in the end zone. If the quarterback hits him with a pass and the receiver drops the ball, that's a pass the quarterback failed to complete.

Interview/The Dallas Times Herald, 9-22:(Sportsweek)5.

Edward Bennett Williams
President, Washington "Redskins"
football team

4

I see the [team] general manager as being responsible for the signing of the players and, therefore, having a tremendous voice and effect on the financial operations of the company. I see him as the principal administrative officer of the company, next to the president. I see him as working closely with the coach in trading, drafting, in supervision of the personnel department . . . It's important to have a general manager who knows the operating heads of all teams, who knows personnel directors, who knows the player personnel of all the teams, who has a relationship with the general managers and coaches around the league, so he will have good intelligence and information—good information about problems other teams may be having, information about where there may be unrest. Where there is unrest, there is fertile ground for advantageous trading.

Interview, Washington, Jan. 23/
The Washington Post, 1-24:(D)3.

Ted Williams
Former baseball player, Boston
"Red Sox"

5

One of the silliest things I ever read is that hitters should do better late in the season because the pitchers are tired. How can pitchers be that tired, with the bullpen picking them up in more than three quarters of their games? Also, why shouldn't the hitters be just as tired? They play in a lot more games than pitchers. If a pitcher is tired in the fall, it only means that he's relieved in the fifth or sixth inning, instead of the seventh.

Interview, Phoenix/
The Christian Science Monitor, 6-12:21.

Maury Wills
Former baseball player, Los Angeles
"Dodgers"

6

The years we [the *Dodgers*] got along well, walked hand in hand, were the years the *Dodgers* did poorly. The years we won were the years we had these fights. To me, that means we cared. Everyone was emotionally involved with the pennant race. Tempers will flare when that happens. When you get so passive that nothing bothers you—whether you win or lose—that means even your own production doesn't bother you. That's bad.

Interview/Los Angeles Times, 3-27:(3)1.

WHAT THEY SAID IN 1978

Sahabzada Yaqub-Khan
*Pakistani Ambassador to the United
States*

1

After polo, every other game is uninteresting, flat and slow. Polo demands, in spite of the speed at which it is played, physical courage. Yet one has to be ice-cold in the midst of a fast-moving crisis; one must also retain serenity and coolness, to prevent the blood from rushing to your head.

*Interview, Washington/
"W": a Fairchild publication, 3-31:12.*

Cale Yarborough
Auto-racing driver

2

I start every race believing I'm going to win it. When I start believing I'm going to run for second, then I'll quit. I think I'll know when it happens. I'll lose some of my reflexes, my quickness; I'll probably dread for a race to start, dread to get into a race car. When that time comes, I'll let somebody else take my place.

Interview/Los Angeles Times, 1-18:(3)1.

Ephraim Yuchtman-Yaar
*Visiting professor of sociology,
Columbia University*

3

[Football is] a modern sport; it's aggressive, more dynamic than baseball. Aggression is the key. People now tend to be passive; they want the product delivered to them, obviously, and football delivers it all. It is highly visible and doesn't require too much imagination. It provides a legitimate opportunity for men and women to express their aggressiveness.

The New York Times, 1-9:(C)12.

Bella S. Abzug
Women's-rights leader; Former United States Representative, D-New York

1

Federal and major legislative branches aren't committed to the rights of women. They did make some commitments of some funding, but it's not enough. Women and their lives should not be sacrificed to inflation. You can't expect them to earn 60 cents on the dollar and not get child care, job training and so on. It's going to have to be a cost that society and the whole Congress pay. Women are moving ahead and there is no chance that this movement won't continue, and that if the demands are not met there will be more action. We've reached the heads and hearts of a lot of people. There is a certain amount of resistance that takes place, economically and politically, but, once we open the doors more broadly, we'll be there. Oh, within 10 years—we're not going to wait another couple hundred years.

Interview/Los Angeles Times, 11-21:(1)5.

Howard H. Baker, Jr.
United States Senator, R-Tennessee

2

I supported ERA when it was first adopted by the Senate. I still support it. But I do not support the extension [of time for ratification] of the amendment by a simple majority [of the Senate] vote. If it were presented by a two-thirds vote—that is, in the Constitutional form—I would consider it, but it will not be. It will be submitted as a simple majority vote. I believe that the active extension should be of comparable, of equal, dignity to the original enactment. Therefore, I would insist on two-thirds; I will vote against a simple majority. On the question of recission [that is, allowing states who had ratified ERA the opportunity to rescind that ratification], if there is an extension, there ought to be an opportunity for states to consider recission.

TV-radio interview/"Meet the Press,"
National Broadcasting Company, 8-20.

Alan Bates
Actor

3

I'm all for women's liberation. I think the sooner we all liberate ourselves and start over again, the better. In my world, acting, we have not had as many problems, because women in the arts have automatically got the kind of independence women are seeking. But what you can't get away from in life is that some of us are women and some of us are men, and nature dictated certain things.

Interview, New York/
Los Angeles Herald Examiner, 4-21:(B)2.

Birch Bayh
United States Senator, D-Indiana

4

[Supporting an extention of ratification time for the ERA]: This arbitrary time period [of seven years] was adopted by the Congress in the assumption that it would be a reasonable time period to assure full and open debate on such an important question. No one in Congress at that time could foresee that parliamentary tactics by a recalcitrant few would prevent the ERA from even reaching the floor for a vote in some state legislatures.

The Dallas Times Herald, 5-18:(A)12.

Simone de Beauvoir
Author

5

. . . our objective as radical feminists is not to take the place of men and to replicate their faults. The special qualities of women are the

WHAT THEY SAID IN 1978

result of their oppression. Women don't have the sense of their own seriousness or of the role to be played that men do; they don't have that frantic competition and taste for power. We don't want women to take on men's character faults.

Interview/San Francisco Examiner & Chronicle,
3-26:(This World)27.

Erma Bombeck
Author; Newspaper columnist

1

When [women's-rights advocate] Betty Friedan came to our town in the mid-'60s and spoke, we roared when she made some comments about how some commercials put women down—captains in the toilet tank and that sort of thing. Friedan was furious that we laughed. "This isn't funny," she shouted, "this is serious." Of course it *was* funny to us housewives. The problem with the women's movement is that it's been too elitist . . . I'm totally for [the ERA], but no one ever asked me to make a stand. Which I think is fairly typical. We housewives were the last to be asked what we wanted. That's probably why the amendment is in trouble today. Finally, the feminists are coming to us and saying, "We can't do it without you."

Interview, Paradise Valley, Ariz./People, 5-22:32.

Edmund G. Brown, Jr.
Governor of California (D)

2

[On a seven-year extension sought by ERA backers in the time needed for ratification of the amendment by the states]: To really invigorate this culture from coast to coast, we need the ERA. Therefore, we need the extension . . . I'll do everything I can to get those other states to ratify it as well as the Congress to give an extention for another seven years. [But] I would like to see equality for women today. Women should not have to wait until 1986 to achieve what men have had for two centuries in this country.

Before "Women For," Los Angeles,
May 18/Los Angeles Times, 5-19:(1)3.

Donna Carlson
Arizona State Legislator

3

[Arguing against an extension of ratification time for the ERA]: Changing and extending the ratification time for a Constitutional amendment is a dangerous precedent to set. Whether or not it is legal to extend the time period to 14 years, it seems grievously unfair to put the ERA monkey on the backs of state legislators for 14 years. What would you think of a football coach who demanded a fifth quarter because his team was behind?

Before House Civil and Constitutional Rights
Subcommittee, Washington, May 17/
The Dallas Times Herald, 5-18:(A)12.

Liz Carpenter
Women's-rights leader; Former Press
Secretary to the President of the
United States (Lyndon B. Johnson)

4

[On the difficulty being encountered in obtaining the required number of state ratifications for the ERA]: A handful of willful and mischievous men—two in Florida, two in North Carolina, five in South Carolina, seldom more than a dozen anywhere, who are blocking the ERA—are using fun and games to maneuver it, deciding to stall justice toward women as the expendable issue which can be used to barter for political mischief.

Before House Judiciary subcommittee, Washington/
The New York Times, 5-28:(1)44.

Claude Chabrol
Motion-picture director

5

[On the women's rights movement]: It's like the colonies when Algeria [tried] not to be French any more and the French [tried] to keep Algeria. Women now have the problem to be free. It's a colonial problem. Woman is a country, like the Third World countries. She has to be careful with the new freedom because it can be a pure-Fascist type government. It would really be too bad if we men have to go and free the women all over again.

Interview, San Francisco/San Francisco Examiner &
Chronicle, 11-5:(Datebook)17.

Sam J. Ervin, Jr.
Former United States Senator,
D-North Carolina

1

[Arguing against extending the deadline for ratification of the ERA]: In the first place, the advocates of the ERA have already had more time to secure its ratification than was given to any other amendment ever added to the Constitution. All the recent amendments have been added within about a year. And the longest ever taken in the history of this country was less than four years. The second reason I oppose it is because it is a perversion of the amendatory process as established by the Constitution ... The Constitution only provides for submitting a Constitutional proposal to the states one time, without going back to Congress for another vote. As a matter of fact, the opinion of the Supreme Court of the United States in the case of *Dillon vs. Gloss,* which was handed down on May 16, 1921, was a unanimous opinion that says, in effect, that the Congress has no power to extend the deadline for ratification of a Constitutional Amendment. That involved the 18th Amendment, which had a deadline of seven years, just like the ERA.

Interview/U.S. News & World Report, 8-14:29.

Oriana Fallaci
Journalist

2

I've often said [the women's movement] was the most important contemporary revolution. Now I must confess that I feel rather disappointed. It announced itself as a revolution, but a revolution did not take place. The feminist movement has become a sort of political party with the inevitable bad consequences. And women have not proved as good as they could have for the simple reason that, after all, they're not much better than men ... Feminism is a way of life, a way of thinking, a way of behaving, or risking, or struggling. I don't see much of this, at least in the individual sense. And revolutions start from the individual. Shouting at a rally doesn't mean a damn thing.

Interview, Rome/
Los Angeles Herald Examiner, 5-7:(F)6.

Betty Friedan
Founder, National Organization for
Women

3

You see now a kind of envy from men toward the women's movement. They envy that women have taken their lives in their hands; they have decided how they want to define life, define what they want to do. Men have had their careers and their rat race, and that's about all. What about a new life and new possibilities for men? There will be new developments in human liberation that focus on men. They will move more and more toward mid-life changes, redefining what they want out of life, in part to accommodate themselves to the changing women in their lives.

To reporters/The Washington Post, 11-24:(C)3.

E. J. (Jake) Garn
United States Senator, R-Utah

4

[Arguing against extension of ratification time for the ERA]: I am absolutely opposed to the extension, simply because the time limit was a rule we established. We must not change the rules when one side hasn't won, and seven years is adequate time for consideration of ERA by state legislatures ... The extension is much like saying "we haven't won so we want another 40 minutes, and only our side can score points" ... There is something wrong in our system when people agree to certain terms, then want to change the rules in the middle of the stream. There is still time before next March to get the Equal Rights Amendment passed, if the people want it. But the distortion of the ratifying process is what I'm objecting to, as well as the fact that granting the extension seems to favor only one side, because states cannot de-ratify.

Washington, July 10/**

Elizabeth Holtzman
United States Representative, D-New York

5

[Advocating extending the deadline for ratification of the ERA]: The Equal Rights Amendment is too important an issue to be cut

WHAT THEY SAID IN 1978

off by an arbitrary time limit. The seven-year time limit was chosen arbitrarily. Nobody had determined that seven years was really appropriate for this debate. Seven years was picked because it had been used in some—but not all—prior amendments. In fact, most of the amendments to the Constitution have never had any time limit placed on them. We now can see that the nature of the debate has been such that seven years is not adequate. I believe that Congress has the power and ought to extend the time period so that there can be a full, informed debate, and so that the decision on ERA can be made by people who are properly informed.

Interview/U.S. News & World Report, 8-14:29.

Barbara Jordan
United States Representative, D-Texas

1

[Responding to those who criticize any extention of the time for ERA ratification as changing the rules in the middle of the game]: Change the rules in the middle of the game? It's no game ... We're talking about the rights of living, breathing, viable, working human beings, individuals. We're talking about the Constitution of the United States and something that needs to be done to make it still more perfect. It's no game.

Before House Civil and Constitutional Rights Subcommittee, Washington, May 18/
The Dallas Times Herald, 5-19:(A)6.

Edward M. Kennedy
United States Senator,
D-Massachusetts

2

[The ERA will be ratified] because America in good conscience cannot preach human rights abroad while over half of our population here at home is denied equality of rights and opportunity. It is going to be ratified because America can no longer afford to waste the talents and energy of millions of women who are left standing at the doors of opportunity still marked "for men only."

At National Working Women's Convention,
Boston, Nov. 4/
The Dallas Times Herald, 11-5:(A)17.

Juanita M. Kreps
Secretary of Commerce of the United
States

3

It will be a long time before women at all levels, high to low—whatever that means—will be treated as full participants in the jobs they're holding. We should be able to lose our tempers without having it attributed to our gender, be as aggressive as men without being dubbed a shrew. I'd like to get to the point where I can be just as mediocre as a man.

Interview/Los Angeles Herald Examiner, 7-18:(A)4.

Clare Boothe Luce
Former American diplomat and playwright

4

[On abortion]: I do not accept the extraordinary proposition that women cannot achieve equal rights before the law until all women are given the legal right to empty their wombs at will—and at the expense of the taxpayer. There is no logical process of thought by which the unnatural act of induced abortion and the destruction of the unborn child in the womb can be deemed to be a natural right of all women.

San Francisco Examiner & Chronicle,
6-4:(This World)2.

Shirley MacLaine
Actress

5

There's a lot of confusion about what a female means in this culture. It's a backlash of women's liberation. When it's a man who's active socially and politically, you're never as intrigued with his personal life; it doesn't smack of any lascivious gossip. With a woman, you want to know if she's feminine at the same time she's politically aggressive. Our idea of what's feminine is questionable.

The Dallas Times Herald, 2-3:(E)11.

Margaret Mead
Anthropologist

1

The women's movement has benefitted women by advancing them politically and economically and in other ways. But it has done harm when it promotes the idea we can do without husbands.

At conference on child abuse, New York,
April 17/The Washington Post, 4-19:(A)8.

Henry Miller
Author

2

[On women's liberation] : I think they're wasting their time trying to imitate men. They should abolish all that, live like women. Women have a world of their own. What we men owe to women and why we should adore them and put them in high places is their intuition. This is what men lack.

Interview/People, 8-21:62.

Adela Rogers St. John
Author, Journalist

3

I think women's lib is complete proof you should not trust women to do anything. They're stupid; they do stupid things endlessly—not just once but forever. They don't know what they're doing. If you ask them what is the purpose of women's lib, they can't tell you. If there is a way of proving that women are the stupidest creatures that God ever created, just take a good look at women's lib.

Interview/Los Angeles Herald Examiner, 3-13:(A)1.

Phyllis Schlafly
National chairman, Stop ERA (Equal
Rights Amendment)

4

Women's libbers are not happy people. They are miserable. They wake up every morning with chips on their shoulders and go out and dare the world to knock them off. Sure, life is full of problems, but society cannot be blamed for them . . . Women's lib is inescapably wrapped up in the lesbian movement . . . Lesbian privileges are one of its primary goals. The women's-lib movement has convinced many women that they are poor, mistreated dumb bunnies, and they walk out on the guy who has been supporting them for years. Women's lib is the cause for the rising divorce rate in this country. The women's movement is a radical anti-family group.

News conference, Dallas, Feb. 1/
The Dallas Times Herald, 2-2:(B)3.

Eleanor Cutri Smeal
President, National Organization for
Women

5

We [women] are a political power, and the message is we are going to make this nation safe for equality. We are moving daily, not only for passage of the ERA but for true equality for men and women . . . We are part of a new and great alliance, an alliance between the civil-rights, labor and women's movements. Each one of us has confronted the radical right. We are peers. We are second to no other movement in this country.

At NOW convention, Washington, Oct. 7/
The Washington Post, 10-8:(A)5.

Jean Stapleton
Actress

6

It is the homemaker . . . who stands to benefit most from the Equal Rights Amendment. Contrary to some misconceptions, she will not have to leave her homemaker job unless she chooses. She will not lose the protection of her husband. Rather, she will gain more, in that her legal rights and standing in the economy, insurance, Social Security, inheritance, divorce, credit, taxes, etc., will be guaranteed.

San Francisco Examiner & Chronicle,
6-11:(This World)2.

Gloria Steinem
Editor, "Ms." magazine

7

[Calling on Congress to extend the ratification deadline for the ERA] : The lawful and peaceful stage of our revolution may be over. It's up to the legislators. We can become radical.

WHAT THEY SAID IN 1978

(GLORIA STEINEM)

If [they] interfere with the ratification of the ERA, they will find every form of civil disobedience possible in every state of the country. We are the women our parents warned us about, and we're proud.

At ERA rally, Washington, July 9/
The Washington Post, 7-10:(A)11.

Thelma Stovall
Lieutenant Governor of Kentucky

1

[Saying she supports the ERA]: I've worked all my life and I've watched what's happened to other working women, through my labor-union work. I've seen people being mistreated. When I ran for treasurer in 1959, I saw lady tellers standing beside male tellers in banks, doing the same jobs. The ladies were drawing $400 a month, while the men were getting $800. I said then that we weren't going to have two different salaries for identical jobs. I thought I'd be beaten, but I led the ticket. Up until about 75 years ago, we considered black people chattel; until then, we didn't admit that black people had brains, or souls, like white people. Now, isn't it shameful that, after 200 years, women still aren't considered first-class citizens?

Interview, Washington, March 21/
Los Angeles Times, 3-22:(4)6.

Barbara Walters
News commentator, American
Broadcasting Company

2

It's a wonderful time to be a woman if you have the courage and something of your own; otherwise, it can be frightening. Either something you can do of your own, or some money of your own, or some husband of your own, something that gives you a feeling of security. Otherwise, it's a turbulent time.

Interview/Los Angeles Times, 1-2:(4)18.

Sarah Weddington
Adviser to President of the United
States Jimmy Carter for Women's Issues

3

When you talk about creating a world in which every option for women is possible, it means that you support the individual who chooses to be a wife and mother as completely and as generously as you support the one who chooses to work outside her home. It means that you are concerned about day-care centers and the quality of care they provide for children. Displaced homemakers, domestic violence, equal credit—these are only a few of the things that will be of primary concern to me.

Interview/The Dallas Times Herald, 9-5:(C)6.

Theodore H. White
Author; Political historian

4

It's about time women had their say in the laws governing them—laws that for 5,000 years have been made by old men, mostly with shriveled-up groins, who have long since forgotten what it was like to be young and never knew what it was like to be a woman.

Interview, New York/
"W": a Fairchild publication, 9-15:41.

Andrew Young
United States Ambassador/Permanent
Representative to the United Nations

5

The issue of women's rights is resounding around the earth today, touching all nations. It can no longer be regarded as a phenomenon occurring only in developed societies.

Before United Nations Budgetary Committee,
New York, Oct. 13/
The Washington Post, 10-14:(A)9.

The Indexes

Index to Speakers

A

Abel, Elie, 325
Abourezk, James, 188, 288
Abram, Morris B., 17
Abzug, Bella S., 475
Ackerman, John E., 49
Adams, Brock, 77, 210
Adler, Mortimer J., 56, 427
Agee, William M., 77, 111
Ajami, Fouad, 288
Albee, Edward, 319, 363, 396
Albery, Donald, 396
Alcott, James A., 405
Aldriss, Brian, 339
Alexander, Herbert E., 188
Algosaibi, Ghazi A., 288
Ali, Muhammad, 451
Allen, George, 451
Allen, Irwin, 363
Allen, James B., 244
Allen, Lew, Jr., 173
Allen, Steve, 405
Allen, Woody, 363, 420
Alperovitz, Gar, 132
Alsop, Joseph, 319
Altman, Robert, 364
Altman, Roger C., 215
Amin, Idi, 223
Amis, Kingsley, 339
Amsterdam, Anthony G., 164
Anderson, John B., 188
Anderson, Lindsay, 364
Anderson, Robert O., 132
Anderson, Sparky, 452
Andreotti, Giulio, 272
Andretti, Mario, 452
Andrews, Allen H., 49
Andrus, Cecil D., 71
Anka, Paul, 386
Anthony, Mark, 27
Antonioni, Michelangelo, 364
Arafat, Yasir, 288
Arbatov, Georgi A., 87, 255
Arkoff, Samuel Z., 364
Arledge, Roone, 325

Arness, James, 405
Aron, Raymond, 272
Ashmore, Harry S., 313
Askew, Reubin, 453
Aspin, Les, 27, 173
Assad, Hafez al-, 289
Astaire, Fred, 420, 427
Atkinson, Richard C., 448
Auerbach, Red, 453
Averoff, Evangelos, 272
Avineri, Shlomo, 289

B

Bacall, Lauren, 427
Bachrach, Peter, 111
Bagdikian, Ben H., 325
Bagge, Carl E., 77
Bailey, F. Lee, 49, 164
Bailey, Herbert S., Jr., 339
Baisinger, Grace, 56
Baker, Howard H., Jr., 87, 111, 173, 475
Baldwin, Roger, 49, 111
Ball, George W., 290
Ball, Lucille, 427
Bamberger, George, 453
Bandeen, Robert A., 27, 56
Bando, Sal, 453
Banowsky, William S., 56
Barletta, Nicky, 244
Barnaby, Frank, 173, 313
Barnard, Christiaan, 223, 351
Barre, Raymond, 272
Barris, Ivan E., 164
Baryshnikov, Mikhail, 319
Basie, Count, 386
Bates, Alan, 420, 475
Bayh, Birch, 475
Bayi, Filbert, 453
Beatty, Warren, 420
Beauvoir, Simone de, 475
Begin, Menachem, 87, 290-293, 313
Bell, Daniel, 112

WHAT THEY SAID IN 1978

E

F

WHAT THEY SAID IN 1978

S

Index to Subjects

A

Ability, 427:4

Abortion–*see* Medicine

Aden, 87:3

Acting/actors, 366:6, 367:1, 367:3, 368:2, 368:4, 369:2, 369:5, 371:2, 371:4, 373:5, 375:3, 375:4, 375:7, 376:4, 376:5, 376:6, 377:1, 377:3, 377:5, 379:1, 380:2, 381:6, 382:1, 382:3, 385:1, 399:5, 399:6, 400:1, 400:6, 401:3, 401:4, 401:5, 402:3, 402:5, 408:2, 409:2, 409:4, 411:1, 414:3, 415:2, 415:4, 418:3, 418:4, 419:1, 419:2, 421:5, 425:2
- acceptance of roles, 365:2
- audience contact (on stage), 377:2, 396:5, 397:4, 398:1, 398:2, 398:6, 399:7, 400:2, 400:6, 403:5, 411:2
- British aspect, 372:4, 378:5
- discovery aspect, 385:3
- faith in self, 381:5
- fulfillment, 372:2
- good roles, 365:4
- growing up/children aspect, 367:4, 376:7
- growth, 384:5
- humiliation aspect, 381:2
- imagination aspect, 369:3
- "method," 380:4
- politicians compared with, 201:1
- salaries, 381:2, 381:4
- sex symbols, 426:4
- "stars," 366:1, 367:2, 372:6, 378:1, 420:3, 422:5, 423:3
- staying power, 368:6
- success, 378:5, 380:1, 381:3
- talent, 372:1
- villains, 371:6
- writing books compared with, 349:2

Adams, John Quincy, 200:2

Advertising–*see* Commerce

Afghanistan, 231:3, 267:6

Africa, 90:5, pp. 223-243
- a battleground, 235:4
- boundaries, arbitrary, 225:2
- Communism, 236:5, 239:1, 242:4, 243:1
- dominant continent of world, 228:5
- foreign affairs:
  - Britain, 223:3

Africa *(continued)*
- foreign affairs *(continued)*
  - China, 223:3
  - Cuba, 90:2, 223:3, 224:4, 225:1, 225:5, 226:1, 226:3, 226:5, 227:1, 227:2, 227:4, 229:2, 231:1, 232:5, 233:1, 236:1, 237:1, 240:1, 240:2, 240:4, 241:4, 242:3, 245:4, 246:2
  - economic aid, 223:3
  - France, 223:3, 228:4, 229:2, 230:4, 233:1
  - Germany, East, 240:1
  - imperialism/colonialism, 224:5, 225:1, 226:3, 227:2, 231:3, 236:2, 236:4, 237:2, 240:1, 242:3
  - Soviet Union, 90:2, 90:3, 91:4, 97:3, 104:2, 223:3, 224:4, 225:1, 225:5, 226:1, 227:4, 228:4, 228:5, 229:1, 229:2, 229:4, 231:3, 233:1, 236:1, 236:4, 237:1, 237:5, 240:1, 240:2, 240:4, 241:4, 242:3, 273:5, 274:5, 280:1
  - U.S., 223:3, 226:1, 227:4, 227:6, 230:4, 231:2, 232:5, 233:4, 236:1, 237:1, 240:2, 240:4, 241:4, 243:1, 243:2
- Horn of Africa–*see* Ethiopia; Somalia
- human-rights aspect, 241:3, 243:1
- languages, multitude of, 234:3
- Organization of African Unity (OAU), 225:2, 236:3, 237:1
- pan-African force, 236:2
- racial/majority-rule aspect, 226:1, 231:2, 236:3
- resources, 228:5, 243:1
- *See also specific countries*

Age/youth, 421:1, 423:4, 424:2, 428:2, 434:6

Agriculture/farming, 45:1, 134:2
- economic aspect, 27:5, 30:2, 137:6, 160:6
  - strikes, 32:6
- family farms, 27:4
- government aspect:
  - Agriculture, U.S. Dept. of, 27:4
  - profit, government guarantee of, 27:5
  - regulation, 28:2
  - subsidies/supports, 30:2, 137:6

Air transportation–*see* Transportation

Albania, 284:4

Alcohol–*see* Medicine

Ali, Muhammad, 466:8

Allen, George, 458:2

WHAT THEY SAID IN 1978

C

D

F

J

K

L

Q

R

Racism—*see* Civil rights
Radio, 412:3, 413:5
Railroads—*see* Transportation
Random House, Inc., 344:7
Rattigan, Terence, 397:2
Reagan, Ronald, 113:3, 195:5
Redford, Robert, 374:4
Reedy, George E., 191:4
Religion, pp. 441-447
  abortion, attitude toward, 444:3
  atheism/non-believers, 444:2, 445:5, 446:5
  Buddhism, 271:2
  Catholicism, 443:5, 445:1
    education aspect, 62:3, 63:2
    Pope, 444:4
      choice of, 447:2
      Communist, 445:4
      John Paul II, 445:4
      non-Italian, 443:1
      Paul VI, 442:4, 447:2
  celibacy/sexual aspect, 443:2, 444:1, 444:3
  Christianity as disaster, 447:3
  Christ, Jesus, 443:1, 443:5, 445:3, 446:3
  compromise of principles, 444:3
  cults and other groups, 441:1, 442:1, 442:3,
    445:2, 446:1, 446:2
    People's Temple suicide/murder, 441:3, 441:4,
      442:2, 443:4
  diversity, 445:1
  divorce, attitude toward, 443:3
  evangelism, 446:3
  freedom of, 443:4, 444:2
  government involvement in, 441:3, 441:4, 443:4,
    447:1
  Judaism/Jews, 285:3, 290:3, 292:1, 298:2, 303:5,
    310:5, 445:1, 446:2, 446:4
    Zionism—*see* Israel
  Moslemism, 302:4, 302:5
  Muhammad, Prophet, 445:3
  organized, 441:1, 442:1
  parish priests, 443:5
  political aspect, 441:2, 442:7, 447:1
  Protestantism, 445:1
  spreading the word, 442:5, 445:3
  tax-exemption, 447:1
  women, ordination of, 444:3
  youth aspect, 442:1, 446:1
Republican Party (U.S.)—*see* Politics
Responsibility, 428:1
Retirement—*see* Labor
Rhodesia, 237:1

Rhodesia *(continued)*
  Communism/Marxism, 238:3, 239:1, 239:5
  foreign affairs:
    Britain, 226:2, 228:3, 230:5, 234:1, 234:4,
      235:6, 238:3, 240:3, 242:1
    Cuba, 231:4, 233:3, 239:5
    sanctions/boycott, 228:3, 229:5
    South Africa, 233:3
    Soviet Union, 231:4, 233:3, 235:6, 239:5
    U.S., 226:2, 228:2, 228:3, 229:4, 229:5,
      230:5, 231:4, 232:6, 233:3, 234:4, 238:3,
      239:5, 240:3, 242:1
  human-rights aspect, 95:2
  Patriotic Front/guerrillas, 226:2, 228:2, 228:3,
    230:5, 231:4, 234:1, 234:2, 234:4, 235:6,
    235:7, 240:3, 242:1
  racial/black aspect, 226:2, 227:5, 229:4, 239:3,
    239:4
    majority rule/internal settlement/one-man, one-
      vote, 228:1, 228:2, 228:3, 229:5, 230:3,
      230:5, 231:4, 232:6, 233:3, 234:1, 234:2,
      234:4, 235:5, 238:1, 238:3, 238:4, 239:1,
      239:2, 240:3, 241:1
    whites, 227:3, 228:1, 230:2, 234:5, 238:4,
      239:2
Robinson, Jackie, 19:2
Rolling Stones, the, 386:1
Romania, 276:2
Roosevelt, Franklin D., 113:5, 120:5, 128:3, 135:4,
  147:4, 200:2, 244:4, 312:3, 335:3
Roosevelt, Theodore, 200:2, 246:5
Rossini, Gioacchino, 391:1
Running (sport), 453:6
Russell, Richard, 126:2
Russia—*see* Soviet Union

S

Sadat, Anwar el-, 92:1, 288:5, 289:1, 289:3, 292:3,
  292:4, 296:1, 296:2, 297:3, 297:4, 298:7, 299:1,
  300:2, 300:4, 303:3, 303:5, 306:4, 306:6, 306:7,
  307:7, 308:3, 309:3, 309:4, 310:2, 311:2, 311:4,
  312:1
St. Louis (Mo.), 217:2, 220:1
Samuelson, Paul A., 157:3
Saudi Arabia:
  defense/military aspect, 293:3, 295:2, 297:1,
    297:5, 298:1, 298:5, 302:1, 304:1, 305:2,
    310:4, 311:1, 311:5, 312:2
  foreign affairs:
    Iran, 312:2

U